169 DAYS
A SPIRITUAL JOURNEY

Buzz W.

Wybuzz Books LLC, Saegertown

Special Thanks to:

Many people supported, encouraged, and believed in the project. They are too numerous to mention them all, but I could not have done this without them. Here are a few that spent many hours dedicated to this book.

Editors -	John Edwards and Marilyn Wykoff
Design & Layout -	Phyllis Lord
Proof readers -	David Acker
	Lauren Lyon
	Nadine Stearns
	Marilyn Wykoff

All photos by the author.

Published by Wybuzz Books LLC, Seagertown
Wybuzz Books LLC P.O. Box 184 Saegertown, PA 16412

ISBN 978-0-9889715-0-9

To the addict who still suffers
both in and out of the Fellowship

CONTENTS

THE DREAM

The idea of thru-hiking the Appalachian Trail occurred to me almost ten years ago when I was on the way home from vacationing in Alabama with my new girlfriend. We stopped to see her cousins John and Danotta in Atlanta when I noticed in small type on the Georgia road map, Springer Mountain the southern terminus of the Appalachian Trail. I had previously heard of the Appalachian Trail, but never gave it a great deal of thought.

John and Danetta took us on a tour of the area the next day. I brought up the subject of the trail and John told me what little he knew. He knew about Amicalola Falls State Park where the nine-mile approach trail to the Appalachian Trail started. The conversation with him seemed to give me some incentive to investigate further.

My injured back was starting to stiffen due to the long hours in the pick-up truck and the lack of walking regularly while on vacation. Besides, we had some extra time before we had to be back to work, so I impulsively said to my girlfriend, "Lets hike on the famous Appalachian Trail."

She said, "We aren't prepared to go hiking."

I said, "Sure we are, I have a pack," which we did.

"I think we need hiking boots."

"I'll buy you some boots if we can go hiking."

She hesitated a little then said, "Deal!"

We stopped at a discount shoe outlet and each bought a pair of hiking boots. We picked up some food, a bottle of water purifying pills, and a few miscellaneous items at Walmart. We packed up two old external frame packs that I previously bought at a flea market for five bucks each. We were, all geared up in my mind.

We bid her cousins goodbye and drove around quite a while before we found Amicalola Falls State Park at the foot of Springer Mountain. We donned old, heavy, cotton, camouflaged, USMC fatigues, our brand new hiking boots, and we were off.

The approach trail up Springer Mountain was much more challenging than we anticipated. We hiked nine-miles up the steep trail to the plaque that marks the southern terminus of the Appalachian Trail. We both had huge blisters on the heels of our feet from the steep hike up Springer. We were chafed you-know-where from the hot cotton drawers and we had the drizzling trots from the water purifying tablets.

We had planned on hiking north two days and then hiking back to Amicalola, but changed our minds, at the top of Springer Mountain. We spent the night in the shelter and then turned back due to all our misery. We met a southbound hiker with his dog who over took us on our way down Springer. They were finishing a forty-five-day section hike from Virginia. He took a break with us for about fifteen minutes to talk about his adventures on the trail. I was so intrigued that he already sold me on the idea of thru-hiking the Appalachian Trail.

We got blisters on our toes from the steep hike down Springer that day. That may sound like an initial negative experience, but I learned to not hike in brand new boots, wear cotton clothing when hiking in hot weather, or use so many purifying tablets to turn the water brown. The best thing was that girlfriend eventually became my wife, which showed she didn't always make the best decisions.

The trail became my getaway for the next ten years. When life would get stressful, I would dream of running away and thru-hiking the trail. That was why I adopted the trail name, Dreamer because I dreamed of thru-hiking ever since that first day on Springer Mountain so long ago. That was how it all started.

February 26, 2006   Day 1   13.6 Miles

We left the heavy snows of the North behind two days ago. The weather in Georgia was clear and cold, but snowless. I didn't sleep a wink at Amicalola Lodge where I stayed with my wife Marilyn, who I nicknamed Scooter. The lodge was a lot higher-class hotel than I was accustomed to and sat nicely on the side of Springer Mountain. We ate breakfast at the restaurant in the lodge. We had the AYCE, which is an acronym for all-you-can eat breakfast buffet and I ate all I could eat. I was so nervous I thought I would puke.

I anticipated that day for so long, but when it finally arrived, it seemed surreal. It wasn't as if I didn't want to go, it was more like pre-game jitters. I had a great deal of anxiety, my heart skipped beats, and I felt dizzy. Scooter played a song by Erica Joe, which best described my situation. The words go something like this:

Sweaty hands,

Quick sand,

I know I should, but I'm scared I can't

It's a big move, everything to lose.

What if it's nothing like the way I planned?

What if?

What if I fail?

What if chasing my dreams is just chasing my tail.

Do I listen to the voice telling me to stay or

Listen to the voice screaming out GO?

This town safe and sound,

I already know my way around.

What if I stay?

Do I really want to spend the rest of my days

on a dead end street in a dead end job?

I can live like that, but my dreams won't stop.

Just forget it.

Everybody said it,

But I know that I would regret it if I didn't GO.

JUST GO WITH YOUR HEART.

GO WITH THE FLOW.

THERE IS ONLY ONE WAY

YOU'RE EVER GOING TO KNOW
JUST GO.

GO

I had a dreadfully strong fear of failure. I came from a small town, where everyone in the county knew I was attempting the thru-hike. How would I look if I failed? I decided to do as the song said, "Just go." We drove back to the Amicalola Falls visitor's center where I registered as a thru-hiker. The young girl who was tending the store couldn't find the Polaroid camera they normally use to take pictures of the thru-hikers that register. Her supervisor had her use a disposable camera to take my picture to post on the bulletin board with my trail name, Dreamer as soon as she got it developed. They gave us a map to a parking lot two miles from the summit of Springer Mountain.

We drove about thirty road-miles to the parking lot on Springer, so I wouldn't have to spend my first day on the steep approach trail to the summit of Springer. The last eight miles were on a narrow, steep, winding, and scary dirt road. We parked in the dirt parking lot with other cars. An extremely extraverted woman engaged us in conversation. She dropped her son and his hiking buddy off to hike to Katahdin only a few minutes earlier. She took my mind off my anxiety as she encouraged me to look out for her son on the trail. We packed up as she chatted, bid her goodbye, and hiked two miles south to the summit of Springer Mountain.

The summit was flat and tree covered. The first time I was there the lush trees made me feel like I wasn't on top of a mountain. I now found the trees barren of their leaves, the ground was winter's brown, and the only green was from a few wild Rhododendron bushes that dotted the forest floor. I could see the valleys, houses, and one large pond miles below. A man took names of the thru-hikers starting at the bronze plaque set in stone marking the southern terminus of the Appalachian Trial. We had him take a picture of us by the plaque and we were off on the adventure.

My anxiety subsided after we got on the trail. It was a crisp, clear, sunny, winter day. We stopped for a late lunch in a beautiful setting on Hawk Mountain. My appetite returned as we sat in the sun on the brown grass of winter that spring would soon turn green. I found myself wishing I ate more sausage and eggs earlier. I was enjoying myself and realized how I loved hiking the trail as my confidence started returning.

My anxiety over the newness of the trail was not abnormal for me. I always suffered from stress, anxiety, and depression as far back as I could remember. Walking or hiking as a way to cope with anxiety was not new to me either. When I was young and life got too stressful, I would go for a walk and dream of running away from home to become a wilderness trapper living as a hermit. I would make a living from selling the fur and no one could tell me what to do.

That worked until I discovered alcohol. I was a teenager when I started using alcohol to enhance my fantasies. I discovered chemicals could take me away from reality to a world far, far away where there was no stress and I was the king. Nobody could tell me what to do in my make-believe world where I was in total control. I would go for a walk as an excuse to get away and sneak a cigarette. I actually discovered, if I smoked a joint and went for a walk, I could enjoy my little fantasies even more. I started compulsively getting high and walking, often several times a day.

I did that for longer than a decade. I loved being intoxicated and spent more and more time under the influence of something. I couldn't remember exactly when, but at some point, I stopped walking and merely got high. The real world eventually became so harsh that I couldn't stand being in it, so I stayed intoxicated. The new problem was chemicals took over my life. I became a slave to the drugs and my life revolved around the drugs above all else. I was truly powerless and the real world became so unmanageable all I could do was try to escape by using drugs. In the end, I lost almost everything, but my life.

The trail turned towards the bright sun that snapped me back to the present. The day was a welcome reminder of spring, which might be a long time away in the north. We shed clothes as the day warmed and hiked on to Horse gap. I had a déjà vu feeling. I began reminiscing back to seven years ago to February of 1999. Scooter and I were hiking from Amicalola Falls to Suches, Georgia on a section hike. Where I now stood at Horse Gap, we encountered a man who called himself Eric Meyers from Florida, who claimed he was a southbound thru-hiker about to finish. He told us he was finishing the trail late because he became ill from food poisoning after eating a bad burrito. He spent time in a hospital and then a family took him in while he recovered. He built a deck to repay them. I asked him, "What is one thing could he tell me to enable me to thru-hike the trail?" He said, "Don't just plan it; survive it." He went on to say the police delayed him in Gatlinburg, because he fit the description of Eric Rudolph. I didn't know anything about Eric Rudolph at the time. He patiently explained that Eric Rudolph was the famous bomber who bombed the 1996 Olympics and the abortion clinics in Alabama. I let it go, we went north, and he went south.

Later, on the way home from the hike I asked Scooter what she thought of him. She replied she thought he gave himself a homemade haircut with scissors. We couldn't say what, but we both agreed something was not right. Six months later the news had a picture of Eric Rudolph, who was still at large. The Eric Rudolph they pictured on television looked like the man we met at Horse Gap, only thirty pounds heavier. I called Scooter and she saw the similarity, but didn't think it was Eric. I thought we should call the FBI, but she said, "You'll only embarrass yourself." They caught Eric Rudolph in 2002. I felt sure the skinny Eric Rudolph who was in handcuffs on television in 2002 and the Eric Meyers I stood face to face with in 1999 was the same man.

That was the first time I had been back to Horse Gap since then. The hair on the back of my neck stood up as I remembered his advice, "Don't just plan it; survive it."

We hiked off Justice Mountain and up Phyllis Spur, which was a short but steep up then a sharp down. I was sure they named it after our daughter Phyllis, who has a kind of steep up and down personality. We hiked on to Justice Creek to an unofficial campsite with a good water supply. We made our home for the first night there. Two other hikers named Nick and Will, who are college roommates taking a semester off and attempting a thru-hike had already made camp. Scooter and I talked to them before we set up our tents a short distance away. We cooked our first meal of cooked tuna and noodles for supper. After supper, all four of us gathered around the fire Will made and talked until the dropping temperature drove us to our tents for the warmth of our sleeping bags. Scooter and I wore all the clothes we had to bed to survive the cold night.

I made it through day one, but I didn't know how many days I had to go. I couldn't even think about Katahdin at that point. I was definitely grateful I made it through day one.

Day 2   13.2 Miles

The temperature dropped down to fourteen degrees and ice was on the inside of my tent due to condensation freezing. My water bottle froze and I got too cold to sleep. I got up to a frost covered forest, but no snow. Scooter and I made hot tea and oatmeal for breakfast, which helped us warm up a little before we packed up. Then she headed south, and I headed north.

I turned to look back and she did the same when we were about fifty feet apart. We both silently waved goodbye. I felt insecure and uneasy as I watched her depart through the wilted, frost covered Rhododendron bushes that splashed some dark green on winter's drab landscape. I knew I wouldn't see her again for four weeks, which seemed like a long time.

The Appalachian Trail is not a typical walk in the park, although it is a national park. The Appalachian Trail is a footpath starting at the summit of Springer Mountain in Georgia, extending two-thousand, one hundred and seventy-five miles north, and terminating at the summit of mighty Mount Katahdin in Maine's Baxter State Park. The idea originated shortly after World War 1, but was not completed until 1937.

The setting for the trail is in the wilderness as much as possible. This is why it snakes its way mostly along the backbone of the Appalachian Mountain range. In many places, it runs from mountaintop to mountaintop. The trail runs through more than seventy-five state, federal forests, parks, and game lands along with other private and public lands. The trail even runs through towns and across highway bridges in places to connect the miles of continuous footpath.

The trail is managed by the Appalachian Trail Conservancy, which is a non-profit organization totally dedicated to protecting the Appalachian Trail and its quarter of a million acre greenway. Many local Appalachian Trail Hiking clubs also work cooperatively with the National Park Service and the US Forest Service. Thousands of private citizens volunteer their time and money to build and maintain the trail. Volunteers have built hundreds of shelters scattered along the trail where a hiker can stay free with the exception of New Hampshire. In New Hampshire, the Appalachian Mountain Club controls the shelters and charges a fee to stay in huts it privately owns.

Volunteers have also built bridges ranging from a log across a stream to some impressive feats of engineering spanning streams and rivers that otherwise would be difficult or dangerous to cross. They have built walks across low lands, bogs, and swamps to keep a hiker's feet dry. Some of the steeper ascents on some mountains even have built in steps. All were constructed by volunteer's love of the trail and dedication to pass the Appalachian Trail experience on to others. I wish I had the words to properly express my gratitude to the many volunteers of the trail.

My feet were freezing from forcing them into the ice-cold boots, so I hiked off at a rather vigorous pace. The endorphins soon started to kick in and my body warmed from the fast pace. I got into the moment and my fears and apprehension of my future for the next six months evaporated. I hiked solo with my thoughts in the solitude of the mountains of northern Georgia. I felt so privileged to be hiking as I reflected on the early 1980's when I started to recover from a life of addiction to drugs and alcohol. I started having so much pain in my lower back that I went to many chiropractors until I figured out there was more to my pain than merely needing my back put in place. I scheduled an appointment with the Cleveland Clinic to see if surgery would help. I found out I had a bone disease partially caused by my addiction to alcohol. The doctor told me walking among other things would help. I remember saying to the Doctor, "It hurts to walk."

He said, "Walk anyway." I walked about two-hundred yards the first day and a half a mile on day two. I built up to three miles a day eventually. I would walk three miles a day before going to work. My back started to feel better, and I felt better emotionally.

I found I could enjoy walking without mind-altering substances in my body distorting my sense of reality. My morning walks became my time to process what was going on in my life. They afforded time to be by myself, to meditate, to escape the stressful world, and to dream. I would walk and my endorphins would kick in and produce a euphoric state of mind, helping me cope without using drugs. You might say walking became my new drug. The best thing of all was a miracle that something as simple as walking was starting to heal my injured back.

Those same endorphins kicked in and I felt the euphoria of the beautiful, cold, sunny, winter's day in God's world with no drugs distorting my reality. I felt blessed to be in Georgia where it was practically spring, as opposed to the three feet of snow back home with more forecast. By noon I hiked six miles in my euphoric state to a parking area at Woody Gap on the road to Suches. The sun had taken the edge off the cold, so I stopped for lunch and made Ramen noodles and hot tea.

We parked the car there at Woody Gap on my first section hike with Scooter from Amicalola Falls to Suches, Georgia. It was also in February because Scooter was changing jobs and wouldn't have any vacation for a while so we took a week off and headed back to Amicalola Falls. We were definitely more prepared as we climbed up Springer for the second time. We spent the first night at Stover Creek Shelter. It was much warmer that year. We had the shelter all to ourselves and I remember I slept like a rock. The next morning we ate high protein sports bars for breakfast because we hadn't started to cook on the trail yet. The second day was when we had the encounter with Eric Meyers.

We also met an Army Ranger who told us about a shelter a half mile off trail, which no longer existed. We pushed ourselves too far to the shelter, so we were exhausted and sore by the time we stopped.

The next morning we awoke to a hard springtime rain, but only had about a half-day's hike to the car. I still remember the sense of accomplishment when I arrived at my car parked at Woody Gap.

That was a huge victory for my bad back as not only had I hiked twenty-nine miles in three days on the trail, I did it with a backpack carrying all my food and a sleeping bag. I was giddy with excitement and anticipation. I still wasn't in shape or ready to thru-hike and didn't know if I ever would be, but I knew it might be at least possible.

A few cars sat parked probably waiting for hikers when I arrived. I made a second pot of tea as I enjoyed a second victory to be there again. I was grateful for the miracle that I could even attempt a thru-hike. My back still hurt, but I felt privileged to be walking. I decided I didn't need anything important enough to hitch into the town of Suches. I eventually moved on at a more leisurely pace in the afternoon. I filtered water for the night at a small stream crossing the trail. I started looking for a nice place to set up my tent. I hiked another three miles before I found a suitable place late in the afternoon.

I stopped for the night on the trail to Woods Hole Shelter. I camped on a flat spot barely off the trail because the shelter was four-tenths mile off trail and I was tired. A long-time hiker named Crazy Horse stopped to talk. We took a liking to each other, so he decided to set up camp next to me. Crazy Horse was a seasoned Desert Storm veteran, who was badly wounded in the war, and collected disability, so he could spend a lot of time on the trail. He proudly sported a beat up old black hat with his Purple Heart Medal pinned next to a patch that said Desert Storm Veteran. He had a poorly fitting glass eye, an even poorer set of false teeth, and long, black, greasy, unkempt, hair that made him look a little crazy. He was grandiose, but he had a sense of self-confidence I vicariously absorbed from him. I mostly listened as he told trail tales. I needed his company to keep me from dwelling of my own fear.

Nick and Will stopped by on their way to the shelter. They joined us for a time, but left for the shelter. They found the shelter full, so soon returned to set up camp with us. The four of us cooked our supper and ate together. The night was clear so the temperature dropped with the sun. Will, who was an Eagle Scout, built a fire and we all huddled close for the warmth. Crazy Horse told many tales of his adventures on and off the trail. He gave us some excellent advice based on the wisdom he gained from survival on the trail. He also raided a hiker box earlier in the day and was willing to share all his plunder with the rest of us. I found myself enjoying the fellowship of the other hikers as we bonded in spite of the cold. We talked until well after dark before turning in for the night.

Day 2   10.1 Miles

I was too cold to sleep again. However, I didn't want to leave my cocoon to face the frigid morning. Eventually, Mother Nature forced me out of the tent. I quickly changed from my warm nightclothes into my hiking clothes. When I put my cold shoes on my feet, they froze instantly, so I started hiking without breakfast to warm my feet. I left as quietly as possible to not wake the others. I stopped an hour after daylight at Slaughter Creek to make oatmeal and hot tea. I had tower, so I called Scooter. She hiked back to her car and drove down the mountain without incident and she was on her way home.

I crossed Slaughter Creek and hiked up Blood Mountain. Both got their name from the fierce battles the Indians fought over hunting territory in the early days, before the white man came along. I felt as if I was hiking on sacred ground, almost feeling their spirits. A stone shelter stood at the summit of Blood Mountain. The hair on the back of my neck stood up when I stepped inside, as if it was haunted. I got the heck out of there at once and wouldn't stay overnight in that shelter for love or money. Blood Mountain yielded a nice view as I looked back at Springer feeling a little sense of accomplishment.

I arrived at Neels Gap by mid morning. An outfitter there was the first place I could get supplies without getting off the trail. I mailed myself a package from home back in January, which they held for me until I could pick it up for a dollar. I bought sunscreen and a coke and moved to an outside picnic table to open my package. I sent myself more food than I was able to carry. My lower back was giving me pain, so I decided to take only what I would need to get me to Hiawassee, which was about two days away.

I went through my gear and found I was carrying about two pounds of first aid things for every possible situation. Some of the stuff I carried for years and never used, so I took out everything I never used to lighten my pack. I would never be too far from my next supply stop and I could always get off the trail at the next road for help in an emergency. I took the leftover supplies and extra first aid gear to the hiker box to leave for any hiker who needed it. Hiker boxes were found all along the trail where any hiker could take what they need and leave anything they didn't need for someone else. I wondered if when I saw Crazy Horse again if he would offer me some of the things I left.

Neels Gap was the first place where a thru-hiker could abort their hike and call for a ride home. One out of every five thru-hikers quit there and unfortunately, I met a pretty, young woman who was waiting for a ride home to abort her hike. I knew she might never get the opportunity to thru-hike again because life has a tendency to get busy. I wanted to say something, but I didn't know what to say. I believed that once I started to quit my goals when things got tough it made it easier to continue quitting the next time I faced adversity. Quitting seemed like a bad habit to get into that would lower my self-worth. She started to explain that she hurt her knee and was twenty-years-old, so she had many years to try another attempt. I saw she already made up her mind, but for some reason, she seemed to be trying to convince me that aborting her hike was the right thing to do. I walked away rudely as she continued to make excuses. I didn't want to listen to her or anyone who might make me believe I couldn't thru-hike or think it was okay to quit. I didn't want to be one of the twenty percent like her. I needed to stick with the winners and positive people to follow their examples.

Neels Gap was the only place the Appalachian Trail passed through a building, so I posed for a picture before I passed through the breezeway. I felt another sense of accomplishment as I hiked on. Katahdin was still over twenty-one hundred-miles away, but I felt like a thru-hiker for the first time as I left Neels Gap behind. I was also on part of the trail I hadn't hiked previously. I stopped to take pictures of mountain scenes at almost every vista. The day was cloudy, but the atmosphere was clear enough to see the vastness of the mountains that lay ahead to the north. I was in awe of God's work.

My first memorable exposure to backpacking was in September, 1995 when vacationing in Colorado's Rocky Mountain National Park. My back was getting better with bone building medication and exercises such as walking. By that time, walking was as big a part of my day as taking a morning dump. I decided to walk on one of the manicured trails leading up a mountain at one of the many scenic stops. Several tourist-types equipped with shorts, T-shirts, sandals, and cameras scurried up the trail as if they were late for something. Normally I avoided such chaos, but my back was starting to tighten up from the long drive from Colorado Springs. I laced up my walking boots, grabbed a bottle of water, and ventured up the mountain with the other tourists to loosen up my back.

I encountered two back packers descending from the park's backcountry. They stood apart from us tourists because they both were obviously in prime physical condition, well equipped, carrying large backpacks, and descending as if they were on a mission. They must have been out for a while because one other little thing I noticed as they passed was they stunk as bad as a ripe, road-killed raccoon. I was as intrigued by the backpackers as I was with the breathtaking views of the park.

The drive across Nebraska on the way home was a little monotonous, so I had some time to reflect on my vacation. I first became incredibly envious of the back packers being able to go on such an adventure. The envy soon turned into jealousy and the jealousy turned into self-pity. I felt that my back injury and bone disease forbid me from ever carrying any weight on my back. I was pissed at God because I felt He took away my strength and ability to carry such weight. I blamed God because it was easier than taking personal responsibility for the bone disease that was a direct result of my addiction.

I snapped back from the past with a new sense of gratitude, realizing with God's help I could live out the dream that I once thought was impossible. I thought maybe, I should thank God, but shrugged it off. I hiked several more miles to Hogpen Gap where a blacktop road led to Helen, Georgia. Nick, Will, and some other hikers were already camped south of the road. I chose to camp on a flat spot across the road alone. I noticed two hikers hitching a ride into town. I had no desire to go into a town, but found it comforting to know I could if I needed to.

I had cell tower, so I made a call to Scooter. She was safe and sound in snow that was still ass deep to a tall Indian back home. I also called my daughter Nadine to assure her I was doing fine. The contact with them helped me feel better emotionally, but I still had a lot of back pain that worried me. I crawled into my sleeping bag and tried to focus on the positive accomplishment of passing Neels Gap. I called and my friend Lady D, who I often looked to for positive reinforcement and support. I felt better after we talked as sleep overtook me.

Day 4   15 Miles

I had a hard time falling asleep, but the temperature was warmer, so I slept in until after the sun came up. I then packed up and made coffee before I took to the trail. I mailed myself some of those new single cup coffee bags that look like an old-fashioned tea bag. The coffee hit the fast forward button and put me in an excellent mood as I trekked out. It turned out to be a splendid day on the trail to hike solo in the sun. My mental state became a lot better with the warm weather. I wore shorts and got a little sun burned. I slowed down, took my time, and enjoyed the trail.

The two hikers who hitched to Helen last night overtook me and said they got drunk and were going to hitch back to Helen again tonight. They asked if I would like to join them, but I declined. The northern Georgia Mountains were steep, but not long, as I spent the day going up and down. Blue Mountain at over four-thousand feet was the tallest, but there were half a dozen other mountains over thirty-five-hundred feet. I found water in most of the gaps, which took away my water worries.

The day was perfect to dream, so I found myself reminiscing about when I came home from Georgia for the second time inspired by my success. I received an income tax return, so I went to a reputable chain outfitter in the local mall and invested in a set of high quality trekking poles for both Scooter and me. I also bought myself a pair of expensive, top of the line, hiking boots. I started a checking account with the leftover money at a bank where I didn't normally do business. I earmarked the money for my future thru-hike.

I carried my pack and poles for three miles every morning before work to train for hiking. I soon began to experience pain in both of my knees. The pain was tolerable at first, but it progressively increased. I did a lot of damage before discovering the expensive hiking boots were the cause of my pain. Apparently, the new hiking boots I tried to break in held my feet and ankles in such a rigid position that it caused the plica bands in my knees to swell. My knees failed to heal even with medication, physical therapy, and rest. The following January I finally had arthroscopic surgery on both knees to remove swollen plica bands.

I remember how demoralized I felt with the serious injury. The worst of the grieving was over losing my dream of hiking the Appalachian Trail. I prayed and diligently followed through with physical therapy and miraculously my knees healed.

I felt grateful to merely be hiking even if I didn't finish, the miracle was to be thru-hiking. It re-occurred to me to thank God. That time I didn't shrug it off, but stopped, bowed my head, and said, "Thank you God for the privilege of hiking. Amen."

I got tired late in the afternoon, so I filtered water at a stream that crossed the trail and looked for a suitable campsite. I hiked about another hour becoming afraid I wouldn't find a place before dark. Luckily, I found a flat place to camp right beside the trail before I really panicked. I camped by myself at Indian Grave Gap. It wasn't a good campsite, but it was flat and it would be dark soon so I didn't have too many options. I hoped the Indian didn't haunt me in the night. It was March first and the landscape was still dressed in winter's drab brown colors. However, with the warmer temperatures, I could smell spring on the way and it felt great. My tent faced south about a foot from the trail, but I didn't think anyone would mind. Besides, I would be able to hear anyone who passed in the night. I saw white blazes several feet away in both directions as I cooked rice and beans for supper. I watched the day slip away as I ate.

Day 5   15 Miles

I slept fitfully because my left knee and back hurt. I awoke to a damp, gray day, which might have been why I had extra pain. I took some ibuprofen and started hiking with only a Snickers bar for breakfast. I wanted to get on the trail, excited by the prospect of spending the night in the town of Hiawassee in a real bed, eating restaurant food, getting a hot shower, and maybe even watching the news on television. Three miles north I passed what they called Cheese Factory Campsite. Two tents were there, but the occupants were not up. I could have camped there and had company the night before, but I didn't know. I passed by as quietly as I could to not wake anyone. I heard some giggling in one of the tents.

I came to a cliff on the side of Tray Mountain where a sign said, vista, but the visibility wasn't the best for vistas. I took a picture of the trees disappearing in the light gray nothingness of the fog. Tray Mountain, at almost five-thousand feet, was one of the highest summits I had climbed so far. The summit was anticlimactic and covered with trees in the fog, which was not what I pictured in my mind. I stopped at Tray Mountain Shelter on the way down the mountain to filter some water so I could cook noodles for lunch. I was eating when a thru-hiker came in to get water. He was at the Cheese Factory Campsite in one of the tents I passed earlier. He called himself the Guns of Jesus and I found him to be a cocky twenty-nine-year-old from New Jersey, who worked in New York City as a paralegal secretary. I couldn't tell if he was Jewish or Italian, but he sure was intrusive, arrogant, self- centered, and over familiar. I don't know why I took an instant liking to him; maybe it's because he sounded positive and sure of himself. I thought with his attitude he might make it to Katahdin. We ate together and hiked out chatting like old friends with something in common.

The weather cleared offering great vistas. We didn't find water in the gaps today, probably because we were above three-thousand feet, so I ran out of water. I wasn't worried because it wasn't a day that I would need a lot of water. We were descending Powell Mountain into

Dicks Creek Gap where we could hitch to Hiawassee. We probably hurried in anticipation of town. I was trying to keep up with Guns and I slipped on a root, which further injured my knee. I broke the rule to never step on any kind of wood because it was always slippery when wet. I felt a sharp pain and went right down. It was getting late in the day, so I told Guns to go on ahead, but he refused and stayed with me. I took two ibuprofen tablets and tested it. The knee hurt, but it held up. The pain started to subside as the medication kicked in and I started to loosen up, but the psychological impact of being hurt was much worse than the physical pain.

The fear took me right back to those old familiar feelings of hopelessness and despair when I had the knee surgery. At times like that, it would be easy to throw in the towel and abort my dream. I forced myself to not panic, look back, and think through of how I overcame my emotions in the past. I stopped to stretch right then and slowed my breathing down.

The following April after I had knee surgery I got spring fever and took a long weekend to venture south to where the Appalachian Trail crossed the Pennsylvania/Maryland border. Scooter and I were on what we have come to call a recon mission and explored the trail by car. My knees were improving, but I probably was not able to hike yet. By May, my knees were healed enough to resume my morning walks. I thought I was ready to test them on the trail, so I took a week's vacation and returned to Penmar on the boarder of Pennsylvania and Maryland by myself to day hike on the Appalachian Trail. I arrived at Penmar by two o'clock on a Saturday morning after driving all night and slept the rest of the night in the back of my truck. The first day I hiked to a landmark three miles south through the Devils Racecourse in Maryland, ate my lunch and returned to my truck. I then spent the rest of the day planning my next day's hike and being a trail angel for other hikers. The rest of the week, I went north into Pennsylvania and hiked to a landmark, then returned to the security of my truck. I would park my truck on a road that crossed the trail and hike away from the truck all morning or until I started to feel insecure. I would then return to sleep in my truck. I hiked a little further with a little more weight each day. I didn't go overnight because my back injury was still so painful. I feared I would further injure my back or knees if I carried enough weight to stay overnight.

The hiking went well and I discovered other hikers were a great inspiration as I made friends easily. I would leave a case of pop and some snacks in the back of my pickup truck and leave the cap unlocked. I told the hikers I met on the trail to help themselves to the treats. Most would leave me a thank you note of appreciation and no one ripped me off or took more than a modest amount. That said a lot for the quality of the character of the folks on the trail.

I met several thru-hikers who inspired me, but one who stood out in particular was a salty older gentleman named Colonel. He spent his entire career in the military until he retired. He wore a walking cast on his leg and was more than a little grumpy.

I asked him, "Did you hurt your leg?"

He looked at me with a little sarcastic impatience, "Stress fracture."

"Doesn't it hurt?" I regretted the question as soon as it came out of my mouth.

He smiled and in a soft voice said, "You're as dumb as you look, aren't ya?" Then he raised his voice a dozen octaves and shouted, "Of course it hurts, ya dumbass I've walked a thousand miles on a broken leg."

I immediately came to attention and saluted him military fashion, "Sir, sorry for being a dumb ass, sir."

He laughed and softened his voice, "Let me tell you something son, if you don't expect much you won't get much."

Those words were worth the whole hike. They left a lasting impression on me as words to live by, "If you don't expect much you won't get much." My back and knees seemed to progressively improve each day with just the weight of carrying water and my lunch, which improved my confidence and motivated me to continue to dream of one day becoming a thru-hiker.

After I thought it through, I felt better emotionally as I limped into Dicks Creek Gap with Guns by my side. Two other hikers were already at the road. They called themselves the Broke Back Mountain Boys. They were the ones giggling in the other tent at Cheese Factory Campsite with Guns this morning. I wasn't about to try hitching a ride with four people, so I bid Guns goodbye and started hitching solo the eleven miles to Hiawassee.

My strategy of hitching alone worked as a man in a pickup truck named Denver, who was a local concrete contractor, stopped to give me a ride. He took me first to the Hiawassee Inn, which had no vacancy. The proprietor said he had a hiker with a dog who wanted a roommate to share the cost, but I declined because the last thing I wanted to do was share a room, especially with a dog. I started to panic, but Denver took me into town to Mull's Motel, where I got a room for fifty-five dollars.

Mull's Motel was an adventure in itself. A Vietnam vet and his ninety-year-old mother-in-law Miss Cordie ran Mull's Motel. Mull's had heat, but if you turned it on it roasted you out. The shower was hot, but it burned you out if someone in another room flushed the toilet. The sheets were clean, but the middle of the bed sagged. The room was equipped with a television, but it only got two fuzzy channels. Over all, it was a crummy room for fifty-five bucks, but it was heaven after being on the trail and sleeping on the cold hard ground. I jumped in the shower and washed five days worth of trail off. I can't describe how much I appreciated a hot shower. I stayed in long enough to run out of hot water.

It was so great to be in town. First, I went to Hardees for two cheeseburgers, a large order of curly fries, and a large cookies and cream milk shake. Then I went to the grocery store to buy enough supplies to get to Franklin, North Carolina, which was about three days north of Hiawassee. I then went to the drug store and bought a knee brace because I worried about my knee knocking me off the trail. I went back to the room, turned on the heat, stripped down, and ate a pint of Ben and Jerry's ice cream while I watched a fuzzy Mr. Ed on television. It was great.

Day 6   8.7 Miles

I slept fitfully because I found the soft bed uncomfortable as opposed to sleeping on the ground. I worried about my knee that stiffened up overnight and gave me a lot of pain. The police busted someone in front of the motel for drugs and the flashing red and blue lights kept me awake for quite a while. The traffic on the highway about twenty feet away didn't help either.

I got out of bed at daylight to go to McDonald's for scrambled eggs, sausage, hash browns and two sausage McMuffins. I sat enjoying coffee until the laundromat opened so I could wash my clothes. I stopped at the dollar store on the way back to the motel and bought baggies for my food. My knee began to feel better as it started to loosen up. I ran into Guns on my way home. He split a sixty dollar room at the Holiday Inn with the Brokeback Mountain Boys. Guns also got a free continental breakfast with his stay. I told him I got my room for fifty-five dollars. I didn't go into detail, but I felt a little jealous. He spent his evening drinking beer in the hot tub and then watched a HBO movie. He said, "The Boys both slept in the same bed, but I don't think they're gay." I thought for a city boy, Gun's was pretty naive, but I just looked at him and said nothing.

I had to chuckle inside because Guns's naive experience reminded me of when I was starting to get a passion for hiking. I tried to learn all I possibly could about long distance hiking on the Appalachian Trial, reading the usual books on the subject and bothering anyone I could who knew anything at all about hiking. I went to a local newsstand and asked the cute young girl who was standing behind the counter if they carried the magazine called, Backpacker.

She replied casually without looking up, "If we do it would be in that section over there." She pointed to a magazine rack at the far back of the little store. I scurried back and started to scan the magazines sporting scantily clad, good-looking young men on the covers.

When I discovered what section I was in and what she was talking about, I quickly did an about face and turned red as a beet saying, "No Missy, you got the wrong idea about me. Backpacker is the name of a hiking magazine; it's about hiking!" I found the magazine in the outdoor sports section after I regained my composure.

I went back to Mull's Motel. When I checked in the day before, the owner said he would shuttle me back to the trail. I arranged the ride, which I honestly thought fifty five dollars for the stay at the fleabag motel covered.

When I got in the car with all my gear he asked, "Do you need change?"

"Change for what?"

"The ride back."

"How much?"

"Twenty-five." I gave the greedy son-of-a-gun twenty-five bucks. Then he talked about the good old days in Vietnam all the way up the mountain. I said nothing because I was nursing my resentment. I was happy to get out of the car and back on the trail.

I ran into Guns at the trailhead. He hitched a ride with a pretty, young girl who asked him to buy some beer and drink it with her. He bought the beer, but got back on the trail. Apparently, after he bought the beer he found out she was in the eleventh grade in high school and was playing hooky. Oh yeah, her dad was also the chief of police in Hiawassee. I didn't say anything, I just took two ibuprofen tablets, tightened up the new knee brace, and took off. I quickly put some distance between him and me, with visions of him hanging from a tree in my head. I didn't know if I would ever see him again, but I didn't want to be around when or if the chief caught him.

I hiked solo out of Dicks Creek Gap and over Buzzard Knob. Two men and a six-year-old boy were catching crayfish in a sizable stream that ran parallel to the trail. I stopped to filter water and engaged them in a short conversation as I rested. They were catching the crayfish to eat later. I thought it was a lot of work for what little meat a crayfish provided, but I wished them luck and moved on.

I soon came upon two Native American women with incredibly large packs and a three-or four-year-old boy moving slowly. I was impressed with the young boy, who was also carrying a pack and apparently not complaining. They said nothing and made no eye contact, so I passed them in silence. They looked out of place. I wondered if they were with the two white men and the older boy I passed a couple of miles back.

The day was cold, clear, and sunny, which I found ideal for hiking. When the endorphins and ibuprofen kicked in, the pain started to subside. I got into a hiking rhythm and my confidence increased. I marched on expecting to reach the North Carolina border that day.

I previously hiked over eight hundred miles on sections of the Appalachian Trail as practice for my thru-hike. I took vacations and hiked anywhere from forty to a hundred-twenty miles on each attempt. I started out either hiking solo or with Scooter. I also recruited two more peers about my age. They all hiked with me on several occasions. We all seemed to catch the same infectious passion for the Appalachian Trail.

Those practice section hikes offered me some trail experience. I found the trail was a lot more challenging in reality than in my dreams. I even aborted one hike when I had an Achilles tendon injury going into a hundred miler, then both Scooter and I got dreadfully ill from a virus we apparently caught before we even started.

An old weather-beaten board with NC/GA carved on it, nailed to a maple tree snapped me back to the present. To my surprise, the tree indicated that I had hiked the eight miles to the Georgia/North Carolina border. A long time ago, someone attached a lead pipe to the side of the old maple tree that grew around it over the years. More recently, someone stuck orange and green plastic ribbons in it. I felt like celebrating my small victory having completed the hike through Georgia. Mount Katahdin still seemed like a million miles away, but I felt a bit more confident. I took a picture of the marker on the tree before I entered North Carolina.

I found a spring with clear, cold water and a lot of flat ground a little further north, so I made camp just inside the North Carolina border. Guns soon came in and joined me. I was happy to see he wasn't rotting in some north Georgia jail or hanging from a tree. Will, who chose the trail name Pyro because he's a good fire builder and enjoyed fire and Nick, who chose the name Grizzly because he sports a thick, full, black beard, came in and set up camp. We all cooked our dehydrated meals on our little compact, high-tech back packing stoves. The two men, two women, two young boys, and the big dog I passed earlier came in and set up camp. I was impressed with the ease and efficiency they went about settling in for the night. They all, even the four-year-old set about their individual tasks interacting with each other like a practiced team. When they started to gather wood for a fire, we all pitched in to help. One man set a couple of traps in hopes of catching a squirrel, possum, or anything they could eat. The other man filled a large kettle with water and put it on the fire. He jokingly said, "This is my cooking kit." I said, "It looks like a lot of work." He smiled saying, "It makes the difference between going to bed with a hot meal in your belly or not."

The water came to a boil and they started adding potatoes, carrots, crayfish, and some other ingredients to the pot. I watched all this unfold in awe. I wondered who carried the twenty-pound bag of potatoes. They were all from Maine. One of the men was the man with the dog at Hiawassee Inn who was looking for a roommate to share the cost of the room. He was single and old friends with the other man. They worked together on a commercial fishing boat among many other things. They didn't have much money, so he ran to the towns to bring back supplies to the rest of the family on the trail. The other man was a former thru-hiker, who was taking his wife and two sons on the trail to pass on his values. The women were sisters who appeared to be Native Americans. The one was single, but I sensed some sexual attraction between her and the man with the dog. I thought they would be together before long. After the food was finished cooking, the father offered to share it with us. Everyone declined because it was obvious they needed all the food they had. Besides, the rest of us already ate. I don't know how to describe in words the respect and admiration I had for these folks from Maine. Their integrity, values, and quiet, humble, strength astounded me.

We all gathered close around the fire for warmth and had a social party in celebration of hiking Georgia. We listened to the men from Maine tell tales of their adventures. The two little boys were lucky to have such fine role models. I found myself enjoying the evening tremendously in spite of the cold. The man from Maine told me to boil water in my cooking pot, pour it back in my water bottle, put the bottle in a sock, and curl up around it in my sleeping bag to stay warm. Gun's also told me, if it's too cold to sleep, eating a Snickers would produce enough energy to warm me up enough to fall asleep. I thought, how unlikely to have two teachers with totally different backgrounds. If I remained teachable, I would find many teachers along the trail.

Eventually we all retired to our tents like a family going to our bedrooms. I don't know who it was who started it, but we all said goodnight to one another from inside our tents. I said, "We're just like the Walton's." Everyone laughed, but I felt a sense of family. My knee seemed to be a lot better, but I worried that I might be taking too much ibuprofen. I sure wish I didn't have to worry all the time about something.

March 4   Day 7   15.4 Miles

It was cold enough that ice formed on the inside of my tent again. I woke sometime before daylight to eat a Snickers, which worked and warmed me up enough that I fell back to sleep until daylight. I got up and made hot coffee to share with Guns. The sun came out and the temperature warmed up before I left.

The hike out of Bly Gap was steep and a rude welcome to North Carolina, but I was glad it was the first thing in the morning. We hiked up Standing Indian Mountain, which was almost fifty-five hundred feet high and rather steep. I hiked with Guns part of the day, but dropped back to separate because he got on my nerves. I met a seventy-year-old German man from Tennessee named John who was hiking to the Smoky Mountain National Park. I hoped I could be still hiking when and if I got to be seventy.

I stopped at Carter Gap with Guns, John, Pyro, Grizzly, a hiker from Maine named Rambler, and others who stayed in the shelter whom I didn't know. More people arrived, which formed a carnival type of atmosphere. The extravert in me usually loves all the social contact, but that night it overwhelmed me, so I picked a spot away from the others for a little peace and quiet.

I remembered learning how to build small cooking fires in Boy Scouts, so I built a cooking fire as an experiment. I cooked a rice dinner to see how hard it would be if I ran out of gas for my stove because I wasn't sure exactly how long my little gas container would last. That night I learned that the fire I built took time and was messy. The temperature was too hot, burned my rice to the inside, and discolored the outside of my new titanium pot. The fire made my clothes smell like smoke and left a small burn mark on my beloved Mother Nature. My conclusion was my four-ounce stove and the twelve-ounce butane fuel canister was much faster, cleaner, and easier. I could also move it and start it in the rain, which alone made the extra pound well worth carrying. However, I felt a little more secure knowing I could always build a cooking fire if I had to.

I spent a lot of money on gear most of which was at home taking up space in my basement. When I first started, I went by what I thought I might need at any point, but soon I discovered I couldn't lift my pack. I learned when I carried everything I owned on my back, the trick was to carry everything I absolutely needed and nothing else. I learned a lot by trial, error, and from other hikers on the trail. I formed a self-imposed rule that if I carried something and didn't use it, I quit carrying it. The truth is the trail itself taught me how to hike it. I only had to be patient and observant and not try to force it or hurry it.

Pyro hurt his knee and my knee felt better, so I traded him my knee brace for two packs of Ramen noodles and a pack of rice. He got the best part of the deal, but I wouldn't have to hitch to Franklin to buy food supplies in two days.

That ended my first week on the trail. I hiked ninety miles. I felt satisfied with my hike so far. Over two thousand miles still stood between me and Katahdin, but I felt a sense of accomplishment because I stuck it out a week.

Day 8   15.2 Miles

I arose shortly after dawn to a cold, clear day. I climbed Albert Mountain, which stood a mile high and was the steepest mountain

I faced so far. An alternate route was on Bear Pen Trail to avoid the steep climb up to the summit, but no thru-hiker would ever think of using an alternate route unless there was absolutely, no other way. A fire tower stood at the summit where I met Guns, Pyro, and Grizzly. We all posed at the tower and took pictures of the Smoky Mountains to the north. I didn't realize how high a mile was until I stood on the stairs below the cabin on the fire tower and looked down at the houses and farmland in the valleys below. I wondered if God felt pleased or pissed when he overlooks what we humans created in his world.

Pyro complained about having poison ivy. He showed me the poison ivy on his side, but I thought it looked as if he had Shingles. I chose not to tell him because he planned to go into Franklin the next day to find a doctor. I decided to let the doctor tell him because I could have been wrong, but I had seen shingles before. I may have been right because I never saw Pyro or Grizzly again after that.

I hiked with Guns most of the day. I did something stupid. I was trying to keep up with Guns and adjust my radio at the same time. I took my eyes off the trail for an instant. I stumbled on an embedded rock and ran hard trying to catch my balance before I fell over a cliff. I wrenched my lower back as I was trying to catch myself. I felt lucky, because it could have been worse if I fell over the cliff. I guess I just needed something to cause me to worry.

I stealth camped with Guns and Taco by a stream close to the highway. Taco and Guns planned on hitching ten miles to Franklin in the morning. I was tempted to join them by the promise of restaurant food and a warm motel bed, but I elected to pass on Franklin. Instead, I planned to push on to Wesser and stay at the Nantahala Outdoor Center. I could buy supplies there in a couple days.

I cooked and ate with them, but retired to rest my back in my tent. I felt a little down and could have used some companionship, but I felt too physically uncomfortable to sit with them. I took three ibuprofen gel tabs before I isolated in my tent. I would truly have liked to end the day in sleep, but I had to wait until the ibuprofen kicked in.

CONVERSION

Day 9   16.3 Miles

We all packed up at daylight and left together in the rain. I bid Taco and Guns goodbye at the road to Franklin. They started hitching together. A trail angel left a case of orange pop at the road. I took two cans, which contained ninety calories each, to add to my pack for later. I hiked five miles mostly uphill, feeling melancholy with my pain and worries. I stopped to use a flush toilet with free toilet paper at a picnic area on Siler Bald Mountain. I wished for some other amenities such as a vending machine or pop machine, but had no such luck.

I was about to move on when a short, muscular, athletic looking man in his early thirties stopped. He was a thru-hiker named Bone Pic. I took an instant liking to him when we struck up a conversation. My mood improved immediately as I hiked on enjoying the company of my new friend. My mood improved even more as the rain stopped and we came upon a trail angel who set up a huge walk-in tent beside the trail. He gave us four Reese's Cups and a Coke each. We spent about half an hour sitting and jawboning about the trail before moving on. I didn't remember his name, but he said he planned to start a thru-hike of his own in a couple of weeks. I told him I would watch for him.

I found myself obsessing more and more about food, probably because I felt extremely hungry most of the time. I was in a situation where I didn't want to carry a lot of weight because I was afraid of further injury. The negative side to that, I wasn't carrying enough food and went hungry.

I deeply regretted not going into Franklin with Guns and Taco. They tried to tempt me into going along to an all you can eat buffet, but I wanted to stay on the trail. I don't quite understand why I didn't go, but for some reason I thought it would take up too much time. The bastards probably ate all they could then slept it off and ate again before they left town. They may have even been so full that they got a motel with a hot shower. I bet that was what they did and they got up, went to breakfast, and ate a couple of orders of eggs and biscuits smothered with sausage gravy before they left. I found myself nurturing resentments towards Guns and Taco. I thought, if Guns rubbed it in, I would smack that smirk right off his smart mouth.

I moved on, hiking with Bone Pic for a while, but he was hiking extremely light and fast. Reluctantly I dropped back. I felt all alone once again because I couldn't keep up with Bone Pic's pace. Alcoholics Anonymous had a slogan, One day at a time. I thought I would be happy when the day was over.

I hiked up and over Wayah Bald to another scenic, stone observation tower. I found myself wishing I had someone to share the view, but since I was all alone, I left without even taking a picture. I found a nice campsite with good water on the way down where I would have liked to stay, but couldn't bear the thought of spending the night alone. I kept moving, hopeful someone would be at Cold Spring Shelter about five miles north.

To my delight I found Bone Pic, a marijuana-smoking hiker named Mathewski, a girl named Juliann and her dog in the shelter when I arrived. I set my tent up on a campsite far enough from the shelter that if anyone snores it wouldn't keep me awake. The rain stopped hours ago and it turned dreadfully cold. I returned to the shelter for the company to cook and eat the last of the noodles that Pyro traded me. Bone Pic ate a cold bagel smothered in peanut butter and jelly. He didn't carry a stove or tent so he could travel light and hike faster. Juliann recently graduated college and was hiking with her Siberian husky. I thought Mathewski and she were together at first, but I now think that was only dreaming on Mathewski's part. I enjoyed socializing for a while until Mathewski started to roll a joint. I then returned to my tent because I never liked being around people smoking weed. While I was at the shelter Juliann's dog lifted his leg and peed on the side of my tent. I always hated dogs on the trail.

I had a small bag of peanuts, two Reese cups and some coffee that I had to save for the next day. Other than that, I was out of food and hungry. I was in my tent, my back hurt, I had all the clothes I owned on, and I was cold, hungry, and depressed. I knew I needed to look at the positive side and be grateful for what I had, so I put my journal away, laid back, turned out the light, and pulled the sleeping bag up over my head. I attempted to make a gratitude list. The only thing I could come up with was that I was grateful the day was over and I was looking forward to hitting Nantahala Outdoor Center the next day and eating until I couldn't move. It suddenly started raining again as if it was Mother Nature saying, F@#% you, as I escaped the day in sleep.

Day 10   11.7 Miles

I awoke shivering because it was extremely cold, but at least it stopped raining sometime in the night. I stayed in my sleeping bag later than I usually would until the sun shone through the walls of my tent. I heard the others as they left quietly then I finally climbed out of my warm bag. I was surprised when I emerged from my cocoon and found a white world. I thought it was raining in the night, but it must have been snowing instead. I hastily made coffee, packed up and shipped out by myself. I was moving a little slow due to the cold, wet night and my old bones.

I climbed Cooper Ridge Bald that stood a mile high with a great vista. It was a beautiful, cold, white, sunny morning. The North Carolina Mountains were breathtaking, but the trail was steep and dangerous. I had to be careful because my low back was still hurting from the near fall two days ago. I saw the Smoky Mountains for the first time from a fire tower on Wesser Bald Mountain. They were white, but so was the mountain I was on.

I hiked to the Nantahala Outdoor Center motivated by food, shower, and a room with heat. I came upon a two-time thru-hiker named Stump Knocker, who apparently fell on his way down the mountain in his haste and severely hurt his shoulder. Bone Pic and another hiker were already there when I arrived. We carried his gear and helped him down to the center so he could get help. I felt bad because it appeared that his hike was over.

He said, "You have to be especially lucky to be able to complete a thru-hike."

I realized my hike could end in an instant at any time. Katahdin was still two-thousand miles north, which seems almost impossible. The closer I got to Nantahala River the more excited I became in anticipation. I could hear the road noise, which was music to my ears. Someone might think I had been living in the wilderness for years. Road construction had traffic backed up, so we had to wait to cross the road. The Nantahala River is a major tourist attraction with its scenic setting and fast white water. An outfitter rented rubber rafts and kayaks to the adventuresome, but also sold hiking supplies and equipment. The Appalachian Trail crossed the river on the only bridge to restaurants and the state office rented rooms and beds at a bunkhouse.

I recalled that Alcoholics Anonymous had a slogan which said, "First things first," so I went straight to the restaurant with Stump Knocker, Bone Pic, Juliann, Mathewski, and two other hikers. We ate supper, family style at a table. I had the AYCE taco bar and I ate all I could eat and then some. Stump Knocker was in a lot of pain, but he ate while he waited for someone to come to take him to a hospital for help.

After I ate, I went to the state office and rented a private room at a motel for the night. Everyone else stayed in a bunkhouse for hikers, but I didn't like sleeping with other people when there was a choice. I paid for the room and they gave me a map to the motel. The bunkhouse was a lot cheaper, but I saved money in the account I started years ago. Every time I received an income tax return, bonus or any extra money, I deposited it in my thru-hiker account. I managed to save plenty of money, not only to pay for my thru-hike, but also to pay all my other bills at home. I also had enough to live on until I could get a job when I returned home. The money alleviated a lot of the stress over money that worried many hikers. I wasn't rich by any means, but I had enough for a private room. Before I went to my room, I stopped by the outfitters and bought fuel and enough food to reach Fontana Dam where I had a mail drop. I purposely ate before I bought supplies, so I wouldn't buy so much that I couldn't lift my pack. I was so full that I might have bought too little food.

The motel was the last place on top of the hill, all by itself. It was a two story building that had a living room with a cathedral ceiling. The private guest rooms were all off the main living room. My room was located on the second floor. I felt like I was being watched as I looked around. I said, "Hello," but the only answer was the hollow echo of my own voice. The hair stood up on my arms as I started to explore the place. My footsteps had a lonely, eerie sound on the hardwood floor. I felt like I was trespassing somewhere where I shouldn't be. I found the kitchen equipped with a refrigerator, microwave, sink, and a Bunn coffee maker. I soon found the coffee and made a pot of good coffee. I found my room upstairs at the end of the hall off the main living room, which was small with a single bed, mirror, and a small desk. A community bathroom with a shower was down the hall.

I thought I heard a couple talking downstairs, so I relaxed, thinking I wasn't alone anymore. I unpacked, left my pack in the room, and went back downstairs to get some coffee and socialize. I called out to the couple to see if they wanted some coffee, but the only response was the echo of my own voice. To my astonishment, no one was there. I got spooked instantly, the hair on the back of my head stood up and I went into an extra alert mode. I was the only guest there, so the place must be haunted. I suppressed the urge to panic and bolt out of there as if the place was on fire. I kept hearing footsteps and voices of other people, but there was nobody else there. I went to the bathroom and locked the door. I took a long hot shower and drank my coffee in the shower. When I came out of the shower, the place was dark. I went straight to my room and turned on the light. I thought a night in this place was scarier than camping at Indian Grave Gap. I locked my door, wondering if I could lock a ghost out.

I gave myself a pep talk; after all, I believed there was no such thing as ghosts, right. Besides if ghosts existed who said they would hurt me anyway? I was a full-grown man and men weren't scared of ghosts, right! I decided to go back to the kitchen to pour another cup of coffee. I armed myself with my hiking pole and my headlamp and ventured out to get a nice hot cup of coffee and shut the coffee pot off. The place was a lot spookier after dark. At first, I thought I had no cell tower, but I discovered, if I turned my phone a certain way and held it high I could get one bar. I put the phone on speaker and propped it up on top of the mirror so I could stand on a chair to call out. I called some friends in Alcoholics Anonymous who calmed me down. They reassured me and laughed as I laughed with them. I felt better afterward, but I would still be happy to see daylight come.

Day 11   11.7 Miles

I slept fitfully in the motel as many unexplainable things went bump in the night, but I survived okay. It was probably only raccoons anyway. I made fresh coffee, and took a shower. The sun was out and it looked like it would be a clear day. I went straight to the restaurant and waited for it to open. I was the first customer of the day and ordered a cheese omelet, toast, and home fries. The waitress, who opened the restaurant, appeared to be hung over. She told me the cook hadn't showed up yet, so she would cook my breakfast. The omelet was an extremely greasy cheese omelet with no cheese and greasy home fries. I complained and she brought another greasy omelet to me as I was finishing the first, but with cheese this time. I ate both omelets and all of everything else. I was about to leave when all my friends came in for breakfast. I stayed to drink coffee and socialize while they ate their breakfast. I wished I could start every day that way because I enjoyed the high from all the coffee and the social fix from my friends.

I hiked solo out of the gap and ascended six miles and three thousand feet steeply up Swim Bald Mountain. I fell into a trail dream in my head and climbed the mountain a little too fast, which aggravated my low back. The trail goes up steeply and then down. I thought the steep climbs made the pain in my back worse and I felt overwhelmed thinking of the two thousand miles left to Katahdin with all the pain. I took extra ibuprofen and tried to block out the pain with trail dreams, but I couldn't get my mind off the pain. I thought I could take it, just for the day.

I passed several southbound section hikers but the one who stood out the most was a heavy, out of shape girl. She was trying to catch up with her companions, who I passed hours before. We both took a break and chatted for a while. She was exhausted and needed to stop for the night, but was afraid to be alone. I tried to encourage her, but secretly didn't think she would catch her friends. She told me about a good water source and flat ground that was suitable for camping at Locus Grove Gap, which was a little farther north. I thanked her and thought I could stop there for the night. I invited her to stay with me and get a fresh start in the morning, but she declined, wanting to push on. I could have used the company, but we parted as she went south and I went north, never to meet again. It wasn't far to Locus Grove Gap where I found the unofficial campsite exactly where she told me it was. I wanted to go another five miles to make it closer to Fontana Dam, but decided to cut the day short due to my lower back pain.

I found the water source and a reasonably flat piece of real estate that I called home. I was stealth-camped alone just out of sight of the trail. I made tuna and noodles for supper and then put on my warm nightclothes.

I was using the last daylight to enter in my journal when someone called out, "Hey Dreamer." I didn't recognize the voice, so I didn't respond.

I heard "Hey Dreamer," again.

I hesitantly responded "Yo."

A formidable looking hiker appeared who I didn't recognize at first and said, "Want some company?" His name was Rambler, a hiker who I met a couple of days before. The girl who told me about the campsite told him I needed company, so he stopped in and set up with me. I was grateful to her and happy for his company. Rambler was forty-one and about the closest to my age of any thru-hiker so far. He was originally from Pennsylvania, but moved to Maine some time ago. We cooked and ate together. I cooked a second supper of tuna and noodles that was for the next night. I hoped I would be at Fontana dam and eating someone else's cooking by the next night.

I continued to be amazed at how fast strong friendships form on the trail. We talked into the night about everything, so I felt as if we were old friends when we turned in. I thought we would stay good friends long after the trail. His company sure got my head off my pain and loneliness. I drifted off to sleep with a renewed conviction that I could be a thru-hiker.

Day 12   17.1 Miles

17.1 Miles, plus two more miles off trail

I slept better than I thought I would and awoke to a cloudy day enthused, refreshed, and inspired. Rambler said his radio predicted thunderstorms as we chatted during breakfast and coffee. I hiked out solo with my thoughts and fears while he was still drinking coffee. The pain in my lower back started increasing as I climbed at a fast pace with a purpose.

I stopped for lunch at Hog Back Gap and cooked macaroni and cheese. It seemed each state in the south had a ridge or mountain named Hog Back. I felt I had good news and bad news. The good news was my pack was light, but the bad news was I only had two small bags of peanuts, a pack of cheese crackers, and some coffee left. That was the consequences I got for gorging before I bought supplies. I looked forward to the mail drop with supplies that waited ahead at Fontana dam, but that was still ten trail miles plus two road miles away. I didn't think I could go another mile let alone twelve miles.

I wasn't sure if I believed in such things, but I heard that God wouldn't give you more than you can handle. I had four coffee bags, so I put two in my pot, filled it with water, and lit my stove. I sat there with tears in my eyes, wallowing in self-pity. God must have known I had more than I could handle so he sent help. I looked up and saw Rambler. Now Rambler was the type who I normally wouldn't want to meet in a dark alley, but he sure was a welcome sight for my sore eyes. Rambler was quick to set up his stove and put on some coffee for himself. He ate a cold lunch while waiting for his coffee. We chatted like old friends who hadn't seen each other for a long time. I hadn't seen him in only six hours, but we talked as if we had been away from each other for a decade.

We packed up and hiked out together. Rambler hiked faster than I did normally, but I kept up with him for the company to stay out of my head and keep my mind off the pain. There even might have been a little male competition as we hiked, so we covered a lot of ground. We arrived at Cable Gap Shelter later in the afternoon. Rambler elected to stay for the night and hike to Fontana in the morning. I took my pack off, made the last of my coffee, and ate my last two bags of peanuts.

I told Rambler the weather was holding, so I decided I was going to push on six miles to Fontana Dam and the motel. He tried to persuade me to stay and hike into Fontana the next morning with him.

He said, "Besides, you're tired and a storm is coming. We will be safe here in the shelter." Rambler was making sense and I would liked to have stayed to rest my back and have his company. I was facing a nine-hundred-foot climb up to the rocky summit of Black Gum Mountain with a thunderstorm predicted. Being caught in a violent storm in the high country was the last thing I wanted to do.

I didn't tell Rambler I was out of food. I was sure if I said something, he would have shared what he had with me. I was too proud to ever ask or even let him know I was hungry. I hated to go to bed hungry, so I took two more ibuprofen, washed them down with the last of my coffee, saddled up, and started my ascent up Black Gum. I tried not to make a big deal out of it, but I had some fear and mental reservations. I sure wish I had the foresight to buy a little more food at Nantahala when I had the chance. I secretly took a vow to myself I would never put myself in a situation where I needed food again. I might have to carry a heavier pack and not eat two meals at once, but I wouldn't have to take risks and move on to get food.

I purposely occupied my mind thinking about food to try to keep from focusing on the pain in my back. A question I had early on was, what kind of food do you take on a hike. I knew I would be limited as to what I could carry and wanted to get the most calories for the weight. Once on an early section hike, Scooter and I both purchased five freeze-dried bacon and scrambled egg meals at Gander Mountain for a five-day hike. About three breakfasts into the hike another hiker spread crunchy peanut butter on a bagel and smothered it with strawberry jam as we were eating our watery scrambled bacon and eggs. That was the first time Scooter ever saw me drool. I remembered Scooter saying, this crap is rancid, as she choked down her eggs.

I discovered that whatever other hikers had to eat always looked more appetizing than the crap I carried. I soon found the food on the trail changed as you got sick of the same old stuff. Ramen noodles were usually one staple because they were lightweight, cheap, filling, and it doesn't take much fuel to cook a hot meal. A can of tuna added to a pack of noodles Alfredo qualified as another nutritious treat on the trail.

I ate most of the different brands of nutrition/protein bars and after a while, they all tasted sort of like chocolate-covered sawdust. A Snickers candy bar in my opinion, stood alone as the best nutrition bar in the entire world. I bought them ten at a time and every chance I got. They made a good desert, breakfast, or any time snack. I especially liked to spread about a half inch of peanut butter over the whole thing and wash it down with a cup of trail coffee late in the day. I could squeeze a couple more miles out of my tired old ass, but I also thought eating so many Snickers may have turned my hair white. I could have used about five snickers right then. I realized once again, I was obsessing over food, but at least my mind was off the pain.

I still had a little over three hours of daylight to hike six miles. I soon found out how big of a climb nine-hundred feet truly was. I tried to focus on how desperately I needed a zero-mile day and all the good things that were waiting at Fontana. The sky got darker and it started rumbling. When I thought I was at the top of my last climb into Fontana, I stopped to catch my breath. I was feeling sorry for myself again and thought what a fool I was to have left the shelter. I was gazing to the west and suddenly realized that the blue I was looking at through the trees was Fontana Lake. I continued to be amazed at how quickly my emotions could go from whale crap at the bottom of the ocean to a pink cloud so high over such a little thing as seeing a lake. A little thing called hope was what made the difference.

I was still four steep downhill miles away from Fontana. The guidebook said there was a campsite with a water source less than a mile away. I could set up off the summit in an emergency if the storm hit. I reached the campsite in no time and took a break to filter water, which was so cold I couldn't drink it fast, but it tasted so good. The storm was coming in any minute, but I already decided to keep on keeping on to a motel. I took a quick look at the guidebook and weighed my options. A house-phone was at the information board in the parking lot at the highway. I could call Fontana Village to pick me up, so that became my next goal.

I faced a steep, fourteen-hundred-foot descent to the road at Fontana Dam. I had to take my time due to the pain in my back and for safety's sake, but on the other hand, I was racing with the oncoming darkness and, to add a little incentive, lightning was starting to light up the not so distant sky. I beat both the darkness and the storm to the highway and felt a little Froggy. I soon found the house phone, but the bad news was it didn't work and I didn't have cell tower. A pay phone was in the parking lot, but it didn't work either. I also found a pop machine that didn't work. The restroom had a heater that worked, so I washed my hands with warm water.

I watched the last of daylight fade away as I started hitchhiking the two miles to Fontana Village. I hate to hitch anyway and hitching in the dark could be dangerous, so after several cars passed without stopping, I decided to suck it up and walk the two miles. I passed a closed convenience store and became discouraged. A lady with a North Carolina accent stopped and said, "Git in before ya drown!" I got in and she took me straight to the Fontana Village office where she worked. I registered and paid eighty dollars for two nights.

I asked, "Where could I get something to eat?"

The girl behind the desk said, "I'm sorry darling, but everything's closed this time a night."

I replied, "No big deal." I had already spotted two vending machines and I had a stash of fifty crisp, new one-dollar bills in my pack for exactly that kind of situation. I bought several candy bars, two small bags of potato chips, and four pops. The clerk at the desk gave me a bag to carry all my high-calorie junk food.

The girl who gave me a ride said, "Git back in the car, and I'll take ya to your room, cause it's gonna storm any second." She drove me through a maze of small condominium-type structures until she pulled up to one and said, "You're home!" I don't think I could have found the place by myself that night.

I grabbed my pack while she carried my bag of goodies and hiking poles in to make sure everything was in order before she left. I thanked her and went to shake her hand, but she grabbed me and gave me a big hug saying, "Have a nice stay, Sweetie." I said to myself, God bless the people in the south.

The room was more like an efficiency apartment with a microwave, small refrigerator, and tiny coffee maker with two small bags of coffee. I started to dive into the potato chips when I stopped. Probably for the first time in my life when I was alone, I bowed my head and said grace. I ate first, then jumped in the shower. The hot water felt so good on by back I stayed in until I ran out of hot water. The storm must have finally hit while I was in the shower. I opened the outside door to watch the thunder, lightning and pouring rain. I felt so grateful to be safe and dry in the motel. I sincerely hoped my friend Rambler was okay up on the mountain. I had no cell tower to call anyone, so I turned on the television and started to watch, but that was the last thing I remembered.

Day 13   Zero Miles

My first zero miles day

I awoke in the night, turned the television off, and went back to sleep until daylight. The morning sun was shining in when I awoke the second time. I felt stiff all over and my lower back was especially tight, but I hoped it would loosen up as I got active. It was my first scheduled zero-day, so I was in no hurry. I started coffee in the little coffee maker then jumped in the shower. I turned the hot water as high as I could stand it and stayed in as long as I could to let the hot water do its magic on my back. The storm in the night passed, so I ventured out into a crisp, clear, sunny, day to forage in the village.

I found the post office beside a camp store and picked up the package

I sent to myself from home on January the fifteenth, which seemed like an awfully long time ago. The lady at the post office was hiker helpful and instructed me on how to send the package ahead, which hikers called, bouncing a package ahead. She gave me an address label to put over my original address so I could use the same box to repack and bounce my package to my next town stop at Hot Springs, North Carolina.

I bought a large coffee and two honey buns at the camp store before I returned to the motel. When I got back to the motel, I opened my package. I felt like it was Christmas because I had forgotten all the things I sent myself. I plugged in my cell phone battery charger first because I had five batteries that needed charged. I refilled my empty food bag with enough supplies from the mail drop to get to Gatlinburg. Gatlinburg would be my next planned resupply. I packed everything I didn't need back into the box. I rechecked my gear again, but didn't find anything else I could leave out. I decided to carry my cell phone battery charger so I could recharge my extra phone batteries any time I came to an electric outlet. The post office closed at noon, so I hurriedly packed up my laundry and off I went.

First, I mailed the package to myself at Hot Springs. The post lady taped the box shut free. She told me she did that for all the thru-hikers. I thanked her sincerely before I went next door to the little Laundromat and washed my dirty clothes. I stopped at the camp store and bought a phone card since I didn't have cell tower. I also bought some frozen dinners I could cook in the microwave in my room. I bought three ice cream bars, three donuts, a honey bun, and a lot of good coffee for a second breakfast as I waited for my clothes to wash and dry. I gorged on the junk food as I finished my laundry.

Rambler limped into town after surviving the storm fine, but he fell, broke his trekking pole, and injured his knee on the descent into Fontana. He already checked into a room and was on his way to the outfitter to see if he could fix his pole. We planned to get together for supper that night.

I stopped at the outfitter on my way back to my room hoping to find Rambler, but he already left. I didn't know what room he was in, but hoped to find him later. I didn't find anything I needed at the outfitter, however, I bought two gourmet backpacking meals as a treat for myself on the trail. I spent the rest of the day in my room making phone calls with a phone card to my friends in Alcoholics Anonymous. My long-time friend, Jimmy 3X5 and I talked for over an hour, which was longer than we talked at one time since he first sobered up years ago.

A unique worldwide society known as Alcoholics Anonymous, which most people fondly call AA for short lives surreptitiously among us almost everywhere, even in most small towns in America. I don't recall where I first heard of Alcoholics Anonymous, but it was most likely in a bar. I do remember a riddle:

Question: What's the difference between a drunk and an alcoholic?

Answer: Drunks don't have to go to meetings.

The first contact I had with AA was on the twenty-third of July in 1977. My first wife had it with my drinking and violent behavior, so she left me. I don't recall how I got the number, but I called a hotline. I had no intention to quit drinking, but I wanted to scam my wife into coming back. The lady on the phone introduced herself by her first name and as an alcoholic. She was friendly and not at all pushy as I expected. She answered my questions honestly and didn't try to sell me something.

AA is a program of attraction, not promotion and does not advertise or try to build its membership through recruitment. Local groups usually supported and maintained hotlines where people could call for help as I did. Volunteer members usually manned these hotlines. Individual members may also visit people who request help, which they call a Twelve-Step Call.

I was amazed to see how many local meetings there were when I first started. Two weekly meetings were in the small town I came from that I never heard of, even jokingly. I found at least one meeting weekly in most small towns around where I lived even in 1977. I attended my first meeting that same day in July and have been attending on a regular basis ever since to recover from my addiction to drugs and alcohol. I relapsed a lot in the first three years, but have managed to stay sober continuously from all drugs and alcohol since May twenty-fourth, 1980. I didn't do it all by myself, but with the help of the many loving people in the program who loved me when no one else could.

I spent the day resting my back, which was giving me big trouble as often as I could. I couldn't find Rambler to eat supper with, so I made microwave fried chicken and pizza, which I topped off with coke and ice cream and ate my supper alone. I worried about the knee injury Rambler received from the fall on the descent, but he was tough. He should be all right.

The only time I could get a shuttle back to the trail was at five-thirty the next morning. I planned to take on the Great Smoky Mountain National Park. I had the alarm set for four o'clock, so I would have the time to take a shower and eat breakfast.

March 11   Day 14   14.9 Miles

I awoke, took a long shower, and tried to eat two pizzas with my coffee, but couldn't get all the pizza down at four-thirty in the morning. Mike, the third shift maintenance man, picked me up at five-thirty on the spot. He took me back through the maze of motels. We chatted all the way to the parking lot. I don't think I would have been able to find my way back to the trail in the dark. He was a great guy and didn't want any money for the ride, but I gave him five dollars anyway.

I filled out my Great Smoky National Park permit I picked up at the trailhead. I went into the restroom, which had an electric heater that kept the pipes from freezing. I wished I would have had to take a dump because I knew it would be the last time for a while, that I found free toilet paper and could wash my hands with warm water. I waited at the dam for daylight, but it was too cold to stand by idly. The guidebook said it was a mile to the dam itself, so I donned my headlamp and started out. I found it wasn't hard to hike in the dark.

My lower back quickly became severely painful, so I contemplated the worst-case scenario. I thought perhaps I had a stress fracture in my spine. I had stress fractures before in my lower back, but not in the last twenty-two years, since I took medication to strengthen my bones. I knew I had to get my mind off the negative thoughts or I might psych myself off the trail. I carefully went slowly with the extra weight of my supplies. I even stopped to leave some food on the trail to lighten my pack. My thoughts focused on aborting the hike and I knew the whole mission was in jeopardy. I was afraid if I didn't quit right then I wouldn't be able to until I got out of the Smoky's or worse, the Park Rangers might have to rescue me. I knew my own thinking was becoming my worst enemy. I felt as if I had more than I could handle again, so I stopped to ask for help. I took my pack off, got down on my knees, and prayed, God, I have more than I can handle alone, please send help right now! Thanks.

I tried to recall some of the pain I previously was able to overcome to continue to carry my dream this far. I was no stranger to the physical pain of hiking. Besides the knee injuries and surgery that followed, I have received several other injuries while hiking that I had to learn to cope with to keep on hiking.

I was on a sixty-five mile section hike in Pennsylvania, which was the longest hike I ever attempted at that time. I twisted my right ankle on the rocks about five miles into the hike. I had to stop and soak the ankle in the icy mountain streams to numb it to keep the swelling down enough to get my boot on to keep hiking. I took a lot of ibuprofen, but managed to finish the hike in spite of the injury. Finishing the hike boosted my confidence in my ability to thru-hike.

On my next hike, I injured the plantar fascia in my left foot. The tendon tightened up and became extremely painful. I eventually went to a specialist to have orthotic inserts made that I wore in my shoes at all times to prevent further injury. I received a stress fracture in my left foot on Maryland's, Devil's Racecourse, which took eight weeks to heal. I strained my Achilles tendon on West Virginia's Roller Coaster, which bothered me for almost two years. I have come to expect blisters and sore muscles as part of hiking. Pain and injuries were an annoying part of all sports and distance hiking was no exception. In spite of all the pain and adversity, I became more and more confidant that one day I could thru-hike. The injuries were a small price to pay compared to the huge mental, emotional, and physical benefits from hiking.

I felt a little better as I thought my past pain was a gift that gave me hope that I could overcome my situation. I knew to quit would be a fatal blow, not only to my dream of thru-hiking, but it would also leave me insecure about any of my future aspirations. I always felt quitting can become a bad habit to get into. The Marines have a slogan, Pain is weakness leaving the body. I guess I'll be stronger after I thru-hike the trail. At least I felt inspired to continue.

I broke out of the woods at the top of a hill and behold there was Fontana Dam at sunrise. I took a picture because it was such a splendid sight. I looked at the sunrise and said another prayer. This time I closed my eyes and simply said, Thank You. I felt more like a grateful winner as I moved on. When I approached closer to the dam, I saw a lone hiker crossing the dam. I identified him from a quarter of a mile away as the seventy-year-old German by his stride and hiking poles that were extended higher than most hikers. I felt a little jealous at first because he was hiking at seventy. Then I thought, now there goes a winner. I would have liked to talk to him for inspiration. I soon went negative again thinking, there was no way I could hike fast enough to catch him.

It was full daylight when I got to the dam and the old hiker was gone. My back was starting to loosen up a little, so I felt better. I was experiencing déjà vu from the first time I hiked the Smoky's in 2004 with a friend. I remembered my back was in pain that day also. I had the insecure feeling about being on my own as his wife dropped us off and drove away. That hike was successful, but I had to overcome the pain involved. I previously section hiked the next seventy-one miles in the Great Smoky Mountain National Park, so I was on familiar ground again as I crossed the dam. I entered the park, and started up the thirty-three-hundred foot ascent in the next three miles up Shuckstack Mountain. The pain in my lower back started to escalate as I climbed, becoming an eight on a scale from one to ten. I could hardly bear it and thought I would have to abort my hike and fail if I had a stress fracture. I thought setting such a grandiose goal as thru-hiking the Appalachian Trail at fifty-five-years-old was stupid. I was contemplating returning to the dam and calling home, but instead with tears in my eyes, I prayed again. That time I said, God I surrender to your will and if it is your will that I turn back, let Thy will be done.

I soon came upon the seventy-year-old hiker, who stopped to catch his breath. His name was Joachim, but he said, "Call me John it's easier to pronounce." John was a red-haired, salty seventy-year-old man from Knoxville, Tennessee who spoke with a heavy German accent. He was rather small in stature, but had an aura about him that commanded respect. He went by the trail name Heaven Bound and I had already heard he was a Christian from Guns. Guns appeared to be an atheist and was rigidly outspoken about it. Guns debated with John over their beliefs and I thought Guns lost.

Joachim asked me what was wrong. I wasn't sure how he knew something was wrong or why I spilled my guts to a stranger, but I did.

He asked me, "Are you a saved Christian?" I thought a minute, knowing the answer had to be as honest as I could be.

I replied, "I would have to say no, but I am seeking." Joachim and I sat down on a log as he got out a small pocket-size, white Bible. He would read some passages and then have me read. We prayed together.

I could remember him asking, "Do you accept Jesus Christ as your savior?"

I responded, "Yes." I didn't feel as if a lot changed right then, but I did feel as if I made a commitment.

Rambler came by, but he could see we were into something, so he simply said, "Hi," then moved on. I had no way of knowing how long Joachim and I sat there praying. We had no water to cook a meal, so we shared a cold lunch before moving on. We hiked to the summit of Shuckstack Mountain together. I knew I was holding him back and could no longer keep up. Joachim was getting off the trail that night and it was getting late. He had to rendezvous with his son-in-law at Cades Cove and daylight was fading fast. I hugged him goodbye and watched him slowly disappear into the woods. I have had contact with Joachim by mail and phone, but as it turned out that was the last time, I would ever physically see him. I have ever since wondered if he was an angel sent from heaven with the trail name, Heaven Bound.

I hiked solo the rest of the day. I reached the summit of Doe Knob at four-thousand, five hundred feet and noticed my back was still hurting, but I wasn't so worried about it anymore because I was lost in prayer and meditation. I felt that if it was God's will I thru-hiked then He would take care of me. I arrived at Mollies Ridge, but it felt too early to stop for the night. I didn't want too much idle time to think, so I moved on two and a half miles to Russell Field Shelter where I stopped for the night. I arrived late and the shelter was full of spring breakers. I set up my tent outside of the shelter along with Rambler, Guns, and Mathewski who were already in their tents.

Joachim had left the Appalachian Trail here before I arrived to take the five mile trail to Cadies Cove. He gave me the little white Bible he inherited from his mother when she died. It must have meant a lot to him and it meant a lot to me. I read from the Bible and then I prayed. I felt like I was praying to someone other than myself that night. I suddenly recalled the words of a Canadian spoken at an Alcoholics Anonymous convention when he said his sponsor told him, Yes, there is a God and it ain't you.

Day 15   16.4 Miles

I started early and hiked solo with my thoughts for most of the day. The mountains and views seemed to be untouched by man. I loved to dream, so when the endorphins kicked in, I started dreaming a trail dream and the miles melted away. My back pain still annoyed me, but it didn't seem as intimidating as before.

With the encounter with Heaven Bound still fresh on my mind, my trail dream turned towards the differences between Alcoholics Anonymous and Christianity. Alcoholics Anonymous is a fellowship made up of people who feel they have a problem with alcohol and wish to stay sober and recover. I often heard outsiders call Alcoholics Anonymous an organization or a twelve-step support group. The fellowship isn't evangelistic, believing in a program of attraction, and doesn't promote itself too often. The fellowship of AA is made up of all walks of life. It doesn't matter if you're a man or woman, rich, poor, black, white, gay, straight or any socioeconomic class in today's society. No matter who you are or what you have done in the past, no one looks down on you. I believe the fellowship is the most open-minded society I have ever had the privilege to be acquainted with. We are non-denominational and not a religion although, we are spiritually based. Individual members ought not to impose their personal religious beliefs on one another. Members often share their spiritual insights and awakenings openly, but encourage new members to find a personal God of their understanding who they can believe in.

I personally found Alcoholics Anonymous attractive because instead of telling me what to believe, what to do, or what not to do they let me figure things out for myself with God's help. We support ourselves through the contributions received from passing the hat and decline any and all outside contributions or donations. Most folks put in a dollar now days, but no one ever chastises anyone for not contributing. The only thing they want to know about you is your first name or whatever you would like other members to call you. I was suspicious in the beginning when I first started to attend meetings. I wondered what they really wanted and thought, sooner or later, this was going to cost me something. I didn't have to fill out an application for membership. The only requirement for membership is a desire to stop drinking. When I first attended, the creed said, An honest desire to stop drinking. They took the word honest out of the creed a short while after I first started to attend. I was so narcissistic at the time I thought they took out the word honest because of me, since I wasn't capable of being honest about anything at the time.

The fellowship tries to stay low key and doesn't wish to engage in any controversy. Long before Alcoholics Anonymous existed, there was an earlier movement called the Washingtonians. They took a pledge that they would never drink again and supported one another at meetings much like Alcoholics Anonymous. The movement worked and the membership built quickly. The Washingtonians became more powerful as their numbers increased and they started to take a stand on politics and other causes such as slavery and temperance. The outside issues caused dissention within the membership and brought on controversy from the opposing sides. That turned out to be fatal to the Washingtonians. The movement failed to survive and soon history swallowed it up. When Bill Wilson and Dr. Bob Smith founded Alcoholics Anonymous in 1935, Bill Wilson never even heard of the Washingtonians. To my knowledge, even the Oxford Group, which was the inspiration for Alcoholics Anonymous no longer exists for the same reason. The early fellowship learned a lesson from the Washingtonians and has no opinion on any outside issues, so their name ought never be brought into public controversy.

The early members decided the fellowship shouldn't own anything so problems of money, property, or prestige doesn't interfere with their primary purpose. They hold meetings anywhere they can rent the room such; as churches, schools, any public, or private building, but landlords do not influence the principles of AA. Sometimes landlords terminate the agreement for some reason or the membership out grows the room, so the home group members simply move.

Alcoholics Anonymous never was a treatment facility, does not affiliate itself with any treatment facilities, and does not lend our name to any therapeutic or other outside interests. We don't get involved in mental disorders, domestic, financial, or legal problems as such. Our primary purpose is to stay sober and help others achieve sobriety. We as a group don't enable others; however, some members often help individuals with other issues. One of the reasons why the program strongly suggests folks get a sponsor is the sponsor often helps the sponsee address some of the outside issues.

I abruptly snapped out of my head when I caught up to Guns and Rambler at the summit of Thunderhead, which was over fifty-five-hundred feet high. They posed for a picture at a man-made pile of rocks called a cairn to mark the summit. They stood there unsmiling with their hands on their hips like two gunfighters looking for trouble, with the magnificent vista from Thunderhead in the background.

I hiked solo over Cold Spring Knob at a mile high and Silers Bald at over fifty-six-hundred feet and made good time. I stopped early at Double Springs Shelter and rested my back for the night. Five section hikers were already in the shelter, so I only took off my pack and rested. I socialized with them to make friends, but I wanted to see how many more hikers came in before I set up.

The Smoky Mountain National Park required reservations to stay at the shelters from all section hikers. Thru-hikers had to have a permit, but reservations weren't required. However, thru- hikers had to yield the shelter to section hikers with reservations if the shelter filled up.

I didn't like staying in the shelters anyway because they were always dirty and stinky. Bugs, spiders, mice, and rats also lived in them. They were sometimes crowded with hikers who snore and when everyone geared up to leave in the morning, it was always chaotic. The shelters in the Smoky's also had a chain link fence over the front to keep the bears out, which gave me a claustrophobic feeling. Many colleges were on spring break, so I anticipated the shelter would fill up before long.

Soon, thru-hikers started showing up one by one. They didn't wait, they just started to pitch tents outside the shelter. They were right, because soon several section hikers filled the shelter and started to squabble over room. Guns, Rambler, Mathewski, Juliann, and I camped on a semi-flat piece of ground about fifty yards from the shelter. We thru-hikers usually preferred to stick together anyway.

The section hikers built a big fire and started to gather around socializing in a carnival type of party atmosphere. We joined them, which made about twenty people all having about as much fun as we could have with each other. I still was amazed at how quickly complete strangers bonded and became good friends on the trail.

A section hiker named John Youngblood gave me two packs of Ramen noodles and Rambler gave me a dehydrated meal, so I wouldn't have to stop at Gatlinburg the next day for supplies. I could re-supply at Davenport Gap in three days. We talked and told stories well into the night. I felt so good it was hard to remember feeling bad only the day before.

I retired to my tent, which I thought of as my bedroom. The sounds of the other hikers went silent, but I could not sleep. I found myself reminiscing over the importance of my meeting with Heaven Bound. I spent a lot of time avoiding Christians because I didn't want to hear what they had to say. I thought they were a bunch of egotistical, self-righteous hypocrites. I didn't see any of that in Heaven Bound and I didn't feel judged by him. He seemed sincere, caring, and had a message to carry.

It occurred to me that maybe I was the judgmental one, judging the Christians. I wondered if the philosophies of Christianity and Alcoholics Anonymous could co-exist. I wondered if they were a lot alike, but presented differently. I had so many questions and wondered where I could find answers I could trust. I knew that I made a decision the day before with Heaven Bound and had some things to do and some questions to ask. I laid in my tent meditating for a long time about what I had to do next to carry out the decision that I made to turn my will and my life over to the care of a God as I personally understood Him.

I didn't have to solve everything then, so I decided to simply say thanks to the God who I was grateful to for the good day. The day was a picture perfect day to hike in the Smoky's, so it was easy to focus on the positive and not the pain or other negative stuff. Things such as back pain seemed worse when I focused on them.

I felt blessed as I eventually surrendered my consciousness to the Smoky Mountain night.

THE PLAY

Day 16   14.2 Miles

I awoke at daylight to the pleasant smell of wood smoke from the fire the night before. I walked out of sight of the others to relieve myself when I heard the familiar sound of a gobbler announcing morning to the world. I happened to have my turkey call in my shirt pocket for just that type of occasion. I called out a few sweet hen yelps and a gobbler fired back a double gobble immediately.

Suddenly Guns appeared from behind a tree pulling up his pants. He ran over to me with wild eyes and whispered, "What the heck was that?"

"Haven't you ever heard a turkey before?"

"In the city we eat them all the time, but they don't say much."

I looked him in the eye and said, "This ain't the city." I called again and two gobblers answered.

"Would you quit that."

"What?"

His eyes were popping by this time as he asked, "What if they come in here? Don't they bite or something?"

Lord, please forgive me because I couldn't help myself when I said, "Bite, Naw! That's the last thing you need to worry about this time of year." I paused for the effect.

Guns, "Then what do I have to worry about"

"This is the breeding season, so all you have to worry about is getting raped"

His eyes popped as he questioned, "Raped?"

I said, "That's why we country folk usually sit with our back up against a tree with a shot gun in our hands when we call um." Once again, I paused for him to ponder what I said before I added, "They're a fat, mean, hateful, bird, but you're the one who's teasin' them."

Guns looked horrified, "Teasing them?"

"Yea, your ges eggen um on when ya dropped your pants an stuck your lily white ass out in front of um." I paused with a straight face for the affect, "After all, everybody knows you have to get off the ground."

His eyes popped once again as his voice rose, "What?"

I know I had him so I continued saying, "When ya poop ya have to get up in a tree so you're off the ground. Everybody knows a turkey can't breed ya if en he can't get his feet on solid ground, so the next time ya have to take a dump just get in a tree and he'll leave ya alone." Guns watched the expressions on my face intently for a hint that I was kidding, but I kept the muscles in my face as smooth as glass. He may not have taken me altogether that seriously, but I noticed him eyeing up a couple of trees as I left. I walked away figuring I gave Guns something to think about while he was on the trail later that day.

Things were buzzing when I returned to camp. Everyone was busy cooking, packing, or trying to sort out their gear from the tangled mess of gear in the shelter. I cooked oatmeal and coffee on the community fire with the others. Someone was cooking bacon; I loved the smell of bacon cooking.

The day was crystal clear, and cold. I broke camp and headed out late for me. Just by coincidence, Mathewski was leaving at the same time, so we hiked together most of the morning. We trudged through a foot or better of old, hard packed snow, which they simply called, hard pack. The hard-pack in the high country was the result of many winter snowstorms, packed by hikers until it was as solid as a rock. The hiking was difficult because it was like hiking on rocks or uneven concrete, but we were careful and hiked slow.

I would always remember that day, as the day I twelfth stepped Mathewski. I knew Mathewski smoked a bowl or two of marijuana every night. He asked me why I never smoked with him. I told him I was a recovering addict. I then shared my story with him as he shared his story with me. He was attempting to recover from a heroin and cocaine addiction. He came from Philadelphia's inner city where he made his living as a male prostitute, a drug dealer, and a thief. He did whatever he had to do to get the drugs he needed to survive.

Mathewski attempted a thru-hike a couple of years ago but had to abort at Neels Gap. He seemed more determined this year because he was HIV positive and wanted to complete the Appalachian Trail before he died. He went to some AA meetings in Philadelphia and had some knowledge of the program. The time with him probably helped me more than him, as it felt right to connect at this high of a spiritual level with another addict. I admired him in the sense he was doing what he wanted to do before the inevitable happened instead of giving up. I often heard Alcoholics Anonymous members say, I know I have another drunk in me, but I don't know if I have another recovery in me.

My thoughts drifted back to the girl at Neels Gap who was aborting her hike because she hurt her knee. I wonder if she would ever be fortunate enough to get a second chance at her thru-hike. I became spiritually aware that God was talking to me through Alcoholics Anonymous, Mathewski, and the girl. Sometimes I got a second chance, but I could never count on it because sometimes I didn't. I made myself a promise that if I had the opportunity to begin anything I must muster the tenacity to strive for succeed to the finish. Things almost never went smoothly for long and often it took courage to endure the adversity that stood before success. My eyes filled with tears of gratitude for my opportunity to thru-hike and the knowledge I may never pass this way again.

The morning passed quickly and before we knew it, we were at the summit of Clingmans Dome, which at six-thousand, six-hundred and forty-three feet tall, was the highest point in not only in the Smoky Mountain National Park, but also the entire Appalachian Trail. The alpine vegetation at that altitude reminded me of the Canadian bush with small pines and thick under growth. An elaborate observation deck, with a spiraling ramp for the disabled sat on the summit of Clingmans Dome. Guns and Rambler were already on top, so I climbed up to take their picture. Mathewski was afraid of heights so he moved on. I left with Guns and Rambler, who planned on hitching to Gatlinburg to spend the night in town. They were hiking much faster than I wanted to hike, so I dropped back to hike solo. Hiking fast aggravated my low back pain.

I had some time alone, so I started to digest some of the food for thought from the last couple of days. I questioned myself again does, Alcoholics Anonymous and Christianity coexist within me?

Then I thought, maybe, God created Alcoholics Anonymous in the first place for alcoholics. History gave Bill Wilson and Dr. Bob Smith credit as the founders of Alcoholics Anonymous in 1935. I thought the story may have started a long time before 1935 and could go something like this:

Once upon a time, a cave man or woman ate rotten fruit and liked the feeling. They liked the feeling so well they started to rot fruit on purpose to drink the juice until life became unmanageable thus inventing the first alcoholic. Now, not everyone liked the feeling. Some people actually hated the feeling, but loved the alcoholic. The first alcoholic's significant other tried to help the alcoholic control his drinking and tried to minimize his consequences thus inventing the first enabler. Who knows, maybe that apple Adam ate was fermented and he got shit-faced drunk. That's how he invented the first sin. Maybe Eve tried to control Adam's drinking and invented the first codependent enabler.

I read in the Gospels about when Jesus told the man lying by the side of the road to pick up his mat and walk. Could that man have been an alcoholic? Jesus could have said, "Drink no more least something worse will happen." Maybe it didn't happen exactly like that and I wasn't trying to rewrite the Bible according to Dreamer. I thought it was safe to say both alcoholics and people who love alcoholics prayed for divine intervention ever since the first alcoholic a long, long time ago.

I arrived at Newfound Gap late in the day. I wanted to hitch to Gatlinburg to buy supplies and return to the trail, so I stood at the end of the parking lot with my thumb out for about an hour. About a hundred cars passed but not one would stop and give me a ride. I guessed that they knew I stunk.

I had given up on getting a ride when an unusually attractive girl named Allie and two hikers stopped on her way into the parking lot and offered me a ride to town. She parked and they all piled out. She introduced me to Brave Heart and Messenger, two thru-hikers who were lucky enough to have met Allie in church.

Brave Heart was about five foot tall with a full black beard and feisty personality. He just finished college to become a preacher. Messenger was tall dark and handsome with no hair at all on his face, who also just finished college. He was rather quiet and I suspected the ladies went for him. They were unlikely hiking partners, but both thru-hikers. They saddled up and scurried off as if someone was after them.

Allie offered to take me to Gatlinburg where I could stay at her house, do laundry, get a hot shower, eat a home cooked meal, and she would return me to the trail the next day, as she did for Brave Heart and Messenger. To this day, I don't know why, but I declined. It might be because I was married and would like to stay that way. Otherwise, I must have been crazy choosing a night on the cold hard ground with Brave Heart and Messenger over a warm soft bed at Allie's house.

I silently saddled up and moved on in hopes I could catch Brave Heart and Messenger before dark. Gatlinburg was where Bill Bryson the author of A Walk in the Woods aborted his thru-hike. I superstitiously wanted to avoid going to Gatlinburg because I was afraid I might not return to the trail.

I arrived at Icewater Shelter about dark. The shelter was full of people drinking, so I set up on a flat piece of ground away from the party. I imagined all my other friends were in Gatlinburg for the night. I regretted not going to Gatlinburg with Allie, but at least now I could call Bryson a wimp.

Day 17   12.6 Miles

The day was my hardest day on the trail since Springer. A bunch of drunks in the nearby shelter kept me awake most of the night. Then a severe thunder and lightning storm moved in during the wee hours and kept me awake the rest of the night. The storm intimidated me because I thought I felt the lightning hit the mountain. I gave up trying to sleep and made coffee and oatmeal in my tent. I had to get up and move out, so I packed up a wet tent and left at daybreak with zero sleep. The temperature dropped and the rain started to freeze. I soon found myself in an ice storm with gale force winds. Hard packed snow and ice from previous storms covered the trail at the higher elevations in the Smoky Mountains. The freezing rain on top made it dangerously treacherous on the mountains and ridges, which slowed my progress way down.

The situation worsened when I got to the ridges by Charlie's Bunion, which in my opinion under other conditions, always was the most picturesque part of the Smoky Mountains. The ridges were narrow, sometimes eight feet wide with steep drops on both sides. The ice and wind stung when it hit my face like rain when I was riding a motorcycle. The wind tried to blow me off the mountain when I crossed the ridges. I was leaning into the wind so hard that I felt if it suddenly quit, I would have fallen off the mountain. I crawled on my hands and knees once because the wind was so strong. I looked over the side and it was almost straight down as far as I could see on the Tennessee side and exceptionally steep on the North Carolina side. I thought, that was one of those places where I shouldn't look down.

I stopped at a sheltered place off the ridge and changed from my shorts to my long pants. I was going to take a break and try to wait it out, but I got so cold I thought I would freeze, so I had to move on. The day was definitely a nightmare except I couldn't snap out of it and find myself safely in my sleeping bag. I wished I were somewhere, anywhere else but where I was. I was afraid my hike might end forever in that cold, white hell.

I stopped to pray in case it might help comfort me. I relaxed and felt better after praying. The ice-covered branches looked as if Mother Nature highlighted them with crystal. I let go of my fear and started to enjoy the adventure. The wind chill must have been in the single digits. I had to keep moving to stay warm, but I found it all breathtakingly beautiful. I even took the time to stop and take a picture of the harsh beauty of the trail. The cold front passed through before midday. The weather cleared and the sun came out, but the temperature stayed in the low teens with the wind continuing. A couple of hours before it got dark, I made it to Tri-Corner Knob Shelter, which was almost six-thousand-feet high. The temperature was ten degrees and all my friends were already at the shelter to greet me. Cedar Moe, Yahtzee, Mathewski, Juliann, Guns, Rambler, and Messenger were huddled together to keep warm. Messenger was worried about Brave Heart because they accidently separated in the morning in the storm. He thought maybe Brave Heart was ahead and might have hiked to the next shelter. I secretly prayed Brave Heart didn't fall off Charley's Bunion earlier in the morning.

The Forest Service was replacing the roof on the shelter. They had torn the old roof off, so the shelter had no roof. We built a fire in the fireplace anyway and huddled together to stay warm. The shelter provided some protection from the wind. We all started telling our experiences of the day. I found myself enjoying the camaraderie among the other hikers even in those adverse, freezing conditions I felt safe.

Most of my family and friends back home warned me it would be dangerous to go on such an adventure alone. Some even suggested I would get homesick and return because I would be alone too long. The thought of going solo on the trail never intimidated me before I set off for my thru-hike. I was okay with being by myself, but I soon discovered I was never alone for too long. I quickly found hikers in general, all had a common bond, but it was especially strong in thru-hikers.

I found the social life on the trail unique in the sense that the people I met had a common interest in hiking the trail with me. Hikers and former hikers shared their adventures and the hardships of the trail with me. I learned to call these accounts of their adventures, trail tales. Hikers who were away from home and their loved ones became close to each other on the trail. Somewhere in time someone said, "Misery loves company." The loneliness and hardships on the trail seemed to be the glue that bonded people together to form a unique society. I found it uncanny that when I became too lonesome I always seemed to run into someone to share a trail tale or two with and made a new friend. With some, the bond was instant, with others, it formed slower, but I haven't found any hikers who I didn't like eventually. The social life on the trail was one of the things that kept me going, which was an unsuspected surprise.

The Ridge Runner, who was an employee of the Park, made us leave the shelter and wait at the junction of the Appalachian Trail and the trail to the shelter, which was about a hundred yards from the shelter, while the Forest Service brought the new roof material in by helicopter. We watched the helicopter deliver the material and tools for the new roof and then take away the old roof and the outhouse.

The Ridge Runner wanted us all to stay in the shelter with no roof. Rambler was the first to take issue with the idea of staying where if it rained there could be severe consequences. The debate started getting so heated that I decided to step between the two of them, facing Rambler. It was an extremely tense moment when our eyes met, but Rambler backed away. I let out a sigh of relief and turned to the Ridge Runner who also turned away. That was the first time I ever experienced any drama on the trail.

Rambler, Guns, and I went up the mountain to a clearing where they tied horses. We set up our tents on the reasonably flat ground. We were well above six-thousand feet and it was incredibly cold, but clear as we cooked and ate together. I had a hot supper of beans and rice Rambler gave me a few days before. The Ridge Runner came up to check on us. He and Rambler apologized and forgave each other after their tempers cooled off. That was the way it was on the trail.

The temperature was ten degrees, so I wore all my clothes, two hats, and gloves to bed. I pulled an emergency solar blanket over everything. I was quite snug, so I read the Bible John gave me and gave thanks to my Creator to still be alive. As I was praying, I started to reflect on the events of the last few days. I thought a great deal changed for me and I felt spiritually blessed with a little insight into my understanding of God.

I could see how God was the one who started Alcoholics Anonymous in the first place so the tremendously spiritually sick could find their way to him. He heard the prayers of the desperate and picked a place called Manchester Center, Vermont to get the ball rolling. God might have handpicked the actors for the first act of a drama that I believed He himself directed. He picked Roland Hazard, Ebby Thatcher, Lois Burnham, and of course Bill Wilson. I wasn't sure how they auditioned, but I don't believe they willingly volunteered for their part. All these folks got to know each other and became friends as they grew up in Manchester Center. I never met any of these folks because they were in the first couple of acts, which took place in the early 1900's before I was born.

I found myself wondering if I too, along with thousands of others recovering in Alcoholics Anonymous were all actors with a small role in the play. I knew I had a lot of spiritual work to do on the trail if I was ever going to play my small part in the real life drama before it closed. I felt grateful for the hardships of the day that made hiking the Appalachian Trail a real spiritual adventure. I closed my Bible, tucked my head under the covers, and pulled the drawstring on my sleeping bag closed over my head and drifted into the comfort of dreamland.

Day 18   16.4 Miles

Considering the temperature, I slept well, but the solar blanket caused condensation between it and my sleeping bag. My sleeping bag was wet and frozen on the outside and I had ice on the inside of the tent again. I made coffee and hot oatmeal inside my tent. The little stove warmed the tent right up. The directions said not to use the stove inside, so I only lit it briefly with the zipper to the door open. I ate the oatmeal, drank my coffee, then packed up to a beautiful, cold, sunny day. I departed in silence to not wake Guns and Rambler.

I climbed up to six-thousand, three-hundred, and sixty feet on Guyot Spur and stayed above six-thousand feet to hike solo in the pristine Great Smoky Mountain National Park. I referred to the guidebook on an exceptionally memorable view to see where I was and found I was on Hell Ridge. I found the ridges were breathtaking with magnificent vistas, but the day before they were so intimidating even I was afraid. I sat there in wonder at how much difference a day makes. They probably named Hell Ridge on a day like the day before.

I ate lunch on the side of a mountain in the sun. It warmed up enough that I changed into shorts for the afternoon. I felt a little sense of accomplishment as I descended out of the Park to a lower altitude and warmer temperature. I pushed to Mountain Momma's Kuntry Store and Bunkhouse where I could get one of her famous, giant cheeseburgers. Cheeseburgers had been on my mind a lot lately. In fact, I had a dream about cheeseburgers the other night and woke up aroused. I always knew I liked cheeseburgers, but I never knew I liked them that much. I wonder what Freud would have had to say about that experience.

I arrived at Davenport Gap late in the day, but to my dismay, I found a sign saying Mountain Mamma's kitchen closed at five pm. It was one point three miles to the bunkhouse, so I elected to move on and camp on the trail. I needed supplies, but I could buy supplies in the morning at Standing Bear Farm a couple of miles up the trail.

I was taking a snack break when Brave Heart came up from behind. I was surprised because I thought he was far ahead. Brave Heart was behind because he got lost in the storm the day before and hiked thirteen miles on the wrong trail. I asked him, if he ever looked up to check for the little white blazes on the trees. He gave me a look and said nothing, so I let it go at that. I didn't think he liked my sense of humor. He was going to Mountain Momma's in hopes of catching Messenger. I told him that Messenger was at Tri-Corner Knob Shelter the night before, but I haven't seen him since. I had the wrong first impression of Brave Heart. I thought he was grandiose, which he might be, but he was also tough. He walked a total of twenty-six miles yesterday, which was as far as I hiked the last two days put together.

I lost track of all my friends and had no idea where they were spending the night, so I stopped on a flat spot by a stream that was cascading down the mountain a short distance before Interstate 40. I set up camp by myself within a few feet of a small waterfall because I liked the white sound of falling water to fall asleep to. I took an exceptionally quick shower under a small waterfall. The ice-cold water was refreshing to say the least. I got phone contact with Scooter for the first time since Fontana Dam and arranged a rendezvous with her at Erwin, Tennessee for the twenty fifth of March. I also made contact with some friends in Alcoholics Anonymous. I almost fell asleep as I was talking to one of my buddies, so I said good-bye and ended the day.

THE CAST

Day 19 16.3 Miles

I had the strangest dream just before I awoke. I felt an evil presence of a demon attacking me in my tent as if I wasn't asleep, but I wasn't awake. The demon and I were wrestling in the tent. I had no idea what the dream meant, but it left me feeling uneasy. I only made coffee because I was all out of food. The place seemed to have taken on a medieval type of aura, so I hastily packed up to leave as quickly as possible.

A beautiful spring-like day greeted me. I walked less than a hundred yards and discovered Rambler breaking camp. We camped so close to each other that we could have heard each other if it wasn't for the sound of the stream. I made another cup of coffee while he finished packing. It was good to have company as we set off together.

We crossed the interstate and started the steep ascent up Snowbird Mountain when we came upon a cooler that someone called a Trail Angel left inside the woods on the trail. Rambler was ahead and opened the cooler which contained a gift called Trail Magic for any hiker, first come first served. He said, "Oh boy, beer!" That time a Trail Angel left a cooler full of beer for thirsty hikers.

Rambler reached into the cooler and pulled out two cold cans of beer. He extended one towards me. I put my hand up and said, "No thanks."

"Come on its cold."

My voice went up about two octaves and I looked him right in the eyes and said, "I'm an alcoholic and I said no!"

He seemed to understand, "Mind if I drink one?"

That seemed to break the sudden tension and I laughed as I shook my head, no and said, "I don't mind."

I felt better as I explained to him while he was drinking the beer what it was like to be an alcoholic and how my addiction almost killed me. In spite of what the booze did to me, it was whispering in my ear, "It has been a long time and no one would know." The intellectual part of me knew that one drink would open the gates of Hell back up, but still it looked good. Alcoholics Anonymous called alcohol cunning, baffling, and powerful. I would have also added sneaky and patient.

He quickly finished his beer, belched, and said, "Sorry, let's move out." I had to admit, I felt a little relieved after we put some distance between the beer and me.

I arrived at a dirt road where a painted rock advertised Standing Bear Hostel. I was a little ahead of Rambler so I waited until he caught up. We walked the quarter mile or so to a house set back from the road with several out buildings. No one was around, which added a ghost town kind of atmosphere to the place. We went to the bunkhouse first. No one was around, but I could smell the distinct odor of hikers. We checked out the shower and laundry, which was also empty. Young children's toys were scattered in the yard by the house. I was about to approach the house when Rambler yelled, "Dreamer, over here" from the porch of an out building. It was the store. No one was at the store either, but it was open and you were on your honor to place the money for what you bought in a locked wooden box. I bought enough supplies to get to Hot Springs in a day or two. I also bought a microwave cheeseburger to heat in the microwave. I devoured it and then I bought two more and did the same thing. I then did it all over again. After I gobbled down five quarter-pound cheeseburgers, even my appetite was satisfied. The cheeseburgers weren't Mountain Momma's giant cheeseburgers, but when you're as hungry as I was for cheeseburgers, they were better than steak. I wasn't hungry at all when I picked up a packaged cherry pie and assessed the weight with my hand. I put it down and said to Rambler, "Too heavy." Rambler just looked at me with a stupid look. We put the money for the food and supplies in the lockbox and hiked on without ever seeing anyone.

We hiked up Snow Bird Mountain and stopped at the summit

for lunch. The summit was bald and as we sat in the warm sun, all we could see was the endless mountains in all four directions. The cheeseburgers that I consumed earlier were only a fond memory and I felt hungry again. I got out the fixings for coffee and already started to regret the stupid decision not to buy the cherry pie when Rambler yelled, "Heads up," and tossed me a cherry pie.

We both ended up taking a short nap, probably due to a sugar down. I left Rambler sleeping as I moved on. With time to myself, I returned to my thoughts of the play. Roland Hazard got the privilege of opening the first act. His family was wealthy and owned a summer cottage around Manchester Center where he stayed. His drinking got way out of control and his life was out of control because of it. The family wanted to groom him to take over their multimillion-dollar business, but his drinking headed him for a sanitarium instead.

Roland wanted to stop drinking, but exhausted all the methods of recovery he could come up with on his own. Money was no object, so as a last resort, his family sent him to Switzerland to the most renowned psychiatrist in the world at the time, Dr. Carl Jung, who had previously studied under the famous Sigmund Freud. Roland spent a year in Dr. Jung's care. He stayed sober and left feeling cured with some knowledge and a strong conviction to never drink again. He didn't even make it back to New York sober. He had one seeming innocent glass of wine in France and relapsed into an uncontrollable drinking binge. He returned to Dr. Jung's care in Switzerland. Dr. Jung told him frankly that no further medical or psychiatric treatment could help. That understandably had an immense impact on Roland, leaving him feeling hopeless and helpless.

Dr. Jung said the only thing that he had occasionally seen was a conversion of a spiritual kind bring about recovery for some alcoholics. He recommended Roland get involved in a religious atmosphere and hope for the best. Maybe that was the conversation led to the passage in the book of Alcoholics Anonymous that says, "No human power could have relieved our alcoholism."

Roland went back to New York hopelessly depressed, but instead of getting drunk he sought help in a religious group called the Oxford

Group, which was an evangelical movement that had meetings to encourage one another. They also placed emphasis on self-inventory, confession, restitution, and helping others. That worked and Roland stayed sober and became dedicated to helping others recover from alcoholism. In a sense Dr. Carl Jung perhaps unknowingly, was Roland's sponsor who guided him into recovery.

Rambler caught up to me at the end of the day on Max Patch Summit, which was another bald. Rambler was going to camp there. I refused to camp above the tree line especially since thunderstorms were predicted. I took pictures and moved on as darkness was approaching. I stopped to set up camp on a flat piece of ground by a small stream. Rambler soon came in so I made room for him to set up his tent. We were eating supper and Brave Heart came in and joined us. Brave Heart hadn't found Messenger, so after he ate he went to Roaring Fork Shelter in the dark, hoping to find Messenger. He was real down, so I prayed for him. Rambler and I turned in before the storm hit. I was sure happy Rambler wasn't on top of Max Patch when it lit up. I thought he was also grateful, but I knew he would never admit it.

Day 20   18.8 Miles

I awoke before daylight to thunder, lightning, rain, and wind. I worried about the rain washing down a tree that started to erode around the roots uphill from my tent. I couldn't put it out of my mind and go back to sleep, so I decided to move out. I packed up as quietly as I possible not to wake Rambler, and left. I hoped that maybe if I left early enough, I could pick up my mail in Hot Springs. I hiked two hours in the dark, which wasn't as hard as it sounded, but I had to go a little slower than normal. The rain quit after daylight, so I then made good time. Rambler overtook me and we ate lunch together. He's only forty-one-years old and hikes faster than I cared to attempt. He was also looking to get to Hot Springs, so he went on ahead. I told him I would buy him dinner that night. I didn't know it at the time, but I would never see him again.

When I looked out from the summit of Bluff Mountain, I saw Hot Springs all nestled in the valley nine miles away. Hot Springs looked so inviting, especially as I got near enough to hear the sounds of the town and cars. I was looking forward to more cheeseburgers, a hot shower, and clean, dry sheets. I hurried to the post office to pick up the last mail drop that I mailed to myself from home in January, the box I bounced from Fontana, and several letters from friends and family. Receiving all the unexpected letters instantly brought tears to my eyes. I planned to bounce my extra things ahead to Damascus, Virginia before I left town.

I met a couple at the post office who called themselves Hit and Miss. They hiked the north half of the trail last year and were hiking the south half this year. I gave them some of my extra things and the box that my mail came in so they could bounce some things ahead. I saw Messenger down the street as I was leaving the post office, but I couldn't get his attention to tell him the whereabouts of Brave Heart.

I rented a room at the Alpine Court Motel, which had a hot shower and television. I took a shower, went to The Paddlers Pub, and bought a lousy cheeseburger and French fries for fourteen bucks. Most of my hiker buddies were in the bar getting drunk. I felt out of place in the bar, so I left as soon as I finished eating.

My room didn't have a phone and there wasn't any signal for my cell phone, but I called Scooter from a pay phone before I returned to my room. I sat up in the dry bed and read every single letter I received two times. I was extremely pleased that my friends back home took the time to write me letters. I was so grateful for all their support that encouraged me to stay on the trail. I tried watching television to pass some time for a while, but I was not into watching TV. I turned out the light and sat in the dark, reflecting back on this wonderful adventure. I felt grateful to my Creator for all His gifts. I sometimes wondered if and why God chose me, but it overwhelmed me to try to understand such things. I simply said a prayer and gave thanks to be part of God's great play before I drifted off to sleep.

March 19   Day 21   11 Miles

I got up early, showered, and called Scooter from a pay phone at the Smoky Mountain Diner. I took my time to eat three eggs over easy, home fries, and toast with lots of coffee for breakfast. I was on my way out of town when I met Hit and Miss as they were packing up, so we chatted for a moment. I stopped by the post office to mail my extra supplies to Damascus and picked up three more letters. Altogether, I received letters from Don, Sherry, Rich, Judy, Paige, Darren M, Nancy, Ryan, Chip and Karen, and Christine. I also received a card from Scooter with a surprise in it. The letters meant more than I had words to describe. I stopped at the outfitters and bought a fuel tank for my stove and a gourmet trail meal as a treat. I also weighed my pack, which weighed thirty-nine pounds. I moseyed out of town facing a steep ascent out of the of the French Broad River valley.

The towns always seemed to be in a valley. I always looked forward to the goal of getting to the next town as soon as I left one and started hiking. I was always out of food, hungry, dirty, stinky, and tired and would descend into a town with a light pack. Even the sound of traffic and sirens became welcome sounds. When I arrived in town, I would eat like a pig, re-supply, take a shower, do laundry, watch television, make phone calls, get mail, and rest. When I left town, I would be melancholy until I readjusted to the trail. I usually was lonely and faced a steep ascent with a full, heavy pack. That cycle has played out since I first started hiking. I met up with the Traveling Dingle-Berries, Taco, Hit, and Miss. We chatted as we hiked a short distance beside the French Broad River. All of them hiked faster than this old dog, so I dropped back and hiked solo as soon as we started the steep ascent out of the river valley. I caught up to a troop of Boy Scouts as I ascended, so I stopped at a stream to filter water and take a break so they could go ahead. I later passed them again as the leader was passing out gorp.

The scoutmaster said, "Hey, Thru-Hiker" then tossed me a baggie of gorp.

I saluted and said, "Thank you sir" as I passed. A civilian calling me a thru-hiker for the first time sure felt good.

The endorphins kicked in, my mind was clear and soon my thoughts returned to the play. Roland Hazard was well on his way to recovery when the second actor, Edwin Thatcher, who they called Ebby entered. Ebby's family was well known, established politically, and prominent in Albany, New York. They came to Manchester in the summer where they also owned a home. His father was once a vice-presidential candidate. Ebby and Bill Wilson first became friends in a Vermont boarding school.

When Bill returned from WW1 a war hero, he and Ebby became close drinking buddies in New York. Once when on a drinking spree in Albany, they remembered that an airfield was still under construction in a cow pasture in their old home town of Manchester. They thought it would be novel to be the first to land at the new airport even though it was another week before the scheduled opening. Ebby roused a friend out of bed who had an airplane and talked him into flying them into Manchester for a handsome price. They sent the town fathers a wire to let them know they would be the first to land at the new airfield about mid-morning. They were still drinking when they took off. By the grace of God, the intoxicated pilot managed to safely land the small plane on the almost finished airfield. Who knows, maybe it was then that the pilot first coined the phrase, Hold my beer and watch this shit. A large crowd, which included the local band, cheered their arrival. The wobbly pilot stumbled out of the plain, but they found Bill and Ebby passed out in the rear of the airplane. The band stopped playing, the crowd grew silent. They had to assist Bill and Ebby out of the plane. The two collapsed on the ground, and they carted them away.

Ebby's drinking became an embarrassment to his political family, so they supported him and his drinking adventures as long as he stayed in Manchester, out of the way and didn't return to Albany. He once ran his father's new Packard off the road and into a farmhouse, smashing into the kitchen just missing a terrified housewife. He thought he could ease the tension, so he smiled and said, "Well, my dear, how about a cup of coffee?"

Ebby decided to paint his house and turn over a new leaf. A bird came along and crapped on his new paint. Ebby got a resentment towards the birds, so he set up a chair in the yard and guarded his fresh paint with a bottle and a shotgun. The poor unsuspecting neighbors thought a war had started. The town father's patience eventually wore thin and they yanked Ebby into court. They were no longer going to tolerate Ebby's lighthearted humor and it appeared as if they were going to put him away in an asylum. Meanwhile Roland Hazard heard of Ebby's fate and convinced the magistrate to parole Ebby to his care. Thus Roland introduced Ebby to the Oxford Group and Ebby got sober.

I hiked in the company of my thoughts for the rest of that day. I set up my tent at Spring Mountain Shelter even though the shelter was empty. Guns came by as I was setting up, so I took a break to chat. I gave him the homemade deer jerky from my mail drop that I promised him. He told me Rambler's wife was pregnant, so Rambler caught a bus back to Maine. A Brown Recluse spider bit Cedar Moe and his ankle swelled. He was in so much pain that he also got off the trail. Guns ate the jerky and moved on to the next shelter nine miles, north and left me alone with the news. I didn't know, but that was the last time I would ever see Guns.

It started to get colder as the sun set, so I cooked mashed potatoes for supper in my tent. The little stove heated the tent and gave me temporary relief from the cold. I felt a sudden overwhelming wave of depression when the news settled in about Rambler and Cedar Moe. I started to weep, missing them both already. I felt a special type of grief and loneliness that I couldn't shake. I had no cell tower, so I wasn't able to escape the loneliness that night. I feared I would never see Rambler or Cedar Moe again. I didn't even know their real names. The bond was instant with both of them. I had to laugh through my tears because it took some time for me to warm up to Guns. They will all always be close to my heart. Not only was it their friendship and support, but they also set the example for me to follow, which inspired me to continue.

They were gone and I felt sorry for myself. I thought that maybe it was time for me to get off of the pity pot. I felt a strong sense of loss, but I needed to continue for them in spirit. A line in my high school yearbook that was dedicated to a student killed in an accident surfaced in my head. It went something like this, To lose someone is the greatest of all losses, but it was still better to rejoice that you were fortunate enough to have touched them than to morn their loss.

I reflected on the good times I had with Rambler and my emotions started changing to the tune of the fond memories. I thought not only of Rambler, Cedar Moe, and Guns, but also of Heaven Bound, Pyro, Grizzly, Mathewski, Crazy Horse, and the many more hikers who I connected with on the trail. I stopped dwelling on my grief and losses and reflected on what I gained from each individual. I believe that maybe God was talking to me through them to teach me. I felt grateful for what I learned from them. I decided to pray and as I prayed, I found faith that I would get the opportunity to meet new friends in my journey. I even started to anticipate the gifts I would receive in the future in the form of new teachers who God sent my way. I slowly drifted off to sleep, ending week three, excited like a child on Christmas Eve who anticipated gifts under the tree the next morning.

Day 22   15.4 Miles

The night time temperature dropped way down, so I awoke to a cold, sunny day. My mood improved when I started to hike. I wasn't sure if I was in North Carolina or Tennessee, but it sure looked beautiful with the mountains, valleys, waterfalls, rivers, and woods. I stopped for water and ate lunch at Little Laurel Shelter. Brave Heart came in and joined me. I watched and listened while he shared his lunch with a bird that was begging. He was emotionally low because he hadn't caught up to Messenger yet. I told him that I saw Messenger in Hot Springs. I didn't get to talk to him before he left town, but I knew for sure Messenger was at least a day ahead of us. I didn't say anything, but I wondered if Messenger was avoiding Brave Heart. Hiking partners don't seem to last long on a thru-hike. They usually got on each other's nerves and parted ways. I thought that Brave Heart invested more in the friendship and partnership.

I made my decision to hike solo on my thru-hike because I didn't want the encumbrances of a partner. I learned from personal experiences on section hikes with others that whenever you hiked with someone else you also hiked with their agenda. The more people you hiked with the more agendas and the more personalities you dealt with. I used to organize hikes with as many as six people that worked out okay, but there was a lot of compromising with six agendas. I also didn't want the responsibility of hiking with anyone else, because I might end up having to take care of the other hiker. Usually some conflict would arise and partners often ended up feeling animosity towards each other.

Brave Heart went ahead and I hiked solo. I stopped for a break at White Rock Cliffs because the view was spectacular. I arrived at Gerry's Cabin late in the day. I had a hard time finding a flat spot with no dead trees around. I finally found a minimal spot to set up my tent. I felt a little uneasy, but rationalized that dead trees didn't kill that many hikers. I got into my sleeping bag and was listening to the radio, which predicted a heavy snowstorm. I thought I had better listen to my intuition, so I elected to take my tent down and move into the cabin before dark. This would be the first time I spent the night in a shelter. I had the place all to myself, so I built a fire in the fireplace to cook supper. After supper, I reflected on my thoughts of the play.

Lois Burnham Wilson was one of the many non-alcoholics who God cast for his play. However, she was one of the most important actors because without her dedication and tenacity, Alcoholics Anonymous might not have happened. Lois was the oldest of six children. Their father was a Gynecologist and surgeon in Brooklyn Heights, New York. The family would spend the summers in Manchester while her father took care of his patients summering there.

Her younger brother Rodger played with Ebby Thatcher and Bill Wilson. Lois came to know Bill, who was four years younger, as her little brother's friend. Eventually, Lois and Bill fell in love and were secretly engaged in 1915. She was well educated, but knew little or nothing about Bill's drinking. She married Bill on January twenty-fourth, 1918 just before he shipped off for Europe to fight the First World War as an army officer.

After the war, Bill's drinking became progressively out of control. She could not bear children because of a series of ectopic pregnancies. They tried to adopt children, but were unsuccessful because background checks revealed Bill's problem drinking. Lois could see the bright future she had hoped for dashed out by Bill's drinking. She was the oldest in her family and was used to taking care of others, so she got a job and supported Bill as his drinking shattered their opportunities and ambitions. She tried many tactics in vain to help Bill to stop drinking, but the result was always the same. Bill got sober in 1934, but it was not due to her efforts. Her life or her marriage didn't get much better after Bill got sober. She sought support to cope among other wives of sober alcoholics.

She played the part in this play so well that I personally thought she should have received an Emmy for best supporting actress of all time. In 1951, Lois Burnham Wilson founded Al-Anon to help the wives and loved ones of alcoholics cope. She patterned Al-Anon after Alcoholics Anonymous and adopted the Twelve Steps with Bill's blessings and encouragement. Al-Anon became a worldwide fellowship that helped millions as the third largest twelve-step program in existence. I believe Al-Anon was the world's gift from Lois, but Lois was the world's gift from God.

Three college boys on spring break from the University of Arkansas interrupted my thoughts shortly before dark. They created a lot of chaos as they set up in the shelter, but I welcomed their company. They never hiked before and carried exceedingly heavy packs with lots of borrowed gear. They brought cans of soup, vegetables, and things only first time hikers would carry. They almost set the cabin on fire trying to get their stove to light, so I decided to help them for my own sake. I built the fire up to make a pot of tea as the boys cooked supper. One gave me a generous hunk of hot pepper cheese and I shared my tea. I found them refreshing, positive, and enthusiastic about hiking. They didn't drink, smoke, or complain about being tired and sore, which would have made things miserable for me. The boys kept up a steady stream of questions that I answered the best I could as we talked into the night.

I had a hard time falling asleep, but finally drifted off well after their breathing became slow and steady. Overall, I enjoyed my first night in a shelter.

Day 23   14.7 Miles

I awoke early and packed as quietly as possible. I still woke the boys, but they didn't get up. One of the boys said, "God Bless" as I left. I headed north and knew I would not see them again because they were going to hike south. The day started cold and cloudy, but dry. The snow started at nine o'clock with a light, warm snow at first that melted as soon as it hit. I didn't put on my poncho, because I thought it wouldn't make a difference. That turned out to be a huge mistake. I stopped at noon to cook noodles and coffee at a small stream where I filtered water. I called Dan, my friend in Alcoholics Anonymous, who happened to be drinking coffee and riding in a warm truck. I jokingly told him that I was jealous, but realized I was wet and cold. The wet snow soaked through my Gore-Tex pants, fleece jacket, and nylon shirt. The snow seemed to gradually become heaver as the temperature dropped. I decided to cut the conversation short because I had to move to stay warm. I quickly checked the guidebook and started to get concerned because the next shelter was about eight miles away.

I came upon a tent with a pack tied to a tree and no tracks in the fresh snow. No one appeared to be around so I called out "Hello." No one answered. I found it disturbing and left with an eerie feeling that stuck with me. I said a prayer for the hiker who owned the gear. I hoped that he or she abandoned it to find a warm, dry place. The snow started to stick to the ground as the temperature dropped. I found a single set of footprints in the snow ahead of me. I took comfort in knowing there was someone else in the storm. I kept following the tracks. The snow was getting deeper as I was getting colder and showing symptoms of hypothermia by late afternoon. My concern was turning to fear. The visibility was only a few yards and I was afraid I might have missed the shelter in the storm because I hadn't seen the footprints in a while. I was so cold I didn't think I could set up my tent, besides there was no place to set it up.

The situation was out of my control and I was losing hope, so I stopped to pray for help. I opened my eyes after praying and saw a little horizontal board on a tree fifty feet away. I couldn't read it, but I knew that it said, "SHELTER" in capital letters. To my delight, the tracks in the snow reappeared on the trail to the shelter. I quickly hiked two-tenths of a mile off trail to the Hogback Ridge Shelter. A sixty-three-year-old Christian named Christopher was all wrapped up in a down sleeping bag waiting there to greet me. The shelter was small, dark, and musty smelling, but it looked like the Hilton to me. My hands were so cold my fingers would not work as if I had no fingers. I took out my stove, but couldn't screw on the fuel tank. I said, "I'm in trouble."

Christopher jumped out of his sleeping bag and started both his stove and mine. I gave him a pack of Ramen noodles to put into my pot. I stripped all my wet clothes off and put on dry long-underwear, two fleece shirts, a down vest, dry socks, and my dry hat. I jumped into my sleeping bag before I ate the noodles. Christopher put boiling water in my water bottle and I curled up in the fetal position around it. He also took off his down jacket and gave it to me. That was a sacrifice on his part, because he was cold also. I ate Snickers and hot soup as I slowly warmed up. After I warmed up, I hung up my wet hiking clothes, and gave Christopher back his jacket. I set up my tent inside the shelter to block the wind and crawled back into my sleeping bag with a new bottle of hot water. I was still cold, but I would survive.

I thanked Christopher through the wall of my tent. He responded, "You don't have to thank me, it was my pleasure." I thought it was so lucky that Christopher was there to help me when I arrived. Suddenly, the old saying, a coincidence is when God chooses to remain anonymous, surfaced in my mind. I got back out of my sleeping bag, got on my knees, and gave thanks to God for answering my prayers on the trail. My faith was still weak, but I took great comfort in the twenty-third Psalm. I now saw that God protected me.

I wondered why God was so good to me. The God introduced me to as a child was punishing and saw everything I did. I didn't deserve his protection and if I got exactly what I deserved, I probably would have burned in hell thirty years ago for the things I did. They must have lied to me because I came to know a loving God who forgave and protected. I only hoped that I could pay him back for his help someday, if I ever got the chance.

I already hiked three-hundred and twelve miles and Katahdin was still almost nineteen-hundred miles away, which seemed like a million miles. I wondered if I had what it took to make it to the summit of Mount Katahdin. I knew I needed God's help and protection. The wind was still blowing, but I felt all warm and fuzzy. My problems of the day seemed as far away as Katahdin. I took out my little white Bible and read the last part of John. I thought the Bible could also be a script for a play written by our creator. That play seemed to end after the crucifixion of Jesus. Just by the day's contact alone, I felt absolutely sure God was alive, well, and with us still. He was still writing plays for us to audition for the roles. Who knows, it might be the same play, only different acts.

Bill Wilson got the starring role in the second act in the beginning of Alcoholics Anonymous. He met Roland, Ebby, and Lois growing up in Vermont. They literally had known each other most of their lives. Bill was born on Thanksgiving in 1895 to Gilman Wilson and Emily Griffith Wilson. They lived in East Dorset, which was a small village close to Manchester, Vermont. Gilman and Emily grew up within sight of each other.

I assume they named Bill after his deceased Grandfather, William Wilson. Bill's grandfather apparently had a drinking problem also and took the temperance pledge several times. Eventually, he asked God for help on the summit of Mount Aeolus and had a blinding light experience like the one his grandson had in Towns hospital years later. History says he never drank again and died sober eight years later.

Bill's father grew up helping his widowed mother run the Wilson House, which was an inn ran by the family. They called him Gilly and he had a reputation for being charismatic and entertaining. Gilly drank and socialized with the guests long before he was fully-grown. He became a talented quarry man in the marble mines, but he too had a taste for alcohol. He had a reputation for having an eager sexual appetite and had a hard time keeping his zipper up. Even after his marriage to Emily, he got involved with other women.

Bill was about ten-years-old when his dad got a promotion to head the Florence Mine in Rutland. The family moved twenty some miles north and away from the influence of the Wilson House and both sets of grandparents. Bill transferred from his familiar rural surroundings and one room school, to one of the largest cities in Vermont. Gilly's drinking continued and the fighting between him and Emily increased. The marriage worsened and ended when Gilly had an affair with a minister's daughter. Gillman moved to work in a marble quarry in Canada and Emily took Bill and his sister back to East Dorset. She left Bill and his sister to live with her parents, Fayette and Ella Griffith. Emily left to pursue an education at Boston College of Osteopathy to become a doctor. Emily got a divorce lawyer and told Bill about the divorce in 1906. A divorce was rare in those days. Bill later in life wrote of how devastated he was, feeling abandoned at first by his father and then by his mother.

I finally became drowsy, so I turned out the light. I judged from Christopher's steady breathing that he fell asleep quite a while before. I curled up around the water bottle and said thanks again. I felt safe in the hands of God as sleep overtook me.

Day 24   10 Miles

I awoke after daylight to rain. The night was cold and wet, but rain instead of snow, indicated it was warming up. Christopher was headed for the next shelter, which was ten miles away. I got up so we could take pictures of each other next to Hogback Ridge Shelter in the wet snow.

I hadn't decided if I wanted to take a zero day there in the shelter where I was dry or attempt to make it to the next shelter. My self-confidence was low after the previous day's experience. The rain stopped a couple hours after daybreak, so I filled my water bottle and prepared mentally to move on. My hiking clothes were still uncomfortably wet, so I was tempted to hike in my dry nightclothes. I decided I wouldn't because it would create a grave situation if I got wet again and had zero dry clothes. I sucked it up, put on my wet hiking clothes, and hit the trail immediately to warm up.

The sun came out by noon and my clothes dried out. I passed Christopher on the trail, but hiked on solo after we exchanged pleasantries. The day was sunny and quite pleasant, but still cold. I warmed up, my endorphins started flowing, and I found myself free to dream again.

Bill's grandparents, Ella and Fayette Griffith were in charge of raising Bill and his younger sister, Dorothy. The Griffiths were only yards from the Wilson House, but in a totally different world. Bill went from an adored son of a popular, social-drinking man to the grandson of a hard working, temperance family.

Ella and Fayette never fought, but they didn't seem to care a lot about each other either. Fayette was embittered over the loss of his only son and seemed to never get over it. He believed hard work built character and had Bill working. Bill was now the brunt of gossip and teasing because his parents split-up. He became prone to depression. Fayette saw the intellectual potential in Bill and applied to a boarding school on Bill's behalf without Bill's knowledge or permission. I wondered if he may have been hoping to snap Bill out of his funk. Bill went away to school in the eighth grade. He was awkward at first, but soon fit in and excelled in both academics and athletics. Bill's depression lifted and he became so popular that his classmates voted him class president in 1912.

The spring of 1912 was when Bill fell head over heels in love with the attractive and popular preacher's daughter, Bertha Bamford. Everything seemed like a fairytale come true for Bill. Bill often acknowledged that his sixteenth summer and early fall were the happiest times of His life. That fall, Bertha and her family went to New York for a long weekend so she could have a small tumor removed. It was the first time Bill and Bertha separated from each other for that long. Bill was never to see her again. She hemorrhaged and died days before Bill's seventeenth birthday. Once again, Bill felt abandoned by the one he loved the most.

Bill went into one of his worst depressions of his entire life. He seemed to give up on everything, His grades crashed, and he quit sports. His Grandfather Fayette, tried to help and took him on a trip the next summer to hear President Wilson speak, but nothing seemed to inspire or even reach Bill. His mother took him to a fine school in Boston where she lived, but he couldn't concentrate and failed out. She sent him to Canada to see his father for the first time in seven years. She hoped that would help him, but he returned to East Dorset still emotionally broken. It appeared that Bill was headed for a nervous breakdown.

I stopped by a small mountain spring, nestled in the snow covered Rhododendrons. Identifying with Bill's pain and depression left me feeling unsettled as I watched the water from the spring hurry by on its way. The water looked clear and pure as it sparkled in the sun. I captured some in my cup and took a drink. I found it so cold I couldn't gulp it. Instead, I had to slowly take small sips, allowing me time to savor the sweet, refreshing liquid that's so precious. I can't remember the last time I really appreciated a drink of fresh water. I moved on to process why I sometimes didn't notice gifts or take for granted gifts like water, that are vital. Maybe the hard times that Bill, myself, and millions of others experienced were gifts also. Gifts that allowed us to respond to the adversity, learn from it, and grow strong.

I stopped on top of Bald Mountain to take pictures. The frost covered mountains in the distance looked like a painting in an art gallery. I was completely dry, comfortable and my confidence returned. Twenty-four hours before, I was cold, wet, and afraid I might die from hypothermia. My mother used to say, "What a difference a day makes." The contrast of the hard days sure made me appreciate the good days.

I arrived at Bald Mountain Shelter early in the afternoon and set up my tent to dry. A couple from Florida, Yahtzee, and an overbearing, talkative, grandiose man named Wee Willie the Prince of Wales were already at the shelter. I wasn't too excited to stay, but the radio was predicting severe thunderstorms. The day was clear and sunny, but I didn't want to risk a repeat of the mistakes of the day before. A sign said, No Camping, so I packed up my tent after it dried out and set up my sleeping bag in the shelter for the third night in a row. Christopher came in and set up later. I talked to Scooter and Phyllis, but was annoying Christopher by talking on the phone. I cut the conversations short, which was one more reason why I would rather stay in the privacy of my tent instead of the shelters.

Christopher and Wee Willie dominated the conversation most of the night talking about religion. I found them annoying and they got on my nerves. I slept on the top shelf next to Yahtzee and disturbed him twice when I got up in the night to pee. The storm hit in the night with rain first, then snow, which reassured me that I made the right decision to stay in the shelter even with the little annoyances. I woke up before daylight to a cold, white world, packed up as quietly as possible, and left in a foul mood without coffee.

Day 25   16.9 Miles

The day started cold, but warmed up to the mid-thirties, which was perfect for hiking. The vistas were clear with snow capping the tops of all the mountains. Being a Yankee, I pictured the south being warmer with no snow. Hiking in the winter even in the south, was not for the fair-weather hiker.

Many times when I meditated, I would simply let my mind wander until it settled on something, but I was already focused on Bill before I got up. Eventually, Bill took interest in sailing and spent his time alone sailing on Emerald Lake in a rented boat rigged with a homemade sail. He started racing with the older Lois Burnham who was sailing alone in her family's new sailboat, dressed in the latest sailing fashions. They knew each other through her younger brother Rodger. Rodger had Bill over to their house on occasion and Bill even dated Lois's little sister Barbara for a while.

The next summer, Lois's brother Rodger was dating Bill's little sister Dorothy. Bill and Lois found themselves together when they chaperoned the younger couple to social events. Bill was depressed and Lois, although she was twenty-three-years-old, had no prospects of marriage. She saw Bill as a poor local who was beneath her socially. There probably wasn't much if any sexual attraction on either part. The attraction may have been more maternal on Lois's part. Bill felt safe enough to confide in Lois. Lois listened and reassured him and they both benefited from their friendship.

Bill was nineteen when Lois opened a type of cafe by Emerald Lake.

Business was slow and Bill would stop to see her on most days. He would talk and she would listen for hours at a time. She continued to reassure and nurture him. Often, he would walk her home after she closed and she would ask him to stay for dinner. Bill became part of the Burnham family in a sense. Some say he still had something going on with Barbara, but Dr. Burnham and the rest of the family also liked Bill.

A wealthy Canadian met Lois that summer on Emerald Lake. He asked Lois to marry him and move to Canada. I don't know why, but she turned him down. She confided the proposal to Bill shortly afterwards. He advanced on her and they became secretly engaged that night. A lot has been written about why they were married, but even they may not have known for sure. I choose to think God wrote it in the script. Whatever the reason, the marriage endured until Bill's death in 1971 parted them. I believe their marriage was a rare gift to all mankind.

I pushed hard to Erwin, Tennessee, lured by the prospect of a restaurant meal and warm, clean, dry sheets. The miles often passed quickly when I immersed myself in trail dreams. I was still lost in meditation when I came to a picturesque viewpoint on a cliff overlooking the Nolichucky River Valley that snapped me out of my trance. I felt like a voyeur as I watched a car the size of an ant make its way over a road that ran parallel to the river until it crossed a bridge and disappeared. The river looked lazy at first glance. I changed my first impression as I picked out several white rapids in the coffee colored water as it snaked its way along the valley. A small settlement, nestled in beside the river, looked especially inviting. I moved out anticipating all the amenities of town.

I stopped at Uncle Johnny's Hostel on the bank of the Nolichucky River right beside the trail. I found the store locked with no one around, but the RV out back looked occupied. I knocked on the door and Frank, who was in charge, greeted me and gave me a private room with a television. He gave me a fresh towel and showed me where the community shower was located. His wife Shelly would settle with me when she got home. I wondered how much it would cost, but I dropped my pack in the room and took a long anticipated, hot shower.

I was the only hiker staying there, so I had a lot of privacy in contrast to the three nights in the shelters. Shelly and Uncle Johnny's wife arrived and let me into the hiker store. I paid for my room and bought enough supplies to get to Carver's Gap plus some needed blister and wart medications. The whole tab came to less than forty dollars, which was surprisingly reasonable. Christopher and Wee Willie badmouthed Uncle Johnny's last night, so the others all planned to stay at Miss Janet's Hostel. I was so happy I decided to stay at Uncle Jonny's by myself.

I settled in my room to watch television when Shelly knocked on my door. She was going into town and asked if I wanted to go to McDonald's drive-thru. I hadn't eaten at McDonald's in ten years, but jumped at the chance. I had been dreaming about cheeseburgers, so I ordered two quarter-pound cheeseburgers, a large order of fries, and a large strawberry milkshake. McDonald's offered a double cheeseburger for a dollar, so I ordered two double cheeseburgers that I intended to eat for a night-time snack.

I tipped Shelly ten dollars for the ride because she and Frank treated me so well. They left their home in Michigan to hike the trail two years ago, but only got as far as Uncle Johnny's when he offered them a job. They have been there ever since. Frank also worked in town as a cook. Trail Angels like Frank and Shelly made it so even an old broken down hiker like me could regroup and go on after a bad experience on the trail. I never met Uncle Johnny, but I didn't think he was as bad as Wee Willie made him out to be. I planned to recommend Uncle Johnny's to the Sobos I met in the future.

I ate the fries on the way back to my room. I watched television and ate everything else including the double cheeseburgers. I was amazed at the amount of food I ate. After I gorged, I took some time in the comfort of the warm bedroom and caught up on my journal.

Bill Wilson married Lois Burnham before he went off to World War I as an officer. She found them an apartment in New York close to Wall Street for when he came home to a hero's welcome. Bill was a hero and respected by everyone, including his men. He took a job on Wall Street and soon his talents took him up the ladder to wealth and prestige. His drinking escalated along with his success, but no one thought a great deal of it. Bill and Lois both thought his drinking was normal at first.

Bill's father-in-law, who liked Bill, seemed to be the first to recognize that Bill's drinking was a problem. He also knew a Dr Silkworth at Townes Hospital who had been working with alcoholics. He gave Lois some fatherly advice and recommended she intervene. Lois did and Bill complied, agreeing to meet with Dr. Silkworth. That was early in Bill's drinking career and Bill didn't take him seriously, but before Bill got sober, he ended up seeing a lot of Dr. Silkworth. Bill's drinking continued to worsen even with success, but when the stock market crashed in 1929, Bill's drinking took over his life. Almost penniless, they eventually had to move in with Lois's father and Lois got a job in a department store to support them. Bill's father-in-law, who was concerned how Bill's drinking affected Lois, tried to convince his daughter to leave Bill.

It felt so good to be warm, dry, clean, and full of cheeseburgers. I could no longer concentrate so I turned on the television and then drifted off to sleep.

Day 26   16.4 Miles

I got up early and took a hot shower, ate three honey buns, and drank two cokes. I bought two cokes out of the machine to take with me because they had enough caffeine to get me started again the next morning. I called Scooter from the pay phone before I left. The day was cold and sunny, but the forecast called for heavy snow later. The first shelter was four miles and the second was sixteen miles, so I set my sights on the second and high-tailed it north. I hiked solo all day, but I ran into Yahtzee who was slack-packing southward without his pack. Miss Janet shuttled him up the trail and made him wear a silly hat, which made him look like Rocky. He was hiking back to Miss Janet's for the night. I had to rip on him a little for being a slack packer.

The trail was a hard sixteen miles with several mountains including Unaka Mountain, which stood at almost a mile high. The good news was, it didn't snow, but stayed clear and cold. By late afternoon, I reached Cherry Gap Shelter, which was a three-sided, concrete block shelter. A married couple from Maine, making their second attempt to thru-hike, were already at the shelter. The man was dreadfully sick with a cold, so I set up in the opposite end of the shelter to stay as far away from them as possible. I considered moving on, but it was starting to spit snow and it was almost nine miles to the next shelter. I didn't want to spend a night in my tent with heavy snow forecast. I cooked and ate a spaghetti meal outside of the shelter to avoid catching his cold. I finished eating, jumped in my bag, and took out my journal. I did it more for an excuse to not talk to them at first, but soon returned to the birth of Alcoholics Anonymous.

Lois was considering having Bill committed to a sanitarium, so she asked Ebby, who was Bill's best friend and drinking buddy, to go to the sanitarium with her for support. She was amazed as she noticed Ebby obviously looked good and seemed to be sober.

She asked Ebby what his secret was. He identified himself to Lois as an alcoholic and confessed that he almost ended up in a sanitarium or jail. He then told her how Roland Hazard helped him seek help through a Christian fellowship called the Oxford Group. They had meetings, prayed, and helped others. The miracle happened and Ebby was staying sober. After Lois heard his story, she gained some hope. She asked Ebby to talk to Bill in one last effort to help Bill before her and Dr. Silkworth gave up and had Bill committed to a sanitarium permanently. Ebby agreed.

Ebby called Bill and arranged a meeting with him. When they met, Bill scoffed and had nothing to do with the idea at first. He practically threw Ebby out of his house, but Ebby had done his job and planted the seed. The next step was up to Bill and God. Bill continued drinking and ended up detoxifying in New York's Townes Hospital by Dr. Silkworth once again. That was when Bill had the famous spiritual experience that they still talk about in the rooms of Alcoholics Anonymous.

After the hospital released Bill, he contacted Ebby and asked to learn more. That was when Ebby introduced Bill to the Oxford Group. Together, they went to meetings and started to pick up alcoholic bums in the Bowery and brought them to Bill's house and preached to them to try to help them. None of them ever stayed sober except Bill and Ebby. The miracle was that Bill learned he could stay sober by helping other drunks.

Bill had been sober four months while Lois was working as a clerk in a department store to support them. She was also cooking and cleaning for all the bums he and Ebby were dragging home. Eventually, she became weary and overwhelmed by all the work. She went to Bill's former boss and business partner, Frank Shaw to ask for help. Frank did Lois a favor and gave Bill a job. He assigned Bill to go to Akron, Ohio to investigate a proxy battle at a tire company for some Wall Street investors.

The man from Maine was snoring, so I closed my journal. I was going to try to get some sleep because I had about eighteen miles to hike to Carvers Gap where I planned to meet Scooter on Saturday. I wanted to hike to Roan High Knob Shelter on Friday, which was only a mile and a half from Carvers Gap. That way, I could clean up to be fresh when I met my bride on Saturday.

ALCOHOLICS ANONYMOUS

Day 27   8.9 Miles

The snow and wind started in the night. I awoke to eight inches of fresh snow and it was snowing hard. I believed that I made a sound decision staying in the shelter in spite of the folks from Maine being sick and keeping me up most of the night with their snoring. However, I wanted to put some distance between us, so I packed up and left without any breakfast or coffee.

The trail was getting hard to follow, because eight inches of snow was hiding the path on the ground. I had to rely on the 2 X 6 inch white blazes painted on the trees to guide me. The snow itself was slowing my progress and made the hike even more strenuous. I was starting to wish I would have stayed at Uncle Johnny's a while longer. The couple from Maine caught up to me, because apparently, I was breaking trail for them. I took a break to make coffee and eat, so they would go ahead and break trail for me. I soon caught back up to them on the road to Bakersville, North Carolina. They lost the trail where it crosses the road. We searched until I found a white blaze on the road covered by the new snow. I let them go first up the incline after Greasy Creek Gap, but soon caught up to them on the mountain. They stopped and were contemplating turning back to Erwin to stay at Miss Janet's Hostel. They were afraid to go up Roan Mountain at sixty-three-hundred feet in altitude. I knew at the time I shouldn't be listening to their negativity, so I moved on up the mountain.

The snow was mounting when I arrived at the trail to Clyde Smith Shelter. I needed water, so I hiked a tenth of a mile to the shelter for water. Since it was lunchtime, I ate in the shelter out of the weather.

The words of warning from the Maine couple kept haunting me.

What if they were right? What if Roan was too dangerous in these conditions? After all, the couple from Maine did have more trail experience. Besides, Clyde Smith at a lower elevation of almost forty-four-hundred feet was a nice, three-sided shelter with four bunks. I would be safe and dry there. I could hear the mind war within myself as I watched the storm outside. I kept asking myself, should I stay or should I go on six miles to Roan High Knob Shelter?

I made more coffee and decided to give myself some time. The coffee put me in a talkative mood, so I called Allie, the trail angel I met in the Smoky's at Newfound Gap. She helped me get out of my head for the moment, as she was a positive person. I enjoyed her attitude and planned on keeping in contact with her even after the trail was over and only a memory. The combination of talking to her and drinking two days worth of coffee put me in a great mood in spite of the situation.

I had eight miles to go to rendezvous with Scooter at Carver's Gap the next day. The memory of getting in trouble a few days ago was still fresh. I thought maybe the snow would let up by morning. I decided to error on the side of caution and stayed put in the shelter. I would write letters to the people who wrote me and talk on the phone for the rest of the day. The temperature was cold, but I was dry and thought I would be okay if I ate a lot of food. I had some extra food and I didn't have to save any because I would be eating restaurant food and drinking good coffee with Scooter by noon the next day.

It was late afternoon before I talked to Scooter. She was on the road, traveling south to rendezvous with me. The temperature dropped and I was having a hard time staying warm. The euphoric effect from caffeine in the coffee had worn off and my mood plummeted along with the temperature. I planned to cook a hot meal and boil water to put in my water bottle to warm my sleeping bag. I thought that would help. I told Scooter I might be late meeting her, but I gave no details because I didn't want her to worry needlessly. I had too much time to think. I knew from experience, that when I was alone in my own head, it was as if I was behind enemy lines by myself.

I deliberately directed my mind to focus on the miracle that happened in Akron, Ohio in 1935, which was somewhat already on my mind.

When Bill Wilson arrived at the Mayflower Hotel in Akron all the tire plants were on a sit down strike, so he had unexpected time on his hands. He knew no one, had nothing to do, and was away from his main supporters, Ebby and Lois. He got thirsty and feared he was going to get drunk if he didn't find another drunk to talk to. A bulletin board in the hotel lobby had the names and phone numbers of churches and ministers in the area. Bill got a dollar's worth of nickels and started making phone calls from a pay phone in the lobby until he got a positive response from a Reverend Tunks.

Reverend Tunks, who by coincidence was from the Oxford Group, referred Bill to a wealthy do-gooder named Henrietta Syberling, who was also in the Oxford Group. She arranged a meeting with Dr. Bob Smith who was a successful proctologist who's drinking had caused him trouble in every area of his life. Like Bill, Dr. Bob's life also became unmanageable. Henrietta and Dr. Bob's wife Annie, coerced Bob into meeting Bill at the Syberling Gate House. Bob was hung-over and shaking from drinking the night before. He reluctantly agreed to the meeting, but he felt forced. He told them he would give the mug fifteen minutes.

Dr. Bob was hostile at first towards Bill. He thought it was another plot by his wife and Henrietta to get him sober. However, he quickly bonded with Bill when he discovered Bill wasn't trying to change or fix him, but came to him to try to stay sober himself by talking to another drunk. Bill didn't give him any advice or tell him what to do, but he shared what his drinking had done to him. Dr. Bob soon joined in with his own personal drinking experiences. They started to share their experience, strength and hope with each other and connected on an intimate level that only alcoholics who have been living the Hell of addiction could understand. The meeting lasted six hours to everyone's delight. A life-long bond formed between the two men at that first Alcoholics Anonymous meeting.

Well after it got dark, a frozen thru-hiker from South Carolina interrupted my meditation. I think God knew I needed company, so he sent a young man by the name of Coconut Monkey in from the storm. He got his name because he carried a coconut with a monkey's face carved into it, as a pet. He was a tough, good-looking boy with coal black hair and bronze skin. He graduated college and decided to take on the trail as an adventure. He didn't know I was going to be at the shelter because snow had covered my tracks. I helped him as Christopher helped me. I was so grateful for his company. He ate and curled up in his sleeping bag. I enjoyed his southern accent as we talked until late into the night. He had hiked twenty-one miles in the snow and planned on hiking twenty-three miles the next day. Coconut Monkey was optimistic and I needed a positive thinker to give me hope. We made a deal that someday I would take him fishing for salmon at the Salmon River in New York and he would take me bass fishing in South Carolina.

Sometimes, when the wind would stop, we could hear footsteps outside the shelter that sounded human. Coconut Monkey called out a couple of times, but no one answered. I finally got curious enough to crawl out of my sleeping bag to look. I don't know what we were hearing, but there were no tracks in the foot or so of new snow.

I suggested, "Maybe this place was haunted."

Coconut Monkey asked, "Who was Clyde Smith anyway?"

I replied, "Maybe he's watching out for us." Eventually, we fell silent and drifted off to sleep with the sound of the storm.

March 25   Day 28   7.9 Miles

7.9 Extremely tough miles

I slept fitfully because it was too cold to sleep, so I got up to boil water to warm my sleeping bag a couple of times in the night. I was also fearful of what the day would bring. It was still snowing and blowing like a good old Pennsylvania blizzard. The thermometer on my pack read eight degrees. My feet became extremely cold as soon as I put my frozen boots on, so I hit the trail as soon as possible to warm up without breakfast.

I checked on Coconut Monkey to make sure he was still alive before I left. He put on all the extra socks he had and a pair of moccasins to keep his feet warm last night. He assured me he would be okay if he kept his warm. I silently said a prayer, bid him goodbye, and wished him Godspeed. I left him sleeping at about daylight. I couldn't see his tracks from when he came in the night before because about two feet of snow was on the ground. I gambled that the weather would get better, but it was still snowing and blowing. I was wrong. I felt pissed at myself for listening to the fearful people from Maine. I prayed a foxhole prayer for God's protection, Lord if you get me through this storm, I will be a good boy from now on.

The going was slow and exhausting. At times, I plowed through snow up to my waist. I was soaked from sweat, but I couldn't stop to rest because I would freeze. I realized that fatigue may also be another unwanted enemy before the day was over. White blazes marked the Appalachian Trail often, but normally I would follow the path beaten down by the hundreds of hikers before me. I mostly used the blazes to make sure that I was not lost on a side trail like Brave Heart. I was having a hard time distinguishing the path in the deep snow, so I had to rely on the blazes that showed me the trail. I had to be careful to not get lost because I was not sure I could survive if I got lost in that big of storm. I backtracked every time I didn't see a white blaze until I found the trail. It was like working out a puzzle that might be fun if I wasn't so afraid.

I realized I would be late getting to the rendezvous with Scooter at Carvers Gap. I had no cell tower to warn her, so I hoped she wouldn't be too worried. Then I started worrying if she could reach Carvers Gap in the storm with her new car. I made it to the ascent up Beartown Mountain, which at fifty-four hundred feet high, was good practice for Roan Mountain. I stopped to get a drink and discovered my water bottles had frozen solid. I was carrying four and a half pounds of ice. I considered tossing the extra weight, but it would be sacrilegious to litter on my beloved Appalachian Trail even considering the situation.

The trail cut through a Rhododendron thicket, which gave me a break. The snow was deep, but the trail was clearly visible and the bushes blocked the wind. I somehow made it to the summit of Beartown and down into Ash Gap. I found a spring that was flowing, but I couldn't filter water because my filter was frozen. I took a chance and drank unfiltered water directly from the spring. I desperately took on Roan Mountain at six-thousand, two-hundred, and eighty-five feet high, which was only about another thousand feet up. The going was steep, but again, the Rhododendron at the higher levels was thick enough that the path was visible. The going actually got easier as I ascended High Roan. I reached what I thought was the summit. I gave a yell of triumph and then gave thanks. I have to admit I was feeling ten feet tall and fairly bullet proof.

An eerie, uneasy feeling soon crept in because the trail didn't descend as quickly as I thought it should. My jubilation was short-lived as I discovered my worst nightmare. When the wind let up for a moment, I could see what lay ahead of me. I stood there stunned by what appeared to be a snow and ice covered wall that reached up and disappeared into the storm. I couldn't describe the overwhelming fear I felt realizing I had been on a false summit and the worst was yet to come. I wondered if I would make it over that one. I said a prayer, put my hiking poles in my pack, and started my assault on Roan. I took one step at a time, one white blaze at a time, and one minute at a time. I focused on the trail, as my entire world became the next few feet. I could only see ahead about twenty feet, which may have been a blessing. It seemed that every time I was about to give up hope another friendly two by four inch white blaze would appear and mark my way. I reached the summit, but didn't believe I was there until I started a steep descent.

The wind was calmer on this side of the mountain and the going became easier as I descended. I came upon the US Forest Service access road to Roan High Bluff. Snow choked the road, but I knew for sure I was on my way down and the worst was over. The trail leveled off as I met some cross-country skiers coming up the mountain.

One said, "Isn't this snow wonderful!" He seemed elated with the unexpected snow.

I suppressed the urge to sucker punch him and asked, "Did you see a small white woman with a black Honda Element at Carvers Gap?"

"Yes, but she was going north."

"Are you sure?"

"Yeah, I'm sure."

I thought Scooter might hike south to meet me, but north was going away from me. I thought of the bald mountains north of here and her lost by herself in the storm. I knew Scooter wouldn't make such a mistake, but it gave me a reason to worry. I suddenly focused on concern for Scooter. I had a lot of confidence in her consistent ability to make sound decisions, but the skier put doubt in my mind. I was horrified by the thought of her alone and lost on the trail to the north. I almost ran in a panic with my new adrenalin charged energy stopping often to yell, "MAR-I-LYN" at the top of my lungs. There was no answer, but I covered the remaining mile fast. I broke out of the pine and rhododendron about fifty yards above the parking lot at Carvers Gap. I was amazed at the number of cars there. Among the cars was the black Element with Scooter pacing impatiently beside it.

Tears immediately blurred my vision. I did an about face to salute the mountain. I stared into the white nothingness of the storm, but in my mind's eye, I could see the summit of High Roan along with the morning's events. I knew that logically, I should not have been able to make it over a mountain like Roan on a day like that as ill-equipped as I was. The story of David and Goliath popped into my mind and I thought logically, David should not have been able to defeat Goliath as ill-equipped as he was. Logically, Goliath should have kicked David's ass. I suddenly came to a spiritual awakening or awareness that human logic has nothing to do with the outcome of anything when God was involved.

I had to ask myself, why did I still have some doubts? I thought back to that day I came out of Rice Gap when I was wet, freezing, and could not go on. I closed my eyes, prayed desperately, cried out for help and when I opened my eyes, I saw the shelter sign for the Hogback Ridge Shelter. When I arrived at the shelter and a Christian was there to take care of me, even a dummy like me could understand God clearly answered my prayer. I recalled that Heaven Bound told me, you will always have doubts, in his German accent, but I didn't recall him saying why. Heaven Bound's response puzzled me because

I couldn't imagine a Christian as devout as him ever had any doubts, but his response sounded like personal experience. The Gospels, in the little white Bible quoted Jesus as saying, "Father why hast thou forsaken me?" as he hung on the cross. Did Jesus have doubts also?

Maybe it was the normal, insecure, human part of me to have some doubts. I wasn't sure I needed to know the answer or if it mattered. I did know when I felt contact with God I felt better than when I was alone. Maybe that's all I need to know at least for now.

O'boy was I happy to see Scooter. I stripped naked beside the car in ten degrees Fahrenheit. I washed with wet wipes and put on clean underwear for the first time since Springer Mountain Georgia. The underwear I started with in Georgia didn't last. It rotted off in the first couple of weeks. I also put on clean cotton socks, blue jeans, flannel shirt and patchouli oil. I felt as if I was sixteen getting ready for my first date. I was a little disappointed when I got in the car and Scooter said, "My God, you stink!"

A Tennessee snowplow sat at the North Carolina and Tennessee border. The road needed plowed, but the plow driver just sat there drinking coffee. We had a terrorizing ride down the mountain on the unplowed road in Scooter's new Element. We descended to two thousand feet and found a completely different world. The snow disappeared, and the temperature was thirty-five degrees. We stopped at a McDonald's in Hampton, Tennessee, so I could get a small snack of three double cheeseburgers, fries, and a large coffee. Scooter said, "I thought you said a small snack."

A NASCAR race was at Bristol that weekend, so all the motels were booked a year in advance. We headed north four hours to Daleville, Virginia to an Econolodge. I took a shower and washed my laundry first thing. I weighed myself at a hundred and fifty-four pounds, which was down twenty-one pounds since I left Pennsylvania. We went to Shoney's to an AYCE buffet and I ate all I could eat and then some. Scooter and I gave thanks together. It was the first time I ever recall praying together. We prayed for Coconut Monkey and all my other brothers and sisters who I left behind somewhere out on the trail. I prayed that they would all be safe and warm.

The day was a little too close of a call, even for me. I lay beside Scooter and listened to her steady breathing, but for some reason I couldn't surrender my consciousness to sleep, so I took out my journal to record the day's events.

That first meeting between Dr. Bob and Bill in 1935 ended when they ran out of cigarettes, but before parting, both men willingly agreed to meet again the next day. Bill and Dr. Bob continued to meet every day. A short time later, Dr. Bob asked Bill to stay at his house with him and his wife Annie, so Bill packed his bags and moved from the Mayflower. I don't know if it ever became official, but Bill became Dr. Bob's sponsor. Dr. Bob was sober a couple of weeks when he went to a medical convention. He was away from Bill and Annie, who were his entire supports to stay sober. All the drinking influenced him into thinking only one drink wouldn't hurt, even after all he had discovered with Bill. Besides, he thought no one would ever know. He relapsed back into an uncontrollable drinking binge at once. He came home drunk, so Bill and Annie had to detoxify him at home. He was going through such violent withdrawal that Bill had to convince Annie to let him give Dr. Bob a drink of alcohol to bring him down slowly so he wouldn't have a seizure and die. Dr. Bob sobered up and the two continued to support one another. Neither man ever drank again for the rest of their lives.

I calmed down, so I closed the book and closed my eyes. That ended week four and I hiked three-hundred and seventy-two miles since I left Springer that day in February. Katahdin was still eighteen-hundred and three miles north.

Day 29   Zero Miles

I awoke to a wet, grey, winter's day. My mood was as gloomy as the day. Maybe the bed was too soft or maybe it was the weather, but everything hurt.

Scooter said, "Are you okay, you're moving like an old man"?

I was a little grumpy when I replied, "I'm okay, and I'm moving like an old man because I am an old man." Then we both laughed.

We went back to Shoney's to an AYCE breakfast and I ate all I could eat again. We packed up to drive south for four hours back to Carvers Gap. I drove most of the time in silence which fit my mood. We stopped at Walmart to buy supplies for my future mail drops. I had a big plastic bin that I filled with food and things I would need on the trail. She took the bin home with her so I could call to let her know what I needed and she could mail it to me on the trail.

The race at Bristol caused nightmare-type traffic, which delayed us and annoyed me. We had to wait in long lines to get off the interstate, but once we got out of traffic, it went smoothly the rest of the way. I found Carvers Gap as I left it the day before. The storm continued to rage in the high country with high winds and cold temperatures. The bald mountain tops north of the gap were all at about six-thousand feet high and covered with waist deep snow. No new tracks were on the trail and I couldn't see mine from when I rolled in twenty-four hours ago. I didn't know what I was going to do, but I knew going out there in the storm might be suicide.

That was by far the lowest I was emotionally since I started on the trail. I briefly considered going home. I tried to quickly put that thought out of my mind, but I understood why many hikers abort at times like that when the adversity seemed overwhelming. I took out my guidebook and found several options. I couldn't find my first choice, which was a bed and breakfast within walking distance of the trail. Hampton, Tennessee was about eighteen miles away, but it had everything, so we went back down the mountain to find a place called The Braemar Castle Hostel. The day was a grey and damp once we got off the mountain. Hampton was a small rural, southern town nestled in the foothills of the Appalachian Mountains. We found Brown's Grocery on the main drag. The guidebook said the owner would open on Sunday for thru-hikers only, but no one was around.

We drove around the town, but found no one anywhere. It was almost like a ghost town. It felt a little spooky, as if I entered The Twilight Zone. I found a unique, three-story, stone-faced building that looked out of place compared to the rest of the town. There were no signs, but I could see why people might call it, a castle. I pulled up in front. I got out, told Scooter to stay there, and locked her in the car.

I knocked on the door and got nada. I didn't know why, but I tried the door and it was unlocked. I opened it enough to stick my head into an entryway. The place looked empty, but I could smell the stale odor of hikers. I called out, "Hello" and the only response was the echo of my own voice. I called out the second time, only louder, but the result was still silence. All the cells in my body were at battle station status. I wouldn't have entered the place for love nor money, so I returned to the car.

Scooter was stiff from being in the car, so she got out to stretch, and walked around. We walked out back where there were several small, one-story houses. Some had toys or bicycles in the yard, but no one was around. I was fully expecting Kujo the Rottweiler to suddenly come charging out of the shadows, when a voice with a friendly southern accent said, "Hiker, can I help ya?"

I puked out the desperate situation I was in to the stranger.

He just said with a grin, "You'll be okay son, I can help ya."

I got a déjà vu feeling of Mull's Motel in Hiawassee, Georgia where the owner exploited me because I was a hiker. I immediately challenged him as to exactly how much his help would cost me. He showed patience, smiled, and went over the cost. He agreed to rent a room and then shuttle me back to Carver's Gap after the storm passed. The price he quoted was reasonable. My intuition told me the guy was okay, so I calmed down and started to like him. I asked him how he knew I was a hiker when he addressed me as, Hiker right off the bat. I wasn't dressed like a hiker because I wore blue jeans and a flannel shirt.

He smiled and said, "I done a little hiken myself."

I stuck out my hand and said, "My trail name is Dreamer."

He grabbed my hand firmly, smiled, and replied "Seiko like the watch." The name Seiko rang a bell in my head, but I couldn't place it.

Seiko said, "Foller me". I grabbed my pack, which was the only luggage I had, and followed him to the third floor of the Castle. Seiko tried to talk me out of taking a private room with a private shower for thirty dollars a night when I could save money by taking a bed in the bunkroom for five dollars a night, since he didn't expect any more guests that night. I would have the bunkroom all to myself, but I declined, thinking that with the luck I had lately, the bunkroom would fill up at the last minute with a troop of cub scouts or something. He led me to a large room with a double bed. He explained the hostel was over full last night with people sleeping on the floor, who were here to go to the race. He told me that was why the town seemed abandoned, because everyone was at the race.

He said, "This here's the biggest day of the year in these here parts." Seiko was busy changing the sheets and cleaning the shower as I chatted with him.

I asked, "Have you ever thru-hiked?"

He straightened up from his work and said, "The trail has been my life for more'n twenty-five years. I hiked it fourteen times complete with a few yoyos thrown in." A yoyo is hiking from Springer to Katahdin and back to Springer.

I had a memory bubble pop as I remembered Crazy Horse, Wee Willie, and Christopher all talked about Seiko, who has hiked more than forty-thousand miles on the trail. I couldn't describe the feeling I experienced as I realized I was standing face to face with an Appalachian Trail legend.

My mood elevated as I chattered away bombarding Seiko with questions as he completed his tasks. He said, "Help yourself to anything the folks from last night left before it spoils and I have to throw it out."

Seiko invited me to join him at his place, but I declined because I didn't want to impose.

I said in my best southern accent "Naw, I'd like to say goodbye to the little woman proper."

He smiled and said, "If'n ya get lonely later jes knock on my door."

We shook hands again and I said, "Appreciate ya." He returned to his modest house that was right behind the castle to watch the race.

I wanted to go to dinner with Scooter, but it was getting late. She was getting nervous, and wanted to get on the road for home. She did agree to take me to the Dollar General we passed earlier so I could get some food to eat there at the Castle for the next couple of days. I bought hotdogs, ham, cheese, bread, and pop to take back to the castle. I bid Scooter goodbye and settled in the spooky old castle all by myself. I found an inviting living room with a television and several big, well-used easy chairs. I opened a pop and turned on the television to the race. I watched my first NASCAR race. I could only get the one channel anyway. I was still a bit down emotionally.

I discovered I left my hiking poles in Scooter's car. I thought I could buy some new poles in town the next morning. I didn't plan on hiking for a few days, so it would give me something to do. I was able to let it go and didn't worry over it anymore that night.

That was the first time since before the storm that I had the time to meditate. I shut the television off and gave thanks for how everything worked out almost magically. Maybe if I included God, things would always happen that way. I let my mind drift and soon found myself in the beginning of Alcoholics Anonymous again.

One day, early on, Bill said to Dr. Bob, "Since this works for us, why not try it on someone else?"

Dr. Bob said. "I'm game."

They went to a hospital that knew Dr. Bob and visited a man named Bill Dodson. He hit a nurse in a drunken rage while being admitted the night before, so they had him physically restrained. Bill and Dr. Bob didn't preach to him or try to shame him into getting sober like Bill tried in New York. They identified themselves as alcoholics and shared their personal experience with him almost the same as the lady on the hotline did with me that day in 1977. Bill Dodson got sober and became the third member of Alcoholics Anonymous. He identified with Bill and Dr. Bob's story as Dr. Bob did when Bill shared his story. That was how Alcoholics Anonymous worked then and how it has always worked ever since.

I hoped that some other hikers would come in, but no luck. I prayed for Coconut Monkey and all my other brothers and sisters caught in the blizzard in the high country. I was lonely, but I needed to remember the Alcoholics Anonymous slogan, This too shall pass.

Day 30   Zero Miles

I awoke early, took a shower, dressed, and ventured into the village to forage. I kept a full set of street clothes, which included blue jeans and underwear, flannel shirt, and cotton socks. I planned to give my street clothes to Seiko when I went back to the trail because he looked to be about the same size as me.

Hampton, Tennessee was a quaint little rural town with a lot of old second-hand stores, an old fashion grocery/general store, diner, and Post Office. Down by the highway was a Dollar General and McDonald's. I walked a mile to the local diner, where I felt out of place. All I had to do was open my mouth to speak and everyone there knew I was a Yankee. I ordered biscuits and gravy, which the waitress, who called me Sugar, recommended. Many of the local men from ages thirty-five to sixty had mullet-type haircuts, which I found strange. The buzz at the diner was all about the race, which I knew nothing about even though I watched part of it the day before on television.

I found the outfitter my guidebook said was in Hampton, but it was permanently closed. I checked out the town trying to find hiking poles with no luck. I stopped at several second hand stores and found the people more interesting than the merchandise. I would have bought a lot of nice junk if I wasn't limited as to what I could carry in my backpack. I bought food and stopped at a computer store/coffee shop for coffee with a shot of espresso. I visited with the lady who ran the store while I drank my coffee. I finished my coffee and went back to the Castle and took a nap to kill time until lunch.

I woke up and went to Brown's Store where Seiko also worked part time to earn a little money when he was not hiking on the trail. Brown's was the largest general/grocery store in town. The owner also owned the Castle Hostel and many other things in town. Browns looked like the 1950s, small local grocery store that existed before the chain stores of today. The store had two checkout isles, but Seiko only opened the second isle when they got so busy they needed to speed things up. They built an addition for an old-time hardware/general store where they sold furniture, lamps, toilets, and almost anything else except hiking poles. Lumber, building supplies, topsoil, coal, and mulch were sold outside. Seiko also delivered whatever needed delivered.

Seiko showed me around the store before he took me back to the diner for lunch. He introduced me to the locals saying, "This here's our hiker. He plans on hiken the Appalatchen Trail." That was how he talked. The race was still the main topic of discussion. A driver named Matt Kenseth bumped Jeff Gordon. Jeff got pissed and pushed Matt after the race and almost started a fight. He may get in trouble for it. The news kept replaying the video clip, which inspired more heated discussion. Half of the customers admired Jeff Gordon and the other half seemed to despise him. Everyone, even the waitress had an opinion, except me. I stayed quiet like a dumb Yankee.

Seiko knew I was bored, so he invited me over for supper at his house that night. He told me, "I'm also famous for my cooken, especially my gram cracker cream pie, which I ain't gonna be able ta make tanight." I said, "My mom sure made good gram cracker cream pie." He took me back to Brown's and I walked back to the Castle to take a nap. My thoughts drifted back to the start of Alcoholics Anonymous as I walked.

Bill returned to New York after four months in Akron to see if he could get Alcoholics Anonymous started at home. He was welcomed home at the train station by Ebby. Ebby lost his main support when Bill went to Akron and he relapsed. He was drunk when he met Bill that day. Lois was miffed that Bill had been gone for over four months and they had an argument soon after he got home. Let's say Bill's homecoming wasn't how he pictured it, but he wasn't discouraged about what he was discovering. Soon the fellowship between drunks started to catch on in New York as it did in Akron. That was how a meeting between two drinks in 1935 grew into the worldwide fellowship of Alcoholics Anonymous.

I couldn't sleep so I took a shower and watched the local news. Finally, it was time to go to Seiko's for dinner. I spent the evening with Seiko. It was as if I went to a hiker workshop. He had thru-hiked the Appalachian Trail exclusively and had incredible knowledge of hiking. I watched and listened as he fixed sweet and sour pork on rice. He shared several trail tales of his past hikes and gave me valuable advice as he went. Best of all, he was positive, which gave me the hope and encouragement I needed to continue my hike. Some of his passion for the trail rubbed off on me. I was quite surprised to find out he was sixty-four-years-old. He looked to be about forty-five because he was in such good shape. I met Seiko's forty-year-old girlfriend, Sunshine, but she didn't stay long. I thought they were having some type of argument because I sensed some tension in the air, but maybe they didn't want to fight around me. She took a plate of sweet and sour pork to go.

Seiko suggested I attempt fourteen miles the next day. He offered to take me to Carvers Gap to drop me off the next morning and pick me up at US 19E and bring me back to the Castle that night. I jumped on the offer because it would get me back on the trail a day sooner. He heard the storm had let up, but there was deep snow for about ten miles until I got out of the high country.

Seiko took out a new pack that some manufacturer wanted him to try, which was lighter than the pack I had. He also got out an antique, bamboo, hiking pole. He said, "Here, I carried this pole on my first ever thru-hike." He then handed me his new pack and the antique hiking pole to use on my hike the next day. I tried to decline the use of his hiking pole, but he wouldn't take no for an answer. I told him how honored I felt, but all he said with a grin in his slow Tennessee accent was, "Shee-it, its jest an old piece a wood."

I went back to my room in the castle so pumped up I couldn't sleep. I recalled Eric Rudolf's words, Don't just plan it, survive it. I felt grateful to both Seiko and Eric. I thought it strange how God used so many different types of angels in a person's journey.

Day 31   13.7 Miles

Seiko took me to another down-home diner for breakfast. He ordered two eggs, biscuits, gravy, grits, and coffee. I had the same. I still wasn't feeling accepted by the locals, but they were friendly and treated me well. Seiko and I were becoming good friends. Seiko tried to teach me to talk country with the accent, but I still sounded like a Yankee. We took our time to finish eating before we left. I had Seiko's pack loaded with my tent, sleeping bag, clothes, and water filter in case the snow delayed me. I had packed six ham and cheese sandwiches, snickers, cookies, and coke for the day's hike.

Two feet of snow greeted me at Carvers Gap when Seiko dropped me off, but the temperature was forty degrees, sunny, and calm. The best thing was hiker tracks were on the trail that I could follow. I soon discovered why Seiko used the term, "Post holing," because I sank up to my thighs with every step. The hiking was exhausting and I was soaked in sweat in no time, but it felt great to be back on the trail again.

I followed the tracks for a half mile to where they split. I took the trail that looked used the most, and followed it for a hundred yards and found no blazes. I was on a bald with no trees and thought the white blazes could be on rocks covered by snow. I decided to continue to the top of Round Bald at fifty-eight-hundred feet high and the tracks stopped. Apparently the hikers I was following were lost and had taken the wrong trail and turned back, so I turned back also. Probably that was why the wrong trail looked more traveled because everyone was walking it twice. I hiked a total of about two miles off trail in the snow. I wondered if the tracks I followed were the tracks of Brave Heart and Messenger, who were experts at getting lost. I felt better when I found white blazes marking the trail on trees below the tree line.

I soon discovered I forgot two truly important things when switching packs. The first was my camera. I couldn't take pictures on Roan Mountain three days ago because it was too cold for the camera batteries to work. The day was clear and picturesque with great views in the deep snow, but my camera sat in my pack back at the castle. I had to record the scenery on the snow-covered mountains with memory and pen only. Oh yeah! The other important thing I forgot to bring was toilet paper, which I discovered at a bad time. The good news was I found out I could substitute snow for toilet paper. The bad news was I experienced a true pause that refreshed more than words could describe.

I hiked over the three bald summits and overtook a bunch of college kids out for the day. A young man who thru-hiked last year was guiding them. I talked with him for a while and he took my picture in the snow. I gave him my e-mail and he said he would mail me the picture. Once I descended to a lower altitude, the snow disappeared and the hiking became a lot easier so I made good time. I arrived at the pickup point in the afternoon as planned. I found Seiko waiting for me with a trail angel named Dragon Slayer and guess who, Brave Heart and Messenger. They were all sitting in Dragon Slayer's SUV drinking pop and waiting for me and the college kids who I passed earlier on the trail. Dragon Slayer gave me a pop and a bag of potato chips. She had thru-hiked last year with the young man I talked to earlier on the trail. The whole atmosphere was like a family reunion.

Brave Heart caught up to Messenger at Erwin. They stayed at Miss Janet's in the storm. They told me thirty-one hikers stayed at Miss Janet's on the floor and porch. Yes, I was following their tracks earlier when I got off trail in the snow. They continued to earn their reputation for getting lost. They filled me in on all the trail gossip as I drank my soda, which we Yankees called pop. Seiko offered to take Brave Heart and Messenger to the hostel at Kincora. That way I could meet his friend Bob. We thanked Dragon Slayer for the trail magic and said our goodbyes. We all piled into the cab of Seiko's truck and off we went.

The hostel at Kincora was owned and run by Bob Peoples, who was Seiko's biggest competitor and closest friend. When we arrived, Bob put the coffee on while Brave Heart and Messenger settled for the night. We all sat around drinking coffee and listening intently to Seiko and Bob tell trail tales for about two hours. I see why they were the best of friends. Character wise, they were two of the finest men I ever had the good fortune to cross paths with. Seiko made a deal with Bob to pick me up at the castle the next morning to shuttle me back to the trial with Brave Heart and Messenger. I planned on spending one night on the trail and arrive at Kincora in two days, where I planned to spend the night.

Seiko and I went back to the castle, where I took a shower before I cooked hotdogs for supper. I got in the clean, white sheets and gave thanks for being back on the trail. I opened my notebook to record the snowy day before it faded from my memory. Eventually my mind returned to the early days when Alcoholics Anonymous didn't even have a name. The program was part of the Oxford Group and a man-to-man, personal survival from alcoholism affair. By the fall of 1937, the membership was about forty sober alcoholics strong. Bill himself said, "It was a time of flying blind."

The Oxford Group in New York started to criticize Bill for his practice of hosting meetings solely for alcoholics. Oxford Group members also constantly criticized Bill personally for his smoking and womanizing. The Oxford Group declared the Wilsons were not what they called, "Maximum," advising members not to attend the Wilson's meetings. Bill was disillusioned with the Oxford Group's aggressive evangelism and intolerance for other religions and non-believers. The Oxford Group said the Wilsons quit, however Lois said, "We were kicked out." In 1937 for whatever the reason, the Wilsons broke away from the Oxford Group and formed their own group.

I grew drowsy from the strenuous day and closed my notebook. The castle didn't seem so spooky anymore, but I still wished some other hikers would stop by for the company.

Day 32   13.9 Miles

I woke early to make ham and cheese sandwiches to eat later that day on the trail. I also packed a bag of supplies to leave with Bob to hold for me until I got to Kincora, so I didn't have to carry extra weight. Seiko stopped early and wanted to take me to breakfast. I jumped at the chance to see him one last time. He wanted to talk because Sunshine broke up with him after I left the night before. I listened and became a counselor for him. I felt honored that he came to me for counsel. I had tears in my eyes as I bid him good-bye and wondered if I would ever see him again. I didn't even know his real name.

Brave Heart and Messenger were already in the truck when Bob picked me up at the Castle. He took us back to the trail where we left off the day before. I noticed piles of trash dumped by the trail. Bob warned us about the former landowner who was resentful, hostile and vengeful. He wouldn't allow the trail to pass through his land, so the National Parks had to take the land from him by eminent domain. He dumped trash, vandalized cars parked at the trailhead, and set booby traps on the trail, all in the name of revenge.

I hiked with Brave Heart and Messenger for protection in numbers most of that morning. We stopped on the bank of Elk River for lunch. I ate the ham and cheese sandwiches. Messenger had tuna fish burritos, and Brave Heart ate peanut butter and honey bagels. We took off our shoes and socks and then napped in the sun after lunch before we hit the trail again. They were hard to keep up with, so I dropped back and hiked solo with my thoughts the rest of the day.

At the end of 1937, after separating from the Oxford Group, Bill went back to Akron to discuss matters with his dear friend Dr. Bob. They decided perhaps a book would be an inexpensive way to get word of the program to the alcoholic who still suffered. Fully committed to the program, Bill started to write instructions in the form of a book. He solicited help from the one-hundred other early members, including Dr. Bob. This in itself became a challenge with so many opinions causing a lot of negotiation in the writing. What a challenge it must have been for Bill. He had a lot of adversity with zero instructions, so he had to ask for help. He was a true pioneer who I wish I could have met.

The day was a warm, sunny, spring day. I hiked at around three-thousand feet enjoying the warmth of the sun. The snow was almost all melted. What a difference a couple of days made. Bob Peoples said he was in the early stages of building a new shelter at Mountaineer Falls. He and some volunteers were going to cable some rocks. He asked me if I would stop and help them when I passed by. I didn't know what the term, cabling rocks meant so he patiently explained how they used cables to move the larger rocks into place for the foundation. It sounded like a lot of work, but I was excited to be involved in the building of a new shelter on the Appalachian Trail. Unfortunately, to my dismay, I hiked past the area he told me about and never saw or heard them. The new shelter would be called Mountaineer Shelter, named after the falls, that I didn't see either.

I found a flat spot in the woods by a stream late in the day to make my home for the night. After I settled in, Brave Heart and Messenger came up from behind and stopped for a minute. They got lost again and I passed them somewhere on the trail. They never found Bob and the volunteers either. They had to move on even though it was almost dark because they left their tents, sleeping bags, and gear at Kincora. They still had to hike another ten miles to Kincora. I hoped they wouldn't get lost again in the dark. I would have hated to beat them to Kincora the next day.

I made poor macaroni and cheese for supper, but enjoyed eating the crap as if it were steak. I quickly learned from the trail, hunger often made the worst food taste like the best. I was surprised to find lots of cell tower, so I called Scooter. I left my checkbook with Scooter so she could pay my bills as they came in while I was on the trail. She warned me that I had a three-hundred dollar cell phone bill. I first felt that old familiar fear of economic insecurity and agreed that I needed to cut back on my calls to folks in the program, but something didn't feel right about it. The subject of the conversation moved on and we let it go. She had a stressful day at work and needed to do a few things before she retired for the night, so we said, good night.

I wasn't sleepy and looked at the time and realized it was twenty-one hundred on Wednesday night and my friends would have just gotten out of the, As Bill Sees It, meeting of Alcoholics Anonymous in Edinboro. I really missed going to the meetings and all my friends who were at the meetings. I wanted to call some of them, but I thought of the three-hundred dollar phone bill.

One of Alcoholics Anonymous's many slogans said, how important is it? I questioned, how important was three-hundred dollars? Was it more important than my sobriety? One of the few ways I could make contact with the people in the program was by cell phone. Contact with Alcoholics Anonymous was always a way for me to stay focused on what was important. One of the most important of all things in my life had to be my sobriety. I observed other Alcoholics Anonymous members pull away from the meetings, sober friends, and their sober support system, then relapse into drinking. When they returned to drinking, some of them even died of their addiction after many years of being sober. Without my sobriety, I would lose everything else including my self-respect, the respect of my friends, and family. I would replace my spiritual relationship with God with the evil chemicals that would call me away and consume my soul.

After some thought, I speed dialed my friend Darren, who went regularly to the Edinboro meeting. He was actually on his way home from the meeting when he answered the phone. I ran my dilemma past him.

He said, "Let's think it through."

I would have saved a little money if I stopped calling Alcoholics Anonymous people. I would start to rely on my own thinking. Eventually, I would start to think I didn't need any help from anyone. I would start to return to the old me all alone once again. I would be miserable, filled with hate, fear, and anger. Eventually I would convince myself it would be okay to take just one drink to escape the emotional pain. After the first drink, I would go to the closest bar, run my mouth, and get in a fight. I would probably get my ass kicked, at my age. I could even end up in jail in Tennessee.

Darren said, "Think what it could cost to get bailed out."

I said, "Not only bail; there would be the cost of restitution, lawyer fees, and other legal fees. Scooter would have to come down and get me. I may even have to do some time." Then I thought of all the humiliation of having to reintroduce and admit I relapsed.

After making contact, and talking it over with Darren I made the sane decision to keep calling other alcoholics as often as I could. After all three-hundred dollars a month was a reasonably cheap price to pay for sanity. I gave thanks to my creator for another great day to be alive and on the trail. I felt so grateful to have a program like Alcoholics Anonymous and friends like Darren.

Day 33   20.1 Miles

The day was so pleasant with temperatures in the seventies and sunny. I put on sunscreen and hiked in shorts. I felt as if I had seen the last of winter. The hiking was easy and I arrived at Dennis Cove and Kincora mid-morning. Brave Heart and Messenger made it to Kincora in the night, but were still sleeping. I didn't want to stop for the night so early, so I took a shower and had a long talk with Bob as I re-supplied from the bag I left with him.

I carried Seiko's antique hiking pole. I didn't want to take it for fear I would break it and couldn't replace it. Seiko, being the guy he was, wouldn't take no for an answer. He said I could leave it at Mount Rodgers Outfitters in Damascus and he would pick it up the next time he was in Damascus. I told my story to Bob and asked if he would give the pole back to Seiko. He said he would and took the antique hiking pole, but returned with a nearly new set of Leki poles for me to use. Bob also wouldn't take no for an answer, so I took the poles to use. At least I could replace them if I broke one. I planned to send them back to him from Damascus.

Bob was a retired military officer, who purposely bought land close to the Appalachian Trail and built a hiker hostel. He was an older gentleman, stocky but not overweight, and looked to be in great shape. He sported a military type mustache and looked like he kept his hair military style, although I never saw him without his hat. He had that tough demeanor of an officer, but inside he had the kind heart of an angel. He only charged four dollars a day to stay at Kincora, which included kitchen privileges, showers, and laundry. He and his wife also shuttled hikers to town free. Hikers left food behind which he welcomed anyone to eat. He made no profit and if you work on the trail with him, you stayed free.

I had to admit I never encountered two more trusting men than Seiko and Bob. Neither man knew my real name, but they both trusted me to return their hiking poles. I had forgotten people of their caliber even existed. Brave Heart and Messenger were awake and got up, so I put on another pot of coffee. I ate breakfast and drank two pots of coffee with Bob, Brave Heart, and Messenger. They were gloating because Seiko came over the night before and brought his famous gram cracker cream pie, which they ate.

Brave Heart, Messenger, and I then hiked out together. We hiked up Laurel Fork Gorge to the spectacular Laurel Falls, which had a magnificent, hundred-foot waterfall by the Appalachian Trail. We all stopped to pose for pictures. The water was far too cold for me to even consider swimming, but later in the summer, I bet many hot hikers end up in the water.

Brave Heart and Messenger moved out, so I followed. The trail ended at an un-climbable horizontal cliff that rose up in front of us. I didn't understand why I was surprised, but we were lost. I did an about face and back tracked to the falls with them following close behind on my heels. They soon took off on another rabbit trail. I decided to take some time until I found the side trail leading back to the white blazes and out of the gorge. I almost kept going when I found the trail, but instead I returned to the falls to wait for Larry and Curley. I took my pack off and sat down a while before they popped out of the brush. They followed as I led them back to the trail. They took off leaving me in their dust. I wondered if they would get lost again.

I hiked solo until I got to Watauga Lake and stopped at a closed beach for supper. Soon Brave Heart and Messenger caught up to me. They got lost and I passed them somewhere on the trail again. I gave Brave Heart back his buck knife with an eight-inch blade that I found on the trail earlier. I was grateful for their company as they joined me for supper. Brave Heart took a jar of Vaseline out of his pack and scooped out a big gob with his finger. He said, "Excuse me" as he dropped his outer shorts displaying a second pair of spandex shorts, the kind bicyclists wear. He took the gob, shoved his hand down the back of his shorts, and rubbed it on his butt.

My eyes almost popped out, "What the hell are you doing?"

Brave Heart sheepishly said, "Chafing." Chafing was always a huge problem, which occurred soon in any long distance hike, magnified by poor hygiene, and the lack of amenities such as a hot shower.

I said, "My advice is to use a lot of medicated powder and go commando."

"Go commando?"

I used a drill sergeant command and shouted, "Ditch the underwear, you would sweat a lot less, besides they would rot off in a week anyway. That grease you rubbed on your ass only lubricates until it absorbs, then it adds to your problem."

He looked at me as if he thought I was kidding and said, "Right." My first instinct was to fire back, but I remembered he was a grown man and I couldn't control him, so I let it go. He would eventually find out for himself anyway, I hoped.

We ate, filled our water bottles from the faucet at the beach, and then we moved on together. I stopped and made camp about a mile farther down the shore of Lake Watauga. Brave Heart and Messenger moved on because they hoped to arrive in Damascus sometime the next day. Damascus was forty miles away, so I wished them luck. It was a good thing God made them as tough as they were.

I made a pot of tea and watched the lake as God slowly dimmed the lights announcing the end of the day. The lake was as smooth as glass as I drank in the serenity of it all. I sat there at peace with myself reading my pocket version of the Big Book. I called it my little big book, which consisted of Part one or the first one-hundred and sixty-four pages of the book called Alcoholics Anonymous.

Eventually, Bill completed a book with the help of other members. Part one of the text explained how the program helps us escape from the imprisonment of alcoholism. Part two was personal stories from different members who shared their experience, strength, and hope. After completion, all those involved took a vote on what to name the book. The majority wanted to name the book, The Way Out, but when they went to get the copyrights, they found several other books had the same title. They took another vote and named the book simply, Alcoholics Anonymous. Bill Wilson first published the book called, Alcoholics Anonymous in 1939. Our fellowship, got its name from the title of the book.

The first edition was physically large so they nicknamed it the Big Book. Part one that describes and explains our program has remained the same since the book's origin. The personal stories in part two have changed some over the years with each new edition.

The Big Book now in its fourth edition, is one of the largest selling books in the world. The book laid down the ground rules which stood as the backbone of our worldwide society. My little Big Book was small and weighed only ounces which made it ideal for backpacking. I had several full-sized Big Books at home. I occasionally gave one to a new member. I read until there wasn't enough light left to see. I have read this book many times over, but still I was surprised how often it talked about a spiritual awakening.

The day was one of my best days on the trail. I could see this adventure was going to be an emotional roller coaster ride. I know I sure had a lot to meditate about in the future on the trail, and I had a lot of time. I was still almost eighteen-hundred miles south of Katahdin.

Day 34   14.1 Miles

I didn't get much sleep, because two resident societies on the lake kept me awake most of the night. The beavers and the geese had a problem with each other. The beavers would hit the water with their tail to send off a danger warning to the other beavers. That would set the geese off honking, which woke me up. As soon as I would start to fall back to sleep the whole process would start all over again. Eventually, I got up and ate two honey buns for breakfast that I washed down with weak, tea bag coffee. I watched the sunrise welcome the new day over the lake became quiet and peaceful after sunup, before I moved out.

I hiked about two miles along the lake to the outlet. I couldn't find any white blazes going across the dam, so I followed a small dirt road that went north along the west side of the outlet from the lake. The road stopped, but I instinctively took a little path to continue north. I must have been in my head, because suddenly I came to the realization I was on a ledge and it was about a hundred feet down to the bottom of the ravine. I couldn't turn around because there wasn't enough room for my pack to allow me, so I had to back up for a little bit before I could turn around. I made myself a promise to pay more attention in the future and never, ever, do that again. When I returned to the dam, I crossed it, found the trail on the other side, and resumed my hike. I climbed out of the valley and back into the mountains, only seeing two southbound section hikers the whole day.

Late in the afternoon, the sky clouded up and looked like it could rain at any moment. The radio was forecasting rain for the night so I pushed to get to Iron Mountain Shelter. I was the first hiker to arrive at the shelter late in the afternoon. I filtered water and settled in as the rain started lightly at first. The first hiker who joined me was a New York City Jew by the name of Woody Crow who taught me to melt peanut butter over ramen noodles. He was thru-hiking and had a June twenty-fifth deadline to summit Mount Katahdin, so he hiked fast for long hours. Yahtzee and Jolly Green Giant came in soaking wet after dark. Yahtzee was a five foot tall, athletic, yuppie-type also from New York City. His hiking partner, named Jolly Green Giant, was a six foot, three inch tall southern boy who used to work for an outfitter. They also were hiking long distances of twenty plus miles every day trying to git-r-done as soon as possible. I wondered if they were taking enough time to enjoy their hike, but I said nothing.

Yahtzee hadn't eaten and wanted to cook in the shelter because it was raining hard outside. He started his whisper light stove, which flared up as they usually did and almost set my sleeping bag on fire with me in it. I got a rush of adrenalin and gave Yahtzee some energetic feedback about all the drama. I told him if he set me on fire, I would cut out his liver, cook it, and eat it for breakfast. He became incredibly careful not to set me on fire. That was yet another reason why I didn't like staying in shelters. The shelter was small, crowded, dirty, and full of bugs, but at least it was dry on a wet, miserable night.

April 1   Day 35   15.9 Miles

I awoke a couple of hours before daylight to the sound of Woody Crow as he packed up and left in the darkness. I knew the chances were slim that I would ever see him again. I rolled over and tried to go back to sleep. Mother Nature made me get up a bit later, so I made some coffee and cooked the last of my oatmeal. I sat in the darkness drinking weak coffee and thinking about spring. It was April Fools'

Day. March was gone and I was glad to see it go. Katahdin was so far away it was only a dream, but I had survived so far. I hoped spring was finally here and temperatures would warm up a bit. I waited until daylight to start hiking and left to the sound of Yahtzee and Jolly Green Giant sleeping in the shelter. The morning was cold, damp, foggy, and had that just-after-a-rain smell that I liked so well.

The fog lifted by noon and it became a pleasant spring day with temperatures in the mid-seventies. I stopped for lunch, water, and a nap early in the afternoon at Double Springs Shelter. Yahtzee and the Giant passed, but didn't pause for long because they wanted to hike twenty-six miles to Damascus. They tried to talk me into joining them, but I declined. I planned on stopping at Abingdon Gap, which would make a sixteen-mile day for me. I assured them Damascus would still be there when I arrived.

I came upon an old, rickety, log shelter not listed in the guidebook. It must have been one of the early shelters on the Appalachian Trail. It was built log cabin style from logs that I assumed were cut right on location many years ago. Most of the mortar had long ago fallen out of the cracks, which would let the wind blow though. It looked like someone replaced the roof with a metal roof sometime later. I stopped for a snack break, closed my eyes, and let my mind go back to the early days of the Appalachian Trail when they didn't have all the light, high-tech equipment designed exclusively for today's hikers.

Earl Shaffer, a World War II veteran of the South Pacific, was the first to hike the entire length of the Appalachian Trail from Springer Mountain to Mount Katahdin all at one time in 1948. I supposed he may have been suffering from posttraumatic stress disorder from the war and was trying to decide what to do with the rest of his life. I was never sure who first came up with the term thru-hike or even if it was proper English, but people started to call what Earl did in 1948 a thru-hike at some point in time. Earl's first thru-hike was from south to north or northbound. Thus, the term nobo became the acronym for a northbound hiker. In 1965, Earl hiked southbound from Maine to Georgia, which people referred to as a sobo.

Earl thru-hiked the Appalachian Trail for the last time in 1998, which was fifty years after his first thru-hike. I often wished I could have met this great man, but in 2002 time ran out for Earl and cancer took away that opportunity. However, I felt a special spiritual connection with him at times when I was on the trail. The admiration I had for Earl went beyond what my words could describe. I had no way of knowing if he ever stayed in that shelter or not, but I felt his presence as if he was there with me. I believe in a way, Earl would always be on the trail inspiring all the thru-hikers.

I packed up and moved out with Earl in my thoughts. I arrived at Abingdon Shelter well before dark. No one was at the shelter when I arrived, but I still chose to set up my tent on a knob far enough away so I wouldn't be disturbed if anyone arrived later. The handbook said the water source was eight-hundred-feet beyond the shelter. The path to it was steep, straight down off the ridge, and every bit of eight-hundred feet. It was another hike to get water, which had been scarce that day. When I came back, a couple of section hikers from Florida named Foot Loose and Fancy Free, who were about my age, had set up in the shelter. I went to the shelter to cook while socializing with them. I had been alone most of the day, so I enjoyed their company. I returned to the privacy of my tent, which by now was my bedroom on the trail. It took some time to unwind from the day.

After Bill completed chapters Three, and Four of the Big Book he decided to form a written summary of the principles of the program. The Oxford Group members already developed six basic principles. Bill thought they should be broken down into smaller segments to make them more detailed, easier to understand, and accept. Bill prayed for Divine guidance. Later, one night while lying in bed where he felt he could think the best, he wrote, and numbered twelve principles. He felt it was more than a coincidence they numbered twelve because there were Twelve Apostles.

Bill then solicited contributions from other early members including atheists. The atheists reined in the religious content and the Oxford Group material, which could and would lead to controversy. They feared members with different religious beliefs would feel excluded and the program would disband, destroying the program itself. That was how the Twelve Steps of Alcoholics Anonymous came about. Bill then detailed the steps in chapter five, How it Works, of the Big Book.

When I was young, I remembered the preacher telling me I was a sinner, to repent, and sin no more. I thought at the time, *How the hell do you do that? How do you repent and sin no more?* I now wonder if God gave the instructions to Bill. Did God answer my question in the form of the Twelve Steps? I started to lose my enthusiasm for thinking, so I said a simple prayer, "Thank you God for the Twelve Steps and good night." I thus ended week five with only seventy-eight trail miles.

Day 36   10 Miles

I was up and on the trail early to a warm, sunny, spring day. The last ten miles to Damascus was easy hiking on a ridge. I stopped to celebrate at the Tennessee-Virginia border by drinking the last of my water.

Boy Scout Troup twenty-three erected an archway over the trail welcoming hikers to Damascus, Virginia. I took a picture of the weather beaten milestone in my journey before I passed through. Damascus was a great trail town that catered to hikers. I went to Mount Rodgers Outfitters first, which was my favorite outfitter on the trail. I bought many dollars worth of hiking gear over the past five years there. I never came to the south without stopping to check it out and I always found I couldn't live without something they sold. The owner, Jeff, talked so slow that I thought he was drunk the first time I met him. He always spent a lot of time with me explaining how I needed certain things. I found him busy with a customer and he only said, "Hi," as if he may not have remembered me. His father, Dave, owned a rooming house for hikers called Dave's Place across the street. A friendly and attractive, elderly southern lady, waited on me and rented me a private room at Dave's Place for ten dollars, which came with a towel.

I went across the street to Dave's Place, settled in my room, and took a shower to wash off the trail smell. I put on my cleanest dirty shorts and went to the laundry mat to wash the trail smell off all my clothes. I talked to a local man about the history of Damascus and their rivalry with Tennessee, while I waited for my clothes to dry.

I felt all spiffed up as I went to an Italian restaurant and ordered a medium pizza with extra cheese. The rather large, southern waitress asked if I would like it cut in six or eight pieces. I sarcastically said, "Cut it in six, because I can't eat eight."

She later returned with the pizza and a box while apologizing for the cook. "I told the cook to cut it in six pieces, but he done went and cut it in eight anyhow, so here's a box in case ya can't eat it all." I managed to eat it all.

The day was a warm, sunny, summer-like day. I spent the rest of it walking around town talking to other hikers. I saw the couple from Maine who were so negative in the blizzard. I pretended I didn't see them to avoid them. I didn't want to hear whatever they had to say in case it was negative. I saw Yahtzee and Jolly Green Giant. Jolly tried to eat the record number of pancakes at a local restaurant, but failed. The restaurant offered all you can eat pancakes and if you break the record of twenty-two, you don't have to pay. The Giant ate eleven pancakes, which was respectable.

I returned to Dave's Place and found a couple of section hikers. His name was Lone Star from Texas, but I never knew her name. We sat in the living room talking when Brave Heart and Messenger came in. They arrived in town at two o'clock in the morning and had to wait to get a room after hiking most of the night. They slept most of the day.

It was Sunday, so I went to the evening service at a small Southern Baptist Church with Brave Heart. Brave Heart was a Christian who had aspirations of becoming a preacher after he finished the trail. We were the only hikers there, but they knew we were hikers and welcomed us. I enjoyed myself and felt like I fit in as a hiker.

I bought a pint of ice cream at a local drug store on the way home and some wart acid to treat a reoccuring wart. I sat in the living room with all the hikers staying at Dave's Place, eating ice cream, and talking until late before I turned in.

ANGELS

Day 37   11.7 Miles

I awoke to a dark, gray, rainy day, which dampened my enthusiasm. I had hoped the weather from the day before was going to continue. I took a shower before anyone else was awake and quietly snuck out to a local diner for breakfast of eggs over easy, biscuits and gravy southern style with lots of coffee, which improved my mood.

I had to wait for the post office to open to pick up my mail. I received the box of supplies I sent to myself from Hot Springs, the hiking poles Scooter sent, and several letters from my friends at home. I carried everything back to my room and read my letters, which were the most important of all. I would answer them all individually after I got back on the trail. Mail was important anytime I was away from home, family, and friends. I found the cards and letters incredibly inspiring. I had no way of knowing how much I would miss the folks I left behind. I received several cards from Alcoholics Anonymous meetings that everyone at the meeting signed. I read the names on every card. Some people would write a few words of encouragement and some names I didn't even recognize, but all the names meant I was not alone. When I came into Alcoholics Anonymous, many meetings displayed a sign that said, You are not alone anymore. I now knew what the sign really meant. I was glad I was in a motel room where I had an unlimited source of toilet paper because this bad ass kept getting something in his eyes that made them water every time he read another letter.

I re-supplied from the box I mailed to myself and packed up to hike out. I re-used the tube Scooter sent my hiking poles in to send the Leki poles back to Bob Peoples. I then re-packed the left over supplies in my box and bounced it ahead to Pearisburg, Virginia. I returned to the post office and mailed everything out.

I stopped for coffee and returned to Dave's Place to pick up my pack. I weighed my pack at Mount Rodgers Outfitters when I went to check out. My pack weight was forty-two pounds. Jeff, who sold me the pack two years ago, yelled at me for having too heavy a pack. He spent about an hour showing me how to pack and gave me some valuable information about packing.

He said, "That there pack shoun't otta weigh mor'n thirty pounds." He sent me back to Dave's Place to leave out some unnecessary stuff. I left out a bag of jellybeans and some hot chocolate. I then snuck out, so Jeff couldn't see me leaving with the heavy pack.

On the way out of town, I bought two subs; one to eat then and one to go, and one last good, large coffee. The rain was letting up, but the temperature was dropping.

My mind went directly to the Twelve Steps of Alcoholics Anonymous as I left town alone. Not any particular Step, but the Twelve Steps as a whole. A member always read the Steps at the opening of every Alcoholics Anonymous meeting I ever attended. I often heard members say they were directions that were suggested as a program of recovery. I interpreted the word suggested to mean I didn't have to do them if I didn't want to. I first thought they were the directions on how to quit drinking.

Step One said, "We admitted we were powerless over alcohol and our lives had become unmanageable." When Alcoholics Anonymous started to become amazingly successful, other fellowships that wanted to recover from other various addictions, dysfunctions, and disorders started to spring up. They also adopted AA's Twelve Steps, changing one word in Step One. They would change the word from alcohol to whatever the addiction or compulsion was that they were powerless over.

I became humbly grateful to Bill Wilson and the other early members who came up with the Twelve Steps of recovery. The Steps not only helped me personally and other alcoholics, but they could help the entire human race and the future of the human race. I believed the hand of God inspired and guided the hand of Bill Wilson.

Meditating on the trail was a wonderful way to spend a day, but I didn't remember too many details of the trail. I remembered I had a hard hike over thirty-five hundred feet up Straight Mountain with a full pack and a belly full of town food. I was half way up the mountain when I realized I sent my mail package to Scooter at home instead of to myself in Pearisburg. I packed my phone charger and other things I needed in Pearisburg. I had no cell tower, so I would have to call her whenever I got tower and have her forward the package to me in Pearisburg. I had one more thing to worry about, as if I needed something.

I paused at the side trail to Saunders Shelter and remembered an unpleasant learning experience from the past. Last year in early November, Scooter and I section hiked from Atkins, Virginia south to Damascus to help prepare me for the thru-hike. We stopped at the first trail to Saunders Shelter to pick up some water. The sign said two tenths of a mile to the shelter, so we dropped our packs at the junction of the Appalachian Trail and the side trail to the shelter. We only took our water bottles and filter to get water. We walked about half a mile and found the water source and filtered enough water for the night, then returned to the trail. When we got back to the junction with the Appalachian Trail, we could not find our packs anywhere. That put us in a precarious situation to say the least. Damascus was ten trail miles south and we had nothing but water and a filter. I had no phone, no money, no credit card, no weapon, and no identification. The temperature was warm, but it was early November at the time and it would drop with the sun and we were only wearing tee shirts and shorts.

I started to panic, thinking someone stole our packs. I went running down the trail trying to catch up to the culprits. Thank God, I didn't find an innocent hiker. I was in such a heightened state I might have attacked first thing. I spent about an hour in a manic state running up and down the trail. Meanwhile Scooter, who was more laid-back than I, went back to the shelter for the third time and discovered where the trail subtly split. She took the northbound branch, followed it for about a half a mile, and found our packs exactly where we had left them in the first place. I could still remember the relief I felt when I saw Scooter coming down the trail carrying both packs.

Apparently, two trails led to Saunders Shelter; one for southbound hikers and one for northbound hikers. The trails were about a mile apart on the Appalachian Trail. We took the wrong trail back. I found our greenhorn mistake embarrassing, so I made Scooter take a vow to never speak of it again. Except for in the book, I never told anyone either.

We had spent about two hours with the whole ordeal. The temperature was dropping and the sun was going down, so we decided to set up out tents by the shelter for the night. I learned two valuable lessons I adhere to adamantly. Lesson number one was to go slow and when I got lost, not to automatically jump to conclusions. Lesson number two was to never separate from my phone, money, identification, and gear when I leave my pack.

I only paused to ponder the learning experience for a few moments. I hiked two more miles to a pristine campsite by a pond that Scooter and I discovered last November on the same hike when we lost our packs. I was alone, which was a contrast from all the hiker contact in Damascus. I was a little melancholy, but happy to be back on the trail. The weather turned bad and I felt the chill, which may have had something to do with my low mood. I got into my sleeping bag for warmth and comfort. I cleared my mind the best I could listening for God to talk. Once again, my personal spiritual awakening quickly became the focus.

I had been thinking a lot about the Steps but I was confused about their purpose. If recovery from alcoholism was not the purpose of the Steps, then what was their purpose? After being sober and recovering for over twenty-five years, I felt confused about what exactly was recovery. I knew the Steps by heart, but I looked them up to read anyway. I read them aloud and tried to listen to the words. I stopped cold when I read, Having a spiritual awakening as a result of these steps.

The Twelve Steps of Alcoholics Anonymous were suggested as a program of recovery from alcoholism, however part of Step Twelve said, "Having had a spiritual awakening as a result of these Steps." I have heard and read the Steps thousands of times over the years, but it was almost as if I never really read or understood this phrase from Step Twelve. I suddenly had a moment of clarity where I understood that the purpose of the Steps was to have a spiritual awakening. Recovery was a spiritual awakening! The Twelve Steps were suggested instructions on how to grow spiritually towards a personal relationship with God. I felt like I discovered something profound, so I got out my little notebook and wrote some of it down in my journal before my memory lost it.

I had to get out of my warm sleeping bag to pee before I could go to sleep. The night was cold and clear. I could see all the stars as I looked to the heavens through the naked branches of winter. Maybe it was not by accident I was alone that night. Maybe God simply wanted to talk to me one on one. My loneliness melted away as my attitude changed. I suddenly became aware of how cold it was and hastily retreated to the warmth of my sleeping bag. I said a prayer of gratitude as the chattering of my teeth subsided.

I found myself too excited about my spiritual awakening to sleep. I wished I had someone like an angel to come down from heaven to explain everything to me personally or someone who traveled down the same road before me to show me the way. The thought occurred to me that maybe real angels don't have wings and a halo. Maybe real angels were simply God's people divinely sent like a salty old red-haired German-born hiker who goes by the trail name of Heaven Bound. When I thought about it on March eleventh, I didn't pick out Heaven Bound. I prayed for help and the next thing that happened, I walked up on him.

I let my mind run with the thought. The first night after Scooter and I separated, I was lonely and depressed and a crazy looking Desert Storm veteran named Crazy Horse walked in and set up camp beside me. I had to admit it was a stretch to call a man like Crazy Horse an angel, but he came along and showed me the way when I needed it. I became grateful for the others like Guns, Cedar Moe, Mathewski,

Brave Heart, Rambler, and so many more angels who helped me stay on the trail.

I thought a lot about the short time I spent with Heaven Bound because he seemed more significant than most. I met other angels who also had a large impact on my life. Alcoholics Anonymous didn't call them angels. Alcoholics Anonymous called them sponsors. I believed my relationships with sponsors like Heaven Bound, appeared spiritually guided. My first Alcoholics Anonymous sponsor was a large, aggressive man, who I called Big Jim. Now I want to tell you it was hard to think about Big Jim as an angel with wings and a halo, but I think God sent him from heaven with the keys to let me out of hell.

In a sense, Sigmund Freud sponsored Carl Jung. Carl Jung was Roland Hazard's angel. Roland Hazard sponsored Ebby Thatcher. Ebby Thatcher was Bill Wilson's angel. Bill Wilson sponsored Dr. Bob Smith. Dr. Bob Smith was Bill Dodson's angel and so forth. It sounded somewhat like begets in the Bible. Therefore, all of us recovering alcoholics are descendants of the early founders.

With those thoughts in my mind, I became drowsy. I curled up in my sleeping bag, pulled the cover over my head to escape the cold, and ended the day in sleep. I said aloud, "Thank you Lord for sending all the angels my way, Amen," I was sure I had a contented look on my face.

Day 38   21.4 Miles

The rain started again in the night, then turned to freezing rain, and then to light before daylight. I lost my thermometer, but the temperature dropped to damn cold. I had ice on both the inside and outside of my tent when I awoke in the morning. Reluctantly, I left my warm cocoon to face the day. The snow stopped, leaving the day clear, windy, and frigid. I cooked hot oatmeal and made instant coffee that tasted terrible, but it was strong and hot. I ditched the weak tea bag coffee in Damascus, replacing it with the old fashioned, powdered instant coffee. It warmed me up and gave me that coffee kick I was looking for to start my day. I quickly moved out to stay warm.

Mid-morning, I passed by Scooter's dream house, which was a brick farmhouse fenced in a cow pasture, within fifty feet of the trail on a remote mountain road. The house still appeared to be structurally sound, but abandoned for quite some time, and run down. The windows were all broken out, but the brick looked to be okay. The paint had peeled off a lot of the trim leaving the gray, weather-beaten wood exposed. The cows kept the grass rather short, giving it a neat appearance. Scooter wanted to restore it and turn it into a hostel for hikers someday after she retired. I would love to have secretly bought the property to surprise her with it one day. I took pictures of the house and noted where it was so I could find it from the road by car in the future. I thought it might be nice to semi-retire there and run a little business someday.

I climbed White Top Mountain at five thousand, five hundred, and twenty feet and Mount Rodgers at five thousand, seven hundred, and twenty feet. I spent most of the day above five thousand feet in the cold wind. The terrain was open and treeless like the grasslands of the west, blessed with plenty of open sky.

I planned to spend the night at Thomas Knob Shelter, but when I arrived, it was full of someone else's gear. No hikers were around, but apparently, whoever left their gear planned on spending the night, so I opted to move on five miles to Wise Shelter. Wise Shelter was lower at about forty five hundred feet and I hoped out of the wind.

I squeezed through Fat Man Squeeze, which was one of the many spectacular rock outcroppings that broke up the highland's grassy terrain. I entered into the Grayson Highlands State Park, which was famous for being home to a herd of feral ponies. I saw many ponies and one even followed me whinnying for about a mile. The ponies were rather tame and appeared to be healthy. I treated some of them to jellybeans, but quit when the word got out and they became obnoxious and nipped at my pack.

I arrived at Wise Shelter, which was in a grove of exceptionally high rhododendrons that sheltered it from the wind. I had it all to myself, so I gambled right that time. I couldn't find a place to put up my tent, so I decided to sleep in the shelter. That way I wouldn't have to take down and pack up my tent in the morning so I could get an earlier start. I cooked tuna and noodles and crawled into my sleeping bag for warmth to eat. After I ate, I interlocked my fingers, behind my head, and stared at the graffiti on the ceiling of the shelter. I felt lonely as I waited for the day to end in darkness.

The first time I was in a hospital detox unit was in 1977. They recommended I go to Alcoholics Anonymous and get a sponsor. A sponsor's job was to guide you into the Alcoholics Anonymous program and through the Twelve Steps. I had no idea that a sponsor in reality, was a spiritual guide. I came to the conclusion that sponsors were angels, but sometimes in real good disguises.

I picked a meeting held in the basement of the chapel on campus at a local university for my first Alcoholics Anonymous meeting outside of detox. I thought wrongly a younger crowd and maybe a few eligible college girls who I could hit on would be at the meeting. I arrived early and to my dismay, there were no college girls, only a bunch of ugly, old men smoking cigarettes and drinking coffee in the basement. I sat down alone at one of the unoccupied folding card tables and lit up a smoke.

A tall man came right over and asked, "Mind if I sit down?"

I was suspicious, but I pushed a chair his way as I exhaled a lung full of smoke and said, "Free country."

He sat and looked at me with a big warm smile and stuck out his hand and said "Jim Pr---." I was skeptical, but shook his hand. He asked, "First meeting?"

"First meeting since I got out of St Vincent." We made some small talk for a while.

Then he said, "There's a meeting on Monday night in McKean. If you want, I'll pick up and you can ride with me."

I got pissed off, "I ain't queer!" His eyes popped out, his face turned red and a purple vein popped out on each side of his forehead.

"Queeeer, I'm not queer you asshole. I can see you're new and I was trying to make your dumb ass feel welcome!" I didn't know at the time, but I would see him do that many times in the next five years.

I pulled in my horns and apologized, "I'm sorry, but you're right, I'm new and don't know what to expect."

The meeting started and we quit talking. I don't remember anything about the actual meeting, but I remember he was so big that I wouldn't even be able to out run him. I never saw wings or a halo on Big Jim, but he was truly an angel.

After the meeting, we talked a while, then went to Perkins and drank coffee while he shared his experience with the program. I felt surprisingly comfortable with him. I didn't know at the time, but I was experiencing the same spiritual connection that I experienced only one time previously on that first day in detox with the speaker. I asked him if he would be my sponsor. I didn't understand his response at the time when he said, "I'll be happy to be your sponsor. It will help me as much as you."

That was how Big Jim became my first sponsor. Big Jim was one of the finest men I ever met. He shared his experience, strength, and hope with me to teach me about recovery. I used to piss him off sometimes on purpose, but he always forgave me and even laughed about whatever the situation was later. He was my sponsor through the last three years of my drinking until I finally stayed sober. He never gave up on me or quit loving me no matter how angry or discouraged he became from my actions. He taught me so many things, but most of all, he taught me to love myself first then love others. He walked like he talked and led me by his example.

The only time he hurt me was when he left me in 1982. I was two years sober by the time he died suddenly while playing basketball. It was the first time I ever remembered crying over losing anyone, but I didn't turn to the bottle. I think the only reason I didn't drink was I knew it would piss off Big Jim if I relapsed over losing him.

I still cried a little at times over my grief, but he will always be with me in my heart. I hoped to see him again one day. I pulled the covers over my head to shut out the cold. Even though I was lonely, I hoped company didn't come late in the night to disturb me.

Day 39   **20 Miles**

A raccoon tried to steal my food bag that I kept beside me in the shelter. The first time he tried, I awoke and yelled at him and he ran off and I went back to sleep. The second time he awoke me, I sprayed him with pepper spray. He didn't return, but I had far too much adrenalin in my blood to go back to sleep. It was close enough to daylight to cook my oatmeal and coffee. I packed up, hit the trail at daybreak, and hiked out of the park by mid-morning. I saw a few wild ponies again and took pictures, but didn't feed them. They soon lost interest in me and went back to grazing as I passed.

I took a break at a closed campground with a modern outhouse complete with free toilet paper and a trash can. I took advantage of both. The concession stand and office were locked and boarded up. No one was around the ghost camp, which caused me feel even lonelier.

A county sheriff's deputy who was posted on guard duty where Fox Creek Road crossed the trail, showed me a picture of a seventeen-year-old man he wanted by the name of Christopher Bell. He told me Bell wasn't considered dangerous. He simply ran away from a military school. I wasn't convinced the cop was telling me the whole story.

I carried several things a criminal would need to escape by foot such as my sleeping bag, jacket, tent, water filter, stove, and food. I felt a little nervous about the situation, so I decided to put as much distance between him and me as I could before dark. I hoped some other hikers would stay at a shelter with me tonight. I hiked to Trimpi Shelter where Scooter and I stayed on our last section hike. I put in another twenty-mile day and it wasn't too hard. I thought that I must be getting into better shape.

Forsythia and Daffodils were all over so it looked like spring, but it was so cold it felt like winter. I thought about starting a fire, but changed my mind because I didn't want the smoke to attract Christopher Bell's attention. I had to accept I was going to be by myself again that night. I kept my guard up. I was prepared to defend myself as a last resort, but wanted to avoid a confrontation if possible. I felt lonely and wished some other hikers would show up. The only person I saw since I left Damascus was the sheriff's deputy. I didn't have cell phone tower to call any friends or family.

I never would have thought that I would get this lonely. I thought maybe God wanted me to be alone for a reason. Maybe he simply wanted to talk one on one and didn't want anyone to distract me. I found some comfort in that thought.

After Big Jim died, I didn't replace him with another sponsor, but I kept going to Alcoholics Anonymous meetings four or five times a week. I thought no one could ever take the place of Big Jim. I didn't have a sponsor to guide me for the first time in my sobriety. I decided to be my own sponsor. I had often heard folks in the program say, an alcoholic who sponsors himself had an idiot for a sponsor. I thought I was different and could pull off sponsoring myself, but soon my ego took over and I started serving my ego. I started to do things I probably knew I shouldn't and things Big Jim wouldn't approve of me doing.

I gradually slipped spiritually into a downward slide that folks in Alcoholics Anonymous called a dry drunk. A dry drunk was the process when an alcoholic reverted to the behavior and attitudes they had when they were actively drinking. A dry drunk often ends in a wet drunk if something doesn't intervene. My character defects, anxiety, depression, fear, and anger returned as if I was drinking, except I wasn't drinking. I could no longer eat and lost twenty pounds in a week. I was sober, but so restless, irritable and discontent that drinking was starting to look good. I was too prideful to humble myself enough to ask anyone for help. My whole world seemed to collapse on October sixteenth, 1985 when I came to the bottom of my dry drunk. I had broken up with my girlfriend, aggressively confronted an Alcoholics Anonymous friend, and my daughter ran away because things were so bad at home. I became the same person I was when I was drinking, but I hadn't started drinking yet.

I called the state police and fire department and they found my daughter, but I was still in a frenzied state of mind. I went for a ride on my motorcycle late that night to calm down. I was riding down a country dirt road going way too fast, not paying close enough attention, missed a curve, and lost control. I dumped the bike in a potato field and dug up a couple of potatoes with my shoulder. I recalled I was so angry with God that I laid there cursing Him. I blamed God for my own self-serving stupidity.

Miraculously, I wasn't hurt too badly, but trashed the bike. I walked about seven miles on back roads to get home. It was a clear, crisp, fall night and all the stars were out. I had lots of time to cool off and meditate. I got the insight that Big Jim was my spiritual advisor and was no longer with me. I needed another spiritual advisor to replace the space Big Jim left when he died over two years ago.

I had some time to decide whom I would ask to be my new sponsor on the seven-mile walk home. I called a man I held in high regard at two o'clock in the morning, named Gallagher and woke him up. I asked him to be my sponsor. His reply was, "Give me a few minutes and I'll be over." He came over and we went out for breakfast to talk. Gallagher became my second sponsor until he died, but this time I replaced him with another sponsor immediately. I have had several sponsors. I had a sponsor killed tragically and I replaced him before the funeral. I learned the hard way to always have a sponsor.

A sponsor, spiritual guide, or mentor, were similar words that meant teacher to me. Big Jim and all my sponsors taught me how to be a sponsor or spiritual guide to others. I desperately needed a spiritual guide to help me work trough the Twelve Steps and coach me in the game called life.

Jesus Christ was the sponsor of twelve lucky men over two-thousand-years ago. He taught them to be teachers and they in turn taught others to be teachers. Thus, millions carry His message even today. An Alcoholics Anonymous slogan said, "You have to give it away to keep it." In Alcoholics Anonymous, I became both a student and a teacher, which meant I had to have a sponsor and be a sponsor. I became a student first and Big Jim was my teacher. I now sponsor some newcomers and sometimes I find myself saying the exact words Big Jim and my other sponsors said to me.

When I gave away what I knew to the newcomer I seemed to learn more. The more I gave away the more I received. I still don't understand why it was that way, but that was how it always worked. I understood what Big Jim was talking about the first time I met him when he said, "It will help me as much as you."

I cooked noodles and listened to the radio until sleep took my loneliness away for that day.

Day 40   22.2 Miles

I was up and on the trail shortly after daylight. The radio said they caught Christopher Bell the day before, so I relaxed. I wish I would have known that before because I spent a restless night on guard. The temperature rose to seventy degrees with sun, which was a welcome change. I pushed hard eleven miles to Mount Rodgers National Recreational Area Headquarters by noon. The guidebook said restrooms and a drink machine were available inside. I lucked out because I also found a vending machine with candy bars and chips. I ate a big lunch outside then took a short nap in the sun. I needed the rest and energy from the food to hike another eleven miles to Atkins where I could stay in a motel.

I went back to the gift shop and bought a gift for Scooter. The clerk was polite, but not too friendly. I made a return trip to the vending machines and bought three more twenty-ounce pops and several candy bars to go. I packed up and trudged on in a better mood due to my good fortune and the prospect of a night in a motel.

I found I had cell tower, so I made a call to Scooter, which was the first time I talked to her since Damascus. It felt great to talk to her and catch up on things back home. I was having trouble with warts on my feet, so I asked her to pick up a kit to freeze the warts at a Walmart and send it to Pearisburg along with the package I accidently sent to her instead of to myself.

The next eleven miles melted away, probably due to all the sugar and caffeine I consumed. I arrived at the Relax Inn at the interchange on the interstate late in the afternoon. A family from India ran the motel. A hiker friendly young man greeted me and congratulated me on having hiked one fourth of the Appalachian Trail. I hadn't thought about that, but he was right. I felt some accomplishment. He told me where I could find the amenities I needed.

The motel had a coin laundry, so I put on my clean shorts and shirt and then put the rest of my cloths in the washer. I took a hot shower before I put my clothes in the dryer. I stopped at a convenience store beside the motel and bought enough supplies for four days on the trail. Everything was so outrageously high priced I felt ripped off. The cost for the supplies was twenty-six dollars. I picked up my clothes from the dryer and went to the only diner around for supper. I was the only hiker at the motel or the diner, so I dined alone. I wondered where all the other hikers went since I left Damascus. I couldn't decide if I wanted a steak or shrimp dinner, so I ordered both. I bought a quart of strawberry ice cream at the convenience store on the way back to my room. I watched television and ate the ice cream. I ate a tremendous amount of food and that was good because my weight was lower than normal.

I bought a phone card so I could call home from the phone in my motel. I was saving my cell phone batteries for an emergency because I didn't have a charger until I reached Pearisburg in about a week. I talked to Scooter and both my daughters before I fell asleep. I put sixty-four cold, lonely miles behind me in three days since I left Damascus.

THE SEDUCTION

Day 41   13.9 Miles

I awoke to heavy rain. I went back to the diner for breakfast of eggs over easy, biscuits, and gravy southern style. I bought two hotdogs and a large coffee at the convenience store on the way back to eat in my room. The rain continued, so I took a long, hot shower and watched an old Harrison Ford movie on television before leaving at noon, which was the checkout time. The rain quit, but the day was dark and gray with more storms predicted. I hiked solo again and still had no idea where all of my friends were. I started hiking with a heavy pack, so I took only a little water with me to compensate for the extra weight. That soon bit me in the butt because I ran out of water and had a hard time finding more on the trail. I was carrying pop tarts, which were heavy, so I stopped to eat some of them, and finally found water to wash them down.

I stopped at Knot Maul Branch Shelter. I spent the night there last July on a section hike with my good friends Chief and Crow. The weatherman predicted thunderstorms, so I elected to stay in the shelter to avoid the storm that threatened. Shortly after I cooked my meal, a violent thunder and lightning storm hit and continued. I was all alone again and found it more boring than lonely.

I opened my journal, but couldn't put myself in the mood to write. I couldn't think of anything positive to write about. I found myself trying to meditate for something to pass the time until I got drowsy enough to sleep. I casually thought I could sure use a drink tonight, which scared me after all those years. I wasn't serious, but that was the way relapses started. I thought I better think the drink through to get it out of my head.

I was twelve years old when I took my first drink. I didn't fit in well anywhere as a child. I always felt like an outsider at home or in school. I was different from the others. I was skinny, ugly, covered with freckles, and so shy I couldn't even talk to girls.

My parents hosted a family Christmas Eve party every year where lots of alcohol was always available. Watching some of my aunts, uncles, and older cousins getting drunk always intrigued me. They did things out of character, laughed and acted like they were having the time of their lives. I remember feeling as if I couldn't wait until I was old enough to join in the drinking festivities.

I was at the Christmas party when my brother-in-law, Jim gave me his empty glass and asked me to put in two ice cubes, a shot of Seagram's Seven, and fill the rest of the glass with Canada Dry Grapefruit. I felt a little awkward, but followed his instruction precisely. I expected an adult to challenge me, but no one seemed to notice. I took the drink back to Jim who was talking to my older cousin, Bill. Bill handed me his glass with similar instructions. I marched back to the liquor table and mixed another drink. After I delivered Bill's drink, I marched back to the liquor and as nonchalantly as possible, and mixed myself a drink.

That happened forty-three years ago, but I still remembered how my hands were shaking as I poured the whisky into the shot glass to measure it out. I could recall in detail how the tea colored liquid hit the ice and spread around the cubes as I poured it from the shot glass. I filled the glass with the Canada Dry exactly as before. I left with the glass as if I was filling an adult's request, but instead I fled to the privacy of my bedroom with my prize. I vividly recalled that first gulp. I didn't like the taste and it burned at first, as if I had swallowed broken glass. Then it hit my stomach and I felt a type of comforting warmth that I never felt before. The special warmth quickly spread to my chest and then my face.

I remember all the low self-esteem, anxiety, depression, and insecurity vanished with the first drink. I could feel the whiskey warming my soul as it hit my stomach and magically I became bigger, stronger, better looking, and I could talk to people without fear. I felt like I fit in for the first time in my life. I could remember thinking I wanted to feel like that all the time, forever. I boldly returned to the kitchen and helped myself to another drink, but that time I didn't measure with the shot glass. I had no idea how much I drank that night, but I became quite intoxicated.

I awoke on Christmas morning in my own bed feeling terrible. I could still taste vomit in my sinuses and feel my heart-beat pounding in my head. I knew I had far too much to drink, but I couldn't remember anything else. I couldn't even remember how the party ended or how I got to bed. I lay in bed trying in vain to piece together the night before when the fear hit. I wondered how much trouble I was in with Mom and Dad. I sheepishly went down stairs and found Mom and Dad sitting at the kitchen table drinking coffee.

They stopped talking as if they were talking about me. The silence was the worst punishment as they looked at me expressionless. I broke the silence by asking, "What happened."

Dad said nothing, but Mom called me by my full Christian name, which she only did when she was really pissed off and said, "You got drunk!" I looked down and she let me have it, "You made a fool out of yourself in front of all your relatives. You embarrassed your father, you embarrassed me, and you embarrassed yourself. Jim had to put you to bed and you vomited all over the floor in your bedroom and you're going to be the one who cleans it up, Mister." She stopped out of breath. The room fell uncomfortably silent again.

I wanted to change the subject, so I said, "I don't feel good."

She silently went into the bathroom, which Dad built right off the kitchen so he only had to run plumbing to one place in the house. She returned with two Alka Seltzers fizzing in a glass of water and said, "Drink this."

I did and ran to the bathroom to throw up until I got the dry-heaves. My stomach finally settled enough to get off my knees. I took a piece of toilet paper and blew my nose. I looked at my reflection in the mirror. Right then, with tears from retching running down my face, I made a resolution to never drink ever again.

I opened the bathroom door to find them both looking directly at me. "I'll never do that again" I promised, and I sincerely meant it.

Dad looked at me and tried to suppress a little giggle.

Mom gave me a stern look and said, "You better not you Shiite-poke." I was relieved as I saw her face soften. Mom could always ream me out, but she also was quick to forgive me.

After a few days or maybe even a few weeks, the embarrassment and the dysphoric memories faded and I remembered euphoric feelings. I made a conscious decision to change my resolution from never drinking to drinking a little in the future, but not to the extent I would lose control. I only wanted to feel that feeling, but next time I wouldn't get too drunk.

I yawned and my mind came back to the present. The thought that a drink would help had vanished, but that was the reason I never kept alcohol around. The thought to drink could still sneak up on me unexpectedly even after almost twenty-six years of not drinking.

I could have used a little company, but I figured no one would be on the trail in the storm. The good news was I would sleep like a baby in violent weather as long as I was warm and dry. I felt warm, safe, and dry, so I ended the day in sleep.

April 8   Day 42   9 Miles

9 Cold wet miles

The storm lasted all night and continued into the morning. I sat in the gloomy shelter watching the storm, eating pop tarts, and drinking hot coffee. I was in no hurry to face the rain, so I made a second pot of coffee before I left. I hiked nine miles to Chestnut Knob Shelter and stopped for an early lunch out of the rain and wind. I ate lunch of more pop tarts to lighten my pack. The weather turned for the worse with freezing rain, so I made a pot of tea and took some time to think about what I wanted to do. I got out of my wet hiking clothes and into my warm, dry, nightclothes. The wind got worse and the temperature dropped. The next shelter was ten long miles away, so I decided to stay until the next day.

Chestnut Knob Shelter was a solid, four-sided shelter made of rock and mortar with a door and metal roof. The shelter sat on top of a bald which was four-thousand-four-hundred and ten feet high. According to the register, it had no mice because the resident snakes ate all the mice. I would believe the register because when I put my mattress and sleeping bag on a top bunk I had to sweep off a snakeskin from a rather large black snake. I hoped it was a black snake and not a rattlesnake. The shelter wasn't a pleasant place, but it was a safe and dry place on a wet, miserable day.

I used all my water and the closest water source was almost two miles south. I didn't want to get my dry clothes wet, so I had to suck it up and put my wet hiking clothes back on and go out in the storm to get water. I returned with plenty of water, put my dry clothes back on, and made a pot of hot tea to wash down more pop tarts. I crawled into my warm sleeping bag and started writing in my journal. I was hoping someone else would come along because I sure could have used the company.

I must have fallen asleep sometime before dark. I awoke after midnight and remained wide awake. I must have slept over six hours. I was alarmed by a ruckus on the table below, so I shined my light down and saw several big fat mice fighting over my pop tart crumbs. Well, so much for the theory of no mice due to there being snakes. It makes sense that snakes stayed here because there were fat mice to eat. Besides, the snakes were hibernating, so when the snakes went away the mice came out to play. I had been spending far too much time alone thinking about things like that.

I purposely changed the subject in my mind to pass the time. My first experience with alcohol was much like all my future experiences with all the drugs I eventually used. I loved the feelings, but could never control the amount once I started to use. I would take a vow to never use again after a bad experience, but always returned with resolve to control my use better. Thus began my love/hate affair with chemicals. An experienced, seductive mistress called Miss Alcohol intentionally seduced me. I experienced a few drawbacks of drinking right from the start, but I would soon forget the pain. I felt the benefits far outweighed any consequences. I loved the feeling to the extent that I was willing to do things I previously wouldn't have thought of doing in order to drink. I quickly learned to drink surreptitiously hiding from my parents and the police. I started to befriend peers my own age or older who were also attracted to alcohol. Together we formed strategies to obtain booze and drink. The party had started.

I obviously couldn't drink all the time early on, but I was always contemplating and planning when I could drink again. Sometimes the opportunity to drink popped up unexpectedly and I always took the drink over whatever else I planned to do. Drinking became my number one priority right from the start. Looking back, I didn't even suspect I was obsessed with the seductress, Miss Alcohol.

I snapped back to the present and realized I was romancing the drink. That was dangerous for me any time, but especially in the situation I was in because it was hard to recall the bad consequences. I realized, even after twenty-five years, I was still susceptible to Miss Alcohol's calling.

The wind, rain, and occasional lightning continued to make the shelter a spooky old place. I wished I had cell tower to call someone in Alcoholics Anonymous, because even at one o'clock in the morning I could find someone who would talk to me. I felt lonely and bored, so I decided to pray. After praying, an old Alcoholics Anonymous slogan that fit came to mind: *This too shall pass.*

That marked the end of my sixth week on the trail. I hiked one-hundred and eight miles that week.

Day 43   22.3 Miles

It was ten degrees according to the thermometer on the door of the shelter when I left early in the morning. I thought it was unusually cold for April the ninth in this part of Virginia, but the day started clear, sunny, and warmed up. My mood rose with the temperature as it usually did.

A few miles into the early morning hike, I disturbed a turkey hunter who was out scouting for turkeys. He told me Virginia's turkey season opened the next day. We struck up a conversation and talked about turkey hunting. He was using a box call. I showed him how to call turkeys with the mouth call I had been carrying since Springer

Mountain. I tried to call in a turkey that was answering my call, but the turkey wouldn't show himself. The hunter gave me the best homemade ham sandwich I ever ate. It was great talking to him and I wished I had more time to spend with him, but I had a trail that needed hiking. I must now be careful when I called turkeys in the mornings, because I didn't want to get shot by a hunter mistaking me for a turkey.

I had to ford Laurel Creek where Hurricane Katrina washed out the bridge last year. They had an alternative blue blazed route for wimps, but I wanted to be a purest thru-hiker and elected to stick on the original white blaze trail. I took off my shoes, tied them around my neck, put my cell phone, camera, and radio in a zip lock baggie, and forded the creek on the slippery rocks in my bare feet. The water was cold, but I sucked it up and crossed.

The cold water hurt the warts on my feet. They continued to be a problem that was getting progressively worse anyway, but the cold water raised the pain level to a point that I could hardly ignore them any longer. I hoped to get rid of them by freezing them when I got to Pearisburg in a few days.

I soon found where a trail angel left Little Debby's snacks and apple juice on the trail, so I stopped for a snack break. I left a thank you note and pushed on. I didn't know why, but I felt guilty about the time I lost the day before, holed up in a shelter. I came to a road leading to a small campground past Laurel Creek where two middle-aged ladies were serving as trail angels. They came out to the trail on Sunday afternoons after church to re-supply thru-hikers. They had a ton of hiker food in the back of a SUV. I didn't want to take anything, but they insisted. I was a little low on food, but I was planning to stop at a convenience store sometime the next day. I took a tube of peanut butter and jelly they had mixed and put into a reusable toothpaste-type tube, some bread, and a few rice crispy marshmallow treats. I sincerely thanked them and started to leave when one angel said, "Here take this" as she held out a large orange.

The people of the south had been so kind and generous to me. Sometimes I found it hard to believe how good people could be to complete strangers. I thought the trail must be trying to teach me to be grateful for the little things in life like an orange. I didn't go far before I stopped and ate the orange.

I thought about part of a prayer we said after all Alcoholics Anonymous meetings, "...Give us this day our daily bread." I looked to the sky and said, Thanks. I didn't recall ever enjoying an orange as much as I did that one. You didn't have to be a hiker to appreciate the euphoria of eating a succulent orange when you were hot, dry, and hungry. I carefully planted the seeds and hoped one day I would help some nameless hiker enjoy their daily bread. I moved on with an attitude of gratitude with the loneliness of all my yesterdays forgotten.

I hiked a long ways that day and it seemed easy. I also ate a lot of extra food. I had a sudden realization that extra food equaled extra calories, which equaled extra energy, which allowed for extra miles. It seemed like a simple equation, but it took me a long time on the trail to understand that fact. It wasn't as if I discovered a great theory, but I knew what I needed to do if I wanted to make better time.

The sun was fading, so I started looking for a campsite to call home for the night when I broke out of the woods onto a sizable blacktop road. I couldn't camp because the Appalachian Trail ran along the road for some distance and my handbook said, "Do not disturb the private residences." An abundance of No Trespassing signs lined both sides of the road, so I snuck down the road in silence so I wouldn't disturb anyone.

I crossed a bridge over an interstate in the last twilight. The cars had their lights on and were coming at me so fast on one side and the red lights were going away as fast on the other side. I felt sorry for the people in the endless lines of cars in a way because they seemed in such a hurry to go nowhere.

I stopped after I got off the road and back into the woods. It was long after dark, so I cleared the Rhododendrons and set up my tent on the first flat spot I found beside the trail. A shelter was only about a mile and a half north, but I was too exhausted to go any further. I heard a hiker as he passed by after I was in my tent.

I called out, "Who goes there?"

He responded, "Hatteris Jack."

I introduced myself as Dreamer through the tent without ever seeing him. It was a short conversation, but I felt better knowing at least another hiker was nearby, even though he moved on to the shelter.

I thought I would fall asleep instantly, but as exhausted as I was, I laid awake. I said the Lord's Prayer and pondered again on the part; give us this day our daily bread. I felt grateful for all the daily bread I received that day.

When Jesus gave his disciples the Lord's Prayer, they didn't have welfare, food stamps, or all the charities that provide food in modern times. They had to depend on God more in those days and He provided. I took eating every day for granted and forgot to be grateful and give thanks to God for my daily bread.

Day 44   24.9 Miles

I awoke long before dawn's first light, and couldn't get back to sleep. I had slept soundly for six hours, so I packed up and hiked out in the dark. I heard a turkey gobble a short time before daylight, so I stopped and tried briefly to call him into sight, but lost interest and moved on when he wouldn't cooperate. I felt more incentive when I was carrying a shotgun and a turkey dinner could be my reward.

I hiked solo all morning, only stopping at Jenny Knob Shelter for water and lunch. I took a short nap after I ate. After getting back on the trail, I experienced a feeling of déjà vu that I had been there before. I tried to ignore the feeling and rationalized it seemed familiar because I section hiked that part with friends last year. My rationalizing ended when I came to a familiar road I remembered crossing earlier in the day. I somehow became confused and turned around after my nap and went south. I was glad no one was watching as I did an about face to the north. So much for my keen sense of direction.

I arrived at the convenience store I planned to stop at by mid-afternoon. I wasn't at the store long when Hatteris Jack arrived. We introduced ourselves for the second time. I could see what he looked like as opposed to how I pictured him from his voice. He was an athletic looking young man from California who stood about five foot, five inches tall. He only had a short time to hike the entire trail, so he was hiking long mile days. We sat down to eat mass quantities of food and coffee while we discussed strategies to hike as fast as possible.

I ate two giant cheeseburgers, a piece of pizza, a pint of chocolate ice cream, and refilled my coffee several times. I didn't need any supplies, but bought a coke to drink in the morning. Hatteris Jack was still eating when I left. He was going to call home from the pay phone before he returned to the trail. I really enjoyed talking to another thru-hiker, but I never was into hiking as fast as he hiked.

I hiked another seven miles before dark to set up on a flat spot in the woods a lot further off the trail than the previous night. I thought I would sleep well because I hiked twenty-five miles and I was exhausted. I hoped to make it seventeen miles to Pearisburg the next day before the post office closed. I was anxious to pick up my mail drop.

HELL

Day 45   17.3 Miles

I packed up to hit the trail long before daylight, hiking with my head light. I felt a sense of urgency to get to Pearisburg before the post office closed. The amenities of a town day also lured me. The leaves were starting to come out at the lower levels and the Virginia Red Bud was in full bloom, accented by the sun. The mountains still had their winter colors, but the new green in the valleys below announced the coming of spring.

I saw Hatteris Jack briefly, when he passed me. We both knew we would probably never see each other again. I hiked on solo as I listened to music. I thought a seventeen mile day would be easy after all the twenty plus mile days I had been hiking, but I was wrong. The last ten miles were on an uneven ridge with unfriendly rocks, which was time consuming to negotiate.

I didn't arrive at the New River until late afternoon. I was disappointed because the post office closed about an hour before. I had called the Rendezvous Motel about noon and they told me I wouldn't need reservations. I planned to stay there because it was within sight of the trail. When I arrived, I couldn't find anyone around , so I walked a mile uphill into Pearisburg. I found a lot nicer room at a large motel right in town where I was close to everything. I asked the clerk where I could find a laundry mat and a well-dressed older lady offered me a ride, but I declined because I didn't want to stink up her car.

I said, "I'm used to walking, and the exercise will do me good."

I thought, first things first, so I went to my room and took a long, hot shower. I put on my other pair of reasonably clean shorts, ventured out to Hardies, bought three double cheeseburgers, large fries and a milk shake. After I ate, I returned to my room, picked up my clothes and hiked to the laundry mat to wash them. I spent the rest of the evening exploring the town and looking for other thru-hikers.

The problem I have been having with warts on my feet started with one wart on my little toe, shortly after I began hiking in Georgia. I tried to treat it with wart removing acid, but had no luck. Probably due to poor hygiene on the trail, one wart soon became seven and the pain progressively became a major issue. Scooter sent me some stuff to freeze the wart that I hoped to pick up at the post office when it opened.

I had cell tower, but my battery was dead, so I made some calls from my room with a calling card. I planned to charge my batteries before I left town when I got my charger out of my mail drop. I returned to the motel and watched television for a little while because I had the chance, but I found it boring. I turned the television off and tried to sleep, but my mind wouldn't shut down. I soon found myself dwelling on past regrets.

I was fifteen-years-old and working as a junior counselor at a summer Boy Scout camp. I had earned all the merit badges to become my hometown's first Eagle Scout ever. One night, I was drinking and smoking cigarettes in an unoccupied tent with two other scouts. Later, after we left, the tent burned up. I took the rap, so they kicked me out of the scouts and I never became an Eagle Scout. I felt noble for not ratting out my friends and blamed the narrow-minded scout leaders. I didn't consider that I was setting a poor example for the younger scouts. It never occurred to me the problem was my drinking. I will always regret not becoming an Eagle Scout. I think that was the first major consequence of my drinking, but I didn't see it as such and brushed it off. Eventually I drifted off to sleep with an uneasy feeling.

Day 46   8.2 Miles

I awoke feeling emotionally better than when I went to sleep. I quickly dressed and went into the village to forage. First, I bought fresh, hot coffee at a convenience store. I then went to a little local bakery/coffee shop for a breakfast sandwich and more coffee while I waited for the post office to open.

I picked up my mail drop and all I could say was, "Wow!" I received several letters from friends back home, which always elevated my spirits. I went back to my room, read my mail, re-supplied my pack, and plugged in my cell phone charger. I planned to carry it with me from now on, so I could charge my batteries any time I found electricity.

I read the directions on the wart medicine and froze the worst wart on my little toe. The pain was severe, which scared me. I hoped the worst was over, but I never had any previous experience with warts.

I went shopping while I waited for my batteries to charge. I bought some first aid stuff at the drug store and a few things at the grocery store. I just browsed a hardware store and a department store to kill time. The best thing I found was an AYCE pizza shop that would open at eleven o'clock.

I considered taking a zero day and I might have if I would have met up with any thru-hikers. I didn't fit in with town people along the trail, so I thought I would leave after lunch. I went back to my room and packed a package of supplies to bounce ahead. I took a shower, taped my feet, and checked out of the room. I went to the post office and mailed my package to Daleville.

I returned to the pizza shop at precisely eleven and pigged out on my way out of town. The pizza was so good and I ate all I could eat. I didn't feel like hiking at all after I finished eating. It was probably a good thing I checked out of my room earlier or I would have returned to take a nap.

I met a thru-hiker by the name of Do-Rag going into Pearisburg as I left. I told her all about the town and especially about the AYCE pizza. She planned on hitting the post office and getting some pizza, but returning to the trail later that day. She too, like many hikers, graduated college earlier and was thru-hiking before she started her career. I hoped to see her again on the trail. It was good to talk to another thru-hiker so I knew I wasn't alone out there.

I crossed the New River and hiked out of the valley. I didn't see any more hikers. I stopped at Rice Field Shelter and read the log. Hatteris

Jack spent the night before there by himself. He left a sarcastic report on the bear in the area that had me laughing until my sides hurt. He must have been lonely and had too much time on his hands. I would miss him, but that was life on the trail. No water source was at the shelter, so I moved on.

I decided to camp by a spring of fresh water in the woods a mile north of the shelter. I camped there last year on a section hike and met a retired marine named Ragman, who was attempting a flip-flop thru-hike. He showed me how a simple two-dollar lawnmower gas filter installed in the intake tube on my water filter would catch most of the dirt that clogs the forty dollar water filter, extending the life of the filter. I used his idea ever since.

A troop of noisy Boy Scouts came in and set up by me as I cooked a large meal of rice and beans. I retreated to the sanctuary of my tent and ate in privacy while remembering my former visit with Ragman. I answered some of my mail and treated the rest of the warts on my feet. I put on some soft music to drown out the annoying Boy Scouts and turned in for the night.

I carried some resentment towards the Boy Scouts for forty years over nothing they did. I was the one who made the choice to drink that night. I still regretted not completing my goal of becoming an Eagle Scout a long time ago, but I needed to quit blaming the Boy Scouts.

Sometime in my recovery, I learned that when I started to focus on past regrets and consequences of my addiction to remind myself that my past was something I couldn't change. I had to accept my relationship with alcohol and see it as an expensive learning experience.

I got a job working nights, so I could buy a car and have some money. The drinking age in New York was eighteen back then, so I stole an ID and drove my slightly older friends across the state line to drink in the bars like a big boy. All of my money went to the car, cigarettes, and alcohol. I managed to stay in school, but because of my drinking, I went from being an average student in the academic class to barely passing the easiest general courses I could take. I graduated high school with little to spare because of absenteeism and failing grades. Dad said I graduated by the skin on my teeth. I gave up on any ideas of going to college, except to party. I had no aspirations for a career any longer. I only wanted to be left alone so I could escape reality with alcohol.

I found myself wishing I could go back in time and do things differently, but that was impossible. Besides, at the time, it all seemed like it was worth the cost. I realized as I tried unsuccessfully to fall asleep, that maybe the consequences and adversity might have been valuable learning experiences also. I did learn eventually to deal with things the way they were and move on without alcohol.

To hike a thru-hike I would have to deal with a lot of adversity and consequences that can't be foreseen or predicted. The little things like warts and Boy Scouts often come up and I had to use my problem solving skills the best I could. Erik Rudolph's words resurfaced in my mind, *Don't just plan it; survive it*. I didn't feel a whole lot better, but I managed to eventually fall asleep.

Day 47   19.9 Miles

I awoke with the bitter taste of regret still in my mouth. I cooked oatmeal and coffee for breakfast then moved out as quietly as possible, trying not to awaken the Boy Scouts, which didn't work. They heard me and started the chaos of beginning their day. I found I still had some fond memories of when I was a scout myself many years ago. I hiked amongst the Boy Scouts most of the morning. We all experienced a violent morning thunder and lightning storm, but kept moving until it cleared up and the sun came out. I lost them where a bridge washed out over Stony Creek. The scoutmaster took them over the detour and I forded the creek.

The cold water really hurt the sensitive warts on my feet again. The warts seemed to have worsened after I froze them, causing me some fear because I didn't know how bad they would become. I found myself in constant pain even with high doses of ibuprofen. I had hoped to see some improvement because it was getting harder to walk.

I crossed Pine Swamp Branch where I once had an up close and personal encounter with a Copper Head while on a section hike. I remembered the exact place in detail. The hair on my neck stood up as I quickly stepped over the same log, but that time I was fully alert.

I came close to the twenty-mile mark again before I stopped for the night at Wind Rock on an unofficial campsite with a great vista, flat ground, and water. A young couple was already camped there for the night, so I politely asked if they would mind if joined them.

Lewis and Elizabeth met in a medical tech school and fell in love. They too graduated and were thru-hiking the Appalachian Trail before they got jobs and settled down. The trail was now their only home. They built a fire and asked me to join them. We cooked, ate, and talked until I turned in for the night to leave them to themselves.

I asked Elizabeth, "How do you like the trail so far?"

She said, "What is there not to like about it?" I enjoyed their company tremendously and found their positive outlook and attitude so refreshing. I would vote for Lewis and Elizabeth as the cutest couple on the trail.

Day 48   15.9 miles

Today was Good Friday. I packed up as quietly as possible to not wake Lewis & Elizabeth. I left before daylight, hiking with my headlamp. I had to stop mid-morning due to a severe lightning storm. I was between Salt Pond Mountain and Lone Pine Peak. I tried to avoid the lightning by leaving my aluminum hiking poles on the trail and going fifty yards down hill below the trail. I sat on my pack until the storm passed, with my poncho covering the pack and me as if I were a hen turkey on a nest.

I later stopped at War Spur Shelter to eat breakfast and dry out. A trail angel left green tea and Halls honey/lemon cough drops with instructions to melt two drops in a cup of tea. O'boy did the tea hit the spot. I found myself enjoying the feeling of the caffeine, so I sat back and relaxed. I recalled the feeling the first time I smoked weed. The memory was pleasant at first.

I discovered marijuana could take me to a fantasy world far, far away where there was no stress and no one could tell me what to do. I loved smoking pot and being intoxicated. I started to spend more and more time in the fantasy world created by chemicals. The real world eventually became so harsh that I couldn't stand being in it, so I drank as often as I could and smoked marijuana almost every day.

I soon found other illegal drugs could provide the feelings I was so seeking. I liked some drugs even better than alcohol. Illegal drugs were easy to obtain in the social circles I ran in and I didn't need any identification. The down side was drugs were expensive, especially when you had an appetite the size of mine. Chemical addiction was a progressive disease and my disease was progressing at an alarming rate.

My thoughts stopped when I noticed my hands were shaking. I was tempted to make another cup of tea, but thought better of it and moved out. I felt ashamed that even after all the consequences, I still romanced the marijuana. I suppose I should have given myself a little credit because I thought it through to the consequences and if presented with a situation where I could use now, I would turn it down.

The fact that I would always be an addict even after all these years, still left me with a negative, creepy feeling. I deliberately put the subject out of my mind as I stepped up my pace to get the blood flowing. The sky cleared up, got sunny, and then darkened as the storm rolled in, which seemed appropriate for Good Friday. I stopped at Laurel Creek Shelter for lunch and re-taped my warts, which seemed to be still worsening.

I hiked past what they call the Keefer Oak, which was a white oak tree that measured over eighteen feet in circumference and was estimated at over three-hundred-years-old. The tree was naked of its leaves, but its skeleton dwarfed all the other trees around it. It looked like it was the mother tree that gathered her little trees around to protect them from the ax. I had to ponder the fact trees like that were once common, but we may never see trees like the big oak again in our lifetime. I took a picture, but without a person in the picture to compare the size difference you couldn't tell how magnificent the tree truly was. I noticed some ominous storm clouds approaching in the background, so I quickly hiked on for the safety of the next shelter.

The storm over took me, drenched me, and passed on long before I arrived at Sarver Hollow Shelter. The shelter was three-tenths of a mile off the trail on a side trail that dropped steeply off the mountain. I was tired, so I set my tent up on the ridge beside the trail. I rested up before taking my water bottle and one hiking pole down three long, steep, tenths of a mile for water. A nice new shelter with a covered porch and good water was at the bottom. I filtered all the water I would need then ascended back to my tent.

Thunder started to rumble and the radio predicted more lightning storms. I decided to take down my tent and move off the ridge, back down the mountain to the safety of the shelter. I set up in the shelter where I felt safe. Besides, all my gear would be dry for the next day. I read the log and saw where my friend Yahtzee spent a zero day there due to an infected blister that he worried would end his hike.

I worried about the wart on my little toe. I wondered if a zero day in Daleville would help heal the warts on my feet. I wondered if the wart on my little toe was starting to become infected. I never thought a stupid wart could knock me off the trail and end my dream of thru-hiking. I slammed the log shut in anger over worrying about the wart. I knew I needed to stop that type of thinking or I would psychologically defeat myself. I would contemplate the worst-case scenario until I was positively sure it would happen. I then would stop trying to solve the problem and start to form strategies to avoid the problem.

I had exactly the same type of thing happen on Roan Mountain when the couple from Maine planted a doubt in my head. They said, Roan was too dangerous to hike in the snow storm that day. I started worrying about the worst thing that could happen until I was so sure I would die if I tried to hike Roan. I made a decision based on fear and avoided hiking over Roan that day.

I believed my worst enemy was not Roan Mountain, the wart, or whatever was wrong at the time. My worst enemy was my attitude about any particular situation. When I let fear and negative thinking take over, I lose hope.

I never have been too superstitious, but it was Good Friday and I also noticed when I read the in the log that the shelter was exactly six-hundred and sixty-six (666) miles away from Springer Mountain. Lewis and Elizabeth showed up as I started to let things play on my mind. Their company took me away from my fears as soon as they arrived. Lewis and Elizabeth were young and so in love with each other it was a joy to be around them. I realized God knew I started to get in trouble by myself, so he sent company and I felt grateful.

I discovered I had lost my headlamp. I probably forgot to take it off when I put my poncho on over my head in the morning storm. I knocked it off when I took the poncho off somewhere on the trail. Elizabeth gave me a little green light to help get me by until I could replace the one I lost at the outfitters in Daleville. Once again, I felt grateful for the generosity of other hikers. We cooked, ate, and socialized into the night. I had grown so fond of Lewis and Elizabeth I could have adopted them.

April 15   Day 49   15.9 Miles

I made a good decision to stay in the shelter because two big thunder and lightning storms struck before daylight. I was sure glad I wasn't camping up on the ridge when they crashed into the mountain. We all awoke before daybreak and ate breakfast together. I quickly packed up and moved out to give Lewis and Elizabeth their space alone. The morning was a delightful spring morning with that after the rain smell in the air. I felt so grateful for Easter Saturday that I thought it was fitting to stop and thank Jesus for the sacrifice he made on my behalf so many years ago. I believed the trail was a spiritual journey for me since the first day on Springer Mountain.

I ate lunch at Niday Shelter, where fire burned the forest. The register said lightning caused a forest fire the night before. The forest service had to drop water by helicopter two times to put it out. I was happy I wasn't involved in that. I blew up my mattress and thought I would take a little nap. My mind wouldn't shut down, so I started to reminisce about my past again.

Time passed and I married and started working as a carpenter. The job paid well, but I still wasn't even keeping up with my bills by working. I found I could supplement my income and get what I needed by stealing and dealing. Thus, my life of crime began. At first, I only sold marijuana to my friends and only stole from my family, but soon I advanced to a world of crime, lust, and violence.

Selling drugs surreptitiously came natural to me. I liked it and it solved a problem because it appeared as if I could use drugs for nothing. At least, that was how I rationalized it anyway. I soon became dependant on the financial benefits of dealing drugs and the business started growing bigger. The downside to living illegally was the paranoia I lived with constantly. I was afraid of the cops, other dealers, and even my customers. Once again, I found getting high would soothe the fear.

Getting high made me not care, but it didn't give me any hope. When I would come down and face reality, the situation would always seem even more hopeless. I would get high again, which solved nothing except it would take away the hopeless feeling. I had tears in my eyes as that negative, but familiar, old unpleasant feeling returned as if it never left.

A beagle came along and befriended me, which snapped me out of my negative thoughts. He was friendly enough like most beagles and he was wearing a collar. I figured he strayed from his owner, who was probably looking for him. God must have known I was getting in trouble with my thoughts, so he sent an angel disguised as a beagle.

I was filtering water for myself to drink when he walked up to his chin in the spring to get himself a drink. I went to slap him and he ran, which caused the water hole to become all muddy. I had to wait until the water cleared before I could finish filtering water. I found the beagle a little annoying, but at least he seemed to comfort me and get me out of my head.

The beagle and I hiked from Craig Creek, ascending fifteen-hundred feet to a memorial to Audie Murphy which had a bench. I had no idea who Audie Murphy was, but I stopped on the bench and took off my shoes and socks. I aired my feet out to cool off as I re-taped my warts and blisters.

I went to pet the beagle and discovered he had been rolling in human feces. He then pissed on my pack right in front of me. Either God had a weird sense of humor or He was testing my tolerance, or the mutt wasn't an angel.

Do-Rag came along as I was cleaning my hands the best I could with hand sanitizer and toilet paper. She distracted me from thoughts of hurting the beagle as she sat down beside me on the bench and took off her shoes and socks. She had blisters of her own that needed attention.

Apparently, AYCE pizza in Pearisburg seduced her. She ended up so sleepy after eating a lot of pizza, she checked into a room and spent the night in Pearisburg. We had quite an intimate chat about addiction. She was trying to recover from an eating disorder that stemmed from being a gymnast. I shared my experience with my addiction to drugs and alcohol. I hoped my story gave her some hope and encouragement. I felt bad that I told her about the AYCE pizza in Pearisburg. She said, "My boyfriend sent me a package of cookies and chocolates."

The beagle, Do-Rag, and I hiked north as a threesome until the beagle ran off after a deer. I bid him good riddance. Do-Rag and I continued with our intimate conversation as if we were old friends. I had to admire women like her who were not afraid to be thru-hiking alone, especially women who were as attractive and in the superior physical condition as Do-Rag. We stopped to get water at Trout Creek and to our good fortune, a trail angel left pop cooling in the water. We rested for a while before the climb out of the creek valley.

It was getting late in the day and I was hot, dirty, and exhausted. I elected to stop at Pickle Branch Shelter because the radio was predicting lightning storms again. The next shelter was almost fourteen miles north. Do-Rag wanted to arrive in Daleville by Easter Sunday, so she moved on. I would have liked to have joined her for her company, but I bid her goodbye, knowing I might never see her again.

Pickle Branch Shelter was half a mile off trail, but easy downhill. A good-sized stream with enough privacy to get naked ran behind the shelter, so I took a bath before I set up in the shelter. I was alone, but it was still early. I hoped I would get some company for the night.

My thoughts drifted back to the hell my addiction. I was never able to pin-point exactly when I got caught up in my cycle of hopelessness, but that was the way I lived in my addiction. It was no longer fun and exciting to use chemicals. I would drink or use some drug to escape my despair and all the time I was spiraling down into a hopeless pit.

I was starting to emotionally go to that familiar hopeless place which was always so uncomfortable. I believed it was necessary to remember because I never wanted to forget where I came from. Never-the-less, I was grateful when an eighteen-year-old, thru-hiker named Bleach came in and interrupted my painful memories. Bleach was fresh out of high school. The previous year, while on summer break, he rode a bicycle from the state of Washington to Maine in forty-six days. He planned on going to college in Wisconsin next fall. He had traveled more than most people twice his age. He gave me some valuable tips about hiking and nutrition on the trail.

I was impressed with Bleach's degree of knowledge and humility. However, he still possessed an eighteen-year-old, I can do anything attitude, that I also found so refreshing. He hiked with Coconut Monkey fifty-two miles in thirty-five continuous hours just to do it, but they were young and dumb. I told him the only way I was going to go fifty-two miles at one time was in a car.

Elizabeth and Lewis came in next with guess who, the beagle. I was happy to see Lewis and Elizabeth, but I had hoped to have seen the last of the beagle. Elizabeth was in love with the damn dog. She called the phone number on his collar and his owner said, "Keep the #@$+^&* %!" She planned to keep him and train him to carry a pack. I thought, yea right, whatever. We all cooked and the beagle successfully begged. They fed him tuna, jerky, gorp, Cliff bars, and anything else they could think of. I fed him nothing.

We socialized into the evening. I realized I was almost as old as the three of them put together, but I felt like I fit in as the old man. Later, when we turned in, the beagle slept between Lewis and Elizabeth until they went to sleep. He then curled up next to me. He stunk, so I pushed him away. He wouldn't go so I slapped him and he ki-yied until he awoke everyone, but he went back to Elizabeth. I went to sleep, but awoke to this awful, eye-watering odor. The beagle curled up next to me again and apparently, the hiker food didn't agree with his digestive system and gave him gas. I escorted him out of the shelter rather rudely by the collar and tail. He yipped, but didn't return. He soon announced he found a rabbit to chase all around the shelter. I put in earplugs to muffle his barking and drifted off to sleep.

Mother Nature awakened me a long time before sunrise to take the old man, pee. I snuck out of the shelter as quietly as possible as not to wake the others. I had forgotten about the beagle. I was relieving myself outside under the stars when he deliberately snuck up on me from under the shelter and licked the back of my calf. I almost lost control of my sphincter and I was sure the others thought I was being murdered. I couldn't get back to sleep due to the excess of adrenalin in my system. The dog spent the rest of the night under the shelter, directly under me, licking who knows what. I only hope the others knew it was the beagle doing the licking. I spent some time plotting his demise before I fell back to sleep. I thought, Elizabeth must never know.

That was how week seven ended after hiking one-hundred and twenty-five miles.

Day 50   14.9 Miles
Easter Sunday

Easter was the day we celebrated Christ rising from the dead. I awoke to a bright, sunny spring day, which seemed appropriate for Easter. I tried to sneak out of the shelter as quietly as possible so I didn't disturb anyone. I had zero luck with that because Mr. Beagle decided I was a threat to the others and sounded the alarm. After Mr. Beagle made sure everyone was awake, we cooked and ate our breakfast together. I enjoyed their company, so I drank an extra cup of coffee before I left.

Lewis and Elizabeth planned to hitch a mile off trail at Catawba to The Home Place Restaurant for a family-style AYCE Easter dinner. They invited me to join them and I considered taking them up on their tempting offer, but decided to decline. I haven't had a shower since

Pearisburg and I didn't want to offend anyone who was all dressed up in their Easter outfit by having to sit with a funky old hiker at dinner. I planned on stopping at a convenience store which was four tenths of a mile off trail to buy junk food anyway. That was more my style and besides I had my heart set on a bunch of chili-cheese dogs.

I left solo, but soon found the beagle followed me. I threw rocks and shouted profanities at him, but he ducked the rocks, ignored the insults, and followed me anyway like a loyal Lassie. I ascended steeply to the summit of Cove Mountain. I took a side trail to a natural rock formation called Dragon's Tooth, which consisted of several large, thin, sharp, tooth-shaped rocks in a row pointing toward the sky. I found Dragon's tooth truly a spectacular point on the Appalachian Trail and well worth the short hike off trail.

A lesbian couple named, Nike and Sara were sitting in the cavity of the main tooth when I arrived. I befriended them and took their picture and they in return, took my picture in the cavity with my camera. They gave me their phone number so I could contact them to mail the pictures to them when I got home.

They left me to myself. I sat in the tooth, which was a cavity where if I took a step forward, it was a long way down. I sat mesmerized by nature's beauty. I actually saw spring climbing the distant mountains as the lush green of the valleys turned to winter's grey and brown half way to the mountain tops. Each day, the green climbed higher on the mountains. Spring was always such a wonderful time of the year.

My mind wandered back to a sad thought. A year ago on Easter Sunday, I lost one of the best friends I ever had.

DONALD STOVER

"A Marine, a Vietnam combat vereran, a truck driver, a scuba driver, a Fish & Wildlife employee, a bee keeper, a naturalist, a fox trapper, a marksman, a farmer, a father of five, a husband..." but most of all to me, one of the finest men I've ever known.

I called him; "Orville." He was the kind of man who had the respect of all who knew him. I was lucky enough to have known him. Our friendship started almost thirty years ago on the trap-line.

The year was 1977, and the price of fur was at an all-time high. I was drinking beer and trapping fox on private land without permission. Orville was trapping fox on the same land with permission. I dispatched a fox I caught and was on my knees busy resetting the trap.

I heard, "You're trespassing."

I stood up and we faced each other like two gunfighters at high noon. I didn't know how ugly it was going to get. He was packing a gun, but so was I.

He caught me red-handed, but I said, "This here's Sainer's land."

He shook his head and said, "Its Andy's land," as he nodded towards Andy's farmhouse.

I took a minute to assess the situation and knew he was serious. I reached down, and pulled the trap and said, "I apologize, do ya want the fox"?

He shook his head, "Naw, but I'd like to see how ya catch em."

Normally I would not have shown anyone anything or given away any trap-line secrets, but I showed him a couple of sets. When we got back to the trucks, I offered him a beer. We ended up getting drunk that day.

Orville didn't have any trapping skill at first, but he was quick to learn and soon began catching fox. We talked about running a long trapline professionally as equal partners, but Orville felt his ability wasn't equal to mine. He would always put it off one more year until he was ready. Eventually time ran out and the price of fur fell to the point that it wasn't economically worth trapping. We always dreamed of running a long-line after we retired and money didn't matter, but time ran out and lung cancer robbed us of the dream.

We hunted, trapped, built things, worked on projects, and invented a fox box. The fox box was a long story in itself. Once we were even allies in a barroom brawl. We drank a lot of beer until I quit drinking beer. We drank a lot of coffee after I sobered up. We would drink coffee on Sunday morning and tell old war stories and other lies. Orville would call it, "Going to Service."

Family was extraordinarily important to Orville and he treated me as if I was part of his family. He was the big brother I never had. His children still called me Uncle Buzz after his death.

I last saw him at the Cleveland Clinic a year ago on the Saturday before Easter. I walked into his hospital room and we both knew what time it was. We had Service for the last time. Orville was positive and had his great sense of humor even in the face of death. I was thankful for his friendship and would miss him until we meet again. I felt Orville's spirit sending me a message on Dragon's Tooth that day.

The loss of Orville devastated me more than I could describe, but it also inspired me to hike the Appalachian Trail while I still had time. I thought time may be about the only thing limited in this world. Time was easy to waste and I could never get it back once it was gone. I realized I do not know how much time I had left. It may have been later than I thought. I would do my best to pursue the dreams that I was inspired to accomplish while I still had time. I was remembering his friendship as I ended the Service with a prayer, which was what he would have done for me. I saluted my friend before I moved out.

I descended Cove Mountain and hiked four tenths of a mile off trial to the convenience store that was in my plans. Bleach caught up to me at the store, so we dined together. I ate four chili-cheese dogs, two pickled eggs, a pint of butter pecan ice cream and a large coffee. I bought enough snickers, cookies and other snacks to last until I got to Daleville the next day. Bleach was on the pay phone when I left.

The weather was picture perfect for Easter Sunday. The Virginia Redbud was in full bloom adding Easter colors to the landscape as I crisscrossed a babbling brook and ascended the valley. I felt a sudden awareness that the beagle was no longer with me. I thought I might have lost him before Dragon's Tooth. The wimp probably couldn't climb up Cove Mountain. He was most likely annoying some Sobo, but I preferred to think someone ran him over. I sure hoped Elizabeth wasn't carrying the little bastard over Cove Mountain.

I was able to call my oldest daughter Phyllis on the cell phone. We celebrated Easter together long distance. She wanted to hike with me over the Memorial Day weekend, so we decided to rendezvous at

Delaware Water gap on the Pennsylvania/New Jersey border. I felt honored that Phyllis wanted to be a part of my hike.

I crossed the road to Catawba and discovered fresh pizza and Pepsi that a trail angel left for thru-hikers. I wasn't too hungry, but I hadn't had pizza since Damascus. I took a break to eat a piece of pizza and left a thank you note with a blessing for the angel. I had no idea if Elizabeth and Lewis were ahead or behind me. They may have pigged out at the restaurant already. They could have even fed the beagle.

I was ascending Catawba Mountain when it started to thunder, so I high-tailed it to Catawba Mountain Shelter. I quickly set up my tent away from the shelter before a violent lightning storm attacked. It felt good to be alone in my tent after two nights in shelters with other people. I had good cell tower, so I caught up in my journal, then called Scooter and an Alcoholics Anonymous hiker-buddy.

I closed my eyes and tried to settle down to sleep, but my mind wasn't ready to shut down. I focused on a significant event in my life that happened when Phyllis was a toddler and my youngest daughter was only a sparkle in my eye. My addiction was starting to get way out of control and life was becoming unmanageable anyway, but one day, everything became public. I was on my way home from selling LSD at an Edgar Winters Concert in New York when my worst nightmare came true. I was the passenger in a van, strung out from partying the night before, when I noticed a cop facing the road as we passed. He pulled out and started to follow us, but stayed way behind. We rounded a curve and two cop cars blocked the road, and the cop behind us pulled right up on our tail.

The crime took place in New York, so I hoped the news wouldn't reach home. The one and only consolation was I felt my anonymity was safe. I had scores of time to think in jail. I felt I was the victim of an unfair legal system. My thinking was re-enforced and supported by other inmates. I was full of remorse because I got in trouble, but not for how I was living. I made a resolution to be smarter and more careful, so they would never arrest me again.

I sat in jail for a while before Dad came up and bailed me out. I was surprised to see him and wondered how he knew I was in jail.

I tried to thank him when he said, "Don't thank me, thank, your mother. I would have left you to rot in jail if it was up to me." That was the only thing he said during the hour and a half ride home. I was ashamed that I disappointed him so often. I silently took a solemn vow on the long ride back to my hometown to never use again. Dad dropped me off at my house and I could tell instantly from the look on my wife's face, she knew also. She was scared and concerned for me, but not angry. She knew about my drinking and marijuana smoking but never realized the whole story.

I grew up in a family with high moral standards, beliefs, and values. I felt guilty because I committed a crime and they all knew about it. The conflict of values created a mental anguish only getting high one more time could extinguish. I had a personal, secret stash of pot at the house, so the first thing I did was roll a joint, only an hour after taking a solemn vow to never use again. My wife filled me in as we smoked the joint. I noticed a cameraman at the magistrate's office at my arraignment, but I didn't think it was important enough to reach home. To my dismay, our local news channels aired the story at six and again at eleven o'clock. They had the film of me in handcuffs escorted by a New York State Trooper. That was how my parents found out their son was an addict and a drug dealer. My arrest also exposed my behavior to everyone else. My lifestyle was no longer a secret, but I laughed about it because the drug I was smoking took my guilt and shame away. Getting high didn't give me any hope, but I didn't have to face my situation, at least for the moment. When I think back, it seems absurd that even after the consequences of the drug bust, I didn't see my usage as a problem. Quite the opposite, I saw the drug as my savior from the harsh reality of life's miseries.

I thought a cold front moved in with the storm. I hoped it would pass in the night and the next day would be clear. I wanted to be able to see the view from McAfee Knob and Tinker Cliffs, which I heard were two spectacular landmarks on the Appalachian Trail in Virginia. I passed both places last year on a section hike, but the weather was so bad it stole my view. My warts were worse, so I decided to take an unscheduled zero-day in Daleville. I was looking forward to a town day in two days to clean up, heal up, eat up, and rest up.

Day 51   15.7 Miles

I awoke and packed up before daylight, but a storm came in suddenly about daybreak. I called Scooter and stayed in my tent talking until she had to go to work. The rain was still coming down in sheets, so I unpacked my sleeping bag, crawled back in it, and slept for another hour. I awoke and packed up the second time when boredom overtook me. I couldn't procrastinate any longer, so I faced the pouring rain, and moved out. The rain lasted all day, which was a déjà vu feeling of the section hike the year before when I passed McAfee Knob in June.

McAfee Knob was a rock formation that jutted out into space. I have seen many pictures of hikers sitting or standing on the overhanging formation. Some were at the tip, but that depended on how much courage the hiker had. In the coyote and the roadrunner cartoon, the rock usually broke off for Wiley Coyote. He would hit the ground hard at first, and then the rock that broke off would hit him.

I was disappointed again when I passed McAfee Knob and Tinker Cliffs. At times, I could only see about fifty feet into the milky-white nothingness. I would have to come back sometime on another section hike to take pictures. I took a pee off the overhang into the fog, hoping no one was below.

I stopped at Lamberts Meadow Shelter to get out of the rain long enough to eat lunch. Coconut Monkey came in and joined me. I hadn't seen him since that awful night in the blizzard on Roan Mountain. He said he went to Miss Janet's hostel later the next day and then went home for a week. We ate and filtered water before leaving together. He wanted to split the cost at a motel in Daleville but I declined. I liked people, but I also liked my privacy. He hiked faster than I did, so he hiked on ahead. I felt guilty that I turned down his offer of going halvers on the motel. I sure hoped I didn't hurt his feelings.

The last ten miles to Daleville were just git-r-done miles accompanied by dropping temperatures, steady driving rain, with thunder and lightning thrown in. I was cold, wet, hungry, and the wart on my little toe was giving me such terrible pain I could hardly walk. I wasn't having fun at all and it seemed like I would never get to Daleville. I paused at an overlook on a power line, overlooking a river in the valley. The view would have been spectacular on a sunny day, but again, the heavy rain and fog dulled the sharpness of detail and color.

I finally reached Daleville early in the evening. The gas stations, motels, and fast food joints where the interstate intersected with another major highway were such a welcome sight. I went straight to the same Econo Lodge Scooter and I stayed at four weeks before. I checked in, paying forty-seven dollars for the room. I put on my only clean shorts and took all the rest of my clothes to the in-house laundry room. I took a long hot shower as my clothes washed.

Once I got clean, warm, and dry, I felt like a human being again. I walked across the interstate to Taco Bell and pigged out on tacos and burritos until I became groggy. I almost crawled back to my motel room. I jumped under the clean, dry sheets to watch television, but not for long before sleep ended my day.

Day 52   Zero miles

I walked to Shoney's first thing for the AYCE breakfast. I decided to take the day off because my toe was swollen and hurting. I hoped the time off would help the wart heal. I was contemplating cutting out the corner of my boot to allow room for my swollen little toe. I went back to the motel and paid for another night. I then walked a mile to the post office to pick up my mail drop. I also sent some things ahead to myself in Waynesboro, Virginia. I impulsively stopped at a local, down-home barbershop and got a short flattop haircut and my beard trimmed. I enjoyed the company and conversation of the old-time, local barber more than the haircut.

The outfitter didn't open until ten o'clock, so I stopped at the grocery store to kill some time. A man delivering donuts recognized me as a hiker, gave me donuts, and struck up a conversation. The people along the trail have been so kind and generous. I ate the donuts before I went into the store. I didn't need anything, but I bought a Fur, Fish, Game magazine, and some antibiotic cream for my wart. I waited outside until the outfitter opened to buy a new head light for sixty dollars and a can of fuel. The outfitters along the trail had everything a hiker would ever need, but you paid top dollar.

I went to lunch and ran into Coconut Monkey. I invited him to join me at a Mexican restaurant; my treat since he was on a tight budget. He found Yahtzee to split the cost of a room with him last night, which helped me feel less guilty for refusing to let him share my room. He said Yahtzee was having major trouble with his infected blister and may have to hold up until it healed. I told him I would pray for Yahtzee. I didn't know what else I could say or do to help Yahtzee.

I went back to the room and spent the afternoon writing letters and resting. I went back to the outfitters to buy a small light like the one Elizabeth gave me. I planned to return her light the next time I saw her. I stopped at Shoney's for an AYCE steak dinner by myself. I spent the evening talking to Alcoholics Anonymous friends and caught up on gossip and everything that was happening in the recovery community back home. All the warts on my feet were gone except the one on my little toe, which was getting worse. I planned to move on the next day in spite of the pain.

Day 53   18.5 Miles

I almost couldn't get my left boot on over my swollen little toe, so I took ibuprofen to help cope with the pain and swelling. I ate eight donuts and drank three cups of coffee at the motel office before I checked out. I stopped on the way out of town and bought two apples and a sub sandwich for lunch. My pack was my all-time heaviest yet on the trail, but my lower back was getting better and stronger.

The weather was clear, cool, and sunny, which I found ideal for hiking. The ibuprofen and coffee kicked in so, I turned up the music on my CD player and hiked out solo. I was happy to be back on the trail on a bright, sunshiny day.

I stopped for lunch at Curry Creek where Scooter and I spent the night two years ago on a section hike. We were there in the first week of July and the creek was drying up at the time, which trapped schools of minnows in the deeper holes. They were starving and tried to eat our feet when we soaked them. They tickled and gave us a type of foot massage. We fed them oatmeal and crumbs and they would swarm the food like little sharks.

I found the water was high and no minnows were there as I ate my sub and one apple for lunch. The other apple would be a welcome treat in the afternoon. I usually ate fruit soon because of the weight. Fruit was heavy to carry, but had zero garbage to carry out. I would plant the seeds, always hoping they would grow and one day produce apple, peach, or plumb trees for the next generation of hungry hikers. Bananas were also a welcome treat and they replenish potassium, which I heard prevented cramps which were common with all hikers. I got cramps often, which I found annoying, especially in the middle of the night. I took a short nap after lunch before I moved on to Wilson Creek.

Wilson Creek was a significant landmark because it was a third of the way to Katahdin. I hiked seven-hundred and twenty-five miles and had fourteen-hundred and fifty miles left to Katahdin. Katahdin still seemed like a million miles away. Ragman, the retired Marine, was hiking a flip-flop. He started at Springer Mountain late that spring and arranged for a girlfriend to pick him up at Wilson Creek and take him to Katahdin. He would then hike south from Katahdin and end his hike at Wilson Creek. I wondered if he ever made it back. I wondered if I would ever make it to Mount Katahdin.

I was surprised I hiked over ten miles since leaving Daleville. Wilson Creek was my goal for the day, but it was still early afternoon and I wasn't ready to stop for the night. I filtered water, took some pictures as the water rushed over the smooth granite, and moved on, crossing the Blue Ridge Parkway for the first time. The afternoon was uneventful, but I hiked seven more miles and stopped at Bobblets Shelter. Bobblets Shelter was two tenths of mile down an extremely rugged descent, but it came equipped with a handicap accessible out-house. I thought, how stupid, because the only way a person in a wheelchair could get there was if someone threw them off the mountain. Then I considered government regulations and it made more sense. I couldn't find a place to set up a tent, so I set up in the shelter by myself.

I hadn't entered in my journal since I got to Daleville, so I spent some time catching up. My mind returned to the powerlessness of my addiction.

I would have thought the humiliation of arrest and incarceration should have been enough for most folks to at least suspect drug use might be a problem, but I couldn't see it. I used addictively for another nine years. My problem was chemicals took over my life. I became progressively more mentally dependant and as my addiction increased, my morals decreased. When I was sober, I felt shame, guilt, and remorse, which manifested in incredible self-loathing and depression. I hated to be sober and vulnerable to those negative emotions, so I tried to stay high.

I hung out in social circles where addiction and crime were normal. I fit in somewhat and shunned my family and old friends. I turned to stronger drugs, which did the trick at first, but I soon started to experience physical withdrawal symptoms. I remembered feeling incredibly hopeless, overwhelmed, and alone.

I realized my meditation triggered feelings of hopelessness over my wart. I always felt powerless over pain, fear, and uncertainty. I became pissed off because I felt alone again and needed some company. I wished I had cell tower to call in some support. I quickly tried changing my thoughts and made a gratitude list instead of staying focused on my negative emotions over the thoughts the situation stirred up. The first thing I thought of was I was still hiking and still sober. I had the love and respect of my family, friends, and myself. I re-focused on everything that was right.

I felt better emotionally, but before long, my mind started to settle on my pain and I started feeling sorry for myself once more. Then I had a moment of clarity and realized I was never all alone. God was with me that night as He watched over me. I prayed, "Thanks God for helping me get through another day. I need your help to carry on if it is your will." I took comfort in believing somehow all this was God's plan as another day ended in my adventure.

HOPE

Day 54   19.5 Miles

I spent a lot of time trying to pad and protect the wart. I took six-hundred milligrams of ibuprofen, pulled on my boot, and sucked up the pain the best I could. I then asked God for help and started hiking. My experience of the insight the night before told me I had to focus on the positive, ignore the pain, and trust God.

I took a picture of a valley below filled with a white fluffy cloud as the mountains rose above the fog. The familiar tinge of green announcing spring was on the way below a crystal-clear, blue-sky, promised a beautiful spring day and gave me hope.

I crossed the Blue Ridge Parkway several times again that day. I passed Cove Mountain Shelter where Scooter and I once stayed. I recalled the shelter had no water source and we became uncomfortably thirsty.

I stopped for lunch at Jennings Creek, which had an inviting swimming hole. After consideration, I stripped down to my shorts and jumped into clear water. The mountain water was as cold as I feared it might be, so I quickly scrubbed with a little bar of motel soap, ducked under to rinse off, and got out in record time. I looked up and a big old friendly looking section hiker named Robo Cop was applauding.

He asked, "How's the water,"

I said "As warm as bath water." He laughed, as he knew I lied through my teeth, which were chattering.

He took a break to chat while I re-taped my blister and packed up. He already hitched two miles to a private campground for breakfast.

He said, "I hitch into towns for a hot meal any chance I get." I enjoyed his company as we hiked together for a little while. He was slowing me down on the hills, so I bid him farewell and left him in my dust.

I hiked to Cornelius Creek Shelter, which was an impressive, new, two-story structure. No one was there, but I set up my tent anyway to be comfortable. Then I made macaroni and cheese for supper. I hoped Robo Cop would roll in, but he must have stopped earlier.

The weather was great that day, which greatly improved my mood, but I still worried about the wart on my toe. I was afraid it might be infected and I needed medical help. I couldn't do anything about it that night on the trail, so I tried to turn my fear into faith by praying. Apparently, praying worked again, because I was able to let go of the fear enough to fall sleep.

Day 55   18.7 Miles

I awoke to a thunderstorm, packed up a wet tent, and hiked out in the rain. I took extra ibuprofen, but my wart pain was almost unbearable.

I wondered, what the hell was I thinking when I decided to drop out of main stream society and hike for twenty-two-hundred miles. The only reward at the end was a wooden sign that said, Katahdin. Scooter would take my picture and that would be the end. Most people back home never even heard of Mount Katahdin. When they would see me training with trekking poles they would ask, "Where are your skis?"

Dark, rainy days always seemed to get me down anyway. Now I had a lot of pain added to the weather, so I felt quite negative. I knew I had to do something to improve my attitude or I would talk myself off the trail. I wondered if this was, The Virginia Blues Seiko and others warned me about.

The highpoint of the morning was a large, round rock wedged between two larger rocks, suspended above the Appalachian Trail. They called it the Guillotine because it reminded everyone of a guillotine. I felt a little intimidated as I walked under it.

I took a break from a thunder and lightning storm at Thunder Hill Shelter. I could see how it got its name. I tried to focus on the things I was grateful for, but it all seemed hopeless. I felt I couldn't do it with the pain. I wished I had something stronger than ibuprofen. I stopped in the middle of the trail when I became aware my situation was more than simply inconvenient; it was dangerously life threatening. It was as plain as the ass on a goat, I was in trouble if I take something stronger than ibuprofen, I could and would relapse. The big book called alcohol, cunning, baffling, and powerful. I believe it was also patient and sneakier than the best cat burglar.

I took some time to remember where I came from. It was a cold, hard, fact that, once you were an addict, you would always be an addict. I was still an addict even after all the time sober. I became a slave to drugs and alcohol. My whole life revolved around the chemicals above all else. In a sense, the drugs were a power greater than myself, that caused me to be insane. Addiction was a demanding, heartless, slave-master who I tried to serve. The older addicts used the old expression, I got a monkey on by back. Well, the monkey's name was withdrawal and the monkey had to be fed above all else. I couldn't describe the hell of withdrawal in words to anyone who never personally experienced it for themselves. However, those who were addicted knew exactly what I was saying. I was truly powerless and the real world became so unmanageable that all I could do was try to escape it by using more drugs. In the end, even the drugs failed to comfort me. I lost all hope and almost everything else, but my life. I was so alone and isolated in the dark, Godless world I created for myself. It was then and only then that I cried out to the God who I had long ago forsaken for the instant gratification alcohol offered so many years ago. I found it was easy at that point to admit I was powerless and my life was truly unmanageable. I had lost all hope.

It seemed like things were out of control, but it was only a silly wart. It surprised me I even thought I could control a painkiller stronger than ibuprofen. Then, as if a bolt of lightning hit me, I experienced a moment of clarity. My insight into what was wrong was I relied on myself to solve the problem. When I was tired of trying to control my addiction, I cried out to God, let go, and things got better. I stopped and looked up into the dark gray clouds while the rain peppered my face. I dropped my pack, got on my knees, and folded my hands. I closed my eyes, resting my elbows on my pack, and said, "God, I surrender my burden to you. Please give me some hope, Amen."

I felt better as soon as the prayer was out of my mouth. I got up and looked in the guidebook and a town called Glasgow was six miles off the trail, but it was fifteen trail miles away. I was not sure I had twenty-one more miles left in me, but the thought of a hot shower sure motivated me. I saddled up and got back on the trail with a new purpose.

I thought I would never reach town as I managed to limp the fifteen miles to the James River. I found the James River was a major river to cross, but there was an impressive, six-hundred and twenty-five-foot steel and wooden bridge constructed exclusively for the Appalachian Trail that spanned the river. I paused in the rain to read a lone plaque at the entrance, dedicating the bridge to a man named Bill Foot.

Bill Foot and his wife Laurie became active in the Appalachian Trail Conservancy after they thru-hiked the trail in 1987. In 1987, the trail crossed the river on a two-lane highway bridge shared by fast moving traffic. Bill noticed five abandoned railroad piers that spanned the James River. Inspired by his thru-hike, Bill proposed building the bridge in 1991. He found the eighty-year-old miner named Henry Smiley, who owned the five piers. Henry had purchased the piers from the railroad for one-hundred and twenty-five dollars so he could dock his houseboat in the middle of the river. One day, Bill and Laurie stopped to see Henry. Over lemonade, Henry offered to sell the piers to the Appalachian Trail Conservancy for one dollar.

Bill had to overcome a huge amount of adversity to get the bridge built. At first, they turned down his grant requests. He had to get a number of government agencies on board to get the grants approved. He even had to host public hearings. Eventually, Bill received one and a half-million dollars in grants, but he had to raise three hundred-thousand dollars in matching funds. The Appalachian Trail Conservancy had to mortgage the piers and solicited donations of volunteer labor and land for the relocation of the trail. It still took an act of the Virginia State Congress to grant an exception to land ownership on a river bottom.

Nine years later, on October fourteenth, 2000 the six-hundred and twenty-five-foot bridge was completed. The Appalachian Trail Conservancy held a ceremony and dedicated the bridge to the memory of Bill Foot. They also named the bridge crossing the James River after him.

Bill also had a personal challenge to face. In the spring of 2000, time ran out for Bill and cancer deprived him of seeing his dream completed. It was unfortunate the man with the dream and the driving force behind the dream, never saw it all come together.

I was impressed by the bridge, but much more impressed by Bill Foot. Bill had to overcome a lot more adversity than I faced as he accomplished a greater goal. I was sure he would rather have a wart on his little toe than cancer. I always knew there would be bad days on the trail; after all, every day ain't Christmas.

I took Bill's story as a personal message of hope from him to me when I needed it most. I was inspired that he could build a bridge that impressive while facing the adversity of dying from cancer. He gave me the hope that I could at least continue hiking with a wart on my little toe. I stopped feeling sorry for myself and moved on feeling humbled.

I looked up to the gray sky and prayed aloud, Thank you God for answering my prayers. As an afterthought I said, Bill, if you can hear me, thanks.

I crossed the bridge and got off the trail onto the highway. I tried hitching the six miles to Glasgow, Virginia. The thru-hikers handbook listed a Mom and Pop Motel with an AYCE restaurant in the motel. The AYCE restaurant seemed too good to be true. I thought I would feel better once I got a room, a hot meal, dried out, and re-supplied.

I couldn't get a ride into town. Two separate cars of young men gave me the finger, but fortunately, they didn't stop. I was intimidated, so I stopped hitching and walked along the left side of the road, facing traffic. Two college kids who were on spring break came to a screeching halt. I was going to either run or fight when they asked me if I would like a ride. I jumped into the car, but sat with my pack in my lap to ride the last mile into town.

The town of Glasgow looked like it hadn't changed since 1950-something. The boys let me out in front of the motel/restaurant. I found the motel office closed, boarded up, and the restaurant looked like it hadn't been open for years. I walked around and found a couple of cars, but no people. I had a phone number, but no cell tower. I felt like I entered the Twilight Zone. I was in a depressed, scared, and lonely state of mind. I told myself not to panic yet.

A grocery store was open across the road. I went in with my pack on and asked the lady clerk if she knew anything about the motel. She nonchalantly said, "I'll give the owner a call in a minute." She took her time to finish whatever she was doing and made a phone call. I couldn't hear what she was saying, but after she hung up, she turned and said with her southern accent "Hey Darlin, Bob will meet ya in front of the motel in bout ten minutes." I was relieved, as I had visions of hiking back to the trail in the dark and setting up God only knows where in the rain.

The owner showed up in an hour, right before I was about to panic again, and rented me a room. It wasn't first class, but it was a step above Mull's in Georgia. The room was dry and had a heater, shower, and a television that worked. Bob told me how great the restaurant was and he always served two AYCE meat dishes and all the sides, but he quit the restaurant business after his wife died. Apparently, it was too much for him to run by himself. He had about two or three permanent residents in the motel and a couple of rooms he rented out to people like me.

I settled in before I took a shower and put on some dry clothes. I then ventured out to explore the town on Friday night. I bought six chili-cheese dogs with onions and mustard and a pint of cherry ice cream at a convenience store.

I went back to the motel to devour my food before going to a coin laundry to wash and dry my clothes. I called Scooter from a pay phone, which brightened my spirits even more. On my way back to the motel, I bought Epson salts and corn pads for my wart at the grocery store. I soaked my feet and watched television until late. I turned off the television and took some time to reflect on the day's lesson of hope.

I wasn't sober long when I went to my first Alcoholics Anonymous sponsored dance. I was still sick and miserable from the effects of withdrawal. The host of the dance was an old man named Wilber P who had been sober many years. He said over the microphone, "Ain't it great to be sober?" The crowd cheered in agreement. I can remember thinking they all drank too long.

The last thing in the world I wanted was to be sober. What I wanted to be was stinking drunk. I hated being an alcoholic and spent most of my time feeling sorry for myself. I had become so chemically dependent that I couldn't envision life without the use of drugs and alcohol. The only reason I was sober was because the only other alternative was death.

Other people like Wilber kept encouraging me saying things like, "It keeps getting better" and "Keep coming back." I wondered what they wanted at the time. The folks in the program continued to reassure me that I would be happy one day. They led by example and they seemed to be happy sober. I didn't understand, but they sincerely wanted me to join them in their newfound freedom. I was not capable of understanding they simply loved me because I was a suffering alcoholic.

I don't know how long it took, but one day I realized what they told me was true because it was slowly happening. Things were starting to get better and I started to value my sobriety. I discovered being an alcoholic was a blessing in disguise. I found my greatest fear became my greatest asset.

I learned to encourage, support, and love the newcomer. I tried to give them what Wilber and the others of yesterday gave to me so freely. I tried to give the new person what I considered the greatest gift I could ever give which was hope.

I snapped out of my reflective state and put my wart situation in perspective. The wart was only a little adversity. I truly believed adversity, when responded to positively, made us stronger. That gave me hope,which was why Bill Foot's story inspired me so significantly. He gave me hope. My little toe was swollen and the pain was unbelievable, but I had hope. I considered taking an unplanned zero miles day, because the pain seemed to subside when I rested the toe.

April 22   **Day 56**   **Zero miles**

I awoke to a violent thunder and lightning storm before daylight. I went back to sleep until it was well after daylight and the rain subsided. I found out the convenience store didn't open until eleven o'clock on Saturday, so I went to the laundry mat and bought Pepsi and candy bars for breakfast. I decided not to hike so I could heal up and rest. I believed I aggravated the wart when I hiked.

I called Scooter on the pay phone. I arranged to meet her on Friday, the twenty-eighth of April at a motel in Waynesboro. Waynesboro was a big town seventy-seven miles away, where I could get medical attention for my wart.

I met a couple from Connecticut who were Sobo section hiking with their car. They were going to a restaurant in a nearby town for breakfast and invited me to go along. I jumped at the chance and enjoyed the conversation and company even more than the breakfast. They wouldn't even let me pay for my breakfast. I felt ashamed because I couldn't remember their names. I thought God knew I was in need of company, so he sent them. Who knows, maybe they were angels. I always felt better when I had social contact with positive people. I had several reasons to be grateful.

They dropped me back off in Glasgow and I knew we might never meet again. I bought my son, Nick a birthday card and a phone card. I sent them with instructions to call me for his birthday on April twenty-eighth. I couldn't call him because he had no phone. I gave him a bike for his birthday before I left, so he already had his present. We normally communicated by letter, but I sure wanted to talk to him on his birthday if we could connect.

I looked up a man in town by the name of Stewart, who I heard shuttled hikers back to the trail for ten dollars. He was an interesting man who was about eighty-years-old. He agreed to take me back to the trail the next morning at seven o'clock.

I bought enough supplies at the grocery store to last until I got to Waynesboro. I found corn pads with the foot stuff that I thought might be able to pad and protect the wart from rubbing when I hiked. I stopped at the convenience store to buy six chilidogs, a large bowl of chili, and a large coffee for supper. I also bought donuts for breakfast in the morning in case the store didn't open before I left town. After I ate supper, I went back to the grocery store across the street for ice cream to eat while I watched television before I went to bed.

Week eight ended and I only hiked eighty-nine miles due to the pain from the wart on my little toe. I took two zero-mile days because of the pain and discomfort.

Day 57   19.6 Miles

The convenience store was open when I got up, so I treated myself to store bought coffee to drink with my donuts before I geared up. I padded the wart with corn pads and took ibuprofen. The weather was sunny, which improved my mood.

Stewart shuttled hikers to supplement his retirement income. I didn't think his old truck would make it up the mountain, but it did. I gave him eleven dollars plus all the change in my pocket. I was hiking by the time the morning sun dried up the trail. I overtook Robo Cop on my first ascent. He was hiking with a hiker he met on the trail. Robo Cop was extremely extraverted, always smiling, and I could hear the joy of laughter in his voice. He couldn't believe he was ahead of me, so I elected not to tell him I took a zero day. We stopped for an early break and took some pictures, before I moved on. He may have been an angel sent to brighten my day because it sure was great seeing him again.

I stopped for lunch at a viewpoint on Fullers rocks with a group of four couples from Philadelphia who were about my age and on a section hike. They asked questions and seemed impressed with my thru-hike, which fed my ego and helped inspire me to hike on with the wart pain.

I later stopped for a break on Punchbowl Mountain and met two schoolteachers from Pennsylvania who were on vacation. They had section-hiked Sobo from Katahdin over the last eight years. They lived by the trail at Wind Gap in Pennsylvania and gave me their phone number in case I needed help when I got there. Wind Gap was a long way off, but their confidence that I would eventually make it there, gave me hope as I moved on. The trail was easy hiking as it meandered through the lowlands and crossed several picturesque streams in the warm spring sun.

I started to ponder Step Two of the Twelve Steps, which said, "We came to believe a power greater than ourselves could restore us to sanity." I had an issue with the power greater than ourselves part when I first got sober. I didn't know if I was atheist or agnostic, but with my self-centered ego, I believed I was at the top of the food chain and there was no power greater than me. Besides, the power greater than myself who they talked about sounded a lot like the God I grew up with.

A new suspension bridge over Brown Creek interrupted my meditation. I continued to be impressed with the amount of work and engineering that goes into the Appalachian Trail. The bridge was not as great a feat as the Foot Bridge over the James River, but took a considerable amount of labor and funds. I followed the trail along the creek for about twenty miles, so I began looking for a creek-side campsite. I had no luck, but I came to the shelter and since I was exhausted, I decided to stay. I was at Brown Mountain Creek Shelter, about a mile south of a highway to a town. I was on the bank of the Brown Creek by myself. I had a beautiful view and the sound of a waterfall to sing me to sleep that night. A trail angel even left pastries there for my breakfast. I cooked Tuna and noodles and ate a donut for supper.

My feet were painful with new blisters and the wart, but I think they weren't as bad as they had been because the corn pads helped pad the wart. Life was good and I had hope.

Day 58   15.8 Miles

I made coffee and ate some pastries the trail angel left for breakfast. I took my time and padded the wart before I moved out. I crossed the highway to face a steep climb from fourteen-hundred feet at the shelter to Bald Knob at over four-thousand feet. I felt rewarded for my efforts with an amazing vista of Virginia. I checked my gauge of the green of spring in the valleys, which advanced daily forcing winters gray/brown to retreat higher on the mountains. I descended, which seemed to be the hardest on the wart, but then ascended Cold Mountain. The trail then seemed to level off for easier hiking after that, so I drifted into a state of meditation.

I have always had spiritual questions from my earliest memories. I grew up in a Methodist church with a punishing God. I felt the religion used guilt, shame, and fear to control me. The neighborhood kids, who were Catholic, told stories, which also helped instill my fear of God. I always felt guilty, as if I was doing something wrong, while listening to what the preacher was preaching on Sunday morning.

My parents forced me to go to church, but eventually I rebelled against God. I was afraid their God was going to punish me. I became, if not an atheist, at least agnostic. I believed that I was here on earth as the highest of all entities and God was a myth conceived by cowards who were afraid to die or take responsibility for the events that controlled their miserable lives. Looking back, I could understand why I developed such a love/trust relationship with drugs and alcohol. The chemicals themselves became my god in a sense.

The miles seemed to slip away when I focused on the early days of my program. I stopped early at the Seeley Woodworth Shelter. My feet needed a short day. I broke a blister that I would bandage before I hiked the next day. The warm weather was cooking my feet and causing blisters in my heavy leather-hiking boots. I asked Scooter to bring new summer boots that I could switch to when we met at Waynesboro.

The good news was, the wart seemed to continue to improve with the corn pads. It then occurred to me that I asked God for help and turned the wart over to Him. Later the same day, I found the corn pads in Glasgow. Could it be God was the force behind me getting better?

I set my tent up on flat ground by the shelter. I was hoping for company to have someone to talk to, but no luck. I felt I was in a good space emotionally, because I passed the eight-hundred mile stone earlier.

I read what Mrs. Gorp entered in the shelter register earlier in the day. She said she passed up her lunch because she was dreadfully sick. I felt a little paranoid about getting sick myself. I was using the same pen to enter in the register she used. I dropped the pen and went to the spring to wash my hands the best I could with no soap.

I was still writing in my journal after dark when I heard footsteps going toward the shelter. I thought it was a hiker, so I said, hello. The footsteps stopped with no reply. After a pause, they started again, so I said, hello, a little louder and once again, the footsteps stopped with no reply. I looked out of the tent and shined my light on a black bear about twenty feet away. I loudly, yelled hey and he bolted away. I thought he was gone for good, but I put my food bag under my head to use for a pillow in case he returned looking for a free meal. I planned to keep my pepper spray handy in case we had a confrontation.

I thought I was going to climb Priest Mountain earlier, but I was wrong. I would climb the Priest early the next day. I hoped the descent off Priest would not be too hard on my feet.

Day 59   20.5 Miles

The bear never returned as far as I knew. I slept well, awoke early, excited about taking on the Priest. I ate breakfast, bandaged my feet, padded my wart, and hit the trail.

In July of 2004, Scooter and I hiked from the Tye River south over Priest Mountain. I remembered the Priest as a steep mountain that hurt my low back going up and I encountered the worst blisters on the side of my little toes going down the mountain. Thoughts of the Priest have intimidated me since I left Georgia.

I must have been in better shape than I was in 2004, as I ascended to the summit of Priest Mountain with no trouble. While taking a break, I met a grandiose local man who had spent the night at the summit. He was hiking up and down the Priest to train to hike out west in the Rockies. We chatted for quite a while until I moved on. I was grateful I didn't spend the night in his company, listening to his boasting. I descended the Priest, which wasn't nearly as bad as

I anticipated. Wow, what a euphoric feeling to complete something that was hanging over my head since Springer.

I crossed the Tye River on another finely engineered suspension bridge before lunchtime. The scene was perfect with the new green leaves, enhanced by the purple of the Virginia red buds. The fast moving river sparkled like diamonds in the sunlight. It was so crystal clear you could see minnows as they darted over the rocks on the bottom. The sun from the cloudless sky filtered down through the trees and dotted the forest floor with splashes of light. The sound of the water rushing over the rocks invited me to drink right from the river. I could even smell the sweet fragrance of spring in the air.

I stopped and took my pack off on the bridge to just enjoy God's world. I was tempted to soak my feet in the cold water, but since it was so early and I felt great, I decided to hike on to the next shelter for lunch. Harpers Creek Shelter was two more miles away.

I was ascending out of the river valley when I came to the Mau-Har Trail, which bypassed Three Ridges Mountain and rejoined the Appalachian Trail at Maupin Field Shelter only three miles from there. I was tempted to take the side trail because the Appalachian Trail goes over Three Ridges and gets to Maupin Field Shelter in seven miles. Like I said, I was tempted, but I was still a purest thru-hiker and I couldn't take the shortcut even if I wanted to. I had to hike every inch of the Appalachian Trial, so I stayed on the white blazes.

I soon realized most hikers took the shortcut, because the Appalachian Trail obviously was far less traveled and poorly maintained. I was also surprised at how run down Harpers Creek Shelter was when I arrived. The shelter sat in a beautifully impressive setting beside Harpers Creek, which cascaded down the mountain within a few feet. I took off my shoes and socks and found my feet were a bloody mess. I soaked them in the creek. The icy water had a numbing effect on the pain and stopped the bleeding. I cooked noodles for lunch and rolled out my air mattress in a sunny spot in the shelter. I ate, and then lay back on my mattress, interlocked my fingers behind my head, and used my pack for a pillow.

My thoughts turned to when I started to attend Alcoholics

Anonymous meetings, I was attracted to how happy the people seemed to be. I wanted desperately to be happy like them. They shared with me some of their personal stories of insane behavior in their addiction, which made me feel like I fit in with them. I didn't feel so alone any more. In the world I came from you didn't tell anyone anything that would be embarrassing. It seemed refreshing to be able to tell the secrets that I felt ashamed of and somehow things no longer seemed so bad when someone else shared the same feelings.

I soon started to listen to how they recovered and became happy. They never preached or told me what to do. They simply shared their experience, strength and hope with me. Soon, their enthusiasm started to rub off on me. I became hopeful that somehow I could do what they did, becoming like them by emulating their behavior. Their stories of overcoming the adversity of their addictions gave me hope and inspired me, like Bill Foot's story. The Alcoholics Anonymous program didn't open the gates of heaven and let me in; the alcoholics in the program opened the doors of hell and showed me how to get out.

I felt so pleasant and serene, I must have dosed off and slept hard. I awoke in about two hours to a flat mattress. I swept a spot in the shelter, but missed a splinter of wood that poked a hole in my mattress. I want to make it over the mountain five miles to Maupin Field Shelter before dark, so I taped my feet back up and started to ascend Three Ridges Mountain. I took a picture of the mountain earlier from an overlook on the Priest as the three ridges ran skyward from the river to the intersection at the summit. I paused to look at the picture to attempt to see exactly where I was, but I couldn't determine my location from the picture, other than I was somewhere on the mountain.

I found the trail up Three Ridges Mountain as formidable as Priest Mountain, but overgrown and poorly marked. The markings were few and so old that most of the time I wasn't sure if I was on the trail or lost. I was losing daylight fast when I reached the summit. I had visions of a steep, poorly marked descent in the dark. I had no water and the nearest water was at Maupin Shelter, which was by that time, three miles away. Right there on the top of the mountain I got down on my knees and asked for help. I found comfort in praying as my fear melted away. I slowed way down because the desperation to get there vanished. I was hungry, so I ate a half-pound of hard salami, three snickers bars, and a bag of peanuts. I took some ibuprofen for the pain, got out my headlight, and headed for Maupin. I was in a positive mood, took my time, and found the descent in the dark quite enjoyable.

No one was at the shelter, but I set up my tent on flat ground anyway. I put my air mattress down and blew it up, hoping it would stay inflated until I fell asleep. The day was warm and sunny, but the temperature dropped with the sun. I looked up at all the stars in the sky and said, "Thank you, Jesus, amen." I crawled into my warm sleeping bag, grateful to be exactly where I was and to have the privilege to get to know God as I understood him.

Day 60   16.1 MILES

The temperature dropped and the rain came sometime in the night. I realized what a luxury an air mattress was on the trail. I awoke stiff and sore from sleeping on the ground. I supposed the rain didn't help. I broke my water filter when I filtered water first thing before breakfast. I had to use iodine tablets that I kept for emergencies to purify water. I didn't like using them because they tasted bad and always without fail, gave me the drizzling shits. I had a rash on my back that was itching. I was a mess. I was cold, wet, hungry, and in a miserable funk, but the good news was my wart and blisters were better in the cold. I decided maybe I should stop complaining and be grateful for the improvement of my wart and other blessings. The high point of the day was Cedar Cliffs Vista, which wasn't too good with the poor visibility. I guess the day was just another, git-r-done day so I would be sixteen miles closer to Katahdin at the end of the day.

I trudged sixteen miles to Paul C Wolf Shelter, which was a nice shelter with top bunks beside a roaring creek. The creek would put me to sleep if I could hear it over the annoying rain beating on the tin roof. I made tea out of brown water. I took a picture of my sleeping bag on a corner bunk in the big shelter. I was out of food and I climbed into in a wet sleeping bag. I felt a little down, lonely, and bored, so

I got out my little notebook because journaling always made me feel better, as if I was talking to someone.

I struggled with staying sober in those early days in Alcoholics Anonymous. I would get frustrated and go out drinking, but I could never wash the program out of my head with alcohol. I would always come back with my tail tucked between my legs expecting to get chastised and criticized. I would reintroduce myself, admitting I had slipped back to drinking yet again. Everyone at the meeting would applaud my announcement to encourage me. No one ever said anything that made me feel ashamed or guilty. They would shake my hand or give me a hug and say things like, "I have been praying you would come back" or "We have been saving you a seat." Some would share their personal experiences with returning to their addiction and coming back to the program and reintroducing repeatedly. The one thing they always said was, "Keep coming back, it works if you work it." They encouraged me by giving me the hope I could recover one day.

The trouble I ran into was, I wasn't ready to give up my self-serving lifestyle altogether. I wasn't ready to give up the social life in the bars. I loved the pretty girls, the music, and the fun. I fancied myself as a pool hustler and bars were the place to hustle. I still sold weed and speed and met most of my customers in the bars.

I would try to go to the bar and drink pop, which would appear to work for a short while. Bill Wilson said, "Remember we deal with alcohol, cunning, baffling, powerful." I found my disease was also patient, because in a short time, I would get comfortable and deceive myself into thinking I could control my drinking.

I would start out telling myself I would drink only one draft beer. The result was always the same because I would get drunk and the trip back to hell constantly became shorter each time I relapsed. The physical, mental, and spiritual pain became progressively more intense. I was either going to die or kill myself by committing suicide.

Since I was such a fast learner, that cycle went on for almost three years. I started to think maybe that was the insanity Step Two talked about. The one thing I did right was, I kept coming back.

I was a firm believer that if I went to Alcoholics Anonymous meetings long enough, some things would slowly start to sink into my thick head. The big book said, "Some of us have tried to hold on to our old ideas and the result was nil until we let go absolutely." I was one of those they talked about in Chapter Five, which they titled, *How It Works,* when Bill said, "Half measures availed us nothing." Judging from my own experience, I can testify that this was true, at least in my case. However, I kept coming back long enough that, I finally understood that if I wanted to do what they did, I would have to let go of my old lifestyle completely.

I caught up on my journal and felt better. The good news was that the next day would be better because I was only five miles from the Inn at Afton where I had a room reserved. A room with a heater you could control, a soft carpet, a hot shower with real shampoo, all the clean fluffy towels I wanted, a television, and a flush toilet with all the free toilet paper I needed. Best of all there would be a warm, soft, dry, bed with four pillows and clean, dry sheets.

Life would be good once again. I planned to take some zero days to heal up both physically and emotionally. Scooter would meet me there on the twenty-eighth and I missed her tremendously. She took a few days vacation so we could spend some time with each other. I looked forward for things to keep getting gooder and gooder.

Day 61   5 Easy miles

The morning was another cold, damp, misty morning. The only thing I had left for breakfast was two Hall's honey/lemon cough drops. I chewed them and took ibuprofen with brown water. I took care when I taped my feet and I was off singing "zippa-dee-duda-zippa-dee-a-my-oh-my-what-a-wonderful-day." I almost ran the five miles to Rockfish Gap where the Inn at Afton awaited me.

I found The Inn at Afton was top of the line at one time, but run down by years of neglect. I suspected half of the rooms were no longer in use. However, it had everything I wanted, so I checked in and got the bottom of the last pot of coffee. I found a coke machine on my way to my room. It wasn't coffee, but it would fix a caffeine withdrawal headache. I bought three cokes.

My room opened onto a balcony that overlooked a large kidney shaped swimming pool that looked like it hadn't been open in years. The carpet in my room was clean, but stained and worn. The bed was perfect, the cable television worked, and the shower got hot. I felt like I was already in heaven compared to the day before.

The closest laundry was five miles away in Waynesboro, so I took off my shoes and jumped in the shower and washed my clothes hiker style while I still wore them. I then stripped down in the shower and washed myself. I put on my clean, wet clothes to drip dry and went into the village to forage for food.

The only thing available was a broken down convenience store that sold some groceries. The clerk was a fat chick who had a cat on a leash in the store. The coffee pot was empty, so I asked if she was going to make more coffee. She simply said, "No" without explanation. I thought she had an attitude toward me or maybe hikers in general. She was nice to other people who came in the store, but they appeared to be friends of hers.

I bought two microwave cheeseburgers which I cooked and ate on the spot. I bought canned soup, potato chips, ice cream, pastries, candy, and pop, which I took back to the room.

Rockfish Gap was the southern entrance to the Shenandoah National Park, with a tourist information center. I stopped in and found it to be a goldmine of information. A hiker-friendly retired man and woman who worked part-time were so helpful. They gave me a list of doctors and hospitals where I could get medical attention for my wart. They provided me with brochures, maps, and a list of names and telephone numbers of volunteers I could call for a free ride into town and arrange shuttles elsewhere. That was a local project called The Trail Angel Network organized to assist thru-hikers. God bless the trail angels for their work.

I returned to my room and called several physicians, but couldn't get an appointment that day and they weren't open on the weekend. I called Urgent-Care and their doctor didn't remove warts, but he would refer me to someone who would. The bottom line was, they would charge me a hundred bucks to look at it and tell me to see a doctor. I talked to the nurse who was helpful and she said it didn't sound like it was infected, but needed more time to heal. I decided to wait until Scooter got there to talk my options over with her. The wart appeared to be healing on its own because I saw some improvement every day since I had padded it with the corn pads.

I spent the rest of the afternoon resting in my room. I watched a good movie on television, took a nap, and called as many Alcoholics Anonymous friends as I could. I considered myself lucky to have good, loving friends who cared about me.

When I first changed my lifestyle, I started to replace the people of the street with people in the program. I missed the action at the bars tremendously at first, but I found my old friends in the bars negative and narrow minded. They historically set a poor example to follow and always tried to take advantage of me. By comparison, the people I met in Alcoholics Anonymous seemed refreshingly positive, accepting, and caring. They set a great example to follow. I wanted to live as they lived.

I came to understand I also had to give up my old lifestyle of frequenting the bars, shooting pool, and selling drugs because it wasn't working. The folks who I admired in the program all had to change people, places, and things when they got sober to recover. I still scoffed when they talked about God. I guess when I looked back, I think I simply wasn't ready for God yet.

I went down to the lobby and discovered an elegant dining room that was open for breakfast and dinner. They had tables in various sizes with white linen tablecloths set up with real silver and water goblets. Huge windows were on two sides that overlooked an impressive view of Rockfish Gap. I would bet they could seat well over a hundred people at one time.

Later, I dressed as formal as I could in my black Under Armor turtleneck shirt, my semi-clean hiking shorts and my black gaiters, to dine. Apparently, I was the first guest to arrive, because the dining room was completely deserted, I wasn't sure it was even open. I didn't see the, Please wait to be seated sign, so I walked in and took a window seat overlooking a magnificent view of the Shenandoah. I noticed other patrons entering all dressed up. I felt a little self-conscious because they seemed to look at me in a funny way. They were probably jealous of my thru-hiker fashion.

A slightly effeminate male waiter dressed in formal attire, introduced himself as James. He brought rolls with real butter and one of those funny little knifes. He poured coffee into a fine china cup and gave me a silver cream pitcher with real cream in it. Then he gave me the menu. My first thought when I looked at the prices was, holy smokes.

When he returned, I ordered a thirty-five dollar porterhouse steak dinner cooked medium rare. He asked if I would like sour cream with a baked potato. I asked him if I could have fries instead. I think they had to kill the cow as it seemed like it took forever, but he returned with one of the best steaks I had ever eaten even though it was well done. He returned to see how it was and I had it half eaten. I told him I ordered it medium rare and it was too done. He turned red, apologized, and went to take it back. I almost stabbed him with my fork.

He said, "The chef would be happy to cook you another steak."

I said "Awh forget it Jimmy, I'm too hungry, besides it sure beat the crap out of tuna and noodles. Hey Jimbo, could you get me some ketchup?"

He brought the ketchup in a little bowl with a silver spoon and a brand new steak cooked medium rare. He had me try it while he stood there. I said, "Wow, that's perfect Jimmy." I ate the second steak.

I know he liked me because he returned with the check on a silver tray and some kind of fancy chocolate desert compliments of the chef. I said, "Thanks Jimmy, I sure hope I don't hurl!" I threw two twenties on the tray and told him to keep the change. I bet he was impressed with a five dollar tip. It took me a while, but I managed to eat the entire desert.

I thought he wasn't allowed to fraternize with the customers, because I tried to get his attention as I was leaving, but he was standing around with a couple of other waiters and pretended he didn't see me, so I walked up to him and shook his hand.

He said, "I hope you enjoyed dining with us sir."

"I ate too much, but I'll feel better after I take a good dump." I didn't think his waiter buddies understood my sense of humor.

I returned to my room, turned up the heat, and watched television while I gave my two-steak dinner a good chance to turn to fat. Later when I woke up, I took a long, hot shower before I went to bed.

Day 62   Zero miles

I went back to the restaurant in the hotel as soon as it opened for breakfast. I returned to my same table by the window. It wasn't nearly as uppity as the night before. An older lady with a southern accent, who called me Sugar, replaced Jimmy as my waiter. I had four eggs over easy, toast, sausage, home fries, and lots of good coffee. I met an older couple from Michigan who were going to see their daughter in Virginia when their car broke down. They were staying at the hotel until the garage fixed their car. I let them use my cell phone to call the garage to check on the progress of their car. I enjoyed their company.

I called a trail angel couple by the names of Francis and Ed Young. I talked to Francis who agreed to meet me at the information center at nine o'clock to give me a ride six miles into Waynesboro, Virginia. Francis Young was a delightful southern bell in her mid-eighties. Her husband Ed had Alzheimer's disease and she took care of him. Francis talked the entire time that she drove me the six miles to the post office in Waynesboro. I tried to give her a twenty-dollar bill, but she refused. I did, after some persuasion, get her to accept five dollars to pay for gas. Francis was a Christian woman who said she would pray for me to be in God's care on my journey. She reminded me of my own mother so much I had tears in my eyes as she hugged me goodbye. I will also pray for Francis and Ed, but I didn't think of it until after she drove away. I said, "Lord watch over them and hold them close. Amen."

I picked up my mail and went to the drug store for some first aid supplies for my feet. I also picked up some Epsom salt. Waynesboro was a little bigger than the other trail towns so far. Waynesboro also had an old section of town where I saw more cops than civilians. I thought something big like a bank robbery had recently gone down.

A cop stopped me from going any further, saying they were shooting a movie and the only people allowed past that point were the people in the movie.

I crossed the street to a little lunch restaurant and ordered a cheeseburger and fries. The movie was the buzz on everyone's mind. The movie called' Evan Almighty was a sequel to Bruce Almighty. A small crowd of local people gathered on a corner to watch a scene, so I joined them after I ate my lunch. Several people would cross the street and two cars would pass by. It was a short scene and they ran it three times before they took a break. A tall black man in a white suit from the movie cast came over and shook hands with all of us who were watching. I recognized him from the movie, Clean and Sober. His name was Morgan Freeman.

The owner of a small gift shop made cross necklaces out of silver spoons. I bought a cross necklace to give to Scooter. I asked him to tighten the loose screw in my glasses for me. He fixed my glasses for two bucks. I then treated myself to a large cherry sundae for dessert at a Dairy Queen.

The outfitter was my last stop on my way out of town to buy a gas canister for my stove. I walked most of the six miles back to the hotel. I wasn't hitching when an older gentleman stopped and gave me a ride the last mile to my motel. He hiked some on the Appalachian Trail in his younger days. He identified me as a hiker by my noticeable limp. He said all hikers limped when they weren't hiking.

I had previously sent my son Nick a phone card, so he could call me on his twenty-third birthday. He called precisely when I arrived at my hotel room. We had a good father-son talk. He was working as a cook in a nice restaurant and bought a car at an auction for six hundred dollars. He was staying out of trouble and appeared to be doing well. I was proud of him.

I took a long bath in Epsom salts to soak my aches and pains. The wart was feeling better and the decrease in the swelling was noticeable. I still padded it with the corn pads even when I wasn't hiking.

Scooter left work at noon to rendezvous with me. She called a moment before and said she should arrive any minute. I tidied up the room a bit and started walking down the highway to meet her. I met her at the entrance to the hotel and rode up the hill with her. O'boy, it was great to see her! I got her settled in the room before we went out to dinner at an AYCE buffet. After dinner, I gave her the little silver cross and got an extremely pleasant reaction in return. We chatted like two teenagers on our first date as we explored Waynesboro. I was thankful for a great day. I felt blessed.

April 29   Day 63   Zero Miles

Scooter and I slept in later than I normally do. We then went to Weasie's Kitchen for breakfast. Weasie's caters to hikers and were famous for their three dollar and fifty cent AYCE pancakes for thru-hikers. The current record was twenty-four set by a hiker named, Twinkle Toes in 2001. We didn't even come close to the record, but felt the spirit of the tradition.

The waitress brought a hiker register with the bill. I read about several friends who were ahead of me who tried to break the pancake record. I entered in the register to leave a message to those behind me. The numerous trail registers all along the trail were how we hikers kept track of one another. It sounds primitive, but it worked amazingly well.

We set out to take care of business. First we went to the laundry mat and washed all my clothes in a real washer and dryer. Then it was off to Walmart where I bought one-hundred and forty dollars worth of hiker food and supplies. We went back to the hotel and packed three boxes for future mail drops in Front Royal, Virginia, Harpers Ferry, West Virginia, and Boiling Springs, Pennsylvania.

We mailed the packages on our way to the scenic Skyline Drive to explore the trail north. We paid a ten dollar entrance fee to the Shenandoah and I picked up a permit to camp in the Shenandoah. The day was warm, sunny, and the mountains were so beautiful. We had a great time being together, although it felt strange to be driving a car.

Scooter had to skip an eight-mile section of the Appalachian Trail north of Rockfish Gap when she got sick on a section hike two years ago. She wanted to hike that section with me on my thru-hike, so I called a man by the name of Bill Gallagher from my list of trail angels. He agreed to shuttle us to the trail head at Blackrock Gap on Skyline Drive, which was twenty miles north of the hotel. That way, we could kill two birds with one stone. Scooter could make up the eight miles she missed and I could hike with her for twenty miles closer to Katahdin.

We stopped at Gavid's Steak House with an AYCE food bar for a late lunch. I pigged out, but Scooter ate her usual moderate meal. We were leaving the restaurant when Messenger and Brave Heart walked in. It was great to see them for the first time since Damascus. I introduced them to Scooter, which was a treat for everyone because they heard so much about each other since I met Brave Heart and Messenger in the Smoky Mountains.

Scooter and I were going to Walmart again to pick up some more things I forgot that I needed. I offered to take them along, but all they needed was to pig out and find fuel for their stoves. I told them I would do my shopping while they ate, then pick them up to shuttle them back to the trail.

We picked them up as planned. They both looked like they ate far too much, which was their intended goal. I realized how awful thru-hikers stunk when they got in the car. They made my eyes water and I was afraid my teeth would rot. We stopped at the outfitters so they could buy fuel before we dropped them off at Rockfish Gap. We left the windows down with the air conditioner on all the way back to the motel to air out poor Scooter's car.

The day was a great zero-day. I thought my wart was starting to heal; maybe all it needed was a little time off the trail. I was looking forward to hiking with Scooter to Blackrock Gap the next day. I ended week nine with only seventy-seven miles.

Day 64   19.8 Miles with Scooter

We awoke, quickly showered, packed up, and left in the pre-dawn darkness. We ate a trail breakfast from a viewpoint watching the most spectacular sunrise ever over the Shenandoah. I felt so happy to be able to share that moment in time with Scooter. We were so excited, anticipating getting on the trail, it was almost like our first hike together.

It was well after daylight when Bill Gallagher arrived as planned. Bill was a sixty-five-plus-year-old, big bear of a man. He and his wife moved here from Philadelphia after they retired. They volunteered to maintain a section of the Appalachian Trail in the Shenandoah and opened their home to thru-hikers. He was one of those guys you took a liking to immediately. I told him I expected to pay for the shuttle. He said he charged two-thousand dollars. I asked him if he would take a check. We laughed, as Scooter and I loaded our packs into his Blazer and piled in.

Bill drove up Skyline drive on that beautiful spring morning. Scooter saw a black bear we almost ran over on the way. We were on the road for almost an hour before Bill dropped us off at Blackrock Gap. Bill did not want to take any money. I gave him forty dollars for the ride, which he felt was too high. I told him it was my contribution for the gas so he could come back to do trail maintenance. He gave Scooter and me a big bear hug when it was time to say goodbye. I still found it amazing at how easy it was to make that good a friend on the Appalachian Trail. It felt great to know people like Bill Gallagher exist in today's world. He took a picture of Scooter and me on his camera for himself and one on my camera for us. I only regret I didn't think quick enough to take a picture of Bill for us.

I hiked that part of the Shenandoah before on a section hike with my friends Chief and Rose, but it was in a cold, hard rain. The day Scooter and I were blessed with was the opposite with clear blue sky, dark green forest, and beautiful views of God's creations as far as my eyes could see. Hiking with Scooter was so inspiring that I couldn't imagine anything better.

The hiking was easy, even though the Shenandoah wasn't flat, as some said, but the hills were gradual and the footfall was soft. We made good time as we crossed Skyline Drive several times. We ran into Messenger shortly after we started hiking south. He told me that Brave Heart was way behind due to his blisters. I worried about

Brave Heart being able to continue. He was tough, but he was hurting extremely bad. I didn't think Messenger slowed down a bit for him either and Brave Heart tried to keep up. I have noticed partners didn't usually last long on the Appalachian Trail, unless there was a sexual connection. Neither Brave Heart nor Messenger appeared to be gay, so there was no sexual connection.

Further south, we met Elizabeth and Lewis. Elizabeth said, "Dreamer you're going the wrong way." Seeing them made my day and I was happy Scooter met them also. I gave Elizabeth my bottle of patchouli oil. I felt bad, I hadn't replaced the battery in the little green light she gave me yet. I would do that first thing when I got to Walmart and give it back to her the next time we met. We also met two new Nobo thru-hikers named Chronic and Fire Fly.

We hiked south to Rockfish gap and arrived at the motel late in the afternoon. We took a hot shower before we returned to Gavid's for supper. I pigged out again and Scooter ate more than her usual meal. We stopped on the way home at Walmart for batteries for Elizabeth's little light and some last minute things. I was so grateful for the privilege to hike with Scooter. We were so worn out by the time we got back to our motel room we went straight to bed.

SANITY

Day 65   16.1 Miles

I took a shower, padded my wart, and taped my feet before we checked out. I was elated the blisters were almost gone and the wart seemed to continue to improve. We went back to Weasie's for breakfast. I had an omelet with pancakes and Scooter had oatmeal for breakfast.

We stopped on the way out of town for gasoline and large coffees to go. I drove up the Skyline Drive to Blackrock Gap. Scooter and I strolled a little way up the trail holding hands and talking. She stopped to take a picture of me all clean-shaven to remember me by until we met again. I posed, twirling my trekking pole with the trail leading away in the background.

I watched her walk back to her vehicle. I found myself melancholy as she drove away because I hated to see her go. I looked forward to seeing her for so long and it seemed like she was only with me for a minute and then she was gone. I wouldn't see her again until somewhere in Pennsylvania. I resumed hiking and soon my mood improved with the great weather, easygoing trail, and super views.

It wasn't long until I was contemplating Step Two, which said, "We came to believe that a power greater than ourselves could restore us to sanity." I had an issue with the word sanity at first. My definition of insanity was those unfortunates who were so out of touch with reality they were locked up somewhere in a sanitarium. I certainly wasn't that bad. I was sober precisely two whole months when God directed a chain of events that explained a power greater than myself, so I could understand what Step Two was saying. God must have known I wasn't ready for Him yet, so He had to break things down so even an idiot like me could understand and accept at least there was a power greater than myself.

Everything started to change on Friday the twenty-fifth of July 1980. I was sober precisely sixty-one days, I only weighed about one-hundred and twenty-five pounds, and the only food I could keep down was raw eggs, Kayro syrup mixed fifty/fifty with orange juice and of course coffee with lots of cream and sugar. I was still a little dope sick and hopelessly depressed.

I was rolling my own cigarettes with cheap tobacco that I had to borrow money to buy when I unexpectedly received a forty dollar check in the mail that afternoon. All I could think of was the euphoric feeling I would get from the first drink. I promised myself I would only get a little drunk this time and things would be different. I was sober sixty-one days and I wouldn't go back to drinking; I would only drink the one last night for a break from the awful sobriety.

I had a plan. I didn't have gas in my broken down car and I didn't want to spend any of my forty dollars on gas, but Neal was coming out that night to take me to a meeting. I would get a ride to the Alcoholics Anonymous meeting with Neal. I would tell Neal a lie and say I had a girlfriend I was going to visit instead of going to the meeting. I would go to the Town Tavern, which was a strip joint, and they would cash my check. I would then get as far away from the unpleasant reality I was stuck in as forty dollars could take me. In those days, forty dollars bought a lot of booze. Now that was insane thinking, but I couldn't identify it as such by my power alone.

Neal was retired from twenty years in the army. He retired and got sober on his fortieth birthday. He had been sober over twenty-three years by 1980. One of the ways he worked his program was to pick a newbie like me who had very little chance of making it and simply take them to a lot of Alcoholics Anonymous meetings for about the first six months of their recovery. I did so well Neal took me to meetings for my first two years.

Now Neal never said a lot, but when I blurted out my intentions of skipping the meeting to see some fictitious girl, he paused as if he was thinking before he said, "There's no problem you'll ever have that taking a drink won't make worse." To this day, I don't know if he knew my intensions or not. He turned and calmly challenged me and said, "Why don't you go to the meeting first and then go see your girl?"

I went to the meeting with every intention of getting drunk right after the f*%#@ meeting. I have to say, I walked into the Alcoholics Anonymous meeting at the Youth Activities building that night with an attitude. I went straight to the coffee pot, poured a cup of coffee, found a seat at the back away from everybody else, and sat my ass in the chair without looking anyone in the eye. I lit up a smoke and looked at the coffee in my cup.

I think everyone knew I had a chip on my shoulder the size of a concrete block. Now, the folks in the program were used to seeing that type of behavior especially from newcomers, so they came over to shake my hand and said things like, Good to see you, Your looking better all the time, or Glad you keep coming back. Some of them even sat beside me.

The chip on my shoulder started melting even before the meeting ever started. I sat through the usual opening rituals and then the chairman introduced the speaker, who was only a little older than I was. Alcoholics Anonymous has an unwritten suggested protocol for lead speakers, which was to share what it was like, what happened, and what it was like in the present.

The man followed the suggestion and shared he had been sober seven years. He first told about his drinking, which was almost the same hell I went through. What happened to him was he lost everything that was important to him. I could also identify with his losses. I actually thought about the consequences of my decision to drink and it didn't sound as romantic as it did earlier when I first received the check. I actually thought through the first initial euphoric feelings of what the drug promised. I couldn't recall exactly what happened to cause him to seek the help of Alcoholics Anonymous, but I felt he was as desperate as I was.

His life sounded better when he told what it was like in the present. Things turned around and were going well for him. He had a good job and recently borrowed four-thousand dollars from his credit union and bought a new bass boat. I thought, if I had four-thousand dollars, I would buy so much alcohol and drugs that I would kill myself. I would love to have a bass boat someday. I saw a glimmer of hope that if he could turn his life around, maybe I could also.

I remembered it as if it was yesterday. I was smoking a store bought cigarette I bummed and drinking a cup of coffee when I thought, this sobriety thing ain't too bad. To go drinking would be the insanity Step Two was talking about. I would throw away the sixty-one days I had suffered withdrawal to stay sober, for one night of drinking and drugging. Besides, I would soon be drinking and drugging where I left off. I didn't think I could have survived that again, even one more time.

I had Neal take me home after the meeting with my forty dollar check still in my pocket. Later that night when I was in bed going over the day's events, I had an amazing insight. It made sense the insanity they were talking about in Step Two was returning to alcohol and drugs. I could no longer deny I was lucky my use of chemicals didn't kill me. If I started using again, it would be suicide and that was insane. That night I accepted the meetings were a power greater than myself that could restore me to sanity.

My meditative state ended as the trail crossed Skyline Drive and I met Dan and Pam, who were schoolteachers on vacation from Norfolk, Virginia. They asked me several questions when they discovered I was a thru-hiker. They gave me fresh strawberries and Dan took a picture of Pam and me for show and tell. Pam put her arm around me and Dan took the picture. She immediately said, "Delete that picture, because he's married and I don't want his wife to come to the wrong conclusion." We posed again with an appropriate distance between us, but I put my arm around her just before Dan snapped the picture. I put them on my mailing list. I was such an extravert, plus it fed my ego so much I felt like a celebrity. I so loved meeting all the new and interesting people on the trail.

I hiked solo all day. The day ended somewhere on Little Roundtop Mountain. I had a hard time finding a place to put my tent due to the regulations in the Shenandoah. I managed to clear a place big enough on a ridge for my tent, that was one-hundred yards from the trail. I was beat, but the wart was okay. I didn't have enough cell towers to call out, but I was able to retrieve my messages. Scooter left a message saying she arrived home safely.

Day 66 18.4 Miles

I stepped out of my tent about daylight, greeted by the birds singing the arrival of a new day. I wish I could start every day like that. The Shenandoah in the spring was so green it drove the winter blues away. A new lush green plant about six inches high carpeted the forest floor. The trail left a picturesque scar from hiker's feet as the path meandered through the fragile plants on its way to Mount Katahdin. The sun shined through the trees that still only showed a green tinge from the immature spring leaves. I thought to myself, days like that more than make up for the bad days. I hiked seven miles before I found water at a spring under a boulder. I was getting a little thirsty, but the pure, sweet water was right where the guidebook indicated. The only person I met that morning was a trail maintenance worker by the name Hiker Cooker. He took my picture and said he would post it on www.whiteblaze.net. He was a former thru-hiker and encouraged me to continue to Katahdin.

I continued to enjoy the beauty of the woods and impressive views of Saddleback and Baldface Mountains until the sky turned gray. I could hear the distant rumbling of thunder so I hiked faster than I preferred. I managed to arrive at the camp store at Lewis Mountain campground before the rain. I bought enough supplies to last until I arrive at Front Royal on Friday or Saturday. I ate a pint of ice cream, an egg bagel with cheese, and a sixteen ounce can of pork and beans. I paid two dollars and fifty cents for ten minutes in a coin-operated shower and moved on. I could have stayed at the campground, but I couldn't find anyone to talk to. I found everything was expensive, so I moved on with the storm still threatening.

I stopped a mile down the trail at Bearfence Hut. The rain started, so I filtered water and made my home inside the shelter. A section hiker named Professor came in for the night. He was a retired schoolteacher from Kentucky. I found him positive and interesting, which was what I admired, so we got along well. I felt grateful for his company on that stormy night. I was happy I followed my intuition and hiked the extra mile from the expensive campground.

Day 67   26.8 Miles

My Longest Day

I ate two honey buns and washed them down with trail coffee to start my day at daybreak. The Professor and I talked through breakfast then, I sadly bid him goodbye. I met Fire Fly at Big Meadows campground where he spent the night. He told me about a restaurant at Skyland, about eight miles up the trail. I estimated I would arrive there by early afternoon and eat a big meal. I was able to hike further when I took in extra calories.

It was cold and windy by lunchtime, so I decided to cook a hot meal. I stopped on a rock ledge overlooking the hills of Virginia when my phone rang. Scooter happened to call as I ate my noodles. What a pleasant surprise. I didn't realize I even had my phone turned on. We chatted like school kids after our first date as I finished my lunch.

The trail ran past a horse stable at Crescent Rock Cliffs. They rented horses and offered guided trail rides. I met a hiker-friendly lady named Pam who worked there. She told me about the restaurant at Elkwallow Gap where her husband, Jim was the manager. She said to mention her and he would give me a discount. I looked in the guidebook and Elkwallow Wayside was eighteen miles away, so it would be a great place to have a late breakfast the next day. I spent the early afternoon making good time, driven by the promise of a restaurant meal and good coffee. I found the views from the Franklin Cliffs and other un-named cliffs worth a pause to take pictures.

I arrived at Skyland restaurant earlier than I anticipated. I ordered a Rueben sandwich with fries and coffee. Skyland was one of the nicer, hiker friendly restaurants. I picked a window seat with an excellent view of a storm as it moved in, which was a little unnerving. I engaged the couple at the next table in conversation while I ate to take my mind off the storm.

I bought pop and candy bars out of a vending machine on the way back to the trail. I needed the extra rest and food for a long distance day. I hiked past the Stony Man Mountain and Cliffs. I felt the view from the cliffs was worth the whole trip. I felt so grateful to be able to see America as originally created before human greed scarred all of its beauty. I sincerely hoped we preserve the natural beauty of our country for future generations.

The storm that had threatened most of the afternoon held off until I arrived at Mary's Rock. The frightening thunder and lightning storm hit when I had no place to take cover, so I put on the Rolling Stones, turned up the music loud enough so I couldn't hear the thunder, and hiked up Mary's Rock. The storm passed in forty-five minutes and then it cleared and turned into a pleasant evening.

I hiked down the Pinnacle into Thornton Gap where I found Fire Fly, his new girlfriend Feather, and a man named Silver Streak. Fire Fly introduced me then added Silver Streak was aborting his thru-hike. Silver Streak started to rationalize why it was a good idea to quit when I disrespectfully walked away. I learned from the couple from Maine that day on Roan Mountain, to not listen to negative people or quitters. I felt bad, but at least I didn't call him insulting names. An Alcoholics Anonymous slogan said, "Stick with the winners." I needed to stick with positive thinkers, but I didn't have to try to fix Silver Streak by insulting him either.

I had a little over a mile to go to make it to the shelter where tent sites were available. The sky cleared and the last of the day's sun was hanging on when I noticed an animal fifty feet ahead of me on the trail. The animal had its back to me going north also. At first, I thought it was a big raccoon, but too big, maybe a coyote. I soon realized by the way it moved, it was a big cat. I was reaching for my camera when it turned broadside and paused. I was looking at the first wild bobcat I had ever seen in its natural home. The cat bolted before I could take its picture, but I would keep the memory forever.

Moments later, I came upon a former thru-hiker named Skyline. He was the maintainer for the Pass Mountain Hut that was less than a mile ahead. He had been hiking in from Thornton Gap to the shelter for eight years and never saw the bobcat. I felt truly blessed to have seen the big cat. Fire Fly and Feather soon came along and the three of us bid Skyline goodbye. I hiked a short distance to the shelter with Fire Fly and Feather.

We arrived at the shelter well after dark. Chris and Matt, who were college kids on break, were already in the shelter. Feather and Fire Fly joined them in the shelter for the night. I went to the tent site Scooter and I previously camped at on a section hike two years ago. I went back to the shelter to cook and socialize with everyone. Chris and Matt built a fire and I made tea to share with all. We talked way into the night before I retired to my tent. I was tired because I hiked almost twenty-seven miles. That was the longest distance I had ever hiked in one day. The day was one of those days that felt like everything simply went right.

Day 68   22.7 Miles

I slept well, but awoke stiff and sore from the long hike the day before. The good news was, I saw improvement in my wart every day. I made coffee and ate in silence before I snuck past the shelter so I wouldn't wake the others. I hiked out in the solitude of the beautiful spring morning with my thoughts.

Three days after the forty dollar check incident I still did not believe God even existed. The urge to drink hit me again suddenly. That time, it was without warning or reason and the urge was as strong as ever. I thought if I made it to a meeting first, I would not take the first drink. It was mid-morning and the only Alcoholics Anonymous meeting I knew of was at a make-shift halfway house for men in a town ten miles away. I already put gasoline in the car from the forty dollar check and it was running, so off I went. I made it a few minutes before the meeting started and asked the members who were present for help.

A man with seven years sobriety said, "Maybe you want to drink more than you want to stay sober."

His statement insulted me and I said, "If I wanted to get drunk I wouldn't come here, I would be at the bar getting drunk, you asshole!"

Gallagher, a man with twelve years of sobriety, whom I respected and eventually asked to be my second sponsor, stepped between us and said, "What he means is maybe you haven't drank or suffered enough yet."

I felt so defeated I thought I might as well go drinking, and get it over with. Just then, a girl who I had a little crush on walked into the meeting sloppy drunk. Normally, I found her so attractive that I could not talk to her because I couldn't make my mouth work when we were face to face. That day, I found her disgustingly unattractive. Her mouth was foul and she puked out profanity with every other word as she told everyone where to go and to do something sexual to themselves that would be impossible.

The focus shifted everyone's attention to her and off me. She was so disruptive that Gallagher and a couple of the other older members took her outside, so the rest of us could start the meeting. After she was outside and things quieted down, I realized the urge to get high had vanished; it lifted from me as if it was never there. I will always be grateful to the girl because she was the one who God sent to carry the message that helped me not drink that day. She was the one who restored me to sanity that time. Again, the power of the connection with Alcoholics Anonymous was the power greater than myself that could restore my sanity or keep me from drinking.

The trail was easy, so before I realized it I had hiked eight miles to Elk Wallow Wayside. I met Jim who was Pam's husband, and the manager of Elk Wallow. He was the salesman-type and gave me the employee discount after I mentioned Pam. I bought a cheeseburger, large fries, and a large coffee for nine dollars. To my surprise, I found Chris and Matt already there and soon Fire Fly and Feather came in, so we had another party. Fire Fly and I drank far too much coffee, to the point we annoyed the others with our constant chattering. I hiked out after about an hour in a caffeine mind-altered state. I was sure I zoomed up the trail for the next five miles.

I stopped in the afternoon for a quick, cold trail supper. I wanted to make it to a hostel at Compton Gap, which was the end of the Shenandoah National Park. I felt a tinge of sadness as I left the

Shenandoah behind. Shortly, I met a former thru-hiker named B-Man sitting on a stump smoking a joint. He played minor league hockey in Pittsburgh at one time. He was an in your face hockey type and used his hockey stick for a hiking pole as a trademark. I stopped to chat and he filled me in on all the trail gossip.

He told me, "A doctor in Waynesboro knocked Yahtzee off the trail due to the infected blister. First, he lanced the blister, squeezed a half a cup of puss out, and prescribed antibiotics. Two days later, with no improvement, the doctor told him if he didn't get to a hospital, he would lose his foot."

B-Man paused for my reaction, but I said nothing, so he added, "Brave Heart also had to abort his hike due to plantar fascia pain." B-Man could see I took the news about both hikers hard.

I mumbled, "They were good hikers who had a lot of heart." The loss of them made me realize how blessed I would be to be able to finish the journey to Katahdin.

I arrived, accompanied by B-Man, at The Terrapin Hostel an hour before darkness. The hostel was in a fine brick house in an upscale neighborhood with the basement remodeled into three big rooms. The bunkroom came with clean sheets and was large enough to sleep twelve people. A roomy kitchen was complete with a stove and sink, so you could cook. They sold pop, ice cream and other things a hiker could purchase. The third room, was a large living room complete with comfortable easy chairs, HBO on a big screen television, and a library of DVD movies. Last, but by no means least, was a large bathroom with a hot shower, clean towels, and a washer and dryer inside to do laundry.

The owner was Mike Evans, who was a former thru-hiker of the Appalachian Trail and the Pacific Crest Trail. His trail name was The Grateful Greenpeace Guy of 95, but everyone called him Greenpeace. He reminded me of a seventies hippie, complete with long hair and sandals. Apparently, B-Man worked for Greenpeace because he had him settle me in while he took care of other business. I took a shower and did my laundry. Fire Fly and Feather came in while I was in the shower.

I called Scooter. She informed me a letter came from my credit union saying I overdrew my account, so they froze my account for thirty days. The news upset me terribly because I had over thirty-five-hundred dollars in the account and it was my main source of cash. I had a secret stash of cash and a credit card, so I would be okay, but it still pissed me off. I knew I needed to defer the problem and get it out of my head so I could sleep that night. Besides there was nothing I could do until morning, but worry anyway.

I cooked tuna and noodles in the kitchen and bought pop and ice cream. All five of us settled in the living room to socialize. Greenpeace and B-Man entertained us with tales of adventure on the trail. They pumped me up to hike like a coach would before a football game. I didn't go to bed until after midnight while the others were still going strong.

Day 69   9 Miles

We all piled into Greenpeace's van first thing in the morning and he shuttled us to Front Royal. He dropped us off at a grocery store. I browsed, but only bought corn pads and blister Band-Aids for my wart, which seemed better every day with the padding. I had a mail drop with food that I planned to pick up at the post office later.

I called the credit union at precisely nine o'clock and asked for Brian, but he wasn't there. That was a good thing because he set up my account and I was all set to go from zero to asshole in no time on him. Bev handled me and we got it all straightened out quickly, she unfroze my account, and took back the overdraft charge. It would be a day before I could get money, but I didn't need any for a while anyway. I felt better and put Bev on my mailing list. Bev took a lot of stress off my mind and I felt better instantly knowing I had all the money I would need.

The four of us went to breakfast at McDonald's where Greenpeace picked us up. The next stop was the post office where I picked up my mail before we went to Weasel Creek Outfitters so Feather could by shoes. She tried on shoes for an hour before she bought a pair while the rest of us stood around waiting. I grew impatient with her, but held my tongue.

We arrived back at the hostel about noon. Greenpeace and B-Man were going to play some kind of combat golf and Feather and Fire Fly were going to take showers. I packed up and hit the trail as thunder clouds moved in. I felt thankful for the amenities of the hostel, the good company of the others, and all the hospitality of Greenpeace and B-Man, but I was happy to be back to the solitude of the trail.

My mind went to the next day after the half-way house meeting. I was sitting in the window of a coffee shop named The Diamond Deli in a university town drinking coffee with an Alcoholics Anonymous friend, named Mac. Mac was sober over three years, but still burnt out from his drinking days. He reminded me of the character Jim Ignakowski on the old sitcom, Taxi.

It was lunchtime and the place was buzzing with students and professors, many of whom I was familiar with. An ex who I previously had a significant relationship with, apparently saw me in the window and felt it was a good time to inform me of some of the resentments she held towards me. She marched in and took my inventory of character defects and wrong doings in a loud voice right in front of everyone.

Mac put his hand on mine and kept saying in a soft voice, "Stay calm." I did and it infuriated her even more. When she advanced on me, Mac who was well over six feet tall and always dressed like a cowboy, stood up and faced her. A pregnant pause followed where she seemed to realize people were watching, so she did an about face and marched out.

I had enough adrenalin in my system to make me shake. I was infuriated at being embarrassed, but I also felt ashamed. I could look across the street and see a bar where I did a lot of drinking in the past. All I could think of was a double shot of Southern Comfort and a pitcher of beer would calm my nerves.

I stood up and said to Mac, "I deserve a drink after that!" Mac grabbed my arm and picked up a dime from the table.

He said, "Call Big Jim first" as he pressed the dime into the palm of my hand and nodded towards the pay phone on the wall. I took one look into his blue eyes and decided I had better comply.

I called my sponsor, Big Jim at work, blurted out part of the story, and said, "I'm going across the street to the Hotel Bar and I'm going to drink."

He said, "Can you wait fifteen minutes before you drink?" I hesitated then said, yeah okay.

I believe I wanted to take a drink more at that moment in time than any other time in my entire twenty-five years of sobriety. I locked myself in the restroom and repeated the Serenity Prayer over, and over again because I didn't know what else to do.

Finally, there was a cop-knock on the door and a familiar voice said, "It's Jim." I opened the door and Big Jim's six-foot-seven-inch frame filled the doorway. I felt instant relief as my eyes began to tear a little. I wanted to break down and bawl my eyes out, but I was still far too macho for that. The three of us had a coffee and I learned connecting with Big Jim and Mac could restore my sanity. That was what Bill Wilson did that day in Akron with Dr. Bob so many years ago.

I continued hiking with my thoughts in light rain through a low, swampy area where the mosquitoes were especially ferocious. I hiked past a National Zoological Park that had a twelve-foot fence which extended for miles, but I saw no animals. I have no idea what was inside the fence, but they don't allow camping along this part of the trail.

I arrived at the Jim and Molly Denton Shelter and stopped for water. The shelter was the most elaborate shelter I had seen to that point on the Appalachian Trail. The shelter had a deck in front, built in easy chairs, a gazebo with a picnic table for cooking, and a shower. Yes, you heard me right, I said a shower. They mounted a red, fifty-five-gallon drum seven feet off the ground on poles. A black plastic pipe coming from a spring higher on the mountain constantly fed the drum with cold, mountain spring water for the shower.

I filled up my water bottles and was prepared to leave when a violent thunderstorm struck. I stayed in the shelter to wait out the storm. I was alone, so I set up in the shelter and decided to stay the night.

The storm passed, and the sun came out to warm things up, so I thought it would be nice to take a shower. Who knows when the opportunity would present itself again, so I got naked and turned on the water. AGAHHHHHH!!!!!! *%#@*&%#& it all was a blur until I turned the water off. I was gasping for breath and it took me a little time to recover from the shock of the mountain ice water. I talked myself into soaping up. That time I psyched myself up before I turned on the water, but only long enough to wash the soap off. The water must have been thirty-two and a half degrees. That was by far the coldest shower I had ever taken. I was numb all over. I made hot tea, but it still took me some time to stop shaking.

I was sitting on the deck thawing out when two brothers, Burt and Dave, who were about my age, from West Virginia arrived from the south. They carried the biggest, heaviest packs I ever saw any hiker carry. Burt looked like he was a fashion model for Columbia, complete with a huge, bright red pack and white nylon hiking pants that were spotless. They both seemed to take an instant liking to me.

They sat down and told me their life's stories. I enjoyed them competing for my attention at first. I liked the way they talked with their West Virginia accent. They have been section hiking for several years, fifty miles at a time. That hike was to Harpers Ferry. Dave went off to set up his tent while Burt stayed to talk a mile a minute. Dave returned and Burt went to set up his tent while Dave talked nonstop. I thought, holy smokes, they were tag teaming me.

Dave told me he was surprised Burt hiked and camped because he was so meticulous about everything and such a neat, clean freak. He would take an hour to wash up before he would be back. I thought Burt might have an obsessive-compulsive-disorder. That gave me an idea.

I went right over to Burt's tent with Dave following me talking all the way. I said, "Burt, did you know there's a shower down by the creek."

Dead silence at first as if Burt was thinking then he said "Shower?"

I said "Heck yea! It's a little on the chilly side at first, but at least ya can get cleaned up a little before ya eat."

Burt soon emerged from his tent in a robe and sandals, carrying a five-pound bag with all his hygiene stuff in it, He was sporting a smile which went from ear to ear. I went back to the shelter as Dave followed me like a puppy and talked continuously. I got my food bag, stove, and moved to the gazebo to cook. Dave thought that was a good idea and got his food to join me.

I was enjoying being by myself for a minute when the silence was shattered by the most blood-curdling, high-pitched, scream I had ever heard. I didn't know of a man or a beast who could scream who long. I swear it shook the ground hard enough to register on the Richter scale. I may have minimized it a little when I said the water was a little on the chilly side.

I was cooking tuna and noodles and eating the fine chocolate Dave shared with me when Burt returned. He was purple and, shuffled like a hundred-year-old man hugging his toiletry bag. I felt a little guilty when he sat down shaking like a dog shitting razor blades. The only thing he could say was "ca, ca, ca, ca, ca, ca…"

An hour later, Burt returned from his tent quite chipper all clean and sporting clean fresh pressed Columbia clothes. He had the biggest food bag I had ever seen on the trail. He decided to cook freeze-dried chicken teriyaki. When he poured boiling water in the packet, it smelled wonderful. He took one bite, made a sour face, and closed it back up.

I said, "What's wrong?"

Burt said, "I can't eat this and now I'll have to carry it out heavy to a garbage can!"

Dave said, "He always does that. He adds water to his food and won't eat it, then carries out a heavier pack than he started with."

I said, "I'll help you out, give it here."

He said, "You don't want this I've already eaten from the pack."

I said, "Just give it here."

Two Sobo college kids section hiking came in and set up in the shelter. That gave me a way out. I waited until they settled and I excused myself to retire for the night. It worked as Dave and Burt went to their tents. I talked a little to the college boys until I fell into a food coma from the chicken teriyaki and all the other food Dave and Burt couldn't eat.

May 6   **Day 70**   **18.9 Miles**

I slept restlessly in the shelter. One of the boys must have been hurt because he moaned in pain all night. I got up early and tried to leave surreptitiously without breakfast, but Burt was awake and busted me. I gave up and cooked oatmeal and coffee in the gazebo with Burt and Dave. Burt made freeze-dried eggs Benedict and Dave made freeze-dried bacon with scrambled eggs.

Dave asked me, "Did you ever try the freeze-dried breakfasts?"

I said, "Yes, but I prefer eggs handled more sanitary than the Chinese do."

Burt said, "What?"

I knew what I was doing when I said, "Burt, I don't want to ruin your breakfast."

Burt and Dave were nice, generous, guys and treated me great, but I could see me getting tired of them. I moved out as soon as I was finished eating freeze-dried eggs Benedict and freeze-dried bacon and eggs. I wanted to try to put some distance between us.

I ran into a busload of day-hikers from Washington, DC about mid-morning. I had forgotten it was a Saturday and the trail was close to the city. I had a hard time getting by them. I found them annoying because they hiked slow and wouldn't yield the trail to me as I approached them from behind.

I wanted to stop at Dick's Dome Shelter for lunch and water, but it was crowded with day-hikers, so I moved a mile farther up the trail to a spring. I was eating lunch when a dozen or so Romanian and Asian day-hikers, also from Washington, stopped. A grandiose man asked to use my water filter to show the others how to get water in the wilderness. I could see him plugging up my filter in the questionable water, so I offered him iodine tablets instead. He refused and said they had plenty of water anyway. They all gathered around to ask questions. I felt like I was an animal at the zoo.

An Asian girl asked me, "What do you eat?"

I told her, "I strangle little furry animals."

A man asked me, "How do you cook them?"

I put on my puzzled look and seriously said, "Cook them?" I could tell they were a little grossed out, so I said, "I don't cook them, I just bite their heads off and suck the guts out of the little ones then throw the skins away." The girl gave me an apple, but didn't ask any more questions before they left.

I hooked up with two section hikers, one was a former thru-hiker, and the three of us moved through the bus-tour hikers more easily. Besides, it was refreshing to talk to some normal hikers. They had a car parked at the highway in Ashby Gap and offered to take me two miles off trail to a restaurant, but I declined. I would have to walk the two miles back. Besides, I had a heavier than usual food bag with all the extra freeze-dried meals. Apparently, Burt and Dave got the impression the Chinese substitute cats and dogs for chicken and beef.

Late in the day, I ran into Skyline, who was the caretaker at Pass Mountain Hut in the Shenandoah. He was out for the weekend with his dog. We talked as we hiked together to Rod Hollow Shelter. We found the shelter full of eight weekenders from the city. Several tents were set up all around the shelter. I was too tired to move on, so I managed to find a reasonably flat piece of ground half a mile from the shelter to call home for the night.

Week ten ended with me hiking one-hundred and thirty-one miles. The wart pain seemed to be subsiding with the padding and the trail provided easy footfall all that week.

Day 71   21 Miles

The weather was perfect as I cooked a hot breakfast, packed up, and moved out, motivated by the prospect of finishing the big state of Virginia. I soon came to the beginning of the famous roller coaster, which was a series of twelve steep ups and twelve steep downs over the next fourteen miles of trail. I was a little intimidated by a sign posted on a tree that said;

"HIKER NOTICE
WARNING

You are about to enter
THE ROLLER COASTER!!!
Built and maintained by the
"TRAIL BOSS" and his merry crew of volunteers
Have a great ride and we will see
You at the Blackburn Trail Center
(IF YOU SURVIVE)"

I knew folks on the Appalachian Trail embellished things a little bit sometimes, but I proceeded with caution anyway. The roller coaster was hard, but it also had an upside to it. I had cell tower at the mountaintops. I took a break to take advantage of the tower. I called a different friend on the top of each mountain. I called Brave Heart first and he shared the story of how plantar fascia pain ended his hike. I missed Brave Heart and wished him the best in his new career as a preacher. I wished I wouldn't have called him after I hung up. The conversation left me down and my plantar fascia started to hurt, which was probably psychosomatic on my part. Brave Heart said he would never attempt another thru-hike, but I hoped he would change his mind someday after the pain went away and he remembered the good times.

I landed on the Virginia/West Virginia boarder late in the afternoon. I befriended a first time day hiker named Brian, who took my picture at the sign welcoming me to West Virginia. I had a feeling of accomplishment having hiked all five-hundred, thirty-five and nine-tenths miles of the Appalachian Trail in Virginia. Virginia had the most miles of any of the fourteen states which made up the trail. I crossed the Tennessee/ Virginia border on April second, which seemed like a long time ago.

The weather turned for the worst with a steady rain. I had eight miles to go to get to a shelter that marked a thousand miles from Springer Mountain, which was my goal for that day. West Virginia greeted me with its version of the Devil's Racecourse with miles of rocks ranging from the size of a football to a car engine. I also noticed an incredible amount of poison ivy, which made me miserable if I touched it. I took it slow because I didn't want to blow an ankle or a knee on the wet, slippery rocks or accidently touch the poison ivy.

I didn't arrive at the David Musser Memorial Shelter until long after dark. The shelter was impressively made from giant logs. I had it all to myself, which was a negative thing that night. I was cold, wet, tired, hungry, lonely, and could have used some company. I changed into dry clothes and cooked a hot meal, which warmed me up. I curled up in my sleeping bag and read the Bible for a while. I turned off my headlight, shut the Bible, and gave thanks for the wonderful opportunity to experience life.

I let my mind drift back to my early experience with restoration of sanity through the program. As was customary in my early days of recovery, the home group gave a newcomer a little address book about the size of a credit card with a dime taped inside the cover. The home group members would put their phone numbers in it. Often other members would ask for your book, add their phone number, and offer to talk any time, for any reason. The following Tuesday, a few days after the incident at the Diamond Deli, I was riding with Big Jim to a meeting.

The subject came up and he asked. "Do you have phone numbers of men in the program to call?" I proudly whipped out my little address book where I had been collecting numbers for longer than I had been sober.

Big Jim asked, "Who do you call?"

"You."

"Besides me?"

"I'm not a phone talker."

Big Jim's patience often wore a little thin with me at times and I could tell by his voice this was starting to be one of those times when he said, "I didn't ask you if you were a phone talker, I asked you who you called besides me!"

I sheepishly said, "No one."

He seemed to calm down and said, "Okay, here's what I want you to do; tomorrow I want you to call another sober alcoholic besides me."

I said nothing.

He looked directly at me, and the car almost went in the ditch as his voice elevated, "Okay?"

I said, "Okay," but I didn't intend to call anyone. I put my seat belt on.

The next day I was riding down a winding, rural road with Jim to a hot dog roast at a meeting twenty-five miles away.

He asked, "Who did you call?"

I had already forgotten yesterday's conversation, but I said, "I didn't feel like taking a drink, so I didn't think I needed to call anyone."

That time we didn't almost hit the ditch. We hit the ditch so hard I bounced my head off the ceiling as we jumped it and came to a stop in a knee-high cornfield. Jim's eyes were wild, his face was beet red and the veins were popping out of his forehead. Bits of saliva were coming out of his mouth and hitting me in the face as he screamed, "Think! Who told you to think? Thinking is what gets your dumb ass in trouble every time you think! Don't think! I'll do all the thinking for you; you just do whatever I tell your dumb ass to do!"

I was so scared because Big Jim was so big I couldn't even outrun him, so I said, "Okay, okay!"

His voice dropped, but was still threatening as he leaned closer to my face and through clenched teeth said, "Tomorrow you call another sober alcoholic on the phone. I don't care if you say, hello, kiss my ass, have a nice day, but you call someone!"

I came back to the present with a lot of gratitude for the grace of God and Big Jim who saw me through those early days of my sobriety. I now realized God loved me even when I denied His existence. After all, He was the one who picked Big Jim to be my sponsor. I also think Big Jim loved me even when he was so pissed off at me he could have wrung my neck.

I felt better and knew when the sun came up, it would be a new day and a town-day. Harpers Ferry was less than ten miles away and I was looking forward to getting a motel with a hot shower and clean sheets.

Day 72   8.8 Miles

I was too cold to sleep well in the night. I wished I still had my warm, winter sleeping bag and the warmer clothes I gave back to Scooter in Waynesboro. I made a hot breakfast of ramen noodles, changed into my wet hiking clothes, and hit the trail hard to warm up. The weather was cold, wet, and windy. I stopped to make coffee on the trail. I spilled the first pot off the rock I was using for a table, so I had to make it again. The coffee warmed me up some so I could continue hiking more comfortably.

The rain stopped as I arrived at Harpers Ferry. I stopped at the Appalachian Trial Conference Headquarters. The building itself was a slightly older stone and mortar, two-story building with a banner that said, Appalachian Trail Conservancy, hanging on the front.

I took my pack off outside and sauntered in. A friendly older lady greeted me, but I didn't remember her name if she even told me. Messenger was already there on their computer. He was planning to go back home for a week to graduate from college. He didn't think Brave Heart would ever get back on the trail and I agreed. I already knew from talking to Brave Heart, but the news still saddened me. I didn't like Brave Heart a lot at first, but I grew to respect and admire him as we shared some hard times.

I registered and the receptionist took my picture outside under the banner. I was the forty-first thru-hiker to arrive at Harpers Ferry from Springer Mountain that year. I wished I would have asked what number I was when I left Springer Mountain in Georgia so I could have had a comparison of how well or poorly I was doing. I guess I was doing okay because I got to Harpers Ferry.

A thirty-five-year-old thru-hiker named Scout from the state of Washington came in, and we struck up a conversation. She guided hiking trips on Washington's Mount Rainier. She took time off to hike the Appalachian Trail to add to her resume. I previously heard about her from Fire Fly and Feather who planned to rendezvous with her. She told me they stopped at the hostel in Front Royal because Fire Fly was sick. The news disturbed me not only out of concern for Fire Fly, but I also could be at risk to get sick, because I shared the hostel with them in Front Royal.

The receptionist gave me a list of the hiker services in Harpers Ferry. The first thing on my agenda was to find a place to stay. Scout and Messenger were staying at the reasonably priced hostel for hikers. I planned to stay there if I couldn't find a private room.

I walked several blocks to the Hilltop House Hotel, which was an elegant old, three-story hotel. The hotel had a huge front porch with eight white pillars holding up the roof, each sporting an American Flag. I felt like I stepped back in time to the Civil War.

They reserve two rooms as hiker rooms on a first-come, first-serve basis for forty dollars each. I considered myself lucky because they still had a room. I believe all the regular rooms were over a hundred dollars a night. The hiker room was small, but it had a small bathroom with a shower. The room was a lot better than a tent in the rain or sharing a bunkhouse with a bunch of smelly hikers. I settled in and took my usual long, hot shower. When I was home and took a shower or two every day, I didn't appreciate them near as much as I did on the trail when showers were a rare treat.

I met Tom, who had the other hiker room. Tom was a quiet, introverted type of thru-hiker. He passed me twice the day before, but never said a word to me.

He said, "I thought you would stop at Blackburn Hostel, so we waited supper for you last night."

Blackburn Hostel was three tenths of a mile off trail in the dark and I didn't know they even had food.

I said, "I wish I would have known about it, because I would have stopped."

I went to the post office and picked up my mail. I received more letters from friends back home who supported me. I also retrieved the package of food I sent myself from Waynesboro. I found an ATM at a Seven Eleven and withdrew some money. I didn't need money, but wanted to see if the account was running. It was, so I felt a lot more secure. I found a little restaurant and ate two cheeseburgers for lunch. The people at the restaurant didn't seem as friendly as the folks further South.

I took my mail and supplies back to the hotel. I still needed to go to the outfitters for some fuel. The map I picked up from the Appalachian Trail Conservancy headquarters indicated the outfitter was located in the old part of town. I ventured into the old part of town where the buildings were probably over a hundred and fifty years old. The narrow winding brick streets were crowded with quaint little shops and stores. The landscaping was impressive with bamboo, flowers, and shrubs, all in bloom. Again, I felt like I stepped back in time to the civil war.

I had a hard time finding the outfitters because it was on the third floor of a rickety old row house. I entered a narrow, doorway at street level marked only by a small sign. I climbed three flights of stairs which were so narrow, I felt claustrophobic. The outfitters consisted of four small rooms packed with everything I could ever want. The storekeeper was so hiker-friendly I bought fuel and a few other things I didn't really need. He even gave me a plastic envelope for my guidebook.

I spent the rest of the afternoon exploring this delightful part of town. Harpers Ferry was an old town rich in Civil War history. I believe a lot of fighting took place there because both the North and the South occupied the town at different times during the war. Today, Harpers Ferry had an atmosphere where I still felt the tension as if I returned to the 1860s. I wouldn't have been surprised if I saw Union or Confederate soldiers marching down the street any minute.

Harpers Ferry was where John Brown, who came from Blooming Valley, Pennsylvania, organized a slave rebellion that sparked the civil war. I always thought John Brown was black, but he actually was a well-hung white man.

I walked a mile back to the Seven Eleven and bought four hot dogs and a quart of ice cream to take back to the hotel for supper, plus a sub sandwich for lunch on the trail the next day. I spent the rest of the evening in my room eating cherry vanilla ice cream, packing, and answering letters to the folks back home. I fell asleep in the warm, dry bed during a thunder and lightning storm outside.

Day 73   16.1 Miles

I awoke stuffed up from all the pollen in the air. I felt like I was coming down with a cold, but I hoped it was only allergies due to all the spring flowers blooming. I went to the hotel's dining room for breakfast. I found Tom reading the local paper as he was eating. He appeared to be an introvert, but I wasn't, so I sat down and started talking. He was from Michigan and planned to hike twenty miles that day. We chatted until he finished his breakfast. He gave me the newspaper when he left. I finished breakfast and checked out. I stopped at the Appalachian Trail Conference office and bought some souvenirs for folks back home. Scout was on the computer and said she planned to take a zero day to wait for Fire Fly and Feather to catch up.

I returned to the post office to mail things to some folks back home. The postman gave me a hard time about my return address, which said, somewhere on the Appalachian Trail. He made me change it to my real home address. He was a small, frail looking, little man who wanted to show his authority. I thought I did well by keeping my mouth shut and not saying what I was thinking.

The sun came out as I crossed the Potomac River on the Goodloe Byron Memorial Footbridge and left Harpers Ferry behind. I entered my sixth state, Maryland. I was alone again with my thoughts of returning to sanity.

Even though Big Jim pissed me off at times, I had a huge amount of respect and admiration for him. I usually took his energetic suggestions eventually and did what he told me to do. I didn't have a phone and my car was out of gas again, so the next day, I peddled a broken down bicycle to a phone booth three miles from my house. I called Mike, who I looked up to because he had been sober a whole year.

I said, "Hi Mike, I don't want to bother you, but Big Jim made me call someone in the program."

Mike said, "Well, thanks for calling me."

I covered my ass saying, "If Big Jim asks, would you back me up?"

He answered, "If Jim asks, I'll tell him you called."

"Okay, sorry to bother you."

I expected him to say goodbye and I would have completed the assignment, but he said, "Hold on a minute. How are you doing?"

"Okay."

Mike pushed me, "I find it hard to believe everything's okay already." Then he shared how it sucked when he was first new in his recovery. He inspired me to share my emotions of my early recovery, which also sucked.

That particular conversation lasted forty minutes and would have lasted longer if I didn't have to pee so badly. I felt great, like I did when I went to an Alcoholics Anonymous meeting. I found by connecting with another sober alcoholic, even if by telephone, I could restore my sanity. That was how I started to use the phone and still use it.

I didn't know at the time, but Mike and I connected on a spiritual level as did Bill W and Dr, Bob at their first meeting. I have never felt alone after I made contact with Alcoholics Anonymous on a spiritual level. I laughed to myself as I thought of the three hundred dollar phone bill I recently incurred making phone contact. I wondered if Big Jim was watching and smiling. I was still agnostic, but I remembered thinking, maybe after all, there was something to this power greater than myself thing they were talking about.

The Appalachian Trail followed the old C and O Canal Towpath for a couple of flat miles then turned back to the mountains. The mountains were not high or steep in Maryland, so the going was easy except for a few rocks. I stopped for lunch at the Ed Garvey Shelter, which was a new, impressive, two-story log shelter. I ate my sub sandwich and moved on to Gathland State Park where Scooter and I camped at one time on a section hike. A war memorial, restroom, and pop machine were the attractions. I used the restroom, but the pop machine didn't work, so I was a little disappointed because I was hoping for a cold coke.

I moved on and returned to my reflections about my early recovery. I didn't think the chain of events that took place in my early sobriety were a coincidence. I believe God chose to direct them and remain anonymous. I knew for sure those events made a lasting impression on me. From that day on I tried to call another sober addict daily if I could.

As alcoholics, we shared our experience, strength and hope with each other to solve a common problem. When a member shared how they survived a situation, it gave me the hope that I could also resolve a similar situation. I thought faith and hope were closely related, but different. Alcoholics Anonymous was all about, sharing experience, strength, and hope with others. When I shared my hope, I received the gift of faith.

I hiked another five miles and stopped for the night at Rocky Run Shelter where I filtered water. I camped in my tent. Nobody was at the shelter for company, but I had cell tower and talked a long time with my friend Crow. I thought all the pollen in the air was what stuffed up my sinuses, but I still felt a little paranoid about getting Fire Fly's sickness.

Day 74   20.5 Miles

I felt terrible when I woke up. I felt like I caught a cold, but I still hoped it could be allergies due to all the flowers blooming. I took a cold pill and forced myself to hike at least to the next shelter. I felt better after I started hiking and the endorphins kicked in.

I saw a sign which said I was entering the Washington Monument State Park, which puzzled me since the only Washington Monument I knew of was in Washington, DC. I was afraid I got terribly lost if I was coming into Washington, DC. I climbed the hill to the monument, which looked like a giant vase built out of stones. I stopped at a restroom with a flush toilet and a sink with soap. I washed my hands and filled my water bottle. I wished I would have had to go because they furnished free toilet paper. I wondered how many opportunities I passed up to use a modern flush toilet because I already shit in the woods. They had a pop machine, but as usual, it was out of order.

I left my pack outside when I entered the stone doorway, guarded by a wrought iron door at the bottom of the monument. A dark and narrow spiral stairway made of stone, led to the top. I had an eerie, medieval feeling as I climbed to the top, but I was rewarded with an impressive view of Maryland on a clear morning.

I took the time and made some hot coffee. I felt better and enjoyed the scenery as I drank my coffee. The citizens of Boonsboro, Virginia first built the thirty-four-foot high monument in 1827. Someone rebuilt the tower in 1920, but I didn't know why. A campground was in the park, which came with showers for twenty dollars a night, but I didn't know if it was even open yet. I only hiked a little over three miles, but felt better as I saddled up to ride off. I made myself a promise I would take my time and not go too far that day.

I found some trail magic left by a trail angel at the bridge over the interstate. I stopped for another break and ate some Slim Jims and Little Debbie's treats. I left the angel a thankyou note before I trudged on towards the next shelter. I didn't go far before I found a nice place to rest for lunch with a great view and a perfect sitting rock. I realized how lucky I was to be able to be in so many different beautiful places each day. I decided I would stop at the next shelter for the day.

I arrived at Ensign Cowall Shelter where I planned on spending the night. I was chatting with a section hiker who was in for the day, when a helicopter spraying for Gypsy Moths flew over several times. All I could smell was bug spray and I became aware my lungs were starting to hurt, which couldn't be good. I packed up and left immediately in a panic, without finishing my snack.

I hiked as fast as I could for five more miles to the Devil's Racecourse Shelter. The fast pace and the bug spray made my lungs worse. I set my tent up on a flat spot close to the trail. Water was available at the shelter three-tenths of a mile off trail, but I could get by without water and I didn't have any energy left to venture down the mountain. I was only five miles from the Pennsylvania border where I knew I could get water in the morning. I got into my sleeping bag and started to enter the events of the day in my journal. I noticed faith and hope kept popping up in my thoughts.

About fifteen years ago, I had a friend who was arrested several times for driving while intoxicated. His probation officer threw him in jail because he kept using cocaine and violating his parole. He had to sit in jail waiting for the judge to decide what his fate would be. While he sat in jail, he suspected his wife was trading sex for drugs on the outside. One day, another inmate was bragging about sleeping with his wife in a trade for crack cocaine. The two men fought viciously and my friend's nose was broken in the fight. He was thrown into solitary confinement, or as we called it in prison, the hole. His situation was bleak, but not permanent. However, he did not have the hope to see any resolution or believe things would ever get better. He did an insane act and hung himself with his laundry bag cord in his cell. He found a permanent escape from a temporary problem. I maintain, if someone would have shared a similar experience with him and how they resolved it, my friend may have found some hope he too could have survived his situation and went on with his life.

I was happy to see a woman come in with her dog and set up not far from me. She didn't appear to be too talkative, but I wasn't either on that night. I still felt better knowing I wasn't alone when I felt sick. My lungs were congested. I wasn't sure if it was from the bug spray, allergies, or a cold, but I felt miserable. I hiked over twenty miles that day feeling ill. I thought, so much for a short day. I took a nighttime cold pill and went to bed without supper.

Day 75   22.8 Miles

I awoke to rain which started before daylight. I packed up early to try to keep my gear as dry as possible, so it wouldn't be so heavy. I was out of water, so I hit the trail without breakfast or coffee. The woman and her dog were southbound, so I bid them farewell and wished them the best.

The good news was the rain must have subdued the pollen in the air, because I could breathe easier and felt better. The rain became heavier and the temperature dropped as I went north. I reached the Pennsylvania border at Pen-Mar Park by mid-morning. I stopped at a pavilion/picnic area with restrooms and got out of the rain. I made two pots of hot coffee with water from the restrooms.

Thoughts of my friend's demise had been on my mind most of the morning. I looked over the wet, rainy, gray morning and wished he had the hope to see past the turmoil he was in temporarily. I reflected on the many wet, rainy, gray mornings in my life when I was up to my neck in alligators and felt there was no hope anything would ever get better. Sometimes I thought the bad times would last forever, but eventually the sun came out, and things got better.

Alcoholics Anonymous used many slogans that said something very important as simply and with as few words as possible, probably so we alcoholics could store them in our damaged brains. One such slogan was, *This too shall pass.* I used that slogan a lot when I talked to others to give them hope when situations weren't going well for them.

I once went to an Alcoholics Anonymous meeting at a local rehab where patients attended the meeting. I noticed a woman standing off to the side, hunched over with her arms folded hugging herself, trying to stay warm. She was trembling and through my own experience, I knew instantly she was dope sick.

I said to her, "I know exactly how you feel. You feel like you are going to die, but believe me, you won't, and one day you and I will laugh about this."

Slowly she brought her eyes up to meet mine and at that instant, we formed a spiritual connection that would last a lifetime. She said to a complete stranger, "You promise?"

I nodded my head as I smiled and said, "Yes I promise, this too shall pass."

Her name was Sheila and that happened almost twenty years ago. We became good friends and we have laughed about the incident many times since that day. Sheila and I both developed faith the hard times would pass. Sheila also learned to share her experience, strength, and hope with other addicts who suffered. Yes, she and I had not only laughed about that painful day so many years ago, we both became thankful for the pain.

The difference between Sheila and my friend who hung himself in jail was Sheila accepted a little hope things would eventually get better.

Things continued to get better for me as I grew spiritually and eventually, my hope turned into knowing things would get better with God's help. Somewhere my hope had turned into faith. I finished my coffee and moved out. I knew this too shall pass.

I trudged on in a steady, cold, spring rain. Pennsylvania was famous for its rocks and has a well-deserved reputation for taking out many thru-hikers with ankle and knee injuries. With the rain, all those rocks were wet, slimy, and even more dangerous. I thought, welcome to Pennsylvania.

I stopped at Tumbling Run Shelters to get out of the rain for a late lunch. Twelve college co-eds were camping and partying in the two shelters. They were celebrating the end of the school year in the rain. They weren't unfriendly, but I felt like an outsider. I cooked tuna and noodles, ate, made coffee, filtered water, and left without saying a word.

I knew of an old-fashioned Italian restaurant ten trail miles away and a half mile down the highway. I stopped at the resturant two times previously on section hikes, so I knew they made the best homemade subs in the world. I hiked on in the rain with a purpose. The entire day was dark and rainy, but it was another day closer to Katahdin. Darkness was setting in as I walked down the highway to the friendly little restaurant. I was cold, wet to the bone, and shaking as I went dripping to the dining room, pack and all.

It was the waitress's first day. She was still in high school, and breaking in on her first job. I ordered coffee as soon as she seated me. When she returned with coffee and the menu, I ordered a salad with ranch dressing, an Italian sub, and a large order of fries without looking at the menu.

I sat there getting colder because I was resting in wet clothes. The prospect of hiking four more miles to the next shelter in darkness and heavy rain was bleak. I looked in my guidebook and discovered a Scottish Inn-Rite Spot Motel was three miles away on the highway, which was a lot better than a cold, wet shelter.

My mood improved even before my food came. I called the motel as I was eating to reserve a room. A lady with a Spanish accent answered the phone and said they had plenty of rooms available and reservations weren't necessary. I told her I was an Appalachian Trail hiker and would be a while because I had to walk three miles to the motel. I could hear her yelling to someone in Spanish in the distance.

She came back to me on the phone and said, "My husband will come pick you up for five dollars."

I wanted to say "I love you," but I wasn't sure how she would react.

I ate my supper and was waiting, when a small, olive-skinned man with a large, round head showed up in an old van. Alfredo could see I was wet and terribly cold, so he took me straight to the room and opened it with his master key. He turned on the heat and told me to warm up, dry off, and then come to the office to pay.

I took off my shoes and jumped in the hot shower with all my clothes on. I washed my clothes in the shower as I took them off. I dressed in my warm, dry Under Armor, fleece, and dry socks. I went to the office and his fourteen-year-old daughter charged me fifty-five dollars for the ride and the room.

I hung up all my wet stuff to dry before I jumped in the dry bed with the heat turned up. I realized how all of a sudden, a bad day could turn around to have a great ending. I got out of bed, got down on my knees, and gave thanks to my creator.

When I sobered up, things still sucked for some time. I didn't know how long it took, but one day I realized what the people in the program told me in those early days was true and it was slowly happening. Things were starting to get better and I started to value my sobriety.

I realized the folks who stayed sober all helped other drunks by sharing their experiences, strength, and hope. They also talked of the importance of their personal relationship with a higher power. Some folks simply called that power greater than themselves, God.

Hope through the experiences of others turned into faith for me over time. Hope may be the gift I received from others when they shared their personal experience strength and success to show me the way. I believed hope was the greatest gift one human being could give to another suffering human being. I believe faith was the greatest gift of all, but I believed faith was a personal gift from God, which led me to believe.

I learned to have the faith to encourage, support, and love the new comer. I tried to give them what others gave to me so freely by sharing their personal stories. I tried to give the new person what I considered the most valuable gift I could ever give; hope. I let God take care of the rest.

I came to understand what Wilber P meant that night at my first Alcoholics Anonymous dance when he said "Ain't it great to be sober." I discovered being an alcoholic was a blessing in disguise. I found my worst nightmare became my greatest dream.

I snapped back from my meditation and called Scooter and Crow on the cell to get my Alcoholics Anonymous fix. Even my cold was gone and my lungs were clear.

Day 76   19.9 Miles

I awoke before daylight and went to a little hometown diner across the road. I had bacon, eggs, pancakes, and lots of coffee with the locals. The morning was clear, crisp, and promised to be a nice day. When I went back to the motel, I discovered I accidently locked the door when I left. I had to wake Alfredo to get the key to my room. I asked him for a ride back to the trail. He told me he would give me a ride at eight o'clock. I took a shower, watched television, and talked on the phone to kill time. I had to wake Alfredo for the second time at eight o'clock, but he took me back to the trail.

I had a mail drop in Boiling Springs, which by my calculations, was three days away. That meant I wouldn't get there until Sunday and would have to wait until Monday to get my package. I called the post office at Boiling Springs and told a man named John my dilemma. He said he would leave my package across the street at the Appalachian Trail Center under the table at closing time on Saturday, so I could pick it up Sunday.

I stopped to rest and cook couscous for lunch. I took my shoes and socks off to let my feet dry out. My wart was heeling nicely. I had some blisters, but only one large blister, which was good. Five co-eds in their late teens or early twenties were camping at Birch Run Shelter. I only stopped for water, but they were so friendly I decided to take a break and make tea to share with them. They were out of school, hiking, and camping for a couple weeks. I found it refreshing to see young folks having fun without using drugs and alcohol.

I moved on to Pine Grove Furnace State Park where a historic furnace, used to smelt iron during the revolutionary and civil wars still stood. I stopped at the famous Iron Masters Hostel, which was a large brick building dating back to colonial times, with every window dressed in old-time white shutters. Rumor had it George and Martha Washington stayed there overnight. The house also had a secret room used for hiding runaway slaves back in the day.

I found a delightful woman named Donna Rozycki, who was seventy something and still managed the hostel. She showed me around before I took a shower and picked out a bunk. A section hiker from Maryland named Greg, was staying there also. Greg stayed off the trail for the previous two days trying to heal a knee injury.

I went to the camp store adjacent to the hostel and bought a half gallon of mint chocolate chip ice cream. I returned to the hostel to take the traditional thru-hiker challenge of eating a half-gallon of ice cream all at one time, to celebrate the halfway point on the trail.

Kitchen privileges went with the stay at the hostel. I found Greg cooking spaghetti and Donna, a baked potato with cheese. We all sat down at the kitchen table and ate. Greg and Donna were impressed at how big a pig I was as I joined The Half Gallon Club in less than an hour. We talked until much later than I usually stayed up.

May 13   Day 77   15.5 Miles

I woke up in the night with low back pain because the bunk I was sleeping on was broken down in the middle and more like a hammock. I had to move to the floor to go back to sleep.

I got up before the others and went quietly into the kitchen to make strong coffee. The smell of the coffee soon called to Greg and Donna. We drank two pots of coffee, caught a coffee buzz, and chattered like three chipmunks on crack.

I gave Greg some extra ibuprofen for his knee. He was still undecided whether to call his dad to come get him and abort his hike or take a zero day and resume hiking the next day. I encouraged him to cowboy up and hike on.

I packed up and wrote Donna a thank-you note. I gave her a twenty dollar tip with instructions the money was for her personally and not a donation for the hostel. I left the hostel full of coffee.

I soon came to the official halfway point on the Appalachian Trail. A sign said one-thousand and sixty-nine miles south to Springer and one-thousand and sixty-nine miles north to Katahdin. That was where most hikers were elated because the hike was half over, but I found myself melancholy because the adventure was half over.

I met two beautiful, but slightly overweight women who started hiking the trail about fifteen minutes before we met. They were south bound to Springer Mountain, Georgia. They were school bus drivers who were laid off for the summer. They considered hiking as cross-training to lose weight and get in shape in the off-season.

I stopped to take a break with them. They had huge packs with a large teddy bear tied on the back of each. I spent about half an hour with them answering their questions. I helped them pick trail names; they picked Slow-Bo and Wild-Thing.

Wild-Thing was sporting a rape whistle on a string around her neck and warned me she was not an easy woman. I assured her it was tempting, but I was a married man and a gentleman. I talked them into posing for a picture, before I bid them farewell.

I hiked on and met a trout fisherwoman, who was catching trout to the dismay of her husband, who wasn't catching anything. Pennsylvania had several nice looking, crystal-clear trout streams. I wished I had a fly rod with me.

I stopped late in the day to buy two subs and two cokes at a convenience store a short distance off trail. I ate a sub and drank a coke at the picnic table by the store, but packed up the other sandwich and a couple of candy bars for supper later that night.

I hiked another seven miles to Alic Kennedy Shelter. The rain started, so I set my tent up. I was four miles out of Boiling Springs and alone with no cell tower. It started raining hard , so I was in for the night.

Reflecting back on my life, I could see I had low self-esteem, poor self-confidence, anxiety, and depression before I ever drank. I started drinking at the ripe old age of twelve-years-old and magically I felt bigger, stronger, better looking. My low self-esteem, anxiety, and shyness disappeared. I loved the intoxicating feeling and wanted to stay that way forever.

I fell in love with chemicals because they made me feel whole, as if everything was okay. I believed that lie for the next seventeen years and medicated with drugs and alcohol until I was physically, emotionally, and spiritually bankrupt. The feeling of wellbeing chemicals provided was only an illusion while my life progressively became a living hell. The reality was drugs and alcohol fixed nothing.

I thought if I stopped using drugs everything would be okay, but to my dismay, when I sobered up the low self-esteem, poor self-confidence, anxiety, and depression came back vigorously. I could no longer escape the shame and guilt with a bottle of Sothern Comfort. My first year sober was worse than the last year of my addiction, because I didn't have Miss Alcohol, who was my first love, to escape the reality I hated.

The fellowship of Alcoholics Anonymous took me in, loved, and comforted me, when no one else wanted to be around me. The people accepted me and promised things would get better. They gave me hope, which was something chemicals never did.

What the Alcoholics Anonymous members said in the early days came true. My life was better than I ever dreamed it could be and was getting even better. Alcoholics Anonymous was truly a power greater than myself, but not God. I believe Alcoholics Anonymous was a gift sent from God, so children who were lost like me could find the God of their understanding.

I drifted off to sleep and ended week eleven after hiking one-hundred and twenty-five miles.

Day 78   11.9 Miles

The day started out a dark, gray, and gloomy Mothers Day. My Mom passed beyond my mortal sight two years ago and I still grieved the personal loss. My mood matched the day. I spent some time in my sleeping bag in remembrance of the good things about my Mom to try to improve my mood.

My Mother was a lifelong Christian whose life was an example of a walk through life with Christ himself. She lived a life of gratitude humility, loving all, and fearing nothing. She never bragged, preached, nor quoted the Bible. Mom simply lived and led by example, silently carrying the message to others by modeling love and service.

She loved all unconditionally, but especially the less fortunate. She was s self-admitted water dog, who loved swimming, water skiing, boating, and anything to do with the water. She taught us kids to swim about the time we started to walk. I didn't remember learning to swim because I was so young when she taught me. Even in her eighties, she went to the YWCA two days a week to assist handicapped and mentally challenged children learn to swim. I think the only one I ever saw her get angry with was me. She would send me to Sunday school and I would skip out and spend the money she gave me for the collection on cigarettes.

The worst was the time she caught me shooting songbirds off her bird feeder with a BB gun. Wow! She was as pissed as Jesus was at the venders in the temple, but she forgave me. She became pissed-off all over again when she found out I was keeping a bird body count because I was competing with my best friend, Tommy. Believe me, I never wanted to feel the wrath of Mom ever again. I could still remember the fear that struck me when she called me by my full Christian name. Make no mistake, my mother was no wimp. I didn't think she was afraid of the devil himself. I can't imagine her denying Christ three times as old Pete did. I think she would have even spit in the Roman soldier's eye. Mom didn't even fear death. I would always remember the last words I heard her say in this world. A stroke put her in a coma for eleven days before the completion of her life. She could no longer communicate. I was sitting at her bedside and thought she would leave in silence at any time. Unexpectedly she opened her eyes briefly and looked me straight in the eye, patted my hand lightly, and said in a feeble voice, "Don't be afraid."

By now, tears were rolling down my face, so I got out of my sleeping bag, and dressed to face the day. Mom's spirit must have touched me because I felt the indescribable comfort of her presence. I simply looked up into the gray morning sky with my eyes wide open and smiling I said, "Thanks Mom."

Although the sky was still gloomy, I felt Mom's sunshine as I hiked into Boiling Springs early on Sunday morning Mother's Day. The trail crossed a trout stream as I entered the town. I stopped and actually saw some impressive looking trout and several gentlemen fishermen with expensive, new gear, sporting fly rods in their seemingly futile attempts to catch the fish.

A dam in the middle of town backed up the water to form a well-manicured, shallow pond. A large old barn-type brick building stood directly beside the dam may have been a grinding mill for the farms at one time.

The fishermen at the pond were more of my class. They wore blue jeans, used worms for bait, and sat on five-gallon buckets. They were catching Bluegills.

I found my mail drop safely stashed under the table at the Appalachian Trail Conference headquarters. I bought four hotdogs and two large coffees at a convenience store for breakfast. I wasn't sure if I would describe the town as high class or high end, but I didn't find it too hiker friendly. I took my hotdogs back to the swing on the porch of the headquarters to gorge on as I watched the fishermen.

I silently moved on after a short break. Most of the Cumberland Valley was rich farmland and lush river bottom. The soft grass footfall and the level trail made for easy hiking. I was making good time effortlessly.

The rain stopped, so I took my pack off and sat on it while I called Rambler, who was home in Maine waiting for his daughter to be born. I also called Guns who was on the trail in New Jersey. They were both doing well and it helped improve my mood and diverted my thoughts of missing Mom. I would like to visit Rambler in Maine and Guns in New York City someday after I finish the trail.

I moved on in a brighter mood. A girl, who recently moved there from Texas, was jogging on the trail. She stopped to walk with me until we got to her car at the highway. I sold her on the idea of going on the Appalachian Trail for a short hike in the near future.

The rain started again, but heavier at about lunchtime. Due to the weather, I decided to head for a Super 8 motel on the highway not far from there. I previously stayed there on a section hike. I remembered the owners were hiker friendly.

I flirted appropriately with the teenage girl from India who checked me in. The first thing I always did at a motel was take a hot shower, so I did and it helped wash away my lingering melancholic mood. I took all my dirty, wet clothes to an in-house coin laundry. I washed them, but couldn't dry them because Mexican migrant workers staying there took all the dryers. I hung up my clothes in my room, turned the heat way up, and left to find some dinner.

I went to large a restaurant across the street and the hostess seated me at a table by myself. Families were coming in after church with their mothers for dinner. I had been missing my mom all morning and being alone watching them seemed to make it worse. I ordered meatloaf with mashed potatoes, ate in silence, and then left.

My clothes were still wet when I got back, but it was too hot to stay in the room, so I walked a mile down the road to a truck stop plaza for something to do. They had an AYCE buffet, which I wished I would have known about before I had the lousy meatloaf. I decided I would come back later to pig out. I walked around, but didn't buy anything because I re-supplied from my mail drop at Boiling Springs. I went back to my room, shut the heat off, and took a nap. I awoke well after dark feeling sick from the meatloaf. I stayed in and watched boring television until I fell back to sleep.

Day 79   17.6 Miles

I awoke with diarrhea several times in the night, but felt better when I got up. I ate three bagels with cream cheese and washed them down with several weak cups of coffee at the continental breakfast in the motel. I packed and got ready to ride, but procrastinated by watching television because it was raining hard outside. It has rained at least once every day since I entered Pennsylvania.

I finally started hiking in the rain through the Cumberland River Valley. The day before, the hiking was easy on short grass and flat ground. However, with all the rain, the trail got muddy. The mud grabbed my shoes and tried to pull them off with every step, which made the going slower and harder. I went from mud to rocks as I left the valley and entered the mountains.

Pennsylvania became famous for its rocks. Many years ago, a glacier melted in the eastern part of Pennsylvania and deposited all the rocks it carried. From there on, the Appalachian Trail in Pennsylvania was a giant rock pile with granite rocks ranging from the size of a football to the size of a car. Many thru-hikers hikes have ended due to injuries on the rocks of Pennsylvania.

The rain subsided in the afternoon and the sun started poking through the clouds as they thinned out. I stopped on a mountain overlooking the farmland of the Cumberland River Valley to take a photo. I twisted my left knee, which was my weak knee anyway, on the rocks. I only had a few miles to go to town, so I put on my knee brace, took two ibuprofen, and limped down the mountain over the rocks into Duncannon. Trail Angel Mary had left fruit chewy snacks and fruit juice on the trail before I hit town, so I stopped for a snack. She left her phone number, so I called and thanked her. We had a delightful fifteen-minute conversation.

I went straight to the Doyle Hotel and checked into a room for the night. The Doyle displayed a huge Coors Light banner on the second floor balcony railing which said, "Welcome Hikers." I felt right at home even before I entered the bar on the first floor. Anheuser-Busch built the Doyle Hotel in 1906. Time has taken its toll, leaving the Doyle a little run down. The landmark was once a fine, four-story hotel with magnificent oak woodwork, stairways, banisters, ten-foot ceilings, and an indoor bathroom on each floor. Indoor bathrooms were a luxury in 1906. It was a stop for thru-hikers from the time of Earl Shaffer. A second story porch wrapped around two sides of the hotel. I could picture the thru-hikers of yesteryear as they sat there and told tall trail tales and embellished the rigorous trail ahead for the greenhorns.

I walked into the bar with my pack still on, twirling my hiking pole like a gunslinger out of the old west. I knew immediately, that was a dangerous place for a sober alcoholic. The bar was full of hikers. I could tell by the way they were dressed they weren't locals. Fire Fly and Feather were the only hikers I knew and they were getting drunk.

The bar maid came up and asked with a wink, "What will it be hiker?"

I said, "I'd like a room for the night."

She got a key and said, "That'll be seventeen bucks."

I paid her and followed her up two flights of stairs. She gave me a tour as she showed me to my room. Her name was Vicky. She and her husband, Frank bought the place and ran it. He was the cook and she tended the bar.

Vicky had me when she said, "Frank cooks the biggest and best cheeseburgers on the trail."

I don't know why, but I blurted out, "Vicky, I'm a sober alcoholic."

She said, "We serve good coffee, you'll be fine." Then she gave me the same wink she gave me in the bar. I felt a little more comfortable. I did wonder if she somehow already knew.

I stayed at the Doyle in the exact same room on a previous section hike and I must say, Vicky and Frank made a bunch of improvements. The room was freshly painted, the bed wasn't sagging in the middle, the blankets and sheets were clean, and the mattress looked brand new. I settled in and went to the shower which even had hot water.

I returned to the bar all clean and fresh. I met three hikers: Stretch, a tall, young, thin geek; Hitch, a fifty-year-old woman from New Mexico section hiking because she had to abort several thru-hike attempts; and Rickety, a fifty-six-year-old Sobo section hiker. I joined them at their table because they weren't drinking as much as most of the other hikers. I ordered two cheeseburgers and fries, but Vicky suggested I order one at a time because they were so big. Fire Fly recommended I have the pulled pork sandwich, but he was getting extremely drunk. Besides, I had my heart set on a cheeseburger.

Feather attempted a thru-hike last year, but aborted in Pearisburg due to a plantar fascia injury. Feather hooked up with a hiker on the trail last year and hooked up with Fire Fly on the trail this year. Well, last year's partner just walked in and she introduced him to Fire Fly. I thought I would see some drama after an awkward moment of silence. Then Silver Streak, who aborted his thru-hike in the Shenandoah several weeks ago, walked in and announced he was back on the trail, which took the tension off for a while.

Frank brought my cheeseburger and fries out with a cup of fresh coffee. He said the coffee was on the house and gave me the same type of wink Vicky did. I took a big liking to Vicky and Frank. They took a picture of me posing with them behind the bar to hang on the wall along with the pictures of other thru-hikers from the past. The bar was hopping and starting to get rowdy. I ate and remembered how ugly drunks could get, so I vanished into my room upstairs. I wrote in my journal, until I fell asleep.

The room was dark when I awoke, but it wasn't too late, so I went out for pizza. I was walking down the street and heard a female voice yell, "Hiker what's your trail name?"

I turned and said, "Dreamer" to the thirty something year old woman.

She said, "I'm Trail Angel Mary" and gave me a hug.

"Can I buy you a drink, Dreamer?"

I said, "No" and held up my left hand, pointing to my ring.

She replied "I'll be in the bar if you change your mind Dreamer."

I went to the pizza shop as it was about to close. They warmed up two pieces of cold pizza for me. I was disappointed in the pizza, but it was far better than ramen noodles on the trail.

I had to go through the bar to get back to my room. I found Fire Fly getting shitfaced drunk. I had a hard time understanding Fire Fly's Alabama accent when he was sober and he was a long way from sober. Apparently, Feather went out for pizza with her last year's hiking partner. Fire Fly was setting out to get over-the-top-drunk with Trail Angel Mary helping him. I didn't know how the whole thing would play out, but I bet it would suck to be Fire Fly in the morning. I know because, I had nights in my past like the one he was having. I went up stairs and called it a night.

THE DECISION

Day 80   11.4 Miles

I awoke to a cloudy, dry day and ventured across the street to a greasy-spoon type diner for breakfast. I found Rickety already eating, so I joined him. I ordered eggs over easy, sausage, toast, home fries, pancakes, and coffee. Hitch and Stretch soon joined the breakfast club. Stretch only had a credit card, which the diner wouldn't accept, so I bought his breakfast. We all talked and drank coffee for two hours. Hitch started to contemplate aborting her hike due to an ankle injury, so I left before I started to worry about the situation with my knee. I seemed to be able to suck up someone else's fear and negativity like a sponge if I wasn't careful.

I went back to the hotel, saddled up, and rode out of town alone. I crossed the Susquehanna River on Clarks Ferry Bridge and started up the steep, rocky incline. I already hiked out of that valley twice on section hikes, so I had been dreading the climb out of Duncannon. The climb wasn't as bad as I expected. I probably was in better shape because I walked from Georgia. It felt good to be on the trail to dream and meditate once again. My dreams quickly took me back in time to more than twenty years ago.

I had been sober and attending Alcoholics Anonymous for about three years. I was spiritually like Guns and felt God was for the weak. I had already asked a Godly man named Gallagher to be my second Alcoholics Anonymous sponsor to replace Big Jim.

Part of a sponsor's job was to help a sponsee work through the Twelve Steps. I was starting to get to know Gallagher as a sponsor and he asked me to read the Third Step, which said, "We made a decision to turn our will and our lives over to the care of God as we understood him."

He said, "What does that mean to you?"

I replied, "God is for pussies."

Gallagher reminded me of Big Jim when he said, "I didn't ask for your opinion on God, I asked what that step meant to you?"

"Okay it means I have to turn my life over to some mystical character invented by cowards!"

Gallagher, in a calmer voice, "Read it again for me." I read it again. He asked again, "What does that mean to you?"

I answered also in a calmer voice, "It means I have to turn my life over to someone or something I don't believe exists."

"It doesn't say that at all, read it again!"

The process went on repeatedly until I thought we were going to come to blows. Gallagher was about my size and I had gained my strength and weight all back by that time, so I was thinking I could take this guy if he gave me too much shit.

Gallagher must have read my mind and said, "Please, read it just one more time."

I read, "We made a decision..."

He put his hand up like a traffic cop and said, "Stop right there!" I stopped and stared at him for a tense moment.

He broke the silence and said in a soothing voice, "That's what Step Three is all about, simply making a decision. That's all." He went on, "I only want you to think about this." He used the example of going bear hunting, "We could make a decision to go bear hunting right now, but could we actually go bear hunting right now?" He paused a minute and answered his own question, "No, we would have to do some things first to get ready, wouldn't we?"

I nodded in agreement as I said, "We would have to do some things to get ready first."

I could see the excitement in his face as he exclaimed, "Exactly, but what you have to do first is make the decision to go!"

I bought into it and said, "We would have to figure out where to go, when, get guns ready, save money."

He interrupted me in mid-sentence and said, "What we would do next is take an inventory of what we would have to do to carry out the decision we made."

He shared, "Yes, I understand you're having a hard time believing in God. Many of us did at first, including me." He looked me straight in the eyes and almost whispered, "For now, don't worry about the word God, solely concentrate on the words, made a decision."

All my animosity was lost and he had my full attention as I questioned, "Made a decision?"

Gallagher: "But in this case you're not going bear hunting, you're making a decision to turn your self-will over to a power greater than yourself."

I couldn't recall what he said next. I wish I would have paid better attention, but it was lost in time. Gallagher had been dead for many years, so I couldn't ask him.

I usually felt a little melancholy after such a positive experience as being with my friends in Duncannon, but I was looking forward to getting to Port Clinton where I planned to rendezvous with Scooter in four days. I did feel some pressure because Port Clinton was seventy rocky miles away, so I had four hard days of hiking ahead of me. I really didn't like schedules or deadlines.

I stopped near the top of the mountain to cook rice for lunch at Clarks Ferry Shelter. Silver Streak came in and joined me. He was a fifty-one-year-old from Michigan, who had a silver streak in his hair. I apologized for the way I treated him in the Shenandoah when he aborted his thru-hike several weeks ago. He explained he skipped from the Shenandoah to Duncannon, but planned on making it up later. We had a good talk and all was okay between us. He was trying to catch up with Scout, who was somewhere ahead of us.

The trail leveled out after the thousand-foot ascent, but it didn't get easier. I came to what hikers called the knife-edge where millions of years ago, it must have been the bottom of an ocean. Due to some big movement in the earth's crust, the bottom heaved and tipped a thousand feet in the air. I was walking on the edge of a steep slope on one side and an abrupt drop off on the other side. I proceeded with caution because on my first solo section hike, I walked up on a copperhead snake sunning himself on that same ridge. I was okay because I saw him before I stepped on him and gave him some space. I didn't have a phobia towards poisonous snakes, but I developed a good healthy respect for them.

No one was at Peters Mountain Shelter when I arrived, so I set up in my tent a short distance from the shelter and took a nap. I awoke to voices and laughter as the shelter was hopping with excitement. I went over to socialize with Stretch, Silver Streak and the others who were cooking and staying in the shelter. I met Spiritual Pilgrim, who I had been following since Georgia, but that was the first time I caught up to him. We all socialized into the late evening. Things were still going strong when I went back to my tent and called it a night.

Day 81   17.5 Miles

I saddled up to a nice day for a change. I had become used to gray, rainy, Pennsylvania days. I was ready to ride, but my intuition told me to stop at the shelter on my way out of Dodge. Spiritual Pilgrim was making coffee and rolling a cigarette as the others were packing up. Spiritual Pilgrim was an ex-Army Ranger and a real tough guy. He had a touch of gray in his beard which made him look wise. Something else was familiar and friendly, buy I couldn't put my finger on exactly what.

Suddenly it occurred to me he was a brother in recovery, so I said to him, "Are you a friend of Bills?" His face lit up and he picked me up, pack and all, and gave me a big bear hug.

He said, "I have been praying for somebody like you to come my way."

The spiritual bond between us was instant, as only other recovering alcoholics could know. I got my stove out of my pack to make a pot of coffee. We had an Alcoholics Anonymous meeting right there in the middle of the woods. The others didn't understand what was going on.

Silver Streak even asked, "Bill who?"

The question, Are you a friend of Bill's? was a universally known way to be subtle when asking a stranger if they were a fellow recovering alcoholic in the program of Alcoholics Anonymous. If the person asked, Bill who, they weren't.

Spiritual Pilgrim had been going through a dry drunk, which meant he was restless, irritable, and discontent, but stayed sober. He stopped in the town of Carlton for six days and went to meetings and made some Alcoholics Anonymous contact. He was hoping to get back on track. We talked and drank coffee for two hours before we moved on together.

A definite spiritual bond formed between us that Bill W. and Dr. Bob discovered in 1935. I thought of how many recovering alcoholics shared the same bond. God may have had a hand in bringing a rough, tough, Army Ranger named Spiritual Pilgrim into my life at such a critical time. Spiritual Pilgrim too struggled to turn his will over to God. Even the name Spiritual Pilgrim shouted that he was seeking.

We hiked together and talked the entire day, which I hadn't done in the past with anyone except Scooter. Meeting him was such a serendipity; it was as if I got an Alcoholics Anonymous fix. I was so involved in our sharing with one another that seventeen-plus miles flew by in a rush that day.

I was camped in my tent at Raush Gap Shelter with Fire Fly and Feather. The shelter was full with Spiritual Pilgrim, Scout, Silver Streak, and four section hikers. We all had a great time sitting around a fire telling trail tales long into the evening. I felt bombarded with so much spiritual information that I hadn't had time to download it all. Before I went to sleep, I gave thanks to God for being so good to me. I thought, God must have sent another angel by the name of Spiritual Pilgrim my way.

Day 82   17.4 Miles

I started my day earlier than anyone else, so I packed up as quietly as possible. Spiritual Pilgrim woke up and drank tea with me before he hugged me goodbye. We were both out of coffee after the coffee binge of the day before. The tea was decaffeinated, which neither of us cared for. You could trust and believe, I would buy plenty of coffee when I got to town, so I wouldn't ever, ever run out again. I left Spiritual Pilgrim and hiked out alone in the early morning sun. I enjoyed hiking with Spiritual Pilgrim, but I needed the time alone on the trail to digest my thoughts from our hike the day before.

I knew I made many decisions in the past, but never followed through. A decision alone was only words if no action followed up. I wondered when I made the decision to turn my life over to the care of God. Was it on Shuckstack Mountain with Joachim Schubert, with Gallagher when we processed Step Three, or maybe when I quit hanging in the bars and gave up my old life-style? I wasn't sure it even mattered when I made the decision. What probably mattered more was what action I took to follow through with the decision.

The rain started around noon so I stopped in the William Penn Shelter for lunch in a dry place. A six-foot-six, fifty-six-year-old thru-hiker who introduced himself as Sun-Dancer from New Mexico joined me. Soon Fire Fly, Feather, Spiritual Pilgrim, Scout and Silver Streak all piled into the shelter as the storm hit. I made tea and we all had a tea party until the storm passed.

Fire Fly and Feather planned on getting picked up at Five-O-One Shelter and traveling back to Damascus for Hiker Days, which was a famous annual gathering of former thru-hikers and present thru-hikers. I planned on attending Hiker Days the next year to renew the friendships I made on the trail. Silver Streak and Scout were going to hitch into Pine Grove, Pa to a motel for the night. Spiritual Pilgrim, Sun Dancer, and I planned to hike to the Five-O-One Shelter.

The Five-O-one Shelter was a large, four-sided building with doors, which was not typical for Appalachian Trail shelters. The shelter even had a shower outside with hot water. I couldn't have picked a better shelter for a rainy night, but the best thing about it was its location was, a tenth of a mile from the highway. A pizza shop in nearby Pine Grove delivered pizza where the trail crossed the highway. We called on my cell phone and ordered three large pizzas. The three of us walked back to the road and waited until a delivery boy brought us pizza and pop. I bought a large pizza with extra cheese and mushrooms then ate the whole darn thing all by myself. It felt good being in a dry shelter with a full belly as the rain pounded on the metal roof so hard I could hardly hear anyone talking. I drifted off to sleep in a pleasant food coma.

Day 83   23.7 Miles

I slept poorly due to Spiritual Pilgrim's loud snoring. Sun Dancer and I left Spiritual Pilgrim sleeping before daylight. I couldn't keep up with Sun Dancer's long legs, so I soon found myself hiking alone. I twisted an ankle on the rocks on a section hike on the trail ahead many years ago, so I slowed down on the wet rocks to try to prevent another injury. The day would be a long day, because I had to hike twenty-four miles to meet my bride in Port Clinton. I planned to stop often and eat a lot for the extra energy, besides, I had no reason to save any food.

Spiritual Pilgrim mentioned the Third Step Prayer previously. I had read and said it many times, but not for a long time. When I stopped to eat, I took the time and got out my little big book and looked up the prayer which said, "God, I offer myself to thee-to build with me and to do with me as Thou wilt. Relieve me of the bondage of self, that I may better do Thy will. Take away my difficulties, that victory over them may bear witness to those I would help of Thy Power, Thy Love, and Thy Way of life. May I do Thy will always." I read it aloud and pondered what it meant. I thought the Alcoholics Anonymous slogan, let go and let God, summed it up so a simple, even a dumb addict like me, could understand Step Three better.

The day was gray and it sprinkled rain at times, but was relatively dry. I hiked alone with few distractions from my thoughts about my decision. The trail was mostly twenty-four, hard, rocky miles to Port Clinton, but nothing spectacular. I called Scooter on the last ridge to tell her where I was and I might not have tower when I descended into Port Clinton. She was two hours or more away and would meet me at the town pavilion where the other hikers planned to spend the night.

I was going down the mountain into Port Clinton when Scout caught up to me a half-hour before dark. She said the others were close behind. We hiked the last half-mile together and then went to the only restaurant in town. The resturant was packed and the hostess wouldn't let us in because we stunk. She said we could eat in the bar instead. We waited outside for the others to arrive, so we all could go in the bar together. Soon Spiritual Pilgrim, Scout, Silver Streak, Sun Dancer, a Sobo named Fast Track and I all piled our packs on the porch of the bar and went inside to eat. The bar was also packed and extremely smoky. I sat between Spiritual Pilgrim and Scout, but Silver Streak, Sun Dancer, and Fast Track had to sit on the other side of the bar because there wasn't room to sit with us. The place was so busy it seemed like forever before we got to order. I was glad I was with Spiritual Pilgrim, so neither one of us was tempted to drink. We all ordered giant cheeseburgers and I bought a platter of fries to share with Scout and Spiritual Pilgrim.

We were eating when Scooter walked in. She went to the pavilion and found no one was there, so she went to the restaurant where the hostess told her we were in the bar. She saw all our packs on the front porch, so she came in and found me at the bar. She tapped hard on my shoulder, trying to be obnoxious. I turned around with an attitude expecting some drama from a drunk and there stood my Scooter. I was so happy to see her that I grabbed her to hug her and she winced in pain. She had put her back out last week and drove six hours in pain to meet me. I finished eating as fast as I could and we left.

We gave Spiritual Pilgrim a ride back to the pavilion. The others were going to stay in the bar and drink for a while. I asked Spiritual Pilgrim if he would be okay alone and he reassured me he would be fine. Scooter and I left to find a motel where I could get a hot shower and a clean bed. It was great to see Scooter, but I wished she wouldn't have driven that far to see me with a bad back.

May 20   Day 84   Zero miles

Our first stop was Dunkin Donuts for coffee with a shot of espresso, then to McDonald's for breakfast and more coffee. After we drank a great deal of coffee, we both talked at the same time. I posed the question, "What is God's will?"

She paused, looking at me with a puzzled look and said, "What?"

I asked, "How do you know what is God's will?"

She shared, "The Holy Spirit lets me know."

That started a long and intimate discussion about separating God's will from our will. We also discussed turning our will over to God. The conversation brought us closer spiritually as a couple. To my surprise, she has been attending church with my daughters on a regular basis ever since I was on the trail.

I came up with the conclusion that Jesus Christ and the Bible focused on how to turn my life over to the care of God. I was still skeptical because I thought religions and individuals often interpreted the Bible. The problem I saw with both individuals and religions was their beliefs influenced their advice.

The Twelve Steps were a set of suggested principles on how to seek to understand God's will. They were our instructions on how to make contact and form a personal relationship with God. The Holy Spirit would let me know what was right or what was wrong if I was open to listening. They were suggestions only, so my ego still had a choice and a person could certainly be a member of Alcoholics Anonymous and stay sober without ever working all of the Steps. I had known long-time members who stayed sober for incredible amounts of time who worked Step One and part of Step Twelve.

The next stop we made was Walmart, where I bought a hundred and five dollars worth of supplies to fill my hiker box. Scooter would take the box home and send me the supplies when I need them on the trail.

We passed a coin laundry on the way to Walmart, so I stopped on the way back to wash my dirty clothes. Scooter came in with me, but a gentleman lit up a raunchy cigar. Scooter had to leave for some fresh air and I swear I intended to put up with the smoke while I washed my clothes. I did well until, as I was putting my clean clothes in a dryer, he came over to use the dryer next to me exhaling smoke in my face. The next few seconds were a little fuzzy in the sense that I didn't remember exactly what I said or how I said it. Somehow, he got the impression I was going to check his prostate with his cigar. The poor fellow ran out of the Laundromat all wild-eyed like the place was on fire. I didn't see hide nor hair of him again until I noticed him sneaking back to get his clothes as I was leaving the parking lot.

We decided to check out the new Cabela's which was only six miles from the Appalachian Trail. We stopped at the shelter on our way by to see if we could give anyone a ride, but my friends had all left. I felt the familiar sense of loss in the pit of my stomach as I wondered if I would ever catch up with any of them again. We found Cabela's overwhelming with so much stuff. We looked all over, but I only bought Delarme's book of maps for Vermont and New Hampshire.

We checked into a room at a better motel to rest Scooter's back. I went back to Walmart by myself to pick up the things I forgot the first time, while she stayed at the motel to rest her back. I felt bad she came all the way to see me with such an injured back. She didn't tell me about her back injury ahead of time because she knew I wouldn't want her to travel when she was hurting.

Scooter said she felt better after resting and wanted to get out, so we went back to Cabela's for supper, and I bought a new tent. We went back to the motel and spent a quiet evening with each other. I finished my twelfth week on the trail, hiking a hundred miles closer to Mount Katahdin.

Day 85   15.2 Miles

We went to Dunkin Donuts again for coffee with a shot of espresso, then to breakfast at 3C's Restaurant. I ate three eggs, toast, and home fries while Scooter had oatmeal. We went back to Cabela's to buy another tent for Scooter. I also bought a Maine Delarme to send home with Scooter, so she could give me directions by phone when I got to Maine.

To my delight, we met Julie Ann and her dog, Thor. I hadn't seen Julie Ann since that ice-cold night in the Smoky Mountains on the fourteenth of March. She picked up the trail name of Clothes Pin, but abandoned her thru-hike and started skipping large sections of the trail. I didn't give her time to try to convince me it was okay to skip sections and still be a thru-hiker. I bid her good luck and good-bye.

Scooter drove me back to the trail and decided to walk a mile with me to loosen her back up for the trip home. We bumped into a swishy, grandiose section-hiker wearing a skirt and speaking with a lisp, by the name of Sugar Foot. He was telling us how much he knew about hiking. I probably could have learned something from him, but I found him annoying and blocked him out.

Scooter assured me her back loosened up some and she would be okay as she bid me goodbye. I still worried about her back being okay on the six-hour drive. I always felt a little down when she left for home.

The day was cold, clear, and perfect for hiking. I took my time over the rocks, hiking solo with my thoughts as I ascended the mountain out of the Schuylkill River Valley. I turned the music up on my MP3 player and enjoyed the miles. I started contemplating what would happen if I completely turned my will over to God. What would God do with me? Would I become a monk on some mountain in Tibet? I liked being me. An awesome view at Pulpit Rock distracted me from my thoughts for a moment. I looked over the land below and thought, maybe serving the creator of all this would be an honor. I continued on the trail pondering what my life would be like after I turned my will over to the care of God.

I hiked a couple miles until I came to a side trail leading to another overlook. I took the trail to a place called The Pinnacle for a break. I felt so confused I prayed for understanding while I gazed at God's landscape. I moved on again feeling relieved to have left the ball in God's hands with the prayer.

I hiked to Eckville Shelter, which was another four-sided shelter with a door. It was like a bunkroom which slept eight. The shelter was a good place to be because the temperature was going to be in the low thirty's that night. The rocky trail of the day didn't do my low back, knees, and ankles any good, but I felt okay.

I said an un-Christian type word when the door flew open and there stood Sugar Foot. He came in and soon filled the air with unsolicited advice as he set up in the lower bunk across the shelter. I wasn't in the mood to put up with a know-it-all right then. I put on my headphones with some soft music, turned up loud enough to drown out Sugar Foot's constant jabbering. I took out my Big Book, opened it and pretended to start to read, hoping he would take the hint. The bookmark was still at the Third Step Prayer, so I read the prayer over a couple of times. The excerpt, Relieve me of the bondage of self, kept popping out to me.

I was amazed my strategy worked and Sugar Foot busied himself reading something of his own. I left the book open as if I was still reading, but closed my eyes in thought and meditation. I pondered on the phrase, relieve me of the bondage of self. I wondered, what exactly did Bill mean, by bondage of self in the prayer? Self, was it my self-will or ego? My perception of my ego was the self-part of me, which told me I was uniquely different from everyone else, including God. My ego was the birthplace of my self-will and gave me permission to do what I wanted to do. I wondered if I was I asking to be relieved of my ego. Sigmund Freud said, "The Ego in psychoanalytic theory is the portion of the human personality which is experienced as self or I and is in contact with the external world through perception."

Maybe Adam invented ego in the Garden of Eden when he ate the apple from the tree of knowledge. Adam's ego discovered he had a choice between his will and God's will. He chose his will and did what he wanted to do, thus he invented sin. I started to plot if I ran across Adam in heaven I would sucker punch him for inventing sin.

My ego was a God given gift where my ambitions to pursue money, property, prestige, social status, and even sexual interests came from. My ego gave me the drive to explore new and different ideas such as quitting my job and hiking the Appalachian Trail. It also caused me to set boundaries with others that protected my family and me. On the other side of the same coin, my ego was the breeding ground for anger, resentment, envy, jealousy, greed, fear, animosity, anxiety, despair, loneliness, and the list went on. My need to try to control situations and other people also stemmed from my ego. I looked back over my life and discovered every time I hurt someone else, I was pursuing my own self-will. I know that like Adam, it was always my ego or self-will that caused me to do stupid shit that I often regretted. My ego or self-will was what led me into the dark hell of addiction. I wish I could have fired my ego, but I couldn't, so maybe that was why we ask God to relieve us of the bondage of self.

I glanced over at Sugar Foot and he seemed to be preoccupied with whatever he was reading so I took the opportunity to call my daughter, Phyllis. I quietly made final arrangements to rendezvous with her at Delaware Water Gap. We scheduled to meet five days and seventy-two miles away on the twenty-sixth of May. We would hike together to Culver's Gap in New Jersey.

I realized I needed to slow down or else I would get there and have to wait for her in a strange town, which was good news because the trail between here and the New Jersey border was some of the hardest fields of broken rocks dropped by the glaciers of prehistoric times I had faced so far. I considered it good not to have to hurry.

I tried to keep my voice down, but Sugar Foot still overheard our conversation. He started to give me all kinds of advice on how to hike with a new hiker. He meant well and had some good advice, so I adjusted my attitude and almost enjoyed his company while I cooked rice and beans with tuna for supper. I listened to him without getting a word in for the rest of the evening. The temperature dropped, so I put on all the clothes I had and jumped into my sleeping bag to stay warm. I put on my headphones, dropped in a Kataro CD, and turned up the music. I might have fallen asleep as he chatted away, which may have seemed rude, but I didn't think he noticed. Besides, the only other alternative I could see was to kill him.

Day 86   13.8 Miles

I awoke when Sugar Foot quietly packed up before daylight. I pretended I was still asleep so he couldn't tell me how to do things. He finally left before my bladder gave out. I waited until I thought he was out of sight before I jumped up and went outside to relieve myself. It was so cold outside that I got back in the sleeping bag and called Scooter. She made it home safely the day before and her back wasn't any worse. I took my time and made an extra cup of coffee before I ventured out.

The high point of the day was in the morning when I saw a timber rattler sunning on the trail. I thought that was odd because the temperature was still in the low fifties. I was grateful he was moving slowly and not a threat as I passed. I took my time on the rocks and stopped for lunch at the Allentown Shelter. I read the register. Spiritual Pilgrim wrote that he fell two times on the rocks the day before and cut his arm badly. I hoped his injury wasn't severe enough to knock him off the trail. I stopped to set up camp by myself at New Tripoli Campsite. The campsite was about a half mile off trail, but it had lots of water. Scooter and I camped there several years ago with our friends, Crow and Maryann.

I had some time to myself to think earlier in the day on Pennsylvania's rocky trail. The will of society seemed to be the topic for the afternoon. I believed societies also had wills. They made rules and laws to maintain their particular society, which was why we formed police and armies to protect and enforce the will of our society. We built prisons to isolate or segregate people from society who committed crimes that went against society. The rules of society haven't always been fair because the self-will of the person or political party in power created the laws. Societies often made laws based on fear to protect itself or those in power. History taught us the rules for some societies were rigid and grossly unfair.

We as a society of colonists, fought England to gain our freedom from the unfair rules and taxes their society imposed on our society. That was why in America, our forefathers set up the Constitution so we the people could decide the rules of our society. My self-will could take priority and supersede the will of society. Years ago, I chose to defy the laws of our society, but I had to face the consequences. I was in constant fear of the consequences for the decisions I was making, such as fines, costs, and incarceration. After I sobered up, I made a conscious choice to comply with the will of society so I could escape the paranoia that went with breaking the law.

Jesus said, "Give to Caesar what is Caesar's," so I thought maybe God wanted me to follow society's laws. Besides, I never liked jail.

I made a new kind of macaroni and cheese and some trail apple cobbler for supper. Both were new experiments that I wouldn't try again. I didn't have cell tower, so I felt a little isolated. The next day I would be in the town of Palmerton, so I had no need to conserve food. Therefore, I medicated my boredom and loneliness with a peanut butter and jelly bagel. I wrote in my journal and read the Big Book until my mind settled down. I then put on my headphones with soft music and drifted off to sleep.

Day 87   11.8 Miles

It was so cold I froze in my light sleeping bag during the night. I ate bagels smothered with peanut butter and jelly in the wee hours of the morning to generate enough body heat to stay warm. I managed to fall back asleep until after daylight. I started my stove and made coffee in my tent to warm up. I sure wished I still had my winter sleeping bag. I ate all my mini-bagels and most of my peanut butter and jelly before I packed up. I didn't need to save food since I was only hiking twelve hard trail miles to Palmerton.

I carefully took my time on the rocks because I didn't want to risk an injury. Again, I marveled at Pennsylvania's surprisingly awesome vistas from the cliffs. On a previous section hike, I climbed up Bear Rocks for the view, but this time I passed in silence because I already saw the view from the top. I felt blessed as bright sun warmed me, which I was especially grateful for after the nighttime's cold temperatures. I hiked three or four miles to another vista overlooking the farms in the valleys below at Bake Oven Knob about mid morning. I stopped on the exposed rocks the sun warmed to make a pot of strong coffee. I started to meditate in God's tranquil atmosphere while I let the sun and warm rocks take away the chill in my old bones.

I had been pondering the Third Step ever since I left the Doyle Hotel. I thought again about how I could turn my will and my life over to the care of God. What did God want? If God didn't want me to have self-will, why did he give me an ego in the first place? I wonder if God ever asked himself, "Why did I give mankind self-will in the first place?" The Serenity Prayer said, "God grant me the serenity to accept the things I cannot change." I have accepted that I have a self-serving ego and I would keep it until I die, because I couldn't change it. I couldn't fire my ego and I surly didn't want to commit suicide to try to get rid of my ego either. Besides, who said you no longer had an ego after you were dead? I always thought one day I would turn everything over to God and I would live happily forever after. I got frustrated because I said the Third Step Prayer and turned my will over to God, and then took my will back. The problem was my self-will stepped back in and took over again. I remembered the preacher's words, "We are all sinners." Maybe ego was what he was talking about on those Sunday mornings many years ago. I popped open my little Big Book to page sixty and read, "Many of us exclaimed, what an order, I can't go through with it. Do not be discouraged. No one among us has maintained anything like perfect adherence to these principles. We are not saints. The point is we are willing to grow along spiritual lines. The principles we have set down are guides to progress. We claim spiritual progress not spiritual perfection." I decided to turn it over to God in prayer and listen for the answer.

I realized I had cell tower, so I called Lady D in Florida as I drank coffee. I always admired the spiritual quality of her recovery. She was one of the people who knew about my dream of being a thru-hiker way ahead of time and encouraged me to pursue the adventure. I would never forget when I told her I was trying to decide if I should attempt a thru-hike. She said, "Go ahead; God was the one who put the idea of thru-hiking in your head in the first place." I asked her about God's will. She was a Christian and went to church consistently. We talked for forty-five minutes and she was great support and still inspired me to continue my spiritual journey. I did believe God had always played an active role in my life as a provider, motivator, protector, and maybe an initiator also. I thought of the people I admired who were close to me like my Mom, Heaven Bound, Scooter, Lady D and my daughters. They all went to church, so maybe the Holy Spirit was trying to tell my dumb ass, something.

Many people turned to the various religions for interpretation of God's will for them. We as a nation have freedom of religion, which may be the reason we have many different religions in America. Religions were always a society, so they also set rules and guidelines based on their particular beliefs. They hired preachers, priests, rabbis, etcetera to teach the rules of their religion or theology. Religions didn't often agree with each other because they formed a society that wasn't God, but what they thought God should be. Sometimes, differences in religious views bread animosity towards one another. Throughout history, religions fought wars with each other over differences in religious theology. Religions like any society, also made rules based on fear to protect them. I believe one of the justifications to crucify Jesus Christ was fear based. I thought the rigid-thinking religious people of the day who believed they were God's chosen people, feared Christ so they crucified him. I first thought Bill Wilson used the phrase, God as we understood him, to include all the religions. As I gained a better understanding myself, I realized maybe he only wanted to allow folks to think and meet God for themselves. I picked up my pack and moved on towards Palmerton with a new curiosity about church.

Again, I found myself on Pennsylvania's knife-edge. As I said previously, my theory was before humans existed, layers of sediment settled on the bottom of an ancient sea. Over time, the sediment turned into stone and for some reason movement in the earth's crust heaved these layers of flat stone up to create the knife-edge. Much of the trail since Duncannon ran along the edge, which made for slow travel. I had to choose each step carefully, because the knife-edge sloped steeply on my left and dropped abruptly far enough on my right that a fall could kill me.

I joined a first-time hiker from Philadelphia eating lunch at Outerbridge Shelter. I decided to stop and chat before I descended the rest of the way into the Lehigh River Valley. He was drinking unfiltered water straight out of the spring, so I filtered some water for him and gave him some iodine tablets for later. He fired questions at me as fast as I could answer them. I wasn't sure if I admired him for his moxie or thought he was foolish for taking on this section of the Appalachian Trail at Lehigh Gap alone for his first hike. I gave him my best advice for quite a while then gave him the trail name, Tenderfoot before I left. I enjoyed the encounter and left Tenderfoot with what food I had left, since I planned to re-supply in Palmerton.

I left the woods and was immediately confronted by the buzzing of rush hour traffic. I decided not to hitch because cars couldn't safely stop on the busy highway. I started to walk two miles into Palmerton beside the four-lane highway. The road cut through solid rock leaving only a little room to walk on the shoulder. I was squeezed between the rock and heavy traffic when an older lady passed me and stopped down the road at a little pull off. I was approaching her car when she got out, put her hand on her hip, and said, "You get in this car right now before you get run over on this road!" I got in the car relieved to be safe. She was a breath of sunshine and talked nonstop while she drove me straight to the police station. I thanked her while I wondered if she was an angel sent to pick me up for my protection.

The police station was where I checked in for a free, one-night's stay at the Jailhouse Hostel. The hostel was in the basement of the old police station, hence the name. The city manager gave me a care package the local girl scouts put together for thru-hikers, which included toilet paper, a granola bar, a phone card, a post card, toothpaste, and a toothbrush. I felt honored.

The city manager drove me two blocks to the old police station, which looked more like an old school. The city still used several offices and an old gym to play basketball. I followed him down an old wooden stairwell with ornate oak railings to the basement. An old-time boiler was running, which kept the place nice and warm. He said I could hang things on a line to dry that stretched across the low ceiling for that purpose. We exited the boiler room through a hole made in the wall by crudely busting out the cement blocks, and entered a rather large room they called the hostel. Parts of old parade floats and other debris I suspect had been stored there for years by the city occupied half of the room. The other half the Boy Scouts built enough bunks to sleep twelve hikers. I settled in a bottom bunk and put the rest of my gear on the top bunk in case more hikers arrived, I had dibs on the top bunk. I didn't want anyone sleeping above me. I hoped at least one more hiker would stop for the night. I didn't want to spend the night alone there because the place reminded me of a setting for a nightmare-causing horror movie.

I got hungry, so I ventured out into the village to forage for food.

I ate a large pizza at a local family-run pizza shop. I went to the local IGA to re-supply while my belly was still full so I didn't buy more than I could carry. They gave me a free apple just because I was a thru-hiker. I went back to the hostel and found it locked with everything I owned inside. I panicked a little, but managed to find the janitor to let me in, so it wasn't a big deal. The janitor showed me how I could leave a door unlocked in the basement so I didn't lock myself out again. He also showed me where I could charge my cell phone batteries. I took a hot shower in an old-time open shower room while we chatted. I felt a little self-conscious. I just hoped he wasn't gay and out window-shopping.

I went back out to find a laundry mat and washed my clothes. I talked to folks back home on the phone while I waited for my clothes to dry. I couldn't find anything else to do in town so I bought four hot dogs for a bedtime snack and returned to the hostel. I had the hostel all to myself, which was a little spooky. The register indicated all my friends stayed there the night before. I found the hiker box and took two freeze-dried vacuum-packed gourmet meals and left some things I could do without for the next hiker.

I finished entering in my daily journal from the comfort of my sleeping bag. I took off my glasses, closed my journal, and reminded myself I would be sober twenty-six years on May twenty-fifth, which was only two days away. At first I didn't think I could stay sober over a couple of weeks, let alone twenty-six years. Alcoholics Anonymous meetings acknowledged the anniversary of everyone who got sober in that given month on the last meeting of the month. I was impressed when members would celebrate from one year to as many as fifty some years. Everyone would clap and the meeting gave them a certificate indicating the number of years. They would pass the certificate around for everyone present to sign. Some folks wrote short affirmations of encouragement and congratulations on the back.

That simple ceremony was encouraging because it gave me the hope that one day, I could stay sober a year and receive my own certificate. I remember how proud I was when that first May finally rolled around and I received a one-year certificate of sobriety. My last thoughts as

I drifted off to sleep were about how great it would be to be sober twenty-six years.

Day 88   15.8 Miles

I shivered as I ventured out in the early morning fog. I ate four eggs and three blueberry pancakes with coffee at Burt's Diner. The sun was busy burning off the last of the fog as I returned to the hostel to pack up. The city manager stopped on his way to the office and offered to take me back to the trail. I wasn't looking forward to walking back on the busy four-lane highway, so I took him up on his offer. On the ride we talked about his aspirations to hike someday. He dropped me off, I shook his hand and sincerely thanked him for all his personal hospitality and told him Palmerton was one of the most hiker-friendly trail towns I have had the pleasure of staying in so far.

I faced Lehigh Gap for the fourth time in my hiking career, which was the steepest climb that far south. I ascended almost nine-hundred feet in less than my first mile. What made the climb unique was smelting from the zinc mines killed the vegetation on the ascent out of the river valley, which exposed the bare rocks on the side of the mountain to the weather. The view of the valley below was fantastic because it was unencumbered by the usual trees and vegetation. The cars crossing the Lehigh River on the bridge looked like little ants. The scary part was you could also see how far you would fall with no trees to catch you on the way down. That made it easy for hikers to embellish the dangers of Lehigh Gap around the campfire, so you would have plenty of time to think about the dangerous climb before you ever got to it. I tied my hiking poles to my pack and used my hands to find hand holds to climb a short distance. I had no problems with the challenge, but still found the ascent intimidating. I stopped at the top and took a picture of myself overlooking the valley below, so I could give the Sobos something to contemplate as they headed south.

I only carried a half a liter of water out of Palmerton to cut my pack weight. The guidebook indicated a spring called Metallica was at the top of Lehigh Gap, but I couldn't find it anywhere. The next spring, according to the guidebook, was another five miles away and unreliable.

I didn't like the situation, but I had little choice other than hike on with no water. I arrived at the next spring, which was three tenths of a mile down the steep mountainside. I was thirsty so I made my way down the mountain. It would be hard to describe the disappointment I experienced when I found the spring was dry as a bone. I had to ascend back to my pack on the trail to check the guidebook. The next spring was two miles north and six-tenths of a mile off trail. I hiked on as fear started to form in the pit of my stomach. Two trail miles seemed as if it was a lot farther when I was in a hurry, motivated by thirst. I wasn't surprised when I reached a sign only saying, "Water," that pointed down a steep, rocky, trail.

I pondered my situation. The next water source was over four miles away. The terrain was rocky and tough. On the other hand, six tenths down and six tenths back up equaled a hard one point two mile climb with no guarantee of any water. I had no idea if I was in danger or not since I was never in a previous predicament where I considered water that critical. My fear helped me decide to stash my pack in the woods and descend with only my empty water bottles, my water filter, my money, my cell phone, and pepper spray. I was praying all the way down to the spring. God was good and rewarded me with a nice little pool of fresh, ice-cold, spring water. I got down on my knees and gave thanks before I drank. The cold, sweet, water was the best I have ever tasted on a hot, dry day. I drank all I could possibly drink and then filled both water bottles. Back home, I could go to the sink and get all the water I wanted by turning a faucet, but I was never grateful. The trail taught me to be grateful and not take the little things I needed to live for granted.

When I climbed back to the trail, I was exhausted and considered setting up my tent for the night. I decided to get out my sleeping mat, lie down, and rest a little while instead. The next thing I knew it was two hours later. I packed up, hydrated and refreshed, so I hiked four miles farther to the Leroy Smith Shelter. The shelter was a long two-tenths of a mile off trail. I arrived to find a pack, mattress, and sleeping bag set out, so I yelled, "Is anybody home," but no one answered.

I was contemplating going a half a mile to the spring when the owner of the gear came up from the spring. Low and behold, it was Cedar Moe! I couldn't believe my eyes. It was so good to see him. Cedar Moe was a Christian from Tennessee. He and I became friends in the Smoky Mountains where times were hard, which made strong friendships. A Brown Recluse spider bit him, so he had to take time off the trail to heal. I thought he aborted his hike at Hot Springs, North Carolina and I would never see him again. He took three weeks off, but returned to the trail as soon as he could hike. I should have known a man like Cedar Moe wouldn't let a little spider bite knock him off the trail for long.

Cedar Moe and I were cooking our supper and catching up when a stranger with four pit bull dogs on leashes showed up. I thought the man may have been a paranoid schizophrenic. He gave us a lecture on nuclear waste, depleted uranium, the evil President Bush, and how bad the Bush Administration was for the environment. Cedar Moe humored him by listening, but I stayed silent and close to my pepper spray. I read the shelter register, as the man continued his tirade. According to the register, the man came to the shelter every day and promoted his cause to any hiker in the shelter.

After the whacko finally left, I tried to convince Cedar Moe to move on with me, but Cedar Moe didn't have a tent and the next shelter was too far. I wasn't going to leave Cedar Moe by himself, so I made a pot of tea while we continued to chat. I was always attracted to positive folks like Cedar Moe, but I had a deeper admiration for him since he overcame such adversity. I had met only a handful of people of his caliber in my lifetime.

A crap load of section hikers showed up about half an hour before dark. The shelter came alive with laughter and chaos as they all scrambled for room in the shelter. I thought it was crowded enough to be safe for Cedar Moe, so I packed up and moved on to be by myself.

I set up my tent in a secluded setting in the woods out of view from the trail where I felt safe from the whacko. I made another pot of tea and sat up against a tree reflecting on the twenty-fourth of May twenty-six years ago.

On the twenty-fourth of May 1980, I awoke or I should say "came to," at about four o'clock in the morning, dope sick, and suffering with the shakes. I must have passed out early the day before from consuming too much drugs and alcohol.

I had nothing to use to get well. I found the last eight dollars in change left from my income tax return and the retirement check that I cashed on January the eighteenth, when I quit my job. The bars didn't open until seven o'clock in the morning, so I had three long hours of being dope sick to think about my miserable life of addiction. I weighed one-hundred and twenty-five pounds and hadn't been able to eat any solid food in months. The sad truth was the most nutritious thing I had been putting in my body in a long time was beer and whisky. I was using drugs and alcohol from pass out to pass out. I didn't go to sleep any longer, I would pass out and piss my pants.

I sat next to the tree physically comfortable, but emotionally, I could recall the hopeless feeling of being all alone. In a drunken rampage the week before, I alienated the few friends I had left. The girlfriend I had been staying with asked one of her friends to talk to me and I broke his nose badly with my fist. She asked one of my life long drinking buddies to talk to me and I banged on his head. He didn't fight back out of respect, which made me feel even worse. I did some things I would always regret. I probably did even more things I have no memory of due to the many blackouts I suffered.

My girlfriend gave me an ultimatum to go to detox or get out of her apartment. I checked into St. Vincent detox, but left against medical advice after three days. I was drunk again the same day. At that point in my addiction, getting high was no longer fun. I was using to feel normal and to cope with the terrible withdrawal symptoms. The withdrawal was so bad, I thought I would surly die without my drugs and alcohol.

I contemplated committing suicide most of the time when I wasn't extremely high. I was mostly atheistic at the time. However, I thought if God did exist I would go to hell for how I lived. About the only thing that kept me from blowing my brains out was my unwillingness to take the chance that I would get stuck in a worse spot than life for eternity any sooner than I had to go. My life was already hell. Looking back, I could see the reason I felt all alone was the fact I was spiritually bankrupt. I replaced my childhood God who I feared with the chemicals that destroyed my whole being and even they were abandoning me.

I waited until six-forty-five that morning to leave for Nick's Tavern because I didn't want to be too early and have to stand outside with the bums waiting for Nick to open. I didn't want anyone to think I was that desperate.

That day was a beautiful spring day with the promise of being a hot, pleasant day. I was going up the hill on Capp Road. The sun was in my eyes and I thought it would be a great day to go fishing on the fingers of Edinboro Lake like I did when I was a kid. I would go out looking like ivory soap and come back looking like a red lobster. A sudden realization came over me that hit me like a sucker punch. I started to cry not only a few tears, but hysterically like a little child. I couldn't go fishing or anything else I wanted to do because I had to get drunk to survive. I was no longer my own man. I was a slave to my addiction, which had become my god.

I finished my pot of tea and decided to make another pot. I sat by the same tree with a full pot of tea and returned to my trance-like state of reflection on twenty-six years earlier.

I arrived at Nick's Tavern at precisely seven o'clock and went in as inconspicuously as possible and bought two six packs of cheap, sixteen ounce beers for four dollars. I returned to my car to drink because I knew from experience, I would puke out the first couple of beers. After I got a beer to stay down, I went back into the bar and bought a double shot of bar whisky, a long neck bottle of Iron City, one more six-pack of cheep beer, and a pack of smokes. I was then officially broke until I talked someone at the bar into lending me five dollars for gas. I spent my retirement and income tax return along with everything else I could borrow or steal on drugs and alcohol since the eighteenth of January of that year.

I rode around drinking my beer. I didn't know why, but that day I couldn't get lost in an alcohol induced fantasy world, nor could I get that all was well with the world feeling. My alcohol had lost its magic. My love of my life, Miss Alcohol, dumped me cold or it probably would be more appropriate to say my alcohol-god had forsaken me.

I rode around until I got low on gas. I then borrowed twenty dollars from an old girlfriend. I bought more beer and gas to drive around some more. I didn't black out that day as I usually did back then, but I actually did some rational thinking while drinking about eight, six-packs of beer. I knew I had only two choices left, quit drinking, or die. I finished my last beer at exactly twenty-three hundred hours on May twenty-forth, 1980.

I finished the last of my tea. Darkness had set in quite some time ago. I felt a chill to the night air, but I didn't think it was the reason I had goose bumps all over. I got down on my knees and gave thanks to God. I tried my best to express my gratitude to Him for loving me even when I was unlovable. I retired to my warm sleeping bag and ended one more day of sobriety.

Day 89   13.8 Miles
My Sobriety Anniversary

The morning sun awoke me by shining through the trees onto my tent, making me happy I was alive, sober, and on the journey of a lifetime. I got to celebrate twenty-six years of continuous, uninterrupted sobriety on the trail. Things were sure different than they were twenty-six years before when I quit drinking. I got sober by the grace God advanced to me. I never knew why God picked me because I never felt I deserved it, but I was grateful.

I made a pot of extra strong coffee and enjoyed the early morning sun. I sat up against the same tree as I did the night before, reflecting on the day that marked the first positive change in my life, the day I sobered up, May twenty-fifth, 1980.

I didn't sleep that night because I was going through withdrawal, shaking like a dog shitting barbed wire. I was so sick, I thought about going out and getting some dope to make me well, but I had no more money and no gas in my car. One minute I was afraid I would die and the next minute I was hoping I would die. I had a gun and was seriously considering using it to end my pain. I was financially, physically, emotionally, and spiritually bankrupt.

I had given up on God many years before, but in desperation I prayed a fox hole prayer as a last ditch effort. I got on my knees and said "Dear God, if you are out there, if you exist, I need your help." Nothing magical happened, so I thought I had been right all those years; there was no God and never was.

I was feeling sorry for myself when someone knocked on the door. I instantly became paranoid, thinking it was the cops. I peeked out a window as surreptitiously as possible. To my relief, it was the old girlfriend who I borrowed the twenty dollars from the day before. I let her in and she convinced me to call Threshold, which was a non-medical, inpatient detox/rehab.

A man named Smoky answered the phone. I knew Smoky from some of the Alcoholics Anonymous meetings I attended in the past. He suggested, I go to the hospital and get a shot of Valium, then check myself in for twenty-eight days. I didn't want any part of the rehab, but the shot of Valium sounded good. The girl tried her best to persuade me to go to hospital until I got annoyed with her and ran her off with my gun. I was going to shoot her and myself, but she talked me out of it.

I curled up on the couch in the fetal position afraid I was going to have a seizure any minute. I heard the door open, but didn't get up because I thought it was the girl returning. I suddenly realized my father was standing over me. I was extremely shaky, but I managed to sit up as Dad sat down beside me and said in a calm voice, "Please, let me help you."

We rode to the hospital in silence. I had a déjà vu feeling. I realized it had been almost ten years since Dad came up to New York to bail me out of jail. Nothing had changed except things had progressively gotten worse. I put my Dad through a lot in those last ten years. I embarrassed and disappointed him many times. I also stole from him on occasion to buy drugs and alcohol. I was sure I pissed him off many times, yet he still loved me unconditionally.

We went to the emergency room and a nurse talked to me first. I told her I was an alcoholic going through withdrawal and I needed a shot of Valium before I had a seizure. I waited what seemed like forever and finally an imported Doctor from India, Pakistan, or somewhere, entered the room.

Speaking in broken English he asked me, "What the problem?"

I was so scared I was starting to panic, so I took a deep breath, stayed calm, and said, "I'm an alcoholic going through withdrawal and I want to quit drinking, but I need a shot of valium so I don't have a seizure. Then I will check into Threshold."

He said, "How much you drink?"

I panicked; I grabbed him by his lab coat and pulled him up to my face so fast our heads bumped. I yelled in desperation, "I need a shot of Valium right Fucking now!"

His eyes were as big as saucers, his lips were about two inches from mine, and he yelled at the nurse, "25MILLAGRAMSVALIUMRIGHTFUCKINGNOW!"

I immediately let go of him and started apologizing. I was hoping they wouldn't call the cops.

He kept patting my knee and nodding his head saying, "Understand, understand."

We both calmed down. I got the shot of valium, which calmed me down even more. He also gave me a prescription for ten Librium capsules to take as needed. I gave him a big hug and we parted friends.

I thought I had better eat, so I swallowed my pride and asked Dad if he would buy me a cheeseburger. We went to McDonald's and Dad bought two cheeseburgers and two milkshakes. He paid with a twenty and gave me the change. It was a humbling experience to be asking Dad for a handout when I was twenty-nine years old, but I knew I had only a small window of opportunity to eat before the Valium wore off and I would be sick again.

That was all the memory I had of my first day sober. I presume Dad took me back home and I stayed sick, but my recollection of the rest of the day was somehow totally erased from my memory. I might have gone into the Delirium Tremens, but no one was around to be a witness. I had Delirium Tremens on two previous occasions, but I didn't remember them either. I only knew because there were people around who told me all about it later.

That was what it was like for me on the twenty-fifth of may in 1980. That was where I ended up, by pouring drugs and alcohol into the God-shaped hole in my sole.

I found myself enjoying the state of reflection I was in so I decided to make another pot of coffee and enjoy my own company for a little while longer before I moved on.

I remembered a joke Gallagher told to me so many years ago about a town being flooded. The town's people all climbed on their roofs to escape the fast rising floodwaters.

A preacher man started to pray to God for help. Later a rowboat came along, but the preacher refused to get in and motioned them on to a group of children on a nearby roof. He continued to pray. Soon a second rowboat approached, but once again, the preacher waved them on to a family on another roof. The waters continued to rise and a helicopter lowered a basket. The preacher had faith God would save him, so he pointed to an older woman on a distant roof. The preacher continued to pray, but the water washed him off the roof and he drowned.

The preacher went to heaven, but when he got there, he was miffed.

He said to the Lord, "Did you hear my prayers?"

The Lord said, "Yes."

The preacher asked the Lord, "Then why didn't you help me?"

The Lord replied, "I sent you two row boats and a helicopter, you're the one who wouldn't get in."

In retrospect, I saw God answered my foxhole prayer twenty-six years ago. The old girlfriend was the first rowboat, Smoky was the second rowboat, and my Dad was the helicopter. I sure felt grateful God granted me the wisdom to get my dumb ass in the chopper.

I also saw how God's love paralleled my Dad's love. I was sure I disappointed God. I even denied his existence. I was sure I pissed God off more than one time, yet like Dad, God still loved me unconditionally.

I packed up to a rather late start for my rendezvous with Phyllis in the Delaware Water Gap the next day. I was on a spiritual high greater by far, than any drug induced high. I started north on the trail at a faster than my usual pace in a dreamlike state of meditation. I hiked for a while, but after consuming two pots of coffee I needed to talk to someone. I stopped on the trail, took off my pack, sat on it in the middle of the trail, and started making phone calls.

I talked to both of my hiking cronies, Crow and Chief, from back home. They planned to hike from Atkins to Damascus in Virginia the next week. I wished them the best. Crow remembered it was my anniversary, so I felt honored. We talked about my first day sober for a little while. I wished I was going with Crow and Chief on their hike in a way, but I was also happy to be right where I was on the trail and in my life.

I moved on towards Wind Gap. The motel at Wind Gap would have been a good place to stop for the night if it was later in the day. I did stop and bought three cokes from the owner. I noticed two pairs of hiking shoes in front of one of the rooms. I was curious, wondering if I knew who owned them, but I moved on because it was far too early to stop for the night.

I hiked nine more miles to Kirkridge Shelter where I found Cedar Moe along with eight section hikers already in the shelter. I set up my tent far enough away so I wouldn't hear them snoring later. I went to the shelter to cook, eat, and socialize. Cedar Moe and I had a very special hiker/Christian bond by that time. We were the only thru-hikers there, so the section hikers treated us like heroes. I only had six miles left go to Delaware Water Gap to meet up with Phyllis the next day. I wanted to get there early enough to settle in before she arrived. I was looking forward to seeing her, my son-in-law Tom, and my grandson Parker.

I returned to my tent for some time alone. The solution to my Third Step dilemma came to me not as a sudden awakening, but a slow recognition that like the trail, the answer was in the journey not the destination. I decided to thru-hike the Appalachian Trail more than ten years ago and I spent those ten years in preparation.

I didn't know exactly when I made a decision to turn my life over to the care of God. I reflected back to the day Gallagher said, "Exactly, but what you have to do first is make the decision to go!" My thru-hike will be over the instant I touch the sign at the summit of Katahdin and the goal I set when I made the decision fulfilled.

In the book of Luke it said the last words Jesus spoke in this life were, "Father, into your hands I commit my spirit." The turmoil of the last nine days since Duncannon all made sense now. The decision to turn my will and my life over to the care of God of my understanding would be a lifelong process. My earthly hike would end the instant I committed my spirit into God's hands, fulfilling my Third Step goal, but I have a lot to do first. I felt a great peace that went beyond serenity as I drifted off to sleep. I felt fortunate and grateful for the sobriety given to me, by grace alone.

INVENTORY

Day 90   13.8 Miles

I planned to rendezvous with my daughter Phyllis at Delaware Water Gap. I looked forward to hiking with her ever since Easter Sunday when we first started to plan the hike. I hadn't spent three consecutive days with her since she left home years ago. I thought it would strengthen our father/daughter relationship even more.

I was in no hurry because I only had a little over six miles to Delaware Water Gap. I leisurely packed up in a light rain, then stopped at the shelter and made coffee and chatted with the others. A section hiker told me Cedar Moe left before daylight. I wasn't disappointed because I hoped to see him again at Delaware Water Gap. Cedar Moe had become a type of Christian mentor for me because he seemed to walk like he talked.

Most of the other hikers packed up and left by the time I finished my coffee and hit the trail. I found the hike to the Delaware Water Gap an uneventful, just get-r-done hike, with lots of rocky trudge. I saw some views of New Jersey across the river valley, but nothing spectacular. I spent the morning anticipating spending time with Phyllis, but the trail was mostly six, boring miles in the light rain. I purposely took my time so I wouldn't get hurt on the slippery rocks.

I arrived at Delaware Water Gap early and went straight to the post office to pick up my mail. I received many cards and letters from friends and Alcoholics Anonymous meetings back home. I found a little diner to buy some breakfast. I killed an hour or more drinking coffee and reading my mail while waiting for Phyllis to arrive. Crow sent me a twenty-six-year anniversary coin, which made my eyes water.

The quaint little Presbyterian Church of the Mountain ran a hostel in part of the church for long distance hikers only. The church has significant importance to me because last August my friends Crow and Maryann got married on the front steps. My friend and other hiking partner, Chief was the preacher, who did the officiating. I was the best man, Scooter read some scripture, and Chief's wife, Rose took pictures. We wanted to have the ceremony inside, but we couldn't find anyone around, so we hitched them on the front steps. Legally, we had to marry them in Pennsylvania due to Chief's license. The six of us then hiked through New Jersey on a section hike to celebrate the union.

I still had more time to kill before Phyllis was due to arrive, so I went to the hostel. Cedar Moe was already there, so I spread out my sleeping bag on a bottom bunk and stashed my gear on the top bunk to reserve it for Phyllis. Cedar Moe waited for me to take a shower and put on my cleanest dirty cloths. We then went across the street to a quaint little café where we drank coffee and chatted while we waited until Phyllis called.

When she got close and called, I walked to the brand new Pennsylvania Welcome Center on the interstate to meet her. The welcome center was celebrating their grand opening with food, television cameras, and politicians. I didn't fit in well and felt self-conscious. I was reasonably clean, but my clothes weren't the attire appropriate for the occasion and they probably stunk. I waited about another half hour until Phyllis, Tom, and my grandson, Parker arrived. It was good to see them for the first time since my birthday in February. Parker had grown a lot since then.

Phyllis and Tom drove separate vehicles so she could leave her car on the trail to drive home after her hike. We gassed them both up and I rode with Phyllis and navigated, while Tom and Parker followed us to a parking lot at Culver's Lake Gap, New Jersey. We supplied from a box I packed last week at Port Clinton and sent to Phyllis by way of Scooter. I would also re-supply from the box before I moved on when Phyllis and I hiked to her car in three days.

Tom and Parker took us back to Delaware Water Gap. The shuttle took about three hours due to heavy traffic, but I enjoyed the time with them tremendously. We stopped at a family restaurant for a prime rib dinner. It felt good to sit down with family for dinner and chat, even if it was in a restaurant. I said the grace and realized the simple things like having supper with family were such a precious gift. I would try to remain grateful for my many blessings.

We chatted over supper in the restaurant for an hour before we said goodbye to Tom and Parker, who left for Washington, DC to spend the weekend with friends. Phyllis and I walked back to the hostel with her pack.

Phyllis said, "I'm a little apprehensive about going to the hostel because it's meant for long distance hikers only."

I told her, "You'll fit right in with everyone else."

She came back, "But I don't stink like a hiker."

I looked at her a little offended and said, "We stink so bad we won't be able to know you don't stink and besides no one in their right mind, who was not a hiker, would ever sniff a hiker to see if they stunk." She seemed satisfied with my logic.

Several weeks ago, Phyllis and I talked about a trail name for her. She was hesitant to pick one and said she would rather not have a trail name. I knew the rules of the trail and informed her if she didn't pick one she liked, someone would pick one for her that might not be so flattering. I gave her the example of Fire Fly who earned his name while lighting his camp stove several years ago. He set himself on fire and had to abort his hike to go to the hospital. The name stuck and his trail name would be Fire Fly forever.

I now asked Phyllis again, "Do you want to pick a trail name for yourself?"

She instantly replied, "Wildflower." I thought about it for a minute to mentally yell it out in my best drill sergeant inflection, and gave my approval. Now, I had to get used to calling my offspring Wildflower.

We found the hostel full of all kinds of hikers. The thru-hikers were Cedar Moe, a new couple I met earlier that day named Zoma and Lug, from the state of Oregon, and Slow Leak, who was the first thru-hiker I met so far who was older than me.

Fire Fly and Feather arrived back earlier that day from Hiker Days in Damascus, Va. A hiker named Pig Pen, who hiked with Feather for a while last year came back with them. Pig Pen skipped some sections and was going to hike with Feather to make up a section he skipped. Some other section hikers were there also, but I didn't remember their names.

Silver Streak came in and announced he was getting off the trail yet again. He was in New Jersey with Scout and Spiritual Pilgrim when he quit for the second or third time. I got away from Silver Streak and Pig Pen because they were rationalizing you could skip sections of the trail, make it up later, and still consider yourself a thru-hiker. I didn't want to hear something that would make me think I could find an easier, softer way to be a true thru-hiker. Many hikers also skip sections they previously hiked on a section hike. Some unfortunate hikers had to abort their hike one year and finish on another year. I personally wouldn't be able to consider myself a thru-hiker if I didn't hike every inch of the Appalachian Trail in one season. I thought I was being very judgmental, so I got off my soapbox. Those rules were for me alone and no one else.

Wildflower and I had an awkward moment over some of my pictures which got misplaced, but we worked it out. I felt badly I had offended her, but she accepted my apology. I had to remember she was no longer a little girl, but a grown woman. She was a lot more responsible than I was at her age, so I admired her for that.

The hostel buzzed with hikers. Some hikers came back from the bar a little drunk. Some former hikers stopped in only to socialize. Wildflower and I went to bed in the bunkroom a little late for me. The bunkroom soon filled up completely and some hikers stayed in the living room. I didn't fall asleep for a long time.

The situation over the pictures with Phyllis continued to haunt me. Not the pictures, but the way I reacted to her left me feeling guilty. I took an inventory of my past interaction with her. My behavior earlier was nothing new to her. I had always attempted to control her in a similar way. I found myself wondering how she felt. I resolved to always treat her as an adult from that day forward.

I felt a little better with my decision and thought about my personal inventory. I wasn't sure exactly when I decided to let go of my will and turn it over to God, but I thought it no longer mattered, when What mattered was, I believed I made a decision to commit to seeking a personal relationship with God. Now the question was, how could I do that? Gallagher pointed out I had to do some things first before we could go bear hunting so many years ago. I could see clearly I had to do some things before I turned my life over to God's care.

Step Four suggested, I make a fearless and searching moral inventory of myself. I believed before I could solve any problem or achieve any goal, I had to know what I had to do, so I had to take an inventory. I took my inventory when I looked at my behavior with Wildflower. I could see I was wrong and decided to make a change. I had to take action to follow through with any decision I ever made to change or solve any problem, but before I could take action, I had to take an inventory.

A good example was one cold, snowy night after work, I stuck my key in the ignition of my truck, and nothing happened. My truck wouldn't start. I wasn't a mechanic, but I started to take an inventory of what was wrong. I had no lights, so I popped the hood and checked the battery terminals. When I went to wiggle the positive terminal, it pulled out of the side of the battery leaving a jagged hole in the battery. I said a few words you might not hear on Sunday morning in church, but I knew what was wrong from the inventory. I did what I had to do and fixed the truck.

In the case with Wildflower, it was my daughter and not some old truck, but the principle was the same. It seemed that I always hurt the ones I loved the most, more than I did other people. I criticized and tried to control my loved ones, which I needed to change.

May 27   **Day 91**   **10.5 Miles**

I didn't sleep well due to all the activity continuing into the night plus, Slow Leak snored loudly. The good news was I had lots of time on my hands to take some inventory. I felt better with my new resolution.

I was the first hiker up before dawn's first light. I packed up in silence by the dim night light, so I could move my gear out of the bunkroom before the chaotic rush when everyone packed up all at the same time.

I had my cell phone charger plugged in right under Zoma's bunk and she stored her gear in front of the charger. I went to quietly retrieve it when she woke up and raised her head up to within an inch of my face. A pregnant moment followed where we were face-to-face, eye-to-eye, inches apart. I whispered, "I'm getting my battery charger and not trying to rob you." Zoma must have misunderstood because she handed me her wallet. I met her the evening before, so I didn't know her well. I thought she was too sleepy to understand, so I would explain later.

Everyone was still sleeping, so I took a quick shower while there was still hot water and walked to a convenience store to buy coffee. I bought four coffees to go and returned to the hostel. I gave a coffee to Wildflower, Slow Leak, and Cedar Moe who were the only ones awake when I got back. Soon everyone got up, so we all went across the street to the little café for breakfast. Ten of us pulled three tables together so we could sit together as a big family. We ate, chatted, and drank lots of coffee for about two hours. I was pleased to see Wildflower started to get the feel of the camaraderie among hikers.

I explained to Zoma what happened earlier in the hostel.

She laughed and said "I thought you were Lug, so I gave you money for coffee." We all laughed.

I found Zoma and Lug delightful as we all bonded. Zoma and Lug were both athletes who cycled. Lug even raced. Zoma's parents had aspirations of being thru-hikers, so Zoma and Lug started the trail to support them. The parents dropped off in Georgia, but by that time, the trail had Zoma and Lug hooked. I thought they had what it took to make it to the summit. They were engaged to be married and so much in love, they inspired each other.

Wildflower and I went back to the hostel to pick up our packs before we went to the post office to mail some letters home. I received three more letters from friends. I bought Body Glide at the outfitters, which Crow recommended, as a lubricant that came packaged like a stick deodorant. Hikers used it on their feet to prevent blisters and other places to prevent chaffing. I picked up some deet because we were about to enter deer tick country. New Jersey, New York, and Connecticut had the highest rate of Lyme disease on the trail. I didn't believe deet was good for you, but I thought the Lyme disease deer ticks carried was worse.

We crossed the bridge on the interstate over the Delaware River into New Jersey. I could feel the bridge bounce every time a big truck sped onto it. I stopped on Jersey soil, turned around, and saluted the rocks of Pennsylvania goodbye.

When I sobered up so many years ago, I thought life would no longer be any fun. I never could have been more wrong. I felt so privileged to be hiking with my daughter that I was unable to even express the feelings of euphoria. My eyes moistened a bit because I felt so grateful.

The weather was perfect for the Memorial Day weekend, so the trail became crowded with day hikers enjoying the hot sun. We hiked through a rattlesnake preserve and proceeded with caution, but only saw one black snake and a deer. I thought, only in New Jersey would they protect rattlesnakes.

We stopped for water at Sunfish Pond, which was the first glacier pond of the trip. We asked a day-hiker to take our picture with my camera as we posed by the pond. The highest point we reached that day was about fifteen-hundred feet above sea level, but never-the-less, we enjoyed some surprisingly fine vistas. Wildflower was packing a four-pound camera, which she had hanging awkwardly low off her waist strap. She stopped at every flower, tree, bug, bird, or rock, called out, "Photo-op," then took several pictures. I thought, Shutter Bug, might have been a more appropriate trail name for her.

We hiked to Mohegan Outdoor Center as planned, where they allowed thru-hikers to camp free. We did pay two dollars each to take a shower. The boy who registered us gave us each a piece of blackberry pie they had left over. We found a nice tent site to set up beside each other before we went back to the lodge to take our showers that were well worth the two bucks.

To our delight, Zoma and Lug set up in the campsite next to us while we were gone. We all cooked and ate at the picnic table between the two campsites. Zoma and Lug were fast becoming good friends. After we ate, Wildflower and I went back to the lodge to listen to a band play old Cat Stevens songs. We only stayed for two songs because there was no place to sit and we were both beat. Wildflower did quite well for her first day on the trail and managed to take over eighty pictures. I felt so proud to have the honor of being her father.

Wildflower fell asleep almost instantly after we retired to our tents. I laid awake listening to her through the tent walls as her breathing slowed to a steady, deep sleep pace. I quietly said, "Thank you Lord for giving me this opportunity to be with my daughter."

We got along well throughout the day, because I consciously suppressed my urges to take control and bark out orders. Phyllis truly was a Wildflower, but she also was a responsible woman who didn't need her dad controlling her anymore. She became a mother herself, who made sound decisions. I could now see clearly that I needed to support her, but let go of trying to control her.

I set a goal to go bear hunting and actually went bear hunting after I was sober several years. What Gallagher said was true. I had to do a lot of preparation first. The goal in the case with Wildflower was to improve my relationship with my daughter. I now had to take an inventory of what stood in the way of my goal. Alcoholics Anonymous called these blocks that stood between us, character defects.

I was giving that some thought when it occurred to me I was also seeking a spiritual awakening and a personal relationship with God of my understanding. Several members of Alcoholics Anonymous told me character defects were what blocked me from a relationship with God. I had a moment of clarity that truly my character defects were what blocked me in my relationships with Wildflower and others as well. I felt better with my new insight as I joined Wildflower and surrendered my day to the nighttime sounds of the New Jersey woods.

Day 92   14.3 Miles

We slept well, awoke early, and ate breakfast with Zoma and Lug before we packed up and hit the trail. We hiked past several scenic glacier ponds and swamps. Wildflower seemed so happy, stopping often to take pictures of wildflowers, dead trees, scenes from the trail, and me. We shared lunch in the woods and rested before continuing in the afternoon.

We stopped for water at an old-fashioned water pump at Blue Mountain Lake road. We were resting when three vans full of Cub Scouts pulled in and stopped. They were lost and looking for the Appalachian Trail. It was a troop of eighteen Jewish Cub Scouts and four of their leaders from New York City. We told them they were on the trail.

The scoutmaster asked me if I would talk to the boys and answer questions. The kids behaved well as I talked about the value of protecting our Mother Nature and the privilege of being in God's country. I spoke of the importance of preserving the Appalachian Trail for Cub Scouts of the future. I answered their questions for about forty-five minutes. They then asked if they could take my picture, so I had all of them, leaders included, pose with me while Wildflower took pictures with several cameras. They seemed grateful and I felt honored. We departed as they hiked south and Wildflower and I traveled north.

We took several pictures late in the day from a ridge on Rattlesnake Mountain with a great vista overlooking the Delaware River Valley. Wildflower wanted to set up camp on the ridge, but I had to say no. I felt bad having to deny her request, but I was too leery of camping on summits or ridges even though the weather looked good. A lightning storm could pop up in the night. We cooked supper and moved on. I had planned to stay in Brink Road Shelter with her to give her the experience of staying in a shelter, but shortly after we descended from the ridge, we found some flat ground in the protection of the woods. I gave Wildflower the choice of staying there or going to the shelter.

We set up camp for our last night together right there in a hurry so we could return to the ridge on Rattlesnake Mountain. We talked father to daughter for a time, but fell silent as we watched a spectacular sunset over God's world. We sat side-by-side watching the day as it became night in silence for a long moment. I wasn't sure who broke the silence, but when the time was perfect, our conversation took an intimate turn toward spirituality. I knew Phyllis, Tom, Parker, Nadine, and Scooter all went to church as a family since I was on the trail. They all said they were Christians and had been praying for me even before I met Joachim on March eleventh in the Smoky Mountains. They all attended a small church called New Hope Community Church, which was a part of the Southern Baptist Conference. Night's darkness settled in as I looked up at the stars and remembered a piece of advice Joachim gave me that day in March. He Said, "Find a church that preaches the truth and get baptized by submersion." I remembered, I asked him where he went to church and he said he went to a Southern Baptist Church.

When I was growing up, I went to a church where sin seemed to be the topic most of the time. At least that was my perception. I called the Ten Commandments, the "thou shall nots." They told me sin pissed God off, so I learned to fear the God they were talking about as a punisher. I became increasingly uncomfortable in church. I rebelled against religion at an early age because they told me what to believe. They had rules and if I went against their rules, God would punish me by burning my sorry ass in a hell fire for eternity. I was only twelve-years-old when I withdrew from all religious beliefs and turned to alcohol because I feared punishment for my sins. Thus, I developed a fear of God and a negative attitude towards religion. I still thought of myself as spiritual, but not religious, probably because of those early core beliefs. I felt maybe I needed to be more understanding and open minded about religion. My mother set an example by going to church almost every Sunday. She must have gotten something out of what they preached.

Early in my sobriety, I heard a woman speaking at an Alcoholics Anonymous meeting say, "I had to divorce my punishing God to marry the loving God I met in Alcoholics Anonymous." I didn't think much about her statement at the time, but she planted a seed that was still growing in me.

I asked Phyllis if her church would baptize me by submersion. She replied, "Yes, Pastor Mike baptized Tom and me by submersion in the church about the same time you were saved in March." I thought of a line in the Big Book that said, *Nothing, absolutely nothing happens in Gods world by mistake.*

I thought, wow, what a coincidence. I immediately had an awakening. Gallagher once told me a coincidence was a series of events where God chose to remain anonymous. I made a decision that I would commit to attending church with the family for at least one year after I returned home. I would also ask the preacher if he would publicly baptize me by submersion.

My eyes filled with tears of gratitude as I came out of meditation and told my daughter about my decision. She hugged me and I realized she too had tears running down her cheek. I looked at her with the same feeling I had the first time I ever held her, soon after she was born. I couldn't have been happier either time.

She sported a plastic, multi-colored, florescent, cross, which she kept attached to the back of her pack. She gave the cross to me and said, "I no longer worry about you when you're on your adventures now you're saved." I have been wearing a medallion of a Wolf my youngest daughter, Nadine gave me before I left to hike the trail, so she could be with me in spirit. I attached the cross to the same necklace. I now had both my daughters with me in spirit on the trail.

We hiked back to our tents in the dark. I bid her good night and crawled into my tent. I felt good and so close to God as I left the day behind.

Day 93   12.4 Miles

I arose before Phyllis and couldn't find my camera. I ran back to the ridge, but couldn't find my camera there either. I did the stationary panic that I teased Scooter about doing because she panicked so well when she couldn't find something. I almost ran back to camp fearing the worst. I tore all the gear in my tent apart in a fit and found my camera in my pack where I usually kept my cell phone. I sure was happy Scooter wasn't here to witness the whole ordeal as it played out.

I vowed I would never tell her about it either.

Wildflower got up and was eating breakfast oblivious to what took place moments before. She asked why I was up and out so early. I told her, but I minimized my manic reaction. We made coffee with the last of the water and hiked out to the day that promised to be another hot, sunny day.

We hiked a short distance to Brink Road Shelter where we stopped to filter water out of the spring. We met a section hiker there who called himself Buzz Lightfoot. I made another pot of coffee to share with him while he told us of his adventures on the trail. He and Wildflower talked about photography, which they had in common. I didn't understand the conversation when they got into the technical, finer points of outdoor photography. He took a picture of us before we moved on.

We encountered a black bear in the woods and spent a half hour stalking him, trying to take his picture with zero luck. I came to appreciate how hard it was to get a good picture of a wild animal. I had successfully hunted bears in the past and I believed I had several opportunities to harvest that particular bear with a gun. The best Wildflower and I could come up with was a large black spot in the woods. Part of the problem was those new fan-dangled digital cameras didn't go off as soon as you pulled the trigger. I had often threatened to go back to the old thirty-five millimeter camera for that reason, but they also had many shortcomings, like running out of film when a great photo opportunity presented itself. Oh well, I was happy to have Wildflower see at least one bear. I was disappointed she didn't see any rattlesnakes. Rattlesnakes were easy to photograph because they didn't move fast.

We wandered terribly off trail and spent some quality time getting lost. I would have liked to have been able to blame the excitement of stalking the bear or the poorly marked trail, but the truth was, I probably wasn't paying attention. The trail I was on suddenly dwindled to nothing and I couldn't recall seeing a white blaze for some time. My ego was about to take a big hit. I would be happier if we were lost in the Presidential Mountains of New Hampshire, or the hundred-mile wilderness in Maine, but not New Jersey. Wildflower has known me her whole life and she was no stranger to drama in her adventures with the old man, but I didn't want her biggest tale of the trip to be getting lost in New Jersey of all places.

I broke the news to Wildflower and she took it in stride as if things were par for the course. I thought she could have at least looked surprised, but she didn't. It took some time, but eventually we found the friendly, familiar white blazes. I backtracked until I recognized things to make sure I didn't miss one inch of the trail.

We soon started to see more signs of civilization as our hike started coming to an end. We bought a sandwich, pop, and ice cream at a sub shop in Culver's Gap before we got to the car.

The car was as we had left it. I re-supplied from the box she brought with her. Wildflower became my daughter Phyllis as I bid her good-bye. I had a tear in my eye as she started her car to head home. I felt a strong sense of love, pride, and sadness as I watched her disappear. I saddled up and turned to the north.

I was down and lonely for the rest of the day. The time with Wildflower passed so quickly it almost felt as if it didn't really happen. I had never been homesick on the trail, but I did miss my family. I had cell tower for a while, so I tried to call my youngest daughter Nadine. I was unsuccessful, which added to my melancholy mood. I hadn't seen her since I left in February, which seemed so long ago. I really missed her smile, which always brought warm sunshine into my life.

A thru-hiker named Ten Speed caught up to me. He stopped briefly at the sub shop where Phyllis and I bought sandwiches, but moved on to a pub so he could drink a beer with his meal. I hiked and chatted with him for a while. He was a positive, goal orientated person, who previously hiked the Pacific Crest Trail. His company was exactly what I needed to get me out of my funky mood. I kept with him as long as I could, but he was traveling light and fast. When I no longer wanted to keep up with him, I dropped back with my thoughts.

I was sober for a while and started to stabilize both physically and emotionally, when Big Jim started to push me towards doing the Alcoholics Anonymous Fourth Step. I realized he was going to continue to annoy me until I gave in, so I did an inventory.

My first inventory was a basic list of some of the rotten things I did that hurt other people. I could still recall the hair on the back of my neck standing up as I found myself experiencing an old familiar fear as I re-lived my painful past. I instinctively wanted to run to the protection of a fantasy world where I would be safe, but that was how I coped as a child. I knew alcohol made it easy to escape into a fantasy and the urge to drink was incredible. It was no wonder alcohol became so attractive.

Sin, the same three-letter word I had been trying to avoid most of my life kept popping up. I forced myself to stay in the here and now and faced my worst fear. I said a simple prayer, "Lord, please walk with me for a minute as I face the sins of my past."

I made a list of the things I had done or my past sins. However, even at the time, I knew I wasn't being completely honest. I didn't come out and tell any out-right lies, but my ego got involved because I knew Big Jim would read it. I left out some of the things I did because I was still too ashamed to admit them to Big Jim and some even to myself. I embellished other things to portray the tough guy image I admired. Besides, I wanted to impress Big Jim.

I worried, Big Jim might know I wasn't being entirely honest. I expected him to do one of two things: he was either going to confront me and catch me in lies or he was going to ignore my dishonesty. In the past, Big Jim always confronted me when I was telling a lie by saying, "Don't try to snow the snow man, bullshit a bullshitter, or lie to a liar."

He surprised me when He said, "I'm Proud of you. You were as honest as you were capable of being at this point in your sobriety." I felt a strange mixture of pride because he said he was proud of me, but I also felt shame because I lied and I knew he knew I wasn't completely honest. Because of the guilt I felt, I immediately committed to doing another Step Four in the future, but the next time, I would be one-hundred percent honest.

Jim smiled a kind, fatherly smile and said, "You will be capable of being more honest each time you do Step Four."

I said, "I was under the impression I only had to do Step Four once."

He looked up as if he recalled a fond memory of his own. He paused a minute, then almost as if he was quoting someone from his past and not talking to me, he said, "Step Four is like pealing an onion. You peel off a layer and all you find is another layer, but you get closer to the center with each layer."

I said, "What happens when you get to the center of the onion?"

He gave out a little laugh and said through a big smile, "I don't know, I'm still peeling away layers myself." He then stood up and playfully punched me on the arm and said, "That's why they say progress not perfection." I could remember, I was still uncomfortable, confused, and fearful, but I felt like I made a little progress. The best thing of all was I had a glimmer of hope.

I had no idea at the time, but Big Jim would die before I could do another Fourth and Fifth Step with him. After he died, I lost my coach and my incentive to pursue the Steps. I continued to attend Alcoholics Anonymous meetings and stayed sober, but I quit growing spiritually and rested on my laurels. I ended up regressing spiritually on a dry drunk and almost relapsing. That was when I asked Gallagher to be my second sponsor. I did Step Four and Five for the second time with him. I learned a valuable life lesson from the experience. I learned I had to keep pealing my onion to continue to grow spiritually towards being happy, joyous, and free.

I arrived at Mashipacong Shelter feeling inspired and hopeful instead of lonely. I found the shelter empty, but set up my tent on a flat grassy place twenty yards from the shelter. The shelter was a dog hole with no water source, but I had enough water for the night and breakfast in the morning. A twenty-three-year-old thru-hiker, who introduced himself as Team Steve, stopped for the night. He too was a new college graduate who was hiking the Appalachian Trail before he started his career. He also set up his tent because of the shelter's poor condition. We chatted a while, but were driven into our tents early to escape the hoards of mosquitoes that descended on us as the sun started to go down.

I couldn't escape my loneliness in sleep, so I had a lot of time to meditate. I was always slow to catch on so God used times like these for me to catch up. I thought over the time Phyllis and I shared. I retraced my time with Phyllis and tried to preserve my memory of our precious time together. I became aware God used my own daughter and Joachim as rowboats to send me the message to get in. People in Alcoholics Anonymous said, God speaks to us through people. I could see how many people besides Phyllis and Joachim in my life have carried the message to me.

I would never forget the image on Phyllis's face when she said, "I no longer worry about you when you're on your adventures now that you're saved."

I didn't think about the statement at the time, but my smile must have faded into a puzzled look as I started to process her meaning. I said to myself aloud, *Saved from what?* I heard many folks talking about the phrase, being saved, from the time when I was a young boy. I thought they meant saved from death so they conceived a mystical character called, God. God was for people who feared death and didn't want life to end at the grave. Religion promoted the fear to control their parishioners and as an added incentive they created a punishment after death that they called hell. I thought it was all a hoax invented by cowards thinking that Lone Ranger-type named Jesus would save them from death or worse, hell.

What happened to me next would be impossible for me to relate in words. I came to what I would say was a heightened state of awareness. I felt like my mind became a computer and the Holy Spirit was downloading a Divine program. The thoughts and realizations came so fast it was hard to follow as if I had no control, but I could only observe. I received the answer to my question. I clearly saw from my personal experience, my pursuit of my self-will could take full control of my behavior. In my addiction, God stepped back and left me to my self-will and I did whatever I wanted to do. I tried to hide my behavior from others in our society to avoid their consequences. I found myself alone, isolated from both God and society by my own choosing. I chose to pursue my will and what I perceived would make me feel good. The Big Book calls that *Self will run riot*. I now called it my personal definition of hell.

I saw hell as living totally separated from God and society. In the depths of my addiction, I was only pursuing my will and my life became hell. I suddenly awoke to an amazing insight that God sent Jesus to save me from my own self-will. The Third Step Prayer said; Relieve me of the bondage of self. I created my personal hell in my pursuit of my self-will.

My animosity towards religion and fear of God suddenly melted away almost as if it was never there. That was what the little white Bible had been saying all along. God sent his son to carry his word to me through him. To pursue God's will instead of my will felt good and that was what Heaven was about. I felt like I was the first mortal to discover the truth.

I got so excited I wanted to tell someone. Actually, I wanted to tell everyone, but Team Steve was the only one around and he was probably fast asleep. I just met him and didn't know him well, so I was afraid if I woke him and blurted out my discovery I would likely scare the crap out of him. I elected to stay in my tent with my thoughts until sometime in the night, I drifted off to sleep.

Day 94   12.4 Miles

I woke to a beautiful dawn feeling renewed as I ate, packed up in silence, and left quietly without waking Team Steve. I hiked to Highpoint State Park where I could get water. I was hoping they would have a vending machine or pop machine, but no luck. The best I received was a restroom with a flush toilet, free toilet paper, free soap, and hot water. I washed my hands with soap and hot water after taking a dump, which was always a luxury on the trail.

An observation platform at the highest point in New Jersey stood at almost seventeen-hundred feet above sea level. It wasn't exactly Everest, but the guidebook said you could see the skyline of New York City from the platform on a clear day. I climbed to the top, but all I saw was sky.

I was in some kind of physical pain ever since I started the trail in

Georgia. It seemed as if I got over one thing and soon something else confronted me. The wart on my little toe healed up, but lately I had replaced it with pain on the sides of my thighs, which seemed to have gotten progressively worse. I stopped for lunch and took some ibuprofen at noon to rest in a hardwood forest by a serene mountain stream, where the sun filtered down through the leaves in bits and pieces. I filtered water from the stream to cook tuna and noodles.

I was tired and felt a little down emotionally. I discovered good cell tower, so I called Jimmy 3X5 who was a long-time Alcoholics Anonymous friend from back home. I sat on my pack in the woods, which by now had become my immense living room and talked to Jimmy as I ate lunch. We talked for about an hour and a half and Step Four came up in the conversation. Boy, I felt so much better both physically and emotionally after I connected with Jimmy. That was how I stayed focused on working my Alcoholics Anonymous program while on the trail.

My first Fourth Step was about twenty-five years ago and now looking back, it seemed quite primitive. I felt pretty shitty at first when I listed my sins, but relieved when I confessed them to Big Jim. I still had no idea why I was a sinner, but it was the beginning of my seeking. I started questioning what I had to change to carry out the decision I made in Step Three. My addiction started with the first time I got drunk at twelve-years-old and progressively worsened. I could now see clearly, I started to seek recovery with my first Alcoholics Anonymous meeting in 1977 and had progressively gotten better as long as I continued to seek change. I moved on after resting and still in some physical pain, but I had hope. I believed Alcoholics Anonymous was still the God given tool that always gave me hope and restored my sanity.

I stopped in the afternoon at Jim Murray's Secret Shelter for water. Jim Murray was a former thru-hiker who built a shelter on his own land, two tenths of a mile off trail for thru-hikers only. The shelter was a two-story cabin with a kitchen, electricity, a sink with hot and cold running water, an electric stove, heater, and even an electric fan for hot nights. It was somewhat early to stop, but I felt exhausted and my thighs hurt, so I decided to stop for the day. The shelter could accommodate several hikers with the second story, but I chose to stay in my tent for the privacy.

Three of my four cell phone batteries were dead, so I took advantage of the electricity and charged them up. I was digging through my pack to get my battery charger when a donkey snuck up behind me and gave out the loudest bray I had ever heard. He scared the beejebers out of me. After my heart returned to my chest, I realized I was sharing a pasture with two resident donkeys who were trying to breed and didn't appreciate my company.

I discovered a shower with hot water on the outside of the shelter. It was on the side of the shelter in the open with zero privacy, but no one was around. I stripped naked and was enjoying a hot shower when Jim Murray drove down his access road and stopped. He waved with a big smile on his face, so I waved back feeling a little self-conscious. He drove on to feed his donkeys. A few minutes later, I looked up and saw Fire Fly, Feather, and Team Steve coming down the road. I was still wearing only what the good Lord gave me. I felt exposed and self-conscious, especially since Feather was of the opposite sex. I hauled my lily-white ass back to the privacy of the shelter as fast as I could and put on some clothes. I came out dressed and still a little soapy, but no one said a word. We all acted as if nothing happened.

Later, Team Steve was looking around and he opened the door on the outside of the shelter and discovered an inside shower. It appeared, I could have taken a shower in privacy if I simply would have opened the door to see what was in there. I assumed it was probably the water heater, but I never looked. Everyone had a good laugh on me and then they all took a private shower.

Jim Murray stopped at the shelter later on to socialize. He was a great guy, who thru-hiked the Appalachian Trail in 1989. He later had a stroke that disabled him to the point where he could no longer hike long distances. He built the shelter with his own money on his own land for thru-hikers with all the amenities. He charged no fees to stay there and wouldn't even accept donations. I thanked and saluted Jim Murray.

Day 95   18.7 Miles

It rained all night, but quit a little after daylight. I started later than usual, packing up a wet tent and moving north. My friends left before I did to go a half mile off trail to a little town called Unionville for breakfast. I agreed that getting some home cooked breakfast with them wasn't a bad idea. Besides, I needed to buy some things anyway, so I planned to meet them somewhere in town.

I hiked less than three miles to Unionville and found a little grocery store and bought the few things I needed. I went to the only diner in town for breakfast and found Team Steve, Fire Fly, and Feather already waiting for their food. I felt like I stepped back into the 1950s. The diner reminded me of the old-time pharmacy in my hometown. When I was a kid, I used to sit at the counter and drink sodas, which consisted of pop and ice cream blended.

I sat at a table with my friends and ordered eggs over easy with toast, home fries, and coffee. We ate and were finishing our coffee when the town's mayor brought his coffee over to our table, pulled up a chair, and welcomed us to Unionville. He invited us all to his house to take a shower, but I declined.

I thanked him and said, "New Jersey was one of the best states I had been in so far."

He gave me a look and said, "You're in New York son."

After I got my foot out of my mouth, I apologized. I left to hike back to the trail before the others. I was embarrassed for the second time in less than twenty-four hours. Apparently, unknown to me, the trail crossed briefly into New York and back into New Jersey. I promised myself in the future, I would make sure I knew what state I was in before I opened my big mouth.

I wanted to put some miles in while it was still cool because I knew I had to cross an old sod farm where I had to hike on a black, gravely sod-type surface which was exposed to the sun. I knew from a previous section hike it would be hot on my feet. I hiked faster than normal to make it across early in the day, before the sod became too hot.

I started getting pain in my left upper thigh, which I thought was from the stress of hiking fast. My son Nick called, so I stopped in a spot of shade and gave it a rest while I talked to him. We talked for over an hour. He bought a car at an auction and was fixing it up. He was making some good decisions and I was proud of him. I didn't make it to the sod farm before the black soil was hot enough to fry an egg, but talking to my son was worth it.

Fire Fly, Feather, and Team Steve caught up with me on a boardwalk across a marshy wildlife preserve. The impressive boardwalk zigzagged for over two miles across an open marsh. The abundance of all kinds of wildlife was dormant in the afternoon heat, except for a multitude of turtles who sunned themselves on logs. We also saw some impressive water snakes. I would like to return some day early in the morning or at sunset and be able to take the time to quietly observe some of the other residents in their world. We found the hiking was easy and made good time, but the boardwalk was extremely hot on the feet as we scampered along. The good news was a store where we could buy ice cream was a tenth of a mile off trail after the boardwalk ended.

We ran into two female animal rights activists, who told us about an aggressive bear who dragged a child out of the Wawayanda Shelter. The New Jersey wildlife commission shot the bear. I said, "Things like that often happen when states ban hunting, because hunting helped manage the balance of wildlife." They stuck up for the poor bear to the point that I wanted to puke. I didn't say what I was thinking in the name of peace. Besides, I thought punching out two women wouldn't be in my best interest.

We hit the store and all bought ice cream and pop for the first round. We sat at picnic tables behind the store, but they were in the sun so we found some bags of fertilizer to sit on in the cool shade and had a party. We ate our ice cream and went back and bought pastries and coffee for the second round. I bought two apples and two oranges for my pack before I left them behind the store sleeping off their sugar down.

I ascended over a thousand feet up Wawayanda Mountain, as the temperature rose to ninety-five degrees in the shade. It was the longest and most grueling climb in New Jersey. I probably burned all the calories I took in from the ice cream and pastries. I hiked four hours into Wawayanda Shelter. I was happy when I got to the shelter before darkness set in because I saw three bears within the last mile of the shelter. One bear was a little too aggressive for my liking, but I made it safely. The shelter was full of hikers, so I found a little flat spot to set up my tent not far from the others, but far enough that their noise wouldn't bother me.

The shelter had no water source, but I had enough water to cook. I could get water at the restroom at the state park in the morning. Normally, I would keep my food bag in my tent, but I elected to put it in the bear box that night. I personally thought, if there was a controlled bear hunting season in New Jersey, it would solve the bear problem. I felt enough people were at the shelter that we should be all safe from the bears that night.

I met several new folks there, but I didn't feel like socializing, which was unusual for me. I was so exhausted I could hardly stay awake long enough to enter in my journal. I forced myself to open my notebook and started to write, which seemed to give me a little energy.

The Oxford Group and many other religions practice confession on a regular basis. I had no idea if they guided or taught people how to change, but that might have been what inspired Bill to write Step Four and Step Five.

The Big Book identified three basic, God-given instincts. They were the instinct for security, social standing, and of course sex. God probably gave us these basic instincts when he gave us humans our self-will, so we could take care of ourselves. Only God knows why and he didn't tell me.

He gave us the instinct for security so we would gather food to be able to feed our family, so we wouldn't starve. That was good, but because of our self-centered, self-will, we became selfish and greedy. We sought money, property, and material value. When I became desperate for the means to feed my addiction, I would steal and deal to satisfy my selfish needs. I wouldn't pay my bills or take care of my obligations to my wife or children. I felt guilt, shame, and remorse, but I did it again and again.

God gave us a social instinct so we would take care of our families to provide, protect, and teach our children. That instinct caused us to seek prestige within our societies. Because of ego, we became codependent, controlling, and inconsiderate to the point that we forced our will on many levels of society. In all my relationships, both sexual and nonsexual, I became either dependant on others or dominant over others. I became grandiose and bragged to try to impress others in an attempt to falsely build my own self-esteem. I always tried any means to manipulate or control others to get my own way.

Our God given sexual instinct was designed so we could reproduce and the human race would survive. Because we humans become lustful, we have caused pain and heartache to both others and ourselves ever since the beginning of mankind. The pursuit of my sexual ambitions did enormous harm to others. I was inconsiderate, purposely deceived others, and made promises I didn't intend to ever keep to temporally fulfill my own lustful needs.

I believe every sin or everything I ever did that went against God or society, stemmed from my own self-serving pursuit of these three basic instincts. My intent usually wasn't to hurt others, but I seldom considered the welfare of others either. Maybe that was why the preacher said we were all sinners, because we all had self-will and those same basic instincts.

I realized I had been writing and meditating for over two hours. I closed the book, took off my glasses, and turned off the light. I must have fallen asleep quickly, because I didn't remember anything after that.

Day 96   18.1 Miles

I awoke to a morning that promised to mature into another scorcher. I retrieved my food from the bear box. The bears left me alone after the encounter on the trail. I quietly packed and left as it was starting to get light without waking anyone else. I slept in New Jersey for the last time because I planned to enter New York sometime later that day. I hiked to the restroom at Wawayanda State Park for water and washed up a little. I was hoping for a pop machine, but no luck yet again. I stopped soon afterward, made coffee, and ate breakfast.

My left upper thigh continued to give me trouble. On a scale of one to ten it was a seven, which progressed from when I first noticed it three days before. The problem was I didn't know what was wrong or how bad it would get. I caught myself still worrying too much and too often about injuries knocking me off the trail.

I already hiked about thirteen-hundred and fifty miles, but I still had very little confidence that I could make it to Katahdin, which was eight-hundred and twenty-seven miles north. I still became overwhelmed when I looked at how far I had to go and what I would go through to summit. To stay positive, I had to turn around and look at how far I already came and what I had to overcome so far.

I had to get my own head out of trying to control the future by letting go and letting God take care of what would lie ahead. All I had to do was keep putting one foot in front of the other, a step at a time, a minute at a time, a mile at a time, a day at a time, and let God take care of the rest. Even after all God did for me, I still had a hard time letting go to trust Him.

I crossed the New Jersey/New York border by late morning. I stopped long enough to take a picture of the line painted on a rock at the border. The rocks seemed to change from small pieces to long, smooth, giant granite rocks. It was almost as if I was walking on the backs of huge, stone whales.

Feather, Fire Fly, and Team Steve passed me. I told them about an ice cream store I knew about from a previous section hike. They were skeptical because the guidebook didn't list the store. However, they said they wouldn't eat all the ice cream before I got there.

I arrived at New York Route Seventeen-A by early afternoon. The significance was because I had hiked from that point south to the Tennessee/Virginia boarder on previous section hikes. I had been on familiar soil since April. I never was north of Seventeen-A on the Appalachian Trail. I felt a little uneasy as I entered virgin territory.

Alcoholics Anonymous had a slogan that said, first things first, so before I moved on, I had a lot of ice cream I had to eat. I hiked a short distance down the highway to the store I told my friends about, which only sold homemade ice cream in many flavors.

I found my friends already there, but apparently, they didn't wait for me. They were sleeping off their sugar down in the shade on the sidewalk in front of the store. I went inside and bought a quart of homemade mint-Oreo Cookie ice cream and sat in the air conditioning as I ate it all myself. I went to the restroom and filled my water bottles before leaving. I found Team Steve awake, but in a stupor as I left. Fire Fly and Feather were still fast asleep in each other's arms on the sidewalk. I took their picture and left the wimps to sleep it off.

I knew if I stopped to nap, the muscles in my thigh would tighten up and I would have a hard time starting again. I also knew from experience if I stopped, the sugar down would put me to sleep, but the same sugar would give me an extra energy boost if I kept moving. I moved slowly because of the pain in my thighs, so all my friends caught up to me in four miles at Fitzgerald Falls. Fitzgerald Falls was a small waterfall in the woods that cascaded over a sixty-foot stone face. We all jumped in to get an Appalachian Trail style shower. The falls were so beautiful and felt so good on that hot, muggy day. I told my friends I was staying behind to wash my clothes. I really wanted to take an afternoon nap to rest my thigh before I continued hiking. I couldn't let my friends know I was wimping out and tarnish my reputation. They would be disappointed.

After my nap, I moved on another four miles until a big thunder and lightning storm hit suddenly. I set up in a hurry beside the trail on a not so level spot I cleared in the woods. I would call this home for the night. I was by myself and had no cell tower, so I spent the time reading about the Fourth Step in the Big Book before I could sleep. Somehow, I didn't feel so isolated when I was listening to what God had to say through the program.

Once I understood my basic God given instincts were my ego's incentive to sin, my Forth Steps became a lot more sophisticated. The things I did to pursue the basic instincts began to manifest in fears, resentments, and harm to others producing shame, which gave me more incentive to use more chemicals to cope with my out of control, Godless life. The drugs were my only relief or sanctuary from the reality of how I was living. The chemicals, in a sense, became a demanding illusion of God. I found myself in a vicious cycle, spiraling down to the pits of hell until one day, I asked for God's help to be free.

In the active stage of my addiction, I thought if I only stopped all the use, everything would be okay. I got sober and my behavior did get better, but I had to face the wreckage of my past without the help of chemicals. My shame, depression, and anxiety worsened once the reality of living in my addiction set in. In other words, emotionally, things became worse after I got sober. The fog of years of chemical abuse started to lift and I could no longer use drugs or alcohol to hide from the painful emotions.

I started the process of forgiving myself with my first primitive inventory many years ago. Time passed and I learned more about self-will before I did my second Step Four inventory with Gallagher. I listed my resentments, fears, and the harms to others first and then wrote down what I did to cause them. I was sober longer and capable of being more honest. I found in each case, I was pursuing at least one and often a combination of basic instincts. My self-seeking caused me to become selfish, inconsiderate, dishonest, or frightened, which were the exact nature of my wrongs.

Alcoholics Anonymous called these defects of character, but I often heard them called mistakes, wrongs, shortcomings or sins. My sins, or the exact nature of my wrongs, were what blocked me from God as I understood Him.

I then understood what Big Jim was talking about when he said, "It's like peeling an onion." I had done several Step Four inventories and planned on continuing to do more formal, fearless, and written Step Four inventories because each time it was like peeling an onion. I peeled off another layer and got closer to the core that resulted in spiritual progress towards improving my relationship with my Higher Power who I came to understand as God.

My strategy of rest, meditation, plus some extra ibuprofen, worked, so with prayer and medication, I finally escaped the pain in sleep.

SPIDERS

Day 97   8.7 Miles

It thundered and rained all night, so I had to pack up a wet tent in the rain again. Section hikers often understandably, aborted their hikes due to rain. I wouldn't abort because of rain, but I grew to appreciate the luxury of packing up a dry tent in dry weather. My upper thigh would barely hold my weight, so I took a double dose of ibuprofen. Doc Turner would probably crap if he knew how often or how much ibuprofen I took. The rain stopped by mid-morning and it turned damp and cool, which I preferred for hiking. I was running low on water and it looked like I would have to go about six miles before I could get water, so I started to conserve.

I crossed an overpass on the New York State Thruway going into New York City. I looked at all the cars hustling into and out of the city like busy little ants. My biggest concern was where I was going to get water next. I wondered which world was real, theirs or mine?

I entered Harriman State Park and found some water a trail angel left. Only a little water remained, so I barley took enough to get by. I left a note to the unknown trail angel thanking him or her and explaining how grateful I was for the water.

The warm sun came out to dry up everything. I hurt my upper thigh more when I slipped on a rock, so I stopped early for lunch at a glacier lake named Island Pond. I set up my tent in the sun to dry out. The lake must have gotten its name from a tiny little island in the middle of the lake. I would bet on a hot day, some hikers swam to the island to privately lay naked in the sun. I felt overwhelmed at the thought of the two-hundred-yard swim, which seemed too exhausting for me that day. I was so exhausted from the morning hike I crawled into my tent and fell fast asleep. I awoke after an hour groggy, so I made a cup of coffee. I had only hiked five miles so far that day. I felt dizzy and exhausted all that morning, but I hadn't hiked far. I decided to go to the lake and take a swimbath before I continued.

The water was cold, refreshing, and as smooth as glass. I was drying off in the sun and I saw my naked reflection in the lake. I was shocked because I was extremely skinny. I looked like I did twenty-six years ago when I first quit using drugs and alcohol. I looked like a Cambodian boat refugee. I smelled my clothes before I put them on and they smelled like ammonia, which I heard could mean I was burning my own muscle. Two plus two started to equal four. That explained why I felt tired all the time and was hiking short days but still exhausted. It may even have been the reason my thighs were hurting so badly. After all, they were my largest muscles, so I could have burned the muscles in them for energy. I started to worry, which I did well and often anyway.

I decided on the spot to take a zero day when I got to the next town, Fort Montgomery. I would rent a room, so I could eat town food and rest. I would stop to re-supply more often and eat more food when I got the chance in the future. I moved on slowly, but had hope because I knew what was wrong and what I needed to do.

New York had some impressive rock formations. I went through one they named the Lemon Squeezer in the early afternoon. The Lemon Squeezer was a single granite rock the size of a building, which split and left a narrow passage between the two sides. The climb through was spectacular. I only hoped the pictures I took did it justice.

I met an excited, panicky French Canadian and his husky-type dog on the trail. He was speaking half in English and half in French, but I translated the best I could. I thought he started a fire in the fireplace in the shelter and smoked out a rattlesnake. Apparently, he was extremely afraid of rattlesnakes, so he was moving to his tent. I arrived at Fingerboard Shelter a few minutes later. I read what he wrote in the register, which said, "I make fire. Snake come out, fuck shelter, move to tent." I laughed until my sides hurt.

A storm hit and a young couple who were section-hiking came into the shelter to get out of the rain and ate lunch with me. I was happy for the company. I warned them about the snake. They laughed and said they saw the Canadian earlier as he passed them.

I was leaving when a familiar looking hiker came in. I recognized him as soon as he said, "G'day," in his Australian accent. He was an Australian named Mountain Goat who I first met in May 2004 at Icewater Spring Shelter in the Smoky Mountains as we sat out a thunderstorm. I was section hiking with Chief at the time and Mountain Goat was attempting a thru-hike. I was on another section hike with Scooter in July of 2004 and I met him for the second time on Priest Mountain in Virginia. He was hiking with a girlfriend by that time.

I didn't think I would ever see Mountain Goat again, but as it turned out, he had to abort his hike at Five-O-One Shelter in Pennsylvania. He thought he had shin splints, so he took eleven zero days at Five-O-One hoping to recover and go on. He didn't get better and found out he was suffering from stress fractures. He went back to Australia to recover. He healed up, returned in 2006 and, started at Five-O-One in Pennsylvania, and was attempting to finish at Katahdin.

Alcoholics Anonymous has a slogan which says, *God won't give you more than you can handle.* That day, I had more than I could handle, so God sent some help. He sent a salty, heathen, whisky-drinking, fist-fighting, rigid, opinionated Aussie who inspired me to continue. I had to admit sending Mountain Goat was positive proof God had a sense of humor. We spent about an hour in the shelter chatting, hoping the rain would quit. Mountain Goat offered me a Lipton Noodles meal because of my situation, but I declined. I had already eaten and besides I would be in Fort Montgomery the next day. I still had enough food to last until I got there. The rain continued and looked like it set in for the night, so we hiked out in the rain. I hiked with Mountain Goat for about half a mile, but couldn't go any further, so I stopped and set up beside the trail. I hiked less than nine miles that day, but I felt exhausted and I had tremendous pain in both of my thighs. Mountain Goat bid me, "G'day."

I was camped in a lush green, hardwood forest in a serene setting.

Camping there would be perfect if I didn't have the pain in my thighs, if I felt better, if I had more energy, and if it wasn't raining. I stopped setting up and took a moment to reflect on the situation.

Five years ago, my wife sent me on an errand to Walmart to pick up some things including five, forty pound bags of cow manure for her garden. My lower back was hurting badly at the time, so when I went to pay for it I told the clerk I needed someone to load it on my truck. She called for a loader from lawn and garden to the cow manure and told me to take my truck to the pallet of bags and someone would be there shortly.

I only waited a short time and a pleasant older man named Stan came out, marked my receipt, and loaded the bags with ease. I asked him his age and he said, "I was seventy on my last birthday." I instantly became envious of the man who was twenty years older than me. I thought to myself, why was he so lucky that he could do things I hadn't been able to do since I was thirty-years-old. Why did I have to go through life with an injured back?

I returned to the store to pick up the rest of my list. I parked my truck and stomped back to the store feeling oh so sorry for myself. As I entered the store, a voice said, "Hi, Welcome to Walmart." I looked at the greeter and saw a twenty-year-old boy in an electric wheelchair whose nametag said, "Bradley."

Bradley inherited a body bent, distorted, and deformed from birth through no fault of his own. His head permanently turned to the side, bobbed up and down as he struggled to hold it up. The only way he was able to get around was by moving a lever on his wheelchair with his twisted hand.

I said, "Hi Bradley, how are you doing?" He said, "Great." My self-pity melted instantly as tears filled my eyes. I realized I was being an immature, self-centered ass, who was ungrateful for all my blessings.

My mind returned to the woods where I sat. I took a deep breath to smell the fresh, wet air slightly perfumed by the pine trees. I looked around at the beauty of the late spring day on the Appalachian Trail with the rich green of the forest, the shine of the wet gray rock formations, and the brown of the woods and forest floor. Spring wildflowers added an occasional splash of color, which the spring rain enhanced. It occurred to me how grateful Bradley would be if he could be in my situation instead of his. I prayed, "Lord, I am ashamed for my attitude. I apologize and ask forgiveness. I give thanks for Bradley, Stan, and the privilege of being here on the trail with the rain and the pain. Amen."

I felt better knowing God had truly blessed me. Nothing had changed in my situation. Katahdin was still eight-hundred miles away. The only thing that changed was my attitude and the way I looked at the situation.

I cooked rice and cheese in the rain. I had two more meals and fourteen miles to go before I came to a store. I would take a zero day when I got to a motel in Fort Montgomery. I took off my wet clothes and crawled into my sleeping bag, which was actually dry for a change. I closed my eyes and enjoyed something as simple as the silky feel of the nylon sleeping bag on my skin. I felt it would be a good time to try to connect with God as I understood him.

Soon my mind went to Step Five which suggested after you completed a searching and fearless moral inventory, you admitted to God, yourself, and another human being the exact nature of your wrongs or defects of character. When I first read Step Five I thought, why couldn't I just admit my shortcomings to God? My ego didn't want another human being to know anything was wrong with me.

Many years ago, I had the privilege of being associated with an inmate named Willy. Willy's addiction on the mean streets and harsh prison life had hardened him. He was still physically formidable in spite of his age. He had been shot and cut in street fights in his younger days, but eventually Old Man Time had mellowed him some and given him the wisdom which only came with experience. Willy and I developed a mutual respect for one another over the years. One day we were discussing trust with some younger fish in a county prison. Trust was something rare in prison, but Willy had an untarnished image of being a bad ass with the younger men both black and white.

All the inmates respected him, so they listened when he said, "I had to have somebody watch my ear for me."

He had the group's attention, so he continued, "My eyes are in front of my head, and my ear is on the side, so I can't see it myself."

He paused before moving on, "If a spider gets in my ear I have to trust someone who can see it to give me the word up before I get bit."

I didn't realize it at the time, but Willy answered the question as to why I need to admit my faults to another human being. Sometimes I couldn't see what was wrong with me and I needed another mortal to point out spiders in my ear.

Earlier in the day, I didn't have anyone to take a close look at me to watch for spiders, so God showed me my own reflection in the lake so I could see the spider myself. Now that I saw the problem, I could form strategies to resolve it, so I could continue. I felt a comfort which comes from feeling cared for by God as I escaped the day in sleep.

June 3   Day 98   13.6 Miles

It rained hard and steady all night, and showed no signs of letting up that day. I made hot coffee and Ramen noodles in the tent to stay dry out of the rain. I was soaked within minutes after I left my tent, packed up, and started hiking. I met Team Steve at William Brien Memorial Shelter about five miles down the trail. He still had his tent set up and was cooking. He couldn't find room in the shelter the night before in the rain because it was full of Boy Scouts. I took the time to cook an early lunch with him. We ate in silence. He seemed almost as down as I was. Days like that must have been where the term, under the weather, originated. I found it so hard to maintain a positive attitude when I was constantly soaking wet and cold. Before I left, I told Team Steve, "This too shall pass."

I put on some music and the miles slowly passed. I saw a sign on Black Mountain saying "NYC visible," but I could only see endless gray nothingness that day. The good news was I felt better physically. I walked up on a man dressed in street clothes, dress shoes, with a garbage bag for a pack. He was laying on a rock as he drank straight out of a stream. He didn't see me coming and I didn't want to alarm him, so in a soft voice I said, "Hi." He jumped up startled anyway. He didn't seem to fit as a hiker, so maybe he was on the run from the law or something. All my intuition said the man could be dangerous, so I never once took my eyes off his.

His name was Frank and he asked me for food. I felt sorry for him and tossed him my last Snickers bar and a small bag of smiley-face-gumdrops, which was all the food I had left. I didn't want to get within his reach because I suspected Frank was schizophrenic and currently psychotic. I didn't like the look in his eyes, but he may have simply been trying to intimidate me. I was determined if I thought it was going to come to blows or he advanced to within reach, I was going to attack first. Fortunately, for me, it didn't come to an altercation and I moved on safely after a few tense moments.

Soon after, I met two attractive, wet, young women from New York City who were out for a day hike. They also had an encounter with Frank and gave him food. They asked if I would hike with them for protection because they were afraid of him. I felt honored and enjoyed their company, plus their request fed my old man's macho ego. We all chatted as I escorted them to their car without incident. I took their picture and they both hugged me goodbye. I soon realized I was in an excellent mood. I am amazed at how two attractive young girls could make an old hound dog like me quickly forget all my problems on a rainy day.

I arrived at Bear Mountain State Park around noon. I realized it was Saturday because hundreds of people came from the city and sat under the cover of several pavilions at Hessian Lake to stay out of the rain. A concession stand was an unexpected serendipity. I paid two dollars and fifty cents for a hot dog with sauerkraut; obviously New York City prices. I didn't find any people friendly enough to talk to, so I moved on because I was wet, cold, and felt like an outsider.

The trail passed through a wildlife center which had native animals caged up for all the tourists to see. I saw bears, bobcats, coyotes, and otters watching me as I quietly walked by. I felt like opening the cages and freeing the prisoners, but I didn't.

I turned off trail at the bridge over the Hudson River and started hiking two miles down the highway to Fort Montgomery. I walked about half the way when an older lady about my age, stopped to pick me up. I tried to decline because I was soaking wet and didn't want to get her car wet. She said she didn't care because she too was hiking on the trail and soaking wet. She wanted to take me to a restaurant for a meal, but I declined because I was wet, cold, tired, and wanted to get to a motel. She dropped me off at the door of the Bear Mountain Bridge Motel.

I rented a room for two nights for one-hundred and forty dollars, which was half what I would have had to pay at the Holiday Express a mile farther down the highway. The owner, an older German gentleman named Doug, was hiker-friendly and settled me in the room. I was wet to the bone, so I felt extra grateful for the hot shower and dry clothes.

The rain let up in the afternoon, so I ventured out to a convenience store for pizza, ice cream, and coffee. After I returned to the motel, the owner came by to check to see if the toilet was shutting off and asked if I needed anything. I asked if there was somewhere I could weigh myself. He took me to his house and on his bathroom scale, I discovered I weighed a mere one-hundred and thirty-five pounds. When I got back to the privacy of my room, I stripped down and took a picture of myself at a hundred-thirty-five pounds. It amazed me at how emaciated I looked.

I took a short nap before I went across the highway to a bagel shop owned and operated by a Mexican family. I bought two sandwiches, one for now, and one to go. I returned to the motel and tried watching television, but I soon became bored with it. I turned the lights off and went to bed. I couldn't sleep, so I started to reflect on Step Five.

Trusting someone, even Big Jim, to admit my sins to, came hard for me in Step Five. I was a drug dealer and one of the requirements of being a dealer was not to trust the wrong person. Besides some of the harms I did were against the will of society and could land me in the pokey. I understood logically why it went against my nature to trust anyone. Then I realized I actually had always trusted certain people in certain areas. I had never been too good of a mechanic myself, so I found a mechanic I could trust to fix my truck. He gained my trust by consistently being trustworthy to fix my truck.

When I was planning my thru-hike, I went to Doc Turner and got my heart tested. He asked me, "When was the last time you had a colonoscopy?"

I said, "Cola what?"

He explained the procedure in enough detail that I said, "Hold on doc, you want to stick what up my what?"

He never even cracked a smile when he said, "A trained surgeon will perform the procedure to check to see if there is anything wrong in your colon."

I was horrified at the thought and said, "Ain't nuttin wrong with my colon, a lot of people have told me I was a perfect asshole."

He said, "Trust me, you don't want to die from something like colon cancer that may have been prevented if it would have been caught in time."

The Doc had always been trustworthy, so I reluctantly agreed. The day arrived and I had to go through some unpleasant preparation starting the day before. They had me take off my clothes and put on a gown that left a revealing draft in the back. The nurse wheeled me into the operating room and hooked me up to an IV.

Several people were present when a masked man with a syringe introduced himself and said, "Roll over." He was going to inject something into my IV port.

"You better give me a lot of that shit or we're going to be wrestling when you go to do what you're going to do!" The next thing I knew I was in the recovery room babbling to Scooter when the surgeon came in and confirmed I was a perfect asshole.

The point was I had to trust others to do for me what I could not do for myself, even if I felt vulnerable. I couldn't see spiders in my own ear and sometimes I couldn't see my own character defects. I always was the one who chose who I trusted. I wouldn't trust my mechanic to shove a camera up my rectum, but neither would I trust the Doc to fix the brakes on my truck.

I always picked what I considered a wise man in the program or my sponsor to hear my Fifth Steps. It had to be someone who believed in God, had a sponsor, and worked the Twelve Steps. I trusted them to a point, but I always changed the names of the others in my Fifth Step to protect their anonymity. I picked a man because I believe only men could understand men's issues. Besides, I didn't think Scooter would be appropriate to do a Step Five of my past with. She wouldn't ever be ready for that. I looked for someone who wasn't afraid of me. People who I intimidated would agree with me and tell me what I wanted to hear. I needed someone with enough courage to stand up to me, look me in the eye, and tell me the truth I needed to hear.

Some of my friends did their Fifth Steps with a counselor or a member of the clergy. I personally felt if the person I did my personal Fifth Step with hadn't been where I had been, I would waste their time and mine. I didn't believe anyone outside the program could ever understand why I did what I did.

I planned to take a zero day, explore the area, and re-supply. I wanted to take in as many calories as I could to try to gain some weight in the next day or two. I was tired enough to sleep, so I rolled over in the fresh, clean sheets and closed my eyes. That was the last thing I remembered.

Day 99   Zero miles

I awoke stiff and sore to a gray, but dry day. I stretched and took some ibuprofen. I walked a mile to a New York style deli which had a counter with stools like an old-fashioned diner. I ate three eggs over easy, sausage, potatoes, toast, and coffee. I enjoyed watching the locals come and go, buy the Sunday paper, eat breakfast, or simply have coffee. They would exchange pleasantries with the owner and the cook or maybe even gossip a little about other locals. I walked around Fort Montgomery, New York exploring the town, which was a small town that had two convenience stores, a bagel shop, and a New York style deli. A small public lake in town had benches where I sat watching ducks and the local folks fishing. I ate as much high calorie food as I could in my attempt to gain some weight back.

I re-supplied as best I could between the two convenience stores.

I bought two, twelve-ounce jars of peanut butter, two eight-ounce packages of hot pepper cheese, and three sixteen-ounce cans of cake frosting because they contain twenty-six hundred calories each. I bought the usual rice, noodles, peanut packets, and the old staple, Snickers bars. I also found some bug repellant, which I needed desperately.

I would be in deer tick country at least until I got to Massachusetts so I had to use a lot of deet. I also ran into what they called no-see-ums, which were little tiny flies who flew closely and directly in front of my eyes. The salt in my tears might be what attracted them. Sometimes they got in my eyes. They didn't bite, but they were terribly annoying. I found they stayed away if I put deet on the brim of my hat.

I was craving about ten double cheeseburgers from McDonald's, so I walked toward West Point looking for a McDonald's and a larger grocery store, but my legs hurt so badly I returned to the motel after a few miles. I took several showers and watched television to kill time. I wanted to rest all I could before I went back to the trail, but I found resting extra boring and lonely.

The owner of the motel gave me permission to set up my tent in his back yard to dry out. I dried out my sleeping bag and all my other gear in my room. Dry gear lightened my pack considerably.

I read my Big Book for a short time before I focused on my first ever Fifth Step. The first time I took an inventory with Big Jim, was a list of my sins. My first Step Five was a confession because that was all I was capable of at that time. I didn't follow the directions in the big book, but as primitive as it was, that was the point where I started. As my recovery matured and I continued to repeat my Step Four inventory, I learned more and discovered many of my sins were for the same reasons. The reasons always boiled down to the same selfish pursuit of my basic instincts, which were money, power, or sex.

Big Jim was right, it was like peeling an onion. The sins were always my self-will trying to meet my needs at the expense of God's or society's will, which separated me from God, society and my fellows. My sins were many, but the reasons behind my behavior that caused me to sin were few. A pattern of the same sin against different people started to emerge. The reasons for my sins were the exact nature of my wrongs or my character defects.

I had to admit the exact nature of my character defects to another live human being for two significant reasons. The first reason was I needed someone else's expertise to give me honest feedback to see what I couldn't see for myself like a spider in my ear. The second important reason was simply to keep me honest. I have a tendency to lie to God and myself. I also got what I called tunnel vision. I only saw a small part of the picture that I wanted to see. The problem was I could convince myself into believing the lie, which I call rationalization.

I got in trouble once when I spoke publicly to about a hundred people and said, "Rationalization was like masturbation, you were only screwing yourself." I was being sarcastic to make a point and lighten things up, but unfortunately, my boss failed to grasp my humor.

I found a few trustworthy folks were out there who worked their own spiritual program to watch for spiders in my ear. They also had a good bullshit detector and enough guts to confront me when I was lying or about to be bit by a spider I didn't see.

I wished I had cell tower to run some of my thoughts past someone in Alcoholics Anonymous for a reality check. I missed the social aspects of Alcoholics Anonymous. I would loved to have gone to a meeting in Fort Montgomery since I hadn't been to one in over three months. I hoped I would be able to get cell tower when I got back on the trail. I would then use my phone to contact my sponsor to do a little Step Five reality check.

I closed my little Big Book and ate a can of cake frosting. Scooter sent me an emergency package with some things I couldn't get on the trail. I planned to pick it up at the post office before I left town. The sugar down from the frosting ended my day.

WILLINGNESS

Day 100   11.8 Miles

Day one-hundred was another dry day. I could also see a strange thing they called the sun. I couldn't think of a better way to celebrate my hundredth day on the trail than with the sun. I showered, dressed, and headed for the bagel shop across the street. I met three hikers, Ric and Sharon, who called themselves the Newly Weds and Eagle Eye. They were already at the bagel shop when I arrived. They recognized me as a hiker and invited me to join them at their table. Wow, the day kept getting gooder and gooder. They stayed at the motel last night and the owner told them I was in room three. Someone had left them a six-pack of beer as a gift. The Newly Weds didn't drink at all and Eagle eye didn't drink alone, so they knocked on my door to ask if I would like to join them to socialize. I must have been in the shower or sleeping. I wish I would have heard the knock because I could have used the company, but not the beer.

The Newly Weds, were a Christian couple who just married and chose the Appalachian Trail for their honeymoon. They started at Palmerton, Pennsylvania and hiked over Lehigh Gap, which was a hard climb first thing. They were attempting to make it to Mount Katahdin before they returned to college in the fall. Ric grew up overseas with his missionary parents. He met Sharon in school; they fell in love and married. They aspired to become missionaries themselves after they finished school. I found them both delightful.

Eagle Eye claims he was a retired Air Force medical doctor who was thru-hiking after retirement. I asked Eagle Eye several questions about the pain in my thighs and my low weight, but his answer was vague. I drank a lot of coffee and chattered away, but they didn't seem to mind.

I welcomed the company of some other hikers, but eventually, they left to head back to the trail.

The post office was open, so I picked up my mail from Scooter. I also received a ton of music for my MP3 player from a good friend in Washington State. My friend sent me music ever since I was in Georgia. I used the music to kill pain, drive away the blues, inspire me, give me courage, and put me to sleep at night. I felt blessed to have a friend like him.

I returned to the deli where I ate breakfast the day before and ate a big breakfast of three eggs, toast, sausage, and home fries. The lady also made a big hoagie to go for my lunch. I went back to the motel with a full stomach, saddled up, and started walking the two miles back to the trail. I experienced tremendous anxiety over my low weight and the pain in my thigh, which seemed better after I rested a day. Eagle Eye said I might be cannibalizing my own muscle but I wasn't sure he knew any more of what he was talking about than me.

I feared as always I would have to abort my hike over an injury. I said a prayer to ask for God's help and realized I had already asked Him the same prayer many times. I felt a little foolish and disrespectful after I prayed the prayer, so I apologized to God. My mind traveled back to the freezing rain in Tennessee when I was wet, cold and thought I would surely die if I couldn't get out of the elements. I stopped and prayed and when I opened my eyes I saw the sign on a tree for the shelter and Christopher was at the shelter to help me.

I don't know why, but I still had a hard time trusting God and letting go of my fears, even after all the times he answered my prayers and calmed my fears. I reminded myself to stay hopeful and trust God. I felt better after I apologized and thought maybe God liked it when I depended on him and asked for help.

I started hiking and my muscles warmed up. When I had idle time I contemplated the worst until I talked myself into believing the worst would happen. I knew I had to let go and let God, but for me, that was easier said than done. I remembered to be grateful for the gifts I received in the present and stop worrying about the yesterdays and tomorrows because God would take care of them.

I stopped for a view from a distance of the Bear Mountain Bridge, which was an impressive suspension bridge. The milky gray mist hid the view on my way into town a couple of days before. I looked over the magnificent bridge and wondered why God chose me for all this. Did God come into everyone's life as He did mine? Did everyone get the opportunity of a lifetime like being able to hike the Appalachian Trail? Why did God bless me? My eyes filled with tears as I felt overwhelmed with gratitude for my creator.

My mind drifted back to Bill Foot. He had cancer and was still willing to build a bridge over the James River. Why did God choose a man who had cancer to give the opportunity to build the bridge? The bridge James Foot built in some ways was larger than the one I was gazing at that crossed the Hudson River. When I eventually came to the Bear Mountain Bridge, I found it quite a bit larger than it looked from the distance, and by far the largest bridge I ever crossed on foot. The cars buzzed by as I made my way at a whopping one and a half miles per hour.

I stopped to watch a huge commercial barge that passed underneath to make its way upstream. I started to reminisce back to when I was a young boy. I used to stay at my sister's house in a small town when my parents would go on vacation. I would fish in the river with other kids about my age. We would all run to the overpass when we heard the sound of the train whistle four miles away. We would line up assuming the position and start peeing as the train was approaching. If our timing and accuracy was precise, the engineer would turn on the wipers and shake his fist at us. As I stood on the bridge in a perfect position, I had the incredible urge to be eleven-years-old once again. I thought I would leave it up to you the reader to wonder, did I or didn't I?

Once I crossed the bridge, the trail entered the woods immediately and climbed a steep, five-hundred and twenty foot ascent, which started my heart pumping. The altitude was only seven-hundred feet, but the steep climb gave the illusion of being much higher. The strenuous climb and the flow of endorphins took away my pain and fears. It felt good to be back on the trail.

I hiked to the entrance road of the Graymoor Friary, home of the Franciscan Friars. Eagle Eye and the Newly Weds planned to spend the night at a pavilion with free cold showers and if they were lucky, the Friars would serve them supper. I paused to consider hiking the two-tenths of a mile for the experience and company, but I had only been back on the trail a few hours. I don't like cold showers and I have a pack full of food, so I ate my hoagie and moved on, hoping I wouldn't regret it later. I hiked another five miles and camped in the woods by myself, a short distance from South Highland Road. I still had some pain in the big muscles in my legs, but as they say, "No pain, no rain, no Maine." The day threatened rain off and on all day but stayed dry, which was a welcome change. I made a cup of coffee and took some time to reflect on the day. I was still wondering why God gave the opportunity to build a bridge to James Foot who was dying of cancer. As I pondered the question, an unpleasant event from my past answered the question.

I was drinking whisky in a little bar in my hometown many years ago. I needed to use the men's room and found the door locked. I pounded on the door and demanded the gentleman inside move it along. An energetic exchange of words about our mothers followed through the door. When the door flew open, I saw how big he was, so I decided to take the first punch. I hit him as hard as I could. He had friends who jumped on me and I had friends who jumped on them. Before long, someone called the cops and they escorted us out of the bar.

I don't believe I even had any remorse at the time. More whisky always helped me cope with guilt and shame anyway. I probably even managed to rationalize somehow the whole thing was his fault anyway. After I sobered up, in early recovery, my past started to haunt me. I could no longer escape such events by temporally washing them away with the booze.

I was over five year's sober and sponsoring Danny, who was sober for two years at the time. We met at the Diamond Deli on a weekly basis for a sponsor/sponsee chat. Danny had talked about a brother who drank, but I had never met him. One day while we drank coffee in the Diamond Deli, Danny looked up and said, "Here comes my brother now." I turned and instantly recognized the man walking through the door as the man I punched many years before. A tense moment followed as our eyes met like two bulls in the same pasture.

Danny said, "Mark, this is my sponsor who I told you about."

I never took me eyes off Mark's as I said, "Your brother and I met a long time ago and I owe your brother an apology." I then extended my hand and said to Mark, "I'm deeply sorry."

Hesitantly, Mark shook my hand and said, "Apology accepted."

I bought Mark a cup of coffee and we all sat down. Danny had no idea what was going on so we both explained the event which took place years before. I found out I broke Marks jaw that night and I felt so guilty, I offered to let him give me a free punch in the mouth.

He declined saying, "Then I'd be as big of an asshole as you." We all agreed and laughed.

Believe it, or not, Mark and I became friends and the three of us went to a few Alcoholics Anonymous meetings together. Mark eventually decided Alcoholics Anonymous wasn't for him. He was happy Danny and I were going, but he wasn't that bad. He did say if his drinking ever got out of control, he knew where to come for help. He wasn't willing at the time to quit, because he felt he was in control of his drinking.

One night about a year later, Mark was walking home after spending some time playing pool at the bar. He had a blood alcohol content which was over two times the legal limit to drive. For some unknown reason he was laying in the middle of a back road and a car came along and hit him. The car dragged and twisted him up under the rear axle before the driver could stop. The accident broke most every bone in Mark's body.

After the funeral, I went to see Neal, the retired career army sergeant. Neal was a wise old man with thirty some years sober. I often went to Neal when I was emotionally in trouble. Neal already knew the story, but he was patient and listened to me as I related it again. I was struggling with the same questions that day.

I said to Neal, "Why did I get sober and Mark who deserved it more than me, didn't?" Neal was not a big talker, but when he said something, I learned it was always worth listening to.

He pondered a minute then said, "Mark made a different choice than you."

I turned away from Neal as he said, "Mark was given the same opportunity to get sober you got."

I choked up and could not talk as he added, "Alcoholics Anonymous was never intended for those who needed it. Alcoholics Anonymous was for those who wanted it. Be grateful you were one of the messengers who helped present him with the opportunity. The choice was his, he just wasn't willing."

I snapped back to the present with a new awareness. I remembered the helicopter story and thought probably God sent all his children helicopters to rescue us when we were in trouble, but he leaves the choice to get in or not up to us. Some folks made a different choice. Neal's words, "He just wasn't willing" stuck with me.

I could see the opportunity to build the bridge was already there, but Bill Foot was the one willing to seize the opportunity. God didn't actually do it for him, but He sent the chopper.

I ate tuna and noodles for supper and a can of cake frosting with a cup of heavily sugared tea for desert. I probably took in over three thousand calories. All the sugar made me so sleepy, I didn't remember it getting dark.

Day 101   14.7 Miles

I ate a toasted honey bun, a twelve-ounce jar of peanut butter, cookies, and a can of tuna for breakfast before I hiked out. My legs still hurt, but a lot less. At least I had the hope they were getting better and I would get past the adversity. I realized, I was starting to psych myself off the trail a few days ago. I had to remember, God grant me the courage to change the things I can. I would eat as much food as I could and leave the rest up to God. I hoped to hike twenty miles, so I could stop at a pizza shop and eat pizza for supper. I could re-supply at a convenience store next door and eat breakfast there again the next morning. I hiked in solitude in the lush green forest at an altitude of only ten to twelve hundred feet. The day was hot and humid, but zero rain. I put on some of my new music, so I could let my mind go into a trail dream.

Neal's words in regards to Mark, "He just wasn't willing" kept haunting me. Willingness appeared to be universally essential, but especially in recovery or any other spiritual quest. Sometimes the opportunity window opens for a short time and sometimes the window stays open. Experience has taught me time ran out on some opportunities never to present itself again. That was exactly what happened to my friend Orville on the trapline. I also missed many opportunities, because I wasn't willing to take the risk, invest, change, or believe in it at the time. My friend Mark missed the opportunity to enter Alcoholics Anonymous because he wasn't willing. I wonder if he ever regretted his decision. I became aware maybe my friends Mark and Orville were sending me personal spirit whispers from their graves.

I unexpectedly came upon RPH Shelter, which interrupted my thoughts. The shelter looked more like a cabin with a mowed lawn. A hiker box inside contained all kinds of goodies. I immediately investigated and ate a small bag of Hersey Kisses. I took a twelve-ounce jar of peanut butter and jelly, and an eight-ounce bag of beef jerky for later. I made a cup of tea to wash down a nutrition bar and read the trail register before I moved on.

I was going to try to hike five more miles to the pizza shop, but decided to make camp at a vista instead, which made things easier for me. I camped off the trail by Taconic Mountain. I changed my plans to stop at the convenience store the next morning, eat brunch, and buy as many supplies as I could carry. I ate ramen noodles mixed with peanut butter and an eight-ounce block of hot pepper cheese for supper. I later ate a sixteen-ounce can of cake frosting for a bedtime snack.

My emotions rose after I got back on the trail. I wondered if the intake of more calories was also boosting my emotions. I would think folks who were starving would be a little depressed. I thought the sun might have also helped. I was hoping to run into some other hikers, but no luck. The cake frosting helped me quickly end the day in sleep.

<h2 style="display:flex;justify-content:space-between">Day 10215.3 Miles</h2>

It rained all night and continued, so I made coffee in my tent. I ate the peanut butter and jelly to go with my coffee, before I ventured out into the weather. Both my gear and I were soaked by the time I finished packing. That didn't help improve my mental state. The good news was I had a lot less pain in my thighs, which gave me hope that I had resolved that problem.

I hiked about four miles to a highway where a convenience store was four-tenths of a mile off-trail. The pizza shop didn't open until the afternoon, but to my surprise, my friend from Australia, Mountain Goat was already at the store. We stood outside under the overhang out of the rain to eat our breakfast sandwiches and drank hot coffee. We chatted in the rain until we started to get cold, then we moved out. We hiked together, talking non-stop from the store to Morgan Shelter where I stopped for lunch. Mountain Goat was negative by nature and never seemed to smile, but hiking with him was a pleasure, especially on a dreary day. His negativity started to outweigh the value of his company, so I decided to stay and rest at the shelter for a while as he moved on.

I made a pot of coffee and ate a huge lunch of eight ounces of hot pepper cheese, twelve ounces of peanut butter, and a can of tuna. After I gorged, I took a nap. I moved on at a slower pace in the early afternoon. It rained hard and steady all that day, so I decided to stay at Telephone Pioneer Shelter. The shelter was only a tenth of a mile off trail and I wouldn't have to crawl into a wet tent.

I was expecting another lonely night, but when I arrived at the shelter, the Newly Weds and Mountain Goat were already there to welcome me. They said misery loved company, which may be the reason my mood rocketed from melancholy to ecstatic immediately.

I was happy to see the Newly Weds again who filled me on the trail news in since I last saw them. They stayed at the Graymoor Friary as they had planned and had a great experience. They told me a leg injury knocked Eagle Eye off the trail. They didn't think he planned on returning. I felt bad, but wasn't surprised because my intuition suspected Eagle Eye wasn't what or who he said he was all along. He sported brand new, top of the line hiking clothes and equipment, which was common in Georgia. We were in New York and his new equipment would have shown a lot of wear from fourteen-hundred miles of trail.

That night was the first time I actually enjoyed staying in a shelter. I dried out and warmed up. I made several pots of hot tea to share as we traded stories and laughed together. It was a strange combination of people God put together for the night. We all talked into the night from the warmth of our sleeping bags. One by one, my friends fell silent in sleep. I stayed awake for quite a while listening to the downpour only a few feet away. I took an inventory of my blessings.

Step Six said, "We were entirely ready to have God remove all these defects of character." God sent Mark the opportunity, but he wasn't ready or willing to step out of his comfort zone and let go of the comfortable to change. I could understand, because I too wasn't willing to let go of my drinking for years.

In discussion meetings about Step Six I had often heard folks say, They didn't want to get rid of all their character defects. I could agree because I liked some of my selfish traits. I was afraid if I gave up everything I would no longer be me. Step Six was more about being willing than anything else, for me personally. Sometimes I was not willing to make changes in my life when the outcome was unknown. I perceived I would be giving up something I needed or wanted.

Maybe the spirit whispered in my ear, I wasn't sure, but I received a sudden awareness fear was usually the reason I was unwilling to change. I was afraid of the unknown result of change. Who would I be if I changed? I was often slow to catch on to things because I said the Serenity Prayer at every Alcoholics Anonymous meeting I ever attended. The second line in the prayer requests, *God grant me the courage to change the things I can.* Nothing changed if I wasn't willing to change and change was how I grew spiritually closer to God. I made a decision to change in Step Three. I wanted to change, but it took courage to step out of the ordinary to change.

I said a prayer, "Dear God, Please grant me the courage to be willing to step out of my personal comfort zone so I can take new opportunities to change and build new bridges. Amen" I relaxed and felt comfortable and grateful for the new insight until sleep overcame me.

Day 103   13 Miles

I awoke before anyone else and made a pot of coffee. The others soon awoke to the smell of coffee filling the shelter. Mountain Goat asked in his Aussie accent "Ay mate, ya mind if I mooch a spot ah coffee." I smiled as I filled his cup. He took a sip and made a face as if he had just accidently drank from a beer can filled with somebody's tobacco spit. He coughed and gasped as he tried to get some air. He couldn't even bitch for a moment. I was laughing so hard I thought I was going to lose control of my bladder.

He said, "I've traveled the world and that sludge is the worst excuse for coffee I ever had the misfortune to experience."

I said in my best Aussie accent "It'll grow on ya mate."

I gestured to the Newly Weds, offering them some coffee and Sharon responded with, "We're good," for the both of them.

I had to admit, my coffee would make your eyes water, your hair curl, and your teeth ache, but it did wake you up. I never drank coffee for the taste anyway. I drank coffee for the feeling I got from the caffeine. I mixed instant coffee fifty/fifty with sugar at the store when I bought it. I put the mixture in a zip lock baggie and threw away the jar. Water was often scarce on the trail, so I would fill my pot half way with the mixture, and then I added a little water and heated it. I waited until it was hot enough to melt the protein powder I would mix in. Protein powder didn't do much for the taste, but it was white, which made it look like coffee with cream. Besides, the protein might be good for me. The result was a concoction that would eat the chrome off a car bumper.

The newly Weds could not get a word in edgewise, as Mountain

Goat and I had about three conversations going at the same time. It was still raining, so we took our time packing. Mountain Goat had a little tripod for his camera, so he set the timer on his camera to delay, and posed with us to take a group picture before we rode out of Dodge.

The Newly Weds dropped back probably because the Goat and I got on their nerves, but I preferred to think they simply couldn't keep up with us old farts. Three miles down trail, was The Appalachian Trail Train Station, where the Metro-North Commuter Railroad Train would take you to New York City for eighteen dollars round trip. We all talked about going to Grand Central Station and Manhattan for the day. I had never been to New York City and said I would never go, but I made a snap decision, probably based on my caffeine high, that I would go with everyone else that day. I thought we would stick out a little with our hiking poles and packs, but I didn't care.

Mountain Goat and I arrived at the train stop first and to our disappointment, it was deserted. The schedule on the sign said the next train was due to stop on Saturday. Neither Mountain Goat nor I knew for sure what day it was, but we thought it might be Thursday. The rain stopped about the time the Newly Weds caught up. We were disappointed we couldn't go to New York City, but the good news was Toni's Deli was only a half-mile down the highway. We took off our rain gear and happily hiked down the road as the sun started to break through the clouds.

To our delight, Toni's Deli was more like a busy truck stop which sold groceries, magazines, papers, and other supplies a hiker could purchase at city prices. First, we all bought large coffees, huge breakfast sandwiches and glazed donuts. I had two sausage, egg, and cheese on a croissant sandwiches and several donuts. I bought two eight-ounce blocks of pepper jack cheese, a twelve-ounce jar of peanut butter, glazed honey buns, and some other food supplies for my pack. I picked up two more cans of bug spray that were thirty percent Deet. One can was for me, and one can I gave to Sharon.

Only the day before, I removed deer ticks that could carry Lyme disease from both Ric and Mountain Goat. I believed I hadn't had any ticks because I had been using a lot of deet since I entered deer tick country. The goat was adamantly against using deet. He said it was too bad for you, but I thought I would continue to use deet until I got to Vermont and out of tick country. I agreed, deet posed a health hazard, but so did Lyme Disease. I tried to avoid putting it directly on my skin, but I used it liberally on my gaiters, clothes, and hat.

The others moved on, but I stayed behind for another cup of coffee and two ice cream sandwiches. I bought the June issue of Fur-Fish-Game magazine, which was an unexpected luxury. The sun had broken through, so I went outside and sat in the sun to drink good coffee and read my magazine. I drifted off for a little nap before I headed back to the trail.

A lady set up a roadside hotdog stand on my way back to the trail. I wasn't hungry, but I loved hotdogs, so I bought two with sauerkraut and mustard for later. The lady and I chatted as I devoured the hotdogs. They were so good I decided to buy two more dogs for later, but I actually saved them for later.

Soon after I got back on the trail, I had to cross a large hay field. The hay was up to my thighs and still wet from the rain. Fields were a prime place to pick up a deer tick, so I sprayed my legs before I entered. The grass made my skin itch as I bulled through. I must have hiked over a mile through the field in the hot sun. When I entered the woods, I stopped to take off my gaiters, shoes, and socks, and did a thorough inspection for deer ticks. The bug spray must have done its job, because I found zero ticks. I sprayed on more bug spray before I moved out.

I hiked solo through second-growth woods with good foot fall to the Connecticut border by early afternoon. I stopped for lunch at the border to celebrate hiking through another state. I ate the hot dogs and a half a pound of cheese for lunch. I felt better as the pain in my thighs was almost gone and I thought I was gaining some weight. I found the hiking easy in Connecticut because the altitude was around a thousand feet and the hills were gentle, but I was surprised and impressed with the several white water rivers.

I caught up to the Newly Weds and Mountain goat at Ten-Mile

Shelter. They were setting up for the night in the shelter. I was contemplating putting up my tent in the grassy yard in front of the shelter when a noisy troop of Cub Scouts landed to spend the night.

I moved on about a half mile to set up my tent on the bank of the Ten-Mile River. The river was a fast, forbidding, white water river with a class four rapid less than twenty yards from my campsite. The sound of the raging torrent would sing me to sleep. That night would be the first time I ever camped in Connecticut. It dried out after the rain stopped, but my clothes, tent, and sleeping bag were still wet. I opened up the tent and hung my sleeping bag in a tree for the breeze to dry as I made supper.

I crawled in my damp, but not wet sleeping bag with my belly full and recorded the events of the day. The promises in the Big Book said, "We will no longer regret the past." I always thought the Promises were talking about the things I did in my past I regretted. Towards the end of his life, my Dad said to me with regret, "I wished I would have become a pilot."

Dad held the same job for forty-four years, raised, and supported four of us kids. He was a devoted husband, father, and friend. He was popular, accepted, and all who knew him respected him. He never did anything to regret or get into even a little bit of trouble. Yet he had regrets, not for the things he did, but for what he didn't do. He regretted the opportunities he wasn't willing to take.

Dad had a good job at a newspaper that paid well, so he wasn't willing to let go of the comfort and security to take the opportunity to become a pilot. Neal's words, "He just wasn't willing," surfaced again.

The thought hit me like a sledgehammer, Would I regret the things I didn't do because I wasn't willing to leave my comfort zone? Would I regret the opportunities I passed up when my life was over, because I was afraid to step out of the ordinary?

I wanted to be willing. I pondered willingness for a while. At the time, I felt good with the pain in my legs subsiding. Katahdin was only seven-hundred and thirty miles away. I had some good friends at the shelter a short distance away. I felt so grateful because I was willing to take the chance to hike the trail. I even got a chuckle when I thought about Mountain Goat in the shelter with a bunch of noisy Cub Scouts. Hee! Hee! Hee! The sound of the forbidding river singing was the last thing I remembered.

Day 104   8.4 Miles

The early morning looked like it was going to turn into a wet, cold, rainy day. Mountain Goat showed up as I finished making coffee, so being sarcastic, I offered him a cup, and to my surprise, he accepted the offer as he whipped out his cup.

I said in my best Aussie accent, "It's startin ta grow on ya, ah mate."

I hiked with Mountain Goat to Schahghticoke Road where an old-time covered bridge called Bull Bridge crossed a white water creek. The guidebook said George Washington crossed the bridge thrice. I was a little impressed, but more impressed at the white water creek that ran under the bridge. I found myself wondering why I didn't see any kayakers on these rivers and creeks. I figured, maybe they were unable to navigate them. The real attraction was a convenience store on the other side of the bridge. We stopped to eat breakfast sandwiches and bananas with good coffee under the overhang of the store, protected from the rain.

I dropped back as the Goat was getting on my nerves and hiked solo. I had a mail drop waiting in Kent, which was about another seven miles up the trail. I hoped to re-supply, get a motel room, hot shower, and dry out.

The rain stopped and the sun came out about noon, which improved my mood the way it always did. I stopped at Mount Algo Lean-to early in the early afternoon. They called the shelters lean-tos in New England, but I wasn't sure why. A thru-hiker named Furious was at the shelter eating lunch, so I joined him. He was hiking fast, and furious to finish the trail. He was far more interested in making miles, getting his hike done, and moving on with his life than I was. He moved on about the time a gentleman about my age showed up. He was looking for his son, who was thru-hiking. He was describing his son to me, when his son arrived moments later. His son's name was Thomas, but he went by the trail name of Tank. Tank was a twenty-year-old introvert who was thru-hiking for the adventure. They soon moved on to hike together for a few days.

I looked in the guidebook and all the motels in Kent were over a hundred dollars a night. It was only three-tenths of a mile to the highway and another half mile road walk to Kent. I decided to set up my tent there in the sun to dry out while I hiked into town. I would buy a restaurant meal, pick up my package at the post office, and return to my tent for the night and save the motel money.

I set up my tent on a flat piece of ground as far away from the shelter as possible. I hung my sleeping bag and air mattress up to dry along with my wet, stinky cloths. I took a bath with wet wipes and put on my clean town shorts, shirt, and touched it all off with a generous splash of Patchouli oil for good measure. I took my empty pack and hiked to the road to Kent where I found a trail angel who went by the trail name of Patti-O. He offered me a ride to town in his van.

Several days before in New York, a trail angel left water on the trail and I left him a nice note thanking him and signed it Dreamer. It turned out Patti-O was the Trail Angel and he still had the note. We became instant friends as he took me straight to the Post Office where I picked up my mail drop from Scooter. I re-supplied from my package and started out to explore the town. I found Patti-O had waited for me to take me back to the trail. I didn't want to say I was going into town and risk hurting his feelings, so I jumped in the van. He gave me a coke and we chatted on the ride back to where he picked me up.

I backtracked to my camp at Mount Algo Shelter. My camp was as I had left it. The bad news was while I was gone, a troop of Boy Scouts came in and set up all around me. I guess I deserved what I got for laughing at the Newly Weds and Mountain Goat when they were with a bunch of Cub Scouts their first night in Connecticut. The trail in Connecticut only allowed you to camp at designated campsites, so I would stay in my tent that night and eat lots of food. I planned to move on at first light the next morning.

June 10   **Day 105**   **13,9 Miles**

It rained all night, which kept the noise from the Boy Scouts down. My spirits were as gray as the day. I should have been used to hiking wet, but I wasn't. I packed up in the rain and started north on the trail. I changed my mind and decided to walk the half mile back into Kent for some town breakfast before moving on. I hoped the rain would stop.

The locals were not too hiker friendly. They even seemed to snub me when I would say "Hey." The guidebook called Kent an up-scale, New England Village, but I thought of it more as a snobby, high-ass, white bread town. I found Mountain Goat in a little deli, all wet and in a foul mood. He didn't have a tent, only a tarp which leaked, and he spent a wet night in the rain. He was waiting for the outfitter to open so he could fix his tarp. I joined him for breakfast sandwiches and coffee.After we finished eating, I asked the Goat, "Where could a bloke get a good cup a Joe?"

He said, "It might be a bit costly."

I said, "I'm buyin" I soon found myself at an expensive coffee shop buying coffees with a double shot of espresso in them. We drank coffee and flirted with the lady who owned the coffee shop for about an hour.

Mountain Goat and the Newly Weds had gotten permission to set their tents up behind a church in town for the night. They were all going to take a zero day and spend it in town getting dried out, but I believed the Goat planned to get drunk as soon as he fixed his tarp.

The newly Weds were still sleeping as I bid Mountain Goat goodbye. I hiked out of town in the pouring rain, all wired up with nobody to talk to. It quit raining in the early afternoon, which greatly improved my mood. I set up my tent on a rock in the sun to dry. I talked to a young couple who stopped and asked me some questions while I was waiting for my gear to dry out. I really loved the image of my thru-hiker status, although I knew I was in danger of being the victim of my inflated ego. I moved on in an excellent mood as opposed to a couple of hours earlier.

I had a stream crossing on Guinea Brook where the high water from all the recent rain made it impossible to ford. The guidebook said a bridge about a half mile downstream was an alternate crossing in high water conditions. I started downstream, but found a log I could use to shimmy across the stream. It was a scary crossing. I was so proud of myself when I made it to the other side with dry feet.

I walked back up stream to the trail where I found a man and woman who were section hiking south for the weekend. They were attempting to ford the river in the dangerous current. I took my pack off and sat down to watch the drama unfold. The man sent the woman out into the river as he stayed high and dry to watch. She soon lost her balance in the strong current and went down with her pack still fully strapped on. He stood there doing nothing as the current took her helplessly. I ran out into the river, grabbed her by the pack, and pulled her out of the current by her pack. He just stood on the bank watching. I wanted to sucker punch him, but didn't. My shoes and socks I kept dry earlier were now soaking wet. She was grateful and thanked me, but he said nothing. Maybe he was trying to off her.

I was still scared and reamed them both a new one before I hiked north. I said in as commanding a voice as I could muster up, "Never have your pack strapped to you when you cross any river!" My shoes were wet, but the weather was dry and everything worked out, so I gave thanks for God's protection and counted my blessings.

I stopped at Caesar Brook Camp Site for the night. I was camping alone, but a young man and his dog set up camp fifty yards away. I welcomed the company and talked to him for a while. He gave me a tip about a restaurant where he worked that my guidebook didn't list. It was only a little ways off trail and I would pass by it the next day.

Once I was alone in the sanctuary of my tent, I thought how hard it was for me to let go of the security of the known. Even if the known was what imprisoned me, it was hard for me to give up because of my fear of the unknown.

An African legend talked about a primitive tribe who trapped monkeys for food. The trapper cut a hole in a coconut, put an apple inside the coconut, and then tied the coconut to a tree. The monkey would see the apple, stick his hand in the hole, and grab the apple, but the hole was too small to allow the monkey to pull his hand out with the apple. The hunter would then bum rush the monkey. Some monkeys let go of the apple and ran to the safety of the trees, but some monkeys would hang on trapped by their own unwillingness to let go until the hunter bopped them in the head with a club. Thus, the successful hunter took the monkey who was unwilling to let go of the apple, home for lunch.

Someone like the monkey who ended up as lunch, probably coined the phrase, a bird in the hand was worth two in the bush. I saw Step Six as more about me being willing to let go of my character defects to be free to become what I could. I could see from my past where I trapped myself with my unwillingness generated by my fear of letting go of the known. I recall, I hung on to my known drinking behavior for a long time even after I knew my drinking sucked. I pondered my own willingness for a long time before sleep ended my thoughts. Another good day ended that started out rainy.

Day 106   15.7 Miles

I drank my own bad coffee before I hit the road early without waking up the man camped with his dog. The weather was clear, so I really enjoyed my morning hike. I found Connecticut surprisingly scenic, especially since the altitude was seldom over a thousand feet above sea level.

I hiked to the Housatonic River where my friend from the previous night told me about the restaurant. I had a little trouble finding it and of course, I got lost, so I stopped at a volunteer fire hall that was preparing for a chicken barbeque. They gave me directions, but wow, the chicken on the grill smelled sooo good. I wished it wasn't going to be two hours before they started serving because I would have stayed. I finally found the Mountainside Café, which was a little more up-scale than I had pictured in my mind.

The day was a Sunday and people came in after church all dressed up for dinner. I hadn't had a shower since Fort Montgomery, which was at least a week before, so I washed up in the rest room and put on some patchouli oil. I felt a little self-conscious, so I sat at a table by myself in a far corner. The other customers pretended they hadn't noticed me. The waitress treated me nicely when I ordered coffee, a cheeseburger, french-fries, and coleslaw. I also ordered a ham and cheese sandwich with potato salad to go. I ate in silence, paid the twenty-five dollar bill, and left without saying goodbye.

I returned to the trail where it ran along the picturesque Housatonic River. Two unleashed golden retrievers aggressively confronted me soon after I entered a park along the river. I reacted defensively and hit the one dog so hard on the top of the head with my hiking pole, he had a seizure on the spot. A lady who I suspected was their owner yelled, "Leave them alone, they won't bite!" I wasn't convinced as I held the other aggressive dog off by swinging my pole. I responded in a commanding voice, "Control your dogs!"

The lady tried hard to get hold of the other dog, but he wouldn't listen. He was in a frenzied state of aggression, but stayed inches out of reach as I backed up the trail still holding him at bay with my hiking poles. The dog finally retreated to his owner, so I quickly backed out of sight. I felt bad for the lady, but I also was worried about the consequences for hitting her other dog. I thought, with my luck, her son was the local sheriff.

I had mental visions of being the outsider, the villain in the local jail. She would be the controlling codependent widow living with her only son Johnny Bill the sheriff. He never married or left home so he could take care of his mother. He controlled the town because they were all afraid of him. The only person he was afraid of was his mother, who he secretly resented. They would have a formal funeral for the dog and everyone in the whole town would attend while I sat in jail eating my last meal, waiting to be hanged publicly in the town square right after the funeral.

I snapped out of my fantasy with a shiver. I told myself it was only a fantasy, but I still thought it was wise to put as much trail between me and the scene of the fight as quickly as possible. I crossed the river on an old bridge by a public beach crowded with people picnicking on a Sunday afternoon. Kids were swimming, people were fishing, and it looked as if everyone was having a great time. I may have stopped for a swim under different circumstances.

The adrenalin started wearing off and I realized I was hiking at super speed and out of breath. I stopped for a moment to take a picture of a hundred-foot waterfall. As I said previously, Connecticut had many spectacular rivers and waterfalls. They called that waterfall, the Great Falls on the Housatonic River. The trail followed an old dirt road along the river for a while, which made for easy hiking, so I made good time.

I hiked another four miles to Limestone Springs Lean-to. I wanted to set up my tent, but a group of inner city adolescents sentenced to hiking by the legal system, occupied all the flat ground. Two not so friendly, tough, quasi drill sergeant adult leaders supervised them closely. These kids would be right at home in the urban jungle, but were way out of their element out there in Mother Nature.

I felt like an English explorer, who walked into a remote African village. My reception was cold at first, but being an extrovert, I soon had a conversation going. I found them delightful, but a little naïve. They hadn't been on the trail long and weren't exactly thrilled with the whole idea. They asked questions and I told them tales of the trail. Soon we were laughing and kidding and even the leaders joined in. All the kids each had their job to do. One of the leaders asked if I would care to join them for supper, but I declined since it didn't look like they had any extra food.

I set up by myself in the shelter, but soon a ridge runner named Marlisa came in and set up with me. Marlisa was a mature, twenty-year-old college student who worked as a ridge runner for the summer. Connecticut hired ridge runners to monitor the hikers on the Appalachian Trail, to make sure hikers followed the rules. She hiked from the border of New York to the Border of Massachusetts and then back. She took two days off every two weeks.

Marlisa was an extremely attractive, black haired girl who looked good even without makeup. We each cooked our own supper and chatted into the night. I enjoyed Marlisa's company. I thought if only I was thirty-five-years younger and single, but I put the thought out of my head since my daughters were more than ten years older than Marlisa and I also just happened to be happily married. The bugs and mosquitoes that infested the shelter kept me awake long after she fell asleep. I still worried a little about Johnny Bill the sheriff, showing up in the night to lynch me as I ended the day in sleep.

Day 107   10.9 Miles

The pleasant smell of a wood fire woke me after daylight. I lay in my bag listening to the chaotic sounds of the kids who tried unsuccessfully to be quiet as they were getting ready to start their day. Soon Marlisa arose and started to pack, so I crawled out of my bag and packed up. She even looked good in the morning. She left as I was still drinking coffee.

I stopped by the fire to say goodbye to the kids on my way back to the trail. We talked only for a few minutes as they bid me farewell. Some would thump their heart with their right fist in a salute type of a gesture and a few bumped fists with me. I told the leader he was doing God's work and he wished me God's speed as he thumped his chest with an open hand. With that, I set sail for Salisbury in the clear, crisp morning.

The hike into town seemed like a little warm up before breakfast. Salisbury was another quintessential, upscale New England town with a shopping common. I had a small emergency mail drop from Scooter with a few things I needed that I couldn't get on the trail. My friend from Washington also said he sent music for my MP3. I didn't need supplies, but I was sure I would find something I needed, even if it was only a good cup of coffee.

I soon found the post office, but it didn't open for another half-hour. I scanned the shops with a purpose and to my delight, I zeroed in on a gourmet coffee shop. I went in, ordered a large coffee with a double shot of espresso, and went back outside to sit in the sun and drank my coffee.

I went back to wait for the post office to open when Marlisea showed up and asked me if I knew where there was a grocery store. I didn't know, but I said to an athletic looking lady passing by, "Mam, could you tell me where we could find a grocery store?" She stopped and patiently took the time and gave us detailed directions to a store, which was not far from where we stood. I introduced myself as Dreamer and shook hands with Franny. I have always been an extrovert and I just drank my fill of high-octane espresso, so we soon had a conversation going as I explained life on the Appalachian Trail.

I paused from talking to get a breath when Franny said, "We live not far from here, and you two could come over to take a shower if you want to."

I was pleasantly surprised at the offer and quickly said, "Sure."

Before I got to town I stopped and washed with wet wipes and put on my town clothes, but I had been on the trail for over a week, around campfires, sweating, and who knows what else. I probably smelled like four-day old road kill in the hot sun. I fully expected Marlisa to also jump at the opportunity, but she declined.

I suddenly felt a little awkward since I wasn't sure how secure Franny felt alone with me. Then I felt a little apprehensive, wondering if Franny had a husband, whose name was Guido and he was a collector for the mob. I had visions of him coming home as I was in the shower and jumping to conclusions.

We soon arrived at a nice, larger home in an upper class neighborhood with manicured lawns perfectly landscaped. She introduced me to her two adult daughters and her son-in-law, who were going to play tennis. It appeared they may have lived with her. They didn't seem surprised or put off when their mother brought home a smelly, unshaven, uncombed old fart with all he owned in a backpack. They treated me with respect and kindness.

Franny briefly left and reappeared with a fleece shirt, shorts and a pair of slippers of her husband's and told me to change and she would wash my cloths with her other washing. I started to protest, but I could see she was determined and already made up her mind to help me. I felt self-conscious, but followed her instructions as she showed me to the downstairs guest shower and gave me fresh towels and a washcloth. The shower was superb with a clear glass door, hot water, and great water pressure. I would like to have stayed in the shower all day, but I didn't want to be rude. When I emerged clean and groomed, Franny was cooking eggs with toast. We sat at the kitchen table chatting as we ate breakfast. I learned her husband was a professor at a prestigious Ivy League college in Massachusetts. We had a delightful conversation while my clothes dried.

I changed and Franny gave me directions on how to get back to town. When she saw the vague look on my face she said, "Just jump in the van and I'll take you back." She let me off in front of the grocery store. I asked for her address and walked around the van to shake her hand and thanked her for her kindness. I then thumped my heart two times with my open hand and said, "God bless." I only wished there were more people like Franny in the world.

I went into the grocery store and immediately identified the pleasant aroma of roasted turkey. One cold, wet night on the trail a few weeks ago, I had finished eating Ramen noodles, crawled into my sleeping bag to get warm and called Scooter. I could hear her eating and asked her what she was eating and she told me she was eating hot, roasted turkey fresh out of the oven. I cried myself to sleep that night and had an incredible craving for roasted turkey ever since. I bought a pound of roasted turkey, a whole fried chicken, two pounds of cheese, two bananas, and a giant bag of potato chips. I sat on a bench outside the grocery store and gobbled down the pound of roasted turkey.

I went to the post office to pick up my mail. My friend David sent two CDs for my MP3 player and Scooter sent the emergency package and a card. I walked across the street to a drug store and bought a card for Scooter and a thank you card for Franny. I returned to the coffee shop and bought another coffee with a shot of espresso. I sat at a table in the morning sun in front of the coffee shop, writing the cards while my turkey digested. I mailed out the cards before I left town.

I caught up with Marlisa on the first mountain as she was talking to three older ladies who called themselves the Golden Girls. They had an eleven-year-old boy named Kiel with them. One of the Golden Girls was his grandmother and the other two were his other grandmothers. Kiel looked bored and seemed to want to attach to me. I took a picture of everyone and moved on as Kiel's three grandmothers were getting on my nerves with their bickering.

Connecticut's Bear Mountain was only twenty-three-hundred feet high at its summit, but sported a rigorous sixteen-hundred-foot climb from Salisbury. Someone or several people built an impressive observation tower out of rocks on the summit. The tower was square, thirty feet wide on each side, more than twenty feet high, and built completely out of native stone fitted together without mortar. I took a picture of a hiker who was standing on the side of the tower to show its immense size in comparison to the person. I had some time, so I climbed to the top of the tower and looked out over most of Connecticut. I paused to say a prayer of gratitude to my maker for the gift of hope.

I found cell tower available, so I called my friend in Washington to thank him for the music. We had a long conversation as I closed in on the Massachusetts border.

After a steep descent off of Bear Mountain I crossed the Connecticut/Massachusetts border late in the day. I stopped at Sages Ravine Brook at an official campsite with a caretaker named Gregg, who was from Canada. Gregg lived at the campsite for the summer months to oversee the hikers. I found him hiker friendly and talkative. We talked for quite some time before I moved on to set up my tent.

I took my choice of campsites and set up on a pristine location overlooking the stream that rushed through the ravine. The sound of the stream would serenade me to sleep later. I tied the giant bag of potato chips on top of my pack to keep them from crushing before I left town. I ate them with some instant peach ice tea, I made from filtered stream water to celebrate entering the new state of Massachusetts.

I stopped eating as I felt a sudden closeness to God while I sat in the world he created. I closed my eyes, listening with every cell of my body for the Holy Spirit to touch me and give me some knowledge of his will. I would truly like to live the rest of my life like that in the close presence of God. It was a bona fide natural high far more wonderful than any drug I have ever experienced. I felt inspired by my insights on the trail. I saw where I was sometimes unwilling to let go because I feared failure or rejection. I had missed many opportunities in my life that because of my fear, I wasn't willing to let go of my apple to face the unknown.

A good example was, I once heard a speaker, whose name I lost in time, share his story at an Alcoholics Anonymous meeting. He had a crush on a girl in his ninth grade Spanish club. He was so infatuated with her that she was the sole reason he joined the Spanish club. He never found the courage to let go of his fear enough to ask her out. He was afraid she would say no and reject him. The window of opportunity passed and life went on for both of them. They both married someone else and didn't see each other until their thirty-fifth class reunion. They both had aged, but he recognized her, so he reintroduced himself to her.

She said, "I must confess, I had a huge crush on you in ninth grade Spanish Club."

I wondered how different their lives would have been if he would have been willing step out of his comfort zone and let go of his apple, faced his fear of rejection, and simply asked her out back in Spanish class when he was in the ninth grade and had the opportunity.

How different would David's life have been if he wasn't willing to let go of his apple of fear and trust God to fight Goliath? How different would everything have turned out if Noah wasn't willing to let go of his apple and build the Ark because of fear of ridicule or failure? I wonder how different it would be if Christopher Columbus wasn't willing to step through his wall of fear and discover the earth wasn't flat after all.

I spent quite a bit of time listing the great accomplishments in history. The list went on, but the one thing they all had in common was they all had to be willing to let go of some type of apple and trust, before something great happened.

Kiel and his three grandmothers barged in and rudely interrupted my meditation. I thought to myself, God really does have a sense of humor, as I helped the golden girls set up camp. They must have discussed me after we met because they seemed to be competing for my attention. At first, their attention was rather subtle, but it soon advanced to openly hitting on me. I was a little flattered, but mostly creeped out by the whole scenario. They settled in and started to cook their supper. I took the cue and retreated to my own campsite to focus my attention back on the bag of chips. Fortunately, I was far enough away from them that I couldn't hear their constant bickering.

I finished eating and went back to the stream to filter more water for the next morning's coffee. I stopped to chat with Greg for a while, so darkness was settling in as I returned to my camp. The night was warm enough to sleep without clothes, so I stripped, crawled in my dry sleeping bag, and used my clothes for a pillow.

I discovered my defects of character I inventoried were what blocked me from a spiritual life. I thought of all the places I didn't go or things I didn't do because of my fear of economic insecurity. I chose to save the money rather than risk it on an opportunity. I thought of how many times I did or didn't do something that would have brought me closer to God because I was fearful of how it would look to others. I couldn't have a meaningful relationship until I was ready to let go of some of my sexual ambitions. I wasn't willing to take the risk because of fear of change from the known, to the unknown outcome.

I could smell the fabric softener Franny used on my clothes as the brook sang to me. I felt as though I was the richest man in the world as I drifted into my world of dreams.

Day 108   14.6 Miles

I woke up in a good mood to a beautiful day. I packed up and said goodbye to Kiel, his three grandmothers, and Greg, before I rode off into the new day. I hoped to hike to Great Barrington where I could buy a fuel canister from the outfitter and maybe get a room in a motel.

I descended steeply into Sages Ravine first and then ascended to the summit of Race Mountain. I psyched myself out from being up high for a long time on a surprisingly steep cliff. The view of Massachusetts was amazing , but I stopped on the edge too long for time to think. I wasn't frozen by fear, but I feared it would get worse. To distract myself, I called the first person in my phone who was my friend, Anita. I calmed down after talking to her for a while and the same place that almost paralyzed me with fear didn't look nearly as intimidating.

After we hung up I took some time to meditate. I then ascended on to the summit of Everett Mountain, which was only twenty-six-hundred feet high. Looking back at my life, I saw clearly what I feared most from the time I was a child, was not usually my present situation. What I feared most was what I projected in the future. I would take the situation, pain, or any problem challenging me, and add my self-imposed fear. I would try to control the future by worrying and make a mountain out of a molehill. I wish I would have discovered that particular character defect fifty years ago. I guess it just took the experience on Race Mountain to break through my thick skull.

I made a cup of coffee and took the time to ponder Step Six. When I first started on the trail, I thought Step Six was all about being ready to have God magically remove my desire to sin. The last few days gave me some time to reflect on my past through prayer and meditation. I saw the many teachers on my path who were teaching me all along, but I never took the time away from the pursuit of my basic, instinctual needs to listen.

I recently came to understand Step Six more as me being not only ready, but also willing to have God remove my defects. The defects I perceived not only to be bad, but also the fears blocked me from improving my spiritual relationship with God. Step Six was where I could definitely understand what Gallagher was talking about when he said, "There are some things you have to do first." Step Six was one of the vital things I had to do to before I could follow through with the decision I made in Step Three. Step Six may be the key to the door where I became willing to, let go and let God.

Dear God,

Thanks for the new insight. Thanks for letting me see my fears were self-imposed by my own ego. I will try to focus on faith instead of fear in the future, to let go of my apple. Please remove my largest character defect of fear so I can get spiritually closer, and be free.

Amen.

Dreamer

I felt better as I moved on with a little better understanding of Step Six. I went from one extreme to another as I descended from the mountains into a bug-infested swamp with big, mean mosquitoes. The trail traveled long distances on boardwalks which snaked their way through the tropical-type swamps. I was amazed and grateful to the volunteers for all the work they did to build the trail through areas like that. They had to be waist deep in smelly swamp muck as they constructed the boardwalks. I didn't know what western Massachusetts was like, but I never expected swamps.

I hiked almost fifteen miles to the highway that led to Great Barrington by mid-afternoon. I called the Monument Mountain Motel and reserved a room for sixty-five dollars. My guidebook said forty-five dollars, but my guidebook was a year old. I started hitching, but had no luck and it looked like I would have to walk all four miles to Great Barrington. Then a former thru-hiker, who hiked in 2004 named Stone Hopper, picked me up. We chatted like old friends and he gave me some good tips while he took me all the way to the motel. I still found the strong bond between thru-hikers amazing.

I settled in my room, took a hot shower, and went to a nearby McDonald's. I ate four double cheeseburgers, an order of fries, and a strawberry shake. McDonald's double cheeseburgers were my favorite food on the trail. I knew they were so caloric I would have to quit eating them as soon as I finished the trail. I took some time to explore a mini mall to let my food digest, before I walked back to the motel.

I went for a swim in the outdoor pool at the motel. The water was refreshing, but I didn't have the energy to do anything but soak. The cool water felt good on my feet, which cooked all day in the heavy hiking boots. No one else came to the pool, so I got board soon and returned to my room.

A 2004 thru-hiker named Paparazzi stopped by my room to see if he could find Mountain Goat, who he hiked with in 2004. Paparazzi and Mountain Goat formed a thru-hiker bond and stayed in touch after the Goat aborted in Pennsylvania. Paparazzi left messages for Mountain Goat on the road crossings, but hasn't successfully met up with him. I thought the Goat was near, but I honestly didn't know where he was. Paparazzi stayed for about an hour telling me trail tales. He warned me about the prices in the Whites of New Hampshire. He also gave me some advice about where to stay in New Hampshire and Maine. I made some notes in my guidebook before he left.

I had good cell tower, so I called Scooter to arrange for her to send a new pair of low-cut hiking shoes to Cheshire, Massachusetts. I would pick them up at the post office in about five or six days. My wart that almost took me off the trail was only a memory, but I was getting new blisters on both feet. I hoped the cooler shoes would keep my feet from getting so many blisters.

Massachusetts had started out a little scary on a ledge on the side of Race Mountain where I enjoyed great vistas, but one carless step could have been disastrous. I was then surprised when the elevation dropped into a swamp with misquotes the size of pigeons.

I put my cell batteries on charge and went to bed before it got dark. I was so tired I didn't even turn on the television. I drifted off to sleep, wondering what the future would bring.

HUMILITY

Day 109   11.7 Miles

I went across the street to a Friendly's restaurant for breakfast. Two section hikers recognized me as a thru-hiker and introduced themselves. I invited them to sit with me and we ate breakfast together, telling hiking stories. I needed the social contact and left feeling inspired.

I re-supplied at a grocery store before returning to the motel to pack up and check out. I walked about a mile into the heart of Great Barrington where small, old shops lined the main street. The main street was a wide, nicely landscaped area with brick sidewalks and benches to sit on which were tactfully placed every few yards bordering both sides of the street. A crowd of touristy people made for a busy shopping mall-type of atmosphere.

I found the post office and mailed my photo card to Scooter. I crossed the street to the outfitter and bought a can of fuel. I bought a pint of Ben and Jerry's ice cream at a small deli to eat as I sat on one of the town benches watching people pass by. I stopped at a Dunkin' Donuts on the way out of town to pee, so I bought a bagel and coffee to go. I hitched out of town and Stone Hopper picked me up for the second time to take me back to the trail by early afternoon.

The Housatonic River was slow and muddy on the flatland in Massachusetts in contrast to its fast moving rapids downriver in Connecticut. I crossed the river on a bridge before I ascended to higher ground. I felt happy to be out of the swamp. I hiked five miles to Tom Leonard Shelter where Tank, Knight Rider, Norm, No Cheese, and a Sobo were socializing.

It was getting late in the afternoon and starting to threaten rain, so

I decided to stay and share their company. I enjoyed myself for a while until they started to drink whisky and smoke marijuana. I decided to move on to a new campsite. I had a standing rule if anything made me uncomfortable, I simply would move on.

I ended up hiking five miles in the rain to Mount Wilcox South Shelter before I could find a flat piece of ground. I camped behind the shelter by myself in the rain. The shelter was empty, but I purposely set up out of sight in the bushes in case Larry, Curley, and Moe came in drunk later.

The rain cooled things off a little as I lay in my tent listening to the steady pitter-patter. I felt a little melancholy, but I was usually a little down after I left the amenities of a town. I closed my eyes, but it was far too early to sleep.

Step Seven said, "Humbly asked Him to remove our shortcomings." I thought, that seemed easy enough after all the work of the first six Steps. I would just let God take my faults away. I sure wished it was that easy. I could simply ask God and he would zap the defect away and I would be done with it. I would be perfect in a short time and have nothing else to work on. I was being sarcastic and I apologize. I found it took a lot of work to barely manage my character defects and they always returned eventually. The truth was I had never aspired to be perfect.

I once talked to a woman heroin addict to help prepare her for parole from prison. The woman declined my help and said, "God took the taste of heroin right out of my mouth, and I don't need no Alcoholics Anonymous." I thought she was using God as a copout because she didn't want to do the work of changing. I too have asked God to fix things many times because I was too lazy or didn't want to invest time or effort into something, so I simply went to God and asked him as if he was Santa Claus.

I thought of all the miracles Jesus preformed and I couldn't recall any he preformed all by Himself. Someone else always did something to help. My favorite was when they ran out of wine at the wedding and the people came to Jesus with the problem. He didn't make more wine appear. He told them to fill the vases with water. Apparently, they had the faith to do it, so he turned the water into wine. I really wished I could do that at one time in my life.

I believed, not only do I have to be willing to have God remove my shortcomings, but I also have to be willing to help God remove my shortcomings or defects of character. In other words I had to be willing to do what I had to do so He could use me. Eventually the rain lulled me into a peaceful sleep.

Day 110   15.8 Miles

The rain continued all night and into the next morning. I made bad coffee, packed up a wet tent in the rain, and quietly left. I was surprised to see some hikers came in and spent the night in the shelter. Either I must have been asleep or maybe I didn't hear them because of the rain on my tent. The rain stopped mid-morning and the sun came out and made an unpleasant day pleasant. The hiking was easy, and the footfall soft, so the miles passed quickly. I thought I entered the Berkshire Mountains, which appeared to be older and less steep. I hiked fifteen miles to a sign on a side trail which read, "The Upper Goose Pond Cabin, half mile."

I had heard about Upper Goose Pond Cabin from trail angel Allie, when I called her in a blizzard back in March from Roan Mountain, Tennessee. Allie had stopped by the cabin on a Sobo section hike a few years ago with friends and had a splendid time. The cabin was furnished with bunks, gas stove, and cooking utensils for hikers. She told me about a place north of the cabin that allowed hikers to pick blueberries for the hikers staying at the cabin. The caretaker of the cabin used the blueberries to make blueberry pancakes in the morning for all the lucky hikers.

I had a tough decision to make, so I took off my pack to look at my guidebook. I was thirty miles from Cheshire, where I had a mail drop waiting. The day was Thursday and the post office closed on Sundays. I planned to hike another ten miles before dark and fifteen more the next day, so I could pick up my mail early Saturday. If I didn't pick it up by Saturday, I would have to wait until Monday to pick up the new shoes Scooter sent. I rationalized if I stopped, dried out my tent, rested, and ate a lot, I could hike a lot further. I compromised with myself, deciding to stop for a late lunch at the cabin. I set up my tent in the sun to dry out on the way to the cabin.

I found several hikers already at the cabin, so I sat on the front porch overlooking the lake to socialize for a while. I enjoyed the family-like camaraderie of the other hikers immensely. A nonprofit hiking club owned the cabin and maintained it with volunteers. The pond offered swimming and canoeing. The club provided a canoe free if you signed a release and wore a life jacket.

I became instant friends with a section hiker from Belgium named Eve, who spoke English as a second language. I wanted to hike another ten miles, but got seduced into staying by the lure of the company and all the pancakes I could eat the next morning . I walked back to my tent, took it down, brought it back, and set it up on one of the wooden tent platforms close to the cabin. I went to the cabin and used the stove to cook lunch and socialize.

The caretaker, Debra and her daughter Marret were Jews from New York City who volunteered to be caretakers for one week every summer as a vacation. They took care of the cabin, collected a three dollar donation for the stay, and made pancakes for the hikers every morning. I was a little disappointed because the blueberries weren't ripe yet, so we would have to eat pancakes without the blueberries.

Debra fits the stereotype of a Jewish, New York City mother for everyone. She took Pick Wick, who was a section hiker, thirty miles to see a dentist because he had a painful abscessed tooth. Her daughter, Marret was a junior in college and on the swimming team. She swam everyday in the lake and talked me into going swimming.

I knew the water would be cold so I was a little hesitant. I walked down to the dock and the lake looked like an unblemished mirror, reflecting perfectly the green mountains and the blue sky with a few white, wispy clouds. I took my camera out of my shirt pocket for a picture then put the camera back in my shirt, took the shirt off, and hung it neatly on a broken tree branch. I walked out on the dock in the sun contemplating a refreshing dip. I checked the pockets of my shorts to make sure there was nothing in them and slipped out of my hiking boots. The dock was hot on the bottoms of my feet, so without further adieu, I leaped off the dock and cannon balled into the glasslike surface of the glacier lake.

The water was so cold I think my testicles retracted clear up to my eyeballs. I let out a soprano type scream and then tried to catch my breath. I swam for a short time after I acclimated to the cold water. I did find it refreshing, but I didn't think I would ever try it again. I returned to my tent to warm up and fell asleep for a relaxing nap before supper.

Seven hikers and two caretakers were sleeping in the cabin that night already and they expected more were on the way. I was happy I decided to sleep in the privacy of my tent. Eve soon came and set up his tent on the platform next to me. He didn't want to sleep in the bunkroom because he said, "It smelled like feet in there."

We both returned to the cabin to cook supper on the gas stove. We ate supper on the front porch sharing trail tales with all the others until late in the evening. I so needed the fellowship, but I returned to my tent a long time after dark, unusually exhausted. The day was a totally enjoyable day on the Appalachian Trail. I ended the day with a prayer giving thanks to my Creator for the privilege of living in His world.

Day 111   8.8 Miles

I slept later than usual in the morning and found most of the others were already awake when I went to the cabin. We waited on the porch, shooting the bull until the pancakes were ready. I ate pancakes and enjoyed the good coffee Debora and Marret prepared. The Newly Weds, Pick Wick, Norm, No Cheese, Knight Rider, Eve and five other hikers all sat at the table and ate family style. It was great to socialize. I had so much fun, I didn't leave for the next shelter until almost noon and had a hard time leaving then.

I hiked solo sluggishly at first, due to my overindulgence of pancakes drowned in syrup. I descended to fifteen-hundred feet then ascended to the summit of Walling Mountain at twenty-two hundred feet. The ascent helped my system process the pancakes and I felt better. I was more than ready for a break when I arrived at October Mountain Shelter by late afternoon. I found the Newly Weds taking a break when I arrived. We sat chatting for a while until they moved on to Dalton to get a mail drop the next day.

I decided to stop there for the night and make it a short day. I also decided to take a short day Saturday and another on Sunday. I would be in Cheshire first thing on Monday to pick up my mail. What the hell, Mount Katahdin would wait for me another day or two.

I set my tent up away from the shelter, so I wouldn't be disturbed in case someone came in. I laid on my back with my fingers interlaced behind my head and watched a fly bounce off the ceiling of my tent, trying in vain to escape.

I often heard folks at Alcoholics Anonymous meetings say, I asked God to remove my defects, and then I took them back. I could identify with their statement because I said and did the same thing. I would ask God to remove a particular defect and believe I meant it, and it would be gone, but the next thing I knew I was doing the same thing again.

I never thought of myself as being fickle, but I seemed to change my mind and take back my self-serving control often. I knew I was moody at times and my moods always seemed to affect the way I saw things. I pondered my thoughts for a moment and said aloud as if I was talking to someone, *Who is the real me?* Sometimes I felt as if I was the center of the universe and everything revolved around me and other times I felt insignificant. I looked at the fly on the ceiling and asked, *Who am I?*

I know my ego was involved, because when my ego got inflated, I became grandiose and felt as if I could do anything as if I was special. That was exactly how I felt when I threw caution aside, quit my job, and took to the trail. That was not the first time I did things others wouldn't even have thought of doing. When my ego deflated, I became depressed, anxious, and afraid to try anything. I had times when I became so depressed, I was afraid to do even simple tasks like go to work. I asked the question once again, *Who am I?*

Mountain Goat interrupted my thoughts by yelling, "Hey Dreamer."

I answered him and reluctantly got up to join him as he set up in the shelter. We cooked and ate supper together. It was good to see him. The Goat was an experienced hiker who had hiked in many countries around the world. He taught me a lot about hiking and camping. I admired him, but wouldn't tell him that because it would definitely inflate his ego more than it was already. Paparazzi managed to catch up with him and they spent some time together. Mountain Goat read out loud in the trail register about a free hostel called the Bird Cage. We decided to try to stay at the Bird Cage in Dalton, which was about twelve miles away. We talked until dark when I returned to my tent. I found enough signal to call Scooter. We talked for an hour about Step Seven before we said goodbye and I fell asleep.

June 17   Day 112   11.8 Miles

I awoke and packed early. I made horrible, but strong coffee. Surprisingly, Mountain Goat mooched some. He came over with his cup in hand and said, "Got any of that mud I have to endure?"

I said, "It's grown on ya, ah mate."

I poured him a cup and said, "Ya owe me one mate." Knowing all along, the Goat was too cheap to ever buy a drink of any kind for anyone but himself and then only if he couldn't talk someone else into buying.

I called my hiking buddy, Chief and put the Goat on the phone. Chief was my hiking partner when I first met Mountain Goat in the Smoky Mountains in the spring of 2004. I woke Chief up on Saturday morning, which I thought was cool because I took the opportunity to call him a slug. Chief remembered the Goat, but the Goat didn't remember Chief. They talked a little while, but neither Chief nor Mountain Goat was very talkative until they got to know someone. The Goat and I cooked breakfast and moved out as it started to rain. I hiked with Mountain Goat until my caffeine high wore off. We agreed to meet somewhere in Dalton before I dropped back to hike solo.

The trail was relatively flat with soft footfall so I made good time. The coffee and the exercise started to work on my system suddenly. I dropped my pack beside the trail and quickly harvested my toilet paper from its special pocket in my pack. I made a hasty retreat out of sight of the trail with a warning clock in my head going five, four, three, two… I relieved the pressure barely in time before I created a problem which would have been hard to deal with on the trail.

I told that story because when I later stopped to read my guide book, I discovered in my haste, I lost my reading glasses. I couldn't read without my glasses, but it was no use trying to find them. They were miles behind and probably off trail where I hid to crap.

I arrived in Dalton by late morning. The rain had stopped and the sun was starting to poke through. I walked through a residential section and felt out of place, but a woman jogging stopped to talk and made me feel right at home. I found Mountain Goat's pack leaning up against the wall outside a little deli on Main Street. I took off my pack and found him inside telling the locals embellished tales of his adventures. We had a second breakfast and drank some good coffee as he talked to the friendly locals, who saw him as a celebrity from Australia.

The folks at the deli gave me directions to a local pharmacy where I could pick up a pair of reading glasses. We said our goodbyes and found the Shell gas station as instructed in the trail register back at the shelter. The station attendant called Rob Bird, who apparently owned the station. Rob soon came by in his van and took us to his house that everyone called the Bird Cage.

Rob was a fifty something bachelor who loved being a trail angel for hikers. He has had over fourteen-hundred hikers stay with him at the Bird Cage over the years. Rob was a father-type caretaker dedicated to helping hikers. He said, "I can sleep twenty-one hikers, but the twenty-first has to sleep with me in my king size bed." I silently hoped I wasn't the twenty-first. He still didn't turn anyone away, but some hikers had to stay in their tent in his back yard when the cage was full.

Rob had us stay on the porch and let us pick out clean clothes he had in many sizes to lend to hikers to wear until he washed our stinky clothes. We then took showers and put on the clean clothes before he would allow us in the house. He threw our dirty clothes in a large washer he had for the sole purpose of washing hiker's clothes.

Tank and the Newly Weds were already there when we arrived. I was happily surprised to see the Newly Weds stayed after they picked up their mail. Rob's big black dog, who was half Labrador and half pit bull and one of the friendliest dogs I have met, also welcomed us as if we were kings.

Rob put Mountain Goat and I on the porch for the night. He assigned the Goat a top bunk and me a couch. Another hiker who was in town already took the bottom bunk. He gave us clean sheets and blankets so we didn't ruin his mattresses with our smelly sleeping bags.

I asked Rob for directions to the pharmacy the locals told me about and he said, "Jump in the van and I'll take you there." He left the others to themselves in his house as he took me to the store.

I said, "You are a trusting man to leave strangers in your home and not be concerned about getting robbed blind." To my amazement, Rob only smiled.

I asked "Do you hike?"

He said "No, I wouldn't want to smell like you guys." We talked like old friends all the way to the pharmacy. Rob waited in the van until I purchased a new pair of reading glasses. We returned to find the house exactly as we left it. I felt privileged to have the one-on-one time with a man of Rob's outstanding character. I wished the world had more people like Rob.

When we got home, Rob took Polaroid pictures of Mountain Goat and I for his album. We each signed our pictures and he placed them in his 2006 album. Rob took pictures of every hiker who ever stayed at the Bird Cage to help him remember them. He had the albums in chronological order on a shelf. I spent some time looking through his albums and recognized several hikers who I met over the years.

Rob had a big screen television and an impressive library of videos. Tank and Ric picked out the movie, The Last of the Mohicans. We all sat in easy chairs and watched the movie as the afternoon passed. When it came time for supper, we all piled in Rob's van and he took us to the Country Buffet. We sat together at a table and ate family style, which I found beyond enjoyable. Rob enjoyed watching us pig out as he ate a moderate meal. I so missed eating with my family back home.

Rob wouldn't take money or donations for staying and wouldn't even let us pay for his supper. He kept a refrigerator stocked with pop, which they called soda in New England. He agreed to stop to let me buy a case of soda for the hikers on the way back. Ric and I went into the store and filled a cart with soda while the others waited in the van.

When we got back to Rob's house, two section hikers who stayed with Rob previously came in for the night. In addition, a hiker named Keith stayed at the Bird House and worked for Rob at the Shell station. We all talked into the night before going to bed.

Day 113   9.3 Miles

I slept well on the porch couch. Mountain Goat was still fast asleep when I awoke. The bottom bunk Rob reserved for the other hiker was still empty. I walked through the house to the bathroom as quietly as possible so I didn't wake the others. I found Ric putting his shoes on when I returned from the bathroom and the Goat was awake too, so the three of us snuck out of the house for some coffee. We were not sure where to go, so we walked towards town hoping we would find something. We walked about a mile before we found a little deli slash convenience store to buy breakfast sandwiches and lots of coffee. When we returned everyone was up.

The day before when Rob took me to buy glasses, I told him I was in recovery. After I returned from breakfast Rob came to me and asked if I would talk to Keith, who's drinking had already gotten him into trouble several times. I talked to Keith, who appeared to be receptive and agreed to try an AA meeting in Dalton later in the week. I would have liked to take Keith to a meeting myself, but I planned on leaving town. I gave Keith my phone number and encouraged him to call me anytime.

I left at noon because I wanted to be in Cheshire first thing on

Monday morning to pick up my mail as soon as the post office opened. Rob tried to lure me into staying by offering to take us swimming, but my Upper Goose Pond experience was still fresh in my mind. I left after we all got together for a group picture.

The guidebook said a Catholic church in Cheshire let hikers stay there free, so I planned to stay there. I hoped to spend the night with some other hikers. Everyone else was taking a zero day to go swimming. The sun was out and the footfall was easy as the trail meandered through the woods. The hike to Cheshire should have been pleasant, but I was angry with myself for leaving the Bird House. I was lonely and filled with regret and guilt for not staying at Rob's with my friends and going to an Alcoholics Anonymous meeting with Keith. I would like to have gone back, but my pride wouldn't let me.

I found myself rushing when there was absolutely no reason to rush. Katahdin was only about six-hundred and fifteen miles north and I was sure it would still be there whenever I got there. I had until October fifteenth to summit, so I would be way ahead of schedule, even if I had a schedule.

I thought about a line in a song which said, I'm in a hurry to get things done; I rush and rush and rush until life's no fun. I have always been goal oriented, which may be a good thing if I just took some time to enjoy my life. I seemed to rush through things until I experienced a lot of self-imposed stress because I felt an unnecessary need to git-r-done. I decided from now on I was going to take the time to smell the roses. I stopped for a break, turned on my cell phone, and saw I had messages. I had forgotten it was Father's Day until I retrieved messages from Phyllis, Nadine, and Nick, all wishing me happy Father's day.

I closed my eyes and started to reminisce about my Dad. I would always buy him a card and a carton of Tareyton cigarettes before I would go to visit him on Father's Day. I felt sorry for myself at first because the time when I could visit with him in this world had long passed. Dad was my mentor, my confidant, and my counselor among other things. I would go to him when I was overwhelmed with life. No matter how busy he was at the time, he would drop what he was doing and focus on me. He would look me in the eye as he pulled his Tareytons from his shirt pocket, shake one up, take it out with his mouth, expertly shake another up from the pack, and offer it to me. I would take it, light his first with my Zippo, and then light mine. We would both take a pull on our cigarettes and he would start to talk. The first thing he said was, "It can't be all that bad." His voice was kind and friendly with a hint of laughter in it. No matter what was wrong or how grave the situation, he had a calming effect on me like no other person ever. Magically, by the time we crushed our butts out, the situation was either resolved or at least manageable. Nothing ever seemed as bad after I talked to Dad. It was Fathers Day and I planned to rejoice because I had a father like him rather than mourning his loss. I tried to focus on how fortunate I was and not feel sorry for what I lost.

I arrived in Cheshire and found it was smaller than Dalton. I bought an ice cream cone at a small stand and sat at an outside picnic table, watching the people come and go, waiting for someone to strike up a conversation. I felt smug when a man about my age came over and sat across from me at the table.

He said in his New England accent, "Hiking the trail?" We talked until he finished his ice cream cone and moved on. He gave me directions to St Mary's church, but said he didn't think the new priest let hikers stay there any longer. I left in a mild panic following his directions. I found the church, but the priest didn't answer the door. I went looking for an alternative place to spend the night and found nothing. I was considering stealth camping out in the woods when I found an Italian restaurant that was open. I went in and ordered a pizza, which I ate while watching their television. I felt out of place when people came in for supper in their Sunday best. I thought for a while and decided to go back and try the church again. A priest answered the door that time. He was friendly and younger than I pictured in my mind.

He said, "Sure, you can stay one night in the hiker's room." I breathed a sigh of relief.

I followed him to the church, which was huge and had a medieval atmosphere. The light that was able to get through the stained glass windows depicted saints or something from biblical times and small candles lit the altar. He showed me the hiker room where I could sleep on the floor. The room was small with a large regular window that looked out over the street. The church stored a few textbooks, student artwork, some literature about the trail, and a framed news article about a local man who thru-hiked the trail in 2001.

I took my pack off and looked around. I found a half of a box of stale donuts left there for a couple weeks. The priest apologized and said he would have to throw them out and clean the room. I assured him it was fine and thanked him for his kindness. I followed him as he showed me to the restroom. We walked down the aisle and crossed in front of the altar, where a few small candles flickering dimly, lit the statues. I thought the church would be an eerie place to spend the night alone, I sure hoped some other hikers showed up before it got dark.

The priest walked me back to the room in silence then bid me goodnight. I settled in and got in my sleeping bag. I turned on my cell phone, but had no tower, so I took the time to catch up my journal and did some reading. I deeply regretted not staying with my friends in Dalton at the Bird Cage and following through with Keith. They were probably back from supper by now nursing sunburns from being at the beach all day and I was alone and lonely in a spooky old church.

I pondered my own question, *Who am I?* The answer I came up with was the real me was controlled by my ego. My ego was my self-will and controlled my moods. When I got my own way I became grandiose, but I became anxious and depressed when things didn't go my way. My next question was, where was the middle ground between grandiosity and depression, between high and low self-esteem?

I wasn't good at distinguishing the difference between my will and God's will. At times, it was my will versus God's will. God never interfered with my will. God kept his promise and let me have my self-will, which my ego controlled. He left the choice between my will and his will up to me.

When I thought back to my addiction I became aware, I denied

God even existed. I purposely chose to keep God out of my life so my ego could take control of my world. I spent all my time selfishly pursuing my will, totally disregarding all costs to everyone including myself. God let me have my way and didn't interfere until I asked him and then he still gave me the choice. The world I created for myself was dark and lonely. I had lost my way, entering a world void of God, filled with spiritual pain or hell.

In the Bible, Matthew quotes Jesus as saying, When you cling to your life, you will lose it, but if you give up your life for me, you will find it. Maybe what old Matt was saying was what I experienced. The insight that jumped into my consciousness was the controlling God I imagined growing up was completely the opposite. My ego was the one guilty of being controlling. God's will only came into my life with my consent and permission. I had to first invite Him and then surrender my will to Him. That probably was why I felt good when I pursued God's Will. The will of God has always been pleasurable to me no matter how difficult the situation seemed beforehand.

Eventually, I must have drifted off to sleep, still lonely and feeling sorry for myself. Mother Nature woke me up in the wee hours of the morning and forced me to venture out to the restroom. The church was even spookier in the dark, only illuminated by several red exit signs and some candles that still burned at the altar. I scurried silently in my bare feet toward the exit sign that marked the restroom. I turned on a light in the restroom and felt safer as I relieved myself. I paused before I turned the light off to mentally psych myself up for the journey back to the safety of the hiker room. I snapped the light off and bolted out into the church, reminiscent of the Upper Goose Pond when I jumped into cold water to git-r-done. I couldn't see because my eyes had not yet readjusted to the dark. I stopped to give my pupils time to open, so I didn't run into anything. As I grew accustomed to the dark, I watched an almost life-size image of the crucifixion appear out of the darkness from behind the altar. I thought, why would God do that to his only son?

I returned to the security of my room, but when I shut the door to the outside, I couldn't shut out the image of the crucifix. I had known the story of the crucifixion and resurrection since my earliest recollection as a boy, but it never made sense to me. It was always the same old questions. Why would God let that happen? Why did Jesus let it happen? Why didn't his disciples fight to the death protecting him?

It would be several hours before I could pick up my mail and return to the trail, but I was far too alert to go back to sleep so I lay in the comfort of my sleeping bag pondering the unanswered questions.

A strange image kept popping into my head. The image was of a woman I met while she was awaiting trial for the attempted murder of her three-year-old daughter. She said, "God told me to do it." I personally believed it was her will and God let her have her own will. She was blaming God for her heinous crime. I had used that example many times when I confronted a criminal who used God as a copout and blamed God's will for their behavior.

I realized, I was doing the same thing. I had been blaming God for killing Jesus on the cross all the time, when God had nothing to do with it. The rigid thinking-Jews asked the Romans to crucify Jesus because of their insecurities. They saw him as a threat. I also blamed God or Christ himself for letting it happen, when Pilate was the one who ordered him crucified because of his social insecurity and political ambitions.

I came to believe when God created Adam, He gave us humans a free will. God was unlike the politicians and never rescinded or went back on his word. He never interfered with the free will of man, even if we mortals used our free will for evil and did such things as kill children, start wars, or crucify his son.

I could accept my explanation, but I had a lot to think about as I ate a stale, two-week old donut and fell back to sleep from the sugar.

Day 114   15.6 Miles

I awoke to the sun coming through the window. They didn't allow cooking in the church or on the property, so I ate the rest of the stale donuts and went without my coffee. I was grateful for the place to stay, but happy to leave. According to my guidebook, a convenience store was only a short distance north and one-tenth of a mile off the trail. I hoped to get some good coffee there later.

I waited on a bench across the street from the post office until it opened, so I could pick up my new shoes. I also received a Father's day card from Christine in my mail drop. The shoes seem lighter and smaller. I found a new wart on my foot, which gave me something to worry about, as if I needed something. I left my old shoes in the hiker box at the post office for some needy hiker.

I was packing up to move out when I heard someone call out, "Hey Dreamer." I looked up and saw Messenger going to the post office. Oh boy, he was a sight for sore eyes. The last time I saw him was in Harpers Ferry, when he left the trail to graduate from college. We chatted as we left town on our way to the convenience store. He stayed in a motel and ate in town, so he moved on when I went off trail to the store for coffee and breakfast.

I was sitting on my pack on the sidewalk outside the store in the sun enjoying my store bought coffee, when a man dressed in a business suit stopped and gave me a five-dollar bill. He must have mistook me for a bum. I felt offended at first, but I didn't know what to say. I paused and realized he was simply being kind to a stranger, so I thanked him and stuck the bill in my shirt. We had a short conversation, but instead of saying good-bye I said, "God bless" as he hurried off to his job. A cop came over and talked to me. He was nice, but I thought he was checking me out to see if I was a vagrant and bothering people. I didn't even let that bother my ego as I ate several donuts and coffees before I ventured north.

I was a little disappointed in my shoes because they weren't waterproof and my feet were wet from the little dew on the grass. I hiked up Mount Graylock, which stood thirty-five-hundred feet high at the summit. Graylock was the highest mountain in Massachusetts and the highest I have been on since Bearfence Mountain in the Shenandoah National Park back on May second. Graylock wasn't nearly as fierce a mountain as the locals made it out to be, but it marked the beginning of some higher mountains. A distinctive war memorial tower stood directly on the summit.

An insight came to me as I gazed at the war memorial. My ego went over emotional mountains all the time. When I was going up on one side of the mountain, my ego inflated with high self-esteem, but when I was going down on the other side of the same mountain, my ego deflated with low self-esteem

I thought, "What's at the summit?" In that case, a war memorial, but often there was only a marker of some sort. The summit was the point where I wasn't going up any longer and not yet going down. I closed my eyes trying to clear my mind so God could talk to me. I asked, what was on top of the mountain? The word humility kept surfacing in my mind. Step Seven said, "We humbly asked Him to remove our shortcomings." I thought maybe Step Seven was more about humility than anything else.

I attended many Alcoholics Anonymous discussion meetings over the years, where the topic discussed was humility. I heard many people's opinions of humility. I wasn't sure I could describe what I thought humility was in words. To me, humility was something more spiritual in nature . Humility was like a spiritual summit where I wasn't grandiose nor depressed. I never got to stay there long, but it felt so good when I was there. I decided humility was at the summit of my emotional mountains.

Many years ago I watched a television series called, Kung Fu. The star character was a Shaolin priest named Caine. I liked to smoke weed while watching the show. Caine never picked a fight, but some bully or bullies would always pick a fight. Caine would use Kung Fu to kick the crap out of them. Caine was a model of a humble man for me, because he wasn't a wimp. Caine seemed to clearly see things realistically as they were. He always seemed to know who and what he was while he kept his ego in check.

My ego seemed to distort the truth. When I was on top of a mountain on a clear day, I could see everything clearly for miles. When I was humble and denied my own ego and self-will, I could see more clearly some things as God saw everything. I thought I had some insight towards the answer to my own question as I looked at the summit of Graylock. At the top of the mountain, my ego was not involved and I could be humble for a short time, until my ego got involved again. At the top of the mountain, I could have contact with God as I understood him.

Reading about Jesus Christ in the little white Bible made more sense now. Jesus denied his self-will and focused on God. He set the example for us to follow of perfect humility. I didn't recall Jesus ever letting his ego take control and he seemed to always have contact with God. Humility was the state of mind at the summit of my spiritual mountain where I had contact with God; where I could see the truth. The Bible said, "The truth will set you free." Humility seemed to set me free of my ego or as the Third Step Prayer said, "Relieve me of the bondage of self."

I snapped out of my meditation when I came to the best part of Graylock, which was a gift shop at the summit. I bought good coffee and some small souvenirs to mail to folks back home. The clerk gave me an apple as we struck up a conversation.

Messenger came in so we sat in the easy chairs of the living room-type lobby to talk and drink coffee. Soon a park ranger, Red Dane, Dodger, a trail angel named Ed, and two girls who were section hiking, joined us. We had a little impromptu party going. We laughed, joked, and told embellished trail tales. We went out to the porch where the light was better so Ed could take our picture to preserve the memory of each other before we departed.

I descended Mount Graylock alone, hiking through a hardwood forest to North Adams. I wanted to find a grocery store to re-supply before dark. I had to hike about a mile off trail on a busy highway with weather threatening to storm any minute, before I found the grocery store. It started to downpour while I was still in the grocery store, buying supplies. I went to a Chinese AYCE restaurant in the little mall and spent about an hour eating. I was hoping the rain would let up, but it didn't.

I eventually had to venture out in the driving rain and hiked a mile back to the trail. I then hiked two more miles on the trail to Sherman Brook Campsite where I set up on a tent platform in the pouring rain. I couldn't have been wetter if I swam there. The storm's thunder, lightning, and heavy rain confined me to my tent for the rest of the night.

I had some time on my hands, so I lay back on my air mat, closed my eyes, and let my mind drift. The sight of the crucifix popped into my mind again. I had many questions and most of them start with why. Why did Jesus have to die for my sins? Did God want to put an exclamation point on the life of Jesus? Why did he have to fulfill a prophecy? Why did God give us mortals our own self-will in the first place?

Then based on my boyhood superstitions, I became afraid I might have offended God by asking all the questions. I could almost hear Reverend McIntire saying in an elevated voice, "Because the Bible said so, that's why!" Why should I trust everything the Bible said? I always wondered why, Reverend McIntire wouldn't allow me to question the Bible? Why should I trust the Apostle Paul who wrote a lot of the New Testament? After all, at times when I read the Bible, I got the impression Paul was so codependent he needed to get his ass to a few Al-Anon meetings.

I felt tormented and discontented so I started to pray. I came up with a why question for myself. Why did I have to know right now? Maybe conversion was not an event, but more of an ongoing progressive process and God wasn't done with me yet. I found some comfort in a slogan that popped into my head, *More will be revealed.* Sometime late in the night, the rain sang me to sleep.

FORGIVENESS

Day 115   18.5 Miles

The rain stopped by daylight, but I still had to pack up a wet tent and sleeping bag. I discovered Pick Wick also spent the night on a tent platform nearby. We talked briefly before I headed north to take on Vermont. I hiked to what I believe was Eph's Lookout, which treated me to a majestic sight of the Green Mountains of Vermont as they rose above the clouds. The morning sun highlighted the mountains in contrast to the top of the fluffy clouds that still clung to the valleys below. It all gave me the impression, I was in God's garden, isolated from the land of the mortals below the clouds. It felt so good to be back in the mountains again.

I hiked two and a half miles to the Massachusetts/Vermont boarder in the morning's dampness, as the sun worked hard to dry out the mountains. The Long Trial started at the border of Vermont and paralleled the Appalachian Trail until Killington. Then the Appalachian Trail turned east towards New Hampshire and the Long Trail continued north to Canada.

I met a thru-hiker named Mango and hiked with him most of the morning. Mango spent the night before with Messenger in Williamstown and said Messenger was only a little ahead of me. I stopped for a long lunch to set up my tent and sleeping bag to dry out. My new shoes seemed to be okay, but they too were soaking wet. I took off my shoes and socks to spread them out in the sun to dry. I blew up my air mattress and laid on my back watching the clouds as they took their time passing by, with no particular place to go.

My addiction went through my life similar to a tornado that went through a mid-western town and left a lot of debris. The aftermath of the tornado's destruction needed cleaned up. The aftermath or debris from my addiction that blocked my spiritual relationships with God and others, also needed cleaned up.

Step Eight said, "Made a list of people we had harmed and became willing to make amends to them all." Making amends was a tool used to help clean up the destruction from my past. I often wished I could go back in time and undo the things I did to others I regretted. The reality was, if I had all the gold in the world I could not buy back a minute of my past.

In Step Eight, becoming willing was not as huge of a problem as becoming ready. I was not ready because I hadn't done Steps Four, Five, Six, or Seven yet. The people on my list who were the closest to me also weren't ready because many had heard numerous apologies already, so why would anything be different that time.

My friend Mark was a small example of the harms I did to strangers while I was drinking. I didn't even know Mark's name until Danny introduced me to him as his brother that day a long time ago in the Diamond Deli. I was fortunate Mark forgave me. I left many nameless others like Mark behind who I wronged in one way or another. I suspect I also did harm to even more when I was in the many blackouts where I had zero memory. I felt guilty about all the victims I left behind, but for now, I had to accept what I couldn't change. Maybe in time, more would be revealed and I would become willing to make amends whenever possible the same as I did with Mark.

I felt closer to God than I did the night before in the pouring rain when I was questioning things. I suddenly remembered Joachim saying I would still have doubts at times. I felt good as I packed up my dry tent and moved out solo after a good rest.

I was nearing the road to Bennington, Vermont when I came upon a hiker's pack and a lot of blood. I feared I would find a dead hiker. My body went into a full, man all battle stations alert, as I proceeded slowly and cautiously, expecting the worst. I started to find clumps of bloody toilet paper discarded along the trail, which actually made me feel better because whoever got hurt was still alive. I heard voices and soon assessed the situation as being an accident and no danger to me. I found some hikers helping the injured hiker. He cut his head and was bleeding badly. They were trying to stop the bleeding, but couldn't. I called 911 with my cell, but someone already called and an ambulance was on the road. The ambulance took the wounded hiker to the hospital.

I moved on to Melville Nauheim Shelter where I found Jamie and Sharon, who were schoolteachers and roommates. They were going to attempt to hike the Long Trail to Canada. Jamie, who was a New York City Jew, was sleeping outside for the first time in her life that night. I was talking to the girls when Norm, No Cheese, and Night Rider came in and set up in the shelter. The conversation was mostly about the injured hiker when a hiker named Bear Bait came in to join us. Bear Bait was a retired nurse from Florida, who assisted the injured hiker. He said the hiker could have bled to death from the cut on his head.

Bear Bait looked familiar, but I couldn't place him at first. We chatted for a while before I realized I had met him last year in New Jersey, only he was skinnier then. I recalled he was taking a zero day to rest an injured back. I was section hiking with friends and he was thru-hiking. He recalled me when I started to refresh his memory. He said, "I had to abort my hike the next morning in New York because I broke my back." He was now attempting to finish the hike. We became friends instantly.

We built a fire before the hiker named Six Pack, who was the injured hiker, came into camp. He had to have seventeen staples put into his head to close up the cut. Bear Bait was surprised the hospital released him so soon, but he said he didn't have insurance and he was medically cleared to go. Judging from his behavior, he was probably taking some major painkillers. We all socialized into the night.

Bear Bait and I set up our tents away from the shelter. I figured it was going to be noisy in the shelter and I liked the privacy of my tent to sleep. After I was in my tent, Bear Bait and I did some catching up through the tent walls until we drifted off to sleep.

Day 116   17.4 Miles

I broke camp as quietly as possible, trying to not wake the others and hiked out silently without saying goodbye. My right ankle was hurting. I probably rolled it yesterday in my haste to descend the mountain after Six Pack got hurt. The adrenalin surge would explain why I didn't feel it until it tightened up in the night. I hoped it subsided soon and didn't become a problem. The good news was, my thighs weren't bothering me any longer. Maybe prayer helps more than I ever realized because it seemed to let me know how to resolve my low back, my wart, and all my other physical issues.

The warm sunshine I only dreamt about in March brought in the first day of summer. Vermont had many beaver ponds and swampy areas, which provided food for Moose and other wildlife. I started to see moose poop on the trail, so I kept my eyes open, hoping for a moose picture.

When I first started to address Step Eight, Big Jim said, "Don't worry so much about the strangers as your loved ones." His words hit me hard like a sledgehammer made of shame. The reality was, I hurt the ones who loved me the most.

My family who loved me unconditionally took the brunt of my destruction. They trusted me and forgave me easily, which made it easy to exploit them. Oh, I was quick to show up all full of remorse with my hat in my hand to apologize, begging their forgiveness. I even thought I really meant it, but I soon turned around to do the same thing again time after time.

Yes, it was expensive to love me. I used to think, I wasn't hurting anyone, but myself. I used to even say to my ex-wife, "You're lucky because I don't beat you!" I would rationalize if I didn't hurt her physically, I wasn't hurting her. My children, whom I was proud of, were afraid of me because I was so volatile. They didn't understand and thought they were the ones who did something wrong. My Mother was too ashamed to go to church for a while because she didn't want to face questions after I made the news at six and eleven on charges. My Dad would try to talk some sense into me at times. He would get frustrated and try to help. I wanted to please him, but always seemed to do the next wrong thing. I couldn't even imagine how big a disappointment I must have been to both of my parents. My one sister tried in vain to help me and I repaid her by stealing from her and taking advantage of her kindness.

As I said, "Becoming willing was not the problem." I was desperately willing at first to make amends and ask for forgiveness to appease my guilt. I had more than my share of guilt and shame on my plate and I could no longer use drugs or alcohol for even temporary relief.

I truly believe my family always loved me, but they were frustrated by years of my inconsistent behavior and countless hollow apologies. When I finally became sober I needed love, understanding, and forgiveness the most, but I deserved it the least. I can understand why my dearest loved ones were hesitant to buy into my sincerity.

I hiked solo, processing my past until lunchtime when I caught up with the teachers, Sharon and Jamie at Kid Gore Shelter. They must have left before me in the morning. They said Six Pack snored so loud he kept everyone in the shelter awake all night. He felt better, but he was taking a zero day at the shelter.

Bear Bait came in while we were eating and joined us for lunch. I hoped he would catch up. The teachers were all thrilled with the wonder of the trail. I could only imagine the contrast between life in the city and life on the trail. I found them innocently refreshing as they told the blow-by-blow story of their first day on the trail.

The teachers planned to stay there for the night. Bear Bait and I packed up after a long lunch and moved out together. Bear Bait was one of the few distance hikers my age and we had a lot in common. He told the story of how he was attempting a thru-hike last year when he fell and broke a vertebra in his back, He tried to go on in spite of the injury. Eventually, he couldn't ignore the pain any longer, so he had to abort his hike.

He got back on the trail late in the spring at Bear Mountain in New York and was determined to finish his hike at Mount Katahdin. He had the support of his wife and kids who thought he was a little off. I admired Bear Bait's determination to overcome adversity and complete his goal. I felt privileged to be in the presence of a man of his character.

We talked like old friends as we hiked to Story Spring Shelter by early evening. It felt good to be friends solely because I liked him, with no ulterior motives, in contrast to my past. When I was active in my addiction, I was incapable of being a friend even when things were going well. I was always in it for what they could do for me. Most of my friends were people active in their own addiction, so we would use each other. I never trusted anyone, often for good reason. Believe me, not many trustworthy, actively using addicts were ever out there.

However, I grew up with some loyal friends and classmates. I did the same thing to them. I took advantage of our friendship and borrowed or swindled to fulfill my need to feed my addiction. In contrast, I only wanted Bear Bait's support and inspiration, which was what I offered to him.

We arrived at the shelter and found it full. Kuwait, who looked like a man, but turned out to be a manly woman, was with her girlfriend, along with a salty, seventy-year-old, retired Marine named Captain, and a young couple in their late teens who were more interested in each other than anything else on the trail, were all crowded together in the shelter.

Bear Bait and I cooked at the shelter as we all listened to the Captain tell war stories. I thought, only on the Appalachian Trail could so many socially diverse people come together. We not only tolerated each other's differences, but respected each other's right to be different. We then became friends in such a very short time. The Alcoholics Anonymous slogan, live and let live, popped into my mind. Tolerance of one another was a daily practice by most on the Appalachian Trail. We sat around the fire until the bugs and mosquitoes caused us to retreat to the safety of our tents. Bear Bait and I set up our tents away from the shelter for a little quiet time, however we made sure our tents were close enough so we could talk through the walls. We talked long into the night until I must have fallen asleep.

Day 117   15.4 Miles

I started out early, but had to go slow because my ankle was still hurting. It was raining hard and steady, which never did my bones or my mood any good. I checked and found I had cell tower as I started the long ascent up Stratton Mountain. I felt lonely, so against my better judgment I made some calls in the rain. I tried to protect my phone from the rain, but it got wet anyway. Then it started to flash on different screens before cutting out altogether, leaving me with a sense of isolation. My phone was my lifeline to my world back home and something I didn't want to have to go without for long.

My mood was grave until the rain subsided by mid-morning. I neared the summit of Stratton and came across a strange type of flimsy netting or type of fence that ran up the middle of the trail which I hadn't seen before. It looked as if it were temporary and even a small animal could easily knock it over. It was annoying, but I did my best to leave it undisturbed as I made my way by hundreds of yards of the fence.

I limped to the summit where I found a caretaker's cabin and a caretaker. I stopped and talked to the caretaker who was about my age with dyed black hair and I suspected, single. I found her pleasantly informative and hiker friendly. She lived alone in the cabin all summer and watched over dummies like me and provided information about the trail in Vermont. She told me the nets along the trail were to catch a certain kind of rare bird for research. The birds migrated through there that time of year and the researchers caught and tagged the entangled birds. She said the migration was about over for the season and they would take the nets down soon. I wished I could have remembered the bird's name.

She warned me to watch for the symptoms of Lyme Disease as they start to show up about now in thru-hikers. I was past the danger zone of New York and New Jersey, but the disease took a while to manifest symptoms. She also told me not to camp on the trail because moose walk on the trail at night and would step on me. I already knew better because I saw moose poop on the trail in several places.

Kuwait came in while we were talking and joined in on the conversation. She spent a tour in Kuwait when she was in the military, thus the name. I ate a snack while I enjoyed their company for a while, but then moved on and left them to themselves.

I hiked solo to William B. Douglas Shelter where I set up my tent. A young man and woman who recently returned from college in Russia were staying in the shelter. I cooked and socialized with them for a while until the black flies and mosquitoes became too annoying. I turned in early to the protection of my tent and gave the couple my bug spray because they didn't have a tent to retreat to for a sanctuary. I would buy more bug spray in Manchester the next morning, I hoped.

I wanted to go to the next shelter to keep up with Bear Bait, but I needed to rest my ankle. I hoped to catch up with him in Manchester Center. The Good news was my phone dried out and appeared to be working fine, although I had no tower to try it.

I killed all the mosquitoes in the tent to find some peace. I took out my journal and read the entry from the day before. When I was using, drugs and alcohol were always my main lover. The sexual relationships I managed to become involved in were usually one sided and superficial on my part. They would only last until my newest girlfriend could no longer put up with the many types of abuse I would put her through in the name of love. I would use women and then throw them away like a Kleenex. Like a tornado, the longer the relationship lasted, the more destruction I caused. Some of the women were also addicts and we used each other. Others knew what I was like and were so codependent they wanted to control or fix me. Some had no idea what they were getting themselves into. They were simply the unlucky ones I mislead into a relationship by my deceptions of who I really was.

In some of those relationships, one of us simply detached and went on with their lives. Some still seemed cordial and spoke on a superficial level if we happened to see each other in a store or on the street. Some still have great animosity towards me for justified reasons. I felt especially remorseful towards those women because their resentment towards me still abused them. I wished I could relieve them of their hate to appease my guilt, but I would reopen old wounds, doing more harm to both them and me if I tried to make amends.

I was lying there feeling down, not because I was alone or in pain, but because I felt I had some unfinished business with Steps Eight and Nine.

Day 118   7.7 Miles

I slept fitfully last night due to the shame and guilt I dredged up from my past. I truly regretted the harms I did to others in my addiction. After twenty-six years, some of the wounds hadn't healed and I still bled when I picked the scab off. The promises said, "We will not regret the past nor wish to shut the door on it." I still regretted the past, so maybe I really did have some unfinished business in Steps Eight and Nine.

A storm came in after dark and cooled things down a bit. The rain continued all night and into the morning. I felt like I had gotten used to packing wet gear and hiking in the rain. I even started to consider hiking a water sport. The rain quit and the weather cleared by mid-morning almost exactly like the pattern of the previous few days. I wondered if it was a weather pattern here in Vermont.

I called the two motels in Manchester that were listed in my guidebook. The owner of one left for his honeymoon and closed the motel and the other had no vacancy. I knew there would be other motels in a town the size of Manchester Center, but I had an uneasy feeling about the whole thing.

I hiked almost six miles to the highway to Manchester Center. I easily hitched a ride to town and tried to find a motel with a vacancy in my price range. I had zero luck, so I bought the supplies I needed at a grocery store. I went to McDonald's to eat and think over my situation. Knight Rider came in and joined me as we ate cheeseburgers and drank coffee. He was trying to find Norm and No Cheese. I parted company with him after we ate. I stopped at a small convenience store and bought more hot coffee and bug spray.

I decided to hitch a ride back to the trail. A nice young man gave me a ride and let me off at the trailhead. I was a little disappointed because I was looking forward to a night in a motel and soaking my ankle in a hot shower.

I felt as if I forgot something and suddenly remembered Spiritual

Pilgrim telling me about the Wilson House. The Wilson House in East Dorset was a type of museum where Bill Wilson, the co-founder of Alcoholics Anonymous was born. East Dorset was about two miles from Manchester. The Wilson House was also an old time Inn, so we planned to spend the night at the house when we first met back in Pennsylvania. I sat down on my pack and tried to call Spiritual Pilgrim, but only got his voice mail, so I left him a message and hung up. I sat there beside the road in a quandary, because half of me wanted to return to Manchester and go to the Wilson House. The other half wanted to move on and forget the whole day. I decided to move on after pondering the decision for a while.

I identified the trail by the familiar white blaze and started down the trail. Being a woodsman, I immediately lost the trail while I was still in sight of the road, which added to my frustration, so I became angry. I retraced my steps back to the road and tried again with the same result. The trail was plainly marked where it entered the woods, then it would go down to a sizable stream and disappear into thin air.

I returned to the road for the third time and was sitting on my pack looking at the guidebook, when two young, athletic-looking men came by in a hurry. I tried to strike up a conversation, but they rudely moved on. I continued to sit on my pack and had to admit I was mildly amused when they returned to the road for the second time also frustrated. I had heard it said many times misery loves company.

The guidebook said a footbridge crossed the stream, so I returned to the stream, but couldn't find the footbridge. I thought it would have to be upstream, so I walked upstream about a hundred yards and found the footbridge and the trail. I backtracked to the road and found the problem was the trail split to go down to the water and a large tree blew down in the storm the night before, which expertly camouflaged the intersection to the Appalachian Trail with its branches.

I told the two thru-hikers who were in such hurry. They were a little more cordial and said they were trying to average thirty miles a day, before they left me in their dust. I thought they must miss a lot of the trail going so fast, but they were young and in good shape.

I limped two miles to Bromley Mountain Shelter. It was only early in the afternoon, but it was hot, humid and looked as if it could storm any minute. I found some nice wooden tent platforms near the shelter, so I set up my tent for the night. The storm hit and drove me to the confines of my tent. I tried to escape my mood in sleep, but my mind wouldn't shut down.

The people in Alcoholics Anonymous helped me tremendously in the dark beginnings of my recovery by sharing their own experiences in similar situations. They would share humiliating details of horrendous harms they committed against their loved ones and how they eventually made sincere amends.

They didn't share to be grandiose or brag. They shared their experience lovingly to give me hope. They gave me hope that one day, I too could gain the trust and respect of my family. They gave me hope by befriending me and reassuring me that one day, I too would have friends and be a friend. They gave me hope that one day, I would be able to have a healthy, interdependent sexual relationship based on love. They just gave me the hope, period.

The recovering addicts in Alcoholics Anonymous welcomed me in with open arms and gave me the love and understanding I didn't deserve, but desperately needed to survive. They understood me because they recognized themselves in me. When I was hopeless and spiritually starving, they spoon-fed me the spiritual food, I so desperately needed, called hope.

I needed a little hope right then sitting there alone and glum in my tent. The rain let up enough so I could hear voices of other hikers at the shelter. My spirits rose with hope, so I looked up to the heavens and said, "Thank You!"

A long trail hiker named Hiker X and a section hiker named Christian were in the shelter. Two more thru-hikers soon showed up, but I couldn't remember their names. We were involved in some technical conversation about gear when Jamie and Sharon came to my rescue. Two more Long Trail hikers named Diana and Em, which she pronounced M, stopped and crowded into the shelter.

The scene was chaotic as the other hikers jockeyed for a place to put down their sleeping bag and gear. I was sure happy I set my tent up prior to the storm. I sat at the table under the roof's protection, amused by all the drama.

The rain stopped, so I made some coffee as the mood turned festive. We had a great time shooting the bull. Hiker X gave Sharon the trail name Bench Hog, because she took up more than her share of room. I thought he was being a little passive aggressive because she crowded him with her gear. Bench Hog gave Jamie the trail name Princess. I suspected a little rivalry going on between them. I gave Diana the trail name Pancake Pounder. She was small and petite, but she ate a ton of pancakes for supper. It was all in good-natured fun, so no one took offense.

Princess's boyfriend and his buddy came in to spend the night. They brought beer and wanted to party, but their girlfriends hiked all day and didn't feel like drinking. The boys set up a tent to party by themselves later, but returned to socialize with us. They didn't seem to understand that hikers didn't last long into the night.

We all had a great time until a violent thunder and lightning storm drove me to my tent. The company of the other hikers did me good that night. I didn't feel lonely as I crawled into my still wet sleeping bag. I reflected on how the day started out disappointing and frustrating, but ended up being another great day on the trail. I listened to the storm outside as I said a simple prayer, "Thanks God for sending me help when I needed it today."

The first thing I did to get ready to make amends was, one day, I didn't drink or use drugs and I went to an Alcoholics Anonymous meeting and listened. The next day, I didn't use and I went to a meeting to listen. I kept going to meetings and staying sober. I suspected it was a while before anyone noticed, but the people closest to me started to notice. They also noticed they saw me more often and when they did see me, I wasn't asking for something. I stopped stealing from them. My violent outbursts stopped and they stopped hearing rumors of bar fights I instigated. I stopped getting into trouble. Eventually, I started to work and paid my bills. One day at a time, I started to become more responsible and trustworthy.

I started to wonder if the feelings of remorse I had lately were a spirit whisper. I questioned what the spirit wanted, as I drifted off to sleep to the sound of the rain.

June 24   **Day 119**   **12.8 Miles**

I awoke to hard rain and packed up wet again. I wasn't previously aware Vermont had a monsoon season. I left without going down to the shelter because I didn't want to wake the others. I soon caught up with Em, who left even earlier than I did. She was from State College, Pennsylvania. We hiked together, chatting most of the morning, until she fell behind. The rain stopped late in the morning and it cleared into a hot, humid day.

I stopped for lunch and set my tent up in the sun to dry at an old shelter. Two Sobo Long Trail hikers were packing up to head south. I filled them in on what the trail was like south and they did likewise about the trail north. I bid them goodbye, knowing I probably wouldn't ever see them again. I would like to hike the Long Trail to Canada with Scooter some day after we are retired.

I thought the spirit was sending me a message about the Eighth Step because it kept returning to my mind when I was alone. Even after being sober twenty-six years and working the Steps many times, I still had a familiar feeling something was wrong or I left something out.

I wasn't sober a long time and I was still completely self-centered, but I was staying sober and stopped creating more debris from my addiction. Eventually, my guilt and shame started to subside. I started to gain a little trust back from the people closest to me. I was rapidly enlarging my circle of friends in the rooms of Alcoholics Anonymous and overall, my life was starting to get better.

One day I was at a discussion meeting and the topic picked was on making amends. Many people shared their experience about making amends. I thought there were good comments, but one gentleman who had a considerable amount of time sober said, "You're making amends just by staying sober." When I heard his comment, my intuition told me what he was saying wasn't exactly right, but it was what I wanted to hear. The persistent sense I had pestering me was similar to the feeling I had then. I suspected I had some unfinished business in Steps Eight and Nine.

Christian arrived and distracted my thoughts. He spread out his wet things in the sun to dry. I offered him a cup of bad coffee and he accepted. I watched his reaction as he took his first sip and he took it in stride and didn't even make an ugly face, so I was impressed. Christian was twenty-years-old and from Boston and hiking from Vermont to Maine. His father was a Native American and his mother was white. Christian was a good looking young man with black hair and darker skin from his father's side. I met Christian the day before, but didn't get a chance to talk to him because of all the other hikers at the shelter. We talked for a short time and discovered, we were both friends of Bill. I thought that explained how he tolerated my coffee so easily.

Christian came to the trail to get out of the city and take some time for reflection to sort things out. We bonded instantly and became big brother and little brother as only brothers in recovery could. We both were grateful to have someone else who spoke the same language. We chattered like a couple of chipmunks on crack. The extra strong coffee probably also helped a little.

He was hiking to Andover, Maine where his grandparents ran a bed and breakfast for hikers. I decided I would send myself a mail drop to Andover, stay with them, and maybe even take a zero day. He gave me their phone number to contact them when I got there. I hoped he and I would arrive together so maybe we could attend some Alcoholics Anonymous meetings in Andover.

Bench Hog, Princess, and Em arrived and stayed for lunch, but moved on, planning to stop at Lost Pond for the night. Christian and I stayed about another hour, enjoying the sun and each other's company until our equipment dried out.

The mountains of Vermont were beautiful, but the hiking was harder than it had been since Pennsylvania, so we took our time. The terrain was rocky and the mountains began to get steeper. However the beauty of the enormous mountains more than made up for the adversity. My ankle was still tender and swollen, so I had to go slow. Christian was new to the trail and not in trail shape, so we were compatible in that sense. I stopped and took a few pictures of Christian with the mountains in the background.

We continued to talk as we hiked to Lost Pond Shelter where we found Bench Hog and Princess already set up in their tent. Em was in the shelter with an older man who didn't fit as a hiker. They were waiting for Norm, No Cheese, and Knight Rider who planned to pack in some wine.

Norm's girlfriend from home met him in Manchester for the night. She was going to shuttle them ahead to a town called Danby. They promised the girls they would get some booze and meet them for a party at Lost Pond.

The girls set their tent in the middle of the only campsite. No other flat ground was suitable to set a tent on, so I crowded in next to the girls. I thought it might be safer for the girls, because I didn't trust the old man at the shelter. I laid on my mat to rest my ankle for a minute and must have fallen asleep. I awoke in an hour to the pleasant sounds of laughter coming from the shelter. Knight Rider and No Cheese as promised, packed in a box of wine and they were drinking with the schoolteachers. Norm stayed with his girlfriend and planned to meet the others in a few days.

I noticed the old man covered his face with his hat when Em took a picture. His behavior immediately arose more suspicion in me. I figured there must be a reason why he was adamant about not having his picture taken. Em wanted a group picture, so I asked the old man if he would take the picture. I gave him my camera and he seemed okay with that and took a group picture of all of us as we posed in front of the shelter.

Later, I noticed the screen on my camera seemed to be broken. No Cheese said it would still take pictures anyway, only I couldn't see the pictures in advance. I never saw him do it, but I wondered if the old man broke my camera on purpose. I decided we all might be better off if I didn't confront him. Besides, maybe I broke it on the rough trail earlier.

I thought he could be on the run from the law or something because he sure seemed out of place. No Cheese, Knight Rider, and Christian were staying in the shelter with Em, so I figured there was enough red meat to protect Em. I would be sleeping next to Princess and Bench Hog to protect them. I still felt uneasy because my intuition screamed something wasn't right.

Christian and I went for a walk to get away from the party. We climbed a hill and found cell tower. I let Christian call his sponsor, his girlfriend, and his Grandpa Paul. Christian had a lot of support from family and friends, which I thought was good.

My ankle was a little better with less swelling, but still painful. I hoped the injury healed soon because it was annoying. I talked to Scooter and she agreed to bring another pair of hiking boots that were more supportive for my ankles when she met me on the fourth of July. She told me she reserved a motel room in White River Junction, which was near Hanover.

The girls returned from the shelter a little tipsy after I was in my tent, but not yet asleep. They giggled for a short while, but alcohol was a good central nervous system depressant, so they soon abandoned me to their personal dream worlds.

I clung to the statement, You're making amends by just staying sober, for a long time. I kept it a secret because I knew it wasn't exactly the right thing to do. I started to rationalize, I was living better and treating everyone better. The people I harmed didn't bring it up, so why should I remind them. The wounds of my past were starting to heal, so like I said, why pick the scabs off. I ignored the people who weren't talking to me. I even blamed, them thinking they needed to get over it. Couldn't they see I was staying sober? I decided to leave sleeping dogs alone.

I purposely changed the subject in my mind to escape the unpleasant feelings that I started to detect. I didn't think my snoring would awaken the girls after all the wine they drank.

Day 120   17.6 Miles

I awoke to the sound of rain on the tent, which seemed to be the normal way days started in Vermont. It had rained almost every day since I was in Massachusetts. I was tired of the rain, but I couldn't do anything about it, but accept it. I took my time packing up before I went to the shelter, cooked breakfast, and made coffee. Everything appeared to go well last night in the shelter. The old man had already headed south and all my friends were going north. I breathed a sigh of relief because I didn't trust him. Something just didn't seem right, but I couldn't put my finger on it.

The folks in the shelter were up and scrambling to start their day. Bench Hog and Princess were the first to move out as they planned to rendezvous with Princess's mother at a road not far from there. I was the next to leave. Christian was dallying, so I hiked out solo to a rainy, gray morning. I passed Bench Hog who seemed to be struggling on the rough trail. The trail in Vermont was picturesque with several mountain creeks, deep gorges, and glacier lakes. I had yet to see a moose, but I startled something big that went crashing through the brush. I suspected it might have been a moose.

I caught up with Princess and her mother at a road crossing while they were waiting for Bench Hog. I met her mom, who was the stereotypical Jewish mother from New York City. Her mom brought bagels and cream cheese from New York and gave me one. She planned to take the girls into town to go shopping. I ate the bagel and thanked her before I hiked on in the rain.

The monotony of the steady rain soon lulled me into a meditative state. I remembered going on for some time semi-content, thinking I was making amends just by staying sober. I expected the annoying feeling that I wasn't being honest would eventually go away. Then one day I made a big mistake.

I was riding with Big Jim and he asked, "Have you made any amends yet?"

I said, "Yep."

A pause followed until he said, "Well," which meant he wanted a little further explanation.

I knew I would be in trouble when I said, "I'm making amends, just by staying sober."

Jim almost put the car in the ditch yet again, but by that time, I was used to his driving. I did get a little concerned when he leaned over and stuck his face about two inches from mine and looked me straight in the eye, since we were still going sixty miles-per-hour.

He quietly, but in a challenging way said, "Good God, you are as f#@*%g dumb as you look." Jim's voice elevated noticeably an octave or two and he gave me some extraordinarily energetic feedback about, doing things my own dumb ass way.

I actually felt some relief because I already knew on some level making direct amends was the right thing to do. I guess I was starting to change and listen to my conscience. Looking back, I thought, having Big Jim as a sponsor also helped.

The rain stopped and the sun came out, which seemed to be the rule rather than the exception most days. I came upon some hiker/campers swimming in a lake who distracted my thoughts. They tried to entice me into jumping in for a refreshing dip. I remembered the cold water of Goose Pond, so I stuck my hand in the icy cold water and said, "I'm good." I could see these people were either extremely tough or extremely stupid.

I took my shoes and socks off and soaked my feet. The icy water had a numbing effect on the pain in my ankle. I sat on my pack watching them and remembered my last shower was at the Bird Cage in Massachusetts, which seemed like a long time ago. Without thinking, I lifted my arm and sniffed my arm-pit to see if I stunk. When I regained consciousness, I made a mental note to never, ever do that again. I started thinking euphorically about a long, hot shower.

I looked in the guidebook. To my delight, I found a reasonable motel almost eighteen miles north. Eighteen miles was a long way on a bad ankle, but possible. I took two ibuprofen tablets and set out with a purpose in mind. I put on some John Denver to help take my mind off the pain and hiked out singing to Country Roads.

Staying sober was only the first thing I did to get ready to become willing to make amends. Only after I was sober and changing did people close to me believe the sincerity of my amends. The first three words of Step Eight were, made a list. I felt it wasn't necessary to make a list of people I had harmed at first. I rationalized, writing a list seemed silly, which allowed me to minimize the importance of a list.

Therefore, the second thing I did was to take a piece of paper and make a physical list of people I harmed. I returned to take a look at the moral inventory I did in Step Four. My Step Four inventory had a name attached to all my resentments, fears, and harms done to others. I found when I came to Step Eight, I already made my list of the people I harmed in my Step Four. I added those names to my list. The list on paper was larger than the one I had in my head, but first on the list were the people I loved the most.

Once I had my list or inventory of names, making my amends became methodical. I would make amends to the easiest first, which was to the people I loved the most like my Mom and Dad. I felt better and gained confidence as I started to face those I had harmed and made amends.

I hiked to Minerva Hinchey Shelter late in the afternoon, where I stopped to take a break. I took off my shoes and socks and gave my poor feet some air. I called the Country Squire Motel, which was less than three trail miles away from the shelter to reserve a room. The lady at the motel told me to buy supper at the Whistle Stop Restaurant before I walked two road miles to the motel. No food was available at the motel.

Tank came in as I hung up the phone. He set up for the night. I told him about the motel and restaurant, but he was beat and wanted to end the day there. Tank was introverted and hard to get to know at first, but I had spent enough time with him that he warmed up to me. We chatted for some time, catching each other up on what had happened since we last saw each other at the Bird Cage. He too was tired of all the rain and wished he could hike only for one day with dry feet, merely to see what it was like.

I packed up and tried to entice him into coming to the motel, but he was adamant about staying at the shelter. He planned on stopping at Killington in a couple of days. I bid him goodbye and hiked the three more miles to the road. I crossed an intimidating suspension bridge on cables over Mill River at a place called Clarendon Gorge. I felt like

I was in an Indiana Jones movie as I swayed and bounced across the bridge. The river below was white with rapids, but no crocodiles.

I arrived at the Whistle Stop Restaurant by suppertime and found it pleasantly busy with the locals. Apparently, a family owned the restaurant. The kids, from ages twelve to twenty-two seemed to run it. My waitress was only about fourteen. Her younger brother was cleaning up the tables as people left. The cook was about eighteen and the boss was twenty-two-years-old. They were all respectful and polite to each other as well as to the customers, which I found refreshing. I ordered one of my all-time favorite meals of a hot roast pork sandwich with mashed potatoes and green beans. My waitress asked if I would like gravy and I said, "Please, over everything." I was on my second cup of coffee when she returned and to my delight, she presented a huge plate with a generous double scoop of mashed potatoes all dripping with thick, tasty gravy. I finished my meal, but couldn't squeeze in desert.

My ankle tightened up with the rest and protested as I reluctantly left, hoping to hitch a ride to the motel. I didn't get a ride, but about a mile down the road was an unexpected, old-type gas station slash general store. I bought barbeque potato chips, Little Debbie Snack cakes, cream filled oatmeal cookies, a pint of chocolate chip mint ice cream, and two sticky buns for breakfast. Then to top it off, they had the new July issue of Fur-Fish-Game Magazine, which was a special treat.

The sky turned dark and started to thunder as I left the store and hurried toward the motel to beat the storm. I hoofed the last mile of the day in record time. I found the motel run by a lady in her late seventies who charged me forty-three dollars for the room, which was very reasonable by Vermont standards. The motel was an older, Mom and Pop type, but the room was nice. I took my usual shower and did my laundry at the same time. A violent storm hit by the time I was out of the shower and safe. I smiled as I watched the light show from the window and said, "Thanks."

The first direct amends I made was to my mother, who loved me always, even when she didn't approve of how I was living. She had been praying for me all along and forgave me probably before I even made amends. My dad took a little longer, but he too forgave me and even started to admire and respect me. Making amends to Mom and Dad felt good and inspired me to continue to make direct amends to others.

The process had been ongoing over the years and continued. As the Big Book suggests, I made direct amends to folks as I became willing, except when to do so would injure them or others. I was sober thirteen years before I got over the animosity I held onto towards my ex-wife and became willing to make direct amends to her. I had to forgive her first to see my part in everything.

I walked to the bathroom, still in meditation, when a sharp pain stabbed me in the ankle. My ankle was sore, swollen, and must have tightened up as I rested. I walked almost twenty miles, including road miles that day, which may have been overdoing it on a sore ankle. I took some ibuprofen so I could sleep.

I plugged in my charger to charge my extra cell phone batteries and discovered I had cell tower. Spiritual Pilgrim called while I was on the trail and left a message. I called him back and we connected. He had a hard time in New Hampshire on Mount Moosilauke, so he skipped the White Mountains. He said no one who he knew of had made it through the Whites. He was so negative that I wished I hadn't called him back. I didn't need the influence of negative attitudes or negative people, especially when I already felt a lot of fear over the issue with my ankle.

The Whites would be hard, but I wouldn't give up until I made it through them. They may be a hundred-twenty miles of hell, but other people hiked them. I thought Spiritual Pilgrim has been psyching himself out over the Whites ever since Pennsylvania. I realized I was doing the same thing he did. I was psyching myself out. I feared the future, which was only in my mind, embellished by my fear. I needed to quit contemplating taking on the Whites until I got to the Whites. Then I needed to only take them on one-step at a time and let go to let God guide me. I recognized, when I worried all I was doing was visualizing the future with me in control instead of God. I prayed the serenity prayer and then called Darren, who was a positive friend from back home. We talked and he encouraged me until I felt better.

I randomly opened the little white Bible to the book of Mark, about Jesus going into the wilderness after John baptized him. It said, The spirit then compelled Him to go into the wilderness, where he was tempted by Satan. I remembered reading the same thing a few days ago so I thumbed back to the book of Mathew and read the same thing in a little more detail.

Severe pain in my shoulder from holding an awkward position to read interrupted my concentration. I took a break and felt pins and needles which intensified as the blood began to circulate in my arm. I closed my eyes, which were burning from reading in the poor light with cheap glasses. I laid on the soft mattress and listened to the sound of the rain in the night as I pondered why the spirit sent Jesus into the wilderness. I asked myself, why did Satan even try to tempt him?

I looked at my watch and it was ten o'clock and way past my bedtime. It was a good thing I bought a waterproof watch with all the rain. I had worn my watch in the rain, the shower, swimming, and it still kept ticking.

A parallel formed in my mind. My watch was water poof, but that didn't mean it wouldn't get wet. It meant water wouldn't destroy it or keep it from working. Just because I became a Christian, didn't mean alcohol, drugs, or the sight of a pretty girl wouldn't tempt me. The gospels said Jesus was tempted, but he resisted the temptation. I wondered if Jesus wanted to show me that I would be tempted, but I still had my free will to choose.

I wouldn't believe my watch was waterproof if I only read it was waterproof on the label. I knew my watch was waterproof because it was wet many times and it resisted the damage water caused.

I pondered my thoughts and wondered if the spirit was sending me a message connected to Step Eight and Nine. Step Eight said, "Became willing to make amends to them all." I was willing to apologize to the folks like my friend Mark who I punched in the bar, because I selfishly wanted forgiveness to sooth my guilt and shame.

The folks who I had resentments towards were extremely hard. In time, after several years of Alcoholics Anonymous meetings, I started to see my part in the drama. I noticed I often did something to cause them to react, which caused me to resent them. I came to accept others also had egos and character defects which caused them to do harm to me, thus causing my resentment. I thought, forgiveness on my part was also a huge part of becoming willing to make amends.

I still wasn't willing to make amends to certain people on my list of resentments who I hadn't forgiven yet. I listed these people every time I took Step Eight and still couldn't see where I did anything to provoke them. I still felt I was the victim and they were the ones who needed to make amends to me. My seventh grade school teacher was the largest example of someone who, after forty some years, I still wasn't willing to make amends to. I also resented a girl who stole three-hundred-dollars dollars from me after I was sober six years. All I could see was how they wronged me. I couldn't see my part in my resentment.

I felt a little more open to forgiving them because I was weary of carrying the resentment for all those years. Chief once said, "Let it go, your resentment holds you back spiritually." I wasn't sure what he meant, but maybe I needed to add those people to the list. I thought the resentment was still too strong for me to trust myself yet not to fall to temptation and seek revenge that would harm them or others. I had considered the possibility, but wasn't quite willing to forgive them yet.

I seemed to be stuck. I thought maybe I should pray because after all, God always answered my prayers. I folded my hands and prayed, Dear God, please send me a message to help me forgive those I resent so I can Move on and live free, Amen.

The ibuprofen did its job on the pain, so I turned off the light. I was grateful to be in a warm, dry motel on a stormy night. I drifted off to sleep as the thunder, lightning, and rain continued.

Day 121   Zero miles

I slept uneasy last night. I thought maybe because the violent thunderstorm lasted all night or maybe because of the conflict within me over Steps Eight and Nine.

The storm persisted and threatened to continue all day. My bed was wet from the leaking roof and my clothes, tent, and sleeping bag were all wet. The thought of going back on the trail in that weather depressed me. I made bad coffee, ate two Honey Buns, and took some time to think things over. My ankle felt better than the day before, but was still swollen and hurt, so I decided to take a zero day to rest. I went to the office and paid for another night. The lady gave me another room that wasn't leaking, so I moved my gear to the dry room.

I read every story and all the ads in my magazine, and then I watched television until boredom overtook me. I could no longer sleep the time away, so I decided to venture out in the driving rain to the convenience store so I could buy food for the day and re-supply.

I ran into Christian at the store. He had hitched a ride with a trail angel, who was waiting in the car to take him back to the trail. He offered me a ride to the Whistle Stop restaurant. I accepted without hesitation and jumped in the back seat.

Christian warned me that Mountain Goat and Fire Fly were going to force me to take a drink when I stop at the hotel in Killington. I was quick to reply, "There will be a lot of bloodshed." I tried to act as if the threat didn't faze me, but on the inside, I could feel the adrenalin rise as I became furious. I suddenly wanted to be alone when we pulled into the parking lot of the restaurant. I thanked the driver and gave Christian a big hug goodbye.

I bought the breakfast special of three eggs over easy, ham, toast, home fries and real coffee. I didn't appreciate the meal as I normally would have due to the huge resentment I was nurturing. I was angry and felt betrayed by my so-called friends.

I thought back to the insight with my watch last night. The watch was waterproof, but that didn't mean it wouldn't get wet. I could see being sober and in recovery didn't make me immune to resentments. It meant I had the tools to cope with my resentments without acting out and harming others or myself.

I hadn't planned on stopping at Killington because I knew it was only going to be another drunken party anyway, but now my ego felt challenged to stop and teach them a lesson. Killington was famous for its popular ski slopes in the winter months. It was the home of, The Inn at the Long Trail, which was the first ski lodge in Vermont, built in

1939. In the off-season, they offered reduced rate discounts to hikers, which included a hiker-size breakfast. The inn also had a bar that advertised Guinness at the correct temperature by the pint. Killington was where the Long Trail and the Appalachian Trail separated. The Long Trail hikers went north and the Appalachian Trail hikers went east, so everyone planned a goodbye party. Apparently, the Goat was planning a goodbye party for me.

I believed God knew I suddenly had more on my plate than I could handle by myself so he sent help. As I was leaving, Zoma and Lug arrived at the restaurant, soaking wet from the driving rain. They temporarily took my mind off my resentment. They stripped down almost to nothing to put on clean, dry clothes right on the porch, before they went into the restaurant. I believed only thru-hikers would do such a thing. I told them about the motel, but they wanted to eat breakfast and return to the trail. They also planned to stop and spend the night in Killington. I purposely didn't mention the Goat as I bid them goodbye and started back to the comfort of the motel. I could have joined them and drank coffee as they ate, but I didn't take the opportunity. I said nothing of the resentment I was harboring because I needed to process it, but not with someone on the trail.

That was not a good time for me to be alone, because my ego took over again. I started to rehearse the bar scene in my mind. I hadn't been in a fistfight since I quit drinking twenty-six years ago. The resentment made me think I rather missed fighting. I was the veteran of enough bar fights to know you attack fast and keep attacking until the bystanders pull you off. I fantasized that I would walk into the bar acting as if I knew nothing and would wait until the Goat started to taunt me. I would surprise him with a sucker punch, a right cross to the Adams apple and follow with a right jab to the nose. In my fantasy, he would go down so I could start kicking him until they stopped me. I would leave Fire Fly alone unless he got involved. I could not focus on anything besides my anger and resentment towards the arrogant Goat. I would end his hike for him, maybe permanently.

I came out of my fantasy and realized I was almost running, my heart was beating a mile a minute, and I was out of breath from all the adrenalin. I was clenching my fists and my jaw was aching with tenseness. I stopped in the pouring rain, looked up into the sky, and said a prayer. "Please Lord, I don't want to live like this."

I took a deep breath to calm down as I walked the rest of the way back to the motel. Bill Wilson once said, "Resentment is a luxury an alcoholic cannot afford." I didn't agree with Wilson on that one as far as a resentment being a luxury, but I knew I couldn't afford to keep the resentment. That resentment clearly stunted my spiritual growth.

I called several AA friends in an attempt to process my resentment. They all said just about the same thing. They told me to pray for Mountain Goat, let it go, and don't go to the bar. I was in recovery long enough to know they were right. I would give someone else the same advice. I felt okay when I was on the phone, but as soon as I was by myself my foolish ego's pride wanted revenge.

I liked watching cartoons when I was a kid. I now felt like Mickey Mouse when he had a devil on one shoulder telling him one thing and an angel on the other shoulder telling him the opposite. I knew my ego was the mouse who wanted revenge, even though I knew revenge was evil and definitely the wrong thing to do.

My mind flashed back to a time I was plotting revenge shortly after I became sober. I went to a meeting in a church basement and on the blackboard, some anonymous angel wrote in chalk, "Nothing promises so much, but delivers so little as revenge." I felt an angel left the message exclusively for me.

One of our many slogans said, Think it through. I tried to think it through. I knew no one could predict the outcome of a fight. I knew my destiny would be out of my control as soon as I reacted emotionally to a feeling such as pride. I knew the worst case was I could kill the Goat and end up in jail or he could kill me. I wasn't too crazy about either outcome. I also knew from experience, I would at least make an ass out of myself no matter what the outcome. Later I would feel shame, remorse and regret if I sought revenge.

I knew I should pray for the Goat because my friends told me. I said, "Lord, Pleasehelpthesonofabitchamen." I thought afterwards, that probably wasn't a prayer I ever heard in church.

I thought God heard the prayer, because, "As we forgive those who trespass against us" immediately popped into my pea brain. Alcoholics Anonymous meetings almost all closed with everyone joining hands in a circle as one and reciting the Lord's Prayer. I said the prayer literally thousands of times in the last twenty-six years. I just mechanically rehearsed the prayer aloud with the others, but I never thought much about the meaning of those words.

I prayed, *Lord, was that the message? Was the reason for all the unrest from within about forgiveness? Was that the answer to the prayer I prayed the night before?* I didn't feel much better, but it gave me food for thought as I tried to calm down.

I spent the rest of the day in the motel with my resentment popping up in my mind like an unwanted guest. I watched mindless sitcoms on television as I lay in bed eating junk food like a nine year old whose parents left him home alone for the first time. I also called some folks back home in an attempt to process my resentment towards Fire Fly and Mountain Goat, without having to forgive them.

I thought my ankle was a little better with the rest. I planned to return to the trail at dawn. I prayed for sunshine, healing, and a better attitude.

Day 122   20.7 Miles

My resentments kept me awake, most of the night. When I managed to nod off, violent dreams haunted my sleep. I packed up and walked the two miles to the Whistle Stop restaurant for breakfast. I ate a big breakfast and then hit the trail to a cloudy, but dry day that threatened rain. I hiked with my thoughts over three mountains. It was a good day to be alone so I could make contact with the God of my primitive understanding.

I spent the day in meditation. I had a déjà-vu feeling of familiarity with my resentment towards Mountain Goat ever since Christian told me about it yesterday. I once worked with a peer who majored in Gestalt Therapy. I remembered her saying any time there was an unusually strong reaction to something it probably was from old, unresolved anger.

It all started to come together at once; something I hadn't thought about previously. I stopped hiking, took my pack off, and sat on it. I hadn't smoked a cigarette in over twenty-five years, but it was one of those times that I sure wished I could smoke a Tareyton with Dad right then.

The old, unresolved anger stems from when I was twelve-years-old. I was the victim of a seventh grade homeroom teacher who was a mean, abusive bully. He had authority and flaunted it. He liked to paddle students in front of the class and I was one of his victims. I not only hated it when he physically abused me, I hated it when he would go into an unpredictable temper tantrum and beat other helpless students. In those days, the bastard got away with it. He used to say, "In the Army they single out an individual and make an example out of them." I didn't think the prick was ever even in the army, but I was the one he singled out and used as an example. One time I studied hard and got an A on his English test, but he gave me an F for cheating.

I held on to such a hatred, I used to think about him when I was drinking and try to hunt him down to make an example out of him. I would have liked to see his reaction when he realized he wasn't facing a seventy pound twelve-year-old, but a full-grown man with a hatred that would kill. I would dream of beating him to death and be a hero to his other victims. Eventually, after I started to recover from my addiction, I thanked God I never found him because it would surely have changed the course of my life and left a dishonorable legacy to my loved ones.

I could see walking as Jesus did was harder than it looked at first. I had to let go of old hatred and follow Christ. The words, "As we forgive those who trespass against us" surfaced again as if the spirit whispered in my ear.

My ego, the mouse with the horns and pitchfork was screaming in my ear, "The greasy bastard doesn't deserve forgiveness, shoot him in the knee, and let him think about it as he bleeds out." The Holy Spirit whispered in the other ear, "Forgive us our trespasses as we forgive those who trespass against us."

I thought I actually heard the words, You have to forgive him so you can stop hating him. I had a moment of clarity where I received a message from the Spirit which said, forgiveness was the cure for all my resentments.

I was still angry, but for the first time ever I made a sincere attempt to forgive the teacher right there, right then. I didn't want to forgive him because I felt he deserved forgiven. I wanted to forgive him so I could be free of the bondage of my own hatred.

I prayed almost a plea, "Dear God, please help me understand how I can forgive those who trespass against me when I feel like I'm their victim."

I didn't feel any different as I hiked on, still with an uneasy emotion. I arrived at the road to The Inn at Long Trail where most of my friends were going to stay. I paused while pondering whether to go or not when the words, "Lead us not into temptation, but deliver us from evil," also from the Lord's Prayer, came into my mind. I knew all along it was going to be a drunken party and as much as I was going to miss my friends, I didn't want to get involved in that mess anyway. My wounded pride was the only thing that wanted to go kick the Goat's ass.

I came upon a clearing where I could see the Killington ski slopes on the mountain. From that far of a distance, they looked like scars on the top of the mountain. I soon passed the Long Trail junction, where the Long Trail went north and the Appalachian Trail turned east toward New Hampshire and the White Mountains. I turned east recalling the line in the Lord's Prayer again that I hadn't given much previous thought, "Lead us not into temptation, but deliver us from evil."

I pondered the line for a moment and I couldn't think of one time ever when God's will led me into temptation. It was always my pride, ego, or self-will that got me into trouble every stinking time. It was as if my Guardian Angel imbedded a thought into my pea brain that my wounded ego was what was tempting me to do something stupid right then. My foolish pride told me they were disrespecting me.

I passed by the Long Trail by putting one foot in front of the other reluctantly at first, but soon it started getting easier. I felt relieved. Besides, in a moment of clarity, I could see them kicking my ass in front of all my homies, which would have been a quick cure for my inflated ego.

I hiked on to a highway where I could stay at a state campground. They had a tent site reserved for thru-hikers for four dollars. I also took a hot shower in a coin-operated shower for four quarters. I felt like I was in a car wash.

I was all alone and lonely again, still obsessed with my resentments, and rehearsing revenge. I got pissed at myself all over again for not going to Killington to confront Mountain Goat and Fire Fly.

I started to pray a simple prayer for clarity and recalled reading the book of Mark a few days ago, I wondered, why was Jesus tempted in the first place? Then by coincidence, Christian told me about the goat's plot to sabotage my sobriety.

I pondered the question and looked at my watch by habit. I was reminded again my watch was waterproof as evidenced by the many times I had gotten it wet and submerged it in water and it still functioned. Maybe one of the reasons God sent Jesus into the wilderness was for the same reason. Jesus was tempted to prove he could be tempted, but not seduced into pleasures of his ego or as they say, sin.

I wondered if God sent Mountain Goat and Fire Fly as messengers to give me the resentment. God may have created the series of events the last few days to give me a chance to overcome my ego and let go of some resentments. I prayed the same prayer I prayed earlier, "Dear God, please help me understand how I can forgive those who trespass against me when I feel like I'm their victim." I thought maybe God didn't hear me, forgot, or didn't take me seriously the first time.

I hiked past the long trail earlier that day, so I realized I may never see any of my friends who were hiking the long trail, which depressed me a little, but I knew tomorrow was another day. My ankle was hurting even more than it did before I took the day off. I had some fear, but I thought I could keep on keeping on at least for a while.

I needed to remember that similar to my watch, I was waterproof but that didn't mean I wouldn't get wet. I had to face my temptations, but like Jesus, I didn't have to face them alone for, "Thou art with me."

I thought back to that time so many years ago, in the Diamond Deli when I wanted to drink and Big Jim asked, "Can you go fifteen minutes without drinking?" I did it one minute at a time. Earlier, I passed the trail to Killington one-step at a time. One foot in front of the other, I went too far both times to turn back.

I felt a lot of gratitude as the day ended because a great burden lifted. God had been especially good to me that day. Chief showed great wisdom years ago when he told me, my resentments were holding me back. I thought it was time to move forward.

Day 123   16.6 Miles

I slept well, but awoke to another wet, rainy day. I made coffee and ate two honey buns for breakfast in my tent to stay dry as long as I could. I laid back on my sleeping bag after I ate, procrastinating facing the driving rain outside. I thought maybe I could go back to sleep. I was idly watching a bug bounce off the ceiling of the tent unsuccessfully trying to escape, which had become a type of sport for me.

Some questions occurred to me. Why would the Goat and Fire Fly even think of getting me drunk in the first place? Didn't they know what it would do to me? What was my part in it all?

I was open about being an alcoholic and I didn't care about being anonymous. I asked myself, was there something wrong with that? I pondered my own question and recalled Dr Bob once said, "We must remain anonymous to keep our damn fool egos from getting inflated."

The light bulb lit up and I experienced an awakening. I was proud of being a sober, recovering alcoholic, so I was quick to break my own anonymity. My damn fool ego got involved and I was bragging about being a sober, recovering alcoholic. I could see how they felt judged by me and they were right because I was judging them. I felt as if my eyes opened to how they saw me. I could understand why they resented me. They wanted to get me drunk to knock me off my high horse.

It was still pouring down rain, the kind of hard rain that normally didn't last too long, so I made a second cup of coffee. I could feel the mist from the rain when I unzipped the opening of the tent before lighting my stove so I wouldn't asphyxiate myself. I gazed out into the driving rain. I sucked in the moist, sweet smelling fresh air. I filled my lungs to the max and held it as I did when I took a hit on a joint in the old days. I always loved the smell of a hard rain, as if God was giving the world a shower at the car wash so everything would be fresh and clean.

I faintly heard the spirit who was whispering, so I tried to block out everything and listen to the spirit take me where it wanted. I found myself pleading my case as if I was in court with old Judge Walker. I said, "Your Honor, in my own defense, I was breaking my anonymity so others could know they too could get sober and find the joy of recovery through Alcoholics Anonymous."

Now old Judge Walker was a big man who didn't often use a gavel. I could almost see him slapping his big fist down on the bench, which sounded like a butcher slamming a slab of beef on the counter. He would then point a fat finger at me while he looked over his glasses right into my core, and then pass judgment. I heard the words as if the judge said them himself, "Alcoholics Anonymous is a program of attraction not promotion, so I find you, young man, guilty of promotion."

I hung my head at the reality of the insight. I recalled the animosity I felt within me from the unsolicited promoting of Christianity by enthusiastic folks. The realization I was guilty as charged of doing the same thing left me with a nasty taste in my mouth.

I reluctantly packed up my wet tent in a driving rain. My left ankle was killing me. I felt miserable and my mood matched the weather. I couldn't remember the last time I hiked with dry feet. I felt guilty and hoped I would see Mountain Goat and Fire Fly not to fight, but to apologize and make amends. I was wet to the bone before I took my first step on the trail towards Katahdin. I soon came to Kent Pond's outlet where the high water from the rain created a sizeable, picturesque waterfall. I stopped to take a picture and soon felt a bit of gratitude because I knew the waterfall was only there due to the flooding from all the rain. I felt privileged to be a witness to God's beauty. I guess when they said, "There is a silver lining to every dark cloud," it was true.

My mood changed as I moved on and the endorphins kicked in. I forded the raging torrent of two un-named streams that I probably could have stepped across most other years. The weather stayed the same, which gave me time to meditate as I trudged on in the rain. I found it easy to forgive Mountain Goat and Fire Fly once I accepted my part in it. Instantly, my resentments melted away. I understood how they felt and making amends to them was the right thing to do. I smiled to myself as that may be the example of the purpose of Step Eight. Bill sure knew what he was talking about when he wrote the Steps. I would make direct amends to them whenever it was possible.

I hiked almost seven miles before I came upon a sign indicating it was a tenth of a mile to a shelter. I was soaked to the bone, so a dry place to cook a hot lunch was a blessing. I took the trail to Stony Brook Shelter, out of the driving rain for lunch. To my good fortune, I found Night Rider, Norm, and No Cheese still in their sleeping bags. They had spent the night and were in no hurry to venture out into the rain on a day like that day. I so welcomed their company.

I cooked a hot meal with them and made a pot of bad coffee. I was proud because my coffee became famous on the trail for being strong and bad. I was in no hurry to leave in the driving rain either. I made a second pot of coffee, which wired me so tight, I had to leave to burn off the excess energy. They said they were going to hike six miles to a cabin called The Lookout, where hikers could stay. However, they were still in their sleeping bags staying dry in the early afternoon when I bid them goodbye.

I thought that was the most time I have ever spent processing Step Eight and Step Nine. I saw how being unwilling to make amends could stand between me and my relationship with God. Amends were not only my attempt to clean up the debris from my past selfish behavior, but also freed me from the past. Amends also helped me avoid the same mistakes in the future. Steps Eight and Nine showed me the impact I had on others such as Mountain Goat and Fire Fly. I realized I never only hurt myself, so I learned to think a little before I hurt someone.

I always felt good when someone understood and forgave me. However, that wasn't always the outcome when I made amends. Some folks didn't forgive me and that never felt good. That would be why we started out all Alcoholics Anonymous meetings with the Serenity Prayer. "God grant me the serenity to accept the things I cannot change." The wounds of my past had healed for the most part. They were much like an old football injury where the pain showed back up to haunt me occasionally. I thought it was a good thing because I didn't want to forget where I came from, for fear I might return and repeat the past.

I continued to hike watching my feet and trudging on in the rain. The hiking was unpleasant, but I knew it wasn't the only reason I felt uneasy. Something far bigger than the rain, was eating away at me. I thought about praying, but there really was no need to pray to ask what it was about. A line in a song of the seventies said, "Oz never did give nothing to the Tin Man that he didn't already have." I would like to deny it, but I already figured out why I felt uneasy for the last several days. I had known for a long time I had unfinished business with my seventh grade teacher.

I stopped in my tracks and almost puked. I had been comfortable for years with being his victim. I was comfortable with hating his guts. The thought of even looking at my part in it and making amends to him literally nauseated me. It would appear to others, if they were watching, that I was gazing into the rain, but I was in deep thought, watching drops of water form, swell, and fall off the brim of my hat. The truth was, my ego had been holding onto the hate and carrying it around for all these years, wallowing in self-righteous shit. I didn't even know if he was still alive. Chief's words came into my mind, "Let it go, it's holding you back."

I felt like I was the monkey holding onto the apple in the coconut as the hunter approached. Only hatred was the name of the apple I was unwilling to let go of to become free. My own ego was what forbid me to let go which held me imprisoned in the coconut. My resentment was the coconut that, like Chief said, was holding me back. I guess Chief and others could see it all along, but my stubborn ego blinded me with foolish pride for over forty years. I was blind, but now I see.

I hiked ten monotonous miles in the monsoon-type rain in a back and forth struggle within my own mind. I arrived at Wintturi Shelter to find standing water everywhere on the ground, which took away the option of setting up my tent.

I set up in the shelter by myself. I found a tasteful picture on the wall of the mountains and the words, "Tough times never last, but tough people do." My friend Taco signed it. I usually found graffiti in the shelters appalling, but it was exactly what I needed to inspire me on that wet, rainy day.

I suddenly came to a spiritual realization that I couldn't hike the trail alone, but I wasn't hiking all alone and I never was. I turned to Chapter Five in my Big Book to page fifty-nine, which said *Without help it is too much for us, but there is one who has all power, that one is God. May you find him now.*

A slogan in Alcoholics Anonymous said, "God won't give you more than you can handle." Well today, I was dreadfully close to the edge of more than I could handle, so God sent help in the form of graffiti on the wall of a shelter.

Nothing had physically changed. My ankle still hurt, I was still wet, it was still raining, the lightning was still frightening, but as it said on page four-seventeen in the Big Book, *Nothing absolutely nothing happens in God's world by mistake.* The trail was supposed to be difficult. That was why most who try alone fail to make it to Katahdin.

I got out my little Big book and read the paragraph on page four-seventeen aloud. The paragraph also said, "When I was disturbed, it was because I find some person, place, thing, or situation--some fact in my life--unacceptable to me." I stopped to ponder what I read and thought, that was why I was so disturbed with my old teacher. I found the situation unacceptable. I read on and it said, *I can find no serenity until I accept that person, place, thing, or situation as being exactly the way it is supposed to be at this moment in time.* I found peace, because I accepted the situation I was in on the trail as being exactly the way it was supposed to be at that moment in time. I then realized to find peace and serenity I had to accept the past situation with the teacher because it was one of my apples in the coconut, which still entrapped me.

I sat on my pack in the shelter, processing my insight when Messenger came in to break my trance. He was wet and miserable, but I was extremely happy to see him. Messenger was one of the thru-hikers I held in exceptionally high regard. We focused on Taco's comment posted on the wall. He too knew Taco personally, which added a touch. We helped each other take our mind off our misery.

Soon No Cheese, Norm, and Knight Rider came in because they hiked to the Lookout Cabin only to find it was flooded out. They hiked on to Wintturi Shelter and hoped to find a dry place to spend the night. The shelter became full as everyone set up. Then Tank came in, so we all made room for him. Normally, I hated to stay in shelters, but that night I welcomed the company. Sharing misery with such great people on a rainy night sure helped.

I was still awake when everyone settled down. I prayed to thank my Creator for loving me as I drifted into a peaceful sleep to the rhythm of the pounding rain on the roof.

Day 124　　　　　　　　20.4 Miles

It rained hard all night and continued as I packed up and hiked out. The others were awake, but still in their sleeping bags. The rain was so hard it soaked me to the bone within minutes. I forced myself to focus on the situation of my resentments in an attempt to finish the business that had gone unfinished far too long.

The truth was, my seventh grade teacher didn't pick on all the kids, he even had some pets. I knew why he picked on me before I even asked myself the question. I brought it on because I did a lot of passive aggressive crap to him. Driven by my ego, I didn't want to let him think he could intimidate me.

I started to make a mental list of the things I did to him. I would bad mouth him just out of his hearing, but he knew I was talking about him. Who knows, maybe his hearing was better than I assessed. Even at twelve-years-old, I knew better than to make fun of someone's nationality, but I was constantly referring to him with ethnic slurs. Maybe he knew or heard me. Even the looks I gave him were so hate filled he had to interpret them as aggression.

Yes, he also had an ego and he did some things which would be criminal now days, but they weren't criminal back then. As soon as I focused on what he did to me, I clenched my jaw and my pace noticeably quickened as the adrenalin poured into my blood stream. I became aware of my reaction, stopped, and gazed out into the fog of the early morning rain. I stood there until my heart rate subsided, to refocus. The Eighth and Ninth Step wasn't about him or what he did to me. Step Eight and Nine were always about me and what I did which was my part in that situation or any other situation.

I continued taking an inventory of some of the wrongs I committed. Even though time had dulled my memory, the list went on in some detail. I believe that was the first time I ever looked at my part in all of it. I started to understand why he did some of the things he did. I couldn't believe I was actually feeling some empathy for him. I mentally changed places with him and I may have reacted similarly had I been in his shoes.

I continued physically hiking on in the rain, but my mind was processing my new discovery. I had known for years I had control issues and when I thought about it, I could see he too had control issues. I snickered aloud when I thought maybe he and I had some common issues.

Sarcastically I thought, in some ways I was exactly like the prick. Then it occurred to me that was the problem all along. We were so similar, we clashed. My problem was he had the upper hand in our little drama. He was an adult with authority and I was a rebellious, twelve-year-old, mouthy punk, challenging, and badmouthing him at every opportunity. I guess I hadn't yet learned to pick my battles better.

I no longer felt like I was the victim because I saw I had a big part in it all. If my ego allowed me to submit, things would have improved forty years ago. I felt like my pack suddenly got lighter as all the weight lifted from me. My resentment toward the teacher didn't disappear altogether, but it melted considerably. I gritted my teeth once again when I thought he most likely didn't even remember my name and had no idea I held on to my resentment all those years. I took some satisfaction in knowing he had to live with his wrongs and his own crap, but that was his problem, not mine.

The heavy fog limited visibility adding an eerie feel to the forest. The rain and mosquitoes were making the hiking miserable in Vermont. I had to ford two more streams swollen by the heavy rain. My feet looked like a dead man's feet from being wet so long. My sleeping bag, tent, and all my clothes were sopping wet. Nothing changed physically in my world, but I was a world away from where I was a few days ago.

I had four zero days coming up, which would give my ankle a rest. Scooter planned to meet me with a new pair of shoes which I hoped would give me more ankle support. I hoped the ankle healed up before I took on the White Mountains of New Hampshire. I still worried because I might be taking too much ibuprofen.

The rain let up by late morning and the thing they called the sun started to shine. I crossed Cloudland Road, which was a dirt road. A homemade sign said, "Farm store, one tenth of a mile," with an arrow that pointed left. My mood improved considerably since my food bag needed attention, so I hurried up the road accompanied by the squishing sound of my shoes.

I found a farm girl who ran the little store out of her barn as a side business. She was working in the garden, but stopped to wait on me. I bought some jerky, honey sticks, and a huge length of smoked sausage to carry in my pack for later that night. I bought homemade ice cream and a strange kind of pop to enjoy there. Wow! What a serendipity.

The girl told me Vermont was in crisis because the rain ruined all the hay and some of the other crops. The farmers were even supposed to get some financial help from the government.

I sat on my pack outside in the sun, eating ice cream, and drinking pop. Her father-in-law, who owned the farm, came by to visit while I ate. He said it was the wettest June in Vermont on record. I tried to cheer him up a little, but he seemed too depressed.

I said goodbye to them and returned to the trail. Messenger caught up to me and I told him about the store. He didn't see the sign in his haste to make miles, but he didn't hesitate to do an about face for some food. I went north as the rain started again.

The rain dampened my spirits a little, but I soon found my new insights on my mind once again. I was grateful for the rain, which gave me the opportunity to continue to process the discoveries of the past several days. I wouldn't have focused as much on my resentments if I had good weather.

I accepted I was no longer the victim of someone else's behavior. I played a huge part in all my resentments. I saw the value in accepting I was powerless over what someone else said or did, but I could change my perception of my resentments and prevent future resentments, by owning my part in all situations. After all, the only things I could control were my behavior and decisions.

I easily added Mountain Goat and fire Fly to my list of people I had harmed. I was more reluctant to add the teacher to the list, but I did, which I considered a major milestone in my personal growth. I was sure as my recovery unfolded, I would add even more names to my list. I saw that would be an ongoing process.

I took a deep breath to fill my lungs with the fresh moist air. I held the air for a few seconds and slowly exhaled as I felt a great sense of relief from the heavy burden being lifted off my shoulders. My work wasn't complete, I owed amends to many, but I hoped someday I would become willing to make amends to them all, whenever possible.

I hiked eleven more miles in the rain to Happy Hill Shelter. I didn't recall anything that stood out about the trail, but I would always remember that day as the day I felt delivered from my own evil. The shelter was a small, two-story shelter. Two Canadians were already set up on the second floor. I scouted for a place to set up my tent for privacy, but the heavy rain continued and the woods were so wet, puddles of water were everywhere. Reluctantly, I set up on the first floor. I had just rolled out my sleeping bag when Messenger came in and set up beside me.

I shared the cooked sausage I bought at the store with him for a snack. We both cooked some ramen noodles and chatted as we ate supper. The shelter was small and crowded with the two of us, so we hoped no one else showed up as the rain continued. I welcomed Messenger's company again that night because I was tired of being alone.

The good news was I planned to meet Scooter in Hanover, New Hampshire the next day. I only had about six miles to trudge to Hanover. I was looking forward to seeing her, a hot shower, dry clothes, dry bed, clean sheets, hot food, and four days off to rest my ankle.

THE PROGRAM

Day 125   5.8 Miles

I started early because I was anxious to get to Hanover. The rain stopped on my way out of Vermont and I ran into some trail magic where an angel left Reese's cups and pop. Vermont treated me harshly with the wettest June on record. My poor feet looked like wrinkled prunes and I was tired of being wet all the time. I looked forward to clean, dry clothes, which was something I took for granted in my world back home.

I crossed the Connecticut River at the border into New Hampshire and saluted Vermont good-bye. I met my first sobo thru-hiker, a man about my age from Kentucky whose trail name was Kentucky. He gave me three packs of tuna because he thought he had an allergic reaction to tuna. I thanked him, but felt bad because I didn't have anything to give him in return. I was all out of supplies. I talked to him for half an hour because he seemed lonely and happy to talk to another thru-hiker.

He enlightened me about some of the details of Hanover and recommended the Dirt Cowboy Coffee Shop, which he said sold the best coffee in town. He also warned me about how hard the Whites were compared to the southern mountains. I felt a little insecure about my ability to climb the Whites. I would face them a day at a time soon, but not that day.

My first priority, once I hit town was to find the Dirt Cowboy Coffee Shop to buy a good cup of coffee with a shot of espresso, which I did. I sat at a little table on the sidewalk outside the coffee shop and watched the people pass by as I relished my coffee. I thought, welcome to New Hampshire.

I called Scooter and she was still about two hours away. I also called Messenger and he was in town trying to find me. I told him I would give him a ride when Scooter got there.

I decided to take a walk around town to look for Messenger. Hanover was the home of Dartmouth University and a true college town. I saw more people in the busy town streets than I saw in one place in a long time. I felt a little self-conscious about being dirty and carrying a pack, but people either treated me well or ignored me. The extravert in me loved being in the city for a change. I checked out all the stores and bought a pizza for lunch. I followed the trail through town to see what the town had to offer.

I talked Scooter into town on the phone, but she still got lost due to a misunderstanding on where to turn right. We finally straightened it out and managed to rendezvous at the drug store.

I found Messenger at the post office with another hiker picking up his mail. He decided he didn't want a ride because he was going to move on with his new companion. Messenger told me last night he was tired of being on the trail and wanted to git-r-done to go on with his life.

Scooter and I went the motel she reserved in White River Junction, Vermont. I took my usual shower first thing, but washed my clothes in a coin laundry at the motel. After I cleaned and spiffed up, we went out to McDonald's and found a Walmart. It was so good to see her for the first time since Pennsylvania. We talked a mile a minute after some espresso. I didn't think we said anything profound; we simply enjoyed being together again.

We went out to a Chinese restaurant that evening, but ended the date early to return to the motel.

July 1   Day 126   Zero miles

We slept in until six o'clock, waking to a beautiful summer morning. We ate a light breakfast with coffee at the continental breakfast the motel provided. Then it was off to Walmart where I bought enough supplies to pack three mail drops. I also bought a new camera and left my pictures to be developed.

We stopped at an old-fashioned diner for a second breakfast. I ate bacon, eggs, toast, and home fries. I felt a little guilty when Scooter ordered oatmeal. I would have to stop eating like I was as soon as I got off the trail or my cholesterol would be off the charts. The people in New England didn't seem as friendly as in the south. Even our waitress wasn't overly friendly.

I had to find a new pack because my old one was shot. We decided to make a day out of looking for a new pack so we went south in Vermont where my guidebook listed more outfitters. I hadn't been in a car for more than a few miles in a long time, so exploring picturesque Vermont while being with Scooter was a special treat.

We found several outfitters who sold ski equipment, but didn't carry many if any hiking packs. We ended up looking all over Vermont for a pack. I finally found one in Manchester Center at a place ironically called, The Mountain Goat Outfitters. Manchester Center was where I stopped two weeks ago to buy supplies.

I didn't like the girl who tried to talk me into a pack that I felt was too small. She was determined she knew more of what I needed than I did, just to sell me a pack. I was getting desperate, so I ended up buying a medium torso pack, which wasn't my first choice. It was the best I could do under the circumstances, because they didn't carry a long torso pack and my guidebook didn't list any more outfitters in Vermont.

Scooter wanted to go to a store called Jones of New York, so I followed her in. I felt a little out of place being the only man in the store. I was browsing the ladies lingerie section and a well-dressed woman asked me if she could help. I felt as if she caught me with my hand in the cookie jar. A pregnant pause followed while my mind raced to find an excuse for holding a ladies thong.

I remembered Spiritual Pilgrim talking about The Wilson House being somewhere around here, so I blurted out, "Have you ever heard of the Wilson House?" She seemed a little irritated, but she gave me directions to East Dorset, to the house where Bill Wilson was born. The lady wasn't friendly, so I decided to wait outside for Scooter while she tried on different fashions. I was afraid the lady was going to call security on me or something.

I looked on a road map and apparently, we passed East Dorset on our way into Manchester Center. Scooter emerged with several packages after what seemed like an eternity. I told her I had a big surprise and we were off to East Dorset and the Wilson House.

The Wilson House was the birthplace of Bill Wilson, the co-founder of Alcoholics Anonymous. Bill Wilson's grandparents originally ran the old fashioned inn. He was born in a room behind the bar, which I thought was appropriate for our founder. The original bar hung on the wall in a room where they held Alcoholics Anonymous meetings. The inn became so run down after his grandparents died that they considered having it demolished. Then a private group of Alcoholics Anonymous members bought it and lovingly restored it to a working inn where a guest could rent a room for the night.

The three-story house sported a fresh coat of maroon paint, accompanied by windows with white shutters. A sitting porch spanned the entire front of the building supported by white, ornate pillars spaced evenly. The entrance was an old-fashioned, wooden door framed by small, eight by ten inch windows. Scooter took my picture on the porch under the sign that said, The Wilson House.

The house was a non-profit foundation and the money needed came from individual donations and by renting the fourteen rooms out to overnight visitors. They had no endowments or large grants. Restorations continued as a work crew was restoring the front porch when we arrived. Volunteer carpenters had parts of the porch roped off as they were in the process of replacing the porch floor. Soon guests could sit on the front porch to share their experience, strength, and hope with each other.

The staff were all recovering members of Alcoholics Anonymous who stayed at the inn. Most of them were volunteers. The inn also served three meals a day for the guests. The house was a museum of old Alcoholics Anonymous relics and provided a peaceful place where a recovering alcoholic could spend some time in prayer and meditation. I could feel the quiet, but powerful spirit of the house as I entered.

A sixty-something woman in recovery greeted us with a big hug and said, "Welcome home!" I felt like I was home as every cell in my body relaxed. I felt welcomed and at peace. She showed us around and put on a video explaining the history of the house.

They never turned the light off by the chair where Bill Wilson would sit and read. I picked up the first addition of the big book sitting there as if Bill himself had just set it down to go get a cup of coffee. I sat down in his chair. Wow, what a feeling to sit where the Big Bill sat. It was sort of like the first time I ever held a real gun. I truly felt blessed to be on such sacred ground. I felt tingly all over as I closed my eyes to let my mind drift into deep gratitude and meditation. I recalled my first Alcoholics Anonymous meeting ever.

The date was July twenty-third 1977. I really didn't see anything wrong with my drinking and drug use, but I had a wife who left me because of all the violence and drama that went with my life. I didn't think my drinking had anything to do with my bad luck. My motive at the time was to convince my wife I was serious about quitting forever. I don't remember how I got the phone number for the Alcoholics Anonymous hotline, but I called. A friendly woman answered the phone and I talked about my drinking to another human being other than my wife, for the first time ever. She told me if I was too bad, I could go to St. Vincent where they had a five-day detox/rehab. I thought, wow, what a wonderful way to scam my wife. If I went to rehab, it would convince her to return home for sure. I had a good job with good health insurance and sick time that would pay for it, so I called the number the lady gave me. The secretary who answered the phone told me in a professional voice to go to the emergency room, register, and they would send a counselor down to assess me. My heart sank as I thought they were never going to accept me after they assessed me because I wasn't an alcoholic. After all, I drank and used drugs every day, but I never missed work, I had a family, I didn't have to have alcohol. I could take it or leave it. I just liked it.

I decided, I would buy a six-pack to drink on the way to the hospital, so I would have alcohol on my breath when I arrived by mid-morning. I drank the six-pack in the forty-minute drive to the hospital and followed the instructions. After a long wait, an attractive, but professional looking young lady called out my name. I followed her to a small room with a desk and two easy chairs. I took a seat and she started filling out the usual demographic data on a form, but the questions soon turned into some personal, intrusive probes towards my drinking behavior.

She asked, "How much do you drink on the average a day?"

I said, "I don-no."

"Do you drink a six-pack a day?"

"Yeah."

"Do you drink two six-packs a day?"

"Yeah."

Her eyes widened as she questioned, "You don't drink three six-packs a day?"

I could tell by her look she thought three six-packs were a lot to drink, so I said, "A little less than three six-packs." I thought if I told her how much I really drank, she would think I really was an alcoholic.

She bought my little act and admitted me, made a phone call, and I followed her out. A cop met us outside the little office and said, "Come with me."

I thought, why in the world did I get myself into this mess? The cop took me to a private elevator and rode up the elevator with me. We said nothing to each other. The elevator doors opened and the first thing I saw in front of me was a poster with capital letters which said, "If you need a drink to be social then that's not social drinking." My first thought was, Oh no, they were going to put me in a ward with all those people.

Nurse Ratchet then entered my life. First, she took my vital signs and then she gave me pajamas to put on in the middle of the day.

I said, "I don't wear Pajamas."

She said, "You do now."

I just looked at her and said, "I haven't warn pajamas since I was four-years-old."

She folded her harry arms and in an intimidating voice, slowly said, "Take off all your clothes and put the pajamas on."

I thought I better comply, but said, "Underwear too."

She nodded and said, "Yes!'

"Are you going to turn your back?"

"No!"

My eyes popped when she got out a needle about the size of a bicycle pump and said, "Bend over."

I said, "Oh, shiitt," as I turned my back and dropped my jammies. She gave out an evil bitch laugh as she gave me a shot of vitamin B in the butt.

After I thought it couldn't get any worse, she took me to the living room where I met the other patients or those people. Wow, what a bunch of losers. We all sat around in a living room and smoked cigarettes and drank decaf coffee. I listened to them as they filled me in on the way things worked. Most of them had been to several detox units, jails, and rehabs due to their drinking.

I met my counselor who was a white bread college graduate, named Rob. He probably hadn't ever been shit-faced drunk in his life. He also asked more personal questions that I thought were none of his business. About the time I had an attitude, he introduced me to Warren. Warren was a one-eyed, recovering alcoholic who had been sober five years. He worked there as a counselor's assistant and calmed me down. I connected with Warren because he didn't judge me. I liked him right off the bat.

Early that evening they rounded all of us up and took us to an Alcoholics Anonymous meeting, which was my first meeting ever. We all piled into the elevator in our pajamas and went to the first floor. I already felt self-conscious enough being in public in pajamas with nothing on underneath. Then we entered the hospital cafeteria and found three hundred people in street clothes waiting for the meeting to start. I felt humiliated, which manifested in anger. I would have run away except I had no clothes, wallet, money, or car keys. I felt like I was living in a nightmare, like the one where I was in high school naked. I was hoping I would wake up soon. I had no choice, but to sit down and endure whatever came next.

The chairman introduced himself as an alcoholic, and everyone who read the rules also introduced themselves with their first name, and stated they were an alcoholic. I thought these people were acting as if they were proud of being an alcoholic. I promised myself that no way in hell would I ever do such a stupid thing in public. After I listened to the opening prayer and ceremonies which were meaningless to me, the chairman introduced the speaker. The speaker was a man with no fingers on either hand, who also introduced himself as an alcoholic. He started to tell what Alcoholics Anonymous called his drunk-a-log, which was a personal life story about his drinking history. I was astounded the dumb ass would tell things that would embarrass him in front of three hundred people, by telling all the humiliating things he did when he was drunk. He worked in a factory running a punch press. One day he was stoned and accidently cut the four fingers off his right hand. He was off work for six months until he recovered. He went back to work stoned again and cut the fingers off his left hand with the same punch press. I was embarrassed for him, but then I started to understand him. I identified with him because I had felt the same feelings he felt. However, I would never admit to anyone else or in public how I felt.

I didn't remember his name, maybe I never knew his name, but I felt unusually close to the speaker. I took his words to heart and never questioned the validity of his story. I identified with him and realized for the first time ever, I was truly an alcoholic. I had a good talk about it later with Warren, who seemed to understand. I didn't know then what I know now, but what I experienced with both Warren and the speaker was a spiritual connection which I since have shared with literally thousands of other recovering alcoholics and yes, even publicly in Alcoholics Anonymous meetings over the years.

I completed the program after five days. Warren, Rob, and the rest of the staff tried to talk me into going to a rehab called Serenity West for twenty-eight days, but I refused.

I said, "I'll be okay because after all, I'm really not bad enough to need rehab. I'll go to Alcoholics Anonymous, which will be enough."

After they released me, I established Alcoholics Anonymous attendance, Big Jim became my sponsor, and I called the Edinboro meeting my home group. I called my wife, told her about the sacrifice I made for her and promised to never ever drink again, which put us on kissing terms because she told me to, kiss her ass.

I only stayed sober seventeen days, but Alcoholics Anonymous and the people in Alcoholics Anonymous left a permanent impression on me that I could never drink away. Continuous, uninterrupted sobriety was a fleeting thing in those early days, as I relapsed on a regular basis. I went in and out of the program many times in the next three years until I bottomed out. I got bad enough to almost kill myself with the lifestyle I was living.

I came back to the present with Scooter asking, "Are you okay?"

I replied with, "I don't think I could ever be better." I felt a strong sense of gratitude for Bill and Dr. Bob, the founders of Alcoholics Anonymous, which extended to the thousands of recovering addicts who helped me in my journey over the years through the thing we call life.

I put the Big Book down and said, "Let's get some coffee."

I could smell the great aroma of roast pork as the staff prepared lunch for the guests at the inn. Soon the guests would sit at two big tables and share a family-style meal. I bet even Bill and his wife Lois would join them in spirit.

We would liked to have stayed for the night, but unfortunately, the Inn had no vacancy. We were disappointed, but I would make reservations the next time I was in this neck of the woods. I heard some guests even saw the ghost of Bill himself in the night.

They were getting ready to serve the resident guest's lunch, but told us about an Alcoholics Anonymous meeting later. Scooter and I left to find a place to get some lunch ourselves before we returned for the meeting. We ate at a nearby diner and returned in plenty of time for the meeting. People were starting to gather in the meeting room.

The meeting room alone was a museum filled with nostalgia from the past. Bill was born behind bar, which fittingly hung on display on the wall. Pictures, slogans, and other memorabilia from Alcoholics Anonymous and Bill Wilson's past, neatly cluttered the room. We helped ourselves to a cup of coffee and found a seat to join the others. We talked to a couple of overnight guests from Florida. They came to stay each year to connect to the principals which kept them sober, sort of like a retreat. We socialized with them until the chairman called the meeting to order.

We introduced ourselves as visitors from Pennsylvania when several others introduced themselves as visitors. People came from all over the country to stay there and attend meetings. That particular meeting was a discussion type. I only listened and didn't make any comments. It was my first Alcoholics Anonymous meeting since I started to hike back in February. I forgot how good it felt to be in a room full of love. We closed the meeting by joining hands and said the Lord's Prayer as one. I realized the Lord's Prayer had more meaning to me now.

They announced a yard sale/auction of stuff from the attic was taking place to raise money. Scooter and I went directly to the yard across the street where it was happening. They were getting ready to auction off the things left from the yard sale when we arrived. I found a small box of old coffee cups and saucers. I asked the lady how old they were, but she didn't know. I wondered if Bill himself could have drank coffee from any of them. I bought the whole box to give as gifts to my Alcoholics Anonymous friends who helped support me while I was on the trail. We stayed for the auction and bought two old paintings. We lost interest in the auction after a while, so we left to return to the motel.

The ride back to the motel took three hours, so we stopped for a bite to eat on the way. We didn't last long after we arrived back at the motel, so we soon went to bed. I felt the time we spent together made an extraordinarily good zero-day.

Day 127   Zero miles

I awoke stiff and sore, from not hiking, but I suspected it was also from riding all day in a car. I took a shower to wash away the stiffness.

I really could get used to sleeping in a bed and taking a shower every morning. We took advantage of the donuts and coffee at the motel's continental breakfast bar.

We spent most of the morning packing three boxes with the supplies I bought at Walmart. Scooter would send one to Gorham, New Hampshire and one to Monson, Maine after she got home. The third we planned to take to a hostel for hikers at Glencliff, New Hampshire to leave there for me to pick up in about four trail-days.

The day was gray and overcast, but not raining as we set off for Glencliff to drop off my supply box. Glencliff was an incredibly small, rural town with only a post office and the hostel. Maybe calling it a town was embellishing things a little bit.

We met two men at the hostel, who seemed to run it for the owner, who was absent for the summer. I thought they might have had a spat because I sensed some tension in the air between them. The one gentleman was giving himself a permanent and dying his hair. Apparently, the other gentleman had helped him, but didn't do something right. They weren't aggressive just pissy with each other. Scooter and I both felt awkward, but they were polite towards us and happy to hold my box until I arrived.

The hostel had two bunkrooms, tent sites, kitchen, television, a hot shower in a tent outside, laundry facilities, and simple supplies for sale. I was a little disappointed because no hikers were there to talk to, but I was impressed with the set up. I would spend the night there before I ascended Mount Moosilauke, which would be my first time above tree line. The White Mountains National Park started north of Glencliff.

We left the hostel and continued north, exploring some of New Hampshire. I pulled off at an overlook and I caught my breath when I saw the awesome beauty of the White Mountains for the first time. The mountains had a bluish tint from the sun burning off the morning mist as it streaked down through the light, fluffy clouds. The majestic mountains stood as far as my eyes could see and beyond. I saw some detail on the closest mountains, but the blue haze dimmed the detail of the distant mountains until they faded into faint shadows. I anticipated the adventure that awaited me.

We took our time going back to the motel to explore more of rural New Hampshire. We stopped at a general store for coffee and donuts. We found the local people not hostile, but not friendly either, which may have been because we were outsiders. We spent the rest of the day together exploring and doing little things. We went out for pizza and then to an Alcoholics Anonymous meeting in White River Junction, Vermont. I was disappointed in the meeting because I felt like I didn't fit in. The people at the meeting weren't as friendly as I hoped, but I found most of the time it took people in New England a little longer to warm up to outsiders.

We stopped for ice cream before we returned to the motel. I wore the new shoes Scooter brought for me, which gave me a lot more ankle support. I thought my ankle was better with the rest. I turned in early because the next day I would take on New Hampshire.

Day 128   11 Miles

We spent the morning together and ate an early lunch at a high-class pizza shop. Scooter had the next day off from work, but wanted to start home because it was such a long trip. We parked her car on the trail in town so she could hike with me for a while before leaving. We talked of future adventures and thru-hiking together some day as we leisurely hiked. She turned back after about three miles. My mood instantly turned to loneliness and depression as I watched her disappear in the summer forest. It was great to see her, but I felt a sense of abandonment when she went home. I wouldn't see her again until I reached Mount Katahdin.

I found a ring on the trail someone about my size lost. I thought it might be Mountain Goat's because I recalled he had a ring something like it. I not only got over my resentment towards Mountain Goat, I forgave him. I understood why he wanted to get me drunk. I would like to make amends and give him the ring even if it wasn't his. I put the ring on and planned to give it back to whomever if someone recognized it and said it was theirs. Otherwise, I would give the ring to the Goat whenever possible.

God may have sent me some help, because I soon caught up with

Zoma and Lug. Oh, boy was I glad to see them. I hiked with them the rest of the day, which was an unexpected, but pleasant surprise. They helped me forget how lonely I felt. We climbed the south peak of Moose Mountain together. Moose Mountain was only two-thousand, two-hundred, and twenty-two feet high, but the steep climb and awesome vista made it seem higher. Lug split an orange three ways so we could celebrate at the summit. Oranges were a delicacy on the trail and it took a lot to carry one up the mountain, so I declined and said, "I'm good."

Lug wasn't going to take no for an answer and said in a commanding voice, "You're part of all this!" He pushed the piece of orange towards me.

I felt honored as I said, "Thanks." I knew it meant more than simply a piece of orange.

Lug held up his piece of orange and said, "To the Appalachian Trail."

Zoma and I followed by holding up our piece of orange, saying, "To the Appalachian Trail!" We touched the pieces of orange together in a toast as if we were toasting with the finest wine Parris had to offer. My eyes misted with gratitude for the privilege of being associated with friends of their quality. In a way, I envied them because I wished I had discovered what they already knew so early in life. I made them pose at the sign marking the summit of Moose Mountain.

Zoma jokingly said, "You already have a ton of pictures of us."

I said, "Yes and I'll cherish every one of them until I die." I wasn't joking.

I realized the trail was going to become more challenging in New Hampshire. It was not because the mountains were steeper or bigger than the mountains in the south. The trail in the south zigzagged up the mountains with what they called switchbacks, but in New Hampshire, the trail went straight up the mountains, which made the trail steeper. The mountains in New Hampshire and Maine also had a tree line, which was a line on the mountain where trees stopped growing above a certain altitude. That far south tree line was just over four-thousand feet, but it became lower farther north.

We stopped for the night to set up at tent sites by Moose Mountain Shelter. Two couples from Dartmouth University and two Sobo hikers were staying in the shelter. After we settled, we went to the shelter to cook our supper and socialize.

I showed everyone the ring I found on the trail earlier that day, but no one knew who lost it. I somehow knew they wouldn't know the owner. Zoma and Lug remembered the Goat wearing a similar ring, but they couldn't say it was his for sure. I liked the ring and would wear it in the meantime to remind me to forgive those who trespass against me.

Zoma, Lug, and I returned to our tent sites and chatted until after dark. Many things happened since Wildflower and I spent the night with them back in New Jersey. We had a lot of catching up to do. It felt good to be back on the trail with friends again. I returned to my tent physically spent, but wide-awake. I opened my journal to catch it up to date, which would be my first entry since I spent the night with Messenger in Vermont. I brought it up to date, but I was afraid I missed some details. I made myself a promise not to neglect my account on paper for so long again.

I re-read what I had written before I met Scooter and it occurred to me, I finished working the first Nine Steps on the trail. After Bill addressed the first Nine Steps in the Big Book he wrote, "We will be amazed before we are halfway through." Then he wrote the Twelve Promises, which started with, "We are going to know a new freedom and a new happiness."

In the first Nine Steps, I learned how to start removing the things in my character blocking me from a relationship with God and all levels of society. After I worked the Steps the first time, my life became noticeably better. The people close to me even noticed. I guess I pealed the first layer off my onion.

I took a deep breath and held on to the air, tasting the sweet pine-filled night air. I slowly let go of the precious air and relaxed every cell in my mortal body. Many years ago, a recovering alcoholic from New Orleans said to me, "Oooow-eeee, it just keeps getting gooder and gooder and I can guarantee that." I laughed aloud at the memory, but he was one-hundred percent right and working the Steps were how I could make it happen.

Step Ten said, "Continued to take personal inventory, and when we were wrong promptly admitted it." In twenty-six years, I went through the Steps several times with other people and by myself. I was always amazed at how much "gooder" my life got each time. The more I learned, the more I let go of my selfishness and the happier, more serene, and free I became.

I never would become Saint Dreamer, but I saw changes for the better come from the decision I made so many years ago with Gallagher in Step Three. I once heard someone in the program say, "If you commit suicide in the first five years of your recovery, you kill the wrong person."

I sat pondering the changes which happened. It was like the metamorphosis of a caterpillar that turned into a butterfly. I wasn't Saint Dreamer, but I wasn't the person I was twenty-six years ago either. I thought I would be more of a moth than a butterfly when it was all said and done anyway. I closed my little notebook, satisfied that I caught up with my rough notes enough to move on. I turned off my light and closed my eyes, ending that bittersweet day with thoughts of Scooter.

July 4	Day 129	17.7 Miles

The birds gently awoke me prior to sunrise, but I stayed in my sleeping bag enjoying the moment listening to their songs. It was the Fourth of July and I anticipated a beautiful day ahead. I soon heard the sleepy voices of Zoma and Lug, so I decided to get up to start my day.

We ate breakfast together. I shared my coffee with Lug who was too polite to make a comment about the quality of the coffee. We packed up our homes and left together.

I got another taste of the Whites as we climbed Smarts Mountain, which was higher and by far steeper than Moose Mountain. Towards the summit, the trail was smooth, solid granite rock. The trail was already more challenging and I wasn't even in the White Mountain

National Park yet. An old fire tower and fire warden's cabin were at the summit of Smarts Mountain. Zoma and Lug planned on staying in the warden's cabin and climbing the fire tower to watch the anticipated fireworks in the valleys and towns below that night. I hoped they weren't disappointed.

Zoma dropped back on the steep ascent up Smarts, so Lug and I arrived at the fire tower first. We dropped off our packs on the porch and went inside the old fire warden's cabin. The cabin was dusty, dark, dingy, and deplorable. I almost puked because the place stunk so bad even by my hiker standards. I thought the sweltering heat didn't help the smell either. The floor gave and squeaked under my weight, threatening to break through as I tip toed to the windows to see the view distorted by years of dust and cobwebs.

The fire tower was of the same vintage, which consisted of rusty angle iron and paint mostly worn off long ago by time and weather. I climbed up two sections of the rusty, rickety stairs and turned back because of either fear or common sense. I would pray for Zoma and Lug who planned to watch fireworks from the top after dark.

Zoma arrived looking more rested than Lug and I because she took her time on the ascent. Lug and I both had far too much testosterone to ever admit she was the wiser of the three of us. I left my pack with them so I could venture out to find a suitable tent site for myself.

I couldn't find a tent site where I felt safe enough to call home. The sites seemed too exposed to lighting or dead trees hung precariously over them. I returned and Zoma and Lug elected to set up their tent on the porch of the cabin. The inside of the cabin wasn't an option according to Zoma. Zoma offered to let me set up beside them on the porch, but I felt it was too crowded and I didn't want to impose on their privacy.

I took a break and told them I was thinking about moving on five miles to the next shelter, so I would only have a fifteen-mile day to Glencliff. I knew from experience on the trail, once you parted with a friend you may never see each other again, so I was a little apprehensive. Lug assured me they were hiking to Glencliff and would spend the night at the hostel, which would be a twenty-mile day for them.

I felt the bite of loneness as I left to hike solo in strange territory. I soon found a concrete post on the trail with four-hundred and twelve miles engraved on one side and one-thousand, seven-hundred and thirty miles on the other side, which meant I had four-hundred and twelve miles to reach the summit of Katahdin. That was the first time Mount Katahdin seemed reachable to me.

I met a Sobo girl who was thru-hiking with an Osprey pack like the one I bought in Manchester. She really liked her pack, which made me feel like I made a good choice after all the hassle of picking my pack. I took another break as was customary, to fill her in on the trail south and she filled me in on the trail north. She planned to go to the fire warden's cabin hoping to see some fireworks. I told her Zoma and Lug were there. I couldn't remember her name, but I wish I would have stayed at Smarts Mountain with Zoma and Lug because it sounded like it would be a good time. I hoped to see some hikers on Cube Mountain where I planned to spend the night.

I had to ford a creek where the bridge washed out some time ago. I lost the trail on the other side, but a group of juvenile delinquent boys and their leaders helped me find the trail. I started worrying about getting to the shelter before dark because I lost a lot of valuable daylight time. I started to hurry as I ascended Cube Mountain, which was a formidable mountain at the end of the day. I made it to the six-sided shelter called Hexacuba Shelter near the summit as darkness ended the day. To my dismay, no one was there.

I set my tent on a tent site and filled up on fresh water. I found a can of peas someone left at the shelter, so I added them as a treat to the tuna and noodles I cooked for supper. I was in the woods with no view to see fireworks and I was alone without cell tower, so I felt lonely. I really wished I stayed at the fire warden's cabin with the others. I guess I simply made a bad choice. I planned to be at the hostel with Zoma and Lug the next day, which helped me feel better.

I was alone with my thoughts, and drifted back to when I started to tell friends and co-workers I was quitting my job and going to pursue my dream. Many of them said things like, "It must be nice." or "Aren't you lucky." I didn't respond, but I never believed it was luck. I had a dream and set a goal, which led to a detailed plan I executed. I started to ponder why I did those kind of things. Why did I get those type of opportunities? Why was I different from other people? I concluded that it was because of the positive example of some positive people in the program and the Twelve Steps of recovery.

I was sober less than a year when a gentleman whose body was ravaged by cancer made a huge impression on me. I was at a Monday night meeting with Big Jim, which was held in a small country church. The church had no plumbing, so we used an outhouse. The man was so feeble it took two other members to help him walk in and sit down.

Big Jim said to me, "The doctors gave him a month to live three months ago, so get your ass over there and shake his hand."

I went over to shake his hand and introduced myself.

He humbly said, "I've heard some good things about you, I feel privileged to finally meet you."

I lied and said, "The pleasure is all mine," but I wasn't sincere.

On the ride home, I asked Jim, "Why is he still attending meetings in his condition?"

Jim simply said, "Stay sober."

I replied, "If I was going to die any minute, I would go out and get shit-faced drunk!" I don't think Jim said a word, but he reached over and firmly smacked me on the back of the head.

I had to chuckle at the memory. I must have frustrated Big Jim a lot. I hoped he could see me now days to know I really was listening back then. I closed my little note book and closed my eyes and instead of feeling sorry for myself because I was alone, I decided to try to be grateful for the opportunity to be alone with the memory of the man who died of cancer while he was still working on his program.

The weather was perfect for the fourth of July with zero rain and lots of sun. The sky was clear and the vistas looked like scenes from a fairy tale. The mountains were steep with solid granite footfall. I hiked almost eighteen miles from daylight until dark. My ankle was tender and sore, but seemed to be doing okay with the extra support of the new boots. I prayed aloud, "Thank you God, I am truly grateful for a program that taught me how to live and a special thank you for the nameless man with cancer who taught me how to die still working the program, amen." I stopped feeling sorry for myself as sleep took me away.

Day 130   14.7 Miles

I was tired, lonely, and escaped in sleep early, so I awoke well before daylight. I packed up and moved out in the dark before dawn because I was anxious to get to the hostel at Glencliff. I stopped on the summit of Cube Mountain, made coffee and ate breakfast as I watched the excitement of a new day begin. Daybreak had always been one of my favorite times of the day. That morning on the summit of Cube the birds sang a welcome to the new gift even before its light began to shine. I closed my eyes and took a deep breath and felt the cool, moist air of the fresh new day. I watched as the darkness of the night began to give way to the gray of pre-dawn as the sun started forcing its way in from the east to awaken the sleepy mountains. A misty fog covered the world in nature's blanket as the mountains started to appear in black and white. The sun then burned off the haze and the miracle of a brand new day appeared magically as it always has since creation.

The fog in my head in the early days of my sobriety took a long time to clear enough so I could appreciate the gift the nameless man with cancer gave me a long time ago. He set an example by walking the walk even in the face of death. I can now understand the reason was because he was still pealing his onion. Two days later, he completed his hike at his summit and surrendered his spirit to God as he understood him.

I remember Big Jim saying, "Alcoholics Anonymous will survive, but we're sure going to miss him." He didn't seem to be saddened by his death.

I asked, "Aren't you pissed off?"

Big Jim, "He's okay."

I was far too immature in the program to understand what made recovering people different was the thing we called, the Program.

I made a second pot of coffee to drink as I enjoyed living in the present. I sat there on the summit of Cube Mountain meditating, drinking coffee for a long time, gazing out over the Whites, and feeling privileged to still be alive.

I felt that I spent the time well, but I eventually hiked on with a completely new attitude. I took my time and enjoyed the solitude of hiking solo in God's world, while feeling the presence of the big G. Zoma and Lug caught up to me before noon. They moved along at a fast pace on a mission to get to the hostel at Glencliff. We chatted for a minute as they described the spectacular fireworks show from the fire tower the night before. I didn't try to keep up with them, but I looked forward to spending some time with them at the hostel.

I eventually descended to the highway which led to the hostel where I met some trail workers. I stopped long enough to help them hang a sign on the trail. Then I walked the half a mile on the road to the hostel at Glencliff. Zoma and Lug had already settled in and showered by the time I arrived. A small, quiet Sobo appropriately named Hobbit was also staying at the hostel by himself.

I took an instant liking to a big man named Phatt Chapp who replaced the two gentlemen who were running the hostel when Scooter and I dropped off my supplies three days prior. He said he was from Florida, but lived there in the summers to help run the hostel. Phatt Chapp was a monster of a man who towered over everyone else. I estimated he weighed over four-hundred pounds. His hair had started to turn gray and his full beard in contrast was already steel gray, which gave him a rugged/distinguished look. He was a gentle, friendly giant, but had an aura which said he didn't take a lot of crap from anyone. Given his immense size, I found it hard to believe anyone would give him any crap in the first place.

He gave me the package I dropped off with Scooter, then showed me around. Zoma and Lug stayed in one bunkhouse and Hobbit in the other. I set up my tent out back for privacy as planned and settled in. I took a long hot shower from a hose mounted on a board in a tent in the back yard. The amenities on the trail like the temporary platform made of cement blocks that I stood on while in the shower may be part of the reason I had to treat Athletes Foot so often.

Phatt Chapp wasn't a hiker for obvious reasons, but he loved hikers and working at the hostel. He was intelligent, knowledgeable, and learned about hiking from all the hikers he helped over the years. He told me to put Vicks Vapor Rub on my feet on wet days before I hiked to help keep the skin on my feet healthy.

I asked Lug to take a picture of Phatt Chapp and me with my camera, so Zoma and I posed standing behind him as he was sitting, which showed his impressive size by comparison.

Phatt Chapp shuttled Zoma, Lug and I to Warren, New Hampshire to the grocery store and pizza shop for five dollars. I didn't need anything, but went along for the ride. I bought a jar Vicks VapoRub for my poor feet. Zoma and I each bought a large pizza at the pizza shop. I shared mine with Phatt Chapp, who to my surprise, only ate one piece to be sociable. Phatt Chapp took us on a tour of the area as we ate pizza. He took us to a view of Mount Moosilauke, which stood looming over all the surrounding mountains. Moosilauke would be the fiercest mountain I had to face so far.

We all planned to ascend Mount Moosilauke early morning on the next day. Mount Moosilauke was four-thousand and eight-hundred feet high and would be my first time above tree line on the Appalachian Trail. The steep ascent might take most of the next day. I heard the decent on the north face was the most dangerous. Moosilauke dropped two-thousand feet in about a mile. I probably would stay by the shelter past the summit, where I could hold up if it was raining and unsafe to descend. The guide book warned you not to descend if it was wet or icy.

I re-packed my pack with the things from my package. My pack weighed forty-two pounds, which seemed heavy to start the Whites, but I wouldn't have to re-supply for quite a while. Zoma and Lug's two packs put together only weighed forty-one pounds.

I said goodnight to everyone and retired to the privacy of my tent, which by then had the familiarity of my bedroom back home. I was still far too excited to sleep, so I opened my journal and started writing. In 1982, a heart attack sucker punched Big Jim. I never even got the chance to say good-bye. I might have got drunk, but folks in the program stepped in and supported me through my grief. I didn't drink, but I had no sponsor. I had no one to watch for spiders in my ear. I admired Big Jim more than anyone, placed him on a pedestal, and felt nobody could ever fill his shoes. I rationalized that he guided me through the first Nine Steps and Steps Ten, Eleven, and Twelve were only maintenance Steps, so I could take it from there.

When I was a child, I used to play on the escalator at the Sears and Roebuck Store when Mom would take me shopping in the city. I would successfully run up the escalator which was going down, but if I stopped to rest, I wouldn't stand still where I stopped, but would start going back down.

The Big Book talked about resting on our laurels, which was exactly what I was doing when I stopped working the Steps after Jim died. It was as if I was on a sobriety escalator going down because I started to descend. I didn't notice a big difference at first, but my disease appeared to be patient. I didn't quit attending meetings, but my self-centered ego started to take over. I started seeking pleasure to satisfy my need to feel good. I spent a lot of time on my motorcycle when I should have been at work. I started to shoot pool in the bars, dating girls who I met in the bars, and doing selfish, self-serving things to feel good. I knew Big Jim wouldn't approve, but he was no longer there to smack me on the back of the head.

I didn't realize I was going down at first, but I was returning to the pit I came from. Slowly at first, but I soon found myself spiraling downward until the night I crashed the motorcycle in 1983, which was a painful lesson. I was spiritually bankrupt. I saw another glimpse of the living hell I came from. I thanked God I didn't drink, but I knew if I didn't get back to the basics of the program immediately, I would seek shelter from the pain with drugs and alcohol. My addiction was calling me back to the black hole I crawled out of with Jim's help. Later in my sobriety I thanked God for that painful experience. I gained the wisdom that I couldn't stop growing spiritually or I would return to the Godless world from which I escaped a long time ago.

I had a moment of clarity that night as I walked home after the motorcycle crash. A spirit whisper told me, *You can't do this on your own; you need someone to watch for spiders in your ear.* That was when

Gallagher became my second sponsor. He took me through the Steps again. At first, I thought it was redundant, but I soon realized I was learning more the second time around. Big Jim's words, "It's like peeling an onion" came back to me as if he were whispering in my ear.

I had grown to like the time at the end of each day to ponder my spirit whispers. I realized I had to continue to work a program to feed my recovery, the same way I had to eat to nourish my body. In New York, I wasn't eating enough food, so I became undernourished, lacked energy, and my muscles started hurting. I could not continue to hike until I fed my body enough food to go on. If I would stop eating now, the same thing would happen again. If I never ate again, eventually I would starve to death. My recovery was much the same, because if I didn't feed my recovery, it too would wither up, similar to my body. What happened after Big Jim died was I quit eating spiritual food and started to starve. In both cases, New York and after I lost Big Jim, I wasn't eating enough and weakened, but once I started eating again I regained my strength. Satisfied with my analogy to food, I closed my journal, and drifted off to sleep sometime late in the night.

Day 131   7.9 Miles

I slept in until the birds and Mother Nature wouldn't let me sleep any longer. I went to the hostel and drank coffee with Phatt Chapp, Zoma, Lug, and Hobbit. I packed up, bid my friends goodbye, and departed. I would miss Phatt Chapp, but hoped to see more of Zoma and Lug. They planned to catch up with me later on Moosilauke because they were staging to leave soon.

The climb up Moosilauke was steep, hard work, but the forest was beautiful as the sun started to warm things up. Zoma and Lug caught up to me below tree line, so we all took a needed breather as we ascended. I didn't try to keep up with them because I had a hard time with my heavy pack. I had to stop every two-hundred paces uphill to give my heart time to slow back down and dissipate the lactic acid from my muscles. I hadn't done that since I was in southern Virginia.

The size of the timber slowly decreased as I climbed higher until the trees were only as high as my head. I ascended more and even the small trees and brush disappeared and turned into bare granite rocks and grass. I was above tree line for the first time. I could see a rock cairn from a distance that welcomed me to the summit.

The views were spectacular above tree line and it felt good to be in the White Mountains. The ascent was steep, but it didn't seem too dangerous; only a lot of hard work. I thought all the stories hikers told me of mighty Mount Moosilauke might have been embellished a bit. I also had some time to worry before I arrived, so maybe I embellished the stories myself with my fear. I reached the summit in time for a late lunch with Zoma and Lug who were waiting at the top. The panoramic vistas of Kinsman, Franconia and the Presidential ranges were breathtaking. We identified several mountains including Mount Washington, but Washington's high summit was covered in clouds. We spent quite some time taking pictures to celebrate the moment. Zoma and Lug left me at the summit because they wanted to descend the mountain to Kinsman Notch. They planned to hitch a ride on the highway to North Woodstock to buy supplies and spend the night. I didn't know at the time, but it was the last time I would ever see Zoma and Lug or I would have left with them.

I stayed because Moosilauke was the most famous for the steep descent off its north face. I wanted to be able to take my time, so I decided to spend the night at the shelter a mile away and descend on fresh legs after dawn in the morning. After Zoma and Lug left, I took some more time at the summit to reflect on what it took for me to come that far. A dog harassed me before I left the summit. The irresponsible dog owner let his dog run loose. The dog decided I was a threat and went to attack. Being a passive sort, I attacked back, but the dog was too good at staying a little ways out of reach, so I couldn't hit him with my poles. I tried to spray him with pepper spray, but he was out of range. The owner finally got a hold on the dog. I said some un-Christian words while commanding the owner to control his dog. He tried to apologize, but I ignored his attempts while moving on more afraid of my own temper than the dog.

I couldn't stay angry long in the splendid place. I spent some solo time enjoying unbelievable views on Moosilauke. The only way anyone got there to see what I saw was the way I did, on foot. The mountain started to fall away as soon as I started my descent. I wondered exactly how bad it really was. Would it live up to all the rumors I heard since Tennessee?

The presence of an oncoming Sobo named Tyvek broke my trance. Tyvek was a man of my vintage with long gray hair, wearing old worn army fatigues. He had made his tent, sleeping bag, part of his pack, and other things out of Tyvek house wrap, hence the name Tyvek. What made Tyvek extraordinary was he wasn't wearing shoes. I was impressed that he ascended the north face of Moosilauke with no shoes. We stopped, took off our packs, and I got out a half pound of crystallized ginger that I almost never shared. I asked him how hard the ascent was. He said, "Not bad." I somehow knew he was minimizing. We ate the ginger as he told me his story. He swore to never wear shoes again, when he came home in 1969 as a tribute to the brothers he left behind in Vietnam. I spent some time with him, feeling both humbled and honored to be in the presence of such a man even though I knew he was half a bubble off of level. We finished eating all the ginger before he went south and I went north. I gave him a hug and wished him God speed. I couldn't comprehend hiking the Appalachian Trail without shoes. I felt like a wimp compared to him because I was on my fifth pair of boots by then.

I dropped about twelve-hundred feet in elevation in two miles before I arrived at the shelter. I knew the worst was yet to come the next day, but I would worry about that the next day. I was so elated by the views of the mountains that I felt overwhelmed as I tried to put what I saw and felt into words. I took a picture from the shelter of the Kinsman Range, naturally framed by two cherry trees. I wondered if the volunteers who built the shelter also planted the trees with the future view in mind. The haze added a blue tint to the rugged beauty of the White Mountains, which appeared to be steeper and sharper than their southern cousins, which may be older, and rounded by time. The Whites were also naked above tree line as opposed to the tree-covered summits of the south. I wasn't sure exactly why the Whites seemed so majestic, but right then, the reason didn't matter.

I had no idea how long I stood on the deck of the shelter drinking in the beauty of God's creations. It seemed surreal, as if I was looking at an enhanced picture of a vista in a book, but it wasn't in a book. I could taste the mountain air God perfumed with the sweet smell of pine as I attempted to etch the moment in time perfectly into my memory to savor always.

I became aware at some point, I was looking at sacred ground God himself created that was still untouched by the human hand. I folded my hands and prayed for God's protection of the Whites. I prayed my descendants could one day enjoy the privilege of what I experienced. I prayed the Whites would always be as they were and never violated by man's capitalistic greed. Eventually, I returned to my tent treading softly to not disturb even one blade of grass. I was alone in my tent at Beaver Brook Shelter writing in my journal as darkness stole the day away. I planned to start my descent at first light in the new day.

I was in the solitude of the wilderness, but not lonely. I wanted to spend some time in meditation, so I said a simple prayer, "Lord, please talk to me." I then let my mind drift and I was soon thinking about Step Ten again. I questioned, what was the real truth? I first thought Step Ten meant to take a daily inventory and if I pissed someone off, I would apologize. Actually that wasn't even close to what it came to mean to me.

I admitted defeat and surrendered in Step One. In Step Two, I came to believe a power greater than myself could help restore me to sanity. I made a decision in Step Three. Steps Four through Nine was where I attempted to remove the things about my character which stood between my personal relationship with God and myself. I went through the Steps the first time with Jim. I learned a lot, and life got better. I went through the Steps again with Gallagher. I learned more, and life became even better. Once after an exceptionally hard time, I formally went through the Steps three times in the following fourteen months and life became even better yet. Every time I took a personal inventory, more was revealed and life always progressively improved as long as I didn't stop on the escalator.

I snapped out of my meditation and wished every one of my friends could experience being in the mountains with me right then. I heard a hiker come into the shelter about dark, but I was too tired to get up and talk to them. Besides, it felt as if it was my private time to spend meditating and talking to my Creator.

I looked at the chicken scratch I wrote about Step Ten and thought, Step Ten was simply working the Program of Alcoholics Anonymous. When I came into the fellowship, I heard about the Program and wondered what exactly they meant when they referred to the Program? That night in the White Mountains after twenty-six years of sobriety, it finally occurred to me that working Step One through Step Nine was the Program and Step Ten was continuing to work the Program. The first sentence in Chapter Five in the Big Book said, "Rarely have we seen a person fail who has thoroughly followed our path."

I believe path and Program were two similar words Bill used when he described the first Nine Steps, which were suggested as a Program of recovery. After he detailed the first nine steps Bill said, "We will be amazed before we are half way through." I had always been amazed each time I worked the Steps to remove what blocks me from my Creator.

My eyes were burning from the dim light of my headlamp and my shoulder went to sleep from holding an awkward position for so long. I suspected a single hiker was in the shelter because I didn't hear anyone talking. He or she must be asleep anyway because I thought it was late. I closed my journal, shut my eyes, and said, "Thanks God for a great day and thanks for the insight, Amen." I must have then fallen asleep instantly.

Day 132   9.1 Miles

I awoke well before dawn to the sound of my worst nightmare, the soft pitter, patter of rain on my tent. Normally, rain only annoyed me, but after planning my descent later that morning, the rain struck fear in every cell in my body. Everyone I talked to and even the guidebook warned me not to attempt the descent if it was wet or icy. The weatherman predicted the day would be partly sunny and dry or I would have descended with Zoma and Lug. I quickly dressed without putting tape on my blisters, packed up in the dark, and prepared to move out as soon as I had enough daylight to see. I wanted to descend Moosilauke's forbiding north face before the rocks became too wet and slippery.

I didn't go up to the shelter since I didn't know the hiker who I assumed was still sleeping. I didn't want to wake him or her, so I left as quietly as possible. I had only hiked a short distance when I came to a sign permanently bolted to a tree which said, "This Trail is extremely tough. If you lack experience please use another trail. Take special care at the cascades to avoid tragic results." I said to myself, Oh shit! I took a picture of the sign thinking, I sincerely hoped it wouldn't be the last picture I ever took.

I descended slowly and stopped often to assess the trail in view. I kept telling myself I had all the time in the world. The steepest places had wooden blocks set in the granite where some skilled craftsman carved out places for the steps. The wood was wet and slippery, but I stayed calm and proceeded with extreme caution. I previously formed a mental picture of the descent, based on fear from all the stories I heard on the trail. I pictured open terrain, bare rock, frightening views, and lethal drops of hundreds of feet. Phatt Chapp even said it was the worst descent on the trail.

Instead, the trail actually snaked its way down the steep mountain through heavy, lush vegetation where I only saw a short distance ahead at one time. The thick brush would catch me before I fell too far. My fear subsided as I realized I could hurt myself, but it probably wouldn't be fatal. I mentally focused only on the task of descending and actually enjoyed the adventure of the challenge.

Beaver Brook cascaded down the mountain parallel to the trail like something out of a travel channel documentary. Wildflower would have loved to take photos of Mother Nature's many beautifully landscaped waterfalls beside the trail. Thinking of her, I stopped often to take pictures before carefully planning my next move.

Mountain Goat told me he asked someone who warned him of the danger on Moosilauke, "If I make a mistake, and fall will I die?"

The hiker replied, "Well you could die if you fell anywhere on the Appalachian Trail."

The Goat and I agreed judging from his statement, the man was embellishing the danger. I thought my fear also exaggerated the danger when I contemplated the descent for a long time.

I took three hours to descend the one-point-one mile down Moosilauke, but I made it safely. I stopped, took my pack off, and gave thanks when I reached the bottom of the mighty mountain. The rain stopped, so I made coffee and cooked breakfast. The sun came out in full and rapidly dried up the trail. I finished eating and sat on my pack, enjoying the sun, drinking bad coffee, and mentally relived the morning's events.

A grandiose sobo thru-hiker came along intrusively interrupting my serene mood asking, "How's Moosilauke?"

I said, "Slippery, but it looks like it'll dry up soon."

He said, "I came from Katahdin, so a little cloud rain don't bother me."

Under my breath, I said to myself, "Shit."

I didn't think he could hear me, but he said, "what?"

"Nothing."

"I thought you said, shit."

"I did."

He ignored it and told me all about himself as I sat there drinking coffee, purposely not offering him any. I listened to him as he boasted about how he hiked the real mountains as opposed to those in the south. I found him annoying, so I didn't respond.

Things got quiet for a short time when he broke the silence, "So, where did you start?"

I paused to take a pull of my coffee for effect and simply said, "Springer."

"So, you hiked eighty percent of the distance, but only did twenty percent of the work."

I suppressed the urge to sucker punch the puke, but said nothing. Things got silent again and he started another sentence with the word so, which annoyed me.

"So, how are the mountains in the south. Mild and boring compared to Moosilauke I bet?"

I had enough of him, so I said, "From here on, a guy like you don't have to worry much about the mountains, but you have to be even more careful."

I paused for effect "Oh, never mind you'll find out soon enough."

He looked befuddled "So, what are you telling me?"

"No, I don't want to worry you, besides you're better off not knowing."

He commanded, "Tell me!"

I knew by that time I had gained control of our little game and I had to admit I was enjoying it immensely so I said, "It's a fifty/fifty chance it won't happen anyway."

His voice went up about two octaves, "Tell me!"

"Okay, okay, okay, did you ever see Deliverance?"

He paused as if he was searching that pea brain of his. His eyes changed in recognition, "You mean that old movie with Burt Reynolds?"

"Yep."

He thought a second, "Didn't they get raped?"

"Yep."

Then I paused, looking him up and down and said in my best southern accent, "They gonna like a purty boy like you."

He shuddered like a horse shaking flies off , "That shit don't really happen does it?"

By then, I really, really was enjoying my little game at his expense, so I looked him up and down again, "Probably not." Then added, "You look like you could run pretty fast."

He grew unbelievably silent acting as if he heard news about something he never thought of before.

He looked at me and was about to say something, so I winked at him and said, "Purty boy liiike you!"

He did an about face and started his ascent up Moosilauke without even saying goodbye. I waited until he was almost out of sight and gave him a catcall whistle. He shuddered again as he disappeared from sight. I figured I gave him a little something to worry about on those lonely nights on the way to Springer. I felt a little guilty, so I looked up as I was still laughing and said, Lord I apologize, please forgive me. I couldn't stop laughing. I wonder if the Lord forgave me when I was still laughing and showed absolutely no remorse, but who knows, maybe even the Lord got a little chuckle out of that one.

I made a second cup of coffee and set up my tent to dry in the sun and drank coffee while I enjoyed the warm solitude of the morning sun. I was in no hurry after my descent and I wanted to savor the feeling of accomplishment.

Eventually, I continued hiking through Kinsman's Notch, where the trail immediately steeply ascended Mount Wolf. I stopped for lunch in the early afternoon and to my delight, Cedar Moe came limping along. I hadn't seen him since Delaware Water Gap. He was the hiker I heard as he came into the shelter last night, but I didn't know it because I was too lazy to get up to see who arrived. He was limping badly because he hyper extended his knee when he descended Moosilauke too fast. I carried a knee brace, so I gave it to him. He had been trying to catch up to Zoma and Lug. I told him I was hiking with Zoma and Lug until only the day before when I stopped at Beaver Brook Shelter. They went on, but planned to get off at the notch to buy supplies and maybe spend the night in Woodstock.

I loved being the bearer of good news as I watched his face light up with excitement.

He said, "If they spent the night it's a good chance they were behind us."

I said, "Yes, and if they didn't stop they couldn't be too far ahead of us either."

I thought the news killed the pain in his knee better than any pill. We hiked towards Eliza Brook Shelter together. I felt bad for him because he wouldn't admit it, but he was in a lot of pain. The hiking was slow and tough for him, but we took the opportunity to catch up as old friends do. The last time I saw Cedar Moe was when Phyllis and I had breakfast with him and a bunch of other hikers before we left Delaware Water Gap. He was going to take a zero day to do laundry and go to church the next day. He met a girl in church and she invited him over for Sunday dinner. They fell in love and he stayed in the town for a week before they parted.

We hiked about three miles before we arrived at the shelter. Cedar Moe set up in the shelter with a Nobo section hiker named Hero and two Sobo thru-hikers. I set up my tent before I joined the others at the shelter. A trail angel left a three-pound jar of peanut butter. Cedar Moe and I took our spoons and ate the whole jar. Several section hikers and a troop of Boy Scouts came in before dark, which turned the place into a festive atmosphere. The social contact was good for both of us, but I was happy for the sanctuary of my tent when I retired for the night.

I took out my notebook to journal the day's events before they faded in time. The noise of the others invaded my serenity, so I put on some soft music to block the intruding sound and started to meditate. I started with the goal to thru-hike the entire Appalachian Trail. The day before I climbed Mount Moosilauke and felt a sense of accomplishment, but I couldn't quit hiking because I didn't reach my final goal at the summit of Katahdin. To achieve my goal I had to get back on the trail and descend Moosilauke. I hiked nine more miles, but I still needed to get back on the trail again and do almost the same thing again and again to reach Mount Katahdin.

In the case of my recovery, my goal was to be spiritually fit, but no matter how spiritually fit I became I still had to get back on the trail to spiritual fitness. Personally, Step Ten, as I said previously, was simply doing Steps Four through Nine over, and over again. I had to keep peeling my onion. There seemed to be many parallels between the trail and my recovery. They both have been personal journeys. The day was Day one-hundred and thirty-two and it was easier than the first day in February when I started because I had a lot more experience and I was in much better physical condition. I believed my journey would continue to become more rewarding as I gained more experience and became more physically conditioned. Sure there would be some adversities before I finished at Mount Katahdin, but I could overcome them with the right help and guidance. I couldn't stop along the way to rest on my laurels for too long or I wouldn't see Katahdin's summit no matter how many miles I did in one day.

No matter where my next hike was, I would take along the experience of my thru-hike and so on. I made some mistakes in all my journeys and had zero control over some obstacles along the way. I tried to learn from the things I did wrong and not make the same mistakes over again. I missed some things like the vista from McAfee Knob because of the weather that day, but I tried not to dwell on the things I couldn't change or control.

I looked at my whole life as a spiritual journey to be with my Creator, who I saw as even larger than mighty Mount Katahdin. The trek would be long with many spiritual obstacles that could block me along the way. However, it got easier as I gained spiritual fitness and wisdom along the way. Step Ten was simply like getting up, bandaging my feet, packing and getting back on the trail, whether it rained or shined. Sometimes I had an easier day and sometimes the trail was hazardous, sometimes it rained or snowed, but I couldn't quit before I reached my summit.

Once again, my analogy to food fit my understanding. I usually ate Thanksgiving dinner until I felt as if I would never be hungry again, but a few hours later, I made a turkey sandwich. I have been so spiritually full at times in my recovery that I felt I would stay spiritually fit forever on what I knew. However, I soon started to hunger and needed to refuel on a spiritual sandwich. I finished writing and the music ended, so I said my thanks and drifted off to dreamland.

SEEKING

July 8   **Day 133**   **11.4 Miles**

The sleepy camp started to buzz with the chatter from the Boy Scouts as I broke camp. I stopped by the shelter to check up on Cedar Moe's knee. His knee was stiff and painful, so he elected to take a zero day at the shelter to try to rest and heal his knee. I hoped he felt better soon. I feared the injured knee could end his hike, but I knew Cedar Moe was not the type who gave up easily. I still felt uneasy in the pit of my stomach and worried because I might not see him again. I told him I would let Zoma and Lug know where he was at if I saw them.

Hero lost his glasses in a crack in the shelter floor, which took my focus off the situation with Cedar Moe. We all tried, but Cedar Moe was the one who fished his glasses out from under the floor with a stick. Hero was grateful because he was almost blind without his glasses. I thought Cedar Moe was the real hero. I decided the trail could wait a little longer and made a pot of coffee and took the time to socialize a while before I left.

Eventually, I reluctantly departed and started to ascend the Kinsmen Range. Hero soon caught up to me so we climbed South Kinsman together. Hero seemed like a grandiose, twenty-two-year-old whose family was in the oil business. He and his mother started to hike from Hanover, New Hampshire to Andover, Maine. His mother couldn't take the rigors of the trail, so she dropped off. She was running support for him and meeting him as often as she could by car. He appeared rich, because he had all the top of the line equipment, including an altimeter that told him exactly how high he was at any time.

We soon had to put our hiking poles in our packs and use our hands on a steep climb up the face of the South Kinsman Mountain. We seemed to be climbing more than we were hiking as we averaged less than a mile an hour. Eventually, we made it past what my guidebook called a rock scramble and summited South Kinsman. I took some great pictures hoping they would turn out.

I didn't like Hero at first because I quickly judged him as a spoiled, self-centered rich kid. I was starting to see him different than my first impression. He was an only child and moved from place to place with his parents so often he never had any long time friends. He's spent a lot of time in the Mid-East where he didn't fit in at all, so he lacked social skills, but I could understand why. I replaced my judgments of him with understanding and my attitude changed completely. We bonded and I grew to like him as we hiked together.

Hero taught me a valuable lesson; that I needed to try to understand instead of judge. I thought about the learning experience in silence as I gazed at the rugged Whites from the South Kinsman summit. Before I broke the silence, I resolved not to quickly judge anyone who seemed different in the future. We started to descend the rugged Kinsman Range and it occurred to me, I climbed the mountain with an obnoxious rich kid, but descended the same mountain with a friend, only because my attitude changed.

We stopped at Lonesome Lake Hut by early afternoon. That was the first time I had seen an AMC (Appalachian Mountain Club) hut. The AMC owned and operated all the huts in the Whites. I was appalled when I first heard they charged eighty-five dollars for a single night's stay, when a hiker could stay free everywhere else on the trail. I thought they had a monopoly going, so they stuck it to you. What I didn't hear was their huts were nothing like the free shelters. Their huts were a clean lodge with a bunkroom that provided soft mattresses, blankets, and pillows. The bathrooms were clean and indoors. A professional staff cooked and served AYCE supper and breakfast at no extra charge. The staff also provided education on conservation to preserve and protect our precious White Mountains for our descendants to enjoy after we are gone. They understood many thru-hikers had limited funds, so out of their generosity; they offered work for stay to thru-hikers only.

I wondered if God was sending me a message because both my

first impression of Hero and my first impression of the AMC were negative, but changed dramatically. I first thought the AMC was out for the money, but they were quite the opposite. The AMC used any profits to help protect our parks from the capitalists who would exploit and destroy our treasure for their own, self-serving lust for money, property, and prestige.

The huts sold AYCE soup for a dollar, which that day came with a piece of homemade bread leftover from lunch. I also bought a piece of pie and all the coffee I wanted for a dollar. Hero and I ate all the soup we could eat. I ate so much I needed a nap, but I had to move on. I filled up on water even though I over hydrated from all the coffee. I bid Hero goodbye, hoping I would see him again soon. He had reservations and settled in for the night. His mom reserved him a stay at every hut in the Whites, so he was going to hike from hut to hut.

I moved on to descend three miles into the Franconia notch. I considered hitching five miles to Lincoln, New Hampshire for the night, but I didn't need supplies and it would probably be expensive. I faced a large ascent up to the Franconia range the next day, so I decided I would climb three miles to a campsite on Mount Liberty below tree line for the night. The hike up Mount Liberty was steep, in the deep woods, and boring with no views, which made for truly hard work at the end of the day. I made the campsite well before dark, which cost eight dollars a night. A caretaker took my money and put me on a tent platform next to another tent. The owner of the tent was not there. I would be sleeping next to an unknown person. I only hoped he or she didn't snore. The caretaker was a former thru-hiker named Cave Man who worked for the AMC. He gave me a tip on how to get work for stay the next night at Galehead Hut.

I read the register and Zoma and Lug stayed there the night before, which meant they were ahead of me and farther ahead of Cedar Moe. I might catch up to them in the future so I could relay a message from Cedar Moe. The next day I planned to hike over the Franconia Range. I would be facing, Mount Haystack, Mount Lincoln, and Mount Lafayette. Hopefully, I would also climb over Mount Garfield. I would be above tree line most of the day. I no longer felt fearful of the Whites, but I had deep respect for their dangers. I believed I could survive hiking the White Mountains if I was careful, took my time, and enjoyed the journey.

I discovered to my surprise, I had cell tower and Guns left a voice mail saying he successfully ended his hike at the summit of Mount Katahdin. I hadn't seen him face to face since the day after I left Hot Springs, North Carolina, but I talked to him briefly on the phone when I was in Pennsylvania. I wondered if he was still an atheist after hiking the trail.

Not many people were around the campground considering the number of tents. Cave Man said, "Most of the campers were on the summit of Mount Liberty to watch the sunset and wouldn't be back until after dark." I suspected my neighbor was on Mount Liberty.

My ankle was acting up again, so I took some ibuprofen and tried to ignore it. I planned to try to stay awake until dark, but didn't think I would be successful. I stripped my clothes off and took a little bath with wet wipes. Boy did I stink! I laid naked on top of my sleeping bag in the privacy of my tent to dry out. I closed my eyes to encourage my mind to return to the Steps.

Step Eleven said, "We sought through prayer and meditation to improve our conscious contact with God as we understood Him, praying only for knowledge of His will for us and the power to carry it out."

I drank and used drugs for relief from the reality of the cruel, unfair world until my life was totally out of control. Finally, on May twenty-fifth, 1980, I came to understand I could not manage my own life. In Chapter Five of the Big Book it said, "That God could and would if he were sought." Now that was a concept to ponder. I asked myself, am I seeking God? Was the whole journey about seeking God?

I recalled struggling with my decision to thru-hike and prayed for knowledge of God's will and the power to carry it out. I wondered if God answered my prayers and sent yet another rowboat through Lady D when she said, "God's the one who put the idea of thru-hiking in your head in the first place." I didn't make my decision solely on her words but they sure helped. I must have drifted off to sleep, because that was the last thought I could recall.

Day 134   10.4 Miles

I awoke before daybreak and packed, trying to be as quiet as possible so as not wake my next-door neighbor sleeping on the platform three feet away. I didn't think I was completely successful, because they stirred, but didn't get up. I never found out if my neighbor was a man or a woman.

I made coffee and sat on the tent platform to listen to the birds while I watched the new day begin. I let my mind go in the predawn chill to meditate, hoping God would talk. My seeking started long before I ever heard of the Appalachian Trail. Alcoholics Anonymous introduced me to God in Step Two when it said "We came to believe." The thought immediately lead me to the realization that seeking God started long before I ever believed.

In a sense, I was seeking when I took the first drink at twelve-years-old. I discovered a euphoric type of wellbeing. Drugs and alcohol gave me the illusion that I found what I was looking for from the first drink. That was only an illusion that I sought for seventeen years until it nearly destroyed me. The Bible said, "Thou shall not put other gods before me." Maybe drugs and alcohol were part of what God was talking about to Moses that day on Mount Sinai. Perhaps my seeking started even before my discovery of alcohol at the party on Christmas Eve so many years ago. I may have been spiritually curious since my earliest childhood memory, but I clearly didn't recognize it at the time as spiritual seeking. I pondered a while about when I started to seek God, but maybe it didn't matter

When I was in my addiction, I thought the only thing wrong with me was I used drugs and alcohol. I thought if I quit using, everything would be okay. I had no idea the biggest thing wrong was I was starving to death spiritually because I had no contact with God.

. The morning sun pushed away the dark of night, so I set out for the day's adventure. I passed a side trail that went three tenths of a mile off trail to the summit of Mount Liberty. I elected to pass it by because I would see other summits on the trail that day. I hiked above the tree line to the Franconia Range. When I got to the summit of Mount Haystack, I stopped in my tracks to behold the ridge to Mount Lincoln. The ridge was breathtakingly beautiful and looked like the backbone of a giant beast. The trail went directly up the backbone to the summit of Mount Lincoln. The wind blew hard when I crossed the ridge, threatening to blow me off the mountain. The three-hundred and twenty-nine-foot ascent in the next seven tenths of a mile across the ridge to the summit of Mount Lincoln intimidated me enough to hold my full attention. I took a breath of relief as I approached the summit of Lincoln only to find another narrower ridge leading to the summit of Lafayette. I thought Mount Lafayette was the most famous mountain in the Franconia Range, because I previously heard about it on the trail.

I looked back at the ridge I crossed and then ahead at the one I faced. I felt trapped between the two. I had to fight off panic for the moment. I inhaled a deep breath of the mountain air and proceeded ahead. I didn't want to give myself too much time to think. I crossed the backbone to the summit of Mount Lafayette without incident and felt relieved. I paused for a moment to let my heart slow down. I was in awe of all the beauty and oh so grateful for the opportunity to be there. The beauty of the Whites got even harder to put into words. I took pictures, but even they couldn't compare to actually being there.

I dropped below tree line briefly after I passed Lafayette's North Peak, until I started ascending Mount Garfield. Garfield was a steep rock scramble. Back in Great Barrington, Massachusetts, Paparazzi gave me the heads-up to where I could stealth camp at Garfield Pond shortly before the summit. I found the little trail to the campsite and soon found a nice place to set up.

I only hiked seven miles that day, but I felt exhausted from the intense trail. The steep gradient, the lack of switchbacks, and the tension made the hiking extremely hard work. Part of me wanted to stay there, but I knew the park didn't allow stealth camping, so my conscience would have bothered me all night. I took off my pack and sat a spell to contemplate my situation. I concluded that I didn't want to face any consequences, so I decided I would shoot for another three miles to Galehead Hut where Cave Man told me to ask if I could get work for stay.

I moved on, rewarded with another fantastic vista at Garfield's summit. I felt like I was in the Swiss Alps so I tried to yodel, with zero success. I never was musically inclined and anyone who heard my attempt would have thought something was killing something. I arrived at Galehead Hut by late afternoon, asked for and to my delight, received work for stay. A Nobo named Riverside and a Sobo named Just Joe were also there working for their stay.

I mingled with the guests meeting an out of shape day hiker with the same last name as me. He was on vacation from New Jersey and was hiking from hut to hut carrying a daypack. We talked for a while, but really didn't have anything in common besides our last name.

Suppertime came so Just Joe, Riverside, and I waited outside until all the guests were finished eating. We then came in to feast on the leftovers. We had stuffed shells, soup, apple cobbler, and homemade bread. I gorged and wanted to sleep it off, but we had to wait until the guests went to bed first. We then set our mats and sleeping bags on the floor in the dining room. I felt a little like a second-class citizen, but I thought it was good for my ego to be humbled a little. I was full, dry, sleepy, and it was all free.

Thank you, AMC.

Day 135   11.8 Miles

The three of us workers awoke before the guests. I poured myself an excellent cup of coffee from a huge percolator and packed up my gear. We waited outside until the guests finished eating breakfast and then we ate the leftover scrambled eggs, coffee cake, and oatmeal. We cleaned and swept the bunkhouse and dining room, which seemed like too easy work for all I received in return. We were then free to go. I bid the staff and my fellow thru-hiker's goodbye and hit the trail. Work for stay was a positive and rewarding experience.

I hiked solo with my dreams above tree line most of the morning in the mountainous wonderland. I arrived at the summit of Mount Guyot by myself. I wished someone was with me to share the wonderful vistas God created. The day was hot, humid, and slightly hazy, which gave the mountains a picturesque blue tint which made them seem as if they were painted by the angels. I took several pictures, but my camera didn't seem to capture the depths of this vast mountainous terrain. I stopped and inflated my mat to lie on for a break. I felt God's presence as I lay in the sun in his world, only God, and me.

I never would have contacted God until I was desperate. I thought that was why God sent me so many rowboats and helicopters. When alas, I cried out, Alcoholics Anonymous was one of the choppers God sent to rescue me from the combat zone of addiction. I would always be grateful to all the understanding members of Alcoholics Anonymous who nurtured me like a newborn in those early days of my sobriety. They spoon-fed me soft bits of spirituality at first until I could digest substantial bytes of understanding.

Eventually, I picked up my mat and left the summit of Guyot feeling privileged. I soon dropped below tree line into the welcome shade of sweet smelling pines. I hiked seven miles to Zealand Falls Hut by mid-afternoon. I stopped for water, hoping for a late lunch. I was in luck and purchased soup and coffee. The young lady I paid gave me several cookies left from desert the night before. I thought it always pays to flirt with the cooks. The few guests still in the dining room were playing board games. They ignored me while I ate several bowls of soup, polished off the cookies, and hydrated with a lot of good coffee before I moved on.

The trail followed an old railroad bed for a while, so I enjoyed a few level, but still scenic miles for a change. I hiked an easy five miles to an eight dollar a night campsite at Ethan Pond where I set up my tent on a wooden tent platform. John and Debbie, who were a local couple from New Hampshire, were camped on a platform within forty feet of me. They were bickering with each other within range of my hearing, which made me feel incredibly uncomfortable. I made tuna and noodles for supper while trying to ignore them because I didn't want to get involved in their drama. John struck up a conversation with me, so Debbie invited me over for some chicken fricassee. I thought it would be rude not to accept so I apprehensively went over to their campsite. I must have inadvertently been the peacemaker because, magically the bickering stopped, and we chatted like three old friends. They came to the mountains for a few days every summer, so they provided some good information about the trail. I also gained some insight into life in New Hampshire while I enjoyed chicken fricassee and their company.

They hadn't seen the caretaker and we all hoped we would skate on the eight dollar camping fee. The day started fading away when a tough looking man about forty with a black beard and no pack showed up.

John assumed he was the caretaker and said, "Caretaker, what is it going to cost us to camp here?"

The man replied with authority, "Fifty bucks each!"

John aggressively stood up and shouted, "Fifty bucks camping fee!"

A tense moment followed as I thought, oh shit, here we go with some drama.

The man laughed and said, "Yeah, but I'm not the caretaker" and broke out in a big friendly smile, which broke the tension and we all shared a laugh of relief. The man's name was Mark and he already had set up in the shelter. He came over for the company.

I said, "You took your life in your hands, charging fifty bucks." He agreed as we laughed again.

Mark was a thru-hiker who spelled his name, Mark with a backwards "R" in the trail registers. I had been following Mark since Georgia, but tonight was the first time I ever met him. I heard quite a bit about him from Mountain Goat and the registers, so I felt like I already knew him. A tick bite infected Mark with Lyme disease. He became extremely ill, so he took two weeks off to rest and recover while he took the antibiotics. I thought I wouldn't have caught up to him if he wouldn't have stopped. He said he was feeling better and gained more strength back every day. I admired him for continuing and not giving up in the face of adversity.

The four of us socialized like old friends until after dark when uninvited mosquitoes crashed out party. I returned to my tent and was about asleep when an annoying young man who apparently had been drinking, interrupted my serenity by yelling, "Caretaker." I paid him the eight bucks fee to camp, but only after I made sure he was the legitimate caretaker. He admitted he was drinking with another caretaker at another campsite and returned only a moment before. I easily forgave him because I understood a caretaker's life could be lonely. We struck up a short, but pleasant conversation. He gave me the impression the other caretaker was an available female. I snickered when he went on to the next campsite. He had a lot harder time collecting the fee next door from John. John wasn't exactly the understanding type.

I couldn't go back to sleep right away so I purposely took the time to focus on the prayer and meditation part of Step Eleven. Step Eleven said, *We sought through prayer and meditation to improve our conscious contact with God as we understand him.*

I thought, wow what a wonderful concept for making contact with God. Gallagher told me, prayer was when you talk to God. Meditation was when you listened to God. In the Big Book, Bill Wilson encouraged us to meet God alone so we wouldn't adopt someone else's concept of God. It came to me that I met God in Step Eleven. I surrendered my will to the care of God and removed enough of my ego that blocked me to make conscious contact with God. Step Eleven was also where I carried out the decision I made in Step Three with Gallagher so many years ago. I was allowed to form my own personal relationship with God as I understood Him, which was probably why I opened my mind and heart to the possibility of the existence of God in the first place.

I understood God's reasoning for putting the idea of thru-hiking in my head. At least part of the purpose of my journey was to make contact with God. I felt God's presence as I laid in my tent in his world, alone with Him. I really didn't want the day to end, but my body didn't give me any other choice. I fell asleep looking forward to whatever adventure the next day had in store for me.

Day 136   9.3 Miles

I was getting better at packing quietly around others. I moved out before daylight as I heard thunder in the distance. I made my way down a steep, sixteen-hundred-foot descent in the dark to Crawford Notch. The thunder increased as I crossed the Saco River on a bridge and started a steep, twenty-eight-hundred-foot ascent on Mount Webster. The violent thunder and lightning storm hit before I reached Webster Cliffs. I feared going any higher in the storm because hikers were warned to stay below tree line when lightning was a threat. I stopped below tree line to sit on my pack covered by my poncho. I put my aluminum hiking poles about twenty yards away so they wouldn't draw lightning. Other hikers passed on their way down to Crawford Notch and two foolish section hikers passed me ascending Webster.

Mark caught up to me and stopped to wait out the storm with me. I wasn't usually intimidated by lightning, but the lightning in the mountains sounded like bombs going off when it hit close. I felt grateful for Mark's company and conversation. The storm finally passed, so we resumed hiking together to Webster Cliffs, Mount Webster's summit, and Mount Jackson. We found the climbing hard with poor views due to the weather. However, in spite of the weather, we managed to harvest a few cloudy pictures of the storm from Webster Cliffs.

Mark and I seemed to bond in the storm, maybe because of the fear. I thought it didn't matter why, but I felt closer to him than before the storm. We were hiking down a narrow path with thick heavy pine brush on both sides. Mark was in front chatting with me as we inched our way north.

Suddenly, we encountered three Sobo moose on the same narrow path. The mother cow was in front, followed by her year-old calf, with her two-year-old calf bringing up the rear. Mark was watching his feet and thought the moose were southbound hikers as they approached.

I said in a calm, but commanding voice, "You might want to move off the trail, right now!"

He looked up and stood face to face with the mother moose. He jumped off the trail and looked to see if I was scared. He told me later, I was smiling from ear to ear and scrambling to get my camera out. Luckily the three big moose all did an about face in the tiny space on the path and vanished as fast as they appeared before I could even take their picture.

Mark was a city boy from Houston, Texas and never even saw a live moose before, even in a zoo. I noticed Mark was visibly shaken by the encounter and still trembling from the adrenalin rush.

He said in disbelief, "I could smell her breath."

I laughed as I said, "I think you should adopt the trail name of Moose Kisser," so I dubbed him Moose Kisser. We hiked together to Mizpah Spring Hut, where we stopped to buy lunch. Captain, the seventy-year-old retired Marine who I previously met back in Vermont with Bear Bait, was eating, so we joined him. We ate soup and drank coffee for lunch as Captain entertained us with war stories.

An attractive young lady named Michelle asked us if we would like work for stay. She got stuck by herself, cooking supper while the rest of the staff were carrying in supplies from the road. The dishes piled up and she desperately needed someone to wash them and help her with some other tasks. Moose Kisser and the Captain refused immediately, but I hesitated because Michelle looked so overwhelmed. It was early afternoon and I had planned to hike six more miles to Lake of the Clouds Hut, so I could start hiking the next day only a mile south of the summit of Mount Washington. I would only have seven more miles to Madison Spring Hut, but it would be all above treeline.

Michelle noticed my reluctance to decide and tried to entice me saying, "I'm baking the best bread in the Whites and homemade lasagna for supper." I could smell the homemade bread, but if I stayed, I had to hike twelve hard, rugged miles all above tree line the next day. She went back to the kitchen and returned with a huge, fresh baked loaf of homemade bread to show me. I decided to stay because the weather was rainy with thunderstorms in the forecast for the rest of the day. Besides, being an old hound dog, I couldn't say no to such a pretty, young lady as Michelle.

I hadn't showered or done laundry since Glencliff, which was five or six days ago. I knew I smelled like not so fresh road kill, so I went to the bathroom sink and took a sponge bath the best I could. I put on my cleanest dirty clothes and topped it off with a generous splash of patchouli oil. I spent a pleasant afternoon washing dishes and chatting with Michelle. She gave me all the cookies and coffee I wanted. Michelle was a college student, who worked there for the summer. The pay was low, but she was single and understood she might not have another chance for such an adventure once she started her career or a family. I told her she would be in trouble if I was thirty years younger and hadn't already found Scooter. She blushed and playfully slapped my arm.

The rest of the staff started returning one by one, and seemed to accept me. They treated me with respect as an older one of them. It was a nice change of pace for me on a cold, rainy, nasty day. I ate a lot more lasagna and homemade bread with a ton of real butter on it than I should have, but it was so good. I thought I was gaining a little weight while I saved the supplies in my pack. I may not have to stop for supplies until after the Whites.

The next day, I would have to face the rest of the Presidential Range with Clinton, Eisenhower, Franklin, Monroe, Washington, Clay and Adams, but I planned to sleep off my supper first. I figured Katahdin would wait for me another day.

Day 137   11.8 Miles

I ate a big breakfast and left earlier than usual, because I did my work for stay the day before. I bid Michelle goodbye and she gave this stinky old hound dog a big hug and a kiss on the cheek which would put a smile on his face for a long time.

I planned a big day to hike twelve hard miles above tree-line over the rest of the Presidential Mountain Range. The sky was overcast with dark clouds, but dry, as I ventured out hiking solo over Mount Clinton, which was spectacular. I thought it was appropriate when they re-named Mount Pierce, Mount Clinton after the man who most people would agree was the greatest President of modern times. I felt like I was on a giant rollercoaster as I hiked over Mount Eisenhower,

Mount Franklin, and Mount Monroe in the first five miles. I was disappointed to be in the alpine wonderland of the Whites with zero views because a dark cloud-like fog socked the mountains in destroying most of the visibility.

I stopped at Lakes of the Clouds Hut by early afternoon and found it buzzing with day hikers, guests, and staff. I blended in and felt a little anonymous in the crowd. Many day hikers came up from the valley below to hike the one point four miles to the summit of the famous Mount Washington. I was hungry so I bought AYCE homemade chocolate cake and coffee for two dollars. I picked a seat out of the way to adjust to the shock from hiking in solitude all morning then blundering into the chaotic social atmosphere at the lodge. I enjoyed resting while I watched the people. I hoped I would see someone I knew. I assumed Moose Kisser and the Captain, who planned to stop there the day before for the night were long gone. I felt a tap on my shoulder. I turned around and to my pleasant surprise, there stood Cedar Moe. I thought I would never see him again, but I should have known Cedar Moe wouldn't let a little knee injury stop him.

He sat down and we began to catch up as old friends did after they were apart. I assumed he had already eaten until he asked, "How's the coffee?" I found out he wasn't eating because he had no money so I paid the two dollars so he could join me for coffee and cake. We ate a ton of cake and coffee as he filled me in on what happened since I last saw him.

He holed up for the day at Eliza Brook where I left him in the shelter to rest his knee. His injury didn't get better, so he hitched into a town the next day to see the local chiropractor hoping to get his knee put back in place. The chiropractor fixed his knee, but robbed him in the process, charging him an outrageous four-hundred dollars. The chiropractor must have known Cedar Moe had no choice, so he stuck it to him.

I said, "That's the reason you don't have money."

He said, "I'll really have to tighten up and hitch back to Tennessee instead of taking the bus."

I was appalled, especially when Cedar Moe told me how the

chiropractor put him on a tenz unit to relax his muscles after he adjusted his knee. The chiropractor hooked him up and said, "Tell me when the electric becomes too much for you."

Cedar Moe said, "I can't feel a thing,"

The doctor adjusted the current, "How's that?"

Cedar Moe, "Nothing."

The quack made another adjustment and turned the dial all the way up. "You have to feel it now?"

"Nuten."

The bone cruncher looked things over scratching his head and suddenly he said, "Ahh, I see the trouble, I didn't turn it on."

The rocket scientist impulsively hit the switch without turning down the electric and poor Cedar Moe had a seizure. I laughed until I thought I would piss my pants. Then I realized Cedar Moe wasn't laughing, so I stifled myself as I mopped the tears of laughter off my face.

Cedar Moe said, "I'm grateful to him for putting me back on the trail." He couldn't keep a straight face any longer and we both broke out in a laughing spasm like a couple of potheads.

I admired Cedar Moe's tenacity for staying on the trail in the face of adversity. He was a devout Christian with strong faith. My self-centered ego thought God may have put him in my life to teach me the ways of a true believer. I gave him a twenty-dollar bill.

He refused to take it saying, "I don't know when I could pay it back."

I said, "It's not a loan, it's a gift, take it!"

He hesitated, so I lowered my voice, put my hand on his shoulder, and said, "For me."

He took it. I said nothing, but patted him firmly on the shoulder to show I approved.

The weather was turning for the worst so we discussed our options. If we left, we would be committed to hiking above tree line for the next seven miles to Madison Spring Hut. If we stayed, we would have to hike the seven miles the next day and the weather could be worse. We had plenty of time to hike seven miles before it got dark. We decided the weather was only wet and foggy, so we ventured out together towards Mount Washington.

Right before we started to ascend the highest mountain in the entire Whites, we came upon an official, bright yellow, weather beaten, White Mountain National Forest sign which read, "Stop! This area has the worst weather in America. Many have died here from exposure, even in the summer. Turn back now if the weather is bad." We moved on, but I had an uneasy feeling that gnawed in my gut, which was fear.

My guidebook said a weather station at the summit of Mount Washington recorded the highest official surface wind speed ever in the entire world. I had Cedar Moe take a picture of me at the sign. I said jokingly, "I hope this is not the last picture ever taken of me."

The weather soon took a turn for the worst and socked us into a cloud of milky white nothingness. I felt cheated out of the famous vistas seen from the intimidating mountain. Only my imagination could conjure up what the view would look like on a clear day. An eerie feeling of isolation overtook me as we proceeded up the harsh, barren rocks of Mount Washington's south face. I was thankful I wasn't hiking alone. I felt a sense of comfort in the company of Cedar Moe although he was in the same boat as me. I so envied his faith, which hopefully would rub off on me eventually. We stopped to gear up for the storm. I put on my Frog Togg rain jacket and covered everything including my pack with a disposable poncho.

We hastily proceeded towards the summit of Mount Washington. Suddenly, as if we awoke from a bad dream, we popped onto the summit at almost sixty-three-hundred-feet high. The whole world instantly changed on the summit. We entered a type of small mall, which included a restaurant, post office, museum, souvenir shop, and weather station. A road climbed to the summit from somewhere below, so tourists could drive up for a fee of twenty-five dollars. Folks could also ride an old coal burning steam engine train to the top and back for forty-two dollars each way. A ton of tourists with shorts, tee shirts, and sandals were at the top. They seemed unprepared and looked cold, but still ran around like little elves in a fairy tale. I thought the scene looked surreal as the train blew out black smoke and gave out a loud whistle.

We stashed our packs in the men's locker-room in the basement which was reserved for hikers. We found many tourists in the basement also. We first bought ice-cold cokes for a treat. I bought a souvenir for Scooter to send to her with my photo card to be developed. We then walked around the museum a little.

My heart stopped cold when I discovered one-hundred-thirty little white crosses on display. They represented the people killed on Washington, mostly of hypothermia and lightning, but less than a week ago, a lady tourist fell while taking a picture. I guess they would have to add another little white cross for her. I left the museum because I didn't want to psych myself out any more than I was already.

We didn't fit in well with the tourists. A line of tourists was waiting to get their picture taken at the sign on the summit. Cedar Moe, which seemed so unlike him, went to the front, cut in line, called me up to join him, and told a tourist to take our picture. We grasped our hands and held them above the sign with a feeling of accomplishment, as several tourists stood by and watched us pose.

The weather was cold, raining, and nasty, but we had no choice but to hike on for seven miles to the safety of Madison Hut, because camping wasn't allowed on the summit of Mount Washington. I could only see fifty feet into the white cloud as we left the summit.

Thru-hikers traditionally mooned the train as it went past them on the mountain. We psyched ourselves into exposing ourselves to strangers, but when we heard the train go by, the fog was so thick the tourists wouldn't have seen us anyway. We both were disappointed. Cedar Moe even said, "I shaved for nothing."

We hiked as fast as we could over the rocks and up the mountains. Several hard miles on slippery rocks, above tree line, stood between us, and the safety of Madison Spring Hut. The trip would take six hours in the best of times, but that day, with the weather, who knew. Silently we picked our way north. I became even more grateful for the comfort of Cedar Moe's company and courage.

I thought things couldn't be any worse when the weather temporarily cleared barely enough to see a dark cloud moving in below us on the mountain. The violent thunderstorm drifted in as we ascended Mount Adams. The storm cloud reminded me of a giant alien war ship in a science fiction movie, shooting at the mountain with bolts of lightning with thunder exploding immediately following, a little ways below us. I was afraid, so I caught up to Cedar Moe and shouted above the wind, "What should we do?" He said, "The first thing you always do is pray!" I stayed closer to him as we scurried along.

They warn you not to be above tree line in a lightning storm. The books and brochures all said to take cover below tree line. I thought, how the hell do you do that? I knew I was in a bad situation to be in, but where could I go? We had been above tree line all day. We couldn't go back because it was way too far. We couldn't simply go off trail and run down the mountain to safety. We would fall off the mountain, which would kill us as dead as the lightning. The best strategy seemed to be to continue on to Madison Hut. I felt trapped.

The storm overtook us and engulfed us in a cloud so thick we only saw a few feet. The wind was gale force, and the lightning was coming in steady succession, seconds apart as if we were under fire from the alien war ship. You couldn't see the lightning itself, only the flash accompanied by a deafening explosion.

I never panicked in my life, but I have been in some tight spots a few times where I was afraid I might panic. That day was one of those tight spots. I knew to panic would be fatal, so I stopped, took a deep breath, and tried to get a grip on my fear. I lost sight of Cedar Moe when I stopped and the milky white monster swallowed him only a few feet ahead. I hurried to catch him, but was careful not to run on the slippery, rugged terrain.

When I caught up to Cedar Moe, I grabbed hold of the back of his pack and spun him around. I was shocked when I saw his face because even in the gale winds his beard and heavy eyebrows were sticking straight out from all the static electricity in the air. At another time, I would have laughed because he looked like the cartoon character, Yosemite Sam.

I shouted above the wind, "Okay what's the second thing we should do?"

He looked me in the eyes with a smile on his face and shouted back, "The second thing you always do is pray."

He then turned his attention back to the trail. Once again, I grabbed him, spun him around, and shouted, "Okay, okay what's the third thing we do?"

He shouted, "Pray!" He then firmly slapped my shoulder as if to say, "You can do this."

I finally took the hint and prayed. I saw the difference between Cedar Moe's attitude and mine towards the same situation. He had been praying and had the faith God was with us; I was full of fear and felt alone. I was afraid and he was cheerful. I realized the difference was fear and faith. I felt fearful and tried to control the situation myself by worrying and it wasn't working. I didn't know why I never figured it out before, but worrying never helped in any situation. Cedar Moe had faith, let go, and left the control all up to God. In Alcoholics Anonymous they often said, "Fear and faith can't live in the same house." Cedar Moe trusted God to protect him. I was afraid God wouldn't protect me. The lesson I learned was to replace fear with faith and trust in God.

I remembered another Alcoholics Anonymous slogan said, *Let go and let God.* I remembered Step Eleven said, *Praying only for knowledge of His will for us and the power to carry it out.* I remembered in the little white Bible in the book of Luke 23:46, Jesus' actual last words he said on the cross were, *Father, into your hands I commit my spirit.* I remembered the words which we said at the end of every Alcoholics Anonymous meeting when we said the Lord's Prayer, *Thy will be done on earth as it is in heaven.*

Another lesson on my hike made sense as my fear seemed to melt away. Even in the midst of the most violent storm I had ever been in, a feeling of calmness came over me as if the Holy Spirit reached out and touched me. I recognized what I believed to be a spiritual awakening as it happened.

I stopped, looked up to heaven and simply said, "Thy will be done."

Lightning exploded as if God himself said, "Are you sure?"

I smiled, looked up and said, "Whatever."

Intellectually, I always knew this life would end one day anyway. If my hike ended that day on Mount Adams then it would be my last day. Besides, lightning seemed like a good way to go out. Lightning probably would hurt real bad, but not for very long. I wasn't the one in control of such things anyway and I never was. One of the major reasons I decided to thru-hike was for the adventure and that day provided an adventure I would remember for a long time. I surely wasn't bored with things, but maybe in the future, I should be more careful about what I asked for.

I hurried to catch up to Cedar Moe because I didn't want to lose him in the storm. The wind blew a brief opening in our gray blindfold to expose a view of Mount Adams, which even at a mile away, looked intimidating.

I stopped Cedar Moe and asked the stupid question "Do we have to go over the summit?" He smiled and slapped me affectionately on the shoulder. I took it as a show of confidence I could do it. He then turned his attention back to the trail without saying a word. I smiled and took the time to get my camera out and took a picture of the mighty mountain before the gray monster swallowed it back up.

We continued towards the majestic Mount Adams. Cedar Moe paused to read a sign posted on the trail and then turned towards me to cheerfully announce in his high pitched Tennessee twang, "We're going over the top." I smiled and nodded in acknowledgement, knowing all the time we were going to go over the top.

We trudged over the top of Adams as the storm stole any views we would have enjoyed on a clear day. I stopped and took Cedar Moe's picture in the rocky terrain when the mountain flattened out near the summit. I caught him on film between two ten foot cairns spaced about twenty yards apart to mark a place fittingly called Thunderstorm Junction. I wanted to show the density of the dark gray cloud from its belly.

The wind and lightning let up some, but the rain became heavier as we picked our way, descending seven hundred feet in a long mile to the safety of Madison Hut.

We arrived as darkness was setting in for the night. We were soaked to the bone and chilled, but we made it to a safe, dry place for the night. Three work-for-stay hikers were already there for the night, but due to the weather outside, the crew chief felt sorry for us and let us stay. He was surprised when we told him we hiked in from Mount Washington in the storm. I realized for the first time we didn't see any other hikers since we left Mount Washington. I wondered where they all went in the storm.

The staff already started to serve dinner to the guests. Normally we would wait outside for them to finish supper, but tonight the weather was so bad, the crew chief led us to the bunkroom where the other three work-for-stay hikers were waiting.

We met a fifty something section hiker from West Virginia named Huff and a lesbian couple from Colorado named Jody and Diane, who were section hiking New Hampshire. They lied to the crew chief and told him they were thru-hikers to receive work for stay. We chatted until the guests finished eating.

I knew Cedar Moe normally hiked faster than I did and he was trying to catch up with Zoma and Lug, so I thanked him for hiking with me.

He humbly replied, "We both needed a little company today." He reached out and lightly slapped my shoulder, which came to mean we didn't know what else to say.

We finished all the leftovers in the kitchen with the crew as they told us tales about life on a crew for the summer. Apparently, a competition among the crews of the huts existed and Lake of the Clouds Hut was Madison's hated rival. They raided each other's hut at night. Our crew had the hut rigged with an elaborate alarm system made up of fishing line and tin cans to alert them in the night if the other hut intruded. I was grateful they showed me because I would use the restroom in the back of the bunkroom instead of going outside and setting the alarm off when I had to get up in the night to take the old-man-pee. We talked and laughed into the night. All had a good time. The five of us set out our sleeping bags in the dining room after the guests went to bed. I felt full of life, grateful I was still alive, and blessed to be able to experience the adventure of thru-hiking.

I was exhausted, but I laid awake to mentally relive the day. My mind was trying to come up with concrete answers for so many questions that I had always been afraid to even ask myself. Why was I so afraid of the lightning? Why was I afraid of death?

A line in the Big Book of Alcoholics Anonymous popped into my mind which said, "We could not manage our own lives, but God could and would if he were sought." I came to understand and believe I was spiritually inquisitive and seeking all my life, even in my addiction when I claimed to be an atheist.

I was new to Alcoholics Anonymous when an old timer whose name I lost in time, quoted Jesus Christ by saying, "Ask and you shall receive. Seek and you shall find. Knock and the door shall be opened unto you." I remembered I thought, bullshit, but now it all made perfect sense. How could I have been so blind? I didn't know if I needed to know all the answers. I knew the more I sought, the more I found and the more I found, the more I trusted God and the more I trusted God, the stronger my faith became. Maybe that was all I had to know to motivate me to continue seeking.

I came out of my meditation type trance with awareness of an Asian gentleman above me sitting at the table reading with his head light.

I said, "Hey, what are you doing?"

He said, "I'm reading."

I thought, okay Dreamer let it go. We don't need you to be causing any drama. I rolled away and drifted off to sleep.

Day 138   7.8 Miles

I slept poorly because of the issue with the guest who was reading. He was quiet enough, but I woke up about every half hour with him hovering over me. I didn't say anything at first because I thought he would go to bed shortly. I had to get up to pee at about three o'clock and couldn't go back to sleep with him so close. Finally, I got so annoyed I couldn't stuff it any longer. I put both my hands on his book, moved my face within two inches of his for effect, and said,

"Look, if you don't go someplace else to read I'm going to rip your ears off!" He moved, but I couldn't go back to sleep anyway then because of the adrenalin rush.

The weather outside still sucked. It was raining hard, but the good news was, I didn't hear any wind or thunder. I helped myself to a hot cup of coffee and everything started to look better. The five of us sat in the kitchen with some of the crew as we waited for the guests to finish eating. We then ate a huge breakfast.

We bid Jody, Diane, and Huff goodbye. They already did their work for stay the day before. Most of the guests had already left in the pouring rain. The crew chief assigned Cedar Moe and me the easy task of sweeping out the dining room and bunkrooms. We drank another cup of coffee before we got to it.

Cedar Moe went to the bunkroom, but soon returned saying a guest was still sleeping. I went in and guess who was still sound asleep with his headlight still on and his book lying on his chest? I pulled his headlight back as far as it would go and let it snap back on his forehead. He jerked awake and I said in a loud cheerful voice, "Good morning, rise and shine!" I pulled the covers off him, grabbed him by his armpits, helped him up, pointed him towards the pisser, and pushed him to the door.

Cedar Moe was unaware what had transpired the night before while everyone else was asleep, so he said, "That was rude!"

I said, "I know, I'm rude when I don't get enough sleep." I then slapped him affectionately on the shoulder. We took our time finishing our task and did a good job. Neither one of us was in a hurry to venture out in the nasty weather. We hit the trail by mid-morning anyway, in the pouring rain.

We caught up to Jody and Diane on the summit of Mount Madison. The rain seemed to let up some, but we still had zero views. I took a picture of the three of them on the summit enclosed by the gray, misty rain. We only talked briefly and moved on ahead of them. Cedar Moe was hiking faster than I could keep up, so I dropped back and began hiking solo at my slower pace as I picked my way down the slippery rocks of Madison towards Pinkham Notch.

I enjoyed the solitude as the rain stopped and the sun came out to burn off the clouds. I hiked in the bright sunshine, which was a huge contrast from a couple of hours before. I descended Madison, the last mountain in the Presidential range. I felt a sense of accomplishment. It was a great day with all the adverse conditions finally over for a while and then I came to Parapet Brook.

Parapet Brook drained Mount Madison and emptied into Peabody River a short distance from there. On a normal day, it was a pleasant little mountain stream. That day, because of the wet season the brook was a raging torrent, swollen from all the rain. The bad news was I might be forced to ford the nightmare. I didn't want to, but I didn't see a bridge.

I stopped to take my pack off because I needed a break. I pondered the situation and decided to explore upstream first because logically, if I didn't find a bridge, at least the stream was smaller upstream. I ventured upstream until Madison became so steep I stopped. I did an about-face, investigating downstream until Parapet merged with the river and found nothing I wanted to chance. I returned to my pack, got out my stove, made a cup of coffee, and ate lunch, which gave me a chance to think things over before I did something stupid.

I believe contact with God might have been what was missing when I was young. Reverend Macintyre told me to obey God and friends told me I would go to hell if I didn't, so I learned to fear God. I heard stories about God, but I had no personal contact with God. It was hard for me to believe in God or have faith when I hadn't met God. All I had contact with was a preacher who told me stories about God and the neighborhood kids who told me how God punished. I doubt the preacher or my friends ever had contact with God. Even at that age, I still thought the preacher was full of his ego and puked out a lot of holy-crapola from the pulpit.

As I grew up, my prayer life was mostly asking God for something. He was like Santa Claus because He knew if you were bad or good, naughty or nice, and if you were good, you got the bike, but if you were naughty, you got coal.

Jody and Diane showed up as I finished my second cup of coffee.

They were more interested in washing out some clothes since they had an unlimited water source for the first time in days. They should have been with me the day before when the storm on Mount Adams washed everything for me.

They settled in for lunch and I felt I wasn't welcome for whatever reason. I decided to cross the creek right there with them watching, so if the river took me home at least someone knew. I thought about the lesson I learned on Mount Adams the day before, that fear and faith couldn't live together in the same house. I said a short prayer and proceeded to cross to the other side.

I had experienced strong current before, so I knew what to expect. I didn't buckle my pack on when I ventured into the white water, which was stronger than expected. I made sure I planted my lead foot firmly on the bottom using my hiking poles to help keep me stable before I would shift my weight to move my back foot.

I felt a deep trench with my pole in middle of the torrent the white water hid from me before I started to cross. I stopped to assess the situation, sticking my pole in but I couldn't touch the bottom. I could see a big rock a few inches under the surface on the other side, a good jump away. I couldn't turn around and go back, so I decided to jump for the rock. I took a deep breath and jumped as far as I could. I cleared the trench, but slipped on the rock. My momentum took me safely to the other side before I crashed. I picked myself up and that was how my big problem became a trail tale.

I looked back and Jody was applauding, but Diane wasn't even looking my way. I tipped my hat to the ladies as I thought John Wayne would, and then turned my attention to the trail. Jody and Diane didn't have poles, so I had no idea how they would get across the torrent. I guess that was their problem, not mine.

I hadn't been alone lately to process my thoughts, so I welcomed the alone time. I admired Cedar Moe's trust in God. I wondered how he came to trust God or even meet God. I never met God or had contact with Him when I was young, so I didn't understand or have a personal, spiritual relationship with God. I recalled I once told God to reveal himself as he did to Moses and give me instructions of exactly what to do. I was young, but the truth was, if a burning bush ever said it was God talking, I would have left a trail of brown spots behind as I lost control of my sphincter muscle, while departing as fast as my legs could carry my carcass. Besides, no one would ever believe me if I said God talked to me in such a way. They would probably commit me or at least put me on psychotropic medication.

I wasn't too old when I understood the difference between right and wrong. I felt guilty when I did something I knew I shouldn't, maybe because I was afraid someone would catch me. I came to know the feeling as my guilty conscience, which I had most of the time. For example, I felt guilty when I spent the money Mom gave me to put in the collection plate at Sunday school for cigarettes. who knows, maybe God was talking to me through my conscience.

One of the things I liked about drinking was it quickly took away my guilty conscience. I stopped maturing when I discovered alcohol until after I sobered up, which was when I could no longer use drugs and alcohol to cope with everything.

Big Jim told me to pray, so I prayed even though I thought no one was out there. I started noticing little feelings or insights at times that paralleled my conscience. I identified them as a sixth sense, but most people called it intuition. I felt special because sometimes, I could sense things before they happened. I began to think maybe God was telling me something important through my intuition. Scooter called those little insights, spirit whispers.

I believed Gallagher was right when he said, "Meditation was when you listen." Eventually, I learned when I meditate I purposely sought a moment of clarity where I could hear God whispering. Sometimes I had to be patient because I wasn't the one in control and it wasn't something I could force or hurry. I found God as I understand him was not intrusive. My God only came into my life when He was invited and welcome. Then, only when everything was quiet, and I was humble, and listening. My reward was a subtle moment of clarity where God whispered to me through my conscience, intuition, or maybe it was really my soul.

I felt grateful to find a solid looking suspension bridge over the current on Peabody River. The bridge bounced with each step as I crossed, so I had to slow down. I admired the early thru-hiker's tenacity to ford rivers like that before bridges crossed them.

I arrived at Pinkham Notch late in the afternoon. Pinkham Notch was a tourist trap, which had a main highway running through it and home of the Appalachian Mountain Club headquarters. A couple hundred cars were in the parking lot, tourists were all over, and I felt out of place. The Appalachian Mountain Club owned and operated the year around resort. A store sold souvenirs, junk food, fuel, books, maps and a few backpacking supplies. They had a dining room attached that served family style meals for supper and breakfast. In a different building was a type of dormitory with two bunks built into each room that came with clean linens. The guidebook said you could get a night's stay with supper and breakfast included for fifty-seven bucks.

I found Cedar Moe sitting on a bench in front of the store drinking coke. I left my pack with him while I bought two cokes, two snickers, and returned to join him on the bench. I handed Cedar another Coke and a Snickers while we watched the sweet smelling tourists pass by. Cedar Moe, in his haste to catch Zoma and Lug fell as he was fording Parapet Brook and the current swept him downstream a ways. I would have paid to have been there to see that.

A man in his forties with his wife and three kids in tow stopped and interrupted us as it was about to get good. He asked, "Are you thru-hikers?"

Cedar Moe said with a smile, "Yes we are, sir."

"Where did you start?"

Cedar Moe, "We started on Springer Mountain, Georgia."

"Can we get a picture of the two of you?"

Cedar Moe spoke for both of us, "We would be honored, sir."

Cedar Moe must have eyes on the side of his head because he never even looked my way when he said to me out of the corner of his mouth, "Be nice!" I smiled for the picture.

Then the guy asked, "Could I get one of you two with the kids?"

Cedar Moe said in his Tennessee accent, "Be delighted."

I thought he even knew what I was thinking when he whispered a commanding, "Keep your finger down" to me out of the corner of his mouth all while he was smiling. We obviously had been around each other too long as I moved over to accommodate the three brats for the picture. The wife crowded in beside me and gagged when she got a good whiff of me. The picture came out as I was laughing and she had her nose wrinkled up from the smell.

I told Cedar Moe I decided to stay at the dormitory-type hut and offered to pay if he wanted to stay with me, but he declined. I hoped to catch up with him in Gorham, New Hampshire in a few days, but secretly, I doubted that would happen.

Jody and Diane showed up while we were still sitting on the bench. They left their packs with us while they went inside and bought supplies. They came out of the store, packed up, and left without stopping to chat. I wanted to ask how they made out crossing Parapet, but they didn't seem to want to socialize.

Cedar Moe asked, "Did we somehow offend them.

I said, "No, I think it was more between the two of them. Jody liked to flirt with us and Diane felt insecure and jealous."

Cedar Moe said, "I wasn't hitting on them."

I arose, slapped him on the shoulder, and said, "A stud like you doesn't have to,"

I then asked again, "Are you sure you won't stay for a meal and a night, my treat?"

He donned his pack as he replied, "Thanks, but I want to catch up with Zoma and Lug." He affectionately slapped my shoulder and departed. It seemed we both knew we would never see each other ever again.

I checked in at the dorm. I asked for a private room, but they had no such thing. The boy checking me in said, "You are the only one in the room so far, so it would be private if no one else showed up. It's close to suppertime and usually no one checked in after supper because the price would be the same." I paid him and found my room.

I took a hot shower in the men's shower room for the first time since Glencliff. I felt so good and still had a little time, so I fit in a little nap before supper. I stopped at the desk to check if anyone else checked in before I left for supper, which was a family style, five-course meal. I was the only thru-hiker there and I ate the most. We had salad, boiled potatoes, cauliflower, and baked chicken. I felt out of place in New Hampshire with the locals and non thru-hikers.

I bought five Snickers at the outfitters for five dollars. The clerk said, "I heard, you could sell them on the trail for five bucks a piece."

I replied in a curt voice, "If I found someone hungry enough to pay five bucks for a Snickers, I would be proud to give them all the candy bars." I felt self-righteous as I took the passive-aggressive shot at him, but I soon felt ashamed because I stooped so low and apologized. I didn't need a lot in the line of supplies because I ate mostly in the Appalachian Mountain Club huts since I left Glencliff.

I returned to my room to lie down and let my huge supper digest. I felt some relief because I still had no roommate. I took the time to give thanks to God for helping me cross Parapet Brook earlier that day. I once heard someone in Alcoholics Anonymous say, "If you pray, don't worry, and if you worry, don't pray." The slogan didn't mean anything to me then, but made sense after a while. If I prayed over a situation and trusted enough or had enough faith to let go and let the will of God take over, I would never need to worry again. That seemed too simple. I must have lost consciousness while enjoying the scent of fresh, clean sheets.

Day 139   5.9 Miles

5.9 Exceptionally Hard Miles.

I slept well in a warm, dry bed and then took a long hot shower. I waited for the dining room to open for breakfast and ate a huge breakfast. I had to admit my ego inflated as some of the other guests asked questions about my thru-hike. I returned to my room after breakfast, packed up, and hiked out.

I bumped into Jody and Diane at the store as I was leaving. They were going to take the ski lift to the top of Wildcat Mountain. Wildcat was a famous ski slope and in the summer, they still ran tourists to the top of the mountain on the ski lift for a fee. I took pride in being a purist thru-hiker and wouldn't even consider riding over part of the Appalachian Trail. I bid them goodbye.

Wildcat's climb was surprisingly, the hardest climb yet on my thru-hike. I was in dense forest, which gave me a secure feeling and an abundance of trees to hang on to and pull myself up. Wildcat was not scary, but it was steep and a lot of hard work. I passed several section hikers on the strenuous climb up which was hand over hand at times. I stopped to chat with a group of five boys who graduated high school last month. I normally wasn't competitive, but the old man found a sense of satisfaction when I left them in my dust. "Dear God, I know I was showing off and I apologize, Amen."

The climb took four hours to go a mile by the time I reached the top of the ski lift. Several tourists who took the ski lift were already at the top. A pet dog who wasn't on a leash harassed me. Apparently, a mother and her ten-year-old son owned him.

She tried to reassure me by yelling, "He won't bite!" He was barking and growling while he advanced on me, so I ended his advance when I successfully sprayed him in the eyes with pepper spray. The lady apologized, but I was still pissed.

I soon forgot the drama on the summit with the amazing panoramic views. I looked back at the north side of the Presidential Range for the first time. The mountains all looked different from that vantage point, but I picked out Mount Adams and Mount Madison. The day was mostly clear and sunny, but a fluffy white cloud still concealed the summit of mighty Mount Adams. I took a picture of the north side to etch the event in my memory before I moved on.

Wildcat had five peaks which took all day to climb only six miles. I was going to stop at a camp-sight I found which Paparazzi told me about back in Massachusetts and stealth camp, but I moved on hoping I could get work for stay at the next hut. Besides, the young men I passed earlier told me they didn't have any money to pay for a night at the hut, so I told them about the hidden camp-sight. I laughed to myself because they were going to add to their adventure by being poorly prepared. No matter what happened, they would learn some of life's lessons from Wildcat. They would also have some trail tales to embellish later when they tell their grandchildren.

I wanted to go farther that day, but after climbing and descending the five peaks of Wildcat, I was exhausted. I arrived at Carter Notch Hut by mid afternoon, which I thought was early enough to ask for work for stay. To my dismay, Jody and Diane arrived first and already took work for stay. I had a resentment towards them because they weren't thru-hikers and they took the ski lift to beat me there. The caretaker was a little, short pecker-type of a guy who charged me twenty-five dollars to only sleep in the bunkhouse. I thought he might have been smitten by Jody's flirting, so I passive aggressively punched him hard in the arm good old boy fashion, winked, and said, "You're outa luck, Stud." He had no idea what I was talking about, but I thought he would understand come morning.

I stopped at the main cabin's makeshift dining room/kitchen with tables, benches, and a propane stove. That was the only Appalachian Mountain Club hut that didn't provide meals or bed sheets which was why it only cost twenty-five-dollars a night to stay. The three separate bunkhouses were dark and smelled like dirty hikers. I had them all to myself, so I set up for the night.

Soon, a bunch of kids in placement barged in, so I moved to the second bunkhouse. Then the boys I met on the trail who didn't have enough money to stay there came in. They talked to the caretaker and the little puke let the five of them stay for ten bucks, which was two dollars apiece. By now, I was really pissed, but I moved to the peace and quiet of the third and poorest bunkhouse.

I went swimming in the lake and then watched two fishermen from Germany. Watching them helped me let go of my resentment, but made me really miss fishing. I moved on to be alone and found a perfect sitting rock on the water's edge. I sat and listened to the silence, enjoying the solitude of the clear blue, mountain lake.

I was impressed with how God seemed to take care of Cedar Moe and me on Adams, but I was even more impressed with Cedar Moe's trust in God that day. I envied his trust in God. I wondered how people like my Mother, Heaven Bound, and Cedar Moe developed such faith and trust in God that they didn't seem to have any fear.

Over a year ago, I was returning from a trip to Virginia and the transmission in my truck blew up on the interstate over two-hundred miles away from home. I rented a car to get home and return to work. I went back to pick my truck up the following weekend after they replaced my transmission. The truck ran fine, but I no longer trusted it. I soon traded it off because I no longer trusted it.

I didn't know if it was my nature or if I learned to be untrusting, but as I said before, I had always had issues trusting anything or anyone. Trusting an unseen higher power was unheard of for me at first. Trusting God has been a big problem of mine all my life. My ego wanted to take over and run things, so my ego told me not to trust. If I did everything myself, I wouldn't have to trust God or others. The problem was I also couldn't trust myself to do some things.

I didn't have the skill or knowledge to fix my transmission, but I got it fixed by trusting a mechanic to fix it for me. I built a house once and I knew very little about the electrical wiring. I asked a friend whom I trusted, to wire it for me because he had the knowledge and skills necessary. I helped him by letting go of control and doing exactly what he told me to do. As a result, we did a fine job. I found by trusting others I didn't need all the knowledge or skill to accomplish my goal or solve all my problems by myself. I did have to let go of control and trust God and others.

The mosquitoes interrupted my serenity as darkness started to overtake the landscape, so I returned to the protection of the dining room where people were socializing. I joined them, talking mostly to my two German fishermen friends for the rest of the evening. The bunkhouse was full when I returned, so I had to sleep with a bunch of tourists. I was lucky they were all adults who quieted down and went to sleep.

July 15   Day 140   13.3 Miles

I awoke and quietly packed before anyone else was awake in the bunkhouse. It looked like it would turn into a hot, hazy day to hike.

I went to the hut and made coffee on their gas stove. I drank coffee with Jody and Diane before leaving them to sweep out the dining room for their work for stay. I wanted to put some distance between us. I found them annoying and grew tired of them because they got on my nerves.

I felt another sense of accomplishment as I left the White Mountain National Park that day. The White Mountains were rugged, but their beauty far outweighed the adversity of hiking them. I climbed and descended Mount Hight, Carters Dome, and Mount Moriah with great vistas accented by the blue tint of the haze. I hiked solo all day and enjoyed the solitude. Some days I liked people around, but I needed some days to meditate and process what the spirit taught me. I didn't recall a lot about the day's actual journey in the mountains, because I dedicated the day to meditating to digest the spirit whispers from the last few days.

It seemed like the spirit used Cedar Moe as an example on purpose. I already had a little insight and trust in God, but Cedar Moe was a fine example of someone who trusted God more and for a longer time. I first started to trust God in a small way to do what I couldn't do for myself long ago. I helped him by doing what I could to live sober from the start. I soon found God to be a trustworthy partner. I didn't know if I developed trust in God or He earned it, but my trust started to grow stronger.

I guess for me trust led to faith and the stronger my faith became, the weaker my egotistical fear was. I looked back on my life and saw my self-will had always caused me negative consequences. Yet I still had a hard time letting go of control and fear. I believed God would still stand back if I chose to follow my own will, but I would also have to face the consequences. I gradually learned by prayer and meditation I made spiritual contact with God, which increased my trust. By seeking God's will I could tap into a resource of a power greater than myself or anything I ever experienced on my own.

My ego got involved at times and I created doubts and fears on my own. My will and God's will also didn't always mix well. I tried to shake them together to mix the two wills as if they were vinegar and oil. I wanted to compromise with God and tried talking him into helping me with my will, but as with vinegar and oil they soon separated. The Alcoholics Anonymous slogan, Let go and let God, meant I needed to let go of my self-will and let the will of God take over. Sometimes I didn't have the courage to let go of control and trust God to handle everything, because my faith wasn't strong enough yet.

My ego created all my fears and only through faith could I find the courage to let go and let God. I had often heard, "The will of God won't take you where the grace of God won't protect you." I most admire David for his faith that God's will was with him when he faced Goliath.

The Marines said, "Pain was weakness leaving the body," which I understood. I also came to personally believe, fear was weakness leaving the soul. Trust seemed to be the only ingredient I required to metamorphose fear into faith. In the Big Book, Bill Wilson Said, "God could and would if he were sought." Alcoholics Anonymous's Step Eleven was where I continued to seek through prayer and meditation.

According to the gospels, the last thing Jesus said was, Father, *I commend my spirit unto you.* Maybe that was where the Alcoholics Anonymous slogan, "Let go and let God" originated. I wouldn't know ahead of the time, but maybe at my moment of death I too would surrender my ego completely to God.

I didn't realize how physically spent I was until I arrived at the Rattle River Shelter. I set my tent up in a secluded spot next to the river, so the sounds of the river could sing me to sleep later that night. I went back to the shelter and found three Sobo hikers who had returned to the trail after a zero day in Gorham. They cooked hotdogs they bought in town. I cooked my supper of tuna with rice while I socialized with them. They filled me in on the details of Gorham and the trail north and I did likewise about the Whites and the trail south.

I returned to my tent to retire for the evening. I only hiked thirteen miles, but the trail was so hard it took me fifteen hours and I was whipped. I jumped in the bag and to my surprise; I couldn't talk my mind into shutting down. Faith and its archenemy, fear kept sleep from stealing my consciousness as if they said, "Dreamer, we have unfinished business." I tried to blank out my thoughts and listen for the spirit to whisper. Soon I heard, "Fear wasn't a bad thing," which provided my food for meditation.

I have often heard pain was the greatest motivator, which I blindly accepted, but I thought fear might be the real motivator. I could see where pain has motivated me before, but usually, even then it was the fear behind the pain that was the motivator for me. I was in pain on March eleventh when I accepted help from Jesus Christ, but in reality, the fear of how bad the pain would become motivated me into action. I talked to Heaven Bound and became hopeful help was on the way, but I was still in pain. The difference was I then had some hope or faith which pushed the fear out and then my pain lost its power over me.

A serene calmness came over me as if the Holy Spirit said, "The day's lesson was over and you are excused now." I was two miles from the highway and then it was another three to the town of Gorham, New Hampshire. I would go into Gorham to the Hiker's Paradise Motel the next morning. I thought about staying two nights to rest my ankle. I was looking forward to a zero day in town. I was out of food, but they told me there was a McDonald's in town, which would definitely be my first stop for a big breakfast and good coffee. I closed my eyes and let my mind drift away with the day.

Day 141   1.9 Miles

I broke camp at first light and hiked two miles to the road. I slipped and fell in a small stream, because I was careless. Thankfully, I didn't get hurt, but learned I must be more careful in the future. I would hate to end my hike over something as preventable as careless hurrying.

I only walked a short distance on the highway, when a young couple gave me a ride to Gorham in the back of their pickup truck with their dog. They let me off at McDonald's, where I bought eggs, pancakes, hash browns, and coffee to start. Then I went back for two sausage McMuffins and more coffee.

I called the Hiker's Paradise Motel and reserved a private room, but it wouldn't be ready until early afternoon. I walked up the main street, window-shopping. I stopped at two other motels, but couldn't find a better deal. I checked into Hikers Paradise and paid for my room.

I met the owner, whose name was Bruno Janicki. I had the impression I wouldn't like him from the trail talk. Bruno spoke with a heavy Polish accent, which led me to suspect he was a polish immigrant. I grew up in a Polish neighborhood where the parents of my friends were immigrants. They often spoke Polish, so we kids wouldn't know what they were saying. We all learned to understand some Polish and I still knew how to swear in Polish.

I took an instant liking to Bruno, but I saw how younger hikers misinterpreted his demeanor. I also knew older Polish folks took zero shit from anyone, especially the young. I didn't see Bruno tolerating any foolish antics from young hikers, but his bark was probably way worse than his bite most of the time. I felt comfortable, as if I was in my old neighborhood. Bruno let me leave my pack on the back porch and lent me a daypack to go to the grocery store.

I hiked a half-mile to the store and bought enough supplies to get me to Andover, Maine. I stopped at a yard sale on the way back from the store and chatted for a long time with an older lady who filled me in on what was going on in Gorham. I was on foot so I couldn't buy anything.

I met Moose Kisser as I returned to town. He took a zero day in town the previous day, so he was on his way back to the trail. I walked with him and we stopped and bought ice cream, then we went to the outfitters. I replaced the plastic spoon I broke on the trail and bought more insect repellant. It was good to see Moose Kisser, but it saddened me also because I would probably never see him again because he hiked fast and wanted to finish so he could return home to Texas.

My room was ready by the time I returned to Hiker's Paradise. I settled in, took my usual shower, and did my laundry. I went swimming in the swimming pool Bruno called Lake Janicki after himself. He yelled at anyone who called it a swimming pool. Lake Janicki was a round, above ground pool which was about five feet deep and about thirty feet in diameter. It was the hottest day since I had been on the trail, so it felt good as I stood in the water and talked to other hikers. I was grateful to be in town and not on the trail, hiking in the oppressive heat. I went to Kentucky Fried Chicken for supper and ate all I could eat. I then went back to my air-conditioned room and wrote in my journal until I could stay awake no longer.

Day 142   Zero Miles

I slept well with the air conditioner on all night. I bought breakfast at the attached restaurant with several other hikers. I met some new friends as the place buzzed with trail tales. I ate two eggs, sausage, several pancakes, and a lot of coffee for six dollars. Bruno waited on the tables while his wife, Mary Ann cooked. He seemed gruff on the outside, but as expected, I found he was kind and caring once I got past his rough exterior. Mary Ann was so quiet, I couldn't recall her saying anything.

A section hiker I met at breakfast offered me a ride to Walmart after I finished eating. I took him up on it to buy a camera card and some hard to get supplies that slipped my mind when I was there the day before. I started to walk the two miles back and another hiker, who recognized me from breakfast picked me up.

My youngest daughter, Nadine called and talked quite a while. She took the day off from work because her dog was having puppies. She was as excited and nervous as any new mom. It was always good to talk to her, but I felt extra privileged because I was able to share her excitement.

I ate lunch at a Chinese restaurant, which was disappointing because it was very poor in quality. I still ate all I could eat and returned to the motel for a nap. The heat was so oppressive I didn't want to do anything. We were having record high temperatures in New Hampshire, so I spent a good part of the afternoon in Lake Janicki. I stood in the water talking to a bunch of other hikers, while we watched the thermometer on the bank reach one-hundred and three degrees. The overbearing heat was so oppressive that it was the perfect day to take a zero.

The temperature started to drop about dark, so I left the pool and got dressed, walked about a mile to a Pizza-Hut, and bought a large pizza. I also picked up a quart of ice cream on my way back to the motel. I sat in my air-conditioned room and ate the pizza and ice cream. That sure beat eating noodles in a hot tent while hiding from the mosquitoes.

I couldn't sleep, so I walked up the hill until I found enough cell tower to call Dan, who became a good friend who I met in Alcoholics Anonymous. I felt we connected on a spiritual level as we talked about contact with God well into the night. We even ended the conversation with the Lord's Prayer, like any Alcoholics Anonymous meeting.

Contact with God was like tapping a vital resource that as a nonbeliever, I didn't even know existed. Intellect always told me I needed food, water, air, and sleep to survive physically. My self-will usually took care of those needs. I now understood, I also had to have contact with God, which I found vital to survive spiritually. The only way I knew how to make contact was by talking to God and taking the time to meditate or listen. I felt grateful for the many friends like Dan who shared my spiritual understanding.

The air conditioned room was nice and cool when I returned. I even had to use a blanket to stay warm enough to sleep. I must have fallen asleep quickly because I couldn't remember anything after that.

Day 143   11.8 Miles

I slept in, which was unusual and caused me to be late for breakfast. All my friends who I made yesterday had already eaten and left by the time I arrived at the restaurant. I ate alone, disappointed because I enjoyed their company more than the food. I returned to my room to pack up before I checked out. I caught a ride back to the trail in a van with six other hikers. The van driver was trying to drum up business for his shuttle service. He gave us a free ride, but gave all of us his business card in case we would like to hire him in the future. I thanked him and took the card.

I was on the trail by mid morning. The temperature was unbearably hot until a violent thunderstorm hit mid-afternoon. A welcomed cold front came in with heavy rain. The trail never went above twenty-seven-hundred feet, staying well below tree line all day. I felt safer, but the lightning still frightened me if I let myself think about it. I hiked solo with few views in a steady, hard rain the rest of the day.

I arrived at Gentian Pond Shelter, only to find Jody and Diane had already set up their tent in the shelter. I thought they were so rude to take up the shelter space with their tent. I had hoped I already saw the last of them. I set up my tent on an outside tent platform in the pouring rain. Hero and several other hikers trickled in soaking wet, but I stayed in my tent to take a nap.

When I awoke the rain had stopped, the temperature dropped, and the evening turned pleasant. I took a stroll to a nearby glacier pond where a cow moose came to feed. She saw me and approached with caution, but didn't seem too afraid of me. I stayed still and soon she moseyed into the water up to her belly as if I wasn't around. She would duck her long nose under the water and come up munching on a mouth full of plants. I took some close up pictures of her feeding before dark. Moose were big and awkward looking, but to the contrary, quite agile in the thick woods. I was so fortunate for the opportunity to see and photograph her.

I returned to the camp to find it buzzing with hikers. I met a 2004 thru-hiker, who started in Gorham to section hike Maine. He liked Maine so well he wanted to take the time to hike it again slowly. He filled me in on the trail in Maine. I didn't remember his name, but he had a tattoo of the Appalachian Trail insignia with 2004 under it. If I finished the trail, I decided I would get the same tattoo with 2006 under it. We socialized well into the night by hiker standards before I returned to my tent.

I was only about five miles from the border of Maine, which gave me a sense of accomplishment since I had completely hiked thirteen of the fourteen states on the trail. I felt excited about what the next day would bring as I drifted off to sleep.

Day 144   9.6 Miles

I packed up my still wet tent to a beautiful morning. I left the sounds of the sleepy camp behind for the serene sounds of morning in the mountains. Once I ascended above the morning fog, I found a clear, blue, cloudless sky. The gray misty fog metamorphosed into white cotton clouds which filled the great valley below to separate me from a distant mountain range. I felt like an early explorer being the first to discover the enchanted land beyond the sea-like clouds.

My ankle still hurt, but vistas helped me tolerate the pain and put it out of my head as I hiked up to the summit of Mount Success. The morning fog had dwindled into a few wispy clouds that still lingered, leaving a panoramic view of what I believed was Maine. I could see purple mountains for as far as my eyes could see as if God was saying, Behold Maine! I stood there trying to process the miracle taking place within me. I thought back to the early days in Georgia when I was afraid to even think of getting to Maine. Mount Katahdin seemed like a mountain that only existed in a fairytale. I stopped there to take a break, made coffee, and ate my breakfast before moving on to the New Hampshire-Maine border.

I said a silent prayer of thanks for all the gifts God had bestowed upon me. I still didn't understand God, but I didn't understand so many things in this world. I didn't understand my little cell phone either, but I knew how to use it. I didn't understand God, but I knew how to pray and meditate. I still wasn't exactly sure how it worked or why, but God seemed to answer my prayers.

Many years ago, I gazed at the Grand Canyon in amazement of the millions of years it took the Colorado River to cut the natural wonder into the face of the earth. The eerie truth struck me that by comparison to the Grand Canyon, I would only be here on the earth for an incredibly short time. I knew the time I was given on earth wasn't enough to understand everything about God, but it was enough time to seek a relationship with the God I understand.

A blue, weather-beaten sign with white hand painted letters that said, Welcome to Maine, the way life should be, greeted me at the border. I was thankful no one was around to watch me do the, I made it and New Hampshire can kiss my ass goodbye dance. The White Mountains of New Hampshire were magnificent, breathtaking, and as tough as expected, but I hiked every inch of the Appalachian Trail through them.

I thought the trail would be easier in Maine, but I discovered I was still in the White Mountains. Hero caught up to me on Goose Mountain, so we hiked together until we got to Carlo Col Shelter. I ate lunch with him and a Sobo at the shelter. They were going swimming in the lake and staying in the shelter tonight. The swimming sounded good, but I only hiked about five miles and would like to camp closer to the Mahoosuc Notch. I wanted to hike Mahoosuc Notch first thing the next morning when I was fresh. I bid them goodbye and moved on.

I hiked by myself over Maine's Mount Carlo and the three peaks of Goose Eye Mountain. The mountains, forests, and vistas were overwhelmingly beautiful to my mortal eyes. I agreed with the sign nailed on the tree at the border. I felt like Maine was the way life should be.

Full Goose Shelter was full and all the tent platforms were occupied when I arrived. I was amazed at the amount of people already there in the early afternoon. I camped on the flattest piece of ground I could find quite far from the shelter. I returned to the shelter to cook and eat for the company of some Sobo thru-hikers who were staying in the shelter. I exchanged trail talk with them to get the feel of the trail ahead. They passed through the Mahoosuc Notch earlier, which started a little over a mile north of there. The next morning I would face the famous Mahoosuc Notch, which had the undisputed reputation of being the hardest mile on the entire Appalachian Trail.

I returned to my tent to find a noisy troop of Boy Scouts came in and set up all around me while I was at the shelter. I wrote in my journal for a while, put on a Kataro CD to drown out the noise, and drifted off to dreamland while still writing in the journal.

Day 145   12 Miles

More Boy Scouts arrived later in the night, woke me up, and kept me awake for half the night. They also woke me up earlier than I would have gotten up that morning. They seemed to have poor leadership.

I stayed in my sleeping bag until well after daylight, until Mother Nature made me get up to start my day. I packed up before I went to the shelter to make coffee and say goodbye to the Sobo hikers. I wasn't in a big hurry, but I wanted to leave before the Boy Scouts. I didn't want to share the notch with a bunch of noisy kids.

I hiked a half-mile up to the south peak of Fulling Mountain, which started my heart. The trail then dropped over nine hundred feet in a mile to the southern end of the Mahoosuc Notch. A tangled mess of rocks and the skeletons of fallen trees greeted me at the notch. A rabbit would have had a hard time getting through that jungle.

Trail talk embellished the difficulty and danger of many places on the Appalachian Trail, but even Earl Shaffer complained about having to take his pack off to crawl through the narrow tunnels under the rocks through the notch. I would soon know if the Notch deserved its reputation or not.

The Mahoosuc Notch formed many years ago. It looked to me as if a giant granite rock named Mount Mahoosuc split and formed a crack about seventy-five yards wide and a mile long. I thought in the beginning, a river started to flow through the opening, but over many years, rocks from the sides fell into the crack thus covering up and hiding the river. The rocks that ranged in size from a car engine to a house formed an obstacle course.

Some snow and ice stay in the notch all year around, so when I entered the notch, the temperature dropped. A fog-like mist from the change in temperature added an eerie effect unique to the notch. I could hear the hidden river beneath me, but I never saw it. The trail gossip said in some places, hikers had to take their packs off and crawl around and under the rocks.

I came upon a small pool of ice. Yes, ice on the Appalachian Trail, on the twentieth of July. How convenient it would be to camp there and let Mother Nature provide a cooler. I looked around and thought I couldn't even find a place to set up a hammock in the rocky, brush-covered jungle. I took a picture of the ice. I stepped over some intimidating crevasses and holes wondering if any dead hikers were below, frozen in ice.

I have been on the trail long enough to stop listening to all the hype, but my heart stopped cold when a short distance into the notch I came upon a hole in the jagged rocks that had a white arrow painted above it, indicating the trail. I would have barely enough room to take my pack off and crawl through. It was as if some demon was saying, "Welcome to the Notch."

I already had goose bumps from the cold, but the hair on my neck stood up as I imagined the hole in the granite was a monster's mouth. The sharp, broken pieces of jagged rocks were the monsters teeth guarding the hole, waiting to chew me up and swallow me. I said out loud, "This too shall pass," as I mustered the courage to enter. Normally I wasn't claustrophobic, but that creeped me out. I made my way over the jagged pieces of granite to the entrance and luckily, I could see some light at the other end of the tunnel. I took off my pack and proceeded cautiously, dragging my pack behind me trying to be as careful as possible. I could hear the eerie sound of the hidden river below and my own heart beating, which added to my uneasiness.

I emerged on the other side of the tunnel to find a Sobo nervously waiting for me to clear. I welcomed his company and we chatted as customary about the trail ahead. He told me to take my time and enjoy the notch. I felt better and started to look at it as the adventure it was meant to be. I immediately crawled through another tunnel and climbed over some huge, jagged pieces of rock. I slowed to a snail's pace inching my way along one obstacle at a time.

I stopped after a while for a break and my friend Hero caught up to me. I was happy to see him and have company to share the experience. We helped each other pick our way through the notch. I took pictures of him crawling on his hands and knees, dragging his pack under the granite rocks. The mile through the notch took an hour and forty-five minutes. The trip was hard work, but well worth the effort.

We exited the notch and to my surprise, found the humid heat terribly oppressive, making it hard to get a good breath, as we immediately ascended the Mahoosuc Arm. The Mahoosuc Arm was a steep ascent out of the notch. It was also a famous, hard climb. We took our time with the Arm and found it to be no more difficult than most of the Whites. We finally stopped for a deserved break at the top of the arm.

Hero was in a hurry to meet his mom, who would be waiting for him six miles ahead at Grafton Notch. She would take him to Bethel, Maine for the night. He offered me a ride, but I declined. I didn't want to keep up with him and didn't want to hold him back. We took each other's picture and I saluted him as he disappeared to the north.

I turned to the south and saluted the Whites goodbye for the final time. As I looked back I discovered I could see what I believe was the top of the notch, where the granite mountain split many years ago to form the Mahoosuc Notch. I took a picture to show Hero because I was sure he was in such a hurry he didn't notice.

I found myself alone again in the solitude of the Maine wilderness. I drifted into meditation letting my mind focus on what I didn't understand about God. I believe knowledge has always been present out there in the universe. Probably, we as mankind had not yet discovered most of it, but the knowledge still existed.

History for example, gave credit to Alexander Graham Bell for inventing the telephone. Bell didn't create the knowledge to make the phone, he only discovered the knowledge that already existed. Christopher Columbus was another example. He didn't invent or create the Americas he merely discovered the continent that was already there.

After Bell's time on earth was over, other knowledge seekers discovered more knowledge to improve on what he discovered. If we could somehow resurrect old Alex Bell and introduce him to the cell phone of today he probably would be more than a little amazed. If Alex had been on earth longer, he probably would have discovered the knowledge to invent the cell phone of today himself.

A section in Step Eleven said, *Sought through prayer and meditation to improve our conscious contact with God as we understood Him praying only for knowledge of His will.* I thought as a mortal human being, I knew only a minute percentage of the knowledge that existed. I wasn't sure how vast the knowledge that actually existed in our universe was. Knowledge may even be infinite.

Alcoholics Anonymous said, *More will be revealed*. One thing I did know was the more I sought God, the more I saw God. I felt that I personally needed to continue to seek and keep my mind open to new information to be revealed about God. I looked over the primitive notes I wrote on the subject and I thought if anyone ever read them they would think I was still smoking weed.

My mind returned again to the old hymn, "Amazing Grace" as I started to hum the tune. I loved the line, "I once was lost, but now I'm found, was blind, but now I see." I thought back to my addiction when I couldn't see God or his work anywhere, but now I saw God and his work everywhere. I was so grateful that I finally started to see. I found it impossible to not believe or have faith in God once I made conscious contact with God. Maybe I was a little like Mr. Bell in a way, because I started to discover knowledge that was already there.

I took my time in the heat. I even took a side trail to the summit of Old Speck Mountain's observation deck that had outstanding vistas. A short distance before I arrived at Grafton Notch I found a sign that marked the official end to the Appalachian Mountain Club's territory. I felt some animosity towards the Appalachian Mountain Club at first because I thought they were capitalizing on the Whites, but now I felt grateful to them. The Appalachian Mountain Club was instrumental in preserving the White Mountains and protected them from future opportunists that would rape the wilderness in the name of progress and profit. We the people as a nation, need more organizations like the Appalachian Mountain Club. So I salute the Appalachian Mountain Club.

I hiked to Baldpate Lean-to where I set up my tent for the night. No one was in the shelter for company, but the next day I would hike eight miles to a road where I hoped to hitch a ride to Andover, Maine. I had a mail drop waiting in Andover and planned to stay at the bed and breakfast owned by Christian's grandparents. I cooked rice, ate, and went right to sleep.

Day 146   8 Miles

I slept soundly, not even getting up to pee, which was unusual for me at my age. I was exhausted after the adventure of the day before, but also at peace for putting the legendary Mahoosuc Notch behind me. I didn't have to be quiet or hurry since no one was around. I wondered where all the Boy Scouts and other hikers disappeared to. Then it occurred to me, the scouts probably only sectioned the Notch and spent only the one night on the trail. At least that made sense to me. I packed up after my coffee and wondered what the day had in store for me.

The adventure for the day was Baldpate Mountain, which I would never forget. Baldpate sported three peaks. The Baldpate's east peak was thirty-eight-hundred feet of granite. From a distance it looked like a giant soccer ball with green patches. The trail was visible a long ways off, but looked like a crack in the forest inching its way to the top of the bald rock. The last twelve-hundred feet was steeply sloped and exposed above tree line. I started to ascend the mountain and put my hiking poles in my pack so I could use my hands to help climb over the steepest parts. I got careless after building a tolerance for heights over the past months of being in the mountains, but I thought I was being careful. I climbed about two-thirds of the way up the rock, using the cracks in the giant granite ball for hand holds when a stone pulled lose under my right hand as I pulled myself higher. The weight of my pack and mean old Mr. Gravity started to pull me backwards into a thousand-foot slide down the steep granite slope. In desperation, I grabbed a second hold and it held.

I had to freeze right there for a minute until I got my heart back in my chest. I felt like I almost lost control of my sphincter, but regained my composure and proceeded up the mountain cautiously. I didn't think the fall would have killed me, but I was sure glad I didn't have to find out. I took a break at the summit, made coffee, and checked to see if I needed to change my shorts.

Zoma often left hearts behind as subtle messages for Cedar Moe, which he would point out to me. On the summit of Baldpate's East Peak, I found little tiny granite stones placed on the solid granite in the shape of a heart. The journals indicate Cedar Moe had caught up to Zoma and Lug, so I thought she may have left the message for me, personally. My eyes became misty as I fondly, but silently wished all of them God speed and the best. I paused to take a picture of the heart to remember my friends. I read in the journal that Cedar Moe had been planning to attend their wedding in Washington after the trail.

I wiped the tears from my eyes before I moved on fearing the descent. Fortunately, the descent was nothing special. It was steep and hard work, but I had descended many other steeper mountains. I hiked on driven by the lure of a hot shower and a town day. I called Christian's grandmother, Elaine from the top of a mountain about a mile from the road to Andover. Christian was hopefully still on the trail somewhere behind me. He hadn't arrived at his grandmother's yet. I was disappointed, but not surprised. I was hoping to see him and attend an Alcoholics Anonymous meeting with him in Maine. To my delight, Elaine was sending his grandfather Paul to pick me up at the trailhead on the highway, which was about an eight mile hitch from Andover.

I made it to the road in about an hour to find Paul waiting for me with a pitcher of fresh, ice-cold lemon aid, and a bag of potato chips. I felt cared for and took an instant liking to Paul. He looked to be of Italian descent in his mid-seventies with gray hair, sporting a goatee. He was from Boston and shut down his Bed and breakfast to return to the city each winter. He spoke with a heavy Boston accent and really hated the Yankees.

We chatted like old friends all the way to town. He filled me in on everything I would need to know about Andover before he took me on a tour of the small town. Andover was surprisingly flat, with few trees, and open spaces, reminiscent of a small town in the mid-west instead of Maine. Paul showed me the two restaurants slash convenience stores and the ice cream parlor. He also stopped at the post office so I could pick up my mail drop before it closed.

I asked him, "Are there any police in town?"

He said, "Naw, if there's any trouble we handle it ourselves." I had a vision of a mob of vigilantes hanging a rustler, but decided not to ask any more questions. I thought there were some things I was better off not knowing.

We went to his house where he and Christian's grandma, Elaine, ran the bed and breakfast for hikers and other travelers in the summer months. I rented a private room, settled in, and took a hot shower. Paul had a washer and dryer in his garage for hikers, so I did my laundry.

I returned to my room, which had no air conditioner and found it sweltering, but a strong thunderstorm hit and cooled things down some. I didn't often have the luxury of being able to take a nap, but laid down on the bed and the next thing I knew, it was two hours later. I felt refreshed as I spiffed up and walked three or four blocks into town.

I stopped at the first diner slash general store, which also had a mid-west flavor. The diner consisted of an open kitchen with a counter where I could sit to watch the food cooking, while I waited to eat. The store part sold groceries, beer, and hardware supplies. The place was buzzing with locals, but I didn't feel too out of place. I took a seat at the counter. The waitress slash cook had her back to me busily cooking. The hound dog in me couldn't help but notice she looked extremely attractive from behind. I hope I didn't show the shock on my face when she turned to wait on me. My heart literally skipped a beat because she had no teeth and whiskers, but other than that, she was an attractive woman. Yes, she was for sure a woman.

I finally got over my shock enough to realize I was staring and said, "Cacacacoffee." I ordered a cheeseburger and large order of fries and enjoyed them while getting used to my waitress. I stopped at the ice cream parlor on my way home. I froze as I went to enter the store because two large, lazy mutts lay on the porch. They weren't good watchdogs because they barely opened one eye to notice me as I stepped over them. I topped off my cheeseburger with a large strawberry ice cream cone which I ate while I walked home.

I returned to my room, kicked off my shoes and flopped down on my bed to enjoy the content feeling. I opened up my journal, so I wouldn't fall asleep before I entered the day's adventure.

Sought, was the first word in Step Eleven, which meant to me that no matter how close I got to God, I had to continue to seek understanding through contact. Alexander Graham Bell didn't stop seeking when he succeeded because he somehow knew more knowledge was out there.

When I was young and starting to drive, I went to town with my dad. He was going to let me drive when we came out of the hardware store, but I couldn't find my keys. I panicked a little and rechecked all my pockets a couple of times.

Dad said, "Do you have an inside pocket in your jacket?" I checked and to my relief they were in there.

I said, "My keys are always in the last place I look."

He said with a little sarcasm, "That's because when you find the keys you stop looking."

Unlike my keys, I had to continue seeking knowledge of God's will, so God could reveal more. God sometimes sent messages through unlikely people so I needed to stay humble and listen. I needed to remember that as soon as arrogance entered, my ego blocked my hearing. My ego allowed me to lock into a rigid, self-righteous type of thinking that made me think I found all the answers and like finding the keys, I stopped looking.

I once said to a preacher, "I think we might be spiritual beings on an earthly journey."

He said, "Screw your philosophy."

I resented him briefly until I realized he was afraid to think outside of what he learned from his religious background.

I talked to many folks who appear to be unwilling to even think outside the realm of what others told them to believe. They act as if they found the keys because of fear. I could identify with their fear. One of the reasons I rebelled against my Christian upbringing in the beginning was because of fear. The preacher told me what to believe and I would offend God if I ever dared to question anything. Religion led me to believe God knew every thought inside my head, so I was afraid to even think outside the box.

My core beliefs of God were of a punishing God, which was why I rebelled. I didn't understand a loving God. I found that even after my understanding of God changed, it took all the courage I could muster to continue to seeking because I felt fearful I would offend God with my questions.

I closed my journal and took off my glasses. I noticed it started raining again and the room cooled off. I turned off the lamp and thought the sound of the rain was comforting when I was safe and dry. That was the last thing I remember that night.

July 22   Day 147   10.1 Miles

Paul had the coffee pot on when I went down stairs. I was grateful for the luxury of having good coffee already made and waiting when I got up. I ate an omelet, home fries, toast, and coffee that Paul cooked for breakfast at the house. Paul dropped me off at the post office to mail a package and some letters to friends, while he went to fill the gas tank. He then shuttled me back to the trail.

I hiked over several mountains that day, the first of which was Moody Mountain. Paul told me the legend of Moody Mountain. A long time ago, the King of England granted a man named Moody the mountain and the adjoining land. Moody climbed the mountain to see all his territory. He fell off his mountain and died, so they named it Moody Mountain. I didn't know if the story was true, but it made a good story and probably a moral truth could be found in there somewhere. I found Moody Mountain extremely steep and at a few points, they even imbedded steel rods in the rock to form a permanent ladder to climb over the solid rock face. I could see how the mountain could have killed Moody.

It rained most of the day. I had to ford my first Maine stream called Sawyer Brook. I remember the first time I forded a stream back in Virginia, which seemed like a long time ago. In Virginia, a bridge washed out, so I stopped, took off my shoes and socks so they wouldn't get wet before I forded. In Maine, I barely paused to check it out before I plowed through. My feet had been wet more of the time than they were dry.

I traveled alone all day to South Arm Road, where Paul was to pick me up to take me back to the house. I arrived early and waited a couple hours until he came along. I met some other hikers there, but only one Nobo thru-hiker named Fast Lane.

Fast Lane was recovering from Lyme Disease. He stayed in Gorham, New Hampshire for two weeks when he was the sickest, while he treated the disease with antibiotics. He didn't have enough money to stay in a motel, but he wasn't going to abort his thru-hike. He lay around the park in the day and slept in the woods close to town at night, until he recovered enough to get back on the trail. He still took antibiotics and hiked slowly. He was only able to hike four miles that day. He didn't have a lot of money, so he couldn't afford to go into town. I wanted to take him with me to Andover, pay for the night, and buy him some food, but he declined and set up his tent right there in the rain. I had to hand it to him because he was tough. I so admired people like Fast Lane. I gave him what little food I still had left.

Paul picked me up and gave me cold lemon aid. Some hikers were at the house when I got back, but no thru-hikers. I took my shower and watched a science fiction movie with Paul and another hiker. I wasn't usually a science fiction fan, but I enjoyed the movie and the company.

I walked into town with the other hikers to the same diner for supper again. I had a big meatball sandwich with a large order of fries. I became a little afraid when I discovered the waitress was giving me a come on look. The hound dog in me flirted back a little. I was happy to be alone so the other hikers didn't witness the moment. I must remember to never tell my hiking buddies, Crow and Chief because they wouldn't ever let me forget it.

I returned to the house and socialized with the other hikers into the night before I turned in. I fell asleep to the sound of thunderstorms again that night.

Day 148   13.3 Miles

Paul cooked eggs, French toast, bacon, and coffee for a bunch of us at breakfast. He then shuttled us back to the trail in his van.

I faced another wet, rainy day on the trail. I hiked up Old Blue

Mountain, which was wet and slippery. They said you could see Katahdin on a clear day, but I could only see twenty feet. I found the top of Old Blue covered with scrub pines about as tall as me and socked in with a gloomy, gray mist. I became soaked to the bone from the constant downpour. The hiking was harder than usual because the steep slopes were so slippery. It took me eight hours to hike eight miles.

I met two Canadian Sobo section-hikers on top of Old Blue. They gave me maps of the trail to the north and filled me in on the details. I felt bad because I didn't have anything to give them in return. I encouraged them to hike on and simply said, "Thank you," then thumped my heart in the gesture I learned from the inner-city kids in Connecticut.

I worried about being hours late to meet Paul at the pickup point. I hiked in a frenzy trying to make time, which I knew was foolish given the conditions. Thankfully, I found enough cell-tower on the top of Bemis Mountain to call Paul and tell him I would be at least two hours late arriving at the highway. I felt better and took the time for a break to calm down.

I was happy to see Paul waiting for me with lemonade and potato chips, when I arrived at the pickup point. I was thankful to be spending the night in a warm, dry bed and not in my wet tent. I asked him if he waited long and he simply said, "I took the chance to catch up on some reading."

I especially appreciated the shower and the chance to put my wet clothes in the dryer. Paul took me on a tour of the area and we checked on some other property he and Elaine owned and rented out. We talked a lot about the Alcoholics Anonymous program. Paul was becoming a good friend who I could connect with on a spiritual level. He had been good for me and I would miss him when I moved on. That night would be the last night I could stay at their place.

I ate at the same local diner, but with other hikers. We had a different waitress, which disappointed me a little. I watched television with Paul for a while before I bid him goodnight and went to bed. I was exhausted from the day's hike, but my mind wouldn't shut down yet.

I felt like I was in such a git-r-done state of mind, that I wasted the day. I should have taken the time to smell the roses. I thought, *why not start your day over right now?* I realized I hadn't been taking time for prayer and meditation for a while, so I said a short prayer and forced my mind to focus on Step Eleven.

One of the reasons I was so attracted to Alcoholics Anonymous was they told me they didn't have the answers to spiritual matters. Instead they encouraged me to be open-minded and continue seeking to find my own answers. It was almost as if Alcoholics Anonymous gave me permission to form a unique personal relationship with God.

The lesson I learned over time was I had to be open to listening to God who talked in many different ways through all kinds of people, as he taught me his will. Sometimes the spirit whisper I got was only a little whisper, so I had to take the time to always be humble and listen closely. Above all else, I needed to keep an open mind at all times and not lock into thinking I had all the answers and stop looking for the keys.

I remembered when I was new in Alcoholics Anonymous an old timer, whose name I lost in time, quoted Jesus Christ saying, "Ask and you shall receive. Seek and you will find. Knock and the door will be opened unto you." I remembered I thought bullshit at the time, but now it all made perfect sense. How could I have been so blind?

I found the Alcoholics Anonymous slogan, "More will be revealed," was true. God always revealed more through other people and the spirit if I continued to humbly listen. I knew I didn't have all the answers. I probably didn't need all the answers, but it seemed okay to ask questions. I knew the more I sought, the more I found, the more I found, the more I trusted God, and the stronger my faith became. Maybe that was all I had to know. I seemed to calm down enough so I rolled on my side and that was the last thought I remembered.

Day 149   8.3 Miles

I sensed something was gravely wrong when I came downstairs. I looked at Elaine's eyes and she paused when our eyes locked communicating in silence on an intuitive level. She dropped her stare and said, "Paul is dreadfully ill this morning. He couldn't even get out of bed, so I'll cook breakfast." I could see the stress of the situation on her face.

I had no words to comfort or reassure her, so I placed my hand on her back. She turned and embraced me. I said, "How can I Help?" She shook her head negative and said, "We'll be okay," as she turned away to start breakfast. Elaine cooked breakfast and ran the shuttles. I offered to take a zero day to run the shuttles for her, but she declined. I waited at the house while she took the other hikers to a closer trailhead. She returned to shuttle me back to the trail where I got off the day before.

I didn't get the chance to say goodbye to Paul, so I said a silent prayer for him. I didn't know what I would have said to him anyway. Elaine dropped me at the trail unusually late in the morning for me, which was completely understandable. The day was cloudy and gloomy, but no rain. She took a picture of me with a large lake and the Maine forest in the background. She then gave me a hug to silently say goodbye. I would miss both her and Paul, but especially Paul because we connected spiritually as two drunks often did.

I met two section hikers starting at the trailhead, but I didn't talk to or hike with them, probably because I was overwhelmed, preoccupied, and depressed with worry. I hiked over Maxie Bald to Little Swift River Pond and found a campsite. I only hiked eight miles, but it felt like twenty on the rough trail with my bad ankle. I felt melancholy after I left the comforts of Paul and Elaine's bed and breakfast. I was also worried about Paul's health.

I ended up camping with the youth group I previously met at Carter Notch at the bunkhouse ten days before. The kids were noisy and things were chaotic. Normally, I would have enjoyed them, but that day they annoyed me. It was crowded, so I picked the best campsite I could, which wasn't very level. That would be the first time in four days I had to sleep in my tent. My ankle was too painful to move on to find a better place to camp.

The section hikers I met earlier came in and wanted to set up next to me. I asked if they snored and the one said, "Like a chainsaw," so I stopped them and strongly suggested they set up somewhere else. They did and I felt a little guilty, but I would have been up all night with resentments if they stayed.

I stayed in my tent and chose to isolate from the others. I took some extra ibuprofen to try to ease the ankle pain. I knew I wasn't being grateful and needed to focus on something positive and quit bitching. The only thing positive I could come up with was the realization I was only two-hundred and twenty-five miles from Mount Katahdin.

I remembered a short, heavy man who was built like a fireplug in the program. His nickname was Twiggy. Twiggy had passed on, but he was an icon in Alcoholics Anonymous, and famous for one-liner words of wisdom. One was, "Give it to God and let Him worry about it. He's got to stay up all night any way and you get a good night's sleep." I said a prayer with Twiggy in mind and turned it over to God, "God, please protect Paul and Elaine and help me cope with the pain in my ankle, Amen."

My thoughts immediately turned to an idea Lady D gave me many years ago. She told me to write the problem or situation down on a piece of paper and put it in a God box. I wrote down any situation that was especially troubling me on a piece of paper and sealed in an envelope. On the outside of the envelope, I would date it thirty days from that time and put it in my God box. I symbolically gave my problem to God. When I opened the envelope in thirty days, the situation was often resolved.

I took a piece of paper from my notebook and wrote, Paul, Elaine, and my injured ankle. I folded my list into a small strip, wrote August twenty-four, 2006 on the back, and stashed it in my money belt. I felt an immediate sense of relief as if God took the burden, only because I gave it to him. I said aloud, as if I was talking to someone, *It's all in God's hands now.* I lay back, calculating that I could hike the two-hundred and twenty-five miles in a lot less than thirty days. I wondered how I would feel by then after completing my hike. I put on a Kataro CD to drown out the noise and tried to go to sleep early to escape the pain. Twiggy also had another slogan, "Everyday ain't Christmas." I guess that day just wasn't Christmas.

Day 150   15.5 Miles

I slept poorly last night and woke up in a foul mood. I packed up and left without breakfast because I didn't want to talk to anyone. My ankle was swollen and painful, so I took extra ibuprofen, put on some music, and sucked it up. I hiked to the highway at Sandy River by late morning. The parking lot at the trailhead was buzzing with day hikers staging to hike to Piazza Rock and the summit of Saddleback Mountain. I hurried past them, purposely avoiding eye contact, because I didn't want to talk to anyone. One young man caught my attention by yelling, "Hey buddy, you thru-hiking?" I made brief eye contact, nodded yes with my best unfriendly expression, and rudely pushed past him. Day hikers normally didn't annoy me, but I was in a mood where everything seemed to piss me off. I think God noticed I was in trouble and sent a rowboat in the form of a day hiker, but I ignored that angel. I hiked to Piazza Rock, to a sign that said, Do not continue or go any farther if after noon. It was eleven o'clock, so I pushed on wanting to out run myself.

God knew my Achilles Heel, so miraculously my path intersected with an extremely attractive, well-endowed thru-hiker limping southward. She stopped and asked how far to the highway where she could hitch to town. I saw she had some trouble by the look in her eyes. I took my pack off and sat down on it to take a break. She must have felt safe because she did likewise. At first we exchanged information in the usual Nobo meets Sobo fashion.

I asked, "Why the limp?

She replied, "I hurt my knee and need a zero day in town to heal up."

Instinctively, I involuntarily blurted out, "There's more to it."

The conversation soon took a more personal turn as she disclosed she was contemplating aborting her thru-hike. She was all alone, lonely, feeling home sick, and missed the friends and family she left behind. She was overwhelmed and depressed with her physical and emotional pain. She only saw the negative side of the unknowns that lay ahead and blind to the positive rewards waiting ahead on her journey.

I recalled an old saying, it takes one to know one. I felt her pain within myself, so I reflected back to when I was two hundred miles into my hike on the seemingly impossible journey that lay ahead. I put myself back into the place where she was at and I could relate to what she felt. Suddenly, I realized I too was emotionally and physically in the same state. I listened to myself as I encouraged her to stick it out, keep on keeping on, this too shall pass, and the rewards would be great. I told her about the emotional difficulties on this roller coaster ride they called the Appalachian Trail. I could tell she was relating to me on a spiritual level.

I felt safe enough to describe my concern over my friend Paul. I purposely did not share my fear regarding my ankle injury because I was afraid I might discourage her even more than she already was. I shared the story of how I almost aborted my hike in the Smoky Mountains due to my back pain. I told her about how out of control and terrified I was over the wart on my toe in the Shenandoah. I hesitated, but changed my mind and decided to take off my left shoe, ankle brace, and sock exposing my swollen ankle.

I said, "I fear this may knock me off the trail, but not today." She reached over with her left hand to grasp the back of my right hand and squeezed it firmly. I looked at her and smiled as I could see the sparkle return to her eyes.

She said, "Dreamer, we both can and will make it."

I turned my hand over, with tears in my eyes and said, "Yes, we will," as we clutched each other's hand tightly, holding on to each other's strength.

I gave her hope by sharing my experience, strength and hope with her the same way I would encourage a new AA member to continue their journey towards sobriety. They say, *you have to give it away to keep it.* I noticed as her mood started changing and she gained confidence, my confidence, strength, and hope, also increased.

I didn't know how long we talked, but I knew when we were done. We stood and I reached out to shake her hand, but instead she pulled me close hugging me as if we had been friends for a long time. I moved on in a better frame of mind. I remembered, God sometimes sent help even before we asked. I thought about the old saying that defines a coincidence as an event where God chooses to remain anonymous. I wasn't sure if God put her in my life or put me in hers for a brief moment in time, but I knew how grateful I felt to have met her and I never even knew her name. Maybe she was an angel.

I paused on the trail, closed my eyes, and said, "Thanks, God." I moved on a short distance before I recalled the hug. I stopped again, closed my eyes in gratitude, and said, "God thanks for sending this lecherous old pigdog sinner the angel with the big boobs, Amen."

I always was amazed at the huge difference a simple attitude adjustment made in every aspect of my life. I went from the verge of assaulting some poor unsuspecting hiker to Dr. Martin Luther King-like. I believed God deserved the credit for that one. I hoped God has a sense of humor as I resumed hiking. I remembered an old Bill Cosby comedy skit where Noah said, "Who is this really?" I snickered at the thought, but the old fear of God punishing me for being a smartass, wiped the smirk off my face.

I continued to ponder, exactly who God is as I hiked in solitude. I was above tree line, but the clouds that enclosed Saddleback stole the views. I knew I was above tree line with zero cover because of the barren rock. I wasn't afraid to the extent I experienced on Mount Adams, but I felt uneasy, so I prayed, not for any particular reason at first. I only wanted to feel the comfort of the presence of God. I stopped on the trail, tucked my poles under my arms to free my hands, closed my eyes, folded my hands, and stood there. I felt the mist on my face that engulfed the mountain and me. I wasn't meditating, but I didn't know what to say. I felt awkwardly embarrassed, because I summoned God's attention and had nothing to ask him. I blurted out the first thing I thought of which was, "Who are you anyway?" I quickly moved on hoping God was busy with some crisis and hadn't noticed me. I didn't know if it was God's answer, but instantly, the first words of the Lord's Prayer popped into my head. We all joined hands at the end of every Alcoholics Anonymous meeting and said, "Our Father who art in heaven." Those words came from Jesus Christ himself.

I could identify with being both a father and a son. My dad always loved me even when he was angry at what I had done. I believed I gave him good reasons to hate me, but I always felt his love. My own children pissed me off at times, but I always loved them even if I didn't approve of their decisions. Phyllis and I didn't speak to each other at one time for almost three years, but I still loved her every second even though I was incredibly angry. I could see the parallel between earthly parents and God plainly now. I smiled when I thought of the line "I once was blind, but now I see." God always made it all simple for me to understand; I was the one who complicated everything.

I spent four hours above tree line in ominous weather. I climbed two-thousand feet up Saddleback Mountain. They said you could see Mount Katahdin from Saddleback on a clear day, but once again, the weather hid the mighty mountain. I took a picture of a weather-beaten sign that marked the summit. I stood peering into the fog, but only saw the closest mountains and then only shadows.

I had a moment of clarity where the spirit rode in on the wind to whisper in my ear, God is with you always, but sometimes your ego becomes so thick like the mist it hides Him from you. I knew from faith Mount Katahdin, like God, was out there even though I couldn't see either one with my mortal eyes. I felt I understood a little more about my God after the insight from the spirit.

The thunder started to rumble in the distance when I was a little ways below the summit of Saddleback. I could see the thunderclouds coming from the west and it looked like they would miss the summit and blow by. I was contemplating whether to move on or hold up when I met a couple of Sobos and they said I could take cover in some trees in the gap between Saddleback and Horn Mountain. I decided to go over the top because it was farther to safety if I went back south.

I climbed and hiked faster as the thunder closed in on the mountain. I reached the summit of Saddleback Mountain and then dropped down about five-hundred feet. I found the patch of trees the Sobos told me about with enough flat ground to pitch a tent. The storm hit so I stopped in the safety of the cover and almost set up my tent. I thought it over and decided to see if I could wait out the worst of the storm. The weather eventually settled into a steady rain and the thunder moved on. It looked like a cold front moved in, so I chose to move on to a safer place.

I came to the summit of Horn Mountain and the clouds cleared enough to see the ridge leading to Saddleback Junior Mountain. The small victory gave me the confidence I needed to keep moving on, hoping the storm passed. I hurried the next mile and a half to the safety of Poplar Ridge Lean-to. Several people had already taken cover in the shelter for the night, so I found a flat place away from the shelter to set up my tent. The storm passed, so I returned to the shelter for the company. I was delighted to find Fast Lane there, looking better physically, along with several Sobo hikers. We cooked and ate together while Fast Lane and I shared trail tales of what the trail was like to the south. The Sobos shared what the trail was like to the north, but they hadn't been on the trail long enough to learn to tell good trail tales yet. The camaraderie made for a pleasant evening of socializing.

I asked Fast Lane to share his story with us. Fast Lane declined, but I encouraged him and the others joined in, so he humbly told his story of how he overcame Lyme disease. He stopped several times to rest and recover, which threw him way behind his schedule and cost more money than he intended. He had very little money left, so he couldn't stay in towns or motels, but he wouldn't ask for or accept any money. He didn't complain, make excuses, or blame. Yet he hung in there and overcame his huge, unforeseen adversity to complete his goal. Fast Lane's story was a true inspiration to all of us. He was the level of person I wanted to influence me. When I looked at his problems, my ankle seemed insignificant.

I returned to the sanctuary of my tent after Fast Lane's story, a completely different man than when I awoke a couple mornings ago at Paul and Elaine's. The day was a particularly difficult day, but as I wrote the account in my journal, I realized it was an exceptionally good day. I had hope inspired by the day, that I too could overcome any unforeseen adversity.

Day 151   13.1 Miles

My air mattress went flat in the night. I would wake up uncomfortable, blow it back up, and it would go flat again. I repeated the process often enough that I didn't sleep well. I stripped the threads on my stove when I tried to make coffee about daylight. My ankle hurt until the ibuprofen kicked in. I started my day with cold coffee, which was the only thing I could think of that could make my horrible, hot instant coffee worse. I stopped to say goodbye to Fast Lane and the Sobos at the shelter before I left.

The day was gray and gloomy, which matched my mood. A violent thunderstorm broke out before I reached the summit of Mount Spalding. I couldn't find anywhere to take shelter, but at least I was below tree line. I kept going because I didn't know what else to do. Fast Lane caught up to me and I found comfort hiking with him. We stopped at Spalding Mountain Lean-to where he stayed to wait out the storm. I moved on because the shelter had a metal roof, which I was afraid to stay under with lightning ripping through the air that high up.

Eventually, the lightning and heavy rain stopped, but the day stayed overcast and glum with the constant threat of rain. I contemplated stopping at Sugar Loaf Mountain Trail, which according to my guidebook, led six tenths of a mile to a summit house with splendid views from Mount Washington all the way to Mount Katahdin. They permitted hikers to stay one night, but I doubted if I would see too far in the gloomy atmosphere and I didn't feel up to hiking that far off trail with no views.

I struggled to ford the Carabassett River, swollen by the heavy rains. Oh yes, Maine sports many fast rivers and few bridges. When the guidebook said ford it wasn't talking about a ride in a truck, it was talking about getting wet. With all the rain, the streams and rivers were all swollen, so I got wet a lot. I hoped Fast Lane would catch up, but he must have stopped for the day somewhere.

The river offered to sing me to sleep if I stayed, so being exhausted from the crossing, I accepted. Fortunately, I found a nice, flat, unofficial campsite within sight of the river to set my tent up. I gathered twigs and the driest wood I could to make a fire to cook tuna and noodles. The woods were soaked from all the rain, so making a fire was more of a task than it normally would have been, but the reward was a hot meal.

I crawled into my wet sleeping bag after darkness ended the ominous red and gray sunset. I started to think about the insight about, Our Father who art in heaven and my dad. When I was almost twelve-years-old, I wanted a shotgun so I could hunt rabbits when I turned twelve. I saved thirty-four dollars and seventy cents, which was all the money I earned from two seasons of trapping muskrats. Now my dad wasn't a gun or hunting enthusiast, but he didn't oppose nor disapprove of hunting. One day he said, "I know a man who has a little Stevens, double barrel, four-ten shotgun for sale. If you want, we can go look at it." I didn't have words to describe how excited I became as I quickly gathered all my money. The man's name was Ed and he originally bought it for his wife who died several years before. When I held it, I thought it was the finest gun ever made. I popped the question as nonchalantly as an excited almost twelve-year-old could, "What do ya have to have for it?" My heart sunk when he said, "Forty five dollars firm, but I'll throw in two boxes of shells."

I remember I was trying to blink away a tear when there was a tap on my arm. Without saying a word, Dad nonchalantly handed me a ten dollar bill with a quarter and a nickel folded up inside. Dad knew I wanted the gun and he loved me enough to help me buy it. I drifted off to sleep with a smile on my face, thinking of how much I loved my dad.

Day 152   8.6 Miles

Late in the night ,a violent thunder and lightning storm struck. The lightning lit up the sky enough that I could see the mountains in the distance. I was alone and frightened in my tent, but I survived and eventually went back to sleep after the storm passed until almost daylight. I packed up a wet tent and sleeping bag shortly after sunrise. Yes, I said sunrise because that strange light they call the sun showed itself. I made cold instant coffee, yuck. I ate the cold Ramen noodles I soaked overnight to soften, double yuck! The pain in my ankle was excruciating, but I could limp.

The good news was the rain stopped and the sun looked like it would turn the gray clouds of the past into a clear sunny day. The promise of a motel with clean dry sheets, a shower, and a soft bed in Stratton, only nine trail miles and a five-mile hitch away, motivated me in a positive way. I could buy food that didn't need a to be cooked at a grocery store and a hot meal at a restaurant.

I took eight-hundred milligrams of ibuprofen, put on some of my new music to drown out the pain before I rode out singing a duet with John Denver. I thought it couldn't get any better when the summit of Crocker Mountain treated me to one of the most splendid panoramic views I had ever witnessed. White fluffy clouds filled the valleys leveling off evenly at the same altitude, which made them look more as if they were a frozen lake covered with pure, white snow or fluffy cotton. The mountaintops looked like distant islands in the majestic sea of cotton. I stopped to take pictures of the beauty of it all. I thought cold coffee and cold soggy noodles were a small price to pay to behold such a magnificent piece of God's artwork. Grateful for the blessing, I dropped my pack, sat down, folded my hands, and gave thanks for the privilege and good fortune to be on the Appalachian Trail. I closed my eyes, feeling the warmth of the morning sun on my body. I welcomed Mother Nature to come in and cleanse my soul. My thoughts drifted back in time to when I was sixteen years old.

I wanted a car more than anything in the world at the time. Dad gave me an old 1953 Chevy with a blown engine, but the body was good. We bought another wrecked 53 Chevy with a good motor for twenty-five dollars. He then took his time to teach me how to change the engine. We worked hard, side by side to make one good car. I never liked doing mechanic work, but I would always cherish the time I spent working on cars with my Dad. I had often heard the saying, "Give a man a fish and you feed him for a day, but teach a man how to fish and you feed him for a life time." I didn't realize it, but now I see, Dad was teaching me how to fish.

The sun eventually burned the clouds away and my view slipped away forever, but my mind would store the memory of that morning until time takes it away from me. The nine miles to the highway seemed to melt away sometime in the morning and I stopped at a stream my Guidebook said was three-tenths of a mile from the highway. I stripped off my clothes and took a bath in the icy mountain stream so I wouldn't be offensive to whoever picked me up hitching. I put on my one pair of clean shorts, my cleanest dirty shirt, a little patchouli oil, and off to town I went.

A Maine native, who made his living as a lumberjack for fifty years, gave me a ride to Stratton. He was a salty old cuss and filled me in on the lumber industry then and now. The ride and the lumberjack seemed to be all part of my journey. He said some things I would have to ponder on later. I checked into a private room at the Stratton Motel for forty dollars. I took my usual shower while I did my laundry my usual way. I went across the street to a restaurant and bought two red hotdogs, French fries, and a cup of good hot coffee. I called Scooter and asked her to send her pocket rocket stove and air mattress to me at the post office in Monson, which was about five days away. I then went to the post office in Stratton and bought a box to mail my stove, flat air mattress, and some other things back home to lighten my pack.

A variety of hikers were in the bunkroom at the motel when I returned. A hiker could stay in the bunkroom at the motel for fifteen dollars. Some of the hikers started the charcoal grill and were grilling steaks. I found the aroma of grilled steak heavenly, especially after eating cold ramen noodles. I crossed the street to the grocery store and bought enough supplies to last until I got to Monson where Scooter was mailing a package to me.

After I took care of all my business, I took my time to browse through all the steaks in the store to purchase the best thick steak they sold. I hurried back and threw my supplies in my room. I then threw the steak on the grill and stood there with my Spork and knife watching it sizzle with the greatest of anticipation. I patiently cooked it to medium rare perfection. I would remember it as the best steak I ever ate. I sat at the picnic table and ate my steak and talked to the other hikers into the night.

Day 153   10.4 Miles

I went across the street to the restaurant for breakfast. I had an omelet, toast, home fries and coffee. It was by far the worst breakfast I had eaten since I had been on the trail. The coffee was good, but don't forget, I was drinking cold, instant coffee before.

When I checked in, the owner of the motel agreed to shuttle me back to the trail, but he went drinking with some hikers and I couldn't wake him up. I waited a while, then decided to hitch a ride. A man who smoked was on vacation in Maine, picked me up and shuttled me back to the trail. I was grateful, but I had a low physical tolerance for cigarette smoke. I said nothing and endured it because he was kind enough to stop out of the goodness of his heart for a stranger like me.

I hiked in solitude, in a driving rain over the Bigelow Mountains. I was disappointed again because the Sobos told me stories about the beauty of the mountains, but only vague, dark gray shadows of mountains appeared throughout the gloomy day. The going was hard on the rugged, rocky trail, which aggravated my ankle. I wanted to stop for the night and rest, but couldn't find a piece of flat ground big enough to set my tent on. I looked in the guidebook and it said tent platforms were at Stafford Notch three-tenths of a mile off trail.

I arrived at Stafford Notch and found the poorly marked trail. The trail was so difficult I had to climb through and over a lot of debris from fallen rocks and trees. In one place, the trail went under a rock about the size of a building. I started to think I was on the wrong trail because it seemed like I trudged a lot farther than three tenths of a mile. I was thinking no one would hike that trail from hell, when I heard voices of young girls in the middle of nowhere. I walked into a surreal encampment of more than twenty young French-speaking girls who wore dresses that could have been part of their religion or culture. Huge tents occupied all the tent platforms that I saw.

I asked them if they knew of any more places to camp, but they only looked at me with blank looks. Apparently, they didn't speak English. I had no idea what they were saying and they didn't understand me either. Just as I started to think I had entered a dream-world that only existed in my damaged mind, they summoned a girl from one of the tents to interpret. She spoke a little broken English, so we communicated the best we could. I thought she indicated campsites were off to the side further on. My heart sunk, but I took the path hoping for the best.

I traveled about another quarter of a mile and found an old, broken down, lopsided tent platform, which was starting to rot. I didn't believe anyone used it for ten years or more, because Mother Nature was starting to digest it. I left my pack on it while I explored further on down the trail hoping to find a better place. I returned with no luck, so I gathered some flat stones about the size of plates, and propped up the side of the platform that was broken down. I leveled it the best I could, bounced gently a few times and it held, so I set up my tent on my new home.

I checked for cell tower, but wasn't surprised to find no signal in the hollow. I unpacked and everything including my food bag was sopping wet. I killed all the mosquitoes in the tent and laid back on my wet bag in wet clothes. I gazed at the ceiling as the rain continued to pound on the tent. I was cold, wet, lonely, and depressed. My ankle swelled causing a sharp pain in it every time my heart beat, and I had already taken enough ibuprofen to make old Doc Turner shit. I thought maybe I should pray, but what would I pray for, gratitude? I was miserable and pissed off, but in a masochistic way, I enjoyed feeling sorry for myself.

I watched a small fly I missed on my killing spree bounce off the ceiling, which became a sport for me sometimes on the trail. I was wallowing in my own shit when a vision of Father Joseph Martin, a salty old alcoholic who I held in extremely high regard, barged into my pity party. He was pointing a finger at me as he said, "Sounds like God gave you a chance to grow and you blew it." I laughed out loud until tears blurred my vision of the fly. I said, "Okay, you're right, I'm lucky to get this creaky old platform. I'm safe and out of the harsh Maine weather, plus I'll soon escape the day in sleep. I'm sure tomorrow will be better."

I ate peanut butter on soggy bagels for supper. I unzipped my waterlogged sleeping bag to cover myself like a blanket. My synthetic bag warmed me up even when it was wet. I realized I was truly grateful to be off the trail and home for the night. I said, "Thanks God and I'm sorry for being such an ungrateful asshole" before I pulled the bag over my head, trying to end the day. My mood completely transformed from only moments before. I realized how lucky I was God forgave so easily.

Dad was also quick to forgive me. I took a full-time night job in a foundry while I was still in high school, making cast iron vises. It was hard physical work, but I was seventeen-years-old and tough. Besides, the job paid well. I fell in love with a 1964 Pontiac GTO. It was three years old, maroon with mag wheels. Under the hood lived a big, eight-cylinder engine with three, two-barrel carburetors that were called three deuces. The car also sported a four-speed transmission with a Hurst shifter. The Beach Boys even had a hit song about a GTO. I lusted after the car, but Dad was adamantly opposed to me buying the car. We argued more over the car than anything else ever.

He said, "You'll kill yourself!"

I remembered reassuring him, "Dad, I promise I won't break the speed limit."

He said, "I was seventeen once too and I'm not stupid."

Our wills clashed in the kitchen one Sunday morning and Dad punched me in my smart mouth out of frustration. I was pretty froggy at seventeen, but I didn't return fire.

I looked him straight in the eye, lowered my voice and defiantly said, "Nice punch." I then did an about-face and walked away with full intentions of never, ever speaking to him again.

I was so pissed it took me about a week to cool off, regret the decision I made, and start missing my dad. My foolish pride continued to keep me away until Mom came to visit, early one morning. I hadn't considered how bad the situation between Dad and me was hurting her. I agreed to swallow my pride and go talk to the old man.

Dad worked nights and usually slept in, but he was awake, sitting in the kitchen drinking coffee and smoking a cigarette when I walked in. He stood up and faced me, but he didn't say a word as he held his face in a frozen stare that I could still see.

I broke the silence by saying, "I'm sorry, I'll never speak of the car again." He never broke eye contact as he put the cigarette down.

I was expecting a punch, but he extended his hand and said, "Your, Mom and me would like you to move back into your room, son."

I shook his hand and said, "Okay, I would like that."

His face softened and he smiled, but didn't say a word as we stood there still clasping hands. The silence got too uncomfortable for me, so I broke eye contact and said, "I got to go to work now, but I'll be home after work." He didn't say a word, but pressed his lips together in a tight smile and nodded his head as he squeezed my hand. Again, I did an about-face, but that time it was so he couldn't see me cry.

The feeling I had that morning as I went to work was hard to describe. It was the same feeling I felt when I started to make contact with God after being away for so long in my addiction. Probably it was the same feeling the prodigal son had when he returned to his father in the parable Jesus told. I had grown to understand hard times like that were not necessarily always bad if I learned from them. The event actually brought me closer to Dad and strengthened our relationship. Dad never raised his hand to me ever again, which said a lot for his patience. You probably find it hard to believe a nice son like me deserved punched a lot.

When I looked back over my day, I saw God actually gave me a chance to grow and I almost blew it. I folded my hands in gratitude and said aloud, "Lord, thanks for blessing me with the day to grow and thank you again for giving me such a great father and mother, Amen." I went to sleep, hoping the morning would be sunny.

July 29   **Day 154**   **12.2 Miles**

I didn't sleep well, because a strong wind woke me up some time in the night. I spent the rest of the night worrying about trees falling on me. I suspected a cold front settled in because the rain stopped, the wind died down, and the temperature dropped considerably. I ate soggy bagels with peanut butter and topped it off with cold instant coffee for breakfast. I packed up as the predawn gray started to push the night away. The bright side was the wind dried my tent so I didn't have to pack a wet, heavy tent.

The side trail was so difficult, I decided to wait until it was light enough to safely see before I left. I swallowed some ibuprofen and stretched my ankle in an attempt to ease my pain. I sat on my pack shivering, wishing I had a hot cup of the tar, I called coffee. I tried to escape in meditation or by dreaming of future adventures, but I was too miserable. At last, the morning light arrived, allowing me to limp away. The French-speaking girls were still sleeping as I silently slipped by their encampment. I believe I went undetected because no one stirred.

The sun gradually burned off the clouds and the day turned into a crisp, clear, fall-like day, which was perfect for hiking. Eventually, a combination of the release of endorphins and the ibuprofen reduced my pain level to tolerable, so I could enjoy my journey. The morning was still young when the trail gave me a full view of Little Bigelow Mountain, which stood about an hour north by trail. I stopped and took a picture of the majestic mountain as a lone cloud still concealed its summit. I began to feel grateful because things changed for the better that morning, but the attitude change from within me opposed to the day before was the change for which I was most grateful.

At home, a timer started brewing my coffee in an electric coffeemaker before the alarm even went off each morning. I would pour coffee flavored with creamer and sweetener, into a clean cup. I drank the coffee while I took a hot shower in a warm, private bathroom, dried off with a clean towel, and put on clean, fresh clothes. I ate rye toast with two eggs, I cooked on a gas stove, and drove to work in a heated car. I would bitch all the way to work, because I wasn't grateful for anything. My mind was completely focused on what I perceived as wrong, what I didn't have, what I couldn't control, or change. I believed I was starting to learn to see the positive side of my life, but I still fell into negative thinking. I would dwell on what I felt was wrong outside myself. I still felt grateful for the modern day amenities, but I saw adversity as a negative thing.

Maybe life on the trail slowed me down enough so I could listen to the spirit whisper softly, adversity was always a gift to be a motivator to grow stronger emotionally, spiritually, and physically. I moved on a different hiker, thankful for the attitude of gratitude from the insight.

I arrived at the summit of Little Bigelow marked by a sign nailed to a scrub pine. I was hoping for a vista, but at only three-thousand feet high, I was too far below tree line, so Mother Nature's garden blocked the views of distant mountains. I thought I was at the end of the Bigelow Mountains, so I took a picture of the sign. I then saluted the sign, thanked the mountains, and I bid them goodbye.

I dropped from the steep mountains to below fourteen-hundred feet for the rest of the day. The topography of the land changed drastically as lakes, beaver dams, swamps, and thickly wooded forests replaced the mountains. I felt as if I was suddenly in another part of the world. I wasn't disappointed and found my new environment equally as enchanting. The beaver dams especially amazed me at how Mother Nature's little furbearers could engineer and construct such an environment so many species called home. Surprisingly, the trail led to a vista overlooking a huge glacier lake. I looked in the guidebook and discovered it was West Carry pond, but to call it a pond was greatly misleading.

I followed the trail to West Carry Pond Lean-to on the lake by early afternoon. I had easily hiked twelve miles with the smooth trail and easy footfall. I felt I deserved a break so I decided to set up my tent and spread out my wet gear to dry on a groomed campsite not far from the shelter. I was a little sleepy, so I crawled in my tent to nap. The next thing I knew it was late in the afternoon.

I made a little fire to brew some hot coffee. I took my coffee to the lake and sat there enjoying the solitude as the fog from my nap lifted. The lake's rough surface sparkled like diamonds in the sun. The morning winds died down, but some white caps remained, as I gazed across the water trying to decide whether to move on or stay for the night. I checked my guidebook, which said it was ten miles to the next campsite. I didn't feel up to ten more miles that day, so I decided to stay. Besides, the lake seemed like a splendid place to meditate and turn my mind loose.

After I moved back into the house with Mom and Dad, I decided to wait until after I turned eighteen and moved out of the house to buy a Pontiac GTO in order to keep the peace between Dad and me. I resigned myself to never bring up the subject again and act as if nothing ever happened.

Dad was a printer all his life and worked third shift for a local newspaper. He would get home from work at two-thirty every morning. Ever since I was a little boy, if I woke up, I would go down to the kitchen and talk to him as he ate toast, drank coffee, and smoked a cigarette before he went to bed. Dad was always in a good mood and we would talk a while before we went upstairs together.

One morning, about a month after I moved back in, I was talking to Dad in the kitchen as he was winding down from work. Dad asked me how much money I had saved. I said, "Seven hundred dollars," but didn't think anything about it at the time. The conversation took a turn and eventually, we went to bed.

The sound of hikers at the shelter interrupted my meditative trance. I went to the shelter and introduced myself to a girl from Georgia named Bloody Mess and a guy from Oregon named Fortune Cookie. They were Nobo thru-hikers, hiking together. Apparently a trail angel left beer in the shelter, so they drank it as we talked. Some section hikers came in along with a Sobo thru-hiker, so the party was on. I was happy for the company and wasn't tempted to drink. My mood improved tremendously. I didn't realize how lonely I had gotten. I didn't go back to my tent until well after dark.

Day 155   19.7 Miles

I awoke before daybreak, startled by the sound of something big outside my tent. A bull moose in velvet greeted me when I went out to investigate. I quietly got my camera and took several close-up pictures. The pictures didn't turn out well, but they were spooky. The flash wasn't strong enough to show the moose, but reflected his eyes glowing like two red-hot coals in the woods. The pictures looked demonic. The flash intimidated him enough that he left. I read a book once that said bull moose wouldn't charge in the early summer, but he might not have read the same book on moose that I did, so I was relieved when he sauntered off.

I ate a cold breakfast, and drank cold coffee while I shivered in the cold of the early morning air. I would be happy when I got a new stove and could drink hot coffee on fall-like mornings. My trail coffee was bad enough when it was hot, but when it was cold it was torture to drink. I packed and left as quietly as possible so I didn't wake the people in the shelter. I was fortunate the trail followed the lakeshore for a while, because the soft footfall on the sand and level trail allowed my ankle time to loosen up. The exertion drove the chill from my bones as endorphins kicked in, which freed my mind from the pain of my body.

I stopped to take off my pack on a beach covered with fine sand to watch the sunrise over the water. I took a deep breath, sucking in all the air my lungs could hold, noticing the slight breeze carried a pleasant scent of the lake to my nostrils. I prayed because it seemed like the perfect time and place to say thanks for the gifts I have already received. I learned to no longer compare myself to others, competing with them, and feeling envious. Instead, I tried to improve my relationship with God as I understood him, and accept what he gave me. My mind returned to where I left off the day before when I met the others in the shelter.

A few days after I had the conversation with Dad at two-thirty in the morning, I was in my room listening to the radio and doing a little homework before supper. I was doing more listening to the radio because I did little if any homework in those days. Dad knocked on the door before he came in. He turned the radio off and sat on the bed. He then pulled out his pack of Tareytons and extended the pack towards me to offer me one. Dad knew I smoked, but I never ever smoked in front of him., When I was younger he told me he would break my jaw if he caught me smoking. I declined, but he shook one out and nodded as if to silently give me permission, but I still declined. He took the cigarette and shook out another one, put them both in his mouth at the same time, pulled out his Zippo, lit them both, and handed me one. I felt odd, but took it, no longer feeling fearful.

He took a drag and asked, "They sold the car yet?"

I blew out smoke and shook my head no.

He said. "The car will pass anything but a gas station and break down all the time." Then he added, "It'll take your paycheck every week to keep it running."

I took another drag on my Tareyton and looked him straight in the eye as I realized he was going to give me permission to buy the GTO.

He said, "Son, I'll never forgive myself if you kill yourself in the damn car."

I reassured him, "I won't, Dad."

He said, "By my calculations you still need about seven-hundred dollars, so you skip school tomorrow and we'll go see Cliff Hipple after I get up. If he'll lend you the money, we'll buy the car." I wasn't sure why Dad had such a change of heart, but it seemed too good to be true. I had a hard time sleeping that night due to the anticipation of owning a GTO.

Dad gave, I accepted; God gives, I need to accept. With tears in my eyes, I picked up my pack with one hand, swinging it on my back as I stood up in one flowing motion. I filled my lungs again, smelling the air. I was sixteen-years-old again as I walked away.

The contour of the land was low, flat, and about the same as the day before. I hiked to Arnold Point which had a sandy beach with a swimming area. I was afraid the water would be too cold for my liking, but I was hoping for a concession stand or convenience store, but no such luck. I stopped briefly to watch the boats and water skiers.

Next was Arnold Swamp, which was a wild, wilderness swamp and a contrast from the lake. That was the kind of diversity Maine added to the trail experience. The swamp would have been intimidating to cross if it wasn't for the hard work of trail volunteers, who constructed log-plank walkways. The elevation dropped even more to below a thousand feet and resembled a tropical paradise with jungle, beaver dams, swamps, and whitewater creeks. I stopped for a brief snack at

Pierce Pond Lean-to, which also had a swimming beach. I was hot, dirty, and a swim would have been nice, but I wanted to move on.

I wanted to get to the Kennebec River as soon as possible, so I could catch the canoe before the canoe service closed for the day. It was fourteen miles to the river from where I started in the morning, but I had already hiked ten of those miles. If I was lucky, I might get across the river before noon when the man who ran the canoe ferry went home for lunch.

The Kennebec River was a large, powerful river with a man-made dam that released water to generate electric power when needed. The trail crossed the river some distance below the dam. The river was unpredictable and had been deadly when the water rose suddenly after being released. They warned hikers they couldn't cross the river faster than the water rose once it started to rise. An unfortunate hiker drowned fording the river, so the Maine Appalachian Trail Club and the state of Maine provided funding for the ferry service. To not take the canoe could be suicide.

I arrived at the river a little after high noon and an empty canoe was on the beach on the other side of the river, but no one was around. The river didn't look intimidating, but I wasn't about to take a chance and try to ford after all the warnings. I had some time to kill because the ferryman wouldn't return until two o'clock. I explored for a while. I guessed the water was low because they weren't releasing any water for power.

I blew up my air mattress, sat down, and took my boots off to soak my ankle. I found the water warm enough to take a little swim to clean up and smell better. I took everything out of my pockets and walked cautiously into the water with my air mattress for safety. I laid on the mattress in the water, relaxing, and washing my clothes while wearing them. I pulled the mattress up on the stony beach and kicked back in the sun to dry. I laid on my back with my fingers interlaced behind my head and gazed up at the clear, blue sky as I released my thoughts to the pleasant past experience with my dad.

The old bank was almost as intimidating as the old church. It was bigger than most of the other buildings in town and made of stone.

Above the front door, carved in stone, were the capital letters BANK. Inside, the floor was made of marble and the fancy molded metal ceiling must have been about twenty feet high. A horseshoe counter about four foot high with Glass windows mounted on top, provided a barrier for the clerks to stand behind and serve customers through their individual windows. Only two clerks were on duty that day.

I followed Dad to the window of an attractive woman about ten years older than me. Dad said, "Hi Maggie."

Maggie replied in a cheerful voice, "Good Morning, Mr. W..."

Dad asked, "Is there a chance we could talk to Cliff?"

She smiled and said, "One moment please." Maggie disappeared and returned a moment later outside the enclosed office.

She said, "This way please." She escorted us to Cliff's office, which was more of a booth than an office, partitioned from the rest of the bank by walls about four feet high you could see over.

Cliff Hipple was a stern looking man, who appeared to be about ten years older than Dad. I thought he was the bank president forever. He stood, shook hands with Dad, then Dad introduced me to Mr. Hipple. He shook my hand, then offered us a seat and we sat down. I expected Dad to fill Mr. Hipple in, but Dad said nothing, so things became uncomfortably quiet.

I took a deep breath to relax, but I was sure my voice trembled when I said, "I'd like to buy a car."

Mr. Hipple interlocked his fingers, leaned back in his chair and said, "Tell me more." I gave him all the details of the car.

Dad interrupted saying, "He's got a job." Cliff turned to an old time mechanical calculating machine and expertly punched in some numbers, pulled a handle, and ripped off the paper with the numbers on it.

He studied the paper and without looking up he said, "Seven hundred dollars with interest would be thirty-three dollars a month for twenty-four months due on the fifteenth of the month." He looked up at me over the rim of his glasses and said, "Okay?"

I said, "Yes."

He looked at Dad and said, "Of course you would have to cosign." Dad smiled and nodded in agreement.

Cliff stretched his neck to see above his office wall and called, "Maggie." She came in and he handed her the slip of paper from his calculator and said, "Could you take care of this for Mr. W...?" I felt all grown up when I realized he was calling me Mr. W... He gave Maggie the slip.

She smiled and said, "Of course" and left without saying another word.

Dad and Cliff shot the bull like old friends until Maggie returned with the paperwork. We signed papers and shook hands. I would never forget when we got in the car, Dad handed me my first payment book.

He looked me in the eye and said, "Son, if you don't pay for the car I have to and I will to save my own credit, but you need to know if I have to pay for your car I'll never help you get another loan."

I felt proud to say, I not only paid the loan off, but years later I too cosigned for my daughter Nadine and my son Nick's first car loans.

The heat of the sun was so relaxing I must have drifted off for a nap. I awoke when long-time ferryman Steve Longley showed up on the other side of the river at precisely two o'clock. He shuttled me across in a canoe. The ferry has been made the official Appalachian Trail Route complete with a white blaze painted on the bottom of the canoe.

Steve was a hiker friendly businessman who owned and operated Rivers and Trails Hostel and Store. He sold food, gear, and catered to hikers and white water enthusiasts. I could also get a shower and move on if I wanted to. He offered me a free ride there if I wanted to wait until four o'clock when he quit for the day, but I elected to move on because the guidebook said a take-out was two tenths of a mile in the other direction. Besides, I had a scheduled zero coming up in Monson, Maine in a couple of days.

I walked two-tenths of a mile east on the highway to a makeshift old trailer, remodeled into a kitchen with picnic tables in a tent called, The Moose Crossing Takeout. I bought two cheeseburgers, an order of fries, and an ice cream cone for fourteen bucks. A family on vacation from Boston, asked me several questions as we ate together. I enjoyed answering their questions and found them amusing.

I ran into Bloody Mess and Fortune Cookie on the way back to the trail. I warned them it was going to be expensive, but they were hungry enough they didn't care. I hiked another six miles to Pleasant Pond Lean-to where I set up my tent in a poor campsite. I had no tower to call Scooter. I was tired and lonely, but I felt better emotionally. The ankle also seemed better. I heard Bloody Mess and Fortune Cookie arrive at the shelter about dark, but I didn't feel like getting out of my tent to socialize. I don't think they even knew I was there.

Day 156   13.1 Miles

I drank cold coffee and quietly packed up so I didn't disturb my friends. I ascended almost twelve-hundred feet in a mile up Pleasant Pond Mountain by headlight before sunrise. I found cell tower from the summit, so I called Scooter before she went to work. I felt privileged to talk to her as I watched the sunrise over the neighboring mountains. We started planning a rendezvous at Millinocket before I would summit the mighty Mount Katahdin. She planned to take a week's vacation and summit with me.

I descended Pleasant Pond Mountain and found myself skirting beaver dams and their swamps the rest of the morning. The beaver were industrious animals who built dams that raised the water around the trees. The high water killed the trees and left their skeletons standing in the water. At first glance, the swamps they created looked like Mother Nature's slum, but when the trees died, the sun nourished new vegetation. That new vegetation provided a food source, which attracted a diverse array of wildlife. I stopped at one such beaver pond and sat quietly observing Mother Nature's genesis. I believe swamps were a type of mother themselves as they supported and provided a home and food for fish, insects, muskrats, ducks, predators, and even moose.

I stopped on the summit of Moxie Bald Mountain where the guidebook said you could view Katahdin. The day was clear and I saw mountains for miles, on the horizon. I couldn't pick out Katahdin for sure, but I didn't know how a mountain the size of Katahdin would look from a hundred and thirty-five miles away. I saw a purple shadow of a mountain on the horizon that looked like the shape of the mountain in some of the pictures I saw of Katahdin, but I couldn't say for sure.

I decided it was a wonderful time and place to meditate, so I took off my pack and ate a late lunch while I studied the mountain. I soon returned to my memories of my dad. I didn't understand, how much Dad interacted with me in the same way as God until recently. He didn't approve of the car. He said it would break down and I would always be working on it in my spare time. The car would drink a lot of gasoline, and take my paychecks. Dad was a hundred percent right on everything and he knew he would be. However, the wise man also knew I would have to find all these things out for myself, so he stood back and gave me my way.

Looking back at my life, I saw God also let me do some real stupid stuff my way. I was sure he didn't approve, but didn't stop me so I would gain the wisdom of knowing for myself. I didn't think Dad ever understood or even thought he was God-like in many ways. I said a simple prayer, "Thanks, Dad." I walked away feeling maybe this Appalachian Trail experience was part of my genesis.

I now pictured God as more of a grandfather-type who taught, guided, and mentored my Dad while Dad raised me. Dad wasn't religious and never once preached about God, but through his example, he showed me God.

I spent a lot of trail time in meditation asking for knowledge of God's will and the power to carry it out. I believe through meditation, I gained a better understanding of at least to whom I have been talking to.

I rested up, packed up, and moved out, hoping to hike eleven more miles so I would have a short hike into Monson the next morning. I took a picture of the sign nailed to a post, marking the summit of Moxie Bald with the Katahdin shaped mountain in the background. I would save the picture to look at after I figured out if the shadow I was looking at was Mount Katahdin.

I hiked two miles to the next shelter on the shore of a rather large lake to find gear strewn all over in disarray. Styrofoam containers with partially eaten deli sandwiches were on the picnic table, but no one was around. I felt uneasy, so I kept my pack on while I cautiously approached the lake. Three men from New York City all wearing skimpy Speedos were frolicking in the sun, which was an ugly sight I wished I wouldn't have witnessed. I would be forced to live with it in my head for the rest of my life. They paddled three brand new, bright yellow Kayaks from somewhere on the other side of the lake. They were on vacation and planned to spend the night in the Appalachian Trail shelter, which was supposed to be for hikers.

Apparently, they all lived together in New York City. I didn't want any more information. I was more than a little creeped out and was leaving, when Bloody Mess and Fortune Cookie came in to read and enter in the trail register. The NYC men must have heard us talking and came up to the shelter with two cases of beer. Larry, Curly, and Moe thought we were going to steal their gear.

Obviously, they had been drinking when Moe said, "We're going to cook some steaks, so if you help us build a fire we'll feed you." I looked questionably at Bloody Mess and she gave a, what the hell steaks were steaks shrug, so we stayed. We helped them build a fire first. I pitched my tent by the lake away from the shelter because we decided to spend the night there. I would need to hike about eighteen miles to Monson the next day, which should be okay.

A couple named Tata and Poncho, who were section hiking, came in while I was down by the lake settling in for the night. Tata was from Brazil and one of the most extraverted individuals I ever met.

Tata said, "We were stealth camped on the top of Pleasant Pond Mountain this morning and overheard you talking to your wife on the phone." I didn't recall seeing a tent.

I asked her, "How do you know it was me you heard?"

She said, "I could smell your perfume." I was wearing Patchouli oil. I hoped I didn't say anything to Scooter that might be embarrassing. Tata and Poncho seemed to fit in with the trio from New York City as they all started to drink wine and beer.

I went to my tent and took a nap when they started to get drunk and obnoxious. When I awoke, I put dehydrated bean stew in water to soak and ate cold crunchy ramen noodles and the last of my peanut butter. My pack was light and my supplies were low, but I only had eighteen miles to Monson and a mail drop there the next day.

I returned to the fire and found another Nobo thru-hiker named Crazy Nut, joined us. He was from California and started his hike in Georgia on May first, which was impressive, since I started on February the twenty-sixth and we were both at the same place on the trail. He too was seduced into staying by the promise of steaks.

The city boys were drunk and seemed to have forgotten the promise to feed us. Tata and Poncho were vegetarians and pretty drunk themselves. I talked to the other straight hikers for a while. We figured it out and shared the same resentment. I said a few un-Christian type descriptive adjectives, then went back to my tent incredibly hungry with the smell of grilled steaks in the air. I put on my headphones to end the day listening to some soft music to drown the bastards out.

KNOWLEDGE

Day 157 17.9 Miles

I got up at o-dark-four o'clock and left before anyone else was up. I drank cold instant coffee and ate the cold bean stew for breakfast. I hoped to eat a good hot meal in Monson later that day. I felt like a victim and wanted to nurse my resentment. I had the incredible urge wake up the Three Stooges, but I suppressed it with thoughts of something more passive aggressive before I left. The good Dreamer had a wrestling match with the bad Dreamer and I leave it to my readers imagination to decide which one won.

Fortunately, I found signal at the top of a small, nameless mountain and called my Alcoholics Anonymous sponsor. I let go of my resentment and felt better after I discussed it with him. I missed catching Scooter before she went to work, but I left her a detailed message. I soon forgot all about my resentment and my ankle pain in the picturesque land of Maine. Bloody Mess soon caught up to me. We talked briefly, but she was hiking with a mission and I couldn't keep up with her. I hoped to see her that night in Monson at Shaw's Lodging, which was a famous hiker stop.

I stopped at the west branch of the Piscataquis River to work up the courage to ford. The river was wide, fast, but shallow. Fortune Cookie came along and waded in not the least bit intimidated by the fast current, so I followed. He too was soon out of sight trying to catch Bloody Mess. I thought, wasn't it a coincidence Fortune Cookie came along unexpectedly just as I needed someone to set an example. I then remembered an Alcoholics Anonymous catchphrase, The definition of a coincidence is when God chooses to remain anonymous.

I really missed having a stove. I sure wanted a cup of bad coffee, so I decided to take the time to build a tiny fire only big enough to heat up a cup of mud. I turned my mind lose while surrounded by the awesome beauty of the church God built. I started to whistle the hymn Amazing Grace. When I came to the line, *I once was blind, but now I see* I remembered a story told to me by Gallagher many years ago.

A man was born totally blind. All his life, he saw nothing but total darkness. One day an old and wise man who saw everything clearly took him to a meeting with other folks who were also blind, but now they saw more clearly. He listened and what he heard there made sense. The miracle that happened to them started happening to him as he started to see shades of gray at first. He was so excited he continued to go to the meetings and soon he started to see shapes, which were blurry at first, but as he continued to attend those meetings, the shapes started coming into focus. The people at the meetings were also blind in the beginning and they shared with him their personal stories of how they came to see. That inspired him with the hope to continue even in the hard times.

Soon he started to see the colors of the grass and sky. The more he attended the meetings the more clearly he saw the world he only imagined existed in his past. Inspired by his discovery he started telling others of his good fortune, sharing his experience, strength, and hope with those who were also blind. He discovered a world even more beautiful than he ever anticipated when he was blind.

I was looking over the majestic world created by the same God who created me and I wondered, how much more could be seen? The Twelfth Step of Alcoholics Anonymous was divided into in three parts. The first part said, "Having had a spiritual awakening as the result of these Steps." The term spiritual awakening was fitting because it was as if I woke up to God. I now believed God always existed and it wasn't me. That came about for me as a direct result of working the Twelve Steps, which were suggested as a program of recovery. To me the Steps were never about not drinking or even about staying sober, they were always about having a spiritual awakening. "I once was blind, but now I see."

I forced down the last swallow of the foul brew before moving out, singing Amazing Grace. The caffeine evidently did its job in my blood stream. I even felt a twinge of guilt stemming from the bad Dreamer's behavior, but I quickly rationalized it away. After all, the New York City boys would eventually find their kayaks somewhere on that big lake.

The Appalachian Trail followed a river for several miles north into Horseshoe Canyon, treating me to the untouched beauty of a wild river rushing through the wilderness. I would like to return some day when I have the time, with a fly rod or even a kayak.

I forded the east branch of the river by myself after the trail dropped below six-hundred and fifty feet above sea level. The trail continued along the river, but degraded into a mud trail through the brushy forest that slowed my progress way down. Hundreds of other hiker footprints were in the mud as it pulled at my shoes every step of the way. Unavoidably, I became muddy and miserable. The mud ended as soon as I started up hill. I soon came across a stream to wash off all the mud and clean up before arriving at the highway that would take me to Monson. I hitched a ride to Monson with an older, local gentleman named Ned, who dropped me off on the main street.

I ran into Fast Lane at Monson General Store, which was an old-time, small store with two huge American Flags hanging on each side of the door. He was smiling and looking healthy, but the bad news was he left town to head back to the trail. He gave me directions to Shaw's and the post office as we chatted briefly. I shook his hand and bid him goodbye. I watched him disappear, fearing I would never see him again.

Monson was the last stop before I entered Maine's famous hundred-mile wilderness and had a reputation for being a great hiker town. It looked like a quiet little town as I watched young children playing in a yard. Monson seemed the type of town where you wouldn't lock your doors at night. I thought Monson was a good choice to spend a zero day before I took on the hundred-mile wilderness. I went to Shaw's, which was a large, two-story, old New England style boarding house that catered to hikers. I found Shaw's meticulous with old, but well maintained, and freshly painted white, wooden siding, accented by light gray trim around the doors and windows. A permanent sign posted on the finely cut lawn said, "Shaw's, Rooms and Meals Available."

The two fine ladies who hosted Shaw's were retired schoolteachers. I had to take my shoes off on the back porch before I could go inside. The house was as neat and clean on the inside as on the outside. The rooms were light and cheerful with new wallpaper.

I rented a private room, which included supper and breakfast for forty-eight dollars. They wouldn't take credit cards, so I paid cash in advance. I felt a little uneasy when she took the money, stuffed it down the front of her blouse, and didn't offer me a receipt. I didn't say anything because I didn't want to offend her. I had to trust her and as it turned out, I had nothing to worry about in the first place.

She showed me to my room, talking nonstop, filling me in on all the rules and procedures. I felt like I was back in grammar school for a little while as she told me with authority, "There will be absolutely no smoking, or chewing in the house. Go outside to smoke and don't throw your butts on the ground. Supper is served family style precisely at six o'clock pm, that's eighteen-hundred our time. Make sure you take a good shower and put on clean clothes before supper. Clean the bathroom after you're finished; you are not the only one who uses it. Don't show up for supper the way you are because you stink and it wouldn't be fair to the other guests. Absolutely no hiking boots permitted in the house. We provide sandals in a bin by the back door. I'm sure you'll find a pair that fits. Clean clothes are in the bins in the mudroom, you may borrow anything you want, but remember they are a loan, and not a gift so return them to the dirty laundry before you leave. You must always wear your shirt when you're not in your room with the door shut. I don't want to see a bunch of half-naked men running around my house, No one is impressed. Absolutely no bare feet allowed at any time in the kitchen. We provide a washer and dryer for four dollars, on a first come-first served basis, but it's not working well, and the laundry mat in town is cheaper and better. Use that if you have the time. Two refrigerators are for guests that you're welcome to use, but make sure you throw out your leftovers before you leave. Do not take anything that's not yours. You can also use the guest stove. Clean up after yourself. Your mother doesn't work here. Breakfast starts at zero-six-hundred. Do you have any questions?"

I thought wow, she never even took a breath as she barked out the orders schoolteacher style. I could visualize her grabbing a badass thru-hiker like me by the ear and marching him right out the door, so I meekly said, "No." Her voice lowered and softened as she said, "Good! Welcome to Shaw's and have a good time." She left, pulling the door shut behind her leaving me to myself in the room.

The room was bright and ultra clean, with white sheer curtains and matching bedspread on a double-size bed. I only took the time to drop my pack off in my room and hurried off. I wanted to get to the post office before it closed.

I picked up my package from Scooter and asked the postmaster, where I could find an ATM.

He laughed and said, "There is none." I must have had a look of disappointment on my face, because he offered to sell me a money order that I could pay for with my credit card and then he would cash the money order for me. I thanked him and purchased a money order for two-hundred and fifty dollars. I had enough cash to pay for that night's stay, but I wouldn't have been able to stay the next day if he hadn't been so kind.

I went back to my room, took a hot shower, and borrowed some clean, cotton clothes that actually fit nicely. I opened my package from Scooter. She sent her new stove, air mattress, and the usual supplies. She also includes a surprise, so I felt a little like it was Christmas each time I opened a mail drop from her.

I put on some patchouli oil and showed up for supper at five minutes to six all clean in my borrowed clothes. I ate supper family style with six section hikers who were about my age. One couple was on vacation from South Africa. I found them all full of themselves and dreadfully boring. We ate fresh salad, meatloaf, chicken breasts, mashed potatoes, and broccoli. I ate noticeably more than anyone else, but I was the only thru-hiker. I raised some eyebrows when I went back for seconds and thirds.

I went back into town to do my laundry and explore Monson. I also needed to walk off the huge amount of food I consumed. I returned to Shaw's and to my delight, found Bloody Mess, Fortune Cookie, Poncho, Tata, and Crazy Nut had arrived. Some new Nobos, Sobos, and section hikers came in also. The place was hopping as a severe lightning storm hit. We were all happy to be dry and safe as we socialized late into the night. I was quite sure everyone had a great time.

Day 158   Zero Miles

I awoke to the sun shining in my eyes through the window. I went straight to the bathroom, then down stairs. I followed the aroma of freshly brewed coffee to the kitchen. I grabbed a coffee cup and poured myself some of the dark brew. The cook looked up and warned, "Don't get caught out here in your bare feet." He laughed as I did an immediate about face and departed.

I put my borrowed sandals on to return to the living room where I waited with other guests, shooting the breeze, and drinking coffee. Breakfast at Shaw's was an Appalachian Trail experience in itself. The cook was a gruff, old, longhair, bearded, tattooed, ex-Navy cook, named Buddy. Buddy looked more like an outlaw biker than a cook. He scared me just looking at him. He started cooking home fries, eggs your style, sausage, bacon, and pancakes at four o'clock to start serving breakfast at six in the morning. You could order a one, which was one of everything or a two, which was two of everything all the way up to the record of nine. You could order as high a number as you wanted, but you had to eat all you ordered. I ordered a five and all the coffee I wanted went with breakfast. I ordered my eggs easy over. I never thought I could eat all that food at one time. I took my time, stopped once I got full, and waited until I could eat more. The veteran hikers warned me to be careful once I got full not to eat too fast or I would puke.

I spent over an hour eating with the rest of the thru-hikers. The section hikers that ordered a wimpy two, were finished eating, and out of the dining room in twenty minutes. All the thru-hikers took their time and gorged themselves. I don't remember ever having more fun at breakfast.

Buddy the cook, was a great guy, once you got to know him enough to get past his rough exterior. He had a great sense of humor and although he would never admit it, he genuinely liked badass hikers. I still wouldn't want to mess with him.

I returned to my room and packed up all the things I didn't absolutely need and took them to the post office to mail home. I planned to carry all the food I possibly could into the hundred-mile wilderness. I wouldn't be able to get supplies again until I arrived at Abol Bridge in a hundred miles.

I was happy I decided to take a zero day at Shaw's because I had a lot of fun and it took my mind off my ankle pain. Besides, the weather forecast predicted severe thunderstorms and it was already starting to rain. My ankle felt better, but another day's rest wouldn't hurt. I planned to spend the day talking to the locals and the newly arrived hikers.

I met four new Nobo thru-hikers: Red Beard, who sported a heavy red beard, Coup, who seemed to be Red beard's hiking partner; Hiker Cycler, who was deaf and couldn't speak, so he was rather quiet; and Jay Bird, who started hiking four years ago and never stopped. He hiked from Katahdin to Springer and back several times and planned to head south again once he summits Katahdin. I didn't know how he could afford it, but I didn't think he ever planned to get off the trail. Also worth mentioning was a section hiker who called himself, Colonel. The Colonel was a paramilitary type who stood about six-foot, five-inches tall and wore a green beret. He was older than I was, but seemed to be in excellent shape. I didn't talk to him other than to say hi because I thought he seemed full of himself. Poncho and Tata packed up and left for Katahdin late in the afternoon. I hoped to catch up with them in the hundred-mile wilderness at some point. Tata and I were becoming especially close friends.

I was now only one-hundred and fifteen miles from the sign at the summit of Mount Katahdin. It seemed surreal that I had almost completed my journey. Several thru-hikers staying at Shaw's, were about to complete their journey and I was proud to be among them.

The anticipation of finishing the long term, seemingly impossible journey, was a big part of what made a zero day at Shaw's such a festive event.

I didn't have cell tower, so I called Scooter after she got out of work from a pay phone. We firmed up plans for her to take a week's vacation and meet me in Millinocket outside Baxter State Park on Saturday, August twelfth, which was in ten days. We would climb Mount Katahdin on the next clear day.

I went to the local restaurant to buy a lobster roll for supper. I was in Maine, so I felt I had to have lobster. A lobster roll was just a hotdog bun filled with chunks of lobster with mayo, served with potato chips. It cost fourteen bucks. I guessed it was okay, but nothing to write home about.

A Sobo with the flu was taking zero days at Shaw's, in an attempt to recover. I avoided him so far, but he came into the restaurant and sat down beside me. He ordered beer and kept offering to buy me a beer. My impression was he only wanted to have someone to talk to, but I ate in a hurry and left. I hope he didn't infect me with whatever he had. I was still hungry, so I bought a half-gallon of cherry vanilla ice cream at the local convenience store and took it home to eat before I went to bed. I planned to leave in the morning.

Day 159   10.4 Miles

It rained all night and into the morning, but cleared by noon. I only ate a Four with a lot of coffee for breakfast that morning. Red Beard ate an impressive seven, so he became everyone's hero of the day. I felt a tinge of grief as I realized I would never see most of those people again. I returned to my room to pack up for the hundred-mile wilderness adventure. Miss Dawn and Buddy both shuttled hikers back to the trail. We all piled out at the trailhead and started hiking in both directions. Hiker Cycler and I were the only Nobos, but He hiked faster, so I soon found myself hiking solo. I felt a little melancholy being alone at first after Shaw's intense social experience.

My mood soon improved as the sun dried things out and my endorphins kicked in. In my opinion, Maine was by far the most spectacular state on the entire Appalachian Trail. It was wonderfully wild and diverse with steep, intimidating mountains, fast and wild rivers, waterfalls, glacier lakes, huge swamps, and breathtaking views everywhere.

Maine wasn't for wimps with its unforgiving landscape. The bridges had no handrails and the trail was often hard to follow. Getting lost or hurt would be easy and could have tragic consequences. The weather could turn on me in an instant with violent wind, rain, thunder, and lightning. The bogs were extremely unstable and I never knew how deep I would sink when I entered one. The mosquitoes and black flies were vicious and hungry. A tiny fly called, no-see-ums attracted to the salt in my tears and flew so close they often got into my eye. Yet, in spite of all the danger, adversity, and perils, there was no other place on God's earth I would rather be, at least on that day.

The rain had swollen the rivers and I had to ford three rivers that day. The first was Goodell Brook and it was nothing special. I felt some relief, which was short lived. I came to Little Wilson Falls, which I could hear roaring long before I came to the sixty-foot waterfall, which was spectacular even by Maine's standards. What made it even more awesome was the falls were tight against an unclimbable vertical, solid granite wall that reached half way to heaven on the other side. I stood there watching the water crash through the gorge in total amazement until reality snapped me out of my trance. I looked at my guidebook and sure enough, it said I would have to ford Little Wilson in two-tenths of a mile.

I worried the long two tenths of the mile until, to my delight, Hiker Cycler was at Little Wilson ford when I arrived. Little Wilson was fast, strong and wide, but at least I wasn't alone. He forded first and waited for me on the other side. I forded and we had lunch together. Hiker Cycler said nothing because he couldn't speak, so he gave the thumbs up sign with a great big smile as he departed.

I moved out with all the adrenalin still in my veins. God probably knew how stressed I was because I soon came upon a quiet beaver dam built in his garden. I took the time to stop, breathe slowly, and let my heart rate slow down. The glass-like water reflecting the occasional cloud as it passed by in the clear blue sky, had a calming effect on me. It was as if God gave me one of his Xanax.

The third challenge was Big Wilson, which was a lot like the Salmon River where I fished in the fall in New York. Big Wilson was larger, but not in such a hurry, and the current wasn't nearly as strong. I forded it solo with great care, because no one was around to help if I did have trouble. My ego inflated a little, and I felt a little froggy after I forded all three rivers.

I have been in the world for a long time and saw some weird things. Still every once in a while, I saw something so out of the ordinary of what I expected. I crossed paths with the Colonel hiking south, wearing his Green Barrett, but he also wore a woman's dress. I quickly suppressed a little nervous giggle that slipped out because even in a dress he still looked intimidating. Now, I wasn't talking about a hiking kilt. I was talking about all six-foot-five inches of him packed into a cotton printed, woman's summer dress. All I said was, "Daaamn," as I didn't even try to hide my surprise. I talked to him as little as I could before moving on as soon as possible. I was more than a little creeped out by the encounter. I was a little disappointed there were roads into the hundred-mile wilderness where the Colonel could shuttle ahead so easily. I had visions of a hundred miles of solitude.

I still had nine days to go before I reached Baxter State Park, which was less than a hundred miles away. I decided to take my time to savor the last miles of the trail. Besides, going slow helped ease the pain in my right ankle, which was giving me trouble again. When my ankle hurt, I tried to let it go and forget about it because I already gave it to God. It was His problem now. I would put up with the pain just for that day.

The weather cleared up and turned into a great day, but it started to slip away, so I looked for a place to call home for the night. I soon found a flat place to make camp in the Wilson Valley. I set up my tent in the shade under the canopy of the Maine forest. I marveled at how the afternoon sun filtered through the leaves and formed a mosaic patchwork of sunlight on the forest floor. With all the social life at Shaw's I hadn't been alone to meditate.

I found a perfect sitting log, made a pot of hot coffee, and took some time to reflect. I now felt grateful for the little things like a cup of hot coffee even though it was bad enough to make your teeth rot and your hair fall out.

It was nice to be alone for time to pray, meditate, and consciously connect with God so I could stay spiritually fit. When I was young, I thought one day I would have a grand revelation about God and everything would be different. I would live happily ever after like in a fairytale. When that didn't happen, I looked to drugs. I actually thought I found happiness in chemicals, but it was only an illusion. I grew weaker and weaker spiritually in my addiction because I substituted the drugs for a spiritual relationship with God. Living without God in my life gave me a taste of living in deep, dark hell that I believed was worse than burning in the mythical fire and brimstone.

Even as I was living the nightmare of addiction, I always came across a few people like my mother. I envied what she had, but I didn't know how to become like her. I always admired my mother's serenity and quiet courage. Things of the world didn't scare her because her faith was so strong she feared nothing. I didn't think the devil himself could have intimidated her. She had a stroke, which put her in a coma for eleven days at the completion of her hike. I was sitting with her in the nursing home close to her departure, not expecting her to ever awaken again, when she opened her eyes, looked in mine, and calmly said, "Don't be afraid." Those were the last words, Mom ever spoke to me. I have come to appreciate how fortunate I was to have a mother like her modeling her faith. I wish she could see me now. I like to think maybe she was watching me as I struggled on my spiritual journey. I felt a presence that I didn't understand, but suddenly I realized somehow she knew, so I simply said, "Thanks, Mom."

All my phone batteries were charged and I had cell tower, so I called Scooter. We talked for a long time about spiritual contact, awakenings, and whispers. I also felt fortunate to be able to process spiritual matters with Scooter, who was a lot like Mom. I stayed awake for some time after we hung up pondering our conversation. I found it comforting that I would see Scooter in nine days.

I felt as if I was in the fourth quarter of a football game with the clock running, or the ninth inning of a baseball game with two outs. I saw how fitting it was to process Step Twelve. It occurred to me that I felt as if I was on Step Twelve of the trail. I drifted off to sleep having had a spiritual awakening as a result of hiking the trail.

Day 160   13.9 Miles

Again, violent thunderstorms lit up the Maine night sky. Thunderstorms were a little more intimidating when I slept in a tent with aluminum poles. The rain kept coming and the streams got bigger and bigger with each rain. I made hot coffee with my new stove, grateful again to have the luxury of hot coffee in the morning. I sure learned to appreciate the little extras like hot coffee that I always took for granted until I had to go without a stove. I started a list in my head of luxuries such as underwear, clean sheets, dry socks, hot food, pure, cold drinking water, hot showers, and being able to wash my hands with soap and hot water after I crap.

I thought about my home with air conditioning in the summer, a gas furnace to keep the house warm when it was cold outside, timed coffee makers that have the coffee ready in the morning, and I suspect the list would go on as long as I let it. I don't recall appreciating or being grateful for any of these things until the trail forced me to go without them. I stopped to ponder that I really didn't need a lot of material things to get by in the world; only food, water, and shelter. What I needed desperately was spiritual food and spiritual shelter.

I shook the rain off my tent the best I could, packed up, and rode out. I descended right off the bat with my injured ankle on rocky trail. The guidebook warned me of a hundred-seventy-five yard long scree field. I never heard the term scree before, so I looked it up. The dictionary defined scree as a mass of loose rocks on a steep slope of a mountain. The scree mentioned in the guidebook was sharp, broken pieces of granite forming uneven trail, which aggravated my ankle. I swallowed two extra ibuprofen and took it slow.

After I passed the rocks, I had three fords in a row in about one mile. The first was Wilber Brook, which was small, but fast with strong current. I explored downstream from the trail until I found a relatively safe place to cross. Vaughn Stream was the second ford, which I would never forget. The guidebook only said falls to the right, but didn't even mention a ford. Vaughn Stream was located at the top of Slugundy Gorge. I suspected most of the time, a hiker could jump across it. Due to all the rain, I had to ford over a small rapid with a fifty-foot waterfall crashing like thunder into the gorge about fifty feet downstream. I wondered how many dead hikers were down there in the gorge. I explored my options and decided crossing where the white blazes crossed was my best chance. I waded out into the stream, fighting the current on the slippery rocks until I came to a deep rut in the middle of the current. I couldn't see how deep it was, but I thought I could jump to shallow water on the other side. I took a deep breath, planted my hiking pole firmly on the bottom, and pushed off to jump across, pushing with my pole. I was almost surprised I made it, but I had a similar experience on Parapet Brook three weeks before in the Whites. I guess my previous experience was the best teacher.

A Sobo man and woman appeared from the north after I crossed. They ignored me as I watched them go upstream and cross with great difficulty. I was happy to see they made it because I didn't want to deal with it if they didn't. I took a picture of the impressive falls before I moved on.

The third ford was the widest of all. Long Pond Stream was fifty feet wide, but it had a rope across that I could hang on to while crossing. It seemed a bit mild after Vaughn. I thought, oh no, I built up a tolerance to fear, which could end up being my demise.

I climbed the Barren Chairback Mountain Range, which was a series of steep mountains that weren't extremely high. The weather took a turn for the worse and the storm robbed me of any vistas. Severe thunder and lightning erupted as I was on the Barren Ledges starting to ascend Barren Mountain. I stopped to wait it out, fearful of going any higher in the storm. Eventually, the lightning stopped and I continued in the rain. An old fire tower still stood at the top of Barren Mountain, but there wasn't any vistas because of the bad weather. I passed on climbing up the tower to see only gray mist.

I arrived at Cloud Pond where a shelter was three tenths of a mile off trail. I contemplated stopping for the night in the rain, but it was still early. I had only hiked a little over eight miles and I didn't know what I would do with all the time alone, so I moved on. I hadn't gone far before I regretted not stopping. The pain in my ankle suddenly increased and I was wet and miserable. I could compare it to not stopping at a rest area on the interstate and then having to pee badly as soon as I was past the exit. I started to look for the next flat spot big enough to set my little tent on with zero luck. I thought I would never find a camp. I hiked another five miles before I came to a flat spot at the base of a rock about the size of a building. I quickly made camp, thinking the rock would help protect me from the nighttime storms.

The rain let up long enough for me to cook hot tuna and noodles. I made a pot of hot chamomile tea after I ate. The rain started again and drove me to my tent. I got into my dry sleeping bag, drank the hot chamomile tea, and wrote about the day's adventures on the Appalachian Trail. The pain in my ankle subsided with medication. Life was so good once again.

I thought about my mother's true courage. Cedar Moe reminded me of Mom's courage that day on Mount Adams in the lightning storm. I was scared shitless as he cheerfully said, "We're going right over the top." I probably always recognized a spiritual connection in others even though I never identified it as a personal spiritual message to me. I had no idea how Mom or Cedar Moe formed their relationship with God. How did they come about having their personal spiritual awakening? I suspected our path to an understanding of God was as unique and individualized as our fingerprints.

Speaking only for myself, when I looked back, I could see my personal, spiritual awakening came as a direct result of working the Twelve Steps of Alcoholics Anonymous. However, I also had the example of others like my Mom, Cedar Moe, Heaven Bound, and the many, many other teachers God put in my path who walked with him.

I closed my journal and laid back contemplating my next adventure. I had at least two fords in the morning that I worried about, but I would face them in the morning. I hoped it stopped raining soon as the pitter patter sound of the gentle rain on my tent lulled me to sleep.

August 5   Day 161   11.6 Miles

The rain stopped in the night, which made for a good start to the day. I started my coffee as I welcomed a red, slightly threatening, morning sky. I ate three Snickers and washed them down with hot coffee. The coffee didn't seem as bad as it did before I broke my stove and drank it cold. I stopped after a couple of miles on the summit of Chairback Mountain to view an amazing vista. I wasn't in a hurry, so I brewed a second cup of coffee. I wished I discovered the sweetness of being in no hurry earlier in life. However, I felt grateful that I was fortunate enough to discover the euphoria of going slow soon enough to enjoy life before it ended. I have seen many people rush and rush to the grave, not taking the time to enjoy their life.

I gazed out over the landscape of the hundred-mile wilderness stretched out before me as if I was taking inventory of what lies in store. The mountains were spaced less densely than the Whites of New Hampshire to the south. I saw only mountains and vast forests, with zero sign of the white man's intrusion clear to the horizon. I understood why the sign at the border said, "Maine, the way life should be." I wondered where Cedar Moe was out there and if he was still hiking with Zoma and Lug.

After the Big Book described in detail the first nine Steps it said, "If we are painstaking about this stage of our development we will be amazed before we are half way through." I became amazed at the spiritual progress I felt each time I worked the Steps. The Steps became my, how-to instructions. The first three Steps taught me how to surrender and make a decision to change. Steps Four through Nine were my instructions on how I removed the debris created by my ego that blocked God out. Step Ten was continuing to work Step Four through Nine to continue growing. In Step Eleven I started forming a personal relationship with God of my own understanding through contact. The result was the greatest gift of all, a spiritual awakening.

The first of the Alcoholics Anonymous Promises says, *We will know a new freedom and a new happiness.* When I have been asked by the newcomer or anyone else, *What is a spiritual awakening?* I simply say, A new freedom and a new happiness.

I finished my now cold coffee and descended Chairback Mountain feeling so happy and free. I soon approached the west branch of Pleasant River, which was a wide, fast river that I worried about fording ever since I read about it in the guidebook the night before. I approached the river and saw tourist-type folks day hiking. I even passed a fat lady wearing flip-flops, carrying a small kick-me type dog. I stopped her and asked "Ma'am, how did you get here?"

She pointed to a well-worn path and said, "From the parking lot right up the path." Apparently, a road access was only a few hundred yards away. That explained how the Colonel got ahead of me and was hiking south wearing the dress when I met him. That also explained the many section hikers I passed since I left Monson.

The hundred-mile wilderness probably got its name forty or fifty years ago when it was actually one-hundred miles of wilderness, but like anything else in this world, progress was intruding. The reputation of the hundred-mile wilderness, enhanced by hiker's fears and embellished by trail talk over years, probably disillusioned many hikers, including me. I felt betrayed and a little disappointed by my expectations.

I arrived at the bank of the Pleasant River and found an assortment of day hikers, section hikers, and tourists with little or no experience fording rivers. The state put a ridge runner on the river crossing to assist hikers, but he was on the other side at the time. I crossed the river without incident with the ridge runner and a bunch of onlookers secretly hoping to see me baptized by the river.

I met Joe, the professional hired to watch the river crossing, when I arrived on the far shore. Since it was getting close to lunchtime, I filtered water, made coffee, set up my tent, and hung up my sleeping bag to dry. I ate lunch and talked to Joe as we watched people crossing the river. To my delight, Poncho and Tata came along and forded the river. I left Shaw's fearing we might never see each other again.

They took their packs off, took out a snack, and joined us. We sat chatting like old friends who hadn't seen each other for a long time. An older couple, who apparently were section hiking with heavy packs, came from the north. They ignored us and immediately attempted to ford the river, going south as if they were late for something. The man seemed inpatient with his wife and took off into the river. The wife seemed frustrated and left in a hurry before she was ready. She was trying to keep up, lost her footing on the slippery rocks, and fell midway across the river in the current. The man continued to cross, oblivious to his wife's situation because he was having trouble himself. She was struggling and couldn't get up, so Tata and I, without hesitation, went out after her.

By the time we got to her, she panicked, and became hysterical. She still had her belt strap on and the wet pack was dragging her downstream. We calmed her down, took her pack off, and Tata took the heavy, wet pack to shore. I escorted the woman to safety, but meanwhile, her husband, who made it across safely and took his pack off, but then decided to come back to help, and fell into the current. Tata had to come back, rescued him, and helped him get back to shore safely.

It occurred to me the Spirit might be telling me something, because that was similar to the same situation I experienced back in Connecticut with a couple fording Guinea Brook. Next, the man yelled at his wife, but that time he triggered something violent in Tata. I had to physically restrain her from kicking his ass all the way to Springer. I wrestled her to the ground before her hot, Brazilian temper calmed down.

We forded the river to the north side away from him, to where Poncho and Joe, the ridge runner watched the whole thing unfold. Joe said, "Things like that happen all the time." We all talked at the same time, processing the drama until our adrenalin rushes subsided. Tata and I high fived and laughed about getting wet, having a good trail tale to tell, and luckily, no one got hurt. I thought, if I'm in a bar fight, I want Tata on my side.

Poncho, Tata, and I packed up our tents that dried in the sun. We bid Joe goodbye and moved on together, as friends with a common goal. Our immediate destination was a mile and a half away to a place called Gulf Hagas. Some referred to Gulf Hagas as the Grand Canyon of Maine, although I couldn't compare it to the Grand Canyon. However, Gulf Hagas was a unique, five-hundred-foot deep gorge about five miles long. The canyon sat off trail, but we ventured into it because we heard how it was such a spectacular place in Maine and well worth the time. Poncho and I stripped down and went swimming below one of the many waterfalls. It was a lot like a scene out of a movie in paradise. The thirty-foot waterfall squeezed itself in between the sides of the canyon to form a deep pool at the bottom. The crystal clear water was a little on the chilly side and refreshing, but not shocking.

Tata sat in the sun and watched. I asked her, "Why don't you jump in?"

She replied, "The water's deep and I can't swim."

I was so surprised all I could say was, "Really!" I especially admired her courage when she went to rescue the woman in the Pleasant River, not knowing how to swim.

I felt refreshed after the swim and decided to hike up the canyon off trail for a while. Gulf Hagas was truly a treat with many spectacular waterfalls and vertical canyon walls. A line on page eighty-four in the Big Book says, "We have now entered the world of the spirit." I truly felt blessed being here feeling God's presence as I entered into the world of the spirit. I hiked about two miles up and did an about face and returned to the trail. The State of Maine didn't allow camping in the canyon, so I needed to find a place to call home for the night before it got too late. With the discovery of an access road within a couple of miles, I started to plan to come back with Scooter after we summit Mount Katahdin, to hike the entire canyon.

I hiked another four miles on the trail before finding a nice flat campsite close to the Carl A. Newman Lean-to. I set up my tent before I went to a nearby stream to filter water. I accidently barged in on Poncho and Tata as they shared an intimate moment in the afternoon sun. I was a little embarrassed with the awkward situation, but acted as if it never happened. They were going to spend the night in the nearby shelter. They invited me over to the shelter to socialize after I settled in. I thanked them, hurriedly filtered water, and departed, leaving them to themselves.

I did the few chores I had left to do at my camp, grabbed my food bag and stove, and went to the shelter to join the girls. I found Red Beard and Coop already set up to stay with the girls. I laughed because I sensed the boys had less than honorable intentions. They were like two old hound dogs practically humping air. I thought I would leave it up to Tata to tell them they were barking up the wrong tree. I ate tuna and rice with them and socialized for a while before I returned to the privacy of my own tent for the night. I left the kids to themselves. I only hoped Tata didn't hurt those boys.

I lay awake in my tent for some time to reflect on the drama at the river and the similar event with a man and a woman way back in Connecticut. I wonder if God sent me a message that day at Guinea Brook in Connecticut and I didn't understand it the first time, so he repeated it again at the Pleasant River. I know both times the men were dominant. The women were in a state of panic trying to please the men, when they made a bad decision. Both men were controlling, self-willed, and seemed to be imposing their will on their partners. Both women seemed obedient, but also seemed to secretly resent their partners.

I could identify with both the men and the women as I have been in both roles at one time or another. I thought about it for some time and decided it was bad to be either dominant or submissive. I would continue to ponder both incidents. I didn't feel quite satisfied with my interpretation of the events, yet I felt content with my insight for now as I drifted off to sleep to end the day's adventure.

Day 162   12.7 Miles

I started my day again with some bad coffee. The day promised to be sunny and warm. I sure hoped the temperature didn't climb too far, becoming unbearably hot. I passed the shelter in silence because the kids were sleeping peacefully. I immediately ascended Gulf Hagas Mountain then dropped down a little, only to ascend another five hundred feet to the top of West Peak. West Peak's summit provided an amazing vista of the Maine landscape. I could see the same lump on the horizon that I felt rather sure was Mount Katahdin. I moved on in a somber mood, thinking the sight of the mountain of my inspiration for so long should have stimulated me more.

A snake in my path distracted me as it coiled and hissed. Red Beard and Coup overtook me as I was playing with the snake. I thought it might be poisonous, but Red Beard said it wasn't. The snake just expanded its head to make it look poisonous to ward off enemies. I thought it worked because I left it alone not knowing if Red Beard knew what he was talking about. Red Beard asked if he could use my phone to call his sister. I had cell tower, so I let him. He was arranging to have her pick him up at Katahdin in three days. That was when it hit me I felt somber because my adventure was almost over.

Red Beard gave back my phone. I knew better, but my curiosity was killing me, so I had to ask the rhetorical question, "How did you guys make out with the girls last night?"

He said, "They were friendly, but they were more interested in each other than us." I couldn't keep a straight face any longer and started to laugh so hard I couldn't breathe.

He was a little indignant and asked, "Why didn't you tell us?"

I caught my breath and said, "You young guys have too much testosterone clouding your vision, so you wouldn't have believed me anyway." They moved on, leaving me alone, but still laughing.

I climbed White Cap Mountain, which at well over thirty-six hundred feet, would be the last big climb before Mount Katahdin. I could see the same mountain I saw from West Peak, which I still believed was Katahdin, only a little closer. The guidebook said I was seventy-three miles away from Katahdin, so I was quite sure I was looking at Mount Katahdin. I felt a chill run up my spine as the reality struck me. It did look like the same lump I looked at last week from the summit of Moxie Bald Mountain.

I snapped back to the present and moved on attempting to enjoy my time on the trail before I had to face the rat race in the capitalistic world once again. Morning soon slipped into afternoon as rapidly as it sometime did on the trail. I arrived at the east branch of the Pleasant River. I was a little worried about the ford, but found the river as laid back as the day. I hopped from rock to rock across the lazy river and didn't even get my feet wet.

A cow moose was feeding in a calm little pool downstream. She raised her head from the lily pads she was feeding on long enough to notice me. I took pictures and moved on without disturbing Miss Moose. A couple hours later, I stopped at a small glacier pond framed with white pines, thinking, that was a perfect picture of serenity. I impulsively dropped my pack because it was the perfect place to set up camp on a lazy afternoon. I set my tent up among the driftwood and a few white pine tree skeletons on a secluded beach, only feet from the water's edge. I made sure I was out of sight of anyone who might pass by on the trail.

The slightly hazy afternoon sky let the sun shine through the trees enough to dry my gear in the gentle breeze that barely wrinkled the lake's surface. The north shore of the lake was covered with older white pine trees, spaced sparsely enough they provide cover, but their lower branches had died and fallen off years ago to yield an open view of distant details in the open woods. I took a picture of my tent on the beach littered with Mother Nature's debris of fallen sticks and pinecones. The sun gave my tent a translucent appearance of being warm and friendly, yet protective.

Most often, I welcomed company, but I wanted to be alone in the little paradise I discovered. I didn't want to isolate; it's almost the opposite because I wanted to invite the spirit to join me alone in my perfect place. Satisfied everything was perfect, I blew up my air mattress, took my clothes off, and walked into the lake. The water was warm enough it didn't shock me, but cool enough it had a numbing effect on my painful ankle. I laid on my mattress and felt the coolness of the water on the front of my body and the warmth of the sun on my back. I simply focused on the subtle sound of the water lapping on my body and the sweet smell of pines. Eventually the water lowered my body temperature enough that I became uncomfortable so I decided to return to the beach. I was surprised at how far off shore I drifted when I opened my eyes. The swim back to camp invigorated me, so it was all good.

I pulled the mattress on the shore and laid naked as the sun melted my goose bumps away. I purposely listened for the spirit to speak to me at the perfect camp. One of the Twelve Promises that immediately stuck out said, "We will no longer regret the past or wish to shut the door on it." I closed my eyes and pondered, what did Bill mean, when he wrote that promise.

I wonder if all the horrendous things I did, all the pain and suffering I caused to the folks I loved, was part of my journey. Maybe all the humiliation I felt due to my behavior was part of my education through the Two by Four University of Hard Knocks. After all, pain was the motivation for me to seek out God in the first place. I wondered if all the things I did that I deeply regretted were necessary for me to learn through my own experience. I had one of those little awakenings when the things I heard for years in Alcoholics Anonymous suddenly made sense. The second part of Step Twelve said, *We tried to carry this message to others.* Alcoholics Anonymous has a slogan that says, *If you want to show your gratitude, you have to give it away to keep it.* I always felt spiritually strongest when I carried the message to not only the suffering addict, but anytime I carried God's message to anyone.

I became both a student and a teacher. Part of my purpose in life was to give freely what I received. I shared my personal experience with other addicts, so I could help them gain the hope that if I could recover, so could they. The Traditions of Alcoholics Anonymous clearly stated, "Our primary purpose is to stay sober and help other alcoholics achieve sobriety." We learned to share our personal experience, strength, and hope with others so we could solve our common problem.

I must have fallen asleep because the sun was dropping when I awoke. I quickly put on my clothes, not because I felt modest or cold, but to protect my bare ass from squadrons of Mother Nature's flying vampires that I expected would attack before it got dark. I cooked tuna and noodles for supper and went to the water's edge to eat while I watched the sunset. I could see a vista of White Capp Mountain, which was seven miles in the distance. The smooth, mirror surface of the lake reflected the silhouette of the proud mountain standing in front of the reddish orange background of the sky. As I gazed at the reflection framed by the natural pines of the north, I realized what I was looking at in awe was exactly as it had been from the time God created it.

That might have been the message the author of the blue weather-beaten sign that greeted hikers at the border meant to send when he posted, "Welcome to Maine, the way life should be." I thought that was the way, at least some of our world should be. The way it was before the days when the white man came and destroyed so much of God's creation with his greed for money, property, and prestige.

I watched the sunset but suddenly, felt uneasy. Maybe I fell asleep before the spirit was finished talking to me earlier today. Maybe the spirit wanted me to use my gifts from my experience to help others like the Appalachian Mountain Club who defended Mother Nature from the capitalistic right.

The stars came out, turning a beautiful sunset into a spectacular panoramic view of more of the wonders of God. I would have liked to continued to listen, but unfortunately, the mosquitoes, which were also God's creatures, came out and forced me to retire to my tent. I was physically exhausted from the rigors of my day, but mentally I was far too stimulated to sleep, wondering how I could ever defend our environment. I guess, like David, I didn't need to know how, I only needed to be willing, have faith, and eventually, God would reveal more. The day was truly beautiful all day long in every way.

Day 163   14.1 Miles

I was simply so thrilled to be closing in on Katahdin that I hiked out before daylight because I couldn't sleep any longer. I climbed Little Boardman Mountain, which wasn't too big of a mountain at two-thousand feet high. Then the landscape flattened out and was dotted with Maine's glacier ponds. I came across another hiker's camp in the woods, but didn't recognize the tent, so I quietly slipped past to not wake them up. The trail led me to a pristine, unnamed stream cascading down Little Boardman Mountain, so I stopped for a second cup of coffee and a snack. The sound of the frothy white water rushing past invigorated me in a calming sort of way.

A thru-hiker named J-Bird came along and joined me. Actually, he walked around me, stopped about twenty feet up the trail, took off his pack, and squatted in the middle of the trail. The camp I passed a few miles before apparently was his. He said he passed my camp at about midnight, but I didn't think he could have seen it even in the daylight. J-Bird was a strange bird indeed. He hiked mostly alone at night. He hiked six continuous thru-hikes and lived on the trail for the past four years. He planned to hike back to Springer as soon as he reached the summit of Mount Katahdin.

He ate dry, flavored cream of wheat packets for his snack. I would like to try them sometime. I continued learning something new every day on the trail. Soon J-Bird moved on and I hiked with him for a short time, but then dropped back to hike solo in the Maine wilderness. I felt as if I stole some energy from the stream, but wanted to use the time selfishly by myself to listen for spirit whispers.

Carrying the message to others was the theme that came up instantly when I started to meditate. It appeared to be turning into a spirit shout. I thought back to my time in the Smoky Mountains when I prayed for help and I met Heaven Bound who helped me, but Heaven Bound had to leave the trail that same night. I had often heard it said, "When God shuts one door He always opens another." Two days after I met Heaven Bound, God sent me a suffering addict named Mathewski. I remembered as I tried to give Mathewski hope by sharing my personal experience, my hope increased. Mathewski actually helped me as much as Heaven Bound, maybe even more in another way.

Father Joseph Martin, the Catholic Priest I knew, once said, "If you want to buy God's grace the coin you use is gratitude." Gallagher often said, "If you're grateful, don't tell me, show me." That may have been why folks in Alcoholics Anonymous said, you have to give it away to keep it.

The Alcoholics Anonymous Creed clearly states, "Our primary purpose is to stay sober and help other alcoholics achieve sobriety." Helping others may go far beyond helping only the addict. Helping anyone might be a more appropriate way to have said it. I thought it might be time I prayed asking for knowledge, so I stopped and looked to the heavens and prayed a simple prayer, "Dear God, how do I carry the message? How do I show my gratitude? Amen."

I continued to hike with my thoughts until I arrived at Antlers Campsite, which was my goal for the day. I heard Antlers was an awesome campsite on the shore of Lower Jo-Mary Lake. To my dismay, I found a troop of Boy Scouts already set up on most of the campsites. As I walked through the camps of the noisy scouts, a scout named Chris told me about a secluded site on the end of the peninsula a short distance past their camp.

I found the site, which turned out to be another perfect place to set up camp. The camp was on a point of land surrounded by water on three sides. Lower Jo-Mary Lake was a huge lake with a sandy bottom. I set up my tent within feet of the water and went for a swim with my air mattress.

After I cleaned up and refreshed, I made a cup of coffee and called my friend Lady D. I caught her at a time when she wasn't busy, so we mutually participated in a long and delightful conversation about how our message was a unique spiritual gift from God too precious not to share.

Shortly after Lady D and I said goodbye, Chris the Boy Scout dropped in to give me a Mountain House meal of beef and potatoes. I didn't particularly like freeze-dried meals, so my first reaction was to decline because they were expensive. He also carried it a long way and was probably counting on it for himself. My second thought was, to show some gratitude and say thank you. I looked him in the eyes and sincerely said, "Thank you, I could use the meal." His face lit up. I was glad I accepted because I realized I needed to be able to receive as well as give.

We had a lengthy talk about Boy Scouts and life in general as I cooked the meal. I felt like I was the old dog passing on my knowledge to the pup. I carefully picked my words, trying to be a role model, and set a good example because I knew I influenced him. We watched as a storm approached from across the lake. Everything ended when the violent lightning storm hit, which sent Chris home, and drove me to the shelter of my tent to finish eating. I felt good and couldn't help but think it was because I shared with Chris. I didn't share because I felt I owed him for the dinner, but because I felt honored I had something to share.

Gallagher said, "If you are grateful you show it by giving what you have to others." Father Martin's words surfaced again, "If you want to buy Gods grace, the coin you use is gratitude." I could see sometimes my ego got in the way of me being humble and gratefully accepting gifts from others.

I was writing the day's events and insights in my journal when I heard Tata's voice above the storm cussing because my lone tent had the last campsite.

I yelled through the tent, "Quit bitchin and set up."

Poncho exclaimed, "It's Dreamer!" They scrambled and set their tent up to get out of the storm.

The storm passed, so I joined Poncho and Tata as they cooked their evening meal. A solo hiker came in looking for a place to stay.

I was about to invite him to set up in our campsite with us but Tata barked out, "What the hell are you looking at?" The hiker quickly moved on.

I hadn't noticed, but apparently, Poncho and Tata were a little cold in their wet tee shirts. I put on my best innocent face, looked surprised, and acted as if I didn't have any idea what she was talking about. She then turned on me and said, "You can put your eyes back in your head too you old fart!"

I tried to look shocked and innocently said, "What?" But I couldn't keep the grin off my face.

She said, "Pervert!" We all broke out laughing.

I said, "You scared the poor bastard so bad, he's probably half-way to Katahdin by now." We all laughed until I started to cry. It was after dark when we quit talking and I retired to my tent for the night. I was now fifty-two miles from the mystical summit.

I couldn't sleep, so I turned on the light and took out my little pocket version of the Big Book. I randomly opened it up to the Promises. I read another Promise that said, *No matter how far down the scale we have gone we will see how our experience can benefit others.*

My mother was a Christian and went to church most Sundays. I wondered if what she was doing was keeping her feet firmly grounded in Christ in order to survive. She set a good example, but I was blind to what she was doing. Mom never walked away from God and didn't go down the scale at all. She did nothing to be ashamed of in her whole life, yet she always, without fail, did what she could to help others. She took me to church, but I hated it. When I was about eleven, or twelve-years-old, she would let me go on my own. I would skip Sunday school and spend the money she gave for the collection on cigarettes. I wonder if she knew and never said anything, but simply kept giving it away to keep it anyway.

I now could see she was subtly planting seeds. Seeds that at the time didn't appear to grow, but she kept planting them anyway. She probably had the faith that one day the seeds would grow. I must have broken her heart with my behavior in my addiction, but she loved me anyway and kept giving it away. I had no idea why she kept giving and didn't give up on me because I was blind, but she was working her type of program. She never heard of Alcoholics Anonymous until I started to tell her about the program and then she never really understood my program.

I paused to pray, out loud and asked, "Is the answer to my prayer that simple? To show my gratitude I try to plant seeds of hope in others by sharing my experience. Should I share with others my horrible experiences of living Godless for so long?" I felt a sense of peace, which I took as a yes answer to my questions.

I turned the light off and pulled the sleeping bag up to protect against the night chill. I thanked God for the privilege of becoming an alcoholic and for my mother. My mind gradually slowed down as if I took my foot off the accelerator. I eventually drifted into sleep.

Day 164   5.9 Miles

The rain stopped sometime early in the night and the sky cleared, but I didn't sleep well anyway. A noisy moose feeding in the lake and a loon's lonesome call disturbed me several times. I woke up long before daylight with my old work from back home in my head. My conservation with Lady D probably triggered my psyche into the thoughts. Lady D was my boss a long time ago and asked me if I was going to return to the agency. I wasn't sure if I wanted to return to my old job or not, but I felt sure I wasn't ready for my hike to end yet. I thought back to when I watched the four lane highway with bumper-to-bumper traffic pouring commuters in and out of New York City. I thought that could be where someone coined the term, rat race. My only concern at the time was running low on water to drink and they were zooming by like a bunch of ants going to and from the city. I wondered, which world was real, mine, or theirs. I now could see the real world was the one I lived in at the time.

I didn't miss or want to return to the world I left behind on the twenty-sixth of February. It was a world full of demanding bosses, meaningless paperwork, and unreasonable deadlines. I constantly had to be on my toes to be politically correct and careful not offend anyone or violate a client's confidentiality. A world of such intense competition among peers that it bred jealousy, envy, and backbiting. I lived with resentments towards the people I worked with for so long that resentments became a normal part of my life. I had only lived on the trail a short time when I realized resentments were what blocked my spiritual growth.

I wanted to go back to sleep, but it was impossible. I got up quietly because Poncho and Tata were still sleeping. I made a cup of coffee, walked to the water's edge, and squatted in the position of a baseball catcher and felt the water. I took a sip of the foul tasting brew, and felt the caffeine as it entered my bloodstream and did its job.

I marveled at the way the still water reflected the stars of heaven in the endless sky. I purposely focused on my insights into the program in an attempt to escape and force my fear of the future from my mind. My thoughts returned to the Promise, "No matter how far down the scale we have gone we will see how our experience can benefit others." My mother couldn't identify with me because she had no experience of living in hell as an addict like me.

I often envied people like Mom, Heaven Bound, and Cedar Moe. Why were they so lucky they didn't have to be beat down by living in a Godless hell before they surrendered their life and will over to the care of God? The spirit didn't whisper to me. It was more as if the spirit slapped me with the awareness that I was the lucky one. I didn't have to have faith to believe hell existed, because I had already experienced living in hell without God. Maybe God created Alcoholics Anonymous and sent my mother and others to let me out of hell because He loved me.

I had the advantage of being able to share with others that I once lived like any addict where drugs were my higher power, and experienced the miracle of recovery. Not to boast as I did to Mountain Goat, but to give hope to others so they may also change.

I drank my coffee as I gazed out into the mist rising from the lake that was smooth as glass, wondering what I should do as I watched the distant shore appear as the day began. It occurred to me to pray to ask God, so I prayed. Magically as if the Holy Spirit put a thought into my pea brain, I intuited, I need to return and carry the message that I so freely received. I thought, maybe I'll even write a book, which was a thought that crossed my mind occasionally since I was on the trail, although I didn't think the idea was worth taking too seriously.

I must have been in the catcher's position a while because I had a hard time standing up at first, but soon loosened up. I packed up and moved out without disturbing Poncho and Tata. I went from a glum mood to being excited about my purpose in life. God was amazing and how great it was to have the privilege to be able to contact Him.

The Boy Scouts started to awaken as I slipped through their camp. I didn't see Chris or I would have stopped and said goodbye. I hiked solo all morning through low land at about five-hundred feet above sea level, which was unusually wet because of all the extra rain we had that year. The night's darkness yielded to the new day as the birds sang their song from the heart as if announcing the miracle of the arrival of the first morning of forever. The trail led me along the shore of Lower Jo-Mary Lake to a soft sandy beach. I wrote a message to Scooter in the smooth, wet sand and drew a heart with my finger. I took a picture of my artwork for a future Valentine for her.

I believed the spirit of Gallagher rode in abruptly on the breeze, leaving riffles in its wake. His spirit reminded me of the story of a diamond that he told me when I still physically saw and heard him, which went something like:

A lump of ordinary coal and a precious diamond were made of the same element, carbon. The difference occurred when nature exposed a common piece of coal to heat, stress, and pressure over a long period of time. The coal most often burned up, but occasionally, the coal adapted to the adversity by becoming harder and more pure over time. The process eventually drove all the impurities from the coal, leaving only pure carbon. The coal's metamorphoses created the hardest and most precious object on earth; a diamond. But it took external forces of adversity. I didn't know why not all coal transformed into diamonds. God probably knew, but he didn't tell me yet. I believe the coal had to be lucky. With that thought, I realized maybe Mom, Heaven Bound, and Cedar Moe weren't quite as lucky as God's recovering addicts. The adversity I hated experiencing in my addiction may have been a blessing in disguise. I felt special and overwhelmed with gratitude.

I hiked six miles, all below an altitude of seven-hundred feet with wet feet on a sunny day, to Mahar Tote Road. The term road was misleading because I found a grassy path that maybe once could have been a logging road a long time ago. The road led to White House Landing Wilderness Camp where I could rent a private room, shower, and breakfast for thirty-nine dollars, which sounded good. The guidebook said to hike a mile off trail to a dock on the lake and blow an air horn. The owner of the lodge would come to pick me up by boat and take me across the lake to the lodge.

I had a lot of time, but knee-deep standing water on the path caused me to hesitate. I was still contemplating whether it was worth getting my feet wetter or not when I heard people talking down the trail. My curiosity took over and made the decision easier, so I braved the water and ventured down Mahar Tote Road. I met Bill and Mary who owned and operated White House Landing. They were collecting sticks as big as they could carry and placed them in the bigger puddles of water on the road for stepping-stones so hikers would come to White House Landing. Their business was down and they were struggling financially. They thought it was in part due to the high water on the trail that caused hikers to pass by who otherwise would stop.

The hiker Tata ran off the night before stopped. His trail name was Day Break and he was a former, two-time, thru-hiker. He taught school and was out section hiking the hundred-mile wilderness on his summer vacation. He pitched in and in no time, we had a makeshift type of a rickety path over the water to the dock on Pemadumcook Lake.

Pemadumcook Lake was an enormous, pristine lake in the wilderness. The lake was too big to see across in some places and except for Bill and Mary's White House Landing, it was untouched by modern day progress. The four of us all piled into Bill's boat with a forty-horse outboard motor and zoomed to White House landing. Bill, Mary, and their eleven-year-old son lived in the main lodge where the kitchen and dining area were located. The bunkhouse was separate and had a shower with water pumped from the lake that was unsafe for drinking. A few yards away stood a large cottage for guests with a common kitchen and four private rooms with two beds each.

We went to the dining room for lunch. Pizza and one-pound cheeseburgers were the only two items on the menu. They sold pop, beer and bottles of wine. Bill gave Daybreak and I a pop for our work on the trail and we both ordered the pound cheeseburgers at ten dollars each. We enjoyed socializing while Mary cooked our cheeseburgers. The cheeseburger was one of the best I had on the trail and well worth the ten bucks.

I took a liking to Daybreak as he and I exchanged trail tales. He rented a bunk in the bunkhouse and I rented a private room to stay overnight, even though it was only noon and I only hiked six miles. I still had plenty of time to finish the trail. My ankle was sore and extremely swollen as always, so the rest would do me good. I resolved to summit Mount Katahdin even if I had to crawl. I only had forty miles to The Birches, which was a base camp for Nobo thru-hikers only. I had lots of time, so spending the day there wouldn't delay my schedule. I would still even have time to take a zero day in Millinocket on Saturday the twelfth, where I planned to meet Scooter.

I took a shower, which was included as part of the stay. Public electricity wasn't available for obvious reasons, but they had a gasoline generator and some solar heating. The sun heated the water pumped from the lake, but they hauled in propane to cook and light the cabins.

The cabin filled up as Poncho and Tata came in, along with a man and his wife from Connecticut and a seventy-one-year-old, whisky drinking man from Boston. My room was the only one that had an empty bunk left, so if anyone else arrived wanting a private room, Bill would put them in the other single bed in my room. My private room wouldn't be so private and I would have a problem. No one was staying in the bunkhouse besides Daybreak, so he may be the only one to have a private room. We all went to the dining room for supper. I had a cheese pizza that was too big for me to eat. Mary saved the leftover pizza for me to take with me when I left.

We all started socializing. Everyone had fun for a while, but they were also drinking bottles of wine and beer. I was still surprised at how quickly alcohol changed a human's personality and soon everyone became an expert on everything. Tata and the whisky drinking man from Boston were starting to get obnoxious, so I went outside to get some air. I feared there was going to be some drama between them soon because of the drinking.

Canoes were available to take out on the lake, so I took one for a ride to look for moose. I started to paddle franticly to escape the voices from the dining room that were starting to escalate. That was an old feeling because I never could stand to be around people who were drinking when I was sober. Even in my drinking days, if I was sober and ran into a drunk I would either get away or join them. When I was as drunk as they were, we got along. I don't drink anymore, so I distanced myself.

The sight and sounds of the cabin soon faded into non-existence as I entered a distant cove, guarded by huge boulders the size of buildings that stuck out of the water about two stories tall. I felt like they were welcoming me into an enchanted world. I felt small and almost as if I was trespassing on sacred ground as I navigated my way around and through the stone sentinels as silently as possible. I tried not to announce my arrival to any moose who might have been feeding on the tender plant-life that grew in the shallow water in the wonderful world I discovered.

I stopped paddling after I passed the shadows cast by the stone guards and gave control to the gentle evening breeze that took the canoe where it wanted. I found the tranquility of the wilderness lake started to relax my mind and body like Mother Nature's sedative. I smelled the white pine and hemlock that stood on the shores like added lookouts as I drifted into their view. Their rich green faded into dark gray as the sun descended from the sky as if it was going to bed after a hard day's work of lighting up the earth. The coolness of the coming night took the edge off the heat of the hot summer's day. I watched as the angels painted the sky with comforting pastels as if God Himself was signing off at the end of the day, "Love God."

The only sound was the gentle sound of the water as it lapped at the side of the canoe, which put me in a hypnotic state perfect for meditation. I let my mind drift with the canoe as my heart slowed down after I stopped the exertion of paddling. I felt a euphoric feeling all day, but now it started to peak. It seemed ironic that I would use the term peak to describe how it felt because peak was the street term addicts use to describe the feeling when they reached the top of the high from a drug.

To no one, I said aloud, This is the high I have been searching for all these years. It was sad to think of all the years I wasted getting high, trying to find it and it was hidden right there in plain sight. I honestly couldn't see it. I became so excited right there on Pemadumcook Lake I shouted, *This is it!* I heard the eerie sound of my own voice as it echoed back to me from the walls of the cove. In the silence that followed it seemed as plain as the ass on a goat, the search was over. This was really it. My ego entertained for a moment the idea that I finally found my keys and I could stop looking. In a moment of clarity, I remembered an Alcoholics Anonymous slogan. I said aloud, Easy does it, Dreamer.

I calmed down, thinking that moments such as those were all part of my journey. I could enjoy them, but like chewing gum, I didn't want to swallow it. I had to keep my ego in check and keep seeking because that wasn't it. At least not yet, but it was progress. I felt I was the lucky one blessed with recovery, but I didn't know why. I believe along with the gift went the responsibility to carry the message to others. If I didn't pass it on to others, I wouldn't be able to hold on to it for long.

The day had been a great day, but I thought like all good things, this too shall pass, as I watched darkness swallow the lake and steal the color from the wilderness as it had every night since God created it. I took one last picture of the bright orange moon rising above the distant shore, which by now was a black line of trees separating the water from the sky. I would look at the picture someday when things weren't so good and remember my experience on Pemadumcook Lake. I didn't see any moose, but I did witness a sensational sunset and had conscious contact with God as I now understood him.

I picked my way back through the granite boulders that have silently stood guard at the entrance of the cove for thousands of years. The moon was full and shed enough light so I could see my way. When I returned to the main part of the lake, I could see the lights were out in the main lodge, but still on in the cabin where everyone stayed. That was both good and bad. The light showed me the way home, but it also meant the others were awake and still up. I purposely took my time, enjoying the trip across the lake. I was grateful when the lights in the cabin went out before I arrived.

It was later than I was accustomed to staying up when I returned to the cabin. I silently made my way to my room and crawled into the clean, dry sheets. I was thankful everyone was asleep. It did occur to me, if anyone else would have arrived before dark, I would have had a roommate. I laid awake for some time, both excited and sad because my dream journey was about to end successfully. The reality was, I would summit Mount Katahdin in less than a week, which seemed almost too good to be true. It occurred to me as my mind drifted like the canoe, that maybe Katahdin didn't mark the end, but maybe it only marked the beginning.

Day 165   15.8 Miles

I awoke in the early pre-dawn hours, refreshed and far too excited to go back to sleep or even lay in bed. I quietly made my trail coffee in the cabin on the gas stove while everyone else was still fast asleep. I put on my jacket and took my coffee outside to watch another day come alive over the lake, as the birds serenaded me.

I continued to ponder how I was the lucky one. I concluded that, why me, no longer mattered anymore, but what I did with my gift from here on out was what mattered. I decided to pray, so with my eyes wide open, looking beyond Pemadumcook Lake and into the future I prayed, "Lord, thank you for the opportunity to become a diamond, but please help me not end my journey at the summit. Let me seek your knowledge and give me the strength I need to follow through, amen."

I believe Gallagher's spirit was who whispered in my ear, "When a diamond was first discovered, it wasn't so attractive until it was polished, so go now, and polish your discovery with care." I intuitively knew how to polish my stone. I had to pass on to others what so many had freely given to me.

Bill and Mary served breakfast family-style at eight o'clock. I was the first to arrive at the kitchen and drank good coffee as I talked to Bill and Mary while they prepared breakfast. They struggled financially to keep their home, business, and dream. They catered to snowmobilers in the winter also, but last winter, they didn't get enough snow to show a profit. I felt their pain and felt badly for them, but it wasn't my responsibility to fix it for them.

The others started to trickle in for coffee. Soon the place was buzzing with conversation. No one mentioned anything about last night. Like any other dysfunctional family, it would appear all was forgiven and forgotten, but I had the feeling some underlying resentments were just under the surface. We all received two eggs, bacon, toast and all the pancakes we could eat. As usual, when all you could eat was available, I ate all I could eat.

We all settled our bill and Mary gave me the pizza I had left over from last night. I also bought a noodle packet and some Snickers bars. I thought back to how intimidated I was as I anticipated the hundred-mile wilderness. I worried if I would have enough food. As it turned out, I had more food than I could eat. It was about a two-day hike away from Abol Bridge on the West Branch of the Penobscot River, which would be the official end of the hundred-mile wilderness.

I went back to the cabin to pack, which only took minutes because I never took my tent and sleeping bag out of my pack. Bill said he would make two trips to shuttle all of us across the lake by boat. I wanted to be in the first trip because I was itching to get back on the trail as soon as possible. Daybreak and I were the first to arrive at the dock, but soon Tata and Poncho came along. Bill started the engine and we all piled into the boat. Bill shuttled us at full speed back across the lake to the trail where we bid him goodbye.

Daybreak and I saddled up and left as the girls were busy getting ready to hike. I followed Daybreak for about five minutes until we ran out of trail. We were lost and had to backtrack to the lake. I was happy to see the girls were gone by the time we got back on the approach trail. That way, we wouldn't have to explain how two seasoned, badass thru-hikers got lost. We started out fresh again, but that time I took the lead so we wouldn't get lost. Guess what? We got lost again.

We met three attractive girls about Daybreak's age at the junction of the approach trail. Daybreak was embarrassing because he went gaga, practically drooling, as I gave them directions to the landing. They were planning on having lunch and possibly spending the night. We filled them in on all the details and bid them best wishes. I thought Daybreak was going to return with them, but he didn't. I sure hoped they didn't get lost.

I hiked with Daybreak for a while, but soon dropped back to be kind to my injured ankle. Besides, I wanted to spend some time in meditation. Once I was alone, I started to ponder my prayer, How would I carry the message? How could I show my gratitude?

I always hated it when someone tried to impose their beliefs on me or convince me to buy something. Even Bill Wilson said to Ebby, "I just can't stomach the way some people peddle God." One Sunday morning, when I was active in my addiction, the Jehovah Witnesses came to my door. I was smoking weed and wanted anyone to talk to so I let them in the house. The problem with that was they came back every Sunday. They never shared any personal experiences. They only tried to convince me of what God wanted me to do from their understanding. I don't remember if I believed them or not at the time.

Finally, one Sunday, I was dreadfully hung over and tried to ignore their persistent knocking, but couldn't. I lost my temper and chased a well-meaning couple back to a carload of them. They jumped in the car and locked the door. I broke off a windshield wiper blade and cursed them as they were making a hasty retreat. I felt better and started to make a game out of it every time they showed up at my door. I soon had zero unwanted solicitors.

I still kept a baseball bat beside my door hoping for the opportunity to scare off a solicitor. I never hit anyone, yet. I only held the bat in a threatening position with wild eyes and yelled, "They just let me out and that proves I'm not really crazy," which always seemed to be enough to send them scurrying away.

Dr. Bob pointed out to Bill that he hated anyone preaching at him, even if he agreed. I believe I caused Mountain Goat to resent me because he felt I was preaching to try to impose my values on him. Preaching seemed to always defeat the purpose of the preacher anyway.

Dr. Bob suggested they should do simply as Bill did with him, share their experience, strength, and hope with others who suffered. I started to wonder, Is that the answer to my prayer? It hit me like a sucker punch. How could it be so simple. Does God want me to share my story as Bill did with Dr. Bob? How could I have been so blind? So many others in the program have modeled that simple principal, but I continued to do things my way. I gave writing a book a little more than a passing thought. I wondered why writing a book kept resurfacing in my mind because I wasn't a writer. I don't know the first thing about writing a book.

I hiked on solo all morning through the low lands of the Nahmakanta Valley with pleasing dreams about writing a book. My feet were so wet that I long ago stopped trying to avoid the numerous bogs and wet areas of the trail. A detour sign interrupted my thoughts that said, "Detour due to high water, trail flooded." A blue blazed detour trail circled around the hazard, which upset me because I was a purist up to that point and strictly followed the white blazes. I ran into two detours in Virginia and ignored both. One was a bridge out, so I had to ford a creek that was only up to my knees. On the other one, I only got my feet wet crossing a beaver dam.

I was less than forty miles from the summit of Katahdin, so I threw caution to the wind and proceeded on the blocked white blaze trail. I felt a gnawing feeling in my gut that I shouldn't be doing it, but my ego wouldn't let me take the detour. The going wasn't too bad at first, which made it a little easier to ignore my intuition. I soon came to a bog with planks to walk on leading across an especially soft looking area. I thought, "How bad could it be?"

That particular bog could best be described as a type of wetland area characterized by wet, spongy, peat-moss type muck that smelled like sewer. Thick moss and red willow bush grew on the surface of the poorly drained, watery slime. That made for a fragile and unstable ecosystem. The northern bogs weren't only in the low lands, but also small ones were high on the mountains where solid granite rock prevented the water from draining. They always seemed to be stagnant, causing the unpleasant order of a privy from the rotten vegetation. In dryer years they were probably firmer, but our unusually wet year made for bogs that were about the consistency of fresh cow poop. They called the larger bogs in the low lands with trees growing in them, muskegs.

When one person walked gently on a bog, they broke through the surface vegetation about half the time. When many people walked on a bog such as on the Appalachian Trail, they completely sawed through the surface. The volunteer trail clubs placed logs or planks over the bogs on the trail for the hikers to walk on. These bog bridges were also called puncheons and were often as short as a few feet, but sometimes they were hundreds of yards long.

When I stepped onto the first plank of the puncheon, the moss and willow bushes floating on the surface moved with my weight. I continued, but a gnawing feeling I shouldn't be there became stronger as the planks started to submerge under my weight into the smelly muck. I unbuckled my pack belt when I was up to my ass in slime. I felt a little secure as long as had the planks under my feet, but I had to keep moving because the slower I went the more I sank.

I was literally up to my waist in sewer-like decaying sludge when I came to the end of the plank. Either I fell off or there wasn't any more planks. I found myself swimming in the foul smelling muck. I had to fight the urge to panic as I slipped off my pack. I tried to back up to the safety of the submerged planks. I grabbed a willow bush to pull myself back until I found the security of the plank, but it seemed even deeper as I was up above my armpits in shit. I had to stretch to grab the strap on my pack and retrieve it before it sank forever. I turned around and fought my way back towards the way I came dragging my pack with everything I owned through the sludge. I was no longer worried about my purist status. I simply wanted to get my ass out of the predicament I put myself in. I paused to catch my breath as soon as I felt safe. I really wished I hadn't done what I just did as I let my heart rate subside and the folic acid clear. It seemed like it took forever as I backtracked to the start of the detour where I made the foolish decision. I sat on my wet, smelly, pack, and took a drink of water.

One of my heroes as a boy was the Lone Ranger, who often fell into quicksand, but his faithful friend and partner Tonto always came to the rescue, roping and pulling him out of trouble with his horse. I had an awful feeling in my stomach as I realized Tonto wouldn't come for me. I foolishly went down a detour where zero help would come to rescue me. It would have been stupid to die that close to the summit of Katahdin because of my foolish ego.

I sat there and recuperated by drinking water for a while until my heart rate slowed back down and I felt rested. I got on my knees and said, thank you, God, before I saddled up and moved out. I couldn't shake the negative feeling that I should have known better. I took the blue blazed detour, which took me back to the white blazes in less than half a mile.

I stopped to check in my guidebook about something I recalled about detours. I read to be able to claim thru-hiker status you had to hike every mile of the Appalachian Trail between the two termini. Blue blazed trails were acceptable substitutes only in the event of an emergency such as high water that required a detour. I felt a little better after reading that I could officially keep my thru-hiker purist status.

Maybe that was where someone coined the phrase, Up shit creek without a paddle. I donned my smelly pack and continued on, trying to put the experience out of my mind. I followed the trail to the south end of Nahmakanta Lake where I found a sandy beach a little off trail and went swimming clothes and all. I was grateful I had the chance to clean up before I ran into any of my friends smelling as if I crawled out of a swamp. I emptied my pack and washed it off. I was fortunate none of my food got wet. I ate my leftover pizza while I sat in the sun to dry out before I moved on as if nothing happened. I decided to never, ever tell anyone about my foolishness that morning.

I left the lowlands as I ascended Nesuntabunt Mountain. The mountain was only a little over fifteen hundred feet high, but I was happy to be on dryer ground. I came upon a sign at a side trail to my right near the top that said, Vista 200 feet. I normally didn't take side trails to overlooks, but for some reason I took the trail to an open cliff. I stopped dead in my tracks to catch my breath when I recognized before me in all its majesty stood Mount Katahdin. The incredible adrenalin rush traveled clear down to my toes, which was even better than my experience the night before on Pemadumcook Lake. I had absolutely no doubt I was looking directly at the mighty Mount Katahdin. I saw the small details of the mountain at only thirty-six miles away.

The green forest leading toward the distant mountain looked as if it was a manicured lawn landscaped by the angels. I saw the tree-line on Katahdin where the green forest turned into the light gray of naked, granite rock. The mountain itself looked like one solid, giant rock standing alone, made strong by defying Maine's harsh elements since its creation by God.

Time seemed to stop as it all seemed so surreal. I actually saw my goal, which was the summit of the mountain. I stood there staring at the mountain, with tears in my eyes in a kind of an emotional trance. There was the mountain that had been in my hopes and dreams for so long. It was hard for me to comprehend that I was looking directly at the real Katahdin. The mountain was no longer merely a picture on a postcard or in my dreams. The mountain did exist and I was looking at it only three days away. I took my pack off and sat down on it to enjoy the feeling. I remembered to give thanks to God. I realized thru-hiking the Appalachian Trail with God's help had always been possible. He may have even sent me on the journey to become closer to Him.

My ego inflated with a feeling of grandiosity that was pleasant. Then the negative, unsolicited memories from the bog that morning flashed into my mind giving me a chill. I suddenly felt humbled as I stared deep in a state of meditation at the mighty mountain as if all the answers lay hidden there.

I said aloud, "What secrets do you have hidden that you are protecting?" I was talking directly to Katahdin as if the mountain would answer. The mountain, as mighty as it looked, was only a symbol of the reward I gained. I believed the gift actually was an unprecedented spiritual awakening. I developed a better understanding of how the relationship between God and me evolved.

I heard Daybreak approach as he interrupted my meditative state, but I didn't turn to look at him. He didn't say a word either. He just put his hand on my shoulder, then left me to my thoughts. Perhaps he had a similar experience when he looked upon Katahdin for the first time right there on the same spot. I knew he knew, as only another thru-hiker could understand what I was feeling. He then departed without saying anything.

I felt contact with the power greater than myself, who I call God, stronger than any other time in my life. That very moment may have been the reason I was inspired to hike the trail in the first place.

Lady D said, God was the one who put the idea of hiking the trail in your head. Maybe she was right. I remember thinking it was odd that I was so enthusiastic about the Appalachian Trail right from the first time I noticed the southern terminus marked in fine print on a Georgia road map so long ago. I wondered if God sent me to the trail away, from the ordinary day-to-day stressors so we could talk. After all, I prayed for knowledge of His will in Step Eleven before I got the inspiration to thru-hike. I closed my eyes and said, "God, what do you want me to do to serve you? What is your will for me now? Amen."

I had no idea how long I sat there, lost in my questions without answers, before a couple of day-hikers who seemed to be in love came along and broke the silence. They asked me to take their picture with their camera, which I did. I answered their questions before I packed up and moved out in a pleasant state of serenity. I felt grateful for the contact I had with God as I understood him.

I still had over six miles to reach the next lean-to, which was my goal for the day. I was in for yet another treat as I approached Pollywog Gorge, which was a deep canyon-type gorge with Pollywog Stream cascading through it. I took a picture, but the picture didn't show how magnificent the gorge actually appeared in real life. I wished I could have spent more time there, but daylight was running out.

Day Break came along again, as I was admiring the view of the gorge. I thanked him for not interrupting my moment on Nesuntabunt Mountain when I was gazing at Katahdin for the first time. He said, "What?" with a puzzled look on his face. I wondered, who put their hand on my shoulder, but I decided to say nothing.

I hiked with Day Break to Rainbow Stream Lean-to, which made the three plus miles fly by swiftly. We found some day-hikers and section hikers already filling the shelter. We chatted with the others for a little while before we set up our tents on reasonably flat ground about a hundred yards away. We were fifty yards off trail so Poncho and Tata went to the crowded shelter without noticing us. I went to the shelter and invited them to camp with us. After they set up their tent, we cooked and ate together, chatting with excitement like a family. We didn't retire to our tents until well after dark.

Alone in my tent, I took the time to say thanks, being grateful for the day. I was exhausted and wanted to sleep, but I couldn't talk my mind into shutting down. I felt a tinge of envy because the others were close enough that I could hear their breathing as it slowed into the even rhythm of sleep. I stayed awake for quite a long time listening to the sounds of the night, sensing the presence of Katahdin. I replayed the tapes of the trail all the way back to the first day on Springer, while anticipating the adventure that laid in store for me the next day. I always wondered what Bill had in mind when he wrote, "We have entered the world of the spirit." I believe I entered the world of the spirit that day.

Day 166   15 Miles

15 Miles closer to Katahdin

I slept fitfully, tossing, and turning all night long probably due to the excitement of being in such close proximity of Katahdin. I was awake most of the night listening to the sounds of the others breathing as they slept. In the early pre-dawn hours, as I lay awake not quite ready to get up to start the day, I got a little spirit whisper. A phrase I have heard many times in Alcoholics Anonymous entered my mind, *Walk like you talk, you may be the only Big Book someone else reads.* Again, I thought, *How could it be that simple?* If I do what I have witnessed others in the program doing all along, I would be carrying the message. All I had to do when called upon was share my personal experience, strength, and hope with others. Then I needed to let go of control to let God do the rest.

Early on in Alcoholics Anonymous, folks told me over, and over, *If you want what we have, keep coming back.* I did, and they led me into recovery by the example of how they lived and what they did. We as humans learn by emulating those around us. For example, I learned to speak English by the time I was three-years-old. No one actually taught me to speak English. I learned English because everyone around me spoke English and I learned by emulating them. We may always learn by following the example set by those around us. When all my peers were active alcoholics and addicts I became exactly like them. I even thought and believed like them. When I became sober and all my peers were in recovery I started to act, think, and believe like them, I had the same hope they did. When I was around positive people like Daybreak, Tata, and Poncho, I became positive, but unfortunately, when I was around negative people I became fearful. I admired Heaven Bound because he walked like he talked. I was attracted to him because he modeled how he lived, which gave me hope. In a way, he was the only Bible I read at the time.

I once had lost all hope. I came to Alcoholics Anonymous when I was hopeless and I received a glimmer of hope from a spiritual connection with others in the program. The first meeting I attended that day in 1977, the man with no fingers gave me the first glimmer of hope and I didn't even know his name. The hope I received was a lot like the hope Dr. Bob received unexpectedly from Bill Wilson that first day in Akron in 1935. I believe hope is the greatest gift one human being could give to another human being. Hope eventually turned into faith for me. I believed faith was the greatest gift of all, but I had to have God's help with faith.

I got up and started my day with a prayer, *"Lord, thank you for answering my prayer. Please, help me walk like I talk and set an example that attracts and encourages others to emulate me. Please teach me to lead by example and not push others with my impatience. No matter how enthusiastic I become, show me when I'm promoting or imposing the message on others. Amen."* I had a warm feeling of gratitude to my creator for prayers answered as I started my stove and made bad coffee.

I welcomed the sound of Daybreak getting up in the darkness. He got his trail name from being on the trail by daybreak every day. I offered him some extra strong, extra bad coffee. I wasn't not sure why, but he passed on the offer. Daybreak and I ate quietly, broke camp, and left the girls sleeping in the dim, pre-dawn light. The day was overcast and looked as if it might rain, which made the light of the day come slower. I hiked with Daybreak, who set a faster pace than I was accustomed to, but I so enjoyed his company. I took extra ibuprofen for my ankle, put the pain out of my mind, and kept up. The miles slipped by as we chatted with caffeine and excitement like a couple of teenage boys.

I found in the far north, the wild blueberries were at their peak in August. They covered the hilltops with bushes yielding an abundance of the plump fruit. We would pause at first and pick a few berries and pop them in our mouth as we passed by, but the eating of anything when you were a hungry hiker soon became top priority. We stopped in a large patch, took our packs off, and began gorging on the sweet berries.

Three French Canadian young men came by and paused. One gentleman who had a puzzled look on his face asked with a heavy French accent, "Are those berries edible"?

I saw the devilish look in Daybreak's eye as he said, "No, poison" with his mouth full. My mouth was so full so I just shook my head no, with a smirk on my face that gave my sarcasm away. We ate our fill of blue berries before moving out. We soon walked up on the French Canadians, who had also stopped to eat the blue berries.

I said, "You must not have blue berries in your part of Canada." I was the only one who laughed at my little joke. I hope they weren't offended.

Daybreak and I stopped for lunch at scenic Hurd Brook Lean-to, which sat on the bank of a fast moving, nameless stream. I thought the volunteer builders strategically placed the shelter so hikers could hear the white sound of the rushing water sing them to sleep. I took a picture, but it didn't turn out well. We took our time eating as the water rushed by. We were only a little over three miles from Abol Bridge, which was our goal.

The pain in my ankle escalated, probably due to the fast pace I hiked to keep up with Daybreak. I considered staying there for the night, but I was enjoying Daybreak's company. I decided to take more ibuprofen and suck it up. Besides, hiking with Daybreak would help me keep my mind off the pain. I limped out and kept up with my hero.

We arrived at Abol Bridge over the impressive Penobscot River by early afternoon. The bridge marked the end of the hundred-mile wilderness. The Penobscot River was the largest river I had seen since the Connecticut River in Hanover, New Hampshire. Unlike most of the big rivers, the Penobscot appeared to have a strong, intimidating current that looked dangerous. The bridge itself was sturdy, but crude by modern standards. Logging companies built the bridge on an unpaved, gravel road that entered Maine's rich natural forests. Mainly huge logging trucks sped by as we were standing there. They went to the forests to pick up logs, then returned loaded with the logs to deliver to the sawmills. I didn't believe any privately owned property existed past the bridge.

The guidebook warned hikers to use a pedestrian walkway provided for hikers. I could see why, because the trucks created a cloud of dust as they whizzed by on their mission. I could understand how dangerous it would be on the roadway in a cloud of dust. I thought, after hiking all the way from Georgia it would be just wrong to get my ass run over by a logging truck in sight of Katahdin, so I took the walkway.

Abol Bridge provided a postcard-type picture of Katahdin, but not on an overcast day like that day. Clouds covered the top of Katahdin, but I took a picture of it from the bridge anyway. I was fifteen miles from the summit of Mount Katahdin and found the closer I got, the more intimidated I became by Katahdin.

Katahdin was a mile high, but it appeared taller because God planted it alone on the forested Maine horizon. Clingmans Dome that stood over sixty-six hundred feet high in the Smoky Mountains, was the tallest on the trail, but you started your ascent at about fifty-five hundred feet high so you didn't get the feel of how tall it really stood. Besides, most of the mountains around Clingmans Dome were over six-thousand feet high.

Katahdin was unique because the trail started ascending at Katahdin Stream Campground at eleven-hundred feet above sea level and climbed to five-thousand, two-hundred and sixty-seven feet in five miles. The tree-line on Katahdin was at about thirty-four-hundred feet, which meant I had to climb over eighteen-hundred feet in the last two and a half miles above tree-line on cold, bare granite. God must have planted Mount Katahdin alone in Baxter State Park to be the perfect northern terminus for the Appalachian Trail.

Once we crossed the bridge, we came to the camp store, which was like Walmart of the wilderness. The store was a little, one-story building made to simulate a log cabin with dark brown siding and a dark green metal roof. The first thing I noticed was a large beer sign mounted on the roof. They sold beer, wine, groceries, souvenirs, magazines, camping supplies, firewood, toys, and gadgets of all kinds. They ran a privately owned campground where they catered to RVs and Camp trailers. They also provided a boat-launching ramp. They might have even rented boats. They had a shower, but it was only for campers that stayed in their campground.

The usual locals loafed outside the store, drinking coffee, and smoking pipes. They told us all we needed to know about how it was before all the tourists, as if we wanted to know. A school bus stopped and kids poured out, dressed in swimsuits, so a beach must have been somewhere close.

Daybreak and I, without saying a word, dropped our packs in unison at a flowerbed guarded by rocks and hurried inside to the smell of fresh brewed coffee. We flirted with the clerk slash waitress who was about seventy-years-young, but she was single and strait. We bought donuts and coffee and went outside to chew the fat with the locals.

A short, pudgy ridge runner with a long ponytail came over to check us out and offered us free advice about the trail and Baxter. Apparently, the entrance to Baxter was only about a tenth of a mile up trail. I didn't think he hiked much. In fact, I didn't think he ever went out of sight of the donuts, but we listened to what he said. I had to admit he looked sporty in his new ridge runner uniform. I was pretty sure he felt honored when I dubbed him, "Sporty."

We socialized with the locals, the ridge runner, and tourist-type campers for a couple of hours while drinking vast amounts of high octane coffee. We finally decided we better set up camp ourselves before a storm that threatened all day finally hit. I bought a package of hotdogs and buns for supper before we left for the primitive, state owned campground on the other side of the road.

Abol Pines Campground was on the bank of the Penobscot River in the shadow of Mount Katahdin. We deposited five bucks each camping fee in a locked box welded to a pipe cemented in the ground. I set up my tent a few feet from the river so I could see the view from inside my tent. Daybreak set up in the shelter. I was alone for the first time since I left that morning, feeling overwhelmed with gratitude for all the blessings coming my way. I didn't deserve any of it and felt unworthy. I said a simple prayer of gratitude.

The last part of Step Twelve said, "Practice these principles in all our affairs." In today's society, we made rules or laws, because it was easier to make rules than teach principles. I was so bad at following the rules of our society that I nearly landed in prison. I also rebelled against the rules set down by the church of my childhood. Once I learned the principles behind the rules, I discovered that when living and practicing the principles, my life was no longer restless, irritable, and discontent, but happy, joyous, free, and filled with love.

When I planned my thru-hike, I worried about how I would practice the principles of the Twelve Steps and work my program on the trail. I knew it was going to be hard or impossible to attend meetings for six months while on the trail. I also knew I had to have both feet firmly grounded in my personal recovery program in order to survive the trail. I guess, where there's a will, there's a way because my cell phone and the friends in Alcoholics Anonymous who I connected with on a spiritual basis, became the way for me.

I also practiced the essence of the principles that day back in the Smoky Mountains when I shared with Mathewski. It felt so good serving that day that I wondered if God was sending a message for me to be a servant. Maybe that was the message Jesus sent when he washed the feet of his disciples. Jesus spent his life practicing the principles by walking like he talked, so people could emulate Him. The simplicity of it all was, if I could truly walk like I talked, I could serve both my God and others.

I laughed as I thought how ironic it was that I always wanted to be in control. I tried that in my addiction. I only served myself and thought I was totally in charge, but my world sucked. Now I found happiness and wellbeing when I served others. I tried to check my laughter because if Daybreak heard me laughing hysterically, alone in my tent, he might think I finally went mad. I wasn't sure I could explain it to him.

My tent was about thirty yards from the shelter where Daybreak was staying. The storm that had been threatening all day finally hit hard, but I was safe and dry. I went to the shelter to cook and share my hot dogs with Daybreak. Daybreak had a large pot by hiker standards, so we used it to boil the hotdogs. Poncho and Tata came in soaking wet as we cooked. They set up in the shelter and cooked their meal with us. I offered them a hotdog, but they were vegetarians and declined the wiener, but Tata did take a bun. I tried to restrain myself, but I absolutely had to make a crude, sexist comment about lesbians. Tata punched me in the arm and we all laughed. Tata and I formed a special relationship and became closely bonded friends. I accepted her as she was and she understood a lecherous old pig-dog like me. We all ate together, sharing intimately with each other as the odd family that we became in the short time we knew each other.

The rain stopped and the sky cleared a little. I didn't have cell tower, but they had a satellite pay phone back at the camp store. I went back to the store where I got four dollars worth of quarters to call Scooter. I hadn't talked to her lately. We already planned all the arrangements in detail, but I needed some reassurance that all systems were a go. The next day was the Friday she was taking off at noon from work to come to Millinocket. She planned to meet me there sometime on Saturday. She would then climb Katahdin with me as soon as we got a clear, safe day. It was so good to talk to Scooter, but my four bucks only bought ten minutes before the phone cut us off. I went back to the store and bought ten dollars worth of quarters to make a call the next morning. I also bought some ice cream for dessert.

With a little daylight left, I walked out to the middle of Abol Bridge for a last look at Katahdin. I stood midway across on the walkway of Abol Bridge as the forbidding current of the Penobscot River flowed beneath my feet. I watched the ominous clouds pass over Katahdin as the day slipped into history where it would be stored forever. I had the strange feeling Katahdin was watching me as I approached, after calling me for over ten years. I took a picture of Katahdin's black silhouette overseeing the end of the day against the cloudy night sky to preserve the moment.

I needed many Alcoholics Anonymous meetings when I first sobered up. I was so blind, I needed the people who were working their program to lead me. In a sense, I was on my road to Damascus in the beginning. They freely shared their experience, strength, and hope with me, which in turn, gave me hope. I really thought drinking was my only problem. I didn't know I was spiritually starving to death, but they knew because they were once blind and spiritually malnourished like me and now they could see. People who modeled the principles by living by the program, nurtured me to spiritual health. I admired them at first and in time came to deeply respect them because they walked like they talked. I was subtly spoon fed spiritually by spiritual people. Eventually the seeds they planted started to grow and I started to see and believe. I learned to do as they did by emulating them. I started to practice the principles primitively at first. I still needed and continued to need a lot of encouragement from the folks in the program.

When I was first attracted to Alcoholics Anonymous in 1977, my sobriety was fragile. Continuous, uninterrupted sobriety was a fleeting thing for almost three years. I would go back to using when I got frustrated, but I kept coming back to the fellowship. I learned from some hard knocks it was better to stay sober even when things were tough. Going back to using never got any easier or better for me.

I established sobriety in 1980 by working the principles of the program and started to gain a little respect from the people in the fellowship, which encouraged me even more. The folks who loved me noticed my change in behavior at first, but soon saw there also was a change within me. Thus, I started to gain the respect of my parents first, which encouraged me even more. I started to practice the principles in the outside world that I learned in the rooms of Alcoholics Anonymous. Everything in my life started to change. The big Book promised, our whole attitude and outlook upon life would change.

I found the change to be contagious, like a wonderful, magical metamorphosis. I liked the new me, but I always had to remember my disease was only in remission and not cured. I was still definitely as much of an addict as I had always been. The selfish, egocentric, self-serving criminal who dwelled within me never died, he was only sleeping.

God would let me return to my addiction if I chose to awaken the beast within me with the first drink. I could jump back in the hole I crawled out of so many years ago and return to that dark, lonely, Godless hell the instant I picked up the first drink. I always found that fact frightening. However, I believed I could make it through any adversity or tragedy life handed me if I stayed spiritually fit.

An athlete had to practice to stay fit and grow stronger. As an addict I had to practice also. I had to practice the twelve simple principles in all my affairs a day at a time, to stay fit and grow stronger spiritually. It was now time for me to also walk the way I talk. The good news always was, I didn't have to do it alone. I believe I never had to do anything alone ever again.

I didn't think to bring my light when I left camp before dark, but now a storm was fast approaching and to my good fortune, the lightning lit up the way home. I just got back to the shelter of my tent and the weather turned violent.

My guardian angel probably had to work overtime often to protect me from myself. Scooter often told me my, guardian angel was a rather large, loving, black woman with an attitude and when I meet her face to face she was gonna pimp slap me back into yesterday. She probably often said to the other guardian angels, "Watch what this dumb ass is going to do next!" All the other angels probably had a good laugh at my expense.

My thoughts turned to the morning when I would enter Baxter State Park for the first time. I doubted if I would be disappointed in what Baxter had in store for me. I gave thanks as the sound of the rain on the tent lulled me to sleep.

THE SUMMIT

Day 167   9.9 Miles

I purposely got up well before daylight, hoping to see Daybreak off, but to my disappointment, he had packed up and left before I awoke. He had to leave early because he planned to hike fifteen miles to the summit of Katahdin, then descend five miles to return to the Birches campsite. I hoped to see him at the Birches campsite that night. Tata and Poncho were still sleeping, so I returned to my tent. I tried to go back to sleep, but my mind had already activated.

Carrying the message or sharing my experience via a book kept re-surfacing intrusively, ever since the idea drifted across my mind. I went negative and started to rationalize excuses. I couldn't call it a prayer, but I said aloud, "God, remember I was the one who hated my seventh grade English teacher. I almost flunked out of English, and I couldn't spell for shit. How could I write a book?"

I suddenly realized, as I heard myself, I was making excuses for why I couldn't carry out what I felt was God's will. After all, I asked God for knowledge of his will and the power to carry it out many times. I now found myself making excuses as to why I couldn't do what He asked me to do. I laid on my sleeping pad, crossed my feet at the ankles, interlocked my fingers behind my head, and closed my eyes. I really felt God gave me knowledge of His will.

A comedy monologue a well-known comedian, Bill Cosby did several years ago came to mind. The skit was an interaction between Noah and God. My memory wasn't the best, but I recalled it went something like,

God said, "Noah!"

Noah looked up and questioned, "Who's that?"

"It's the Lord, Noah."

Noah, "Right!"

The Lord tells Noah, "I want you to build an ark."

Noah, "Right! What's an Ark?"

Lord, "Get some wood and build it three-hundred cubits by eighty cubits."

Noah, "Right! What's a cubit?"

"Go collect sets of all the animals in the world and put them in the Ark."

Noah Asks, "What's going on? Why do you want me to do all these weird things? Who is this really?"

The Lord confides, "I'm going to destroy the world."

Noah, "Am I on candid camera?"

I snickered to myself at Cosby's skit, but I wonder what the world would be like today if Noah refused to build the ark. Would we even be here? In Alcoholics Anonymous I often heard it said, The will of God will never take you where the grace of God will not keep you.

I made a commitment to God right there in my tent to do my best to write a book to carry my experience to others even after I leave this world. I thought, no matter how impossible it sounded, if I had the help of God and trusted Him, it would come to pass. The purpose was still the same, to stay sober and help others achieve sobriety, but now, I had a plan. I would have a book as a new vehicle to execute my goal. All I needed was the power to carry it out, which I prayed God would also provide.

The rain stopped about dawn as I was packing up. I still had to pack a wet tent, but even wet, it was still lighter than usual. I checked in on the girls, but they were still fast asleep. I set out, inspired by all that was around me. I searched a long time, so I had to beware my ego didn't take over and tell me I had all the answers. I hadn't found the keys, but I felt spiritually okay and on the right path.

I called Scooter from the satellite pay phone before she left for work. She had the car all packed and arranged for the cats to be taken care of while she was gone for a week. She was so excited she would have a hard time working until noon. She would spend the night in our fishing camp in upstate New York, then drive to Millinocket to meet me sometime Saturday. She trained all summer to be in shape to summit Mount Katahdin with me.

I only had ten miles to hike to Birches Campsite, but it would be through Baxter. The thought of fresh coffee and donuts seduced me into waiting until the camp store opened at eight o'clock. I took my coffee and walked out to the middle of the river on the bridge to drink it as I gazed at Katahdin. The day was cold and windy, but the rain stopped and it was clearing up. I hoped the sun would warm everything up soon. I took several pictures of the mighty mountain as it stood overlooking its domain, the Maine forests.

I stopped back at the store for one last coffee before I hiked out solo. I was about to enter Baxter when I ran into a bird watcher returning to the road. I asked her to take a picture with my camera of me standing in front of Katahdin, which she did.

I carefully read the sign that marked the entrance to the park, which stated no overnight stay, camping, or fires for the next ten miles. To protect and not disturb the resident wildlife, visitors were not allowed to bring their dogs into Baxter. Park rangers vigorously enforced the park's regulations and violators received heavy fines. The rangers also escorted them out of the park. I didn't plan on taking anything but pictures or keeping anything but my memories. I planned to leave only my scent as I passed by as unnoticed to all the park residents as possible.

I entered Baxter alone, which was perfect for me because I felt as if I was on sacred ground with my creator. The famous Baxter State Park was over a two-hundred-thousand-acre wildlife sanctuary presented to the people of Maine by the late Governor Percival Baxter. He gave it with stipulations, so it would remain preserved as a pristine wilderness forever, with the wildlife forever free. Baxter had no paved roads, showers, stores, electricity, or phone lines, and there would never be. Hopefully, no Godless oil barons would ever be able to buy enough politicians to get their greedy hands on Baxter and destroy it for its resources. We the people have an important responsibility to protect

Baxter as a gift for our unborn descendants.

I crossed Abol Stream on a footbridge a few feet before it merged with the Penobscot River. I came upon an information board where thru-hikers signed up to reserve one of the twelve overnight camping spaces available for thru-hikers only at The Birches Campsite. If all twelve spaces were already filled I had to sign up for the next day and return to Abol Bridge. I was in luck because the only name ahead of mine was Daybreak's.

The weather cleared up, warmed up, and turned into a beautiful day. The previous night's storm was only a memory. I stopped to take off my jacket and took a moment to pause and reflect. The sunlight filtered through the overhead canopy formed by the trees and painted a patchwork-like mosaic spotting on the forest floor. The warmth dried up the evidence of the rain from the day before. The now familiar sweet smell of pine filled the air like Mother Nature's perfume. I could hear the morning birds singing as they accompanied the distant sound of water rushing off Katahdin in a hurry to get to the sea.

I broke out in goose bumps even though the heat of the morning sun warmed my skin. The forest seemed dreamlike as if I was in an enchanted land, living in the world of the spirit. My eyes filled with tears of gratitude. I felt so privileged just to be there. I wished I could share the moment with everyone. I continued my journey, taking my time, trying to preserve all the details of the world around me. I stopped to take a picture of a sizeable stream cascading over huge granite rocks, worn smooth as marble from centuries of being polished by the strong current.

I snapped out of my dreamlike trance rather suddenly. I couldn't go any further because the trail I was following ended. I was blocked by a vertical canyon wall on my side of the stream. The same benign stream I passed a half hour ago now looked like it would be impossible to ford. The stream roared through an unmovable mass of granite rock, forming white, turbulent current, which was all framed by hemlocks. I quickly felt isolated from the rest of the park. I took a quick scan of my environment and saw zero white blazes. I said oh crap out loud as I felt a little twinge of fear when I realized I might be lost. I stopped to assess the situation. I ate a snack and made a cup of trail coffee. I took an inventory of my food and had way more than enough food to get to the Birches Campsite. I didn't want to get lost and end up having to eat bugs and worms to survive because I was an idiot. I took a photo from where I stood when I felt lost.

I carefully backtracked until I found a well worn trail that came up along the stream. I followed the trail downstream for about two-hundred yards before I found a comforting white blaze. I stopped to chastise myself for not paying attention to where I was going in the first place. I returned to the trail, did an about face and soon ran out of white blazes again. I carefully backtracked to where I saw the last known blaze, and took out my guidebook to try to figure out where the trail went. I thought I was on the Lower Fork of Nesowadnehunk Stream. The guidebook indicated I should be looking at a footbridge, but I didn't see a bridge of any kind.

I began to think, maybe some vandals changed the trail. I heard it sometimes happened, although I hadn't experienced it for myself. I dropped my pack, took out my bear mace, and decided to backtrack on the white blazes for at least ten minutes. I gave myself a little talk and reminded myself to take my time and be observant, which was a quality that came hard for me, especially at times like that. I carefully backtracked at least a mile, looking for any sign of where or how I lost the trail and found nothing.

I returned to my pack and the trail that went upstream was heavily traveled as evidenced by it being well worn, so I took it back to where I first discovered I was off trail and turned around and returned to my pack. I walked downstream a short way and to my relief, I found a white blaze. The bad news was, it was on the other side of the river. I continued downstream hoping to find a footbridge, which I soon found. The bad news was, it was only a heap of twisted boards piled in the stream.

By the way the evidence looked, the bridge washed out a long time ago. I instantly resented the portly ridge runner for not warning me when I spent a lot of time listening to him tell me what an expert he was on the park. He needed to hike a little and quit spending all his time eating donuts and thumbing his nuts.

The first thing I always had to do with any problem was take an inventory to identify what I had to do to resolve it. I took an inventory, so I knew I had to ford the river before I could continue north. I went back to my pack and made the decision to go downstream to find a safer place to cross. I soon found a place, so I stopped, took my pack off, fell to my knees, and started praying. I laughed as I thought how ironic it would be if this little creek took me out. I didn't think my prayer was wasted. I put my camera, and phone in new zip lock baggies. I then put them in each of my shirt pockets and closed the Velcro straps. I made sure my wallet was zipped in my pants, unbuckled the waist belt on my pack, and proceeded out into the current.

Granite polished by centuries of water rushing over it laid on the creek bottoms. The soles of my boots had become smooth from the miles of hiking up and down granite-covered trail. The current in the creek was strong as the water descended to lower ground. All three dynamics added up and I went down in the middle of the creek. I easily slipped out of my pack and soon regained my footing, but the creek attempted to steal my pack. I had to run downstream to tackle my pack that held all my gear. The good news was, I got to the other side of the creek. I checked my camera and phone, and they survived the ordeal fine in their baggies, so all was well. I sat there picturing how funny it would have been to watch this old codger as he franticly ran down the creek, chasing his pack that appeared to find a life of its own as it attempted to escape.

I chuckled a little and then, I imagined Mom and Dad watching that last little escapade from heaven. I could clearly see the scene as Dad would take his time getting out a Tareyton, put it in his mouth, put the pack back in his shirt pocket, fish out his Zippo, light it, and take a pull on his cigarette. He would exhale the smoke as he took the cigarette out of his mouth before he said "Dolly, I think the boy will be moving back in with us sooner than we thought."

I started to laugh aloud as I pictured them shaking their heads. My laughter escalated to the point of hysterical as I tried to stop laughing, but couldn't and started all over again several times. I finally regained control of my emotions, thinking how wonderful it was to spend a few moments remembering the two people who gave me life. I regretted I never told them how much I truly appreciated them when they were alive, so before I moved on I looked up and told them, "I love you, appreciate you, and I'm honestly grateful you are still my parents." As an afterthought I said, "Oh, by the way, it will be a while longer before I move back in, I hope."

Since I was already wet, I decided to take a sponge bath. I took off my shirt and shoes and tried to wash some crud off. The water was cool, but not shocking. I blew up my air mattress to lie in the warm sun to dry myself off. I looked to the sky as if it held all my answers. I have grown to love the cleansing feeling of sun on my body after a refreshing bath. I reflected, what a wonderful spiritual journey the hike has been.

A friend of mine went into the wilderness of Alaska by himself for a winter. He told me to take the time to smell the flowers, because it will be over before you know it. I finally understood the value of what he said as my journey on the trail came to a close. I would look back on my time spent on the trail as one of the highpoints of my life.

I believed the spirit wanted to talk in that pleasant atmosphere because I involuntarily started to listen, reflect, and meditate. I found it amazing my dream of ten years was fast becoming a true memory. I guessed it would be that way when I was about to complete my life. My yesterday's dreams became today's reality, which would form tomorrow's memories.

I looked up as I watched a light wisp of a cloud drift slowly across the sky with no place in particular to go. I asked myself the question, *Well Dreamer, now that your hike is almost over, what message has the trail revealed to you?* I tried to clear all of my own thoughts from my mind so I could listen. Maybe the simple things like the clouds above were sending a message. The cloud had no control, so it surrendered to the wind and took all the time it needed to go where the wind called. I needed to let go of control and take my time to go where God's will called me.

I knew yesterday was gone, but I would remember its experiences.

I would benefit from both the good and the bad experiences. Unfortunately, I couldn't go back and change any of my yesterdays, but I could positively incorporate yesterday's experiences into all I do from that moment on and share my experience, strength, and hope. The Promises said, "We will no longer regret the past or wish to shut the door on it."

I didn't move on for some time, but when I did, I still had some unanswered questions. I soon came to a magnificent waterfall, which probably was on the same stream I had been crossing. I stopped and took more pictures. The trail took me above the same waterfall and I took even more pictures. I felt like a tourist. If I was only given one sentence to describe Baxter I would have said, Baxter was where serenity met excitement.

I felt so inspired by the park. I hoped I would get the opportunity to bring my grandson Parker to Baxter someday when he was old enough to appreciate it. I also hoped I lived long enough to thru-hike with him. I heard the spirit softly whisper, *Your written words could send a message to your grandson and help defend our wilderness from man's greed after you are gone.* I shivered as chills made the hair on my neck stand. Another good reason to write the book was in case I died before I got the opportunity to physically share my experiences with Parker. I could do that through the written word even after I died. I could also share such things with Parker's grandson and his grandchildren.

I had to ford the stream again farther up the trail. I marveled at a little different view of Katahdin from an angle I hadn't seen. I took the time to filter a liter of the cold, clear, water after I crossed the stream without incident. I sat in the sun to dry out and enjoyed the refreshing liquid. It was truly a gift to be in God's church.

The idea of thru-hiking felt selfish to me at first. I wouldn't be working or earning money. I had to depend on Scooter to do everything at home by herself. I wouldn't be there for the rest of my family either. I felt guilty that I even entertained such a self-centered idea. Suddenly, everything appeared to fall into place so I could leave and hike. I hoped that would happen with the book.

I was struggling with the decision to thru-hike when Lady D said,

"God is the one who put the idea in your head in the first place." I thought maybe God also put the idea of the book in my head and inspired me to write. Maybe the idea wasn't mine or maybe a book was the answer to my prayer for knowledge of God's will. God may be telling me, Okay, you want a job? I want you to write a book. Then I thought how grandiose of me to think I was special. I remembered I needed to always check my ego before it became too inflated.

I recalled I started to tell folks back home of my intentions of hiking the trail. Many of them asked, Why would you quit a good job and walk twenty-two hundred miles for no apparent gain? Throughout the ten years that I dreamed of hiking the trail, I struggled with the same question. I had several reasons to hike, but I also had reasons to stay home. I was burned out from having the same stressful job for over twenty years, but on the other hand, my job was secure. I learned how to handle most situations on the job and comfortably made a living that paid my bills. I could easily slip into retirement without changing anything.

As the song said, *This town safe and sound, I already know my way around. What if I stay? Do I really want to spend the rest of my days on a dead end street in a dead end job? I can live like that, but my dreams won't stop.* I reflected back to every time I got ahead in life I had to stick my neck out a little, take a chance, and step outside of my comfort zone. I also felt I needed to take the opportunity while there was still time.

I spent my life searching for something. I first looked to chemicals and thought I found it, but as things turned out, it was only an illusion. Looking back on my life, even in my addiction, I was seeking to live a spiritual life. I remembered clearly when I first discovered I could find a type of euphoric contentment from the use of drugs and alcohol, I thought I had found the secret to happiness. To my dismay, that special feeling evaporated into a dysphoric feeling as soon as the effect of the drug wore off. Thankfully, my addiction eventually led me to Alcoholics Anonymous. The last twenty-six years, I have tried to follow the Twelve Suggested Steps to recover from my addiction.

The hike was more than just an adventure, it was an experience. It gave me time out from the distractions of the busy world for prayer, meditation, and some time alone with God. I wonder if Jesus went into the wilderness alone for the same reason. The little white Bible didn't say a lot about it. I believed his forty days was a time to talk to God in God's church away from all distractions of his day. He took some time to be humble and listened for the spirit to whisper in his ear.

At first, I felt it was egotistical and narcissistic to think God chose me to hike the trail, but then I remembered an old timer in Alcoholics Anonymous named Wilber, often said, "Ask and you shall receive." I felt very humbled when I started to believe God gave me the opportunity to listen to what He had to say. I felt even more humbled thinking God may have given me the inspiration to write the book, simply because I asked for a job. The big Book, on page four-seventeen said, "Nothing, absolutely nothing happens in God's world by mistake"

I don't know how long I sat there meditating. I may have even fallen asleep because my shorts had dried out in the sun. I finished my water and filtered more to go. I took out my camera and took another picture to preserve the memory before I moved on. I couldn't say I was hiking because I mostly just moseyed on, taking my time to drink in the whole experience. My feelings were hard to put into words. The great thing was, I had a wonderful feeling, and there would be no negative consequences because I wasn't drinking or doing anything wrong. I never felt satisfied when I used alcohol or drugs because the chemicals left me always wanting more. Every time I used I hoped I would reach the ultimate high, but the ultimate high always eluded me. Addicts call that, Chasing the ghost, but the ghost was only an illusion.

I had to catch my breath when I came upon Daicey Pond, with Katahdin watching in the background. I saw many pictures of Daicey Pond because everyone put that postcard-type picture on the web or in books. I had to say, the pictures didn't capture the scene as I saw it from the trail. I felt like I was looking at God's oil painting that was a special gift for all to see. Magically, at that moment in time, I felt as if I was in the painting and it wasn't just an illusion. I too took several pictures before I moved on. I felt a comforting sense of serenity as I proceeded towards the Birches campsite. I thought about a famous poem that I had hanging in my bathroom at home. A man looked back at his life and saw two sets of footprints in the good times and one set in the bad times where the Lord carried him.

A set of footprints from a pair of hiking boots were in the sand, but a set of prints from a worn pair of sandals were beside them on that day where I believed the greatest of all sponsors walked beside one of His pigeons. I felt the personal contact. Yet, I had no words to describe my gratitude, but maybe no words were necessary.

I felt a tad bit melancholy as the trail broke out of the wilderness and took me straight to Katahdin Stream Campground where the park had a row of lean-tos along Katahdin Stream where visitors from all over the world could reserve a place to stay in the park.

I checked into the ranger station to register as a thru-hiker and paid the fee to camp at the Birches campsite. The two rangers there reminded me of Mutt and Jeff; one was fat, and one was skinny. The skinny one talked for an hour and gave me a lot of good information. They provide a place for thru-hikers to leave their heavy backpack and they would lend me a small daypack to climb Katahdin if I wanted. The other ranger informed me that I was the one-hundred and eighth thru-hiker to register as making it from Springer Mountain, Georgia in 2006.

I walked the quarter mile to the famous Birches Campsite, which was a one-night base camp for Nobo thru-hikers staging to summit Mount Katahdin. The campsite consisted of the two small shelters and two tent platforms about a hundred yards off the road. I was a little disappointed because no one was there, but I looked up and recognized Daybreak's pack hanging on the bear cables. I smiled because it meant Daybreak stopped, left his pack to climb Katahdin, and would return sometime that night. I set my tent up on the tent platform furthest away from the shelters. I went into my tent and started to write in my journal as I tried to remember every little detail of my experiences that day.

That was the last thing I remembered until I awoke to Tata's voice saying, "Wake up Dreamer, your snoring is scaring the bears." To my delight Daybreak, Poncho, and Tata were set up in one of the shelters. A couple of section hikers and some visitors came to socialize with us, so I made some trail coffee and we all sat around as Daybreak shared his adventure on Katahdin.

Daybreak climbed to the summit of Mount Katahdin for the third time in his life. He descended on the Knife Edge trail, which was by far the most spectacular, but most dangerous trail on Mount Katahdin. The knife-edge was a narrow ridge along Katahdin's backbone with steep drops on both sides where one false step would be fatal. A fall of hundreds of feet there would mean certain death. We all listened intently to every little detail.

The next morning, Daybreak would start south through the hundred-mile wilderness. Tata and Poncho would attempt to summit if the day was clear and I would hitch to Millinocket to rendezvous with Scooter. The outsiders all eventually went their way and Poncho started to doze off, so I reluctantly retired to my tent. I knew I may never see any of them again.

I had no cell tower to call Scooter, so I didn't know where she was, but I trusted she was okay and on her way. I would take my time in the morning. I hoped I wouldn't have a hard time hitchhiking twenty miles to Millinocket with my pack. Scooter reserved a room at the Appalachian Trail Lodge where we would spend at least two nights.

I spent a long time listening to the Maine wilderness night and thinking about my commitment to write a book. The challenge overwhelmed me as I thought about the project. I wished I wouldn't have told God I would write a book. I remembered the old cartoon, Mickey Mouse would have a devil on one shoulder whispering in one ear and an angel on his other shoulder whispering the opposite in the other ear. I could identify with the mouse. I felt inspired and enthusiastic but at the same time, insecure and negative about writing a book. I prayed, "Please God, help me write the book, Amen." I didn't know if it was a divine intervention, but almost instantly, I listened to myself making excuses. I thought all my excuses were negative and my negativity was always fear based.

I recalled the lesson I learned on Mount Adams that day with Cedar Moe about fear verses faith. When I fed my fear, the fear won as evidenced by that day on Roan Mountain. The negative, fearful couple from Maine infected me with fear. I fed the fear and made a fear-based decision that almost cost my life.

When I focused on the positive and positive people I fed my faith and could do the seemingly impossible as evidenced by the fact that I was going to sleep at Katahdin's base camp that night. I thought thru-hiking was impossible at first when I focused on my diseased back. I had many fears, but with support and encouragement, I started to believe I could hike the hike. Once I started to believe, everything fell into place to hike the Appalachian Trail.

David focused on faith because otherwise he could never face Goliath. I believe a positive attitude was fertile ground for faith to grow. I needed to focus on the positive. True, I may not be a writer, but neither was anybody else when they first aspired to become a writer.

All my goals, large or small, started with an inspiration. I was the one who decided to feed the inspiration with faith or destroy the same inspiration with fear. I realized, if I wanted to be a writer, I needed to take the opportunity and start writing. If it was God's will, he would provide what I needed.

I turned on my lamp, took out my journal, and started to list the positive reasons why I could write a book. I had been journaling for years now. I could use the journal as a basis for the book. I did meaningless paperwork that no one ever read for years. Documenting progress, forming treatment plans, and writing biophychosocial evaluations was all writing in a sense.

The list went on and the more I wrote, the more inspired I became. Magically, all my insecurities melted and my attitude turned confident and positive. The last thing I listed I took from the book of Philippians which said, "I can do all things through Christ who strengthens me."

I laid there, too excited to sleep at that time of night, so I turned on my head light, and took out the little white Bible. The bookmark was at the twenty-third Psalm. I read the words, "He leads me in the paths of righteousness for His name's sake." I stopped to ponder a question, was I being lead or was it merely my inflated ego talking?

I read on, "Yea, though I walk through the valley of the shadow of death, I will fear, no evil; for you are with me." I thought, I admired David, Noah, and Cedar Moe, because they let go of their fear and replaced it with faith. Eventually, sleep overtook me sometime late in the night.

Day 168   Zero Miles

I packed up early for the last time. Daybreak came over to talk as I was making coffee. I was pleasantly surprised because he was normally on the trail by daybreak. We talked as if we had been friends forever. We could hear an occasional car that passed as it left the park. Finally, in a big brother kind of way, he said, "You know when the last car leaves there will be no more until the park closes tonight."

Reluctantly, I bid Daybreak goodbye. Tata and Poncho were still asleep as I passed the shelter. I wished I could have said goodbye, but it would be selfish of me to wake them. They looked sweet and innocent as they slept, so I blew them both a kiss and departed. I felt melancholy with grief because I knew I would never see my friends again.

My mood soon improved as I started walking to Millinocket. The day promised to be clear, sunny, and warm as soon as the sun did its job and burned off the cool mist of the night. The walking was easy on the gravel road, so I carried my poles and stepped up the pace a couple of notches. The endorphins started to elevate my spirits as the sounds of morning whispered in my ears.

My thoughts returned to the question I asked myself the day before as I fell asleep in the sun. I said aloud, *What else has the trail taught you?*

Autie came to mind. At first, I thought it odd because I always thought Autie was a fool. He died violently long before I was born so I never met him, but I saw him as willful, rigid, self-centered, and controlling. He took command and never surrendered. It worked out so badly for him that he made an infamous name for himself in history.

My quest to hike the Appalachian Trail started out as a personal challenge. I was a great deal like Autie, because I felt I could handle it on my own and prevail. I marched away from Springer in full command. I didn't ask for help because I felt I knew best and didn't need or want help. I wanted to do everything my way. I soon found my way didn't work. Unlike Autie, when I could no longer go on alone, I surrendered that day in the Smoky Mountains to a power greater than myself. When I surrendered, I was no longer in control and my whole list of strategies changed.

An angel came to me in the form of a salty German born Christian named Heaven Bound. He re-introduced me to an unemployed carpenter. After making personal contact with God, I made a decision to turn my command over to him. I let him lead and magically, the trail turned into a spiritual journey on that grey day in March. I learned to trust and depend on my new Commander's protection and guidance. I found truth in the Alcoholics Anonymous slogan, God could and would if he were sought.

I found it uncanny how often my adventures on the Appalachian Trail reflected a mini version of my life. Both times, I started out exactly like Autie. I saw everything as a personal battle. I took full command and led my way, without help. I did as I determined was best by thinking I knew what was best more than anyone else. I marched into battle in full control, not listening to anything but my ego.

Another angel appeared in the form of a huge, recovering alcoholic named Big Jim. Big Jim introduced me to the program of Alcoholics Anonymous. I made a decision to turn my command over to the others in the program and let them lead. Both times, when I surrendered, my life got better and I became more serene.

Surrender may be one of the many messages the trail has been so patiently carrying to me. The trail had answered my questions and whispered, Dreamer, surrender your will and your life to your loving God. Turn your life over so you don't have to control everything. Learn to serve and you would never be alone again.

I could see I would have to continue to surrender to serve. I didn't ever want to do as Autie did and end up like him. By the way, Autie was a nickname for General George Armstrong Custer.

I walked about three miles before the first car came along. A woman from South Carolina, who ran a shuttle for her boyfriend earlier, picked me up. She was going back to a state campground where they stayed, but she gave me a ride all the way to Millinocket, which was way past her camp. We talked trail talk all the way to town. I offered to fill her tank or buy breakfast for the ride, but she declined. I never even knew her name. She was simply a good person or who knows, maybe she was an angel.

The first thing I did when I hit town was call Scooter. She estimated she was about four hours away. I went to a local diner and ate a big breakfast of four eggs, bacon, toast, and a huge mound of fried potatoes. I drank several cups of good coffee, gave my waitress a good tip and left.

I found the lodge we were staying for the next two nights and checked in. The lodge was an old house run by a pleasant, older couple. The room was simple with a television. The guests all shared a bathroom, but no other guests were there yet, so the first thing I did was take a long, hot shower, getting rid of four days of trail smell.

I took my clothes to a coin laundry for a good washing with detergent and fabric softener then returned to my room. It felt good to be clean. I had cell tower, so I called Scooter again. I still had a lot of time to kill, so I made some phone calls to catch up on things back home. I walked two miles to McDonald's and checked out the area. A rainstorm caught me on the way home. I guess I never liked or got used to getting wet.

Scooter arrived about mid-afternoon and it was great to see her. We went to the dollar store and bought food for the ascent tomorrow. We then picked up a pizza at a local pizza shop to eat in the car as I drove her to Abol Bridge to show her Mount Katahdin for her first time. I never would forget the look on her face as she said, "Wow, I hope I can climb this." I assured her those were also my exact thoughts the first time I laid eyes on Katahdin. We walked up the Appalachian Trail for about a mile with the mighty mountain in view. At ten miles away, Mount Katahdin looked closer and enormously intimidating.

We went back to the bed and breakfast. The owner asked us if we would take another hiker to Katahdin in the morning. Of course I said yes, because I always like to meet new hikers. He introduced us to Dave, a young man from Colorado, who planned to hike south from Katahdin to Monson. I spent some time describing my stay at Shaw's in Monson to Dave. Scooter and I went to bed late by hiker standards, but I couldn't sleep thinking about what the thirteenth of August would bring.

August 13   Day 169   5.2 Miles

August the Thirteenth, Two-Thousand and Six - My last day

I wanted to sleep the night away to make the time go faster, but I didn't sleep a wink because my mind just wouldn't shut down. I had anticipated the day that I climbed Mount Katahdin for ten years. I hadn't been that hyped since I was a kid on the night before the first day of muskrat trapping season.

Finally, o-dark-three-o'clock rolled around, so I woke Scooter up, then went to Dave's room and woke him. The three of us dressed and left for Baxter, which opened at five o'clock in the morning. The guidebook said the small parking lot at Katahdin's Ranger station filled up early on the weekends. It was the only place to park, so it was imperative that we got there early to insure a spot.

We took a quick pass through Millinocket looking to buy coffee, with zero luck. I anticipated that ahead of time and came prepared with a quart of strong, cold, instant trail coffee. I took a large pull of the foul liquid, before I passed it to Scooter who took a sip and said an, unchristian-type word. I took another drink and agreed with Scooter. I offered Dave the bottle, but he said, "I'm good."

We were the fifth car waiting in line at the park entrance. The park opened the gate and let us in at precisely five o'clock. We arrived to an empty parking lot, but it filled quickly. Dave left us to go register at the ranger station, leave his large pack, and pick up a daypack. We had our own daypacks, so we saddled up to start our ascent at dawn.

Mount Katahdin held a mystical status from the first time I heard about the unique, Maine landmark. I had yet to ascend Katahdin, but I heard countless tales of how Katahdin lived up to the reputation of all I dreamed it would be. I would build a trail tale for myself as I climbed more than four-thousand feet to reach the summit at over a mile in the air. I looked at Scooter and said, "The name Katahdin means Greatest Mountain, tread softly because we are sacred ground."

We found the trail easy at first with a gentle slope on fine gravel that had been washing off the mountain for millions of years. The vegetation was so thick you couldn't walk through it off trail. The trail became steep and rocky long before we reached tree-line. Some of the time, we had to use our hands to climb. I wondered if Scooter would have trouble reaching the handholds and footholds on the way down, but she claimed to be six-feet, five-inches tall. I thought she might have embellished the six-foot, five inches a bit, but she was in top shape and had been training all summer for the assault on Katahdin. I only took the zero yesterday to wait for her to get there, because I wouldn't summit without her by my side.

The terrain changed abruptly above tree-line. The undergrowth turned to granite with little fungus-like scales. The boulders were much larger as we faced a harder climb. We solemnly picked and wiggled our way up the mighty mountain. The adrenalin flowing through my veins made the hike up the mountain seem effortless.

The temperature dropped noticeably above tree-line with a strong wind. We stopped to put on our jackets, collapsed our hiking poles, and put them in our packs to free up our hands for the climb. The granite was so cold it had a numbing effect on my hands, but I didn't wear gloves for fear of slipping and losing a handhold. We took our time, stopped often to rest, and took lots of pictures. I could see miles upon miles of untamed Maine wilderness below. I was in no hurry because the vistas were breathtaking beyond words and I wanted to preserve every moment of the day as much as I possibly could.

We met a Nobo thru-hiker named Dubie who overtook us above treeline. He was only twenty, but I felt a spiritual connection, even though I never met him before. I sensed he felt exactly what I felt as he passed.

Scooter was right by my side, but I also felt the presence of all the men and women who supported and encouraged me right from the start. I also felt an awareness that hikers like Dubie, Earl Schaffer, and everyone else who had ever thru-hiked the entire Appalachian Trail were with me in spirit. Only those who experienced what I was experiencing felt what I was feeling. I wished I could have described the feeling for my journal, but the feeling was something I couldn't see, touch, or describe.

Alcoholics Anonymous meetings often displayed a welcoming sign saying, *You're not alone anymore.* When I was living on my self-will without God or man, I felt terribly alone. I didn't fit in anywhere, felt no one cared, and the world was a cold and loveless place. The only comfort I found was in the chemicals I was abusing that were killing me. I seldom felt lonely anymore because even when I was alone physically, I wasn't truly alone anymore. I felt spiritually connected to God and my fellow man. I felt love beyond what I ever could have comprehended in my active addiction.

The trail started to follow Hunt Spur, which looked like the edge of a giant pyramid with huge boulders. Scooter dropped behind and took pictures of my ascent. Some ominous clouds blew in and blocked out the sun, which set my nerves on edge until they harmlessly passed. Scooter reassured me they were harmless, however she wasn't an expert and hadn't ever been in a lightning storm above tree-line. I sure didn't want to be on Mount Katahdin when it lit up.

Scooter stopped me in front of a rock formation to pose for her. My eyes blurred with tears of love and gratitude as I watched her scramble to take the picture as if the moment would escape. I realize the personal sacrifice she made in the name of love to allow me the time to pursue my dream. She literally had to do all the upkeep of our home, take care of our two worthless cats, and work a full time, stressful job. She mailed me anything I needed, managed my finances, and wrote checks from my account to pay my bills.

She always seemed happy to hear from me and dropped whatever she was doing to talk to me. She listened to my wimping and whining when things got tough for me on the trail. Without fail, she supported and encouraged me to continue pursuing my dream. She gave me a

Dutch uncle-type of pep talk at times, but always ended it by telling me how she admired and respected my courage.

She worried and prayed for me lot, but I didn't know why. Our son-in-law said my last words on earth would be, "Hey Scooter, watch this shit!" I thought the only bad choice she ever made was to marry me. I wished I could find the perfect way to express my gratitude, but I had the faith time would eventually provide me with an opportunity.

The higher we climbed, the further we could see across the Maine landscape. We stopped often as we scrambled over the boulders and took pictures of the views of the lakes, forests, and streams, which appeared to be as God left them, untouched by man's progress.

Katahdin from a distance, appeared to be one magnificent, solid granite rock, so I was surprised to find up-close, it was individual pieces of granite. The dirt washed away over time by runoff water, millions of storms, and spring snow melts, which only left rocks behind. Small alpine bushes appeared in a few places where a little dirt remained.

The trail became gentler at forty-six hundred feet when we reached the Gateway where the Tableland began. The Tableland was a plateau where the mountain's steepness started to yield towards the summit. The mountain let me catch my breath, however my heartbeat continued to pound, fueled by pure adrenalin. The Tableland was dotted with smaller rocks with gravel-like soil that supported a type of alpine brown grass and small, frail looking plants that looked as if they could be in a pot on someone's windowsill. A small sign asked hikers to stay on the well-marked path to protect the fragile alpine environment.

We said nothing to each other as we solemnly closed on the summit, sensing the spirit of the mighty mountain. I had yet to see the summit that was still over six-hundred feet higher, due to a cloud that covered it like a blanket, as if the mountain was still trying to conceal its secrets. I silently ventured across the plateau toward the summit. That was the first time since I left the parking lot, that the mountain didn't demand my full attention. I started to reminisce and let my mind wander back to the day I left Springer Mountain in Georgia, which seemed like a lifetime ago. I would always fondly remember the past 169 days for the rest of my life.

I hiked two-thousand, one-hundred and seventy-five miles since I started many footsteps ago. I journeyed a great deal more spiritually since that cold, February day on Springer Mountain. My dream would become a memory when I touched the sign at the summit. I would keep those memories for as long as possible, but they too would eventually fade in time. My life on the trail would become a memory all too soon. However, I gained some wisdom from my experience both on the trail and in my life's journey.

The wind blew the clouds on by and the weather briefly cleared enough to see the pointy mound of rocks piled up by hikers of the past to create a cairn to mark the summit. A half-mile before I reached the top, I could see some people were on the green and gray tableland moving toward the summit as if on a pilgrimage. My emotions started escaping my control as tears started involuntarily forming in my eyes as I approached the summit. I didn't know if the tears were of joy or grief. I was completing a monumental goal, but at the same instant, my nomad lifestyle would end.

The trail was my home. My tent was my bedroom. I slept on a mat on the ground. I ate almost every meal outside in a different place each day. I drank from the springs. I bathed in the lakes and streams. I pooped in the woods. When it was cold, I froze. When it was hot, I sweated. When it rained, I got wet. I thought of the terrifying thunder and lightning storms, the blizzards, the fierce mountains, the swollen rivers, the swamps and bogs, the mosquitoes, ticks, and spiders. I remembered the fear, the joy, the good times, the bad times, the pain, and the blisters. I felt grateful for the friendships and the fellowship both on and off the trail.

I perceived the time on the trail as time to process the painful lessons from my past and heal spiritually. I still had spiritual questions that I would seek answers to. I probably would continue to seek answers as I approach the final day when I totally surrender my will to my creator.

I kept asking some questions that I often asked such as, What has the trail taught you? What secret has it revealed? I could see the trail gave me many insights and answered many questions, but the journey was never-ending and I needed to continue seeking knowledge of God's will.

The Marines have a slogan, The change is forever. The change I decided to make in Step Three wasn't forever, but only as long as I continued to seek God's will and surrendered my will to God. God seemed to help when I asked Him, but He would let me manage my own life if I chose.

I didn't know how much time I had left in the world and I would like to make whatever time I had left count for something. I would like to leave something behind when I die. I felt called to share my life's journey with future addicts, my yet unborn descendants, and anyone else who suffered alone. I found a book was the vehicle I could use to accomplish such a goal.

Maybe if I passed on my experience, strength and hope to others who were blind, they would vicariously gain the hope that one day they could see also. Passing on my experience might have been the purpose of my mission right from the beginning of my life.

Trying to give others hope seemed like a worthy cause to spend whatever time I had left. I felt old, but maybe it wasn't too late for me to be of service to God. Who knows, maybe even writing a book wasn't such a farfetched dream after all. At least I found a purpose for my life. I committed to show up, do the footwork, and write the book, which was my part and the only thing I could control. I would do my best and then let go to let God do whatever he wanted from there on out.

I stopped a few feet from the summit to take it all in as I looked down on Katahdin's, intimidating knife-edge. I shivered with chills as I gazed at the three-foot wide spine with sides dropping thousands of feet that promised death with one misstep.

The final few yards presented a panoramic view of Baxter's landscape below where the lesser mountains seemed to point to Katahdin in a salutation. I first noticed the ten-foot cairn up close at the summit itself and shamelessly broke down crying like a four-year-old, when I saw the sign that ended it all. Through eyes blurred by tears, I turned to Scooter, swallowed the lump in my throat, and simply said, "It's going down." I could only read one word on the wooden, weather-beaten sign through my tears, but that one word was my goal for ten years. All it said was,

"Katahdin!"

REFERENCES

Alcoholics Anonymous, Fourth Edition, 2001.
Alcoholics Anonymous World Services, New York.

The Language of the Heart, 1988.
The Grapevine, Inc., New York.

My Name Is Bill,
By Susan Cheever, 2004.

The Thru-hiker's Handbook.
By Dan Bruce, 2005

The Steps We Took.
By Joe McQ, 1990